Dear Becky

Love from

Glenda

xxxx

Cultural Interactions
Studies in the Relationship between the Arts

Edited by J.B. Bullen

Volume 49

PETER LANG
Oxford • Bern • Berlin • Bruxelles • New York • Wien

Glenda Youde and Robert Wilkes (eds)

Pre-Raphaelite Sisters

Art, Poetry and Female Agency in Victorian Britain

PETER LANG
Oxford • Bern • Berlin • Bruxelles • New York • Wien

Bibliographic information published by Die Deutsche Nationalbibliothek.
Die Deutsche Nationalbibliothek lists this publication in the Deutsche Nationalbibliografie; detailed bibliographic data is available on the Internet at http://dnb.d-nb.de.

A catalogue record for this book is available from the British Library.

Library of Congress Cataloging-in-Publication Data

Names: Youde, Glenda, 1955- editor. | Wilkes, Robert, 1993- editor.
Title: Pre-Raphaelite sisters : art, poetry and female agency in Victorian Britain / Glenda Youde, Robert Wilkes.
Description: Oxford ; New York : Peter Lang, 2022. | Series: Cultural interactions : studies in the relationship between the arts, 1662-0364 ; vol. no. 49 | Includes bibliographical references and index.
Identifiers: LCCN 2022007591 (print) | LCCN 2022007592 (ebook) | ISBN 9781800795648 (paperback) | ISBN 9781800795655 (ebook) | ISBN 9781800795662 (epub)
Subjects: LCSH: Pre-Raphaelitism—Great Britain. | Pre-Raphaelites—Great Britain. | Women artists—Great Britain—History—19th century.
Classification: LCC NX454.5.P7 P74 2022 (print) | LCC NX454.5.P7 (ebook) DDC 700.92/52—dc23/eng/20220517
LC record available at https://lccn.loc.gov/2022007591
LC ebook record available at https://lccn.loc.gov/2022007592

Cover image: *The Little Foot Page*, by Eleanor Fortescue-Brickdale (1905). Oil on canvas. In the public domain.

Cover design by Peter Lang Ltd. Series design by Mollie Tearne.

ISSN 1662-0364

ISBN 978-1-80079-564-8 (print)
ISBN 978-1-80079-565-5 (ePDF)
ISBN 978-1-80079-566-2 (ePub)

Published by Peter Lang Ltd, International Academic Publishers, Oxford, United Kingdom
oxford@peterlang.com, www.peterlang.com

This publication has been peer reviewed.

This collection of essays is dedicated to Jan Marsh and Elizabeth Prettejohn, who have both inspired and persuaded us to bring the women of the Pre-Raphaelite movement out of the shadows.

It is not sufficient merely to add some women to the Pre-Raphaelite canon. Instead it is a matter of writing a wholly new, and different, story about Pre-Raphaelitism – a story in which the activities of women are no longer incidental, but necessary to the plot.

– Elizabeth Prettejohn, *The Art of the Pre-Raphaelites*

Contents

Illustrations

Acknowledgements

The editors would like to thank all those who have been most influential in bringing this project to fruition. Firstly, our thanks go to Jan Marsh for raising the profile of the women of the Pre-Raphaelite movement by curating the *Pre-Raphaelite Sisters* exhibition (October 2019 to January 2020), and for proposing the idea of an accompanying conference to Liz Prettejohn. Many thanks also to Liz, who had the confidence to place the organisation of the conference in the hands of the editors, and to Marjorie Coughlan for her help in staging the event. The two-day conference, *Pre-Raphaelite Sisters: Making Art*, was held at the University of York in December 2019, with support from the Paul Mellon Centre for Studies in British Art. It was extremely successful and generated a great deal of interest in the women of the Pre-Raphaelite movement. It was this success that led Barrie Bullen to approach us with the idea of a publication, and we owe our thanks to him for his interest. We are grateful to Christiana Payne and Dinah Roe for their assistance in preparing the introduction to this volume. We would also like to thank all our contributors, without whom this collection would not have been possible. Finally, our thanks must go to our long-suffering families and friends, who have given us their unfailing support throughout.

Glenda Youde and Robert Wilkes
September 2022

ROBERT WILKES

Introduction: 'A Silent Passing By' – Pre-Raphaelite Women in Context

In her preface to the latest edition of her book *Pre-Raphaelite Sisterhood* in 2018, Jan Marsh reflected that

> since [...] 1985, there has been a vast expansion of research and writing about the women of the Pre-Raphaelite circle from a feminist perspective. [...] [T]he lives detailed in these pages are no longer as obscure as they were when I first began.[1]

First published in 1985, Marsh's *Pre-Raphaelite Sisterhood* quickly became a field-defining text. It was the first book to consider, in detail, the lives and works of individual women associated with the Pre-Raphaelite movement, whether they were artists, writers, artists' models or creative or romantic partners.[2] The book was followed in 1989 by *Women Artists and the Pre-Raphaelite Movement*, co-authored by Marsh and Pamela Gerrish Nunn; and in 1997–8 by Marsh and Nunn's exhibition *Pre-Raphaelite Women Artists* (with an accompanying catalogue that was an expanded

1 I am grateful to Professor Christiana Payne and Dr Dinah Roe for their constructive comments on an early draft of this introduction, and to Glenda Youde for her assistance with information about Pre-Raphaelite exhibitions.
Jan Marsh, *Pre-Raphaelite Sisterhood* (1985; 3rd edn, London: Lume Books, 2018), Kindle edition, loc. 44.

2 A much earlier book is Mrs Matthew Woods's *Some Women of the Pre-Raphaelite Movement* (Philadelphia: Browning Press, 1914), but it is scarce, and it has not been possible for me to consult it. William E. Fredeman, *Pre-Raphaelitism: A Bibliocritical Study* (Cambridge, MA: Harvard University Press, 1965), 228, states that it is the published text of a lecture which Woods delivered in Philadelphia in 1914.

version of their 1989 book).[3] These texts challenged the received idea that women contributed little to the development of Pre-Raphaelitism beyond their capacities as artists' models, inspiring the languid female figures that have long been synonymous with Pre-Raphaelitism. Modelling is a valuable part of the artistic process – many Pre-Raphaelite paintings would not exist without their female models – but the women's other talents and achievements were frequently overlooked until feminist scholars like Marsh, Nunn, Deborah Cherry and Griselda Pollock shone new light upon them in the 1980s.

During the earlier waves of Pre-Raphaelite scholarship in the twentieth century, scholars devoted most of their energies to individual male painters like Dante Gabriel Rossetti, William Holman Hunt, John Everett Millais, Ford Madox Brown and Edward Burne-Jones, who were honoured with memorial exhibitions, catalogues raisonnés, biographies, scholarly articles and film biopics. William E. Fredeman's *Pre-Raphaelitism: A Bibliocritical Study* (1965), published at a critical point in the development of Pre-Raphaelite studies in the mid-1960s, included bibliographies for sixty-five individual figures. Only two of these were women, and both with a close connection to D. G. Rossetti: Christina Rossetti and Elizabeth Siddal.[4] The broader survey exhibitions of Pre-Raphaelite art were also almost exclusively male. An exhibition at the Tate Gallery in 1923 contained 338 works, thirty-three of which were by women: eight by Siddal, twenty-four by Joanna Boyce Wells and one by Florence Caxton.[5] The centenary of the PRB's founding in 1948 saw a flurry of exhibitions featuring predominantly male artists. Those at Birmingham Art Gallery and the Whitechapel Art Gallery included only one woman each: Siddal.[6] (Nicolette Gray, reviewing the

3 Jan Marsh and Pamela Gerrish Nunn, *Women Artists and the Pre-Raphaelite Movement* (London: Virago, 1989); Marsh and Gerrish Nunn, *Pre-Raphaelite Women Artists* (Manchester: Manchester City Art Gallery, 1997). The exhibition toured Manchester City Art Gallery, Birmingham Museum and Art Gallery and Southampton City Art Gallery in 1997–8.

4 Fredeman, *Pre-Raphaelitism*, 176–82 (Rossetti) and 209–11 (Siddal).

5 *Loan Exhibition of the Paintings and Drawings of the 1860 Period*, Tate Gallery, London, April–July 1923.

6 *The Pre-Raphaelite Brotherhood (1848–1862)*, Birmingham City Museum, 1947; *The Pre-Raphaelites: A Loan Exhibition of their Paintings and Drawings held in*

Birmingham show, wrote that the Siddal works on display demonstrated that 'the view that she was just an imitator of her husband [Rossetti] is not tenable'.[7]) Forty years later, the situation had changed little: out of the 250 works included in the major Pre-Raphaelite exhibition at the Tate Gallery in 1984, there were only three works by one woman – Siddal once again.[8]

These twentieth-century exhibitions perpetuated an overarching narrative of masculine genius (or geniuses), beginning with Millais, Hunt, Rossetti and Madox Brown in 1848–53, then introducing figures like William Morris and Burne-Jones in the late 1850s, before petering out in the 1860s, by which time Pre-Raphaelitism in its original form, often summarised by the creed of 'truth-to-nature', was merged with Rossettian bohemianism and the Aesthetic Movement. Women who did more than simply model for the men's paintings (although, as mentioned, we should not disparage this role) were not sufficiently integrated into these broader narratives as anything more than one-dimensional 'muses' and 'mistresses'. As Cherry has highlighted, Alan Bowness's introduction to the 1984 Tate catalogue even attributed the dissolution of the PRB in 1853 to the fact that '[g]irls had now entered the Pre-Raphaelite circle' (distracting the men from their aesthetic goals), and Bowness dwelt at length on Rossetti's romantic affairs – a subject which, even by the 1980s, had received more than its fair share of attention.[9] These accounts typically did not mention that Jane Morris was a prodigious embroider, Georgiana Burne-Jones a draughtswoman or Maria Terpsithea Cassavetti Zambaco a skilled metal worker and sculptor.[10] Conversely, Christina Rossetti was thought of solely

---

the Centenary Year of the Foundation of the Brotherhood, Whitechapel Art Gallery, London, April–May 1948.

7 Nicolette Gray, 'The Pre-Raphaelite Exhibition at Birmingham', *The Burlington Magazine* 89/532 (July 1947), 192–93 (193).

8 See Leslie Parris, ed., *The Pre-Raphaelites* (London: Tate Gallery, 1984), 266, 279, 283.

9 Deborah Cherry, 'In a word: Pre-Raphaelite, Pre-Raphaelites, Pre-Raphaelitism', in Michaela Gibelhausen and Tim Barringer, eds, *Writing the Pre-Raphaelites: Text, Context, Subtext* (Aldershot: Ashgate, 2009), 41; Alan Bowness, 'Introduction', in Parris, *Pre-Raphaelites*, 11–26.

10 For Jane Morris's embroideries, see Tim Barringer, Jason Rosenfeld and Alison Smith, *Pre-Raphaelites: Victorian Avant-Garde* (London: Tate Publishing, 2012),

as a poet, but rarely as an artists' model (she sat to her brother for two paintings and numerous portraits) or as an illustrator of her own poems.[11]

Women were therefore denied a multiplicity of creative roles; they were often 'one thing or the other', *either* an artists' model *or* a painter, but never both. (Meanwhile, scholars were quick to demonstrate William Morris's skills in multiple creative fields, or D. G. Rossetti's double talents as a poet and a painter.) An exception to this pigeonholing tendency was Siddal, whose reputation as an artist and poet sat, if a little awkwardly, alongside her known capacity as a model – we have seen that she was often the woman artist of choice for the twentieth-century survey exhibitions. Pre-Raphaelitism's immediate association with the art of painting in the popular imagination meant that women's contributions to other creative fields, such as literature, sculpture, architecture, the decorative arts and sartorial practices, received even less acknowledgement – an imbalance which some of the chapters in this book also aim to redress.

Paradoxically, female creativity was valued and encouraged in the women's lifetimes. Alison Smith has highlighted the fact that the PRB's unconventional social structure, removed from the public sphere, 'allowed women, as amateurs, to be admitted on more equal terms than they would have been at most art schools of the time'.[12] In an article about Siddal from 1903, William Michael Rossetti observed that her artworks were likely to be treated with undue harshness by post-Victorian audiences:

> [I]n the present day, when vigorous brush-work and calculated 'values' are more thought of than inventiveness or sentiment, [Siddal's] performances would secure little beyond a sneer at first, a glance afterwards, and a silent passing by. But in those

---

203–5. For Georgiana Burne-Jones's drawings, see Jan Marsh et al., *Pre-Raphaelite Sisters* (London: National Portrait Gallery, 2019), 124–34. For Maria Cassavetti Zambaco's sculptures, see Marsh, *Pre-Raphaelite Sisters*, 146–55.

11 See Lorraine Janzen Kooistra, *Christina Rossetti and Illustration* (Athens, OH: Ohio University Press, 2002), 21–43; Dinah Roe, '"Come and See": Christina Rossetti's Illustrations for *The Christian Year*', in Susan Owens and Nicholas Tromans, eds, *Christina Rossetti: Poetry in Art* (New Haven, CT: Yale University Press, 2018), 83.

12 Alison Smith, 'The Sisterhood and its Afterlife', in Marsh, *Pre-Raphaelite Sisters*, 182.

> early 'Præraphaelite' days, and in the Præraphaelite environment, which was small, and ringed around by hostile forces, things were estimated differently.[13]

Siddal showed her drawings and watercolours in the Pre-Raphaelite exhibition at Russell Place in 1857, while the Exhibition of British Art which toured the United States in the winter of 1857–8 included, according to Cherry, 'a substantial number of works by women', Siddal among them.[14] Holman Hunt, writing in 1905, recalled complimenting Siddal's 'stunning drawings' when he saw them in the Russell Place exhibition (although he had little to say about them otherwise).[15] Enthusiastic responses to Siddal's designs by the likes of Alfred and Emily Tennyson, Robert and Elizabeth Barrett Browning, William Allingham and John Ruskin are all recorded in documentary material from the time. As Cherry has shown, the tendency to devalue artworks by women that had formerly been admired in the 'early Pre-Raphaelite days' of the 1850s continued well into the twentieth century.[16]

As Marsh mentioned in 2018, the situation has greatly improved in the present century, which has seen even more exhibitions, scholarly monographs, biographies and articles devoted to the lives and works of individual Pre-Raphaelite women artists, writers and designers. An exhibition devoted to the artworks of Lucy and Catherine Madox Brown was recently held at the Watts Gallery in Surrey.[17] Between 2012 and 2019 there were solo exhibitions dedicated to Eleanor Fortescue-Brickdale, May Morris, Christina Rossetti, Marie Spartali Stillman and Barbara Leigh Smith Bodichon held in Britain and the United States.[18] The last two shows were curated and

13 William Michael Rossetti, 'Dante Rossetti and Elizabeth Siddal', *The Burlington Magazine for Connoisseurs* 1/3 (1903), 273–95 (278).

14 Cherry, 'In a word', 42.

15 William Holman Hunt, *Pre-Raphaelitism and the Pre-Raphaelite Brotherhood*, 2 vols (London: Macmillan, 1905), I, 97–8.

16 Cherry, 'In a word', 42–3.

17 *'Uncommon Power': Lucy and Catherine Madox Brown*, Watts Gallery, Surrey, September 2021–February 2022.

18 *A Pre-Raphaelite Journey: Eleanor Fortescue-Brickdale*, Lady Lever Art Gallery, Liverpool, 2012; *May Morris: Art and Life*, William Morris Gallery, Walthamstow, 2017–18; *Christina Rossetti: Vision and Verse*, Watts Gallery, Surrey, 2018–19; *Poetry in Beauty: The Pre-Raphaelite Art of Marie Spartali Stillman*, Delaware

co-curated by Margaretta S. Frederick, whose chapter in this volume presents further research into Barbara Bodichon's artistic and political ideals. These monographic studies have served as a corrective to the earlier survey exhibitions which omitted women artists – and even to more recent examples like the Tate's *Pre-Raphaelites: Victorian Avant-Garde* (2012–13), which included a small number of works by women: four by Siddal, two by Rosa Brett, one by Florence Caxton and three embroidered pieces (all for William Morris's bed) executed by Jane and May Morris, Lily Yeats, Maude Deacon and Ellen Wright.[19]

In literary studies, new monographs have either given Pre-Raphaelite women writers due credit for the first time – Serena Trowbridge's scholarly edition of Siddal's poetry from 2018 is a notable example – or offered fresh perspectives on known writers, like Emma Mason's *Christina Rossetti: Poetry, Ecology, Faith* (2018) and Anne Woolley's *Poems of Elizabeth Siddal in Context* (2021).[20] New 'lives' of Pre-Raphaelite women have examined them with the biographical techniques previously reserved for the male figures: 'Effie' Gray Millais by Suzanne Fagence Cooper, Fanny Cornforth by Kirsty Stonell Walker and Frances Graham by Andrew Gailey, to highlight a few.[21] The publication of original letters by Christina Rossetti, Jane Morris and Joanna Boyce Wells has also allowed the private textual voices

---

Art Museum, USA, 2015–16; *Politics and Paint: Barbara Bodichon and the Pre-Raphaelite Brotherhood*, Delaware Art Museum, 2018–19.

19 See Barringer, Rosenfeld and Smith, *Pre-Raphaelites*, 73–75, 107, 203–204. This exhibition toured from Tate Britain, London to the National Gallery of Art, Washington, DC and the Pushkin State Museum of Fine Arts, Moscow.

20 Serena Trowbridge, ed., *My Ladys Soul: The Poems of Elizabeth Siddall* (Brighton: Victorian Secrets, 2018); Emma Mason, *Christina Rossetti: Poetry, Ecology, Faith* (Oxford: Oxford University Press, 2018); Anne Woolley, *The Poems of Elizabeth Siddal in Context* (Manchester: Manchester University Press, 2021).

21 Suzanne Fagence Cooper, *The Model Wife: The Passionate Lives of Effie Gray, Ruskin and Millais* (London: Duckworth Overlook, 2010); Kirsty Stonell Walker, *Stunner: The Fall and Rise of Fanny Cornforth* (2006; 3rd edn, Lewes: Unicorn Publishing, 2022); Andrew Gailey, *Portrait of a Muse: Frances Graham, Edward Burne-Jones and the Pre-Raphaelite Dream* (London: Wilmington Square Books, 2020).

of Pre-Raphaelite women writers, models and artists to be read and studied for the first time.[22]

To this layering of representations can be added the fictionalised versions of some Pre-Raphaelite women in films, television shows and the performing arts. The BBC series *Desperate Romantics* (2009) included portrayals of Siddal, Annie Miller, Fanny Cornforth, Jane Morris and Effie Gray, while the film *Effie Gray* (2014) focused on the titular character's relationship with Millais during her marriage with John Ruskin. The recent re-releases of an earlier BBC series about the PRB, *The Love School* (1975), and of Ken Russell's phantasmagorical film *Dante's Inferno* (1967), have enabled viewers to revisit twentieth-century interpretations of several Pre-Raphaelite women.[23] 'Lizzie Siddal', a stage play about Siddal's life by Jeremy Green, ran at the Arcola Theatre in London in 2013, while contemporary artist Margje Bijl has reinterpreted Rossetti's images of Jane Morris in a variety of media, including performances and works on paper, as part of her ongoing project *Reflections on Jane Morris*.[24]

In an essay accompanying the Tate exhibition in 2012, Elizabeth Prettejohn challenged the popular idea that Pre-Raphaelite art 'fell out of fashion' in the post-Victorian period before being 'rediscovered' by critics, art historians and collectors in the 1960s.[25] Similarly, there is still a tendency in the present century to repeat the claim that Pre-Raphaelite women, particularly in their creative roles, are only *now* being plucked from obscurity and given their critical due, having always been 'overlooked',

22 Jan Marsh and Frank C. Sharp, eds, *The Collected Letters of Jane Morris* (Woodbridge: Boydell, 2012); Sue Bradbury, ed., *The Boyce Papers: The Letters and Diaries of Joanne Boyce, Henry Wells and George Price Boyce*, 2 vols (Cambridge: Boydell Press, 2019); Anthony H. Harrison, ed., *The Letters of Christina Rossetti: A Digital Edition*, University of Virginia Press, 2006, <https://rotunda.upress.virginia.edu/crossetti/>, accessed 9 September 2021.

23 Jeremy Green, *Lizzie Siddal* (London: Nick Hern Books, 2014). *The Love School* was released on DVD by SimplyMedia in 2019; *Dante's Inferno* by the BFI in 2016 (*The Ken Russell Collection: The Great Passions*, DVD, British Film Institute).

24 Margje Bijl, *Reflections on Jane Morris*, 2009–present, <https://www.reflectionsonjanemorris.com>, accessed 14 June 2021.

25 Elizabeth Prettejohn, 'The Pre-Raphaelite Legacy', in Barringer, Rosenfeld and Smith, *Pre-Raphaelites*, 231–6.

'marginalised', 'neglected' and 'forgotten'. This was noticeable in the press coverage surrounding the exhibition *Pre-Raphaelite Sisters*, held at the National Portrait Gallery in 2019–20 – taking place after the aforementioned exhibitions and scholarly research devoted to female creativity. One review described the exhibition as 'the first to focus on the role of women in the famous Brotherhood', while another stated that it would 'explore the untold stories of 12 women who contributed to the Pre-Raphaelite movement' – even if some of these stories had already been 'told' by earlier scholars and curators.[26] The *Guardian*, meanwhile, claimed that this was 'the first dedicated exhibition' about 'the female painters and makers of the pre-Raphaelite [sic] era'.[27] Marsh and Nunn's *Pre-Raphaelite Women Artists* exhibition from 1997, for example, was not always mentioned.

On the one hand, these comments demonstrate that Pre-Raphaelite creativity is still perceived as predominantly masculine, despite the efforts of feminist scholars over the past forty years. On the other hand, by repeatedly asserting that these women have been marginalised, we also risk perpetuating a myth of obscurity, the shades of which began to be dispelled by Marsh and her colleagues back in the 1980s. It can now be said with confidence that Pre-Raphaelite women are no longer completely obscure and do not all require rescuing from the shadows – the work facing scholars today is to unapologetically continue this research.

The exhibitions, publications, media and artworks cited above – and there are many more besides – have presented the women as individuals – and rightly, vitally so. Although this book does not claim to be the first

26 Francesca Wade, 'From Dolls to Models to Partners: The Women of the Pre-Raphaelite Brotherhood', *Times Literary Supplement* (22 November 2019), <https://www.the-tls.co.uk/articles/pre-raphaelite-sisters-national-portrait-gallery-review-francesca-wade>, accessed 14 September 2021; review in the *Belfast Telegraph* (13 December 2018), <https://www.belfasttelegraph.co.uk/entertainment/news/national-portrait-gallery-to-explore-untold-stories-of-pre-raphaelite-women-37623009.html>, accessed 14 September 2021.

27 Kathryn Hughes, 'More Than Tragic Muses: Female Pre-Raphaelite Artists Finally Take Flight', *Guardian* (12 October 2019), <https://www.theguardian.com/artanddesign/2019/oct/12/more-than-tragic-muses-female-pre-raphaelite-artists-finally-take-flight>, accessed 14 September 2021.

book ever published on Pre-Raphaelite women, it is the first edited collection of chapters devoted to this topic.[28] Moreover, few publications have offered a collective examination of Pre-Raphaelite women and their diverse contributions to the development of Pre-Raphaelitism – a problem which this book aims to address. As described earlier, the general surveys of Pre-Raphaelitism have been at fault, particularly the museum exhibitions and their catalogues which represent the dominant artistic branch of the movement. Acknowledging that Pre-Raphaelite creativity did not confine itself to the fine arts – specifically, painting – our collection includes contributions from other fields: literary and political studies, fashion history and social history.

It is here that the term 'sisters', used in the titles of the National Portrait Gallery exhibition and this book, becomes useful, although it is contentious. As Smith has pointed out, it 'is very much a retrospective appellation', coming into common usage in the 1980s.[29] Prettejohn titled a chapter of her book *The Art of the Pre-Raphaelites* (2000) 'Pre-Raphaelite Sisterhood', the term previously used for the title of Marsh's book.[30] More recently, Heather Bozant Witcher and Amy Huseby proposed a 'resistance to the gendered language of the Brotherhood or Sisterhood', suggesting that these terms risk segregating the men and the women into separate groups, when in fact the Pre-Raphaelites constituted a diverse social circle.[31] There never was an official Pre-Raphaelite Sisterhood, although a 'non-familial sisterhood of painters and poets' was proposed by Anna Mary Howitt, whose 'sisters in art' included Barbara Bodichon, Bessie Rayner Parkes and Jane

28 For a similar theme, see Clarissa Campbell Orr, ed., *Women in the Victorian Art World* (Manchester: Manchester University Press, 1995), although this book does not focus on the Pre-Raphaelite circle.

29 Smith, 'The Sisterhood and its Afterlife', 183.

30 Elizabeth Prettejohn, *The Art of the Pre-Raphaelites* (2000; 2nd edn, London: Tate Publishing, 2007), 67–86.

31 Heather Bozant Witcher and Amy Kahrmann Huseby, 'Introduction', in Heather Bozant Witcher and Amy Kahrmann Huseby, eds, *Defining Pre-Raphaelite Poetics* (Switzerland: Palgrave Macmillan, 2020), 1–26 (11).

Benham.[32] Howitt maintained friendships with Siddal, D. G. Rossetti, Millais and the poet William Allingham, and her paintings show clear Pre-Raphaelite influences.[33] In a letter in October 1850, Howitt first used the phrase 'the sisters', in Alexandra Wettlaufer's words, 'to link the ideas of art, education, and independence into a metaphorical structure of artistic sisterhood'.[34] Two years later, Howitt published a novella, *The Sisters in Art*, about a group of female painters who use the concept of 'sisterhood' to promote collaborative working and female solidarity.

Using 'Pre-Raphaelite Sisters' as a collective term for the women included in this book is therefore not as anachronistic as might be supposed. This book does not propose a historically valid 'Sisterhood' of creative women, but uses 'Sisters' to suggest that these women were united by their mutual interest in Pre-Raphaelitism. Although 'Sisters' and 'sisterhood' may seem overly broad or generalised, the PRB itself turned out to be a less rigid grouping than its members originally intended. When James Collinson resigned in 1850, the two men mooted to replace him were Walter Howell Deverell and Charles Allston Collins, who were practically thought of as Pre-Raphaelite Brothers anyway, despite not being official members. A similar unofficial status was given to other male friends like the sculptors Alexander Munro, Bernhard Smith and John Lucas Tupper, who were on close terms with the PRBs and even attended some of their meetings.[35] Finally, of course, the Brotherhood itself disintegrated by the end of 1853, after Thomas Woolner emigrated to Australia. The broad homosocial network surrounding the central Brotherhood means that proposing a similarly wide grouping of Pre-Raphaelite 'Sisters' is not unreasonable.

The Sisters' personal names can also have complications. Some women are typically referred to using only their married titles: Jane Morris (née

32 Jan Marsh, 'Introduction: The Sisters and the Movement', in Marsh, *Pre-Raphaelite Sisters*, 10; Alexandra Wettlaufer, 'The Politics and Poetics of Sisterhood: Anna Mary Howitt's *The Sisters in Art*', *Victorian Review* 36/1 (2010), 129–46.

33 See Marsh and Nunn, *Women Artists*, 31–46.

34 Wettlaufer, 'Politics and Poetics', 133.

35 These meetings are documented in William E. Fredeman, ed., *The PRB Journal: William Michael Rossetti's Diary of the Pre-Raphaelite Brotherhood, 1849–1853* (Oxford: Clarendon Press, 1975).

Burden), Evelyn De Morgan (née Pickering), Georgiana Burne-Jones (née MacDonald), Maria Zambaco (née Cassavetti) and Fanny Eaton (née Antwistle/Entwistle). For others, we prefer to use their birth names: Elizabeth Siddal (later Rossetti), Effie Gray (later Ruskin and Millais), Lucy Madox Brown (later Rossetti) and Anna Mary Howitt (later Watts). For others still, both names are used: Marie Spartali Stillman, Joanna Boyce Wells, Barbara Leigh Smith Bodichon and Mary Seton Watts. These combinations seem to have been arrived at randomly over time: why, for example, have names like Jane Burden Morris and Georgiana MacDonald Burne-Jones never stuck, while Marie Spartali Stillman and Joanna Boyce Wells have? Familiar pet names are also adopted, so that Euphemia Gray, Jane Morris, Elizabeth Siddal and Georgiana Burne-Jones often become *Effie*, *Janey*, *Lizzie* and *Georgie* in the popular literature.

This 'name question' may be a moot point. We still know which woman we are referring to when using the names listed above, and the women may have chosen the titles themselves. However, if the women's very names are subject to change (other combinations like 'Marie Spartali' or 'Evelyn Pickering De Morgan', for example, are sometimes used), their identity is less firmly fixed than the male figures. Like D. G. Rossetti's stylised depictions of real women, the different names become multiple reflections of an historical individual; Jane Burden fractures into Jane Morris, Janey Morris or just 'Janey'. A similar problem faces other historical women, such as the eighteenth-century artist Rosalba Carriera, who, according to Rozsika Parker and Griselda Pollock, is frequently referred to as 'Rosalba' in modern studies of the eighteenth century, reflecting a trend of 'casually patroniz[ing] women' by using only their first names.[36]

The naming of Pre-Raphaelite women is also mentioned here because of Elizabeth Siddal, for whom there is an additional scholarly issue which some of our contributors have had to address. The ongoing debates around the spelling of Siddal's surname – 'Siddall' or 'Siddal' – began in the 1980s, when Cherry and Pollock proposed that the traditional spelling of the

36 Rozsika Parker and Griselda Pollock, *Old Mistresses: Women, Art and Ideology* (New York: Pantheon Books, 1981), 28. My thanks to Christiana Payne for bringing this to my attention.

surname, 'Siddal', was a construction imposed upon her by D. G. Rossetti in opposition to her birth name, 'Siddall'. In Cherry and Pollock's view, 'Siddal' came to represent a 'cipher for masculine creativity', while 'Siddall' was an historical individual with agency of her own.[37] The latter spelling has now become standard in academic writing, although the extant historical documents complicate matters. At least two primary sources made by or belonging to Siddal use the 'one L' spelling: her 1853 drawing *The Lady of Shalott* and her personal copy of Walter Scott's *Minstrelsy of the Scottish Border*, both inscribed by her.[38] I have therefore opted for the traditional 'Siddal' spelling in this introduction, in keeping with how Siddal chose to sign her name. Other writers in this book may have chosen differently, and if so, they will justify which spelling they have chosen. Once again, the question of Siddal's agency is revaluated by a new generation of scholars.

In the first part of this book, 'Making Art', the careers of four artists are considered. Sarah Hardy's chapter on Evelyn De Morgan calls attention to a series of dazzling drawings by the artist which have seldom been considered as a coherent body of work, demonstrating both De Morgan's distinctive techniques (gold paint on dark paper) and the Christian teachings which inspired her. Christin Neubauer presents a detailed visual analysis of two less familiar paintings by Eleanor Fortescue-Brickdale, situating them within the context of female emancipation at the turn of the century. Mary Seton Watts's hymn in stone, the Watts Cemetery Chapel in Compton, is the subject of Caroline Giddis's chapter, which deconstructs Seton Watts's complex iconographical scheme and the Chapel's primary function as a community project. Of the various artistic fields to which Pre-Raphaelite women contributed, architecture is perhaps the least familiar, so Giddis's chapter is a welcome addition. Margaretta S. Frederick looks at Barbara Leigh Smith Bodichon, whose radical politics frequently informed her artistic production. Common to all these chapters is a spirit of defiance,

37 Deborah Cherry and Griselda Pollock, 'Woman as Sign in Pre-Raphaelite Literature: A Study of the Representation of Elizabeth Siddall', *Art History* 7/2 (June 1984), 206–27.

38 Volumes three and four of Scott's *Minstrelsy*, once belonging to Siddal, are now in the Fitzwilliam Museum, Cambridge. I am grateful to Nat Reeve for this information.

whether defying standard artistic practises (De Morgan's distinctive golden drawings), the lack of women's suffrage (Fortescue-Brickdale's incorporation of 'New Woman' visual motifs into her paintings), women's limited access to art education (Seton Watts's campaigns for female art schools) or the male-dominated landscape genre (Bodichon's landscapes as documents of her personal experiences). Moreover, Hardy, Neubauer and Giddis take us beyond 1901, the year of Queen Victoria's death, to show that women artists continued to develop the Pre-Raphaelite style into the early twentieth century.

Recognising that Pre-Raphaelitism was not limited to the visual arts, the second part, 'Poetry and Writing', examines innovations in women's writing. Although three of the four chapters feature the same woman – Elizabeth Siddal – two of these consider Siddal's creative partnerships with her contemporaries: Georgiana Burne-Jones in Nat Reeve's essay and Christina Rossetti in Glenda Youde's. Rosalind White sees in Siddal's texts a 'poetic resistance' to the male poet's gaze, inverting the standard literary trope of the female figure inert before a male spectator. In Nat Reeve's insightful comparison of Siddal's poem 'True Love' and Georgiana Burne-Jones's drawing *Death and the Lady*, female collaboration is finally given its due. Typically, only all-male Pre-Raphaelite collaborative ventures have received recognition – for example, the Oxford Union murals and the Moxon Tennyson. Reeve uses Siddal and Burne-Jones's planned book of fairy tales as a starting point for considering how the two women's female protagonists defy impending disasters. Next, Glenda Youde unpicks the tense relationship between Siddal and Christina Rossetti using their 'literary remains' – letters and poems – thereby reminding us, as is sometimes forgotten, that Siddal and Rossetti were eventually sisters-in-law. Lastly, Carey Gibbons illuminates the intriguing relationship between Evelyn De Morgan's experiments with automatic writing and her painting practices, providing new insights into how De Morgan's art was informed by her Spiritualist beliefs.

The third part, 'Female Agency', presents other means by which Pre-Raphaelite women asserted their creativity. Laure Nermel's chapter explains how Siddal appropriated one of the traditional 'male' Pre-Raphaelite principles, 'truth-to-nature', to effect in her own artworks. The field of fashion history informs Robyne Calvert's analysis of the sartorial practices of Elizabeth Siddal and Jane Morris, often described under the capacious term 'Artistic Dress'. By questioning this label, Calvert also challenges the received idea that Pre-Raphaelite women only ever dressed 'unconventionally'; women can be innovators regardless of what they wear. Next, Helena Cox's chapter relocates us from Britain to the Czech Republic, as Cox considers the influence of the Siddal–Rossetti relationship on Ela Švabinská (1878–1967), whose husband, Max Švabinksý (1873–1962), was a prominent Czech painter. Georgiana Burne-Jones's skills as a biographical writer form the topic of Charlotte Gere's chapter, which disentangles Georgiana's self-portrait from her biography of her husband and so presents a new account of her life.

A coda section, 'Personal Perspectives', includes chapters by Brian Eaton and Hannah Squire, which, as the section's title suggests, offer more personalised accounts of engaging with and recovering women in history. They also highlight the practicalities of researching these women and displaying their findings for a broader audience. In Eaton's case, this meant conducting painstaking genealogical research about his great-grandmother, Fanny Eaton, through visits to the National Archives – research that aided the section devoted to Fanny in the *Pre-Raphaelite Sisters* exhibition in 2019–20.[39] Squire, formerly curator at the Pre-Raphaelite 'palace of art' Wightwick Manor, outlines her process in curating the second solo exhibition devoted to Siddal's art, *Beyond Ophelia*, at the Manor in 2018.[40] Squire also examines Sir Geoffrey and Lady Rosalie Mander's collection of works by women artists at Wightwick, formed in the twentieth century. Our inclusion of these more personal chapters was partly influenced by previous edited collections like *Pre-Raphaelite Papers* (1984) and *Haunted Texts: Studies in Pre-Raphaelitism* (2003), which both conclude with personalised 'views', 'recollections' and 'retrospective anecdotal accounts'

39 See Marsh, *Pre-Raphaelite Sisters*, 102–9.

40 *Beyond Ophelia: A Celebration of Lizzie Siddal, Artist and Poet*, Wightwick Manor, West Midlands, 2018. The first solo exhibition about Siddal was curated by Jan Marsh in 1991; see Marsh, *Elizabeth Siddal: Pre-Raphaelite Artist 1829–1862* (Sheffield: The Ruskin Gallery, 1991).

written by Diana Holman-Hunt (Holman Hunt's granddaughter), Jeremy Maas and William E. Fredeman.[41] Eaton's and Squire's chapters remind us of the future work on Pre-Raphaelite women still to be done: the personal histories to be uncovered, the exhibitions to be curated.

This book is by no means a comprehensive survey of every Pre-Raphaelite woman artist, writer, designer and thinker. Like Marsh's *Pre-Raphaelite Sisterhood*, Marsh and Nunn's *Women Artists* and the recent *Pre-Rapaelite Sisters* exhibition, it is a starting point for new research and fresh perspectives on the women's lives and works. Our hope is that the chapters collected in this book will contribute to the existing field of knowledge on the women of the Pre-Raphaelite movement and inspire new generations of scholars, continuing the scholarly work begun by Marsh and her colleagues nearly four decades ago.

Bibliography

Barringer, Tim, Jason Rosenfeld, and Alison Smith, *Pre-Raphaelites: Victorian Avant-Garde* (London: Tate Publishing, 2012).

Belfast Telegraph (13 December 2018), <https://www.belfasttelegraph.co.uk/entertainment/news/national-portrait-gallery-to-explore-untold-stories-of-pre-raphaelite-women-37623009.html>, accessed 14 September 2021.

Bowness, Alan, 'Introduction', in Leslie Parris, ed., *The Pre-Raphaelites* (London: Tate Publishing, 1984), 11–26.

Bozant Witcher, Heather, and Amy Kahrmann Huseby, 'Introduction', in Heather Bozant Witcher and Amy Kahrmann Huseby, eds, *Defining Pre-Raphaelite Poetics* (Switzerland: Palgrave Macmillan, 2020), 1–26.

41 Diana Holman-Hunt, 'The Holman Hunt Collection, A Personal Recollection', in Leslie Parris, ed., *Pre-Raphaelite Papers* (London: Tate Gallery, 1984), 206–25; Jeremy Maas, 'The Pre-Raphaelites: A Personal View', in Parris, *Pre-Raphaelite Papers*, 226–34; William E. Fredeman, 'The Great Pre-Raphaelite Paper Chase: A Retrospective', in David Latham, ed., *Haunted Texts: Studies in Pre-Raphaelitism* (Toronto: University of Toronto Press, 2003), 211–36.

Bradbury, Sue, ed., *The Boyce Papers: The Letters and Diaries of Joanne Boyce, Henry Wells and George Price Boyce*, 2 vols (Cambridge: Boydell Press, 2019).

Campbell Orr, Clarissa, ed., *Women in the Victorian Art World* (Manchester: Manchester University Press, 1995).

Cherry, Deborah, and Griselda Pollock, 'Woman as Sign in Pre-Raphaelite Literature: A Study of the Representation of Elizabeth Siddall', *Art History* 7/2 (June 1984), 206–27.

——, 'In a word: Pre-Raphaelite, Pre-Raphaelites, Pre-Raphaelitism', in Michaela Gibelhausen and Tim Barringer, eds, *Writing the Pre-Raphaelites: Text, Context, Subtext* (Aldershot: Ashgate, 2009), 17–52.

Cooper, Suzanne Fagence, *The Model Wife: The Passionate Lives of Effie Gray, Ruskin and Millais* (London: Duckworth Overlook, 2010).

Fredeman, William E., *Pre-Raphaelitism: A Bibliocritical Study* (Cambridge, MA: Harvard University Press, 1965).

——, ed., *The PRB Journal: William Michael Rossetti's Diary of the Pre-Raphaelite Brotherhood, 1849–1853* (Oxford: Clarendon Press, 1975).

——, 'The Great Pre-Raphaelite Paper Chase: A Retrospective', in David Latham, ed., *Haunted Texts: Studies in Pre-Raphaelitism* (Toronto: University of Toronto Press, 2003), 211–36.

Gailey, Andrew, *Portrait of a Muse: Frances Graham, Edward Burne-Jones and the Pre-Raphaelite Dream* (London: Wilmington Square Books, 2020).

Gray, Nicolette, 'The Pre-Raphaelite Exhibition at Birmingham', *The Burlington Magazine* 89/532 (July 1947), 192–3.

Harrison, Anthony H., ed., *The Letters of Christina Rossetti: A Digital Edition*, University of Virginia Press, 2006, <https://rotunda.upress.virginia.edu/crossetti/>, accessed 9 September 2021.

Holman-Hunt, Diana, 'The Holman Hunt Collection, A Personal Recollection', in Leslie Parris, ed., *Pre-Raphaelite Papers* (London: Tate Gallery, 1984), 206–25.

Hughes, Kathryn, 'More Than Tragic Muses: Female Pre-Raphaelite Artists Finally Take Flight', *Guardian* (12 October 2019), <https://www.theguardian.com/artanddesign/2019/oct/12/more-than-tragic-muses-female-pre-raphaelite-artists-finally-take-flight>, accessed 14 September 2021.

Hunt, William Holman, *Pre-Raphaelitism and the Pre-Raphaelite Brotherhood*, 2 vols (London: Macmillan, 1905).

Kooistra, Lorraine Janzen, *Christina Rossetti and Illustration* (Athens, OH: Ohio University Press, 2002), 21–43.

Maas, Jeremy, 'The Pre-Raphaelites: A Personal View', in Leslie Parris, ed., *Pre-Raphaelite Papers* (London: Tate Gallery), 226–34.

Marsh, Jan, *Pre-Raphaelite Sisterhood* (1985; 3rd edn, London: Lume Books, 2018).

——, and Pamela Gerrish Nunn, *Women Artists and the Pre-Raphaelite Movement* (London: Virago, 1989).

——, *Elizabeth Siddal: Pre-Raphaelite Artist 1829–1862* (Sheffield: The Ruskin Gallery, 1991).

——, and Pamela Gerrish Nunn, *Pre-Raphaelite Women Artists* (Manchester: Manchester City Art Gallery, 1997).

——, and Frank C. Sharp, eds, *The Collected Letters of Jane Morris* (Woodbridge: Boydell, 2012).

——, et al., *Pre-Raphaelite Sisters* (London: National Portrait Gallery, 2019).

——, 'Introduction: The Sisters and the Movement', in Jan Marsh, *Pre-Raphaelite Sisters* (London: National Portrait Gallery, 2019), 8–11.

Mason, Emma, *Christina Rossetti: Poetry, Ecology, Faith* (Oxford: Oxford University Press, 2018).

Parker, Rozsika, and Griselda Pollock, *Old Mistresses: Women, Art and Ideology* (New York: Pantheon Books, 1981).

Prettejohn, Elizabeth, *The Art of the Pre-Raphaelites* (2000; 2nd edn, London: Tate Publishing, 2007).

——, 'The Pre-Raphaelite Legacy', in Tim Barringer, Jason Rosenfeld, and Alison Smith, *Pre-Raphaelites: Victorian Avant-Garde* (London: Tate Publishing, 2012), 231–6.

Roe, Dinah, '"Come and See": Christina Rossetti's Illustrations for The Christian Year', in Susan Owens and Nicholas Tromans, eds, *Christina Rossetti: Poetry in Art* (New Haven, CT: Yale University Press, 2018), 82–107.

Rossetti, William Michael, 'Dante Rossetti and Elizabeth Siddal', *The Burlington Magazine for Connoisseurs* 1/3 (1903), 273–95.

Smith, Alison, 'The Sisterhood and its Afterlife', in Jan Marsh et al, *Pre-Raphaelite Sisters* (London: National Portrait Gallery, 2019), 182–7.

Stonell Walker, Kirsty, *Stunner: The Fall and Rise of Fanny Cornforth* (2006; 3rd edn, Lewes: Unicorn Publishing, 2022).

Trowbridge, Serena, ed., *My Ladys Soul: The Poems of Elizabeth Siddall* (Brighton: Victorian Secrets, 2018).

Wade, Francesca, 'From Dolls to Models to Partners: The Women of the Pre-Raphaelite Brotherhood', *Times Literary Supplement* (22 November 2019), <https://www.the-tls.co.uk/articles/pre-raphaelite-sisters-national-portrait-gallery-review-francesca-wade/>, accessed 14 September 2021.

Wettlaufer, Alexandra, 'The Politics and Poetics of Sisterhood: Anna Mary Howitt's The Sisters in Art', *Victorian Review* 36/1 (2010), 129–46.

Woolley, Anne, *The Poems of Elizabeth Siddal in Context* (Manchester: Manchester University Press, 2021).

PART I

Making Art

SARAH HARDY

1 Evelyn De Morgan: Visions in Gold

ABSTRACT

Evelyn De Morgan made no fewer than eighteen drawings in brilliant gold on dark paper between c. 1885 and 1902. Almost completely unique to her practice, these radical drawings have rarely been considered, and then only as preparatory sketches for her paintings. Examining this body of her work in isolation reveals the gold drawings to be rare and beautiful artworks in their own right, and De Morgan to be an experimental artist who deserves recognition for her technical achievements.

*****

The sale of Victorian enthusiast Joe Setton's collection of Pre-Raphaelite artworks at Christie's, London in December 2020 brought to light an Evelyn De Morgan drawing which quite literally outshone the other auction lots: *The Light Shineth in the Darkness, and the Darkness Comprehendeth It Not* (Figure 1.1). Emblazoned in gold across the paper floats an ethereal being, an oil lamp burning bright in one hand, the other giving the sign of the benediction, whilst a serpent, alligators and a vulture loom in the craggy landscape, illuminated by her light. The sale catalogue essay positioned the drawing as a developmental tool made by the artist between two oil paintings,[1] *Lux in Tenebris* (1895; De Morgan Collection) with which it shares a composition, and her later painting of the same title, *The Light Shineth in the Darkness, and the Darkness Comprehendeth It Not* (1906; De Morgan Collection).

Assuming De Morgan's gold drawings were sketches for later oil paintings relies on the rather limiting assumption that a hierarchy exists in the visual arts where oil painting supersedes drawing. Adopting this view fails to recognise that the artist considered the piece an artwork in

1 *The Joe Setton Collection: From Pre-Raphaelites to Last Romantics* (London: Christie's, 2020), 10.

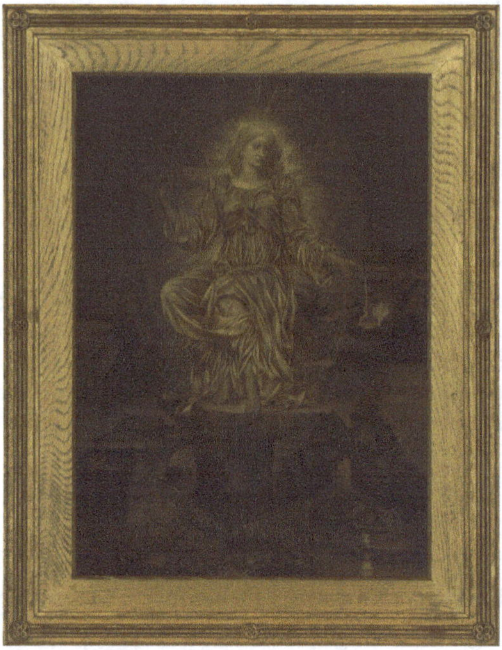

Figure 1.1. Evelyn De Morgan, *The Light Shineth in the Darkness, and the Darkness Comprehendeth It Not*, gold pigment on dark wove paper, c. 1890, © Christie's.

its own right. I have identified eighteen gold drawings made by Evelyn De Morgan during this research. Eleven are in the De Morgan Collection,[2] founded by the artist's sister; one in the collection of the Royal Borough of Kensington and Chelsea,[3] held at Leighton House; one at the Art Institute

2 Listed here followed by the De Morgan Collection accession number in brackets. *Soul's Prison House* (D_EDM_0401), *Boreas and Oreithyia* (D_EDM_0221), *Hero Watching for Leander* (D_EDM_0388), *Mercy and Truth Have Met Together, Righteousness and Peace Have Kissed Each Other* (D_EDM_0321), *Earthbound* (D_EDM_0228), *The Thorny Path* (D_EDM_0336), *Opes* (D_EDM_0416), *Gloria in Excelsis* (D_EDM_0126), *The Valley of Shadows* (D_EDM_0423), *Saint Francis and Holy Poverty* (D_EDM_0334), *Study of an Angel* (D_EDM_0410).

3 *Victoria Dolorosa*, gold pigment on dark paper, c. 1900, Leighton House Museum, London, LH0240.

Chicago;[4] and five in private collections or untraced.[5] Four are dated, which show this body of work was made between at least 1885 and 1902. Although they are almost unique to her practice, these beautiful artworks have rarely been considered by De Morgan's commentators. In 1889, De Morgan exhibited some of the gold drawings at the Fine Art Society's exhibition of 'studies for pictures', where a critic writing for *Portfolio* was intrigued by 'imaginative designs [...] apart in medium and manner' from others on view.[6] More recently, Mark Bills has recognised the unique value of De Morgan's gold drawings as 'finished works with their completed compositions in gleaming golds'. With three exceptions, the gold drawings are versions of subjects and compositions which De Morgan also realised as oil on canvas paintings. Other commentators have provided socio-historical and feminist readings of such paintings to demonstrate her pacifist, Spiritualist and feminist agenda, resulting in a lively discussion of her unique visual lexicon.[7] Whilst these important readings offer rich interpretation of the

4 *Angel of Death*, gold pigment on dark paper, 1885, Art Institute Chicago, Chicago, 2019.925.

5 *Black and Gold Head (Medea) and Luna* (both sold by Rupert Maas June 1989), *The Light Shineth in the Darkness, and the Darkness Comprehendeth It Not* (sold by Christie's, December 2020), *Attainment* (listed in the catalogue of Evelyn De Morgan's artworks shown at Leighton House in 1919, a copy is extant at Leighton House Museum Archive ref. LH/7/1/3/1), *Standing Draped Female Figure* (last sold Sotheby's, April 1978).

6 Philip Gilbert Hamerton, ed., 'Art Chronicle', *Portfolio*, January 1889.

7 There are very few publications entirely dedicated to the study of De Morgan's life and work. Elise Lawton Smith's *The Allegorical Body* (2002) explores De Morgan's expressive and symbolic use of the human form, including an intelligent presentation of the erotic in De Morgan's painting. Cathy Gordon and Judy Oberhausen's 1996 catalogue raisonné includes essays on De Morgan's responses to the Spiritualist movement, war and literature, framing her artworks as painting with moral purpose. The earliest and most recent publications do not take De Morgan in isolation, but rather explain her life and work as inextricably linked to her husband. *William De Morgan and His Wife* (1922) by Evelyn De Morgan's sister Wilhelmina Stirling is a brilliant anecdotal account of her sister's life from childhood to professional artist describing her painting, but lacks critical appraisal of her working methods, whilst *Suffragist Artists in Partnership* (2018) by Lucy Ella Rose, the most recent publication on De Morgan's work, presents her paintings as Suffragist propaganda.

artist's paintings in the context of her contemporaries and lived experience, they neglect to focus specifically on her skill, artistic process and technical experimentation. The focus of this chapter is to build on Bills's understanding of De Morgan's gold drawings as artworks in their own right. An examination of the material construction of her gold drawings reveals much about De Morgan's hitherto overlooked success as a master of a range of artistic media.

De Morgan's early education and subsequent formal training at the Slade School of Art are examined to determine how she became such a proficient draftswoman and reveal why she may have developed her interest in using gold. The materiality of the gold drawings is assessed using her letters, unpublished ledgers of her art materials supplier Charles Roberson and evidence from the De Morgan Foundation's condition reports, providing a tantalising glimpse into her technique and methodology. The range of media in which she excelled at mid-career (1883–1902) set her apart from her peers, and this is discussed at length to demonstrate her experimental approach and locate the gold drawings within her practice. Finally, an overview of the critical reception of De Morgan's gold works is provided, showing them as fully formed, successful artworks in their own right. Here, De Morgan is recognised as a trailblazing, experimental and accomplished professional artist, whose broad achievements in art, drawing, craft and painting amount to more than the painter of Spiritualist and feminist canvases in a Pre-Raphaelite style for which she is usually best remembered.

Going for Gold: Early Education and Formal Training

Of those which are dated, the earliest gold drawing is *Angel of Death* (1885), suggesting the reason De Morgan decided to create works in this unusual medium was profoundly spiritual. The angel of death was De Morgan's *leitmotif*, a constant companion throughout her artistic career. Her juvenile poetry reveals her use of this morbid heavenly creature from the tender age of 13. An untitled poem by the artist describes grief at the loss of true love. It begins:

My love lies deep
Under the ground
And Autumn's gloom
Is gath'ring round

Seventeen stanzas later, it ends:

Soft thy kisses
Warm thy breath
Vision of love
Angel of Death.[8]

The angel of death was not to be feared but rather welcomed and celebrated, according to De Morgan's early prose, and she followed this vision throughout her development as a professional artist with unfaltering determination.

In 1880, De Morgan first realised her spiritual companion in an oil painting, *Angel of Death I* (De Morgan Collection). It is a sensitive, tender meeting between two women. Their touch is light, yet earnest, as the woman reaching the end of her life looks hopefully to the face of the more mature, grey-haired angel for guidance towards her fate. In so realistically capturing the most delicate of gestures of her sitters, De Morgan successfully communicates spiritual ideas.

It seems that De Morgan was dissatisfied with her first attempt at creating the angel of death and turned to experimentation with media and colour to develop this deeply personal image, realising the figures in gold on dark wove paper five years later (Figure 1.2) and a second version in oil in 1890 (De Morgan Collection, destroyed by fire in 1991).[9] In this case, the drawing postdates the painting,[10] demonstrating De Morgan's use of certain materials to progress her ideas and fulfil her artistic vision, even if that meant rejecting the generally accepted narrative that an artist should progress from drawing through to painting.

8 Evelyn De Morgan, *Volume 7. No cover Evelyn's childhood verses. Inventory of paintings in Mrs Stirling's possession with locations noted at the very end*, c. 1870, MS_0009, De Morgan Collection Archive, De Morgan Foundation, London, 1–6.

9 Drawing signed and dated 'EP 1885'.

10 A second oil version of this image was made by the artist. The date of *Angel of Death II* is unverifiable, but generally accepted as 1890.

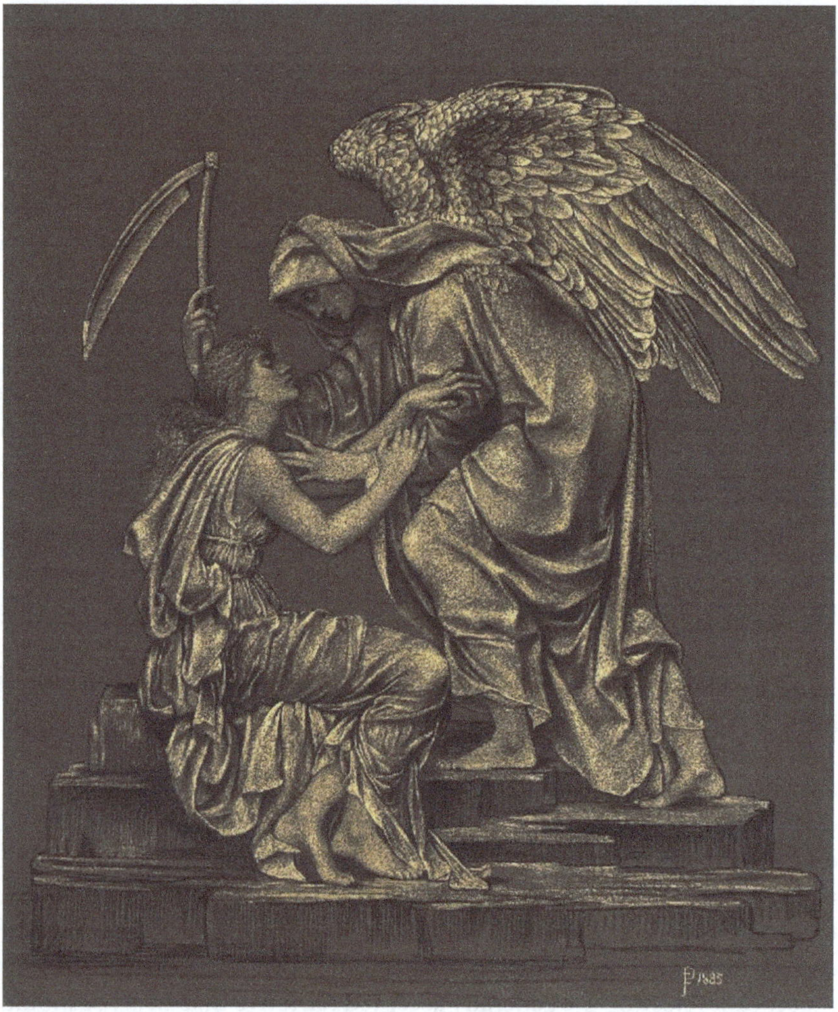

Figure 1.2. Evelyn De Morgan, *Angel of Death*, gold pigment on dark wove paper, 1885, Chicago, Art Institute Chicago © Art Institute Chicago.

Perhaps it was a desire to successfully communicate the importance of these figures that led De Morgan to enshrine them in luminous gold, a colour which she believed to be of the highest spiritual order. Her allegorical picture *The Love Potion* (1903; De Morgan Collection) has been read as one which 'deals with the progress of the soul towards enlightenment'.[11] In it, a chemist mixes her love potion, as a couple seen out of the window of her study embrace. She owns an enviable selection of volumes on the occult, science and philosophy, of which Paracelsus is an important inclusion. Paracelsus believed in the alchemical order of symbolic colours to illustrate the progress of the soul, from black (earthly, of guilt and sin), through red, to gold (salvation). This can be read as lending De Morgan's gold drawing talismanic properties for her own private devotion. She did not intend to sell this drawing, pasting a label on the reverse reading 'The Angel of Death, Not for sale, De Morgan, 1 The Vale, Kings Rd, Chelsea',[12] indicating this vision in gold was one she cherished.

De Morgan's earliest known sketch, *Childhood Watercolour of a Gypsy (female)*, was painted when she was around 13 years old.[13] It shows a confident ability to capture life and manipulate a pose to reveal personality. The girl is depicted leaning on one shoulder on a wall covered with cloth, her tambourine held loosely in her spare hand, as she looks coyly out at the viewer. The pose allows the subject's clothes to stretch diagonally across her body. De Morgan realistically illustrates the appearance of white fabric drenched in sunlight. Her early artistic experimentation and talent was honed through formal art training, providing her with the skills to realise her unique ideas. Although some commentators have reported that De Morgan suffered a lack of support from her upper-class parents in her decision to become an artist,[14] the diary of her father reveals that he employed three tutors for her in 1871 when she was just 15 years old,[15] and ultimately

11 Elise Lawton Smith, *Evelyn De Morgan: Evelyn Pickering De Morgan and the Allegorical Body* (Madison and Teaneck, NJ: Fairleigh Dickinson University Press, 2002), 108.

12 Dominic Winter Auctioneers, Antiques, Antiquities & Textiles, 8 November 2018 (Cirencester: Dominic Winter Auctioneers, 2018), Exhibition Catalogue. <https://www.dominicwinter.co.uk/Auction/Lot/458-De-Morgan-Evelyn-1855-1919/?lot=322825&sd=1>, accessed 30 January 2021.

13 Evelyn De Morgan, *Childhood Watercolour of a Gypsy (female)*, c. 1860s, De Morgan Collection Archive, De Morgan Foundation, London, D_EDM_0088.

14 Wilhelmina Stirling, *William De Morgan and his Wife* (Macmillan: London, 1922).

15 Percival Pickering, *Diary of Percival Pickering QC*, De Morgan Collection Archive, De Morgan Foundation, London, 1871, MS_0382.

allowed her to train at the South Kensington National Art Training School until December 1872, prior to her enrolment at the Slade School of Art in January 1873.

De Morgan attended the Slade School of Art from January 1873 to the 1876/7 academic year,[16] proving herself outstanding when she won the competitive Slade Scholarship in 1874 which waived her fees and awarded her a £50 per year stipend for three years of study. Those submitting themselves for the scholarship examination 'ordeal' had to prove themselves competent in 'elementary knowledge of the English Language and History, of Greek and Roman History, of Ancient and Modern Geography, of Arithmetic, and of a foreign language, to be selected by the Candidate, or of one Book of Euclid',[17] before even being considered for their 'proficiency in drawing, painting, and sculpture'.[18]

In putting herself through such a demanding process in which she would be judged by her peers and superiors alike, De Morgan can be understood as an artist who craved perfection in her craft and sought to be recognised, which might account for her later turn towards the distinctive materials of gold pigment on dark paper, marking her as unique among her peers.

De Morgan continued to excel at the Slade under the instruction of Sir Edward Poynter, a master who rejected the academic method of perfecting the craft of drawing from the antique model in favour of drawing from life. The Slade believed in an interdisciplinary approach to teaching fine art, encouraging its students to take additional classes from other schools at the university, namely geometry, classical archaeology and anatomy.[19] It was in anatomy that De Morgan excelled, creating detailed and accurate scientific studies of sinuous hands and legs in her sketchbook of 1874, now in a private collection. Her meticulous note-taking and detailed diagrams reveal an astute pupil determined to perfect her drawing

16 University College London, *University College London Calendar 1874* (London: Taylor and Francis, 1874), 170.

17 *University College London Calendar 1874*, 170.

18 *University College London Calendar 1874*, 46.

19 *University College London Calendar 1874*, 46.

from life. De Morgan's talent for drawing – rather than painting – the human form is proven by her winning a silver medal for drawing from life in 1876, and the lesser award of a certificate for painting from life in the same year.[20]

At around the same time as De Morgan created her first gold drawing, *Angel of Death*, she opened an account with Charles Roberson of Long Acre, Piccadilly, an artist's colourman and supplier to around 9,000 individual artists between 1820 and 1942, including Burne-Jones and G. F. Watts.[21] De Morgan chiefly purchased canvases and brushes from Roberson and her purchases were sporadic over the years, which strongly suggests she also used other suppliers. She is known to have purchased canvases from other suppliers due to the prolonged periods she spent in Italy, for example. The canvas for her masterpiece *Flora* (1894; De Morgan Collection) was purchased from an Italian supplier, evidenced in the 'sprigging' holding the canvas to the stretcher, a method particular to Italian suppliers.[22] What she did favour Roberson for was his well-known willingness to work with the customer on experimental materials for specific projects.[23] For example, in June 1902, De Morgan was charged by Roberson for his 'specially preparing [a] piece of open canvas with paraffin wax at back and plaster of Paris ground surface [and] experiments with same on stret[cher]'.[24] The unstretched canvas potentially became her painting *The Cadence of Autumn* (1905; De Morgan Collection), which has an 'inherent weakness in bond at the interface of the priming and the paint

20 *University College London Calendar 1874*, 170.

21 The Roberson Archive, Hamilton Kerr Institute, Cambridge.

22 Bent tacks which hold the canvas to the wooden frame.

23 Kirsty Sinclair Dootson explores Watts's relationship with Roberson in her recent publication: Kirsty Sinclair Dootson, 'The Texture of Capitalism: Industrial Oil Colours and the Politics of Paint in the Work of G. F. Watts', *British Art Studies*, Issue 14, <https://doi.org/10.17658/issn.2058-5462/issue-14/kdootson>; Fiona Mann discusses Burne-Jones's relationship with the same supplier in '"Opaque with a vengeance": Burne-Jones's later watercolours, 1880–98', *The Burlington Magazine* 161/1391 (February 2019), 128–39.

24 *Sales Ledger for William De Morgan*, 1900–1904, 133 193-4a, The Roberson Archive, Hamilton Kerr Institute, Cambridge.

layer', which has been identified through examination as 'an absorbent gesso type', which could be the plaster of Paris ground surface prepared for De Morgan by Roberson.[25]

It was no wonder, then, that De Morgan enlisted Roberson's help to realise her visions in gold. Between 1891 and 1916, De Morgan made seven purchases from Roberson's for a 'cake of gold', four of these being between 1896 and 1899 when at least five of the drawings were made. Since her first purchase of a 'cake of gold' recorded in the ledger postdates her earliest dated gold drawing by some sixteen years, it can be assumed that she also bought this material from other suppliers. This record, however, is important for understanding De Morgan's method for making her gold drawings, as it documents the particular material she used. A 'cake' was a dry pellet of pigment prepared by Roberson's and offered for sale as an alternative to their 'moist' paints, which were advertised to artists who might wish to sketch on the move (made available 'in Japaned boxes for the pocket').[26]

One of De Morgan's most accomplished gold drawings is *Gloria in Excelsis* (c. 1895; Figure 1.3). She sketched the outline and rendered some of the darker areas of shadow in Conté crayon,[27] creating an ambitious arrangement of thirteen winged seraphim, executed in minute detail, presiding over two angels in billowing drapery. This gold drawing is noteworthy for the three distinct applications of the gold pigment to achieve varying textures and visual effects.

25 Carol Willoughby, Paintings Condition Report for *The Cadence of Autumn*, 2009, De Morgan Collection Records, De Morgan Foundation, London.

26 'Advertisement for Charles Roberson & Co.', *Home News for India, China and the Colonies*, 7 July 1847, 401.

27 These were purchased from Roberson's by De Morgan at the same time as she bought a cake of gold on four occasions, suggesting they were bought to be used together on the same pieces.

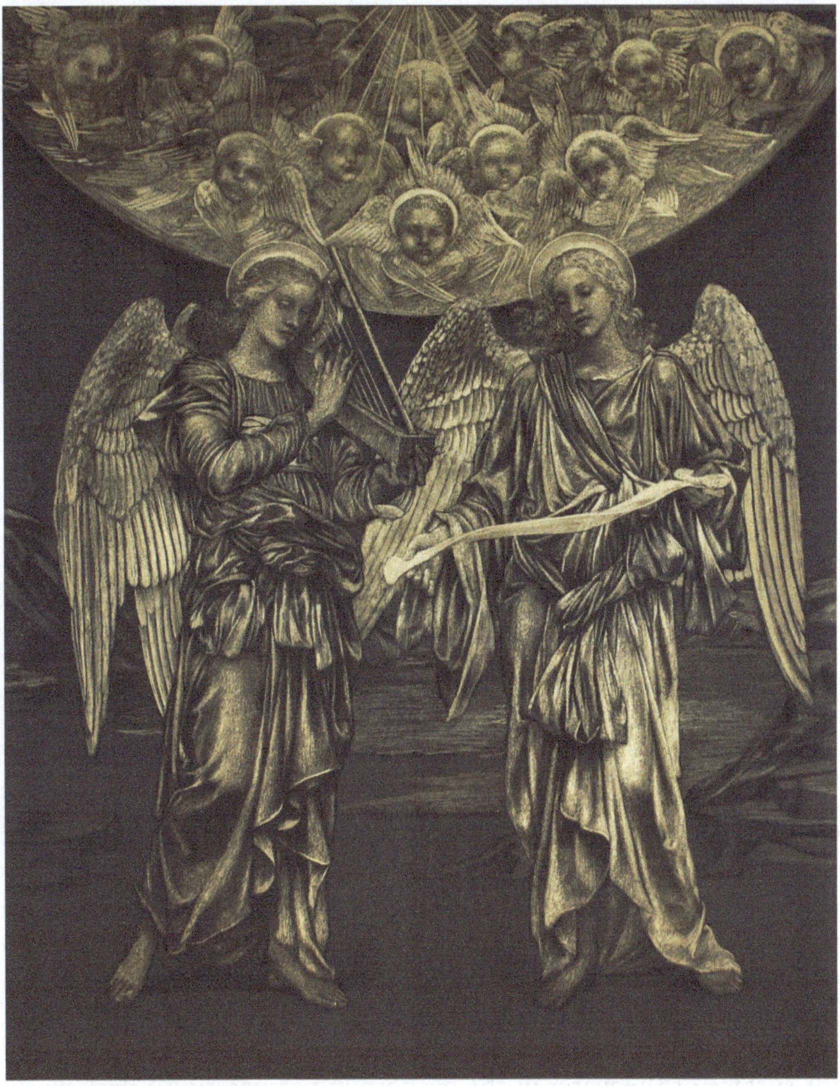

Figure 1.3. Evelyn De Morgan, *Gloria in Excelsis*, gold pigment on dark wove paper, c. 1895, London, De Morgan Foundation © De Morgan Collection, courtesy of De Morgan Foundation.

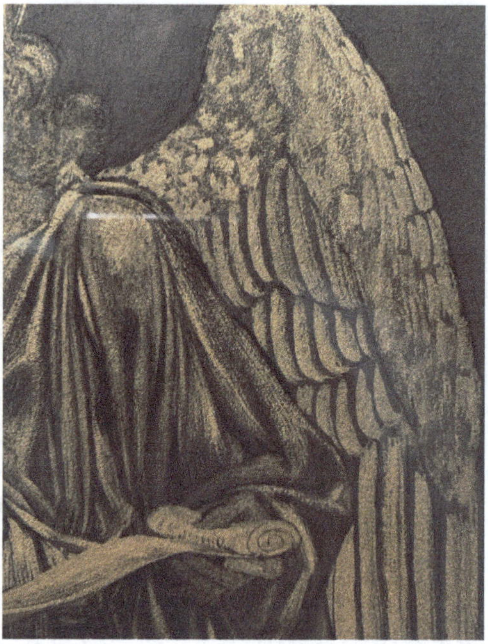

Figure 1.4. Detail of Evelyn De Morgan, *Gloria in Excelsis*, gold pigment on dark wove paper, c. 1895, London, De Morgan Foundation © Sarah Hardy, 2019.

One angel holds a scroll, most likely 'The Gloria' – the very word of God announcing the birth of Christ to the shepherds. For this most sacred element of the drawing, De Morgan ground the cake of gold into a thick paste with a binding agent, most likely gum Arabic, to form a gouache-like paint which she deftly applied in long singular strokes to give the illusion of single feathers in the angels' wings (Figure 1.4).

De Morgan used this same thick gouache applied with a much thinner brush in regular hatched lines across some of the rocks and the surface of the water in the background, suggesting a dark world gently warmed in the glow of the ethereal beings and the glad tidings they bring. In other areas, such as the angels' hair and the seraphim's fluffy wings, De Morgan diluted the gold gouache and applied it with a hard brush in a scratching motion before adding minute details in

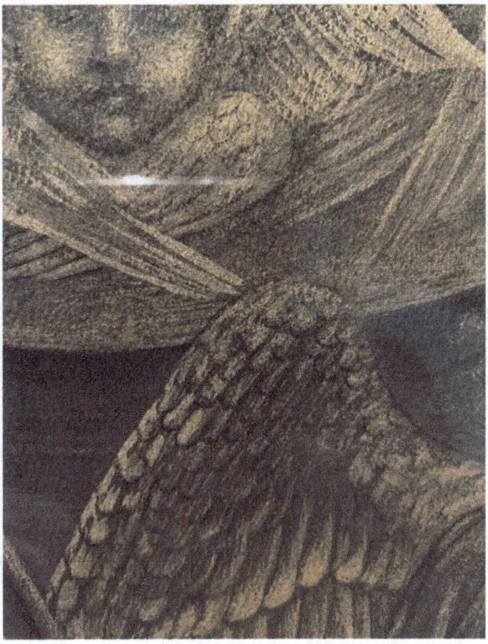

Figure 1.5. Detail of Evelyn De Morgan, *Gloria in Excelsis*, gold pigment on dark wove paper, c. 1895, London, De Morgan Foundation © Sarah Hardy, 2019.

black Conté crayon, which gives movement and realism to the scene (Figure 1.5).

Prior to painting the highlights, De Morgan moulded the round, fleshy faces of the seraphim and folds of fabric almost as though sculpting the figures from the paper. In order to do this, she most likely made her own crayon, or soft, brittle solid, from the dry pigment. She has burnished the gold lightly in areas which appear deeper, and harder – creating a brighter gold – for the protruding features. Burnishing adds texture to the drawing, as the mottled surface of the paper becomes smooth during the rubbing process and so takes a more uniform layer of gold pigment than the textured surface of the paper normally would. This yields a particularly realistic effect in the downy feathers of the angels' wings. De Morgan also experimented with burnishing in at least two of her paintings: *In Memoriam* (c. 1900; De Morgan Collection) and *The Waters of Babylon* (1883; De Morgan Collection). She probably used a gilder's burnisher to burnish the faces in these paintings, creating a realistic appearance of smooth skin. An undeliberate consequence is that the pressure on the canvas caused a 'quilting' effect which gives a sculptural texture to the faces.[28]

The burnishing method in *Gloria in Excelsis* has also revealed the watermark of Canson and Montgolfier on the paper. This French manufacturer was popular with Burne-Jones, who favoured their distinct terracotta-coloured paper,[29] and with Edgar Degas, who appreciated the smooth texture of the wove paper in preparing pastels.[30] Of De Morgan's gold drawings, *Gloria in Excelsis* is the only one in which the paper has been identifiable. It has a distinct, rather cold, deep grey tint, whereas the others in this series are executed on a warmer brown paper, probably the 'brown cartoon paper' which De Morgan bought from Roberson's.[31] The heavier Canson and Montgolfier paper lends itself well to the gold material; *Gloria* is more successful than the other gold drawings which lack its subtle depth.

Four in the series of gold drawings include the use of additional colours for dramatic effect (*The Valley of Shadows*, *Opes*, *Soul's Prison House* and *The Light Shineth in the Darkness*). *The Valley of Shadows* (c. 1899; Figure 1.6) suggests the influence of Mantegna's trompe-l'oeil paintings which imitate marble friezes. De Morgan is known to have copied from paintings at the National Gallery; her study of Catena's *Saint Jerome* is notable for its colour and likeness to the original.[32] She

28 Carol Willoughby, Paintings Condition Report for 'The Waters of Babylon', 2014, De Morgan Collection Records, De Morgan Foundation, London

29 Fiona Mann, '"Opaque with a vengeance": Burne-Jones's later watercolours, 1880–98', *The Burlington Magazine* 161/1391 (February 2019), 131.

30 Edgar Degas, *Deux Danseuses (Two Dancers)*, pastel on Montgolfier vellum paper, 1883–98, Chicago, Art Institute Chicago.

31 *Sales Ledger for William De Morgan*, June 1896–October 1898, 121–71, The Roberson Archive, Hamilton Kerr Institute, Cambridge.

32 Evelyn De Morgan, *Study after Catena St Jerome*, c. 1870, De Morgan Collection, destroyed by fire in 1991.

would have seen Mantegna's *The Introduction of the Cult of Cybele at Rome* (1505–6) which was purchased by the Gallery in 1873,[33] just as De Morgan began at the Slade. The Mantegna features monochrome figures, looking as if carved from stone, arranged across a landscape panel decorated to imitate marble. The dramatic stance and arrangement of robed figures in various groupings around a central procession of the Goddess Cybele are clearly recalled in the colours and compositions of De Morgan's gold drawings. *The Valley of Shadows* is a complex allegory in which a rugged landscape brims with fourteen draped figures in active poses, picked out in gold and black Conté crayon. De Morgan has set them across the landscape, under a red and pink chalk sky suggesting the marble of Mantegna.

Saint Francis and Holy Poverty (Figure 1.7, 1902; De Morgan Collection) is the last in De Morgan's series of gold drawings. In it, Saint Francis rejects material wealth to metaphorically marry the personified form of poverty under a crucifix. Christ's limp body hangs on the cross from the nails through his hands with weighty realism. De Morgan accurately captures the pull of his muscles and his lolling, heavy head, proving an ability to render life and death and to manipulate the most challenging materials to create movement and record gesture in her figures. In this case, the drawing is more successful for its realistic depiction of the figures than the oil of the same scene (1902; De Morgan Collection, destroyed by fire in 1991), in which Christ is rendered more as a monument than a body at the end of its life.

33 Andrea Mantegna *The Introduction of the Cult of Cybele at Rome*, oil on panel, 1505–6, London, National Gallery, NG902.

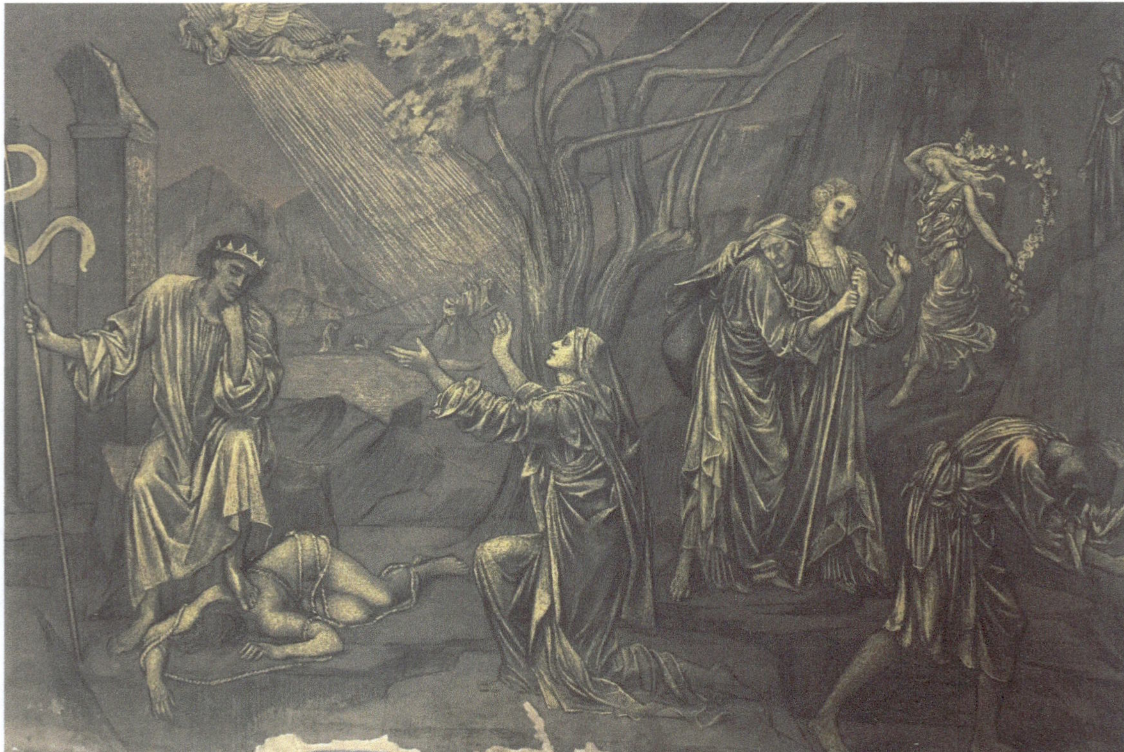

Figure 1.6. Evelyn De Morgan, *Valley of Shadows*, gold pigment on dark wove paper, c. 1899, London, De Morgan Foundation © De Morgan Collection, courtesy of De Morgan Foundation.

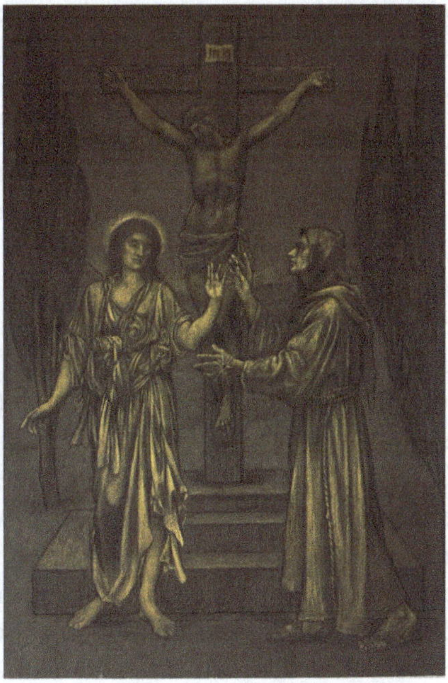

Figure 1.7. Evelyn De Morgan, *Saint Francis and Holy Poverty*, gold pigment on dark wove paper, 1902, London, De Morgan Foundation © De Morgan Collection, courtesy of De Morgan Foundation.

The Midas Touch: De Morgan's Success across Artistic Media

Four of the gold drawings are dated and initialled, showing these were made over seventeen years between 1885 (*The Angel of Death*) and 1902 (*St Francis and Holy Poverty*), a period during which De Morgan excelled at experimental media.

The start of De Morgan's experimental period could be due, in part, to the extended time she spent working with John Roddam Spencer Stanhope in 1883. Her maternal uncle and a close ally to the Pre-Raphaelites, as a pupil of G. F. Watts and friend to Burne-Jones, Spencer Stanhope had an innovative approach to painting which he encouraged his niece to uphold.

Love and the Maiden (1877) had long been considered Spencer Stanhope's highest achievement in the British tempera revival.[34] He was an artist of the forefront of this media and founded the Society of Painters in Tempera in 1901. However, recent scientific analysis of the painting did not detect any egg protein in the paint, revealing this picture to be crafted in oil on paper adhered to board. Spencer Stanhope thus successfully mimicked tempera painting in a method of his own invention, in which he 'built up his composition in many layers. He first drew with fluid brown paint, then sculpturally under modelled with thick white paint, and finally painted each compositional element in color [*sic*].'[35]

Evelyn De Morgan's depiction of *The Salutation* (1883; De Morgan Collection) – the Biblical story in which the Virgin Mary and Saint Elizabeth become pregnant with Christ and John the Baptist – has the same chalky aesthetic of a Renaissance fresco as *Love and the Maiden* and was painted at a time when De Morgan was in regular contact with Spencer Stanhope. A conservation assessment and recent treatment to the flaking paint on the painting's surface revealed that layers of oil paint had been applied to a particularly absorbent base layer added by the artist to soak up the glossiness of the oil,[36] leading the paint to become dry and brittle.[37] It is possible that De Morgan and Spencer Stanhope discussed methods for replicating the beauty they saw in fresco and tempera using alternative modern materials.

De Morgan spent the Christmas of 1883 at her mother's ancestral home, Cannon Hall in Cawthorne, South Yorkshire, upon the invitation of her uncle and John Roddam's brother, Sir Walter Spencer Stanhope.[38]

34 John Roddam Spencer Stanhope, *Love and the Maiden*, oil on canvas, 1877, The Fine Arts Museum San Francisco.

35 Elise Effmann Clifford, 'Behind Truth and Beauty: Paintings Conservation', Legion of Honor, <https://legionofhonor.famsf.org/behind-truth-and-beauty-paintings-conservation>, accessed January 2021.

36 It is possible that the paint is not oil. Without scientific testing, it is impossible to identify the medium with certainty.

37 Carol Willoughby, Paintings Condition Report for *The Salutation*, De Morgan Collection Records, De Morgan Foundation, London.

38 Wilhelmina Stirling, *Mrs Stirling's journal dated 1883–4. Black soft cover*, 1871, De Morgan Collection Archive, De Morgan Foundation, London, MS_0387.

Although she had before spent Christmas away from the family's London home at 48 Bryanston Square, this Christmas there was special occasion to be in Cawthorne. The Spencer Stanhope family had paid for the renovation of the All Saints' church by Arts and Crafts architect G. F. Bodley, under the artistic direction of John Roddam Spencer Stanhope. De Morgan had been engaged by her uncle to create organ panels for the new church interior scheme, which were unveiled on Christmas Eve 1883.[39]

These panels mark De Morgan's first departure from fine art to craft and her first use of gold as a material. Each organ panel features an angel in classic drapery with symmetrical feathered wings clutching a shield emblazoned with an attribute of one of the four Evangelists: Matthew, Mark, Luke and John. The angels are painted in oil on panel prepared with a gesso ground, giving a pastel, chalky finish to the colours. The attributes have been shaped under the gesso, possibly using a build-up of other materials, or simply carved out of the gesso and panel. These and the backgrounds have been coloured with gold leaf, burnished to ensure a dazzling, long-lasting brilliance. De Morgan finished the individual backgrounds with unique schemes of repeat patterns, applied by punching the gold surface with tiny, repeated indents. The panels were fitted into two wooden structures decorated in reds, blues and greens to flank the organ in a church with decorative interior schemes and windows by Spencer Stanhope and by Morris & Co., placing her artwork at the centre of the Arts and Crafts movement within this Cawthorne church.

De Morgan's meeting with her future husband William De Morgan at Walter Bagehot's fancy dress ball in August of 1883 might have been the catalyst for her to consider artistic options beyond the canvas and encourage her pursuit of craftwork as a viable route.[40] William De Morgan, seventeen years her senior, was an experimental artist and craftsman working as a designer of ceramics when the couple met. He had come to this career through the fine arts, taking lessons at Cary's Drawing Academy before entering the

39 Cawthorne Parish Council, *Cawthorne Parish Council Magazine*, January 1884.

40 Emilie Russell-Barrington, *Unpublished manuscript of 'William De Morgan: The Potter As I Knew Him'*, c. 1930, MS_0047, De Morgan Collection Archive, De Morgan Foundation, London, 36.

Royal Academy Schools in 1859. In 1863, upon meeting William Morris, he changed direction to a career as a designer and craftsman, enjoying a successful period working in stained glass providing designs for Morris & Co., Powell & Sons and J. T. Lyon.[41]

William De Morgan had only ever submitted one oil painting to the Royal Academy Exhibition: *Head of a Girl* (1865; De Morgan Collection). Although the surface of the painting has a glossy finish, the varnish layer is thin and matte areas are visible, suggesting that an additional material was used. The reverse of the canvas is stained, again suggesting a method other than traditional oil on canvas. The physical marks of its creation are directly comparable with Evelyn De Morgan's painting *The Soul's Prison House* (1888), which her letters reveal was made in an innovative method of her husband's creation which they called 'the process'.[42] It is probable that William De Morgan invented this method for his own painting and encouraged his wife to attempt it twenty years later. Evelyn De Morgan described the method in a letter to its first owner, Thomas Brocklebank: 'The colours were ground in glycerine and spirit which, of course, never dried. When finished, the glycerine was sucked out by a sort of poultice on the back on the picture, and the picture was finished with transparent oil-colour.'[43] Despite De Morgan having more success at 'the process' than her husband, this painting being largely indistinguishable from her other oils, particularly in terms of its structure, colouring and stability,[44] De Morgan only made two paintings in this way,[45]later describing it as a 'ticklish business'.[46]

41 William Waters and Alastair Carew Cox, *Saints and Symbols* (Abbots Morton: Seraphim Press, 2020), 128–203.

42 Evelyn De Morgan in a letter to Thomas Brocklebank, 7 February 1911, in *Evelyn De Morgan: Oil Paintings*, ed. Catherine Gordon (London: De Morgan Foundation, 1996), 18–19.

43 Letter to Brocklebank in *Evelyn De Morgan*, ed. Gordon, 18–19

44 Carol Willoughby, De Morgan Foundation Conservator, in conversation, 2020.

45 Letter to Thomas Brocklebank, 7 February 1911, in Gordon, *Evelyn De Morgan: Oil Paintings*, 18–19. The artist stated that the other is *Clytie* (1885), now in a private collection.

46 Evelyn De Morgan, *Letter to May Morris*, 1917, 45347, British Library, London.

In around 1884, De Morgan took on the lease of Studio 8 at the purpose-built block of artists' accommodation at Trafalgar Studios, Manresa Road, Chelsea.[47] This was among the first of its kind in an area in which the artists' studio became popular, leading to Chelsea being considered an artistic hub in London with nine in every thousand men being listed as an artist by 1921.[48] What drove De Morgan to depart from the large family home of which she had almost exclusive use to work in a communal building of fourteen other studios which served a dual purpose as homes for most residents is undocumented, but it was potentially due to having met William De Morgan, whose home and business was in Cheyne Row, Chelsea.[49] As well as painters John Percy Cook and Nelson Dawson, De Morgan worked at Trafalgar Studios alongside the sculptor Albert Toft. Toft's elegant bronze figures arranged in effortless, delicate poses somehow recall De Morgan's arrangement of figures in some of her paintings, such as *Phosphorus and Hesperus* (1881; De Morgan Collection). It is possible that her connections at Trafalgar Studios had made De Morgan aware of the potential of sculpture and piqued her interest in the medium. She submitted her bronze *Head of Medusa* to the Arts and Crafts Exhibition Society's first exhibition at the New Gallery in 1888, adding another artform to her impressive portfolio.[50]

Although other commissions and artists had perhaps nudged De Morgan towards experimentation with gold drawings, it was most likely the example of Edward Burne-Jones which first attracted her attention and intrigued her to develop her own. Indeed, De Morgan and Burne-Jones are the only two artists from this period who are known to have created these

47 *Sales Ledger for Evelyn Pickering, 1884*, 110–1993. 449, The Roberson Archive, Hamilton Kerr Institute, Cambridge.

48 Giles Walkley, *Artists' Houses in London 1764–1914* (Hampshire: Scolar Press, 1994), 86.

49 De Morgan's address on her marriage certificate of 1887 is the family home at 48 Bryanston Square, suggesting she did not live at Trafalgar Studios but had it solely as a work-space.

50 Number 256, First Exhibition of Arts & Crafts Exhibition Society, The New Gallery, 121 Regent St., London, 1888 (now in a private collection).

distinct gold drawings. Burne-Jones had been fascinated with producing bright gold on dark paper since the book dealer Bernard Quaritch had enlightened him with illuminated manuscripts, and he became actively interested in Byzantine design through his travels in Italy.[51] He worked in this technique from as early as 1862, gradually coming to gild everything from pianos to his ambitious *Perseus Series* of mixed-media murals for Arthur Balfour in the 1890s.[52] Whilst working on this large series, and *The Sleep of Arthur in Avalon*, he took breaks in the form of a return to his stunningly simple gold works on dark paper.[53]

Burne-Jones had been a close associate of Spencer Stanhope since the late 1850s, when the two had worked together on the Oxford Union murals. They had remained in contact, Burne-Jones being one of the first invited to Spencer Stanhope's new home, Villa Nuti, in Florence in 1873.[54] This was the same year in which the ambitious young Slade student Evelyn De Morgan also visited her uncle at Villa Nuti, and possibly the first time she met Burne-Jones.

It seems De Morgan strove to impress Burne-Jones, taking portfolios to his studio for him to opine on. Rather than nurture her talent, Burne-Jones was supposedly 'particularly frightened' of De Morgan, calling her 'a plain lady whom I never look at when I talk to'.[55] Nevertheless, De Morgan maintained a close association with Burne-Jones stylistically, seeking to visit his exhibitions where possible, and applying herself to develop his novel methods.[56] While Burne-Jones's gold drawings were intended as intimate

51 Samantha Timm, 'Illuminated in Gilt: Byzantium and Gold in the Later Watercolours of Edward Burne-Jones', 'Reassessing Burne-Jones' conference, Ashmolean Museum, Oxford, 21–22 February 2019.

52 Numbers 1–14, Christie, Manson & Woods, *Remaining Works of That Eminent Painter, Sir Edward Burne-Jones* (London: Christie, Manson & Woods, 1898), 8.

53 Timm, 'Illuminated in Gilt'.

54 Wilhelmina Stirling, *A Painter of Dreams and Other Biographical Studies* (London: John Lane, 1916), 338.

55 Thomas Rooke as quoted by Penelope Fitzgerald, *Edward Burne-Jones* (revised edition, London: Harper Collins, 2014), 203.

56 Russell-Barrington, 'William De Morgan', 48.

studies for figures in his paintings,[57] and an opportunity to experiment with materials,[58] De Morgan seems to have developed the method as an end in itself, to produce highly finished attractive arrangements of allegorical figures in landscapes.

Her allegorical work *Mercy and Truth Have Met Together, Righteousness and Peace Have Kissed Each Other* (1896; Figure 1.8) is the largest and among the most ambitious of De Morgan's gold drawings. The four fractions of human emotive action taken from Psalm 85:10 have been transformed into confident, assured women by De Morgan. Each is posed in the gesture and with the attributes of her namesake; Truth with her mirror and palm leaf

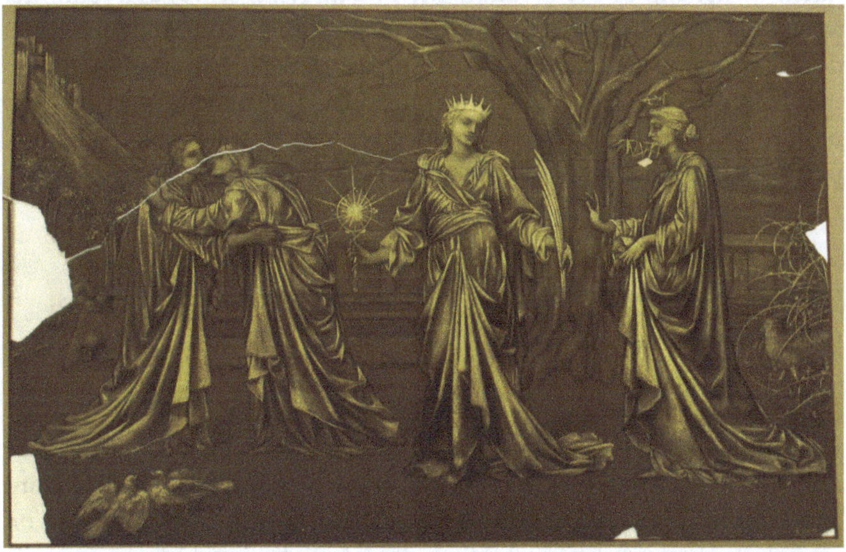

Figure 1.8. Evelyn De Morgan, *Mercy and Truth Have Met Together, Righteousness and Peace Have Kissed Each Other*, gold pigment on dark wove paper, 1896, London, De Morgan Foundation © De Morgan Collection, courtesy of De Morgan Foundation.

57 Edward Burne-Jones, *A Woman Playing a Cithara*, gold pigment on dark paper, 1896, Tate Gallery, London, N05175.

58 Roberson's named several art materials after Burne-Jones which had been developed by the artist. De Morgan purchased items such as 'Burne-Jones Sketchbook'.

dominates the space, outshining the others in a bold statement about the power of veracity. This is one of only four of the drawings which De Morgan deftly initialled and dated in vivid gold in the lower right corner: 'E De M 1896'. In April 1896, an exhibition of Burne-Jones's drawings was held at the Fine Art Society in Bond Street, where his *Sketch in Gold* was hailed as demonstrating the 'ceaseless experimentation of the master'.[59]

De Morgan's Truth holds up her mirror's surface to the viewer. It reflects blinding gold. De Morgan's reason for choosing this relatively unknown Psalm for an 1898 oil painting has puzzled art historians,[60] but considering the clearly and deliberately dated drawing as a direct response to Burne-Jones's exhibition of his gold drawings reflects De Morgan's confident ownership of the medium. *Mercy and Truth* serves as a reminder to all that she first exhibited gold drawings at the Bond Street Gallery a decade earlier, and Burne-Jones's attempts are mere reflections. Burne-Jones may have noticed this arresting drawing on a visit to De Morgan's studio months later, perhaps accounting for his bitter review of her paintings, particularly her handling of the human form.[61]

Glowing Reviews: The Critical Reception of De Morgan's Gold Drawings

De Morgan's experimentation across media shows that she opposed the traditional academic hierarchy of the arts which asserted that oil paint and sculpture were superior to craft. In addition to working in oil on canvas, she perfected her art in a range of media, working successfully

59 Catalogue number 136; 'Sir Edward Burne-Jones' Studies', *Glasgow Herald* (13 April 1896), 9.

60 Patricia Yates, 'Evelyn De Morgan's Use of Literary Sources in her Paintings', in Gordon, *Evelyn De Morgan*, 64.

61 Thomas Rooke, *Burne-Jones Talking: His Conversations 1895–1898 Preserved by his Studio Assistant Thomas Rooke,* ed. Mary Lago (London: John Murray, 1982) 148–50.

in gesso, watercolour, pastel, bronze and stained-glass designs, in addition to her drawings in gold. She never submitted paintings to the outdated Royal Academy, which conservatively maintained the supremacy of 'high art', exhibiting instead at the avant-garde Grosvenor Gallery, at the Royal Institute of Painters in Watercolours and with the Arts and Crafts Exhibition Society.

In 1907, De Morgan became a founder member of May Morris's Women's Guild of Arts,[62] a society formed by women art workers of the Arts and Crafts Movement who were rejected from the elitist and male-dominated Art Workers Guild on the basis of their gender. Her allegiance to such a group aligned her with professional women art workers who determinedly set about proving the place of their art not just amongst their male peers, but in an art world which viewed craft as second rate.[63]

Against these tensions in the art world, De Morgan exhibited seven of her seventeen gold drawings at the Fine Arts Society exhibition in 1889. A contemporary review cites the drawings simply as studies for paintings. De Morgan affixed labels on the reverse of her drawings with her name and address and advertising them for sale (or not, in the case of *Angel of Death*), making her view on the matter clear: her gold drawings were works of art in their own right. She had a working knowledge of the art market and some business acumen, advertising these drawings for sale for £15,[64] while her painting *Love the Misleader* sold for £55 in the same year.[65]

The second most comprehensive show of De Morgan's gold drawings was in an exhibition at Leighton House in 1919 held to commemorate her recent passing. The exhibition was organised by the artist's friend Emilie Russell-Barrington and drew from her collection as well as that of De Morgan's brother Spencer Pickering. Four gold drawings were a highlight of this exhibition, noted in the catalogue for the extreme skill required to create them. The author assures us that 'in this process no erasures can ever

62 *List of Actual Signatures of Authorised Names for the Roll*, 1912 (?), Women's Guild of Arts Archive, William Morris Society, Hammersmith archive.

63 Zoe Thomas, *Women Art Workers of the Arts and Crafts Movement* (Manchester: Manchester University Press, 2020).

64 Label pasted on reverse of *Lux in Tenebris*.

65 Gordon, *Evelyn De Morgan*, 29.

be made. The artist has to do each stroke correctly in the first instance',[66] recalling the method employed by the Renaissance masters De Morgan hero-worshipped in their application of egg tempera paint, and explaining the long brushstroke feathers in *Gloria in Excelsis*. It is interesting to note that Russell-Barrington lists the present location of each painting corresponding to the gold drawings on display, referring to the painting as 'the original of this drawing',[67] implying that at this time the gold drawings were understood to have been created after the paintings, as unique artworks in their own right.

Modern interpreters have begun to appreciate the artistic merit of De Morgan's gold drawings. Mark Bills' essay of 1997 is the most comprehensive study of De Morgan's drawings to date, and her gold drawing *The Valley of Shadows* provides the lead image for his article. Bills alludes to the calibre of this drawing:

> The quality of these drawings is exceptional and they appear as finished works with their completed compositions in gleaming golds and silvers. In the case of this picture [*The Valley of Shadows*] the majority of figures are identical to the finished painting. Some background figures, however, are completely different and the tree in the drawing is not present in the painting. It appears, in this case at least, that the drawing was produced before the painting.[68]

Hero and Leander and *Opes* (Figure 1.9) were produced independently of any known oil painting. A watercolour version of *Hero and Leander* is extant but no painting by the name *Opes* was known to have been exhibited in De Morgan's lifetime,[69] left in her studio at the time of her death,[70] or to have emerged on the open market in recent years. *Hero and Leander* was given by the artist to Audrey Bulwer, a family friend of the Spencer Stanhopes, upon her marriage in 1912 to celebrated Scottish neurologist

66 *Catalogue of Pictures by the Late Evelyn Pickering De Morgan*, 1919, Leighton House Museum, London, LH/7/1/3/1, 14–15.

67 Leighton House, *Catalogue of Pictures*, 14–15.

68 Mark Bills, 'The Drawings of Evelyn De Morgan', *Antiques Collecting Magazine* (March 1997), 22.

69 *Evelyn De Morgan*, ed. Gordon, 28–31.

70 The Last Will and Testament of Evelyn De Morgan, 1919.

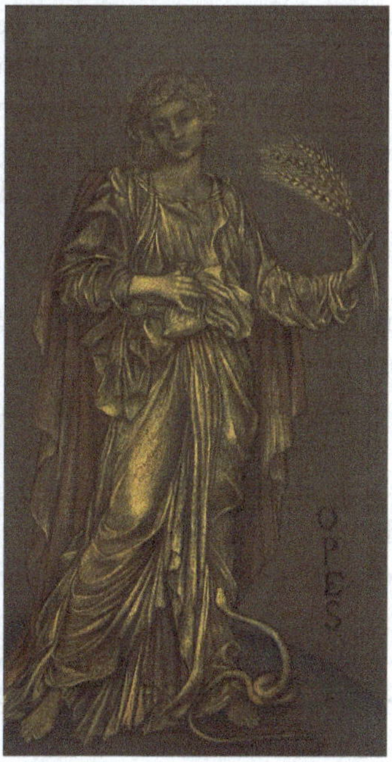

Figure 1.9. Evelyn De Morgan, *Opes,* gold pigment on dark wove paper, c. 1895, London, De Morgan Foundation © De Morgan Collection, courtesy of De Morgan Foundation.

James Crichton-Browne. The unwavering devotion of Leander to Hero led her to wait for his ship to come in each night and to be devastated when at last he came no more. This delicate study of eternal love in beautiful gold seems a fitting wedding gift and was treasured by the Crichton-Brownes in their lifetime before it was returned to the De Morgan Collection as a bequest.

Opes is completely unique among the gold drawings. The fertility deity does not appear to have been conceived by De Morgan as an oil painting or in any other medium. The artist has given the goddess a red cloak and positioned her as Mother Earth atop a blue planet in cool pastel hues not found in any other gold drawing. She is clearly identifiable, clutching at plentiful ears of corn and a bag of gold, but De Morgan has included the inscription 'OPES' vertically in the bottom right-hand corner to ensure that we are in no doubt as to who the drawing depicts, a feature lacking in all De Morgan's other artworks. It is tempting to think that an oil may one day resurface, but based on the evidence presented, it is more likely that this was one of the last gold drawings De Morgan made. Perhaps it reveals a longing seldom discussed of her personal life: the fact that she perhaps wanted but could not have children. This mysterious depiction of fertility in the gold De Morgan saw as of the highest order is perhaps the finale in a series which began with the *Angel of Death* and represented another private, talismanic work to the artist.

De Morgan did create a vast body of preparatory work for each of her oil paintings,[71] but the gold drawings with their singular beauty stand apart and, as I have argued, should not be counted in this number. Rather, they should be considered as outstanding artworks in their own right, which attest to De Morgan's perseverance and determination as a pupil at the Slade School of Art, her wide interest in the arts regardless of their perceived hierarchical position in the art world, and her commitment to experimentation in a range of media to develop her skillset and produce outstanding artworks.

Bibliography

Bills, Mark, 'The Drawings of Evelyn De Morgan', *Antiques Collecting Magazine* (March 1997), 22–6.

Cawthorne Parish Council, *Cawthorne Parish Council Magazine* (Cawthorne: Cawthorne Parish Council, 1884).

Christie, Manson & Woods, *Remaining Works of that Eminent Painter, Sir Edward Burne-Jones* (London: Christie, Manson & Woods, 1898).

De Morgan, Evelyn, *Volume 7. No Cover Evelyn's Childhood verses. Inventory of Paintings in Mrs Stirling's Possession with Locations Noted at the Very End*, c. 1870, MS_0009, De Morgan Collection Archive, De Morgan Foundation, London.

71 The De Morgan Foundation archive alone has over 800.

Dominic Winter Auctioneers, 'Antiques, Antiquities & Textiles, 8th November 2018' (Cirencester: Dominic Winter Auctioneers, 2018), Exhibition Catalogue, <https://www.dominicwinter.co.uk/Auction/Lot/458-De-Morgan-Evelyn-1855-1919/?lot=322825&sd=1>, accessed 30 January 2021.

Effmann Clifford, Elsie 'Behind Truth and Beauty: Paintings Conservation,' Legion of Honor (2018), <https://legionofhonor.famsf.org/behind-truth-and-beauty-paintings-conservation>, accessed 30 January 2021.

Fitzgerald, Penelope, *Edward Burne-Jones* (London: Harper Collins, 2014).

Gilbert, Philip, ed., 'Art Chronicle', *The Portfolio* (1889).

Glasgow Herald, 'Sir Edward Burne-Jones' Studies', *Glasgow* (13 April 1896).

Gordon, Catherine, ed., *Evelyn De Morgan: Oil Paintings* (London: De Morgan Foundation, 1996).

Home News for India, China and the Colonies, *Advertisement for Roberson's & Co.* (Wednesday 07 July 1847).

Mann, Fiona, '"Opaque with a vengeance": Burne-Jones's Later Watercolours, 1880–98', *The Burlington Magazine* (February 2019).

Pickering, Percival, *Diary of Percival Pickering QC*, 1871, MS_0382, De Morgan Collection Archive, De Morgan Foundation, London.

The Roberson Archive, *Sales Ledger for William De Morgan* (1900–1904), 133 193–4a, Hamilton Kerr Institute, Cambridge.

Russell-Barrington, Emilie, *Unpublished manuscript of 'William De Morgan: The Potter As I Knew Him'*, c. 1930, MS_0047, De Morgan Collection Archive, De Morgan Foundation, London.

Sinclair Dootson, Kirsty, 'The Texture of Capitalism: Industrial Oil Colours and the Politics of Paint in the Work of G. F. Watts', *British Art Studies* (2020), <https://doi.org/10.17658/issn.2058-5462/issue-14/kdootson>, 30 January 2021.

Stirling, A. M. W. D., *A Painter of Dreams and Other Biographical Studies* (London: John Lane, 1916).

——, *Mrs Stirling's Journal Dated 1883–4. Black Soft Cover*, 1871, MS_0387, De Morgan Collection Archive, De Morgan Foundation, London.

——, *William De Morgan and his Wife* (London: Macmillan, 1922).

Timm, Samantha, *Illuminated in Gilt: Byzantium and Gold in the Later Watercolours of Edward Burne-Jones*, Reassessing Burne-Jones Conference, Ashmolean Museum, Oxford, 21–22 February 2019.

Thomas, Zoe, *Women Art Workers of the Arts and Crafts Movement* (Manchester: Manchester University Press, 2020).

University College London, *University College London Calendar 1874* (London: Taylor and Francis, 1874).

Walkley, Giles, *Artists' Houses in London* (Hampshire: Scholar Press, 1994).

Waters, William and Carew Cox, Alastair, *Saints and Symbols* (Abbots Morton: Seraphim Press, 2020).

Willoughby, Carol, *Paintings Condition Report for 'The Cadence of Autumn'*, 2009, De Morgan Collection Records, De Morgan Foundation, London.

——, *Paintings Condition Report for 'The Salutation'*, 2014, De Morgan Collection Records, De Morgan Foundation, London.

——, *Paintings Condition Report for 'The Waters of Babylon'*, 2014, De Morgan Collection Records, De Morgan Foundation, London.

CHRISTIN NEUBAUER

2 New Woman in Disguise: The Art of Eleanor Fortescue-Brickdale and the Woman Question at the Fin de Siècle

ABSTRACT
The long-overlooked Pre-Raphaelite artist of the third generation Eleanor Fortescue-Brickdale was a successful painter and illustrator at the transition from the Victorian to the Edwardian era.[1] Brickdale's life coincided with remarkable shifts in the Victorian understanding of gender roles, such as the emergence of the 'New Woman' and suffragism. A close visual analysis of her artworks *The Pale Complexion of True Love and the Red Glow of Scorn and Proud Disdain* (1899) and *The Little Foot Page* (1905) reveals a New Woman in the disguise of a medieval narrative. I argue that with these images, Brickdale addresses an imbalance of power structures between men and women of her time as a visual contribution to the debate on the late Victorian Marriage Question.

* * * * *

> The pale complexion of true love
> And the red glow of scorn and proud disdain.[2]

This quotation from Shakespeare's play *As You Like It*, printed on the second page of the Royal Academy's catalogue for their annual Summer Exhibition of 1899, guided the visitors to a picture depicting a medievalised scene in the first room of oil paintings right after the vestibule (Figure 2.1).[3] In the picture, a man is devotedly kissing the hem of a young

1 In this chapter, I address the artist by the name of Brickdale since the spelling is inconsistent throughout contemporaneous and modern literature. She was, however, listed under Brickdale in the registers of the Royal Academy and Walker Art Gallery catalogues until 1915.

2 *The Exhibition of the Royal Academy of Arts: The One Hundred and Thirty-First* (London: William Clowes and Sons, 1899), 8.

3 *Exhibition of the Royal Academy*, 6.

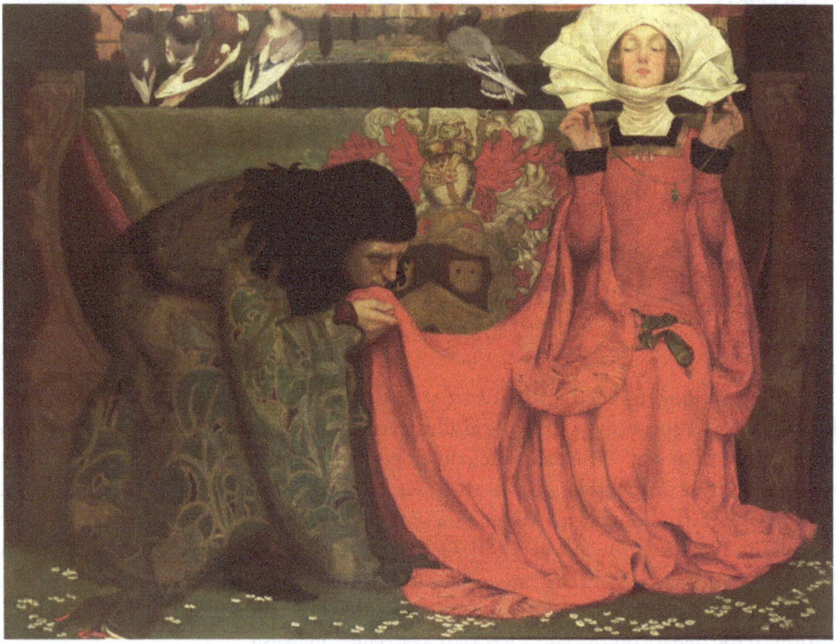

Figure 2.1. Eleanor Fortescue-Brickdale. *The Pale Complexion of True Love and the Red Glow of Scorn and Proud Disdain*, 1899, Oil on canvas, 71.4 × 91.8 cm. Private Collection. Photo © Whitford & Hughes, London.

woman's dress that strikes the viewer's attention by its vivid red colour. The love-struck man and the disparaging gaze of the young woman, together with the quotation from the catalogue, raise the question of the nature of their relationship. The woman's visual rejection of her suitor seems particularly intriguing, considering the rising force of first-wave feminism around the time of the exhibition. In the 1890s, a group of authors fuelled a public discussion on women's conduct and emancipation, using the stereotype of the New Woman as a role model for women's empowerment and self-determination.

The Pale Complexion of True Love was the first oil painting exhibited by the 27-year-old artist Mary Eleanor Fortescue-Brickdale, who started her artistic career during the turbulent transition from the Victorian to the Edwardian era, when art and society headed towards modernism. An obituary in *The Times* defines her as the last Pre-Raphaelite who 'deserves to be remembered for her consistent fidelity to the tradition [of Pre-Raphaelitism]'.[4] Brickdale's oeuvre reveals a strong focus on romantic, medievalised imagery according to the visual language of Pre-Raphaelite principles, which she carried into the first half of the twentieth century. Like the first generation of Pre-Raphaelite artists, Brickdale seemed to engage with contemporary societal issues through her art under the guise of narratives of the past. I argue that *The Pale Complexion of True Love* reveals imagery of the New Woman, mocking courtship behaviour in a visual contribution to the discourse on the late Victorian marriage question.

Brickdale's interest in the gender controversy of her time is also visible in the oil painting *The Little Foot Page*, which she exhibited at the Walker Art Gallery, Liverpool in the Autumn Exhibition of 1905 (Figure 2.2).[5] The image displays a young woman dressed in men's attire cutting her long hair in the middle of a forest landscape. The element of cross-dressing addresses the aspects of gender inequality related to the societal advantages for men during a time when women activists were on the rise to claim the male privileges of work, money, suffrage and a self-determined love life. I contend that this painting depicts a New Woman disguised as a medieval page boy, reacting to gender norms that were still a major topic in public debate and popular press at the time of its exhibition.

4 'Obituary: Miss Fortescue-Brickdale; a Versatile Artist', *The Times* (14 March 1945), 7.

5 Walker Art Gallery, *Thirty-Fifth Autumn Exhibition of Modern Art* (Liverpool: Lee and Nightingale, 1905), 50.

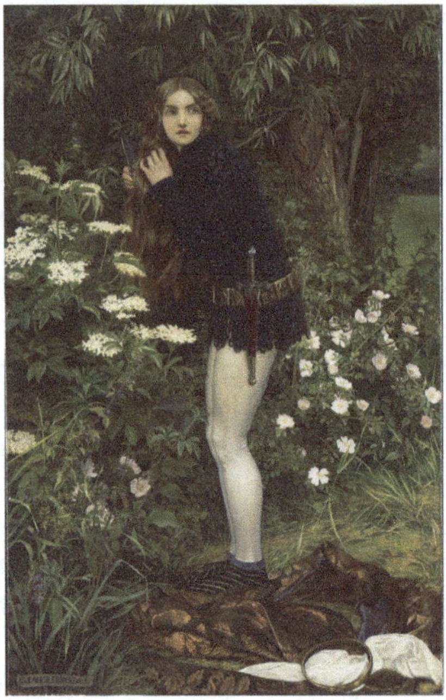

Figure 2.2. Eleanor Fortescue-Brickdale, *The Little Foot Page*, 1905, Oil on canvas, 90.8 × 57.0 cm. Walker Art Gallery, Liverpool. Photo by Walker Art Gallery. © National Museums Liverpool.

In order to examine New Woman-related imagery in Brickdale's works, it is first necessary to briefly discuss the emergence and nature of this gender stereotype and locate Brickdale's own involvement in the debate about the woman question of the fin de siècle. I then analyse the connections between the representations of women in the paintings and imagery of the New Woman, exemplified by *The Pale Complexion of True Love* and *The Little Foot Page*. Addressing these questions proves constructive not only because it reveals potential relations between these pictures and the social debates of the time, but also because Brickdale and her works have been largely excluded from the critical discourse on Pre-Raphaelitism. Although she was praised as an aspiring artist during her lifetime, Brickdale disappeared from the canon of art history after her death.[6] While the Pre-Raphaelite Brotherhood and most of its (male) followers have been widely discussed in critical literature, the art of women within the movement received little attention until 1984, when Griselda Pollock and Deborah Cherry criticised the sole focus on the artistic achievements of the male members with their collaborative paper 'Patriarchal Power and the Pre-Raphaelites'.[7] Besides a retrospective on the occasion of Brickdale's centenary at the Ashmolean Museum in Oxford in 1972 and the exhibition *A Pre-Raphaelite Journey* guest-curated by Pamela Gerrish Nunn at the Lady Lever Art Gallery, Wirral in 2012, the art historians' focus on the 'male geniuses' mainly ignored Brickdale and her Pre-Raphaelite sisters.[8] Since critical literature hardly offers systematic image analyses of Brickdale's artworks, the examination of the female figures depicted in her paintings aims to widen the critical discourse about an overlooked Pre-Raphaelite artist and explore the extent of Brickdale's engagement with the idea of the New Woman as a social phenomenon of her time.[9]

6 See, for instance, Percy H. Bate, *The English Pre-Raphaelite Painters: Their Associates and Successors*, 2nd edn (London: George Bell and Sons, 1901), 90, 114; Walter Shaw Sparrow, *Women Painters of the World: From the Time of Caterina Vigri (1413–1463) to Rosa Bonheur and the Present Day*, in Walter Shaw Sparrow, ed., *The Art and Life Library*, vol. 3 (London: Hodder and Stoughton, 1905); Walter Shaw Sparrow, 'On Some Watercolour Pictures by Miss Eleanor Fortescue-Brickdale', *The Studio* 23/99 (1901), 31–44.

7 Griselda Pollock and Deborah Cherry, 'Patriarchal Power and the Pre-Raphaelites', *Art History* 7/4 (1984), 480–95.

8 G. L. Taylor, *Centenary Exhibition of Works by Eleanor Fortescue-Brickdale 1872–1945* (Oxford: Ashmolean Museum, 1972). Pamela Gerrish Nunn, *A Pre-Raphaelite Journey: The Art of Eleanor Fortescue-Brickdale* (Liverpool: National Museums Liverpool, 2012), 12.

9 A rare example of critical and methodological engagement with Brickdale's art is Nunn's article on the issue of time in Pamela Gerrish Nunn, 'Time and Tide Wait for No Man: A Victorian Apocalypse', in Christian Heck and Kristen Lippincott, eds, *Symbols of Time in the History of Art* (Turnhout: Brepols, 2002), 85–97.

From the Old Woman to the New: Eleanor Fortescue-Brickdale and the Woman Question at the Turn of the Century

> Who or what was the New Woman? A literary construct, a press fabrication and discursive marker of rebellion, or a 'real' woman? A writer, social reformer, or feminist activist? A middle-class daughter eager to study for a career, a married woman chafing against legal inequality, a woman-loving spinster, a reluctant mother, a sexual libertarian?[10]

These questions, raised by Ann Heilmann in her book *New Woman Fiction*, exemplify the mutable connotations of this gender ideal. The somewhat indistinct definition of the New Woman 'derives from the multiplicity of agents who had an ideological stake in constructing her'.[11] The term New Woman was initially coined in the article 'Belles Lettres' which appeared in *The Westminster Review* in 1865 and discusses the emergence of a 'new creed about woman' in literature and considers her the opposite of the 'Angel in the House'.[12] Literary examples, such as Ibsen's play *A Doll's House* (1879) or Elizabeth Barrett Browning's epic poem *Aurora Leigh* (1879), characterise the New Woman as emancipated, independent and determined, going beyond the limits the patriarchal society imposed on women during that time. Main issues were better education, self-fulfilment and responsibility for one's own life and sexuality.

By the end of the nineteenth century, the term spread via public debate in *The North American Review*, fuelled by advocates and opponents of this newly emerged gender ideal. A prominent proponent of the New Woman and a central figure within this debate was Sarah Grand. In her contribution 'The New Woman and the Old' for the *Lady's Realm*, she attempts to describe the physique and character of this gender ideal, emphasising

10 Ann Heilmann, *New Woman Fiction: Women Writing First-Wave Feminism* (New York: Palgrave Macmillan, 2000), 2.

11 Heilmann, *New Woman Fiction*, 2.

12 'Belles Lettres', *The Westminster Review* (1 October 1865), 568; Coventry Patmore, *The Angel in the House* (London: John W. Parker and Son, 1858).

features such as being tall, slender, young and enthusiastic about cycling.[13] Grand also aimed to protect traditional values, and her ideal New Woman cares for her husband and child while also enjoying her own life.[14] Heilmann points out that 'in harnessing domestic values to the dictates of civic duty and the New Woman's desire for self-improvement, Grand reconfigured the patriarchal concept of femininity by both politicising and glamorising its "New Aspect" under modern womanhood'.[15] Measures to gain equality and power also included to some extent the adaptation of stereotypically masculine behaviour, mirrored in Grand's description of the New Woman as having some boyish manners.[16] Juxtaposing this characterisation with stereotypical illustrations in the popular press, such as Phil May's visual depictions of New Women, it is evident that the latter focused heavily on masculine fashion and behaviour – in this case, smoking (Figure 2.3).

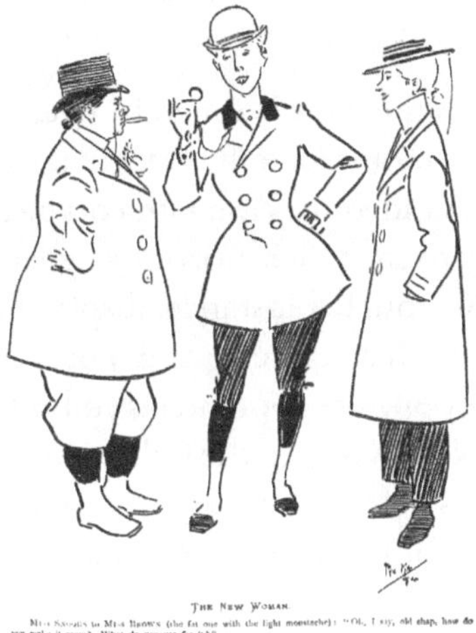

Figure 2.3. Phil May, *The New Woman*, illustration, *Phil May's Illustrated Winter Annual* (1894), 11, Public Domain.

13 Sarah Grand, 'The New Woman and the Old', *Lady's Realm* 4 (1898), 466.

14 Ann Heilmann, *New Woman Strategies: Sarah Grand, Olive Schreiner, Mona Caird* (Manchester: Manchester University Press, 2004), 13.

15 Heilmann, *New Woman Strategies*, 17.

16 Grand, 'The New Woman and the Old', 469.

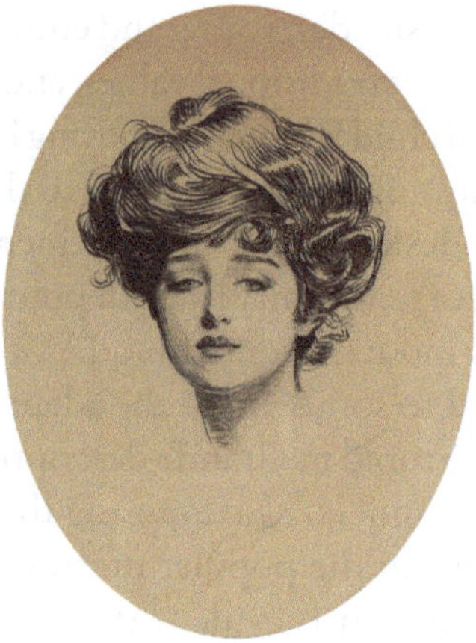

Figure 2.4. Charles Dana Gibson, *The Gibson Girl*, ink on paper, 31.75 × 24.13 cm, Public Domain.

May's image mocks the New Woman by overemphasising masculine features, such as the tiny moustache above the left woman's lip. Despite the teasing, the New Woman advocates used stereotypical masculine attributes to assert their equality to men. Self-portraits by American photographer Frances Benjamin Johnston, for instance, display her in a stereotypically manly sitting posture with a cigarette and a beer mug or in men's attire with a moustache. The opposite approach is embodied by the most iconic visual imagery of the New Woman: the Gibson Girl. Her creator, Charles Dana Gibson, emphasised female beauty instead of masculine features to create a gentler version of the New Woman and make her more acceptable to critics.

An illustration of a head of *The Gibson Girl* (Figure 2.4) reveals a voluminous and fashionable Edwardian hairstyle, a pretty face and an elongated neck as her distinctive characteristics. The woman in the image is holding her head up high as an expression of determination and confidence. Other illustrations present the Gibson Girl as tall and slender with an hourglass figure. Martha Patterson argues that Gibson's images 'promoted a measure of women's personal independence, self-actualization, and sexual assertiveness'.[17] The Gibson Girl entered the male-dominated spheres in subtler ways, by pursuing education or taking part in physical activity. One reason for the Gibson Girl's success was her good marketability, since she personified the fashionable, independent, White upper middle-class woman with her own purchasing power.[18] In their search for liberation and independence, women were 'exploiting and being exploited by the complex ideology the Gibson Girl images promoted'.[19]

Grand lamented the suppressive circumstances women still had to endure and declared a rising awareness among women of the idea of female empowerment:

> What [a woman] perceived at the outset was the sudden and violent upheaval of the suffering sex in all parts of the world. Women were awaking from their long apathy, and, as they awoke, like healthy hungry children unable to articulate, they began to whimper for they knew not what.[20]

A cynical answer to Grand's advocacy of the New Woman is Ouida's article 'The New Woman', in which the novelist claims that '[t]he error of the New Woman […] lies in speaking of women as the victims of men, and entirely ignoring the frequency with which men are the victims of women'.[21] Most of the criticism of the New Woman was rooted in the opposition to her nonconforming behaviour; this behaviour was emphasised by male opponents such as E. S. Scott and E. B. Hall, who debased this gender ideal in their 'Character Note' on the basis of her presumed haughtiness and her habit of wearing manly clothes.[22] Scott and Hall perceived the New Woman to be a threat to woman's mission and the patriarchal system.[23]

17 Martha H. Patterson, *Beyond the Gibson Girl: Reimagining the American New Woman, 1895–1915* (Urbana: University of Illinois Press, 2005), 31.

18 Patterson, *Beyond the Gibson Girl*, 31–2.

19 Patterson, *Beyond the Gibson Girl*, 33.

20 Sarah Grand, 'The New Aspect of the Woman Question', *The North American Review* 158/448 (1894), 271.

21 Ouida, 'The New Woman', *The North American Review* 158/450 (1894), 615.

22 E. S. Scott and E. B. Hall, 'Character Note: The New Woman', *Cornhill Magazine* 23 (1894), 365–8.

23 Scott and Hall, 'Character Note', 368.

The term 'woman's mission' refers to the alleged female duties of being a wife and mother as propagated in conduct books, such as John Angell James's *Female Piety*. Basing his writing on Scripture, the author declares that as soon as a woman is married 'her sphere of labor [...] is the family; and it belongs to the husband to earn [...] not only his own bread, but that of the household'.[24] Throughout the book, the author stresses the subjection of a woman to her husband.[25] Thus, social constraints made it hard for women to reject the traditional path, even if they had financial security. The close connection between a woman's respectability and her sexuality made it harder to live by the progressive ideals that were put forward as alternatives to marriage.[26]

Brickdale's life and career were rather nonconforming regarding marriage and income. Born into a wealthy middle-class family, she lived a privileged life in Upper Norwood, surrounded by parents, three siblings, servants and her own governess.[27] Her father, Matthew Inglett Brickdale, was a barrister married to Sarah Anna Lloyd, the daughter of a judge. In families like this, sons would usually pursue a professional career while daughters would aim for a good marriage. However, none of the daughters in the Brickdale household ever married or had children. Nunn is tempted to 'see this departure from the norms' as a sign of significant changes in the construction of gender at the turn of the century.[28] When Brickdale's father died in an accident in the Alps in 1894, the family lost their guardian and principal earner.[29] Brickdale did not seek financial security in marriage but instead aspired to become a professional artist. In 1889, she enrolled at the Crystal Palace School of Art, Science and Literature.[30]

24 John Angell James, *Female Piety: Or, the Young Woman's Friend and Guide Through Life to Immortality* (New York: Robert Carter & Brothers, 1853), 74.

25 James, *Female Piety*, 80, 85.

26 Lynda Nead, *Myths of Sexuality: Representations of Women in Victorian Britain* (Oxford: Basil Blackwell, 1990), 28.

27 England and Wales Census, Surrey, Upper Norwood, RG 11/822, 14 (1881).

28 Nunn, *A Pre-Raphaelite Journey*, 12.

29 Taylor, *Centenary Exhibition*, 3.

30 Taylor, *Centenary Exhibition*, 3. Initially, the Victorian education system was highly gendered, which 'helped to inculcate children into their gender roles for which they were destined as adults', see Susie L. Steinbach, *Understanding the Victorians: Politics,*

Although the school was not as prestigious as other institutions run by popular artists or the government, female and male students were welcome.[31] In the following years, Brickdale applied to the Royal Academy three times and joined in 1895.[32] Since the academy had opened the nude classes to female students two years earlier, Brickdale had access to what Linda Nochlin describes as 'the very essence of History Painting' and thus enjoyed a quality art education as good as that of her male counterparts.[33] Brickdale proved to be a successful student and she became the first female member of the Institute of Painters in Oil in 1902.[34] When she exhibited her first two oil paintings at the Royal Academy in 1899, she was able to sell both for £35. As Tim Barringer stresses, Brickdale 'forswore the conventional roles of wife and mother and pursued a career as artist and teacher, creating ambitious historical paintings as well as decorative panels and stained glass in a long and distinguished career'.[35] When the Byam Shaw and Vicat Cole School of Art was founded in 1910, she became involved in teaching composition and watercolour to prepare students for the Royal Academy in addition to her extensive schedule as an artist.[36] Working in both fields, Brickdale held the supposedly male

Culture, and Society in Nineteenth-Century Britain (London: Routledge, 2012), 139. From the mid-nineteenth century onwards, it was common that wealthy upper-class women founded secondary schools for girls or both sexes to provide a more equal educational system. One example is the Scowles School in Gloucestershire, founded by Brickdale's eponymous aunt Mary Fortescue-Brickdale in 1858; see Cyril Hart, *Coleford: The History of a West Gloucestershire Forest Town* (Gloucester: Alan Sutton, 1983), 351–2.

31 Nunn, *A Pre-Raphaelite Journey*, 12.

32 Royal Academy, Register of Admission of Students, RAA/KEE/1/1/4, July 1890–January 1922, 6 no. 4479.

33 Linda Nochlin, 'Why Have There Been No Great Women Artists?', in Linda Nochlin, *Women, Art, and Power and other Essays* (New York: Harper & Row, 1988), 158.

34 'The Ladies Column: Gossip for Women', *Lichfield Mercury* (14 March 1902).

35 Tim Barringer, *Before and After Modernism: Byam Shaw, Rex Vicat Cole, Yinka Shonibare, MBE* (London: Central Saint Martin's College of Art and Design, 2010), 48.

36 Nunn, *A Pre-Raphaelite Journey*, 25; Barringer, *Before and After Modernism*, 58–63.

duty as the principal earner for the household she shared with her older sister Kate, thus emerging as a New Woman herself.[37]

In addition to her independence in terms of marital status and career, Brickdale's life also appears interwoven with New Woman ideologies, as it seems likely that she kept company with supporters of this movement. In an amendment to Grand's obituary in *The Times*, Brickdale's eldest brother Charles refers to the author and New Woman advocate as his 'distinguished relative' and suggests certain corrections to the eulogy.[38] Since Charles seemed to have known Grand well and saw the importance of setting specific records straight, it can be assumed that his sister Eleanor, who was close to her brother Charles, also belonged to the circle of the author and early feminist.[39] Moreover, Brickdale was one of the artists that the New Woman advocate Marion Hepworth Dixon praised in her series 'Our Rising Artists' in *The Magazine of Art* in 1902.[40] In this article, Dixon draws attention to Brickdale as a Pre-Raphaelite painter by briefly contextualising her within the movement and emphasising her talent and hard-working attitude.[41] Marion Hepworth Dixon and her sister Ella worked as authors and journalists.[42] Like Grand, Ella was an author of New Woman fiction, and she also participated in the public debate about the New Woman in the late Victorian era.[43] Brickdale's potential connections to the advocates and ideas of the New Woman movement raise the question of whether and how she engaged with ideologies related to this gender ideal in her work. A close and critical account of selected paintings examines the extent of

37 Taylor, *Centenary Exhibition*, 3.

38 Charles Fortescue-Brickdale, 'Obituary: Sarah Grand', *The Times* (24 May 1943).

39 Jan Marsh and Pamela Gerrish Nunn, *Women Artists and the Pre-Raphaelite Movement* (London: Virago, 1989), 143.

40 Marion Hepworth Dixon, 'Our Rising Artists: Eleanor Fortescue-Brickdale', *The Magazine of Art* (1902), 256–62.

41 Dixon, 'Our Rising Artists', 256, 260.

42 Valerie Fehlbaum, 'Sisters in Life, Sisters in Art: Ella and Marion Hepworth Dixon', in Margaret D. Stetz and Cheryl A. Wilson eds, *Michael Field and Their World* (High Wycombe: The Rivendale Press, 2007), 108.

43 Ella Hepworth Dixon, 'Why Women Are Ceasing to Marry', *Humanitarian* 14 (1899), 391–6.

New Woman imagery in Brickdale's artworks to ascertain whether they can be perceived as visual contributions to the late Victorian marriage question.

The Pale Complexion of True Love and the Red Glow of Scorn and Proud Disdain in the Context of the Late Victorian Marriage Question

In 1898, Brickdale used the prize money of £40, won for her lunette *Spring*, to work on an oil painting with which she participated, for the first time in oil, in the Royal Academy's summer exhibition of 1899.[44] Brickdale's painting was well-received by the international press, which considered it to be a highly skilled and clever interpretation of Shakespeare's drama.[45] The 1899 issue of *The Academy Notes*, an accompanying series to the Academy's summer exhibitions which provides illustrations of what they claim to be the 'principal paintings', even included an illustration after Brickdale's oil painting.[46] Thus, *The Pale Complexion of True Love and the Red Glow of Scorn and Proud Disdain* must have made an impression on the editors.

The 'red glow' that is mentioned in the accompanying quotation is literally visible in the painting's colour palette (Figure 2.1). The beholder's gaze is drawn to the bright red dress of the female figure on the right. This slender woman is sitting straight and frontally on the outer edge of a wooden pew. Her hands are raised to shoulder height and are holding a long golden necklace with a precious gemstone, which she seems to have

44 Marsh and Nunn, *Pre-Raphaelite Women Artists*, 152.

45 'The Royal Academy (II.)', *St. James's Gazette* (10 May 1899); Jarno Jessen, 'Moderne Präraffaeliten', *Die Kunst für Alle* 19/ 4 (1903), 86; Hermann Muthesius, 'Kunst und Leben in England', *Zeitschrift für Bildende Kunst* 37 (NF 13) (1902), 68; Henri Frantz, 'Les Salons Anglais en 1899: Royal Academy, International Society, New Gallery', *Gazette des Beaux-Arts* 22/4 (3rd Period) (1899), 347.

46 *The Academy Notes 1899 with Illustrations of the Principal Pictures at Burlington House: Originated by the Late Henry Blackburn* (London: Chatto & Windus, 1899), 38.

just put around her neck. The pose of her arms reveals the sleeve lining of her medievalised garment, which is patterned with golden thread. The woman's face is framed by a bright white, layered headscarf, which also covers her long, slim neck. This elaborate wimple strongly resembles a particular German bonnet, the so-called 'patrizische Kirchenhaube', which was fashionable among upper-class women in Renaissance Nuremberg.[47] Records of this churchgoing accessory are preserved in various drawings and prints by Albrecht Dürer, such as the woodcut *The Marriage of the Virgin* (c. 1504; Metropolitan Museum of Art, New York). A contemporary copy after Dürer's drawing of a costume, which served as a study for this woodcut, was exhibited at the British Museum in 1895, the year Brickdale became a student at the Royal Academy.[48] Although the young woman faces the beholder frontally, her gaze is fixed to her lower right. With eyes almost closed, she is looking down towards a man who is bending over and devotedly kissing the seam of her gown with his eyes closed. The man's head is covered by a black medieval-style hood. His garment is decorated with rich green floral ornaments and fastened with a black belt around his waist. Apart from the opulent decoration, his clothing resembles that of medieval clergymen, suggesting he may be an ecclesiastic. The man seems considerably older than the woman, as revealed by wrinkles around his eyes and forehead.

The accompanying quotation, which belongs to the third act of Shakespeare's play *As You Like It*, suggests that the two figures should be identified as Silvius and Phoebe. The lines are from the scene in which the shepherd Corin explains the current situation of his young comrade Silvius to the Duke's daughter Rosalind and her cousin Celia:

> If you will see a pageant truly play'd
> Between the pale complexion of true love
> And the red glow of scorn and proud disdain,

47 Jutta Zander-Seidel, *Textiler Hausrat: Kleidung und Haustextilien in Nürnberg von 1500–1650* (Munich: Deutscher Kunstverlag, 1990), 113–6.

48 Sidney Colvin, *Guide to an Exhibition of Drawings and Engravings by the Old Masters: Principally from the Malcom Collection in the Print and Drawing Gallery*, 2nd edn (London: British Museum, 1895), 55.

> Go hence a little, and I shall conduct you,
> If you will mark it.[49]

This passage describes Silvius's mental state and introduces his desperate attempts to woo the shepherdess Phoebe in the subsequent scene. Although Brickdale's painting depicts a besotted man and a seemingly aloof woman, the figures do not portray the poor shepherds of Shakespeare's drama but people of nobility. This impression is further supported by the opulent coat of arms in the centre of the tapestry whose golden cartouche is crowned by the type of helmet used to represent aristocratic heraldry.[50] This reading challenges the assumption that the painting is a direct visual adaptation of Shakespeare's play. Moreover, the inscription on the frame that reads 'A Midsummer Night's Dream' beneath the quotation from *As You Like It* also indicates that the figures in the painting carry a broader meaning, as both comedies focus on the absurdity of courtship and marriage.

The assumption that the figures represent an exaggerated and almost comic portrayal of courtship becomes even more evident with an examination of the symbols Brickdale included in her painting. The humble pigeons on top of the wooden fence behind the bench are a satirical element as they have their backs turned to the couple. Although pigeons are associated with Venus as a classic symbol of love, the tradition of portraying the goddess with the birds always displays pure and white doves.[51] A book bound in brown leather, carelessly discarded next to the man's foot, evokes the narrative of Paolo and Francesca from Dante Gabriel Rossetti's visual representation of *Paolo and Francesca da Rimini* (see Figure 11.4). The picture refers to the fifth canto of Dante's *Inferno*, when Francesca tells the tragic story about their romance and emphasises that they 'read of Lancelot', a hero who, like Paolo and Francesca, suffered for his beloved.[52]

49 William Shakespeare, *The Complete Works of William Shakespeare*, eds Stanley Wells and Gary Taylor, 2nd edn (Oxford: Clarendon Press, 2005), Act III, scene V, 671.

50 John Guillim, *A Display of Heraldry*, 6th edn (London: Printed by T. W. for R. and J. Bonwicke and R. Wilkin, 1724), 442.

51 Chevalier and Gheerbrant, *The Penguin Dictionary of Symbols*, 753–4.

52 Dante Alighieri, *Dante's Inferno* (New York: Cassell, Petter, Galpin and Co., 1866), 27.

That the book in *The Pale Complexion of True Love* is lying on the ground face down seems to be a bad omen for a potential relationship between the figures. Brickdale also draws on the Pre-Raphaelite tradition of including flower symbolism in her artwork to enhance the semantics of the image. The daisies, which grow in front of the figures, are associated with innocence and might refer to the considerable age difference between the man and the woman.[53] Traditionally, women, often married at a young age, were considered to be innocent in the meaning of chaste, while their husbands were older and experienced.[54]

This element evokes the pictorial tradition of the 'ill-assorted couple', displaying an older man devoted to a young woman, which was particularly popular in the fifteenth and sixteenth centuries. An engraving by Israhel van Meckenem, *The Ill-Matched Couple*, portrays the corruptness of such a relationship by drawing attention to the woman's hand reaching for the man's coin pouch (Figure 2.5).

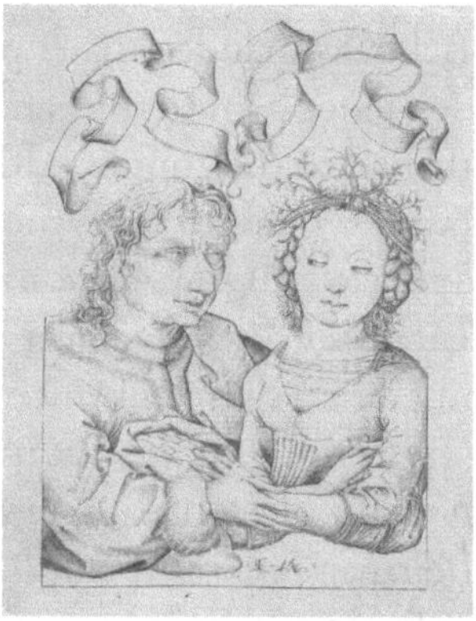

Figure 2.5. Israhel van Meckenem, *The Ill-Matched Couple*, c. 1480–90, engraving, 14.7 × 11.4 cm, The Metropolitan Museum of Art, New York City, NY. Photograph by the Metropolitan Museum of Art, Public Domain.

53 John H. Ingram, *Flora Symbolica; or: The Language and Sentiment of Flowers* (London: F. W. Warne and Co., 1869), 266.

54 Stephen Kern, *Eyes of Love: The Gaze in English and French Paintings and Novels 1840–1900* (London: Reaktion Books, 1996), 18.

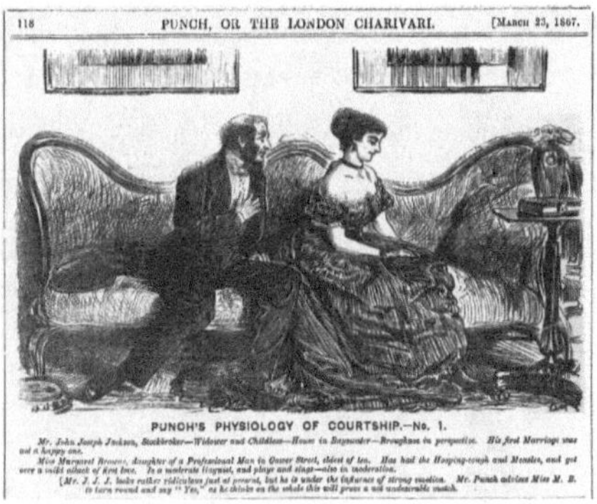

Figure 2.6. *Punch's Physiology of Courtship – No. 1*, illustration, *Punch* 52 (1867), 118. Public Domain.

Images of that genre draw on the topic of love for sale as part of the iconography, indicating the unreasonableness of the male figure's courtship behaviour. Brickdale's reference to this tradition in her painting is the golden necklace, most likely a gift the young woman received from her suitor. A more conspicuous reference is the phallic object on her lap that looks like a coin purse. Here, Brickdale draws attention to the act of buying love, with the young woman being persuaded to give in to the man's proposal. The woman's acceptance of the gifts and her unapproachable demeanour seems to critique her behaviour, exploiting the situation. From the middle of the nineteenth century, contemporaneous adaptations of the ill-assorted couple became a common topic of many paintings, such as Edmund Blair Leighton's *Till Death Do Us Part* (1878; Forbes Magazine Collection, New York) and illustrations in the popular press. *Punch* published a picture entitled 'Punch's Physiology of Courtship No. 1' where a middle-aged widower is wooing the eldest daughter of a middle-class family (Figure 2.6).

Although the transactional nature of the relationship is relatively concealed and wealth is implied only in the man's clothing, the image draws attention to the age difference between the couple. What is striking is the disinterested body language of the woman, who has her back turned towards her suitor. Gibson's illustration *The Ambitious Mother and the Obliging Clergyman* visually exaggerates these absurdities of courtship

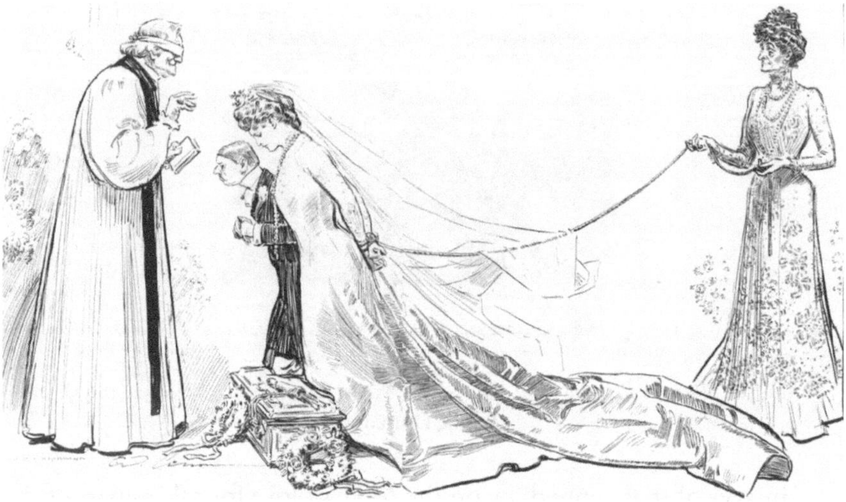

Figure 2.7. Charles Dana Gibson, *The Ambitious Mother and the Obliging Clergyman,* illustration, *LIFE* 39 (1902), 488–9. Public Domain.

and marriage, depicting a woman as a slave to her husband and mother (Figure 2.7). The picture reveals a blindfolded pastor who is conducting a wedding between a short middle-aged man and a tall young Gibson Girl whose wrists are tied by a rope her mother is holding. With this illustration, Gibson criticised the practice of arranged marriages of young daughters to older men on the grounds of their wealth or title.

Towards the end of the nineteenth century and in the wake of the New Woman movement, an increasing number of male and female authors started to question the principle of marriage. Ella Hepworth Dixon's article 'Why Women are Ceasing to Marry', for instance, emphasises that the improvement in women's education contributed to a critical reflection on the disadvantages of marriage. Dixon claims that her time was 'a transition stage [...] [where] a certain amount of misunderstanding [...] between the sexes [...] make[s] marrying and giving in marriage a somewhat hazardous enterprise'.[55] Grand also contributes to the debate and, although

55 Dixon, 'Why Women Are Ceasing to Marry', 392.

she seems to be an advocate of marriage and parenthood, she contends that a marriage can only be successful when partners are equal and mutually respectful.[56] The growing interest in equal rights and alternatives to conventional marriage was also discussed in *The Woman Question*, a book written collaboratively by Eleanor Marx and her partner, Edward Aveling. They blame the organisation of society for the enslavement of women, an argument which was strongly supported by the concept of marriage.[57] Their solution consists of 'equality for all, without distinction of sex', which would lead to the liberation of women in potentially alternative models to conventional marriage, and they even suggest polygamy as a possibility.[58] Therefore, the last decade of the nineteenth century, just as Brickdale was starting her professional art career, marks a turning point in the perception of traditional courtship and marriage.

Considering the satirical illustrations in the press and the critical debate on courting and matrimony, *The Pale Complexion of True Love* appears to be Brickdale's visual contribution to the discourse. This assertion becomes even more probable when the painting is contextualised within Stephen Kern's theory of 'proposal compositions'. In his book *Eyes of Love*, Kern constructs this term for pieces showing a man and a woman in similar arrangements from the mid-nineteenth century onwards. He claims that in these kinds of paintings, the focus lies exclusively on the face of the female figure, which is typically shown from the front while the man is depicted in profile. Kern argues that the male figure is always looking at the woman, but she herself is looking away. The facial expressions of the female figures vary but often reveal a melancholic mood in a moment of contemplation.[59] An example for this theory is Frederic George Stephens's painting *The Proposal* (1850–1; Tate, London), in which a man is proposing to his beloved and actively looking at her while she is staring at the ground, avoiding his gaze in a moment of reflection. According to Kern, this moment is the

56 Sarah Grand et al., 'Does Marriage Hinder a Woman's Self-Development?', *Lady's Realm* 5 (1898), 577.

57 Edward Aveling and Eleanor Marx Aveling, *The Woman Question* (London: Swan Sonnenschein, Le Bas and Lowrey, 1886), 5.

58 Aveling and Aveling, *The Woman Question*, 15.

59 Kern, *Eyes of Love*, 7–9.

'unprecedented moment of power' for the woman since, in this particular instant, the man entirely depends on her answer.[60] In terms of Victorian gender constructions, it is questionable to what extent a woman's position really was one of power on a social level since an agreement as well as a rejection could have severe consequences for her.

Considering the arrangement and pose of the figures in Brickdale's painting, the picture seems to follow the tradition of proposal compositions. The painting focuses on the intriguing interaction between the two figures whose body languages could not differ more from each other: the man is bending extremely low as a sign of his severe subjection to the woman. The woman, in contrast, sits upright and frontally, not turning in the slightest towards her suitor. Although the scene aims to depict a medieval setting, the appearance of the young woman, with the emphasis on her pretty face, slender figure, her long, slim neck and her head held high evoke the stereotypical features of the New Woman and the Gibson Girl. Her highly symmetrical appearance and contemptuous facial expression emphasise her superiority over the situation. A crucial element of the painting which differs from traditional proposal compositions is the aspect of gaze. Here, it is the man who is looking down, not in a moment of consideration but devotion. In contrast, the woman's gaze is directed at her suitor. The inversion of the roles and gazes in Brickdale's painting suggests that in this case it is not the woman who is in a moment of thought since she seems to have already made her decision. The evident emphasis on the woman's superiority links the depicted act of courtship to more progressive ideas of the New Woman movement, which stress a woman's independence in her decisions about relationship and marriage. This aspect supports the argument that Brickdale's painting serves as a visual parody, disguised in a medievalised setting, of courtship behaviour and traditional concepts of matrimony at the turn of the century and seems to provide an insight into the artist's own thoughts on the late Victorian marriage question.

60 Kern, *Eyes of Love*, 15.

Gender Transformation through Aspects of Cross-Dressing and New Woman Imagery in *The Little Foot Page*

The New Woman imagery also seems to be reflected in Brickdale's most popular oil painting, *The Little Foot Page*, which she exhibited in the Autumn Exhibition at the Walker Art Gallery in Liverpool for a listed price of £105 (Figure 2.2).[61] The painting soon found a purchaser in Harold Rathbone, a student of Ford Madox Brown and co-founder of the Della Robbia Pottery.[62]

The title of the image refers to the narrative of the medieval Scottish ballad 'Child Waters'.[63] Although there are various versions of the poem, the one entitled 'Child Waters' was spread through Thomas Percy's collection of ballads and popular songs *Reliques of Ancient English Poetry* (1765), which influenced writers such as William Wordsworth and Walter Scott.[64] With the publication of Francis James Child's book *The English and Scottish Popular Ballads* (1892–8), the story of Child Waters not only gained popularity again, but also appeared in ten different versions.[65] The main narrative hardly varies throughout the poems. The female protagonist Ellen confesses to her lover, Child Waters, that she is pregnant with his child. The knight reveals that he must travel to the North to marry the fairest lady he may meet there, but offers land to Ellen as compensation.

61 Walker Art Gallery, *Thirty-Fifth Autumn Exhibition*, 50.

62 Marsh and Nunn, *Pre-Raphaelite Women Artists*, 154.

63 The archaic word child or childe refers to a title for young noblemen, aspiring to knighthood. The term is related to the Saxon word cniht which is a cognate for knight. See Thomas Percy, *Reliques of Ancient English Poetry: Consisting of Old Heroic Ballads, Songs, and Other Pieces of Our Earlier Poets; Together with Some Few of Later Date*, 2nd edn, vol. 3 (London: Henry Washbourne and Co., 1857), 59; in several versions of the poem the female protagonist is also referred to as Helen or Fair Margaret. For other versions of the poem see *English and Scottish Popular Ballads,* ed. Francis James Child, vol. 2, part 3 (Boston, MA: Houghton Mifflin, 1885), 83–100.

64 Nick Groom, *The Making of Percy's Reliques* (Oxford: Clarendon Press, 1966), 3.

65 Child, *English and Scottish Popular Ballads*, 83–100.

Ellen rejects his offer as she would rather have his love and begs to follow him as his foot page. The conditions of this agreement are set by the man:

> If you will my ffootpage be, Ellen,
> As you doe tell itt mee,
> Then you must cut your gownne of greene
> An inche aboue your knee.
>
> Soe must you doe your yellow lockes,
> Another inch aboue your eye;
> You must tell noe man what is my name;
> My ffootpage then you shall bee.[66]

The male protagonist thus forces Ellen to disguise herself as a male page. While he rides on horseback, the pregnant young woman must follow him on foot, swim through a cold river and take care of his horse while Child Waters enjoys pleasures with other women. Throughout the whole journey, Ellen behaves modestly and never bothers the knight. She even finds him a 'fair lady' for the night while she sleeps at the foot of his bed. Only after she gives birth to his child alone in a stable does he acknowledge her as the fairest of all ladies and announces that he will marry her.

However, Brickdale's visual adaptation of the narrative does not show the male protagonist Child Waters but depicts a young woman standing in the centre of the painting in front of a close backdrop. Her body is turned sideways. It is only her head that points frontally towards the viewer, but her eyes do not encounter those of the beholder. Instead, she is looking beyond the right border as though not wanting to be discovered. The white tights and pointed shoes the figure wears evoke medieval fashion.[67] Her attire is clearly that of a man's typical of this period, which is also suggested by the golden belt and short sword. Carelessly discarded on the ground beside the young woman lies her own gown, on top of which the white headdress and golden circlet indicate her wealth and nobility. The dress is embroidered with floral arabesques of fine bronze yarn. Brickdale had undoubtedly dedicated herself to the original Pre-Raphaelite principle of

66 Child, *English and Scottish Popular Ballads*, 86.

67 Scott, *Medieval Dress and Fashion*, 120–1; Zander-Seidel, *Textiler Hausrat*, 182.

meticulously displaying minute details such as the single threads of the embroidered foliage of the dress. No longer covered by the white cloth, the maid reveals her long brown hair, which she is about to cut off with a massive pair of scissors. The hair on her left side seems already shortened. The act of hair-cutting and the discarded female dress indicate that Brickdale has captured a moment of gender transformation, a scene not directly described in the poem.

By rejecting conventional Victorian womanly features, such as long hair and the lustrous dress, Brickdale's partly androgynous heroine stands in contrast to the favoured Victorian gender ideal of the 'Angel in the House'. This argument is supported by the depiction of the young woman in nature, symbolising her escape from the domestic sphere as the start of a long journey. Following the Pre-Raphaelite style and principles, Brickdale's depiction of nature in *The Little Foot Page* is not only skilful but also full of symbolic meaning, although little is known about her working practice. The elderflower, growing to the maid's right side, symbolises zealousness and Ellen's determination to endure the gruesome challenges of her forthcoming journey.[68] The wild musk roses to Ellen's left side in the lower ground are a symbol of capricious beauty.[69] They may hint at the gender transformation she is about to undergo and the true beauty that remains present regardless of her outer appearance. According to Ingram's nineteenth-century guide *The Language and Sentiment of Flowers*, a book Brickdale would have probably known, the white colour of the musk rose is a statement of being worthy of somebody, something Ellen has to prove throughout the whole poem.[70] The right background of the image reveals a crack willow, a common symbol of melancholy and forsaken love.[71] Moreover, the nettles at the right border represent the cruelty of Ellen's lover.[72]

The story was widely known at the time of the exhibition, and the audience probably connected the title of the painting and the medieval

68 Ingram, *Flora Symbolica*, 349.
69 Henry Phillips, *Floral Emblems* (London: Saunders and Otley, 1825), 86.
70 Ingram, *Flora Symbolica*, 360.
71 Phillips, *Floral Emblems*, 210.
72 Phillips, *Floral Emblems*, 104.

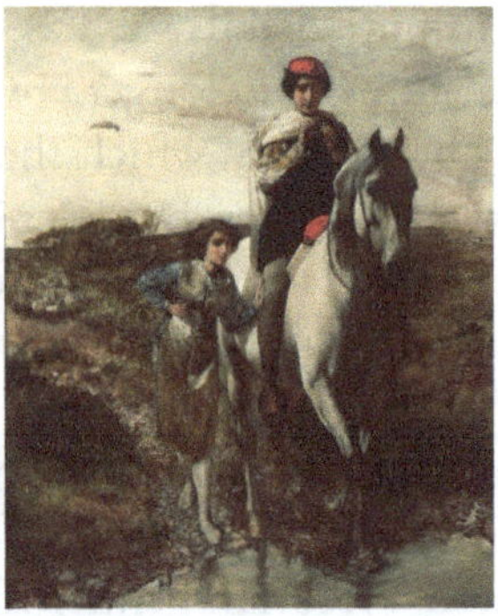

Figure 2.8. William Lindsay Windus, *Burd Helen*, 1856, Oil on canvas, 84.4 × 66.6 cm, Liverpool, Walker Art Gallery. Photo by Walker Art Gallery. © National Museums Liverpool.

setting with 'Child Waters', which was already the subject of William Lindsay Windus's painting *Burd Helen* (1856; Figure 2.8). His painting depicts Child Waters as a nobleman in expensive garments on top of a white horse accompanied by his foot page Helen to his right. The folds of the garment in the woman's womb area indicate her pregnancy. Windus's figures are located in a barren landscape, walking on a stony path and facing a stretch of water. The picture received much praise from John Ruskin, although he had 'a special dislike to pictures of a slate-grey colour, as well as of girls in dresses of pages'.[73] The painting has nothing of the vibrant colour scheme of *The Little Foot Page*. Rather, what Ruskin describes as slate-grey colour reflects the misty and cold weather conditions of autumn in the North and emphasises the cruel treatment of Helen by her lover. In opposition to the young woman in Brickdale's painting, Windus's display of Helen focuses on her suffering. She is holding her stomach in pain from the long and rapid part of the journey she has already endured. Windus captures the harshness of the narrative in his more literal adaptation of the poem, which Ruskin admires as 'thoughtful and intense in the highest

73 John Ruskin, 'Academy Notes: Notes on Prout and Hunt and Other Art Criticisms 1855–1888', in Alexander Wedderburn and E. T. Cook, eds, *The Complete Works of John Ruskin*, 36 vols (London: George Allen, 1904), XIV, 85.

degree'.[74] However, Windus's depiction of the young woman conveys a message of weakness and distress, which emphasises the misogynist treatment by her lover.

Brickdale depicts the young heroine in an entirely different way. The focus lies exclusively on Ellen and her transformation into a young male page. The act of cross-dressing has not only been a popular literary device but was also a common practice among women throughout the Middle Ages.[75] In Christian Europe, female cross-dressing violated the biblical verse of Deuteronomy 22:5 and the First Epistle to the Corinthians 11:6, which claim that God detests all women who put on men's clothes and cut off their hair.[76] The aspect of pregnancy adds another dimension to the genre of disguised or cross-dressed female heroines.[77] As Valerie Hotchkiss emphasises, if a 'page [had] been brought before the London magistrates, bearing a bastard and wearing male apparel, [it] would have been more than enough evidence of her moral depravity'.[78] Cross-dressing was classified as sexual misconduct and was often linked to prostitution. In 1351, a London ordinance restricted what prostitutes could wear to make them distinguishable from the rest of the population and made it illegal for them to wear noble women's clothing.[79] This phenomenon was not limited to England but was widespread throughout Europe to mark the social status, gender roles and sex of the individual.[80] Cross-dressing, of course, posed a threat to those regulations and was only allowed for licenced actors on stage, where it was undoubtedly popular.[81]

74 *Complete Works*, eds Cook and Wedderburn, XIV, 86.

75 Vern L. Bullough and Bonnie Bullough, *Cross Dressing, Sex, and Gender* (Philadelphia: University of Pennsylvania Press, 1993), 94.

76 Valerie R. Hotchkiss, *Clothes Make the Man: Female Cross Dressing in Medieval Europe* (New York: Routledge, 1996), 55.

77 Hotchkiss, *Clothes Make the Man*, 53.

78 Hotchkiss, *Clothes Make the Man*, 56.

79 Michael Shapiro, *Gender in Play on the Shakespearean Stage: Boy Heroines and Female Pages* (Ann Arbor: University of Michigan Press, 1994), 16.

80 Marjorie Garber, *Vested Interests: Cross-Dressing and Cultural Anxiety* (New York: Routledge, 1992), 20, 26.

81 Garber, *Vested Interests*, 35.

Since the discarded dress of the female figure in Brickdale's painting belongs to an upper-class woman, it can be assumed that the young lady belongs to a wealthy family and is not dependent on the additional income of prostitution. Thus, the aspect of cross-dressing is not intended to arouse someone's interest. Ellen is doing so because it is her only chance of not being rejected by the father of her unborn child and left behind as a dishonoured woman. However, the sexual aspect does play a role in medieval cross-dressing stories since, although unintentionally, other female characters often feel attracted to the disguised woman. This is the case not only in various Shakespeare dramas but also in 'Child Waters', when the knight's sister wants to spend the night with the little foot page. In this medieval context, the cross-dressing allows Ellen to leave the domestic sphere and adopt a new identity and gender to be in the position of solving 'masculine' tasks. Transferring this subject matter to the nineteenth century links it to the Victorian Woman Question. Having children outside of legal marriage would have condemned the woman and her offspring since, as Vern L. Bullough stresses, 'a woman's social identity was defined primarily by her marital status [and] entwined with that of her husband'.[82] The act of cross-dressing is a direct reference to the construction of gender classifications since it 'offers a challenge to easy notions of binarity, putting into question the categories of "female" and "male", whether they are considered essential or constructed, biological or cultural'.[83]

While Windus clearly indicates pregnancy in his visual adaptation, Brickdale does not draw attention to this aspect in her painting. One could argue that the moment in *The Little Foot Page* suggests the initiation of the journey when the pregnancy is still not showing, but the way Brickdale depicts the young woman avoids drawing attention to any womanly features. This is supported by Elizabeth Prettejohn's argument that *The Little Foot Page* makes a 'self-conscious reference' to Millais's painting *Ferdinand Lured by Ariel* (1850; The Makins Collection, USA).[84] Both images refer to

82 Bullough and Bullough, *Cross Dressing, Sex, and Gender*, 145.

83 Garber, *Vested Interests*, 10.

84 Elizabeth Prettejohn, *The Art of the Pre-Raphaelites* (London: Tate Publishing, 2007), 87.

medieval narratives and reveal a circular foreground with the central figure surrounded by nature. The resemblance of fashion and posture between the two figures is apparent. Ellen's pose corresponds to that of Ferdinand since both are slightly bent over and turned to the left. Both are wearing pointed shoes and bright white tights with fine folds at the knee area. Thus, Brickdale's role model for her depiction of the young woman seems to have been a male figure. This is particularly interesting regarding the number of 'masculine' features the young woman is showing. Her upper body is slender and androgynous. No attention is drawn to her chest since this area is hidden by her left arm. Unlike Millais, Brickdale does not emphasise the waist of her figure as the waist band shapes Ferdinand's torso like an hourglass, but Ellen's belt is positioned low and creates a straight line across her back and stomach, de-emphasising any feminine features or signs of pregnancy. Only when comparing the legs of the two figures is it apparent that Ellen's thighs are softer, reflecting the female physique.

Arthur Hughes's painting *As You Like It* from the early 1870s also displays a young woman, Rosalind, disguised as her alter ego Ganymede (Figure 2.9). Although both figures represent women in male attire,

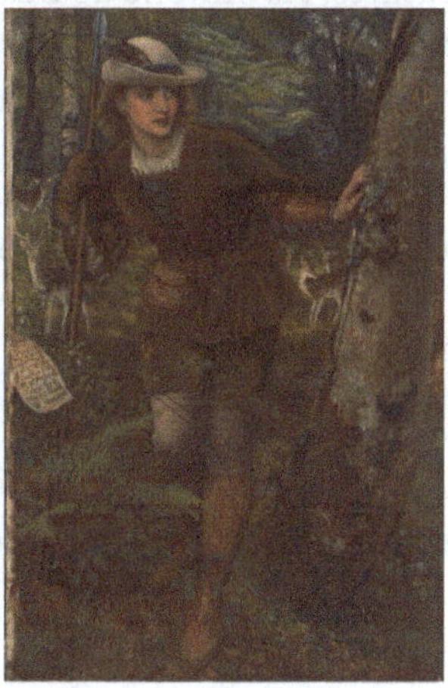

Figure 2.9. Arthur Hughes, *As You Like It*, 1872–3, Oil on canvas, 72.0 × 46.0 cm, Liverpool, Walker Art Gallery. Photo by Walker Art Gallery. © National Museums Liverpool.

Hughes's depiction emphasises the female features more than Brickdale's representation of Ellen. Ganymede's hair is longer than Ellen's not-yet finished pageboy haircut, indicated by the left side of her head. Moreover, Ganymede's waist belt emphasises her hips and chest, and her facial features are highlighted with bright red lips and blushing cheeks. The gender transformation in Hughes's painting has already happened; the alleged man clearly reveals female characteristics, or what in terms of nineteenth-century gender constructions was deemed to be feminine. In a subtler way, the face of the female figure in *The Little Foot Page* also reveals blushed cheeks and a slightly opened mouth with bright red lips. Brickdale's representation of Ellen, therefore, is by no means entirely free of sexual connotations. In her essay 'Women, Art, and Power', Nochlin argues that in a male-dominated society every depiction of a female nude is problematic.[85] Continuing this idea, even depictions of clothed females are in most cases controversial as, considering the theory of the male gaze, clothes still emphasise or de-emphasise body parts. In *The Little Foot Page*, the white tights draw attention to Ellen's feminine legs, and her beautiful face is a central element of the composition.

However, the woman's posture and the emphasis on the men's attire foreground masculine features. As Simone de Beauvoir argues, a woman's orientation towards men, or rather what was considered to be a male attitude, is rooted in an envy of phallocentric advantages within a patriarchal society.

> [T]he girl envies the phallus only as a symbol of the privileges granted to boys; [...] the universal predominance of males, and upbringing all confirm her idea of masculine superiority. [...] She reacts by a 'masculine protest'; she either tries to masculinize herself or uses her feminine wiles to go into battle against man.[86]

Brickdale exhibited *The Little Foot Page* in 1905, the year of the suffragettes' first public protest. Against this backdrop, the aspect of cross-dressing as a

85 Linda Nochlin, 'Women, Art, and Power', in Linda Nochlin, *Women, Art, and Power and Other Essays* (New York: Harper & Row, 1988), 30.

86 Simone de Beauvoir, *The Second Sex*, trans. and ed. H. M. Parshley (New York: Vintage Books, 2010), 77.

gender-performative act in Brickdale's painting links the motif to the New Woman and suffragette movements. The suffragettes used nonconformity in their battle against a significant male privilege: the right to vote. Susan Gubar argues that in the context of drastic changes in women's fashion at the turn of the century, clothing not only fulfilled the role of personal expression but was also a sign of political protest against the patriarchal system. Men's attire was thus often associated with escapism and freedom by some women of that time. In this sense, cross-dressing was an opportunity to redefine femininity. The first-generation Pre-Raphaelite artist Barbara Leigh Smith Bodichon perceived fashionable clothes as restrictive and insisted on wearing boots and loose, comfortable clothes.[87] Other women, such as Dr Mary Walker, had already worn bloomers and pantaloon trousers in the mid-nineteenth century, claiming that women's clothes should be equally comfortable and practical as those of men.[88] Another famous example is the French artist Rosa Bonheur, who not only wore trousers but also fought for the right of two independent women to marry.[89] The French police even granted Bonheur a cross-dressing permit.[90]

By the end of the nineteenth century, more women used 'mannish' clothing to liberate themselves 'from the restrictions of corsets and allowed them to climb astride bicycles'.[91] The bicycle became a symbol of the self-driven New Woman. Public fears were the potential emergence of 'manly women' and the interference of women in the male-dominated public sphere.[92] Guidebooks for lady cycling emphasised the importance of functional clothing, which provide legroom for mobility.[93] The

87 Pam Hirsch, *Barbara Leigh Smith Bodichon 1827–1891: Feminist, Artist and Rebel* (London: Chatto & Windus, 1998), 37.

88 Susan Gubar, 'Blessings in Disguise: Cross-Dressing as Re-Dressing for Female Modernists', *The Massachusetts Review* 22/3 (1981), 478–80.

89 Gretchen van Slyke, 'The Sexual and Textual Politics of Dress: Rosa Bonheur and Her Cross-Dressing Permits', *Nineteenth-Century French Studies* 26/3 (1998), 325–7.

90 van Slyke, 'Sexual and Textual Politics', 321.

91 Patricia Marks, *Bicycles, Bangs, and Bloomers: The New Woman in the Popular Press* (Lexington: University Press of Kentucky, 1990), 142.

92 Marks, *Bicycles, Bangs, and Bloomers*, 147.

93 F. J. Erskine, *Lady Cycling: What to Wear and How to Ride* (London: The British Library, [1897] 2014), 9.

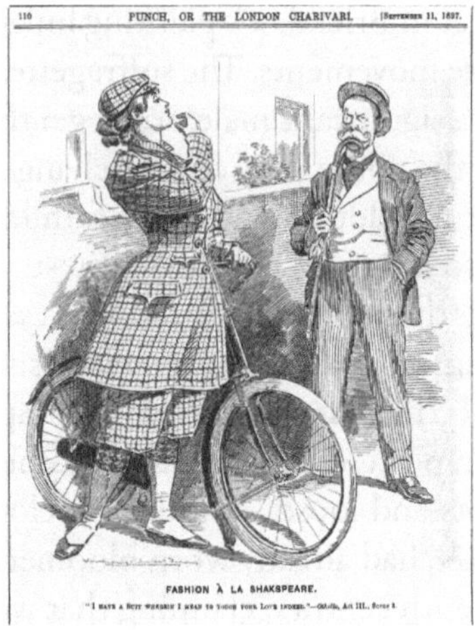

Figure 2.10. *Fashion à la Shakespeare*, illustration, *Punch*, 11 September 1897. Public Domain.

growing interest in cycling attire shows how fashion allowed women to escape their assigned domain and role. Contemporary caricatures reveal how women wearing bicycle outfits were mocked in the popular press as being mistaken for men. An illustration in *Punch* magazine even linked the fashion of the New Woman to the cross-dressing practices on the Elizabethan stage by labelling the woman's clothes as 'fashion à la Shakespeare' (Figure 2.10).

Brickdale's depiction of the medieval heroine emphasises her transformation into a young man, highlighting cross-dressing and the act of cutting long hair. Since the left side of the woman's face is already transformed into a page, the emblematic act of gender transformation, which is half-finished, can be read as women's desire to be equal with the male sex, particularly regarding legal rights such as suffrage and independence, which were reserved for the male heteronormative part of the Edwardian society. Using the Pre-Raphaelite ideology of referring to sources of the past, the female figure in *The Little Foot Page* appears as a New Woman under the guise of a medieval narrative.

Conclusion

The representation of femininity in Brickdale's examined artworks draws analogies to the gender stereotype of the New Woman. The analysis of the female figure in *The Pale Complexion of True Love* reveals a type of femininity that is reminiscent of the Gibson Girl. By emphasising features such as a beautiful young face, an elongated neck, a tall and slender figure as well as a head held high, Brickdale adapted the beauty ideal of the Gibson Girl, transformed according to the Pre-Raphaelite visual language and dressed it in a medievalised narrative. With their exaggerated pose and countenance, the figures in the painting mock the absurdities of courtship behaviour and matrimony and thus serve, together with the contemporaneous satirical illustrations in the popular press, as a visual contribution to the late Victorian Marriage Question. The examination of the woman in Brickdale's painting *The Little Foot Page* reveals cross-dressing to be an important aspect of gender transformation, analogous to the practice of wearing men's clothes by members of the New Woman and suffragette circles. By referring to a medieval ballad, the artist seems to have created a positive visual adaptation of the New Woman in the form of a medieval heroine. The examined paintings address gender-related issues around the turn of the twentieth century, such as the debate on the New Woman and alternatives to marriage, which were widely discussed during the late 1890s. By engaging with the ideologies of first-wave feminism through her artwork, Brickdale appears to have linked contemporary social issues to medieval tales and Pre-Raphaelite role models to establish her unique conception of art within the third generation of Pre-Raphaelitism.

Bibliography

Alighieri, Dante, *Dante's Inferno* (New York City, NY: Cassell, Petter, Galpin and Co., 1866).

Aveling, Edward, and Eleanor Marx Aveling, *The Woman Question* (London: Swan Sonnenschein, Le Bas and Lowrey, 1886).

Barringer Timothy, *Before and After Modernism: Byam Shaw, Rex Vicat Cole, Yinka Shonibare, MBE* (London: Central Saint Martins College of Art and Design, 2010).

Bate, Percy, *The English Pre-Raphaelite Painters: Their Associates and Successors* (London: George Bell and Sons, [1899] 1910).

Brickdale, Charles Fortescue, 'Obituary: Sarah Grand', *The Times* (24 May 1943).

'Belles Lettres', *The Westminster Review* (1 October 1865).

Bullough, Vern L., and Bonnie Bullough, *Cross Dressing, Sex, and Gender* (Philadelphia: University of Pennsylvania Press, 1993).

Chevalier, Jean, and Alain Gheerbrant, *The Penguin Dictionary of Symbols*, 2nd edn (London: Penguin Books, 1996).

Child, Francis James, ed., *English and Scottish Popular Ballads*, vol. 2, part 3 (Boston, MA: Houghton Mifflin, 1885).

Colvin, Sidney, *Guide to an Exhibition of Drawings and Engravings by the Old Masters: Principally From the Malcom Collection in the Print and Drawing Gallery*, 2nd edn (London: British Museum, 1895).

de Beauvoir, Simone, *The Second Sex* (New York: Vintage Books, 2010).

Dixon, Ella Hepworth, 'Why Women Are Ceasing to Marry', *Humanitarian* 14 (1899), 391–926.

Dixon, Marion Hepworth, 'Our Rising Artists: Eleanor Fortescue-Brickdale', *The Magazine of Art* (1902), 256–62.

England and Wales Census, Surrey, Upper Norwood, RG 11/822, 14 (1881). <https://www.myheritage.com/research/record-10154-31924401/mary-e-f-brickdale-in-1881-england-wales-census?s=499190911#household>, accessed 26 February 2018.

Erskine, F. J., *Lady Cycling: What to Wear and How to Ride* (London: The British Library, [1897] 2014).

Fehlbaum, Valerie, 'Sisters in Life, Sisters in Art: Ella and Marion Hepworth Dixon', in Margaret D. Stetz and Cheryl A. Wilson, eds, *Michael Field and Their World* (High Wycombe: The Rivendale Press, 2007), 107–16.

Frantz, Henri, 'Les Salons Anglais en 1899: Royal Academy, International Society, New Gallery', *Gazette des Beaux-Arts* 22/4 (3rd Period) (1899), 343–52.

Garber, Marjorie, *Vested Interests: Cross-Dressing and Cultural Anxiety* (New York: Routledge, 1992).

Grand, Sarah, 'The New Aspect of the Woman Question', *The North American Review* 158/448 (1894), 270–76.

——, 'The New Woman and the Old', *Lady's Realm* 4 (1898), 466–70.

——, et al., 'Does Marriage Hinder a Woman's Self-Development?,' *Lady's Realm* 5 (1898), 576–86.

Griffin, Ben, *The Politics of Gender in Victorian Britain: Masculinity, Political Culture and the Struggle for Women's Rights* (Cambridge: Cambridge University Press, 2012).

Groom, Nick, *The Making of Percy's Reliques* (Oxford: Clarendon Press, 1966).

Gubar, Susan, 'Blessings in Disguise: Cross-Dressing as Re-Dressing for Female Modernists', *The Massachusetts Review* 22/3 (1981), 477–508.

Guillim, John, *A Display of Heraldry*, 6th edn (London: Printed by T. W. for R. and J. Bonwicke and R. Wilkin, 1724).

Hart, Cyril, *Coleford: The History of a West Gloucestershire Forest Town* (Gloucester: Alan Sutton, 1983).

Heilmann, Ann, *New Woman Fiction: Women Writing First-Wave Feminism* (New York: Palgrave Macmillan, 2000).

——, *New Woman Strategies: Sarah Grand, Olive Schreiner, Mona Caird* (Manchester: Manchester University Press, 2004).

Hotchkiss, Valerie R., *Clothes Make the Man: Female Cross Dressing in Medieval Europe* (New York: Routledge, 1996).

Ingram, John H., *Flora Symbolica; or: The Language and Sentiment of Flowers* (London: F. W. Warne and Co., 1869).

James, John Angell, *Female Piety: Or, the Young Woman's Friend and Guide Through Life to Immortality* (New York: Robert Carter & Brothers, [1852] 1853).

Jessen, Jarno, 'Moderne Präraffaeliten', *Die Kunst für Alle* 19/4 (1903), 83–92.

Kern, Stephen, *Eyes of Love: The Gaze in English and French Paintings and Novels 1840–1900* (London: Reaktion Books, 1996).

Marks, Patricia, *Bicycles, Bangs, and Bloomers: The New Woman in the Popular Press* (Lexington: University Press of Kentucky, 1990).

Marsh, Jan, *Pre-Raphaelite Sisterhood* (London: Quartet, 1985).

——, and Pamela Gerrish Nunn, *Pre-Raphaelite Women Artists* (London: Thames and Hudson, 1998).

——, *Women Artists and the Pre-Raphaelite Movement* (London: Virago, 1989).

——, et al., *Pre-Raphaelite Sisters* (London: National Portrait Gallery, 2019).

Muthesius, Hermann, 'Kunst und Leben in England', *Zeitschrift für Bildende Kunst* 37 (NF 13) (1902), 13–21, 49–69.

Nead, Lynda, *Myths of Sexuality: Representations of Women in Victorian Britain* (Oxford: Basil Blackwell, 1990).
Nochlin, Linda, 'Why Have There Been No Great Women Artists?', in Linda Nochlin, *Women, Art, and Power and other Essays* (New York, NY: Harper & Row, 1988), 145–78.
——,'Women, Art, and Power', in Linda Nochlin, *Women, Art, and Power and Other Essays* (New York: Harper & Row, 1988).
Nunn, Pamela Gerrish, *A Pre-Raphaelite Journey: The Art of Eleanor Fortescue-Brickdale* (Liverpool: Liverpool University Press, 2012).
——, 'Time and Tide Wait for No Man: A Victorian Apocalypse', in Christian Heck and Kristen Lippincott, eds, *Symbols of Time in the History of Art* (Turnhout: Brepols, 2002), 85–97.
'Obituary: Miss Fortescue-Brickdale; a Versatile Artist', *The Times* (14 March 1945).
Ouida, 'The New Woman', *The North American Review* 158/450 (1894), 610–19.
Patterson, Martha H., *Beyond the Gibson Girl: Reimagining the American New Woman, 1895–1915* (Urbana: University of Illinois Press, 2005).
Percy, Thomas, *Reliques of Ancient English Poetry: Consisting of Old Heroic Ballads, Songs, and Other Pieces of Our Earlier Poets; Together with Some Few of Later Date*, 2nd edn, vol. III (London: Henry Washbourne and Co., 1857).
Phillips, Henry, *Floral Emblems* (London: Saunders and Otley, 1825).
Pollock, Griselda, and Deborah Cherry, 'Patriarchal Power and the Pre-Raphaelites', *Art History* 7/4 (1984), 480–95.
Prettejohn, Elizabeth, *The Art of the Pre-Raphaelites* (London: Tate, 2007).
——, *Modern Painters, Old Masters: The Art of Imitation From the Pre-Raphaelites to the First World War* (New Haven: Yale University Press, 2017).
Royal Academy, Register of Admission of Students, RAA/KEE/1/1/4, July 1890–January 1922, 6 no. 4479.
Ruskin, John, *Academy Notes: Notes on Prout and Hunt and Other Art Criticisms 1855–1888*, in Alexander Wedderburn and E. T. Cook, eds, *The Complete Works of John Ruskin*, vol. XIV (London: George Allen, 1904).
Scott, E. S., and E. B. Hall, 'Character Note: The New Woman', *Cornhill Magazine* 23 (1894), 365–68.
Scott, Margaret, *Medieval Dress and Fashion* (London: The British Library, 2009).
Shakespeare, William, *As You Like It*, J. W. Holme, ed., 4th edn (London: Methuen and Co., 1940).
Shapiro, Michael, *Gender in Play on the Shakespearean Stage: Boy Heroines and Female Pages* (Ann Arbor: University of Michigan Press, 1994).
Sparrow, Walter Shaw, 'On Some Watercolour Pictures by Miss Eleanor Fortescue-Brickdale', *The Studio* 23/99 (1901), 31–43.

——, 'Women Painters of the World: From the Time of Caterina Vigri (1413–1463) to Rosa Bonheur and the Present Day', in Walter Shaw Sparrow, ed., *The Art and Life Library*, vol. III (London: Hodder and Stoughton, 1905).

Steinbach, Susie L., *Understanding the Victorians: Politics, Culture, and Society in Nineteenth-Century Britain* (London: Routledge, 2012).

Taylor, G. L., Centenary Exhibition of Works by Eleanor Fortescue-Brickdale 1872–1945 (Oxford: Ashmoleon Museum, 1972).

The Academy Notes 1899 with Illustrations of the Principal Pictures at Burlington House: Originated by the Late Henry Blackburn (London: Chatto & Windus, 1899).

The Exhibition of the Royal Academy of Arts: The One Hundred and Thirty-First (London: William Clowes and Sons, 1899).

'The Ladies Column: Gossip for Women', *Lichfield Mercury* (14 March 1902).

'The Royal Academy (II.)', *St. James's Gazette* (10 May 1899).

van Slyke, Gretchen, 'The Sexual and Textual Politics of Dress: Rosa Bonheur and Her Cross-Dressing Permits', *Nineteenth-Century French Studies* 26/3 (1998), 321–35.

Walker Art Gallery, *Thirty-Fifth Autumn Exhibition of Modern Art* (Liverpool: Lee and Nightingale, 1905).

Zander-Seidel, Jutta, *Textiler Hausrat: Kleidung und Haustextilien in Nürnberg von 1500–1650* (Munich: Deutscher Kunstverlag, 1990).

CAROLINE E. GIDDIS

3 New Light Upon the Soul: Mary Seton Watts's Legacy of Progressivism and Late-Pre-Raphaelitism in the Watts Cemetery Chapel

ABSTRACT

Scottish artist Mary Seton Watts (1849–1938) actively subverted the gender roles and artistic divisions of the nineteenth and twentieth centuries, acting as a powerful proto-feminist icon who extended the legacy of the Pre-Raphaelite movement and added the Celtic Revival to its lexicon. While Seton Watts's connection to the movement has been underacknowledged, her greatest creation, the Watts Cemetery Chapel in Compton, Surrey, is a pinnacle of late-Pre-Raphaelitism, Arts and Crafts aesthetics and Celtic-Art Nouveau design. Utilising terracotta and gesso, Seton Watts shaped a vibrant, complex and anachronistic map of symbols to express messages of equality, freedom, progress and rebirth throughout her structure. By examining Seton Watts's *The Word in the Pattern* (1905), diary entries, letters and artworks together, the full impact of her previously overlooked avant-garde fusion of art and craft, proto-feminism, passion for education and artistic practices rooted in Pre-Raphaelitism may be realised for the first time.

* * * * *

> A fresh wind astir. I feel it calls to me saying 'be up, the working world has need of your life.'
>
> – Mary Seton Watts, July 11, 1904.[1]

1 Mary Seton Watts, *The Diary of Mary Seton Watts* [1904], transcribed Desna Greenhow (unpublished archival material, Watts Gallery Trust), 10. This essay is a shortened version of the author's masters thesis titled 'The Morning Cometh: Mary Seton Watts and Her Symbolic Display of Progressive Artistry and Proto-Feminism in the Watts Cemetery Chapel' (Savannah College of Art and Design, 2020) and was the inspired result of attending the *Pre-Raphaelite Sisters: Making Art* conference in 2019.

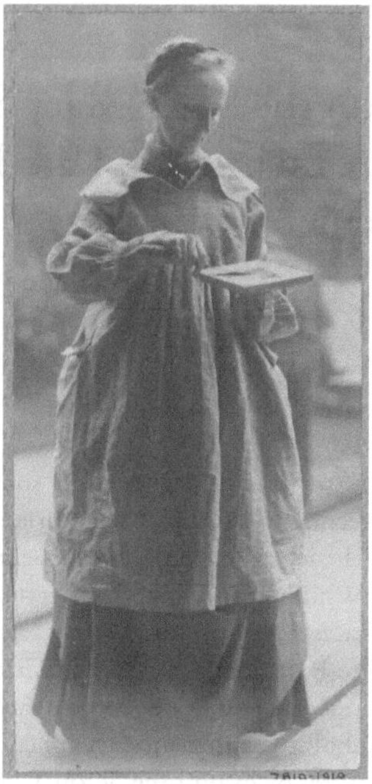

Figure 3.1. Frederick Hollyer, *Mrs G. F. Watts*, c. 1890, platinum print, 15.2 × 6.8 cm, Victoria and Albert Museum, London. 7810–1938. © Victoria and Albert Museum.

In April 1904, in the village of Compton in Surrey, England, a mortuary chapel was finally completed when the focus of its golden gesso altarpiece – a symbolic painting entitled *The All-Pervading* (1887–90) by George Frederic Watts (1817–1904) – was placed in the central panel.[2] Although G. F. Watts, the portraitist and Symbolist painter, was given one of the most prominent placements in the chapel, it is his wife, Scottish artist and architect of the Watts Cemetery Chapel, Mary Seton Watts (Figure 3.1), whose work dwarfs his with its bright gravitas, as her masterpiece is the chapel itself. Within the interior (Figure 3.2), which is adorned with the opulence of an illuminated manuscript, G. F. Watts's painting is barely noticeable despite its enthronement in a golden shrine, due to the expanse

2 The painting has since been removed for conservation purposes.

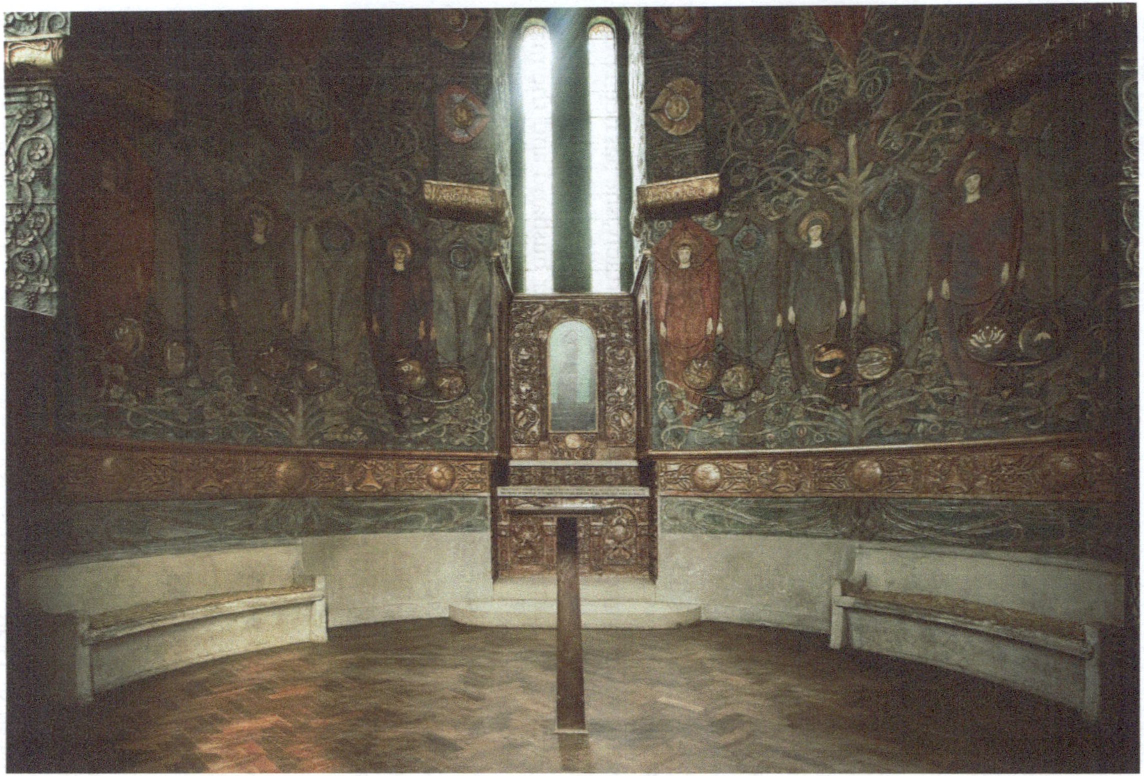

Figure 3.2. Interior of Watts Chapel, 2014, photograph by Ann Ayerst, Watts Gallery Trust.

of intricate gesso relief which surrounds it. Seton Watts's amalgamated pinnacle of late-Pre-Raphaelite, Arts and Crafts, Art Nouveau and Celtic-revival design, the Watts Cemetery Chapel is a complex map of symbols which communicates reformist narratives of hope, equality and rebirth to inspire the fin-de-siècle spirit and redefine its artistic movements.

The chapel structure is embellished with both secular and religious symbolism, which Seton Watts carefully explained in her textual accompaniment to the chapel, *The Word in the Pattern: A Key to the Symbols on the Walls of the Chapel at Compton, Surrey* (1905).[3] A progressive Victorian woman, Seton Watts was an active early supporter of women's suffrage and expressed her proto-feminism in private journals and public artwork. She dedicated much of her life to campaigning for equality and inclusivity in all areas, especially when it came to art education, which she was able to reform in her own way through the Home Arts and Industries Association (HAIA). In 2016, Seton Watts's diaries from 1887 to 1904, held in the Watts Gallery Archive, were finally transcribed and published, revealing her private thoughts and artistic practices.[4] Regrettably, she has been overlooked and undervalued as a trailblazing artist until recent decades, but is now finally marching out of the shadow of her husband and the male artists who preceded her in the art movements to which she also significantly contributed. By examining Seton Watts's *The Word in the Pattern* (1905), diary entries, letters and artwork together, the full impact of her previously overlooked avant-garde practices and personal beliefs on the ecosystem and legacy of the turn-of-the-century art world may be realised for the first time.

While Seton Watts's connection to the Pre-Raphaelite Brotherhood has been underacknowledged, her career and artwork, which uniquely emulated their original tenants of progressivism, social commentary and revolutionary design, are vital to the movement's history and perpetuation.

3 Mary Seton Watts, *The Word in the Pattern: A Key to the Symbols on the Walls of the Chapel at Compton, Surrey*, 2nd edn (London: Astolat Press, 1905). The book has two print editions with a modest original print run but nevertheless had appeal for fellow artists, locals and architects.

4 *The Diary of Mary Watts 1887–1904*, eds Desna Greenhow, Lucy Ella Rose and Gail Naughton (London: Lund Humphries and Watts Gallery, 2016).

Her career broke with Victorian expectations, her artistic process deviated from the norm, her iconography expressed messages that commented on contemporary struggles and her work praised the natural and religious worlds. As an artist who actively subverted the gender roles and artistic divisions of the nineteenth and twentieth centuries, Seton Watts acted as a powerful proto-feminist icon who extended the legacy of the Pre-Raphaelite movement well into the twentieth century, adding Celtic elements to its lexicon along the way. As this is the first examination of Seton Watts's chapel which uses her writings, proto-feminist activism, and myriad of artistic influences to argue for her place among the Pre-Raphaelite pantheon, it is imperative to immediately and scrupulously introduce her greatest artistic triumph: the Watts Cemetery Chapel.

The Chapel

Deciphering the interior and exterior of the Watts Chapel is a labyrinthine process; however, subjecting its symbols and creator to deep investigation is a worthy endeavour for establishing its importance in the artistic multitudes of Pre-Raphaelitism, the Arts and Crafts movement, Symbolism and late Victorian art as a whole.[5] The chapel combines art forms, religions and dimensionalities to create a place of palpable emotion. Forming an equilateral Celtic cross, the overall circular architecture is a mixture of Byzantine and Romanesque styles, perhaps inspired by Seton Watts's previous travels to Rome and Constantinople, with the exterior consisting almost entirely of brick and handmade terracotta tiles.[6]

5 Seton Watts's tie to the Symbolist movement is characterised by a use of iconographic messages and abstract colour, while her husband's symbolic work was more emotionally representational; for more information, see Andrew Wilton, *The Age of Rossetti, Burne-Jones and Watts: Symbolism in Britain, 1860–1910* (London: Tate Gallery Publishing, 1997).

6 Veronica Franklin Gould, *The Watts Chapel: An Arts & Crafts Memorial* (Surrey: Arrow Press, 1993), 15–16; Seton Watts, *Diary* [1887], 46; Seton Watts, *Word in the Pattern*, 4, 24–5.

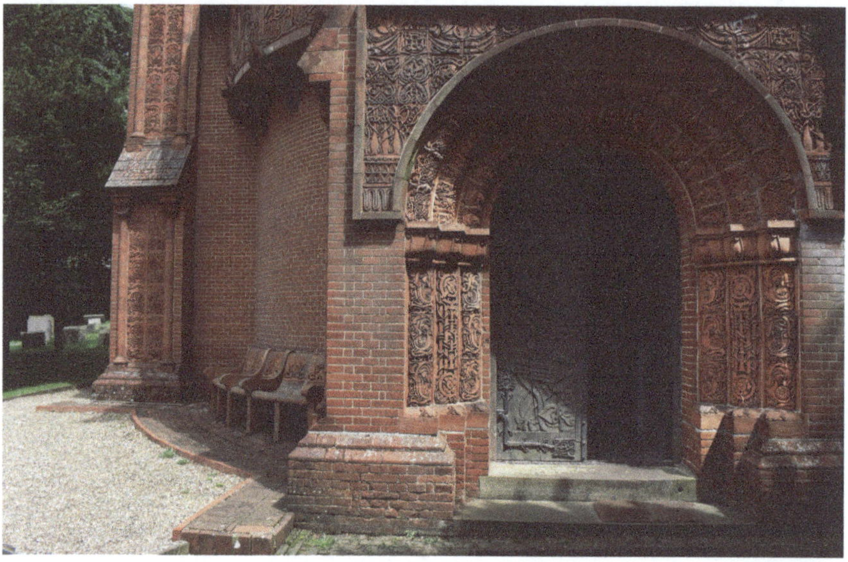

Figure 3.3. Watts Cemetery Chapel, Surrey, 2016, photograph by Mark via Flickr (CC BY 2.0).

The smooth texture and strict linearity of bricks provide a harmonious counterpart to the languid curvilinearity of Seton Watts's Celtic-knotted terracotta tiles.

The most prominent architectural feature is the receding doorway with archivolts supported by ornate jamb columns (Figure 3.3). Enveloping the archivolt above the doorway is an intricate spandrel, or 'wall veil'. The spandrel – titled *The Garment of Praise* – imitates a hanging textile and is derived from the tradition of a baldachin, which separates the living on earth from the divine realm of Christ.[7]

In the veil mosaic, diagonal from the corners, along the rounded edge, sits a curious motif: the phoenix. Captured at a significant point in its

7 The tiles represent passages from Isaiah 61:1–3 (King James Version) to comfort mourners; Margaret Barker, *Great High Priest: The Temple Roots of Christian Liturgy* (New York: T&T Clark, 2003), 205–8; Seton Watts, *Word in the Pattern*, 12–14.

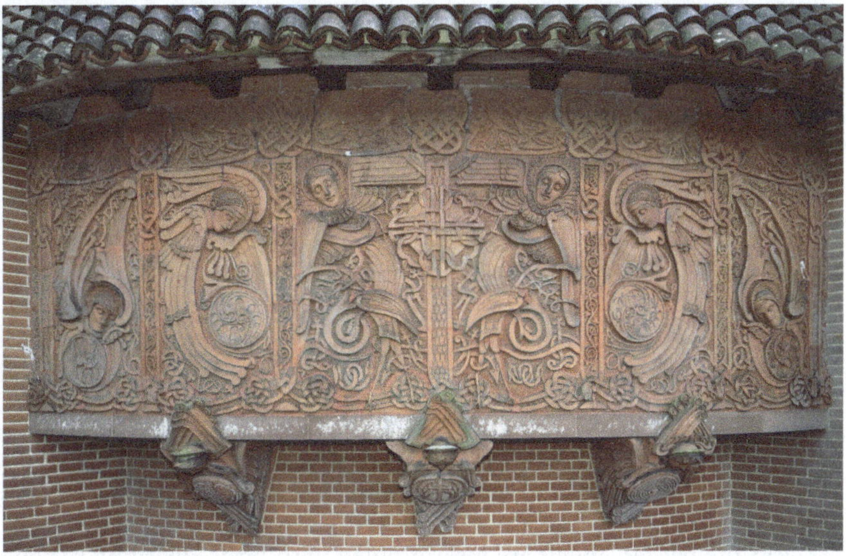

Figure 3.4. *The Spirit of Love* frieze, Watts Cemetery Chapel, 2009, photograph by Anne Purkiss, Watts Gallery Trust.

mythical life cycle, the bird rises from the flames as it is reborn.[8] Conveying a strong message of comfort in the afterlife or – in a more modern sense – personal renewal, the phoenix is one of Seton Watts's first powerful symbols that a visitor might encounter.[9] Below the veil sit the double doors of the chapel, which are made of oak encased in chestnut held with wrought-iron mounts to form a Celtic cross, a design that Seton Watts specifically copied from a gravestone in Argyleshire, Scotland.[10] Stretching around the chapel drum is a projecting terracotta relief frieze, each section resting on three angel-corbels. These overhanging sections hold the four parts of Seton Watts's *The Path of the Just*, which includes *The Spirit of Hope, The Spirit of Truth, The Spirit of Love* (Figure 3.4) and *The Spirit of Light*.[11]

8 Seton Watts, *Word in the Pattern*, 12–14.
9 Seton Watts, *Word in the Pattern*, 12–14.
10 Seton Watts, *Word in the Pattern*, 24.
11 Seton Watts, *Word in the Pattern*, 21–30.

Each frieze was designed to feature a bird species that best represented the respective spirits. With a strikingly proto-feminist edge for the time, artists like Seton Watts and Evelyn De Morgan used avian symbolism in their work to directly address the problems and social impact of common Victorian tropes of 'caged bird', reclaiming the use of birds to instead symbolise the achievement of freedom.[12] Seton Watts's stylised birds are not caged, but alert, mid-action or pre-flight. As she explained, the peacock stands for *Hope*, a symbol that suffragists and the Arts and Crafts movement both adopted; the owl for *Truth* because of their strength of vision; the pelican for *Love* for its myth of self-sacrifice; and the eagle for *Light* because of its connection to the sun and Saint John the Evangelist.[13] Although birds often embody freedom, Seton Watts believed the flying fish – featured as a medallion on the *Spirit of Truth* – to be the ideal symbol of liberty, as the species defies its biology to take flight like a bird, finding freedom in air and sea.[14]

On the friezes, angels are intermingled with birds, guarding various medallions composed of a fusion of words, Celtic knots, animals and vegetative patterns. Seton Watts's love of ornate manuscripts like the *Book of Kells* (eighth century CE; Figure 3.5) may have been due to their extraordinary fusion of text and illustration in a way that gave equal weight to line and form, a technique that she replicated in the friezes to equally magical effect.[15] Victorian audiences rediscovered this phenomenon when Edward Moxon published his edition of Alfred Tennyson's *Poems* in 1857, which fused illustrations by Dante Gabriel Rossetti, William Holman Hunt and John Everett Millais with Tennyson's text, creating an ethereal art object.[16]

12 Lucy Ella Rose, *Suffragist Artists in Partnership: Gender, Word and Image* (Edinburgh: Edinburgh University Press, 2018), 84–7; Elise Lawton Smith, *Evelyn Pickering De Morgan and the Allegorical Body* (London: Associated University Presses, 2002), 138–41; For more information, see Madeleine Kennedy, ed., *The Enchanted Interior*, exh. cat. (Newcastle Upon Tyne: Laine Art Gallery, 2019).

13 Seton Watts, *Word in the Pattern*, 19–22.

14 Gould, *Watts Chapel*, 23.

15 Seton Watts, *The Diary of Mary Watts*, 1887–1904, 163.

16 Anne Anderson, 'Pre-Raphaelite Values', in Anne Anderson, ed., *Beyond the Brotherhood: The Pre-Raphaelite Legacy*, exh. cat. (Bristol: Sansom & Company, 2019), 24–7.

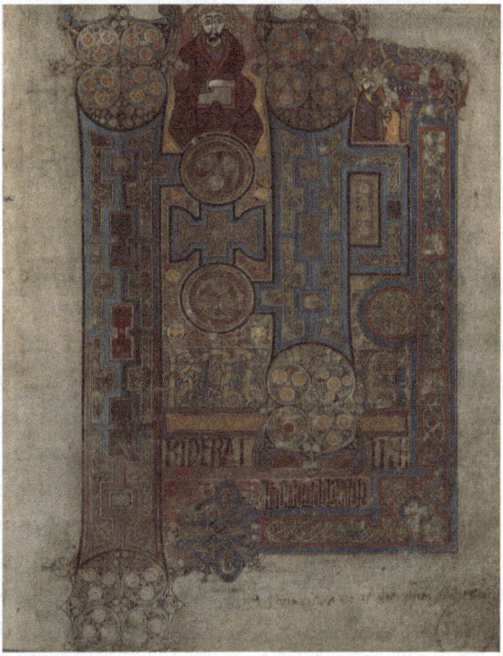

Figure 3.5. Unattributed, Folio 292r: John; In p/rinvi/pio erat uer/bum [et] uer[b]um 'Gospel of John, Chapter I:I', in *Book of Kells*, c. 800, coloured ink on vellum, 33 × 25 cm, Trinity College Dublin, IE TCD MS 58.

William Morris's *Kelmscott Chaucer* (1896) had a similarly stirring impact, especially due to its strong relationship to medieval manuscript illumination.[17] Seton Watts's friezes are, in practice and essence, sculpted pages of an ancient Celtic manuscript with an iconography of their own.

While the periphery offers intricate, subtle beauty, the crown jewel of the Watts Chapel is its dazzling interior (Figure 3.2). In an attempt to describe the intimate inner chapel space, Seton Watts wrote: 'In these lines no endeavour is made to fix particular thoughts to the old

17 *The Works of Geoffrey Chaucer now newly imprinted* [ed. F. S. Ellis; ornamented with pictures designed by Sir Edward Burne-Jones; engraved on wood by W. H. Hooper] (Hammersmith, London: The Kelmscott Press, 1896).

symbols, but only to name them, so that the thoughts may remain free within them, to suggest as much or as little as a song without words.'[18] Here, she was not simply replicating old styles with predetermined meanings but fusing multiple motifs together to transform them into a wholly new and openly interpretable melody. On the interior walls, heaven and earth are united in a plane of rich teal blue with a golden Celtic banner that binds the walls in a never-ending circle. The interior architecture is constructed with intersecting arches that spring from the chapel walls to form a dome-like shape with a gabled roof.[19] The adornment of the interior originates at the ceiling apex with the 'Circle of Eternity' and trickles down to engulf the walls in a spectrum of light, colour and texture (Figure 3.6).

Seton Watts populated the chapel with heavenly beings of Christianity such as angels, seraphim and cherubim. She also added various ancient and pagan Celtic motifs in addition to a prominent symbol found in most creation myths: the Tree of Life, split into four sections within the chapel.[20] All life – heavenly, earthly or symbolic – is connected to Seton Watts's Art-Nouveau-whiplash tree. Here, she used the Tree of Life to physically connect all forms within the chapel, manifesting a symbolic unity in the process. The branches spread over each wall panel and are embellished with vegetation, extending onto the window reveals in whirls. Under the golden belt, the tree's roots weave together.[21]

In 1888, Edward Burne-Jones, artist and close friend of the Watts family, created *Tree of Life* (Figure 3.7), a mosaic apse design for G. E. Street's St Paul's Within-the-Walls (1872–80), a similar neo-Byzantine structure in Rome. In his Italian-Symbolist style, he presented the tree as a blue, lung-like arborescent on which Christ is being crucified within an empty landscape flanked by Adam and Eve. Although there is no current record of Burne-Jones and Seton Watts discussing his design, it may have resurfaced when

18 Seton Watts, *Word in the Pattern*, 28.

19 Gould, *Watts Chapel*, 28–9.

20 W. R. Lethaby, *Architecture, Mysticism and Myth* (London: Percival, 1892), 512.

21 Gould, *The Watts Chapel*, 28.

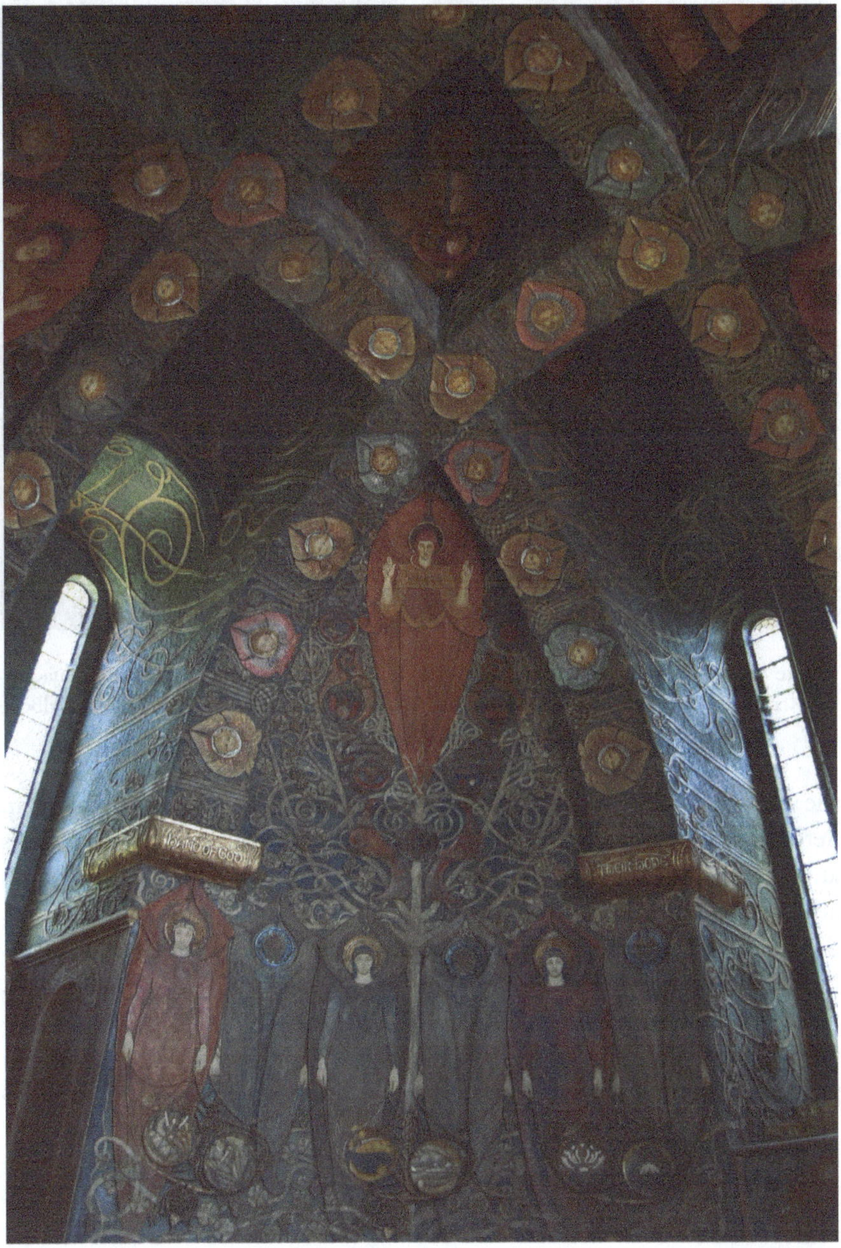

Figure 3.6. Watts Chapel Interior, 2011, photograph by Girish Gopi via Flickr (CC BY-SA 2.0).

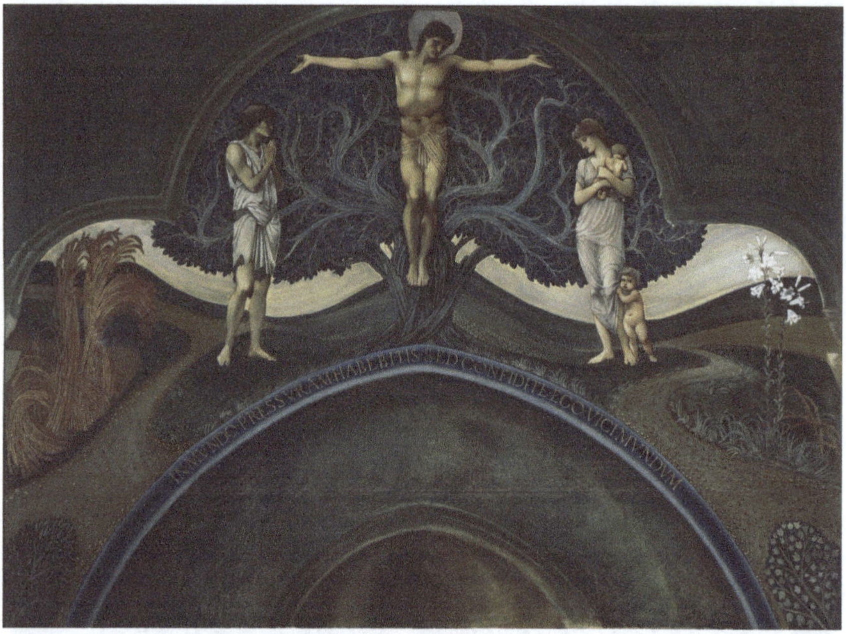

Figure 3.7. Sir Edward Coley Burne-Jones, *Tree of Life*, 1888, watercolour and gouache, 181 × 242 cm, Victoria and Albert Museum, London, 584– 1898. © Victoria and Albert Museum.

she was researching motifs. While the colours and ideas are perhaps similar, Seton Watts's tree is three-dimensional, includes multi-religious symbols and is overwhelmingly Celtic rather than Italian, a change from themes and styles found in even the latest materialisations of Pre-Raphaelitism. Seton Watts's evolution of Pre-Raphaelitism included an allusion to styles far predating Early Italian art, including ancient religions and cultures, while incorporating new developments in fin-de-siècle design. For example, aspects of her Celtic, Art Nouveau style reflected that of an emerging movement at the Glasgow School of Art among 'The Four': Charles

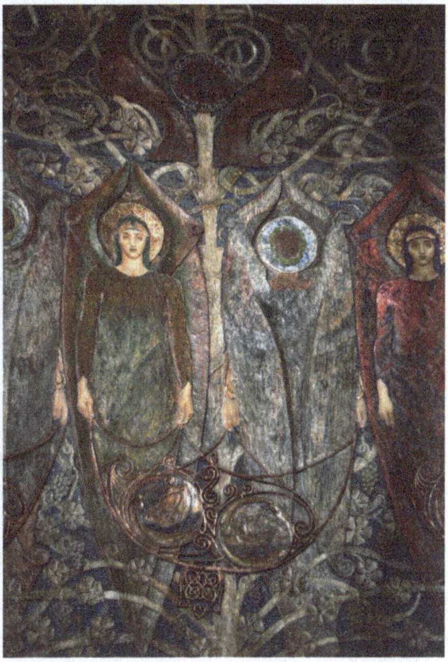

Figure 3.8. Angels, Interior of the Watts Chapel, 2019, photograph by Caroline E. Giddis.

Rennie Mackintosh, Margaret and Frances Macdonald and James Herbert McNair, and epitomises her continued passion for Scotland.[22]

On the four wall panels between each window float crimson seraphim who hold their arms in gestures of benediction and blessing. Surrounding them, medallions depict various 'symbols of the truths which, like footprints of a beneficent Creation, are here to aid man in his search after the spiritual existence'.[23] Wreaths of winged cherubim faces in varying shades of blue, yellow and pink extend around the dome while burgundy peacocks perch on the Tree of Life. Most strikingly, pairs of angels encircle the space, fixing a piercing gaze onto the viewer (Figure 3.8).

22 See Roger Billcliffe, *Charles Rennie Mackintosh and the Art of the Four* (London: Frances Lincoln, 2017).

23 Seton Watts, *Word in the Pattern*, 29.

Individualised by variations in their Egyptian-inspired headdresses, kaftans, deep-hues and front- and away-facing positions, the twenty-four winged figures are a source of reverent magnitude. The angels act as messengers, holding Celtic cords woven with medallions that represent opposing forces of the universe.[24] Seton Watts explained that the angel facing the viewer carries a symbol of light while the other carries a symbol of darkness to 'suggest the earthly conditions in which the soul of man finds itself'.[25] Each angel has a feathered design on their garments and wings, which recall the peacock-and phoenix-feathered angels of Evelyn De Morgan's *Gloria in Excelsis* (1893; see Figure 1.3) and G. F. Watts's *The Dweller in the Innermost* (c. 1885–6; Tate, London). Unlike the delicate, overtly feminine faces of the angels in these works, Seton Watts's angels have more androgynous features of deep-set eyes, wide jaws and Roman noses. While their faces may be ungendered, the angelic bodies display silhouettes of feminine busts and curved hips, emphasised by the fitted tailoring of their kaftans, giving them an overall woman-like appearance. The angels are dominant, formidable beings of the heavenly realm; thus, by feminising them, Seton Watts has given power to the feminine form, elevating it to the status of the divine.

Centred between the angelic pairs, directly across from the front doors, sits a golden, throne-like altar, above which hangs G. F. Watts's altarpiece. Made from terracotta and Portland stone with a layer of gesso and gold tempera, the altar proclaims on a central plaque: 'This chapel designed by Mrs Watts, wife of G. F. Watts, OM. R.A. was built in 1896 by her and the people of Compton: It is dedicated to the memory of all who rest near its walls.' Glowing with golden intensity, the sculpted Celtic knots, angels and words on the altar's base and frame are worthy of scrutiny of their intricacies.

In *The Word in the Pattern* Seton Watts wrote: 'A symbol may well be compared to a magic key. In one hand it is nothing more than a piece of quaintly wrought iron, in another it unlocks a door into a world of enchantment.'[26] The interior of the chapel is earthly and celestial, abstract and geometric, overwhelming yet comforting and is certainly capable of

24 Seton Watts, *Word in the Pattern*, 28–9.
25 Seton Watts, *Word in the Pattern*, 28.
26 Seton Watts, *Word in the Pattern*, 27–8.

enchanting viewers to see the power of beauty and even, perhaps, of grief. As a mortuary space to honour the cemetery and cloistered mausoleum near it, locals likely visited the chapel before or after a funeral or upon visiting the grave of a loved one.[27] In this type of environment, people are prone to contemplate life, death, existence and purpose, giving Seton Watts every reason to permeate the space with philosophical themes to comfort and motivate the living to seek a higher purpose while still alive. One such higher purpose obvious to Seton Watts was achieving equality.

Pre-Raphaelite Progressivism and Proto-Feminism

While the chapel contains layers of proto-feminist symbols and Pre-Raphaelite influence, Seton Watts's life prior to the chapel also reveals an artist of immense skill and undeniable agency, who continually pursued a progressive lifestyle. Her earliest professional artistic training occurred at the Inverness Art Training School at the age of 17, near her home in Scotland.[28] She later studied in Dresden and Rome before enrolling at the South Kensington Art Training School in London.[29] In 1872, Seton Watts attended the Slade School of Art in London, which had opened in 1871 as a co-educational arts school.[30] She originally studied to become a portraitist but later found an affinity for ceramics and sculpture. In 1874 she secured private tutelage under the exiled French sculptor Aimé-Jules Dalou to further her studies in sculpting and pottery. Terracotta would eventually become Seton Watts's preferred medium and was used to

27 The ashes of both Mary and G. F. are interred at the mausoleum cloister, which she also designed and built after G. F.'s death; Historic England, 'Compton Cemetery (Also Known as Watts Cemetery)', Historic England (n.d.), <https://historicengland.org.uk/listing/the-list/list-entry/1417498>, accessed 15 January 2021.

28 Veronica Franklin Gould, *Mary Seton Watts (1849–1938): Unsung Heroine of the Art Nouveau* (Over Wallop, England: Watts Gallery, 1998), 18.

29 Gould, *Mary Seton Watts*, 15, 22.

30 Gould, *Mary Seton Watts*, 15.

create her first professional sculpture, *Mother and Child* (1873–9; Watts Gallery). Historically, women were not considered professional sculptors or painters, more often categorised as 'amateurs'. During the nineteenth century, not only were women becoming professional, successful artists, but they were also actively competing against male artists, which was a revolutionary change. Some members of the art world initially viewed this as a comical endeavour, but soon saw women as a threat to male art-world dominance.[31] From 1875 to 1882, Seton Watts was focused on a career as a professional portraitist in London and Edinburgh, becoming G. F. Watts's student in 1876 after meeting him through photographer Julia Margaret Cameron. Because G. F. Watts was Britain's foremost portraitist at the time, it made sense for her to study under him. They eventually married in 1886 and the two shared a relatively progressive partnership, as evidenced through her diaries and pre-marital letters.

Seton Watts filled at least eight diaries over the course of seventeen years, beginning in 1886 and covering the events of her life until G. F.'s death in 1904.[32] These diaries reveal that she was a reformist and believer in social change, arguing for gender equality, egalitarianism and access to art education as necessities. In 1909, at the age of 60, Seton Watts became President of the Godalming and District Women's Suffrage Society, her local affiliate of the National Union of Women's Suffrage Societies (NUWSS).[33] In 1913, she participated in the famous NUWSS's July pilgrimage, marching through the streets alongside Gertrude Jekyll and more than one hundred other suffragists, with banners designed by Jekyll leading the procession.[34]

Although most of these events were carried out peacefully, those in favour of women's suffrage and especially those who publicly campaigned

31 That is, Burne-Jones's private opinions on Evelyn De Morgan infantilised her even as she rivalled him in skill, see Jan Marsh et al., *Pre-Raphaelite Sisters*, exh. cat. (London: National Portrait Gallery, 2019), 176.

32 Seton Watts, *Diary* 1887–1904, 5–9; Lucy Ella Rose, 'The Diaries of Mary Seton Watts (1849–1938): A Record of Her Conjugal Creative Partnership with "England's Michelangelo", George Frederic Watts (1817–1904)', *Life Writing* 14/2 (2017), 218.

33 'County Jottings', *The Surrey Mirror and County Post*, 2 March 1909, 2.

34 Rose, *Suffragist Artists*, 47.

for it, faced backlash and ridicule. As Lucy Ella Rose noted: 'Mary's bravery in her dedication to the women's cause – in public, in the face of danger in older age – should not be underestimated'.[35] Even before her active involvement, Seton Watts's diaries show that her life had been grounded in the pursuit of a progressive lifestyle. Entries detail her political opinions on controversial subjects and first-hand glimpses into the lives of other influential Victorians, including Oscar Wilde, Josephine Butler and George Meredith. Seton Watts greatly admired Butler for her lifelong dedication to equality and social reform – matters also close to her heart. In one entry, Seton Watts recorded a Butler quotation that most inspired her: 'The kingdom of heaven is for all, even the downtrodden, mud besmirched', a message that she would later echo throughout her chapel.[36] Years of entries, such as this, reveal Seton Watts's evolving religious beliefs. With a solid foundation in Christianity and biblical knowledge, Seton Watts's personal philosophy transcended strict doctrine into deep, universal spiritualism; she held a theologist's reverence for world religions, including Greek mythology and Buddhism, and included them in her own spiritual practice.[37] Bearing an inquisitive mind, Seton Watts was prone to thoughtful questioning about the iconographic histories of the religious symbols she used, revealed powerfully in an entry about the Celtic Cross:

> Signor & I sat & looked at the Celtic cross on our fireplace & saw how in pre-Christian times it was the symbol of unity. God in all from point to point, east and west, north and south. In early Celtic times the symbol of love & self-sacrifice, bound within the double hearts! Why did it ever in Christian hands lose its proportion, a change from cross to sword? The symbol of disseverance & disunion. Shall we end this parenthesis of darkness, misconception, a disunion in the name of Christ, some day not far off?[38]

Seton Watts's diaries also shed light on how she strove to lead by example in navigating a creative life, recognising when she struggled with inspiration and comparison. Although these are typical hardships for an

35 Rose, *Suffragist Artists*, 49.
36 Seton Watts, *Diary* 1887–1904, 162.
37 Seton Watts, *Diary* 1893, 11–14.
38 Seton Watts, *Diary* 1893, 200.

artist, they were exacerbated by her gender, marriage status and Victorian norms of female submission. In 1893 Seton Watts wrote: 'My days slip by without a scrap of artistic work being done. Why women fail in art is answered to myself, "because of the little things in life".'[39] As she surely had experienced, women were expected to handle the minor details of life that inconvenienced men. This frequently prevented them from working on their own professional goals and identities. Seton Watts recognised this phenomenon as such: it was rarely outright, unjust institutional rejection that prevented women artists from succeeding; instead, it was the minor social duties, unwritten rules and subtle infantilisation of women that made professional ambitions difficult. Despite the many possible obstacles, Seton Watts's pages are brimming with drive and victories, such as the completion of symbolic plaster ceiling panels, a gilded gesso reading niche, a Promethean fireplace mantel and many ceramic projects.[40] These were, somewhat surprisingly, supported by Walter Crane and Burne-Jones, who had both advised her early in the creative process and whose work served to inspire her.[41]

Similarly, Seton Watts's writings detail the development of her creative ideas and map her influences, which she would translate into imagery on the walls of the Watts Chapel. On 29 July 1887, Seton Watts wrote: 'Went to see Mr Burne Jones, found him painting his sleeping Beauty, a wonder of colour & detail.'[42] During this visit she probably saw Burne-Jones's work on the panels for *The Legend of Briar Rose*, like *The Rose Bower* (1885–90; Figure 3.9).

Upon close comparison, the panels' visual themes are reflected in the Watts Chapel interior. *The Rose Bower* is set in an overgrowth of vines and branches and painted in rich colour, including deep teals and intricate golds, and even features a Celtic motif on the balustrade on the far right of the composition and a vibrant peacock-patterned rug on the floor. While it is clear that Seton Watts shared many aesthetic affinities with

39 Seton Watts, *Diary* 1887–1904, 124.

40 Seton Watts, *Diary* [1891], 29–30.

41 Seton Watts, *Diary* [1887], 94, 124–5; Seton Watts, *Diary* [1891], 159–60.

42 Seton Watts, *Diary* [1887], 94.

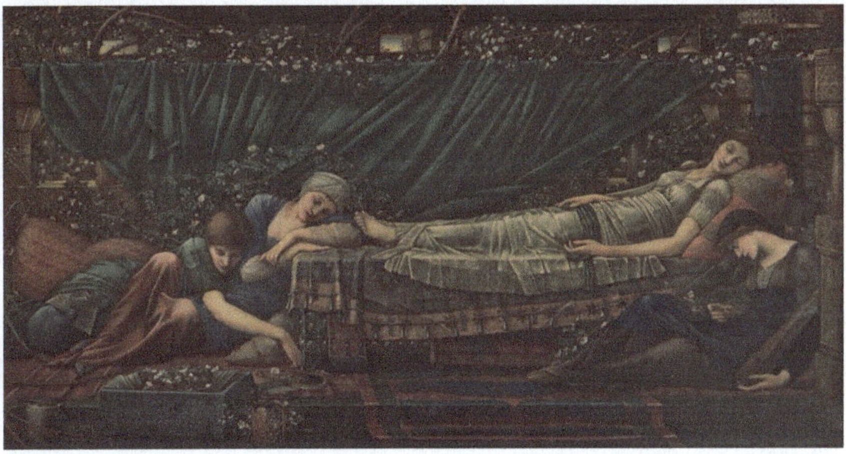

Figure 3.9. Sir Edward Coley Burne-Jones, *The Rose Bower*, The Legend of Briar Rose series, 1886–90, oil on canvas, 125.1 × 228.6 cm, Buscot Park, Faringdon, Oxfordshire. © The Faringdon Collection Trust at Buscot Park.

Burne-Jones, even divulging inspiration from him, her process for producing these similar designs differed greatly and owed much to her beliefs. A fundamental aspect of the chapel that mirrored Seton Watts's inspirations and creeds – in a more powerful manner than even the symbols on its walls – was its educational collaborative creation by the hands of her friends, neighbours and students.

Art and Activism in Education

In a rare compliment that Wilfrid Blunt paid Seton Watts in his biography of G. F. Watts (1975), he said:

> The Watts Memorial Chapel is a creation of genius, unique in England. One may love the Chapel, or (as many still do) one may hate it; but no one can fail to be amazed that so complex, so professional a building could have been produced by a woman

> with no architectural training, assisted (as far as we know) only by the local builder and blacksmith and a handful of enthusiastic but ignorant villagers.[43]

Here, Blunt is most amazed that such a remarkable feat could be accomplished by a woman and insinuates that anyone willing to be led by a woman, such as the Compton villagers, must be 'ignorant'. Since she had more than seventy students, Seton Watts clearly had the ability to inspire and instruct.[44] Even though Blunt insulted the Compton villagers, it is important to note that most began with little to no skill in clay, but, as evidenced by the chapel's precise and intricate ornament, they became skilled artists by the end of the project. From the beginning, Seton Watts had recognised the Arts and Crafts Movement as a gateway through which men and women could become self-sufficient creators by way of access to community art education. In 1884, she established a clay-modelling class for shoeblacks in Whitechapel, one of her earliest efforts to bring art to the working classes.[45] Later, she founded modelling and pottery classes to support the HAIA which were extremely popular and held in day and night sessions at Limnerslease, the Watts's home and studios in Compton.[46] By 1895, her HAIA class had evolved into the fully operational Compton Pottery and Aldourie Pottery in Scotland, through which artists produced professional work.[47] For Seton Watts, the realms of art and social activism were not separate, a belief that she made clear

43 Blunt vilifies Seton Watts on several occasions, accusing her of destroying letters and paintings after G. F.'s death, calling her 'jealous by nature' and 'very demanding', and suggests that she was a sad spinster who worshipped G. F. blindly and was willing to give up her career to be his nurse. In rare sections, however, mostly when he discusses her artwork, he writes of her remarkability and ambition; Wilfrid Blunt, *'England's Michelangelo': A Biography of George Frederic Watts, O.M. R.A* (London: Hamilton, 1975), xvii–xviii, 117, 130, 170, 224–6.

44 Seton Watts, *Word in the Pattern*, 28.

45 Gould, *Mary Seton Watts*, 27–8.

46 Designed by Sir Ernest George and completed in 1891; Gould, *Watts Chapel*, 13.

47 These two potteries united to form the Potters' Arts Guild in 1904; Hilary Underwood, 'Compton Pottery', in Mark Bills, ed., *An Artists' Village: G. F. Watts and Mary Watts at Compton* (London: Philip Wilson Publishers, 2011), 103–7.

through her choice of media, iconography, artistic process and establishment of her own teaching practice.[48]

In 1873, a member of Parliament, The Right Honourable H. A. Bruce made a statement arguing against women's suffrage by using their art careers as evidence of their ineptitude for government. Suggesting that others believed women lacked the traditionally male nugget of genius, his statement included:

> I cannot explain the causes of the differences between the two sexes in matters where equality might have been expected. I cannot say why it is that women, having paid so much more attention than men to the art of music, have never produced a great composer. Again, why is it that women, notwithstanding that they have turned their attention so much more to painting and drawing, have never produced a really great artist?[49]

As Linda Nochlin has rightly argued, the idea that women had insufficient talent was blatantly false – they were simply barred from attending the most basic art institutions for centuries.[50] Because Seton Watts believed in equality of the sexes, she did not limit the participants of her classes to women, although she did support women-only organisations.[51] For example, she was a member of the Women's Guild of Arts, founded by May Morris in 1907 – first appointed as Honorary Chair and then as the Honorary President in 1914.[52] Women were barred from joining the exclusive Art Workers' Guild – founded in 1884 – so this was May Morris's way

48 Lucy Ella Rose, 'Subversive Representations of Women and Death in Victorian Visual Culture: The "M/Other" in the Art and Craft of George Frederic Watts and Mary Seton Watts', *Victorian Culture in Britain* 17/1 (2016), 61–2.

49 H. A. Bruce quoted in Thomas C. Hansard, *Hansard's Parliamentary Debates, Third Series: Commencing with the Accession of William IV: Comprising from the Period from the Twenty-Fourth Day of March 1873 to the Fifteenth Day of May 1873*, 215/2 (London: Cornelius Buck, 1873), 1233–4.

50 Linda Nochlin, 'Why Have There Been No Great Women Artists?', in *Women, Art, and Power and Other Essays* (New York: Harper & Row Publishers, 1989), 145–75.

51 Gould, *Mary Seton Watts*, 53.

52 Rose, *Suffragist Artists*, 49.

of creating an equally prestigious art organisation for women.[53] Arguably, organisations formed as women's clubs or women-only artistic groups tended only to increase the disparity between genders – prolonging the tradition of separate spheres and sometimes harming any efforts to gain true equality; but in many cases, this was the only way to prove their equal worth and share their voice. Stepping in a new direction, Seton Watts saw the beauty that could come from equitable collaboration.

William Morris's utopian vision of a collaborative artist village, on which he founded Morris & Co., was likely an inspiration for Seton Watts.[54] Quixotically expressed through *News from Nowhere* (1893), Morris desired to establish an artistic community in the style of medieval guilds with workers fuelled by passion and the collaborative creation of beautiful things – a foil to dismal mass production.[55] Morris & Co. also employed talented women artists and designers, including Kate Faulkner and Jane and May Morris, to create embroideries and ornament furniture. In this way, the Arts and Crafts movement had opened doors, allowing women to become profiting creators. Similarly, William De Morgan, husband of Evelyn De Morgan, employed and educated women in his pottery workshop, and Ford Madox Brown was one of the first to teach women in his studio, possibly the result of his daughters, Lucy and Catherine Madox Brown, showing promise as artists from a young age.[56]

Similarly, Seton Watts taught in a manner that combined atelier and medieval-guild-like settings, both of which originally involved a male master artist or craftsman teaching male students in a studio, thereby subverting antiquated gender roles to create a new method of teaching.[57]

53 Jan Marsh, 'Feminist, Socialist, Embroiderer: the Untold Story of May Morris', Royal Academy (20 September 2017), <https://www.royalacademy.org.uk/article/may-morris-art-and-life-william-morris-gallery>, accessed 20 May 2021.

54 Hilary Underwood, 'Mary Watts, the Home Arts and Industries Association and Compton', in Mark Bills, *An Artists' Village: G. F. and Mary Watts at Compton* (London: Philip Wilson Publishers, 2011), 56–8.

55 William Morris, *News from Nowhere: Or an Epoch of Rest, Being Some Chapters from a Utopian Romance* (Kelmscott, England: Kelmscott Press, 1893), 130–41, 252–5.

56 Rose, *Suffragist Artists*, 76–7.

57 Melanie Unwin, 'Significant Other: Art and Craft in the Career and Marriage of Mary Watts', *Journal of Design History* 17/3 (2004), 244; Rose, *Suffragist Artists in*

Seton Watts had grown tired of the traditional instruction she received from Slade and Dalou, choosing instead to establish her own artistic pedagogy.[58] In an illuminating photograph from 1902, Seton Watts is seen with three students painting the gesso angel panels that would later be installed in the chapel (Figure 3.10). These students appear to be assisting, learning and even painting their own sections with some independence. With this choice of educational style, she broke down the 'hierarchal binary', as Rose has put it, between genders, mediums, styles and roles to educate a new era of artists who hailed from all classes and backgrounds.[59]

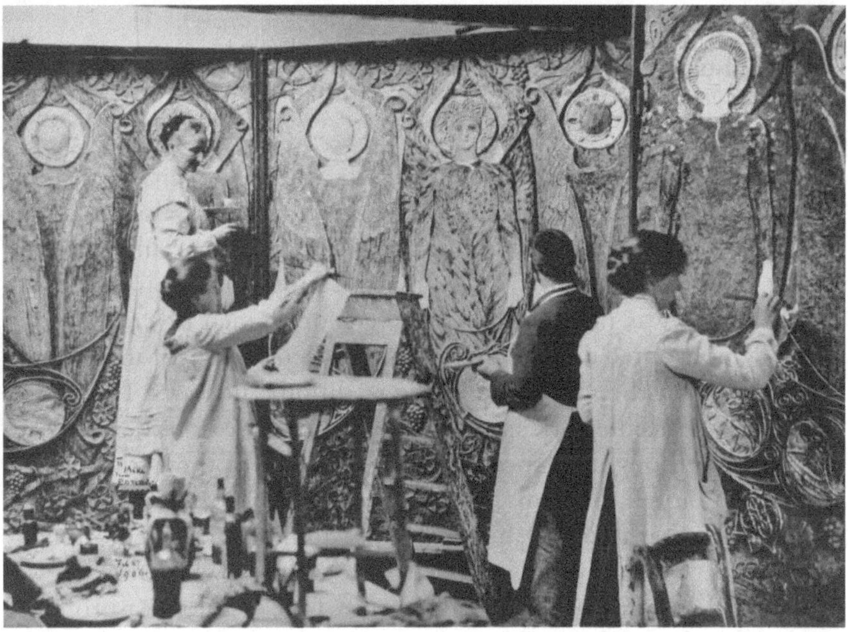

Figure 3.10. Mary Watts and students of her Home Arts and Industries Association class decorating interior panels for the chapel in her studio, c. 1902, photograph, Watts Gallery Trust.

Partnership, 176; Stuart Macdonald, *The History and Philosophy of Art Education* (Cambridge: Lutterworth Press, 2004), 271.

58 Gould, *Mary Seton Watts*, 23.

59 Rose, 'Subversive Representations', 61–2.

The Watts Chapel became a project that Seton Watts and her students could work towards in a collaborative, co-educational environment, resulting in a structure created for the community, by the community. In *The Word in the Pattern*, she wrote that the chapel was 'modelled in clay of Surrey, by Compton hands, under unusual conditions – much of the work having been done gratuitously, and all of it with the love that made the work delightful'.[60] Her gift to the community was not the chapel itself, but the skills she taught her students along the way which helped them to navigate their own creative lives.

Artistic Fusion as Gender Subversion

As evidenced in her teaching style, Seton Watts's pursuit of breaking down boundaries applied not only to human roles but also to artistic rules and gendered hierarchies through craft mediums like clay and plaster to act as symbolist vessels. By educating community members in a way that was not typically reserved for women or crafts, Seton Watts demonstrated a belief that craft and decorative art forms should be esteemed on the same level as the traditional fine arts. Decorative arts, such as needlework and ceramics, were not considered fit to express deep thought or speak messages because of their status as accessory, feminine art forms, while painting, sculpture and architecture remained masculine, hierarchically dominant and emotionally stimulating. Decorative art was tied to usefulness, while fine art was for purely aesthetic or thoughtful purpose. One of the most profound reasons for placing Seton Watts among the greats of her respective art movements, is her ability to reject this restriction and give thunderous voice to pattern through her chapel. Seton Watts wrote: 'The patterns can claim to be no more than are the letters of a great word; hieroglyphs, and very inadequate as representations of the possible reach of

60 Seton Watts, *Word in the Pattern*, 5.

the underlying thought suggested by them.'[61] She evidently saw patterns as abstract entities that could be combined to reveal a larger meaning, similar to the way in which letters, which are abstract lines, combine to form words. Likewise, words have and create meaning through their combinations and context. Through the very title of her book, *The Word in the Pattern*, Seton Watts empowered pattern with the ability to speak, merging artistic dominions. This may have been her first inkling of the movements to come in which abstraction would prove its ability to communicate as meaningfully as figurative art.

Only decades before, the fine line that had existed between high art and decorative craft began to blur in the work of male artists such as Crane, Rossetti, Morris and Burne-Jones, who had the stability of being professionally trained fine artists; yet these men could engage with craft-centred textile and furniture design without experiencing professional or gendered hierarchal minimisation. Interestingly, it should be acknowledged that – unlike Seton Watts – these revered male artists were rarely involved in creating the lauded art of exterior ornamentation, let alone the architectural design of an entire structure, and were mostly tied to the design of rooms. Although women artists were being included in collaborative workshops, their skills were still applied to embroidery and metalware for home interiors – a 'space of femininity' according to Griselda Pollock.[62] As Norma Broude explained, diction is incredibly important when describing these artistic entities, and 'decorative' can be a considerably troublesome term due to the reflex to categorise it as secondary.[63] John Ruskin, Owen Jones and other art philosophers who have concerned themselves with the embellishing elements of art and architecture, exclusively use the term

61 Seton Watts, *Word in the Pattern*, 5.

62 See Griselda Pollock, 'Modernity and the Spaces of Femininity', in *Vision and Difference: Feminism, Femininity, and the History of Art* (London: Routledge, 1988; rev. edn 2003), 70–127.

63 Norma Broude, 'Miriam Schapiro and "Femmage": Reflections on the Conflict Between Decoration and Abstraction in Twentieth-Century Art', in Norma Broude and Mary D. Garrard, eds, *Feminism and Art History: Questioning the Litany* (New York: Westview Press, 1982; Routledge reprint 2018), 326–8.

'ornament'.[64] Ornament is thus powerful, sculpted and masculine – appropriate to be displayed on the exterior of a structure or a divine object. Conversely, decorative art (according to past definition) is intricate, small, formed from delicate material and feminine – suitable for use in interiors and home environments inhabited by women. None of these designations mattered for Seton Watts, who used fine and decorative materials and methods interchangeably, elevating each to the high status of religious and spiritual art. Regardless, Elaine Paterson recognised that scholars who have written about the chapel interior have had a tendency to use terminology that would apply to a textile or tapestry.[65] Julian Holder wrote that the chapel interior is 'woven into a mystical garment'.[66] Seton Watts even described the interior intricacies as the 'clothing of the walls'.[67] By describing the chapel in this way, it is relegated to a piece of embroidery, a traditionally feminine artform, and not the complex architectural structure and intricate bas-relief that it really is. Requiring immense artistic clairvoyance and dexterity, Seton Watts's materials and process speak the loudest for her artistic subversion.[68]

Terracotta, a craft material, was used for the exterior ornament of the Watts Chapel, directly engaging in discourse with the history of terracotta and its artistic value in the hands of Italian masters Donatello, Bernini and Luca della Robbia.[69] The seam of red clay discovered on Seton Watts's

64 See Owen Jones, *Grammar of Ornament* (London: Day and Son, 1856) and John Ruskin, *The Stones of Venice*, J. G. Links, ed., 2nd edn (London and Cambridge: Da Capo, 2003).

65 Elaine Cheasley Paterson, 'Decoration and Desire in the Watts Chapel, Compton: Narratives of Gender, Class and Colonialism', *Gender & History* 17/3 (November 2005), 720–1.

66 Julian Holder, 'Architecture, Mysticism and Myth and its Influence', in Sylvia Backemeyer and Theresa Gronberg, eds, *W. R. Lethaby, 1857–1931: Architecture, Design and Education* (London: Lund Humphries, 1984), 62.

67 Seton Watts, *Word in the Pattern*, 27.

68 She also did this by using the term 'veil' for the *Garment of Praise*; however, she sourced this term from Ruskin's writings and religious tradition.

69 Seton Watts, *Diary* (1887–1904), 111, 136; Victoria and Albert Museum, 'Italian Terracotta Sculpture', Victoria and Albert Museum (n.d.), <http://www.vam.ac.uk/content/articles/i/italian-terracotta-sculpture/>, accessed 15 June 2021.

home property in 1895 provided her with the ability to render the organic designs – vines, birds, trees, flowers – in a natural element, paying homage to the earthly materiality of the red clay and a truth to nature that transcended Ruskinian beliefs.

For the interior, Seton Watts used a technique of painting and gilding *gesso duro* – a gesso substrate mixed with plaster which she covered over felt and cord to create the bas-relief effect – a method she had first experimented with when creating ceiling panels in 1891.[70] Because of the brilliance of the plaster, the *gesso duro* created a white ground on which Seton Watts could paint, parallel to the way the original Pre-Raphaelite painters primed their canvases with white to achieve a higher saturation of colour.[71] She found that it indeed enhanced the vibrancy of the paint and metal leaf that she applied over it, creating a resemblance to an enamelled piece of jewellery or Celtic bronze.[72] In *Ideals in Art* (1905), Crane wrote: 'Decorative design in gesso stands, it may be said, midway between painting and sculpture, partaking in its variations of the characters of each in turn.'[73] Seton Watts's work in gesso is neither fresco nor sculpture, but both. By using an intermediate medium, she symbolically enhanced the liminality of a mortuary chapel space. Despite its decorative connections, the interior adornment is anything but small or delicate, as it covers every inch of the space in sculpted masterwork. Broude wrote that for the decorative arts, scale can be used 'to precipitate that which has previously been categorized and dismissed as modest'.[74] For example, the larger-than-life scale of the chapel's angels enhances their divine nature. The viewer can look into the faces of the massive angels towering above them and feel minuteness, fear or comfort from their power. The scale and intensity of Seton Watts's relief ornament shake off any notions of dainty, decorative elements and, instead, add gravitas and monumentality.

70 Walter Crane, *Ideals in Art: Papers, Theoretical, Practical, Critical* (London: George Bell & Sons, 1905), 249; Seton Watts, *Diary* [1891], 6–7.

71 Elizabeth Prettejohn, *The Art of the Pre-Raphaelites* (2000; 2nd edn, London: Tate Publishing, 2007), 140–44.

72 Gould, *Watts Chapel*, 30.

73 Crane, *Ideals in Art*, 247.

74 Broude, 'Miriam Schapiro and "Femmage"', 325.

Colour also added to the chapel's magnificence. When the late Victorian enamellist Alexander Fisher visited in 1902, Seton Watts showed him the panels she was working on for the chapel's interior. His criticism, she wrote, was that 'the colour of the angels is not quite monotonous enough' – perhaps imagining that it should resemble more of a faded fresco than his own bright enamelled metalwork (likely an effect of the white base layer previously mentioned).[75] As Patricia L. Reilly has suggested, there are art historical periods in which colour was thought to be a crowd-pleaser instead of a serious artistic tool, a reproach that the original Pre-Raphaelite Brotherhood experienced.[76] Reilly wrote: 'Thus, colors were considered beautiful only when they conformed to expectation, and were described, as were women, as subject to the rigors of decorum.'[77] Again, the difference between art forms was reinforced as binaries of masculine/feminine, fine art/craft, form/colour, with the latter elements often described as weaker and requiring less talent. The chapel's mortuary purpose counteracts attempts to see the colours as garish; instead, their presence is a form of an early Aestheticist worship of colour itself and its creator, which perhaps lift visitors' spirits. The enamel-like lustre of the gesso process enhances the golden and jewel-toned sheens to create a heavenly aura of the angels, presenting the chapel to the viewer as a holy or mystical vision. Using vibrant colour, scale and a crossover of mediums, Seton Watts composed a manifesto for the equality of genders, artforms and education written in a visual language to ornament and exalt her mortuary chapel.

75 Seton Watts, *Diary* [1902], 14.

76 Patricia L. Reilly, 'The Taming of the Blue: Writing Out Color in Italian Renaissance Theory', in Norma Broude and Mary D. Garrard, eds, *The Expanding Discourse: Feminism and Art History* (New York: Harper Collins, 1992), 87–9.

77 Reilly, 'The Taming of the Blue', 91.

Ongoing Legacy

Although it can be visually intimidating at first, the aim of the Watts Chapel was to welcome, in a warm and egalitarian manner, those experiencing grief or looking for purpose, much like the quotation Seton Watts loved from Josephine Butler: 'the kingdom of heaven is for all, even the downtrodden, mud besmirched'.[78] Looking closely, the chapel declares that death is just another form of freedom, a comforting thought to mourners, but it also spreads messages of strength to motivate the living. Seton Watts's involvement in the women's suffrage movement and her leadership in HAIA classes makes it abundantly clear that she desired for people to have equality in this life, not just the afterlife. In *The Word in the Pattern*, she wrote: 'These little [symbols] dwelt upon earnestly and lovingly have a fire of thought within them which has power to flash new light upon the soul.'[79] A hope for her chapel symbolism was to transform the perspective of the viewer, which might, in turn, motivate them to act for causes of freedom and justice during a tumultuous time. Seton Watts never says this explicitly, but based on her theories and methods of expression, she was confident that symbols could do that for her.

Along with building the chapel, Seton Watts accomplished several artistic projects and designs in various media. Sundials, grave ornaments, bookbindings, a banner for the Governor General of Canada, garden pots for Liberty & Co. and rugs for Alexander Morton & Co. are all part of her wide-ranging oeuvre, infused with her magical intensity.[80] Until her death, Seton Watts never stopped working, designing or campaigning. Her career reflected an ingenious fusion of art and craft into something altogether revolutionary in its theoretical and practical creation. Motivated by her cornerstone belief that art can transform lives, Seton Watts's instruction had a great impact on the entire community, as well as herself. On the last

78 Seton Watts, *Diary* (1887–1904), 160.

79 Seton Watts, *Word in the Pattern*, 27.

80 Underwood, 'Compton Pottery', 106–11.

two pages of *The Word in the Pattern*, she thanked every single student or worker who had a hand in the creation of the chapel, listing their names.

In many ways, the Watts Cemetery Chapel is an architectural and artistic manifestation of Seton Watts herself: layered and complex, not adhering to any one category of existence, a beacon of hope and an innovative inspiration. The chapel's permanence as an architectural structure, connection to the Watts Gallery Trust and recent preservation all allow the Watts Chapel to continue to introduce visitors to artistic movements and styles of the late nineteenth and early twentieth centuries, permeated together in one space.[81] The chapel and galleries perpetuate the legacy of those styles, inspiring new scholars and fans among the more than 35,000 visitors each year.[82]

Seton Watts put an extraordinary effort into the Watts Cemetery Chapel and her spirit is present in every Celtic loop. To create her masterpiece, she defied sexist Victorian restrictions and expectations about the levels of professionalism to which women were allowed to rise. She combined gendered media of paint, sculpture, textiles and architecture to empower feminised methods, using them all to create a sanctified religious structure that speaks a message of freedom and equality. Seton Watts adds another chapter to the narrative that began with the Pre-Raphaelites by carrying on the legacy of believing that nature and religion are the greatest sources of inspiration, commenting on social issues and promoting egalitarianism, living and creating in ways that broke with contemporary norms, honouring styles of the past and trailblazing ahead to establish new possibilities for all artists.

81 Emma Coburn, 'The Conservation of the Watts Chapel', Watts Gallery (2020), <https://www.wattsgallery.org.uk/about-us/news/conservation-watts-chapel/>, accessed 10 May 2021.

82 School of Hospitality and Tourism Management, Faculty of Arts and Social Sciences, 'The Economic Impact of Watts Gallery – Artists' Village, Compton, Guildford, Surrey: Final Report', University of Surrey (4 March 2016), 2, <https://www.yumpu.com/en/document/read/62391925/the-economic-impact-of-watts-gallery-artists-village-final-report>, accessed 15 April 2021.

Bibliography

Anne Anderson, 'Pre-Raphaelite Values', in Anne Anderson, ed., *Beyond the Brotherhood: The Pre-Raphaelite Legacy* (Bristol: Sansom & Company, 2019), 24–7.

Barker, Margaret, *Great High Priest: The Temple Roots of Christian Liturgy* (New York: T&T Clark, 2003).

Bills, Mark, ed., *An Artists' Village G. F. Watts and Mary Watts at Compton* (London: Philip Wilson Publishers, 2011).

Blunt, Wilfrid, *'England's Michelangelo': A Biography of George Frederic Watts, O.M. R.A.* (London: Hamilton, 1975).

Broude, Norma, 'Miriam Schapiro and "Femmage": Reflections on the Conflict Between Decoration and Abstraction in Twentieth-Century Art', in Norma Broude and Mary D. Garrard, eds, *Feminism and Art History: Questioning the Litany* (New York: Westview Press, 1982; Routledge reprint 2018), 315–29.

Coburn, Emma, 'The Conservation of the Watts Chapel', Watts Gallery (2020), <https://www.wattsgallery.org.uk/about-us/news/conservation-watts-chapel/>, accessed 10 May 2021.

Crane, Walter, *Ideals in Art: Papers, Theoretical, Practical, Critical* (London: George Bell & Sons, 1905).

Gould, Veronica Franklin, *The Watts Chapel: An Arts & Crafts Memorial* (Surrey, England: Arrow Press, 1993).

——. *Mary Seton Watts (1849–1938): Unsung Heroine of the Art Nouveau*, exh. cat. (Over Wallop, England: Veronica Franklin Gould for the Trustees of the Watts Gallery for the Mary Watts Centenary Exhibition, 5 June to 6 September 1998).

Hansard, Thomas C., *Hansard's Parliamentary Debates, Third Series: Commencing with the Accession of William IV: Comprising from the Period from the Twenty-Fourth Day of March 1873 to the Fifteenth Day of May 1873* 215/2 (London: Cornelius Buck, 1873).

Historic England, 'Compton Cemetery (Also Known as Watts Cemetery)', *Historic England* (n.d.), <https://historicengland.org.uk/listing/the-list/list-entry/1417498>, accessed 15 January 2021.

Julian Holder, 'Architecture, Mysticism and Myth and its Influence', in Sylvia Backemeyer and Theresa Gronberg, eds, *W. R. Lethaby, 1857–1931: Architecture, Design and Education* (London: Lund Humphries, 1984), 52–63.

Lethaby, W. R., *Architecture, Mysticism, and Myth* (London: Percival, 1892).

Macdonald, Stuart, *The History and Philosophy of Art Education* (Cambridge: Lutterworth Press, 2004).

Marsh, Jan, 'Feminist, Socialist, Embroiderer: The Untold Story of May Morris', Royal Academy (20 September 2017), <https://www.royalacademy.org.uk/article/may-morris-art-and-life-william-morris-gallery>, accessed 20 May 2021.

Morris, William, *News from Nowhere: Or an Epoch of Rest, Being Some Chapters from a Utopian Romance* (Kelmscott, England: Kelmscott Press, 1893).

Nochlin, Linda, 'Why Have There Been No Great Women Artists?', in Linda Nochlin, ed., *Women, Art, and Power and Other Essays* (New York: Harper & Row Publishers, 1989), 145–78.

Parry, Linda, 'Donegal Rugs of Ireland,' in Linda Parry, David Cathers, Diane Boucher, Ann Lane Hedlund, and Dru Muskovin, eds, *Arts and Crafts Rugs for Craftsmen Interiors: The Crab Tree Farm Collection* (London: W. W. Norton and Company, 2010), 73–93.

Paterson, Elaine Cheasley, 'Decoration and Desire in the Watts Chapel, Compton: Narratives of Gender, Class and Colonialism', *Gender & History* 17/3 (November 2005), 714–36.

Pollock, Griselda, 'Modernity and the Spaces of Femininity', in *Vision and Difference: Feminism, Femininity, and the History of Art, with a New Introduction by the Author* (London: Routledge, 1988; rev. edn 2003), 70–127.

Prettejohn, Elizabeth, *The Art of the Pre-Raphaelites* (2000; 2nd edn, London: Tate Publishing, 2007).

Reilly, Patricia L., 'The Taming of the Blue: Writing Out Color in Italian Renaissance Theory', in Norma Broude and Mary D. Garrard, eds, *The Expanding Discourse: Feminism and Art History* (New York: Harper Collins, 1992), 87–99.

Rose, Lucy Ella, 'Subversive Representations of Women and Death in Victorian Visual Culture: The "M/Other" in the Art and Craft of George Frederic Watts and Mary Seton Watts', *Victorian Culture in Britain* 17/1 (2016), 47–74.

——, 'The Diaries of Mary Seton Watts (1849–1938): A Record of Her Conjugal Creative Partnership with "England's Michelangelo", George Frederic Watts (1817–1904)', *Life Writing* 14/2 (2017), 217–31.

——, *Suffragist Artists in Partnership: Gender, Word and Image* (Edinburgh: Edinburgh University Press, 2018).

School of Hospitality and Tourism Management, Faculty of Arts and Social Sciences, 'The Economic Impact of Watts Gallery – Artists' Village, Compton, Guildford, Surrey: Final Report', University of Surrey (4 March 2016), <https://www.yumpu.com/en/document/read/62391925/the-economic-impact-of-watts-gallery-artists-village-final-report>, accessed 15 April 2021.

Seton Watts, Mary, *The Diary of Mary Seton Watts*, [1870–86, 1887, 1891, 1893, 1896, 1898, 1902, 1904, 1906–8], transcribed Desna Greenhow (unpublished archival material, Watts Gallery Trust).

——, *The Word in the Pattern: A Key to the Symbols on the Walls of the Chapel at Compton, Surrey*, 2nd edn (London: Astolat Press, 1905).

——, *The Diary of Mary Watts 1887–1904*, ed. and transcribed Desna Greenhow, Lucy Ella Rose and Gail Naughton (London: Lund Humphries and Watts Gallery, 2016).

Smith, Elise Lawton. *Evelyn Pickering De Morgan and the Allegorical Body* (London: Associated University Presses, 2002).

Underwood, Hilary, 'Compton Pottery', in Mark Bills, ed., *An Artists' Village: G. F. Watts and Mary Watts at Compton* (London: Philip Wilson Publishers, 2011), 102–19.

——,'Mary Watts, the Home Arts and Industries Association and Compton', in Mark Bills, ed., *An Artists' Village: G. F. Watts and Mary Watts at Compton* (London: Philip Wilson Publishers, 2011), 47–65.

Unwin, Melanie, 'Significant Other: Art and Craft in the Career and Marriage of Mary Watts', *Journal of Design History* 17/3 [Dangerous Liaisons: Relationships between Design, Craft and Art] (2004), 237–50.

Victoria and Albert Museum, 'Italian Terracotta Sculpture', Victoria and Albert Museum (n.d.), <http://www.vam.ac.uk/content/articles/i/italian-terracotta-sculpture/>, accessed 15 June 2021.

MARGARETTA S. FREDERICK

4 Politics and Paint: The Life Work of Barbara Leigh Smith Bodichon

ABSTRACT

Despite a thirty-year exhibition record in England and America representing over 200 works, Barbara Leigh Smith, later Bodichon (1827–91) is best remembered for her work in the women's reform movement. This chapter investigates the juncture between Barbara's[1] activism and her art profession, suggesting a symbiotic relationship between politics and paint in which each nourished the other. The subject of her landscapes encompassed a broad geographical spectrum encountered through extensive travel, often to locales of colonial and/or imperial contestation. Here Barbara's landscapes are interpreted as a reflection of her desire for the empowerment of the "other", most prominently, the enslaved she encountered in America and the colonised peoples of Algeria. Her compassion for the outsider was strengthened through her own position of exile. Born into illegitimacy, her empathy for those who were vulnerable or defenceless, was grounded in her own unique experience negotiating British societal proscriptions. Complicated by limited extant examples and further clouded by historic gender bias, the work of Barbara Leigh Smith Bodichon deserves fresh evaluation.

* * * * *

> She had a large scheme of what she calls the Outer and Inner Sisterhood. The Inner, to consist of the Art-sisters bound together by their one object, and which she fears may never number many in their band; the Outer Sisterhood to consist of women, all workers and all striving after a pure moral life, but belonging to any profession,

1 I have deliberated over to how to refer to Barbara Leigh Smith Bodichon throughout this chapter. Gender sensitivity could preclude using her married name until she was married, but the use of her married name makes references to her husband confusing and awkward. With some hesitancy I have chosen simply to use Barbara, although I acknowledge that recently this option has been criticised as patronising.

> any pursuit. All should be bound to help each other in such ways as were most accordant with their natures and characters.[2]

So wrote the young Pre-Raphaelite painter, Anna Mary Howitt, of her friend Barbara Leigh Smith, later Bodichon, feminist, landscape painter and social reformer. Today, Barbara's work in the women's reform movement has somewhat detracted from her artistic production, despite a thirty-year exhibition record in England and America representing over 200 works. More often than not these dual avocations have been interpreted as limiting her full engagement with either and, specifically to criticisms of amateurism in her painted work – a view which is challenged below. What is clear is that both passions were enhanced through Barbara's lifelong assemblage of a network of like-minded women who shared a belief in female empowerment.

In this chapter, I investigate the juncture between Barbara's activism and her art profession, suggesting a symbiotic relationship in which each nourished the other.[3] Her passion for reformist causes and championing of the outsider was strengthened through a prolific written corpus, a tool utilised to significant effect for the revision, synthesis and enrichment of both. The subject of her landscapes encompassed a broad geographical spectrum encountered through extensive travel, often to locales of colonial/imperial contestation. I suggest these landscapes were a reflection and manifestation of her desire for the empowerment of the 'other', most prominently, the enslaved she encountered in America and the colonised peoples of Algeria. Her compassion for the outsider[4] was undoubtedly strengthened through

2 Anna Mary Howitt, *An Art-Student in Munich* (London, 1853; Boston: Ticknor, Reed and Fields, 1854), 95.

3 Pam Hirsch writes: 'Nor, in my view, did she experience any sense of disjunction between herself as artist and herself as feminist activist'; in 'Barbara Leigh Smith Bodichon: artist and activist', in Clarissa Campbell Orr, ed., *Women in the Victorian Art World* (Manchester: Manchester University Press, 1995), 167.

4 Barbara's close friend, travel writer and novelist Matilda Betham-Edwards, described her compassion for all: 'The basis of Madame Bodichon's character was that very rare, I am tempted to say rarest, quality in my own sex, namely, a sense of abstract justice. Nationality, racial distinction, religion, even colour, for her were nonexistent. A human being, whether Christian or Jew, foreigner or English, White-skinned or Black, remained a brother or sister. As little she cared for demarcations

her own position of exile within Victorian social and cultural conventions. The empathy for those who were vulnerable or defenceless was lifelong, grounded in her own unique position within British society. She was sensitive to political, cultural and economic imbalances in gender empowerment; writing wistfully when in America, 'This is really a free country in the respect of having no privileged class – excepting the class of white over black [...] One is so little used to freedom, real freedom, even in England that it takes time to understand freedom, to realize it [...] Until I came to America, I hardly felt the strange want of rational liberty in England.'[5]

Barbara was the eldest of five illegitimate children of the radical MP, Benjamin Smith, and Anne Longden, a milliner. Her parents were not married, Benjamin believing the laws governing a woman's rights after marriage were unjust. This circumstance of her illegitimacy was encountered and negotiated throughout her life. The Leigh Smith family were historically liberal and reformist, 'members of the nineteenth-century "intellectual aristocracy" '.[6] The Smiths embraced Unitarianism, a faith which encouraged individual freedom and equality for all, a belief reflected in their political activism, while further positioning them outside the mainstream.[7] Benjamin Smith provided all of his children with an independent living, allowing Barbara a rare degree of freedom and choice in her adult life.

Independent means did not, however, grant her liberty from the societal restrictions and social biases decreed by her gender and illegitimacy. For reasons of birth, Barbara and her siblings went unrecognised by most of the Smith family as well as in many social circles. Her ardent and unwavering

of fashion or routine. This immense largeness of sympathy and independence of mind, showed itself in the least little thing. Injustice she could never forgive.' Matilda Betham-Edwards, *Reminiscences* (London: G. Redway, 1898), 266–7.

5 Joseph W. Reed Jr, *An American Diary, 1857–1858* (London: Routledge & K. Paul, 1972), 72.

6 Pam Hirsch, 'Bodichon, Barbara Leigh Smith', in *Oxford Dictionary of National Biography* (2007), <https://doi.org/10.1093/ref:odnb/2755>, accessed 15 July 2021.

7 For a cogent analysis of the importance of Unitarianism in supporting the Leigh Smith family's activism, see Sheila R. Herstein, *Mid-Victorian Feminist, Barbara Leigh Smith Bodichon* (New Haven, CT: Yale University Press, 1985), 2–4.

feminism, as manifested in a forthright character and reformed dress, were also a mark of social unsuitability in the eyes of many. Even those whom she championed, such as Elizabeth Blackwell, a pioneer in the medical profession, wrote critically: 'She will not wear corsets, she won't embroider, she reads every heretic book she can get hold of, talks of following a profession, and has been known to go to an evening party without gloves.'[8]

Undoubtedly, Barbara's lifelong social activism contributed to the disharmony with social convention. Her involvement in reform was prodigious. She is described as 'the sower of seed. She scattered ideas broadcast, leaving others to tend the flowers that grew from them.'[9] In 1854 she founded the Portman Hall School in Paddington,[10] a secular co-educational institution for all children without reference to class or economic level. Also, within this decade she began work towards the passage of the Married Women's Property Act, publishing *A Brief Summary of the Laws in England concerning Women* (1854). With her friend and fellow activist Bessie Rayner Parkes, she founded the *English Woman's Journal* in 1858, providing accurate information on women's issues with articles written by and for women. The journal offices at Langham Place in Westminster became the centre of the women's movement, including the administration for the Society Promoting the Employment of Women. Barbara and her reformist colleagues came to be known as the 'Langham Place Group'.[11] In 1864, at a meeting of the Kensington Society, a women's reform collective, Barbara and fellow feminists Emily Davies and Jessie Boucherett proposed the formation of a Women's Suffrage Committee to petition Parliament for the enfranchisement of women, thereby initiating the march towards gender representation.

8 Cited in Pam Hirsch, *Barbara Leigh Smith Bodichon 1827–1891: Feminist, Artist and Rebel* (London: Chatto & Windus, 1998), 54 (Microfilm reel 142, Blackwell Family Papers, Library of Congress).

9 Hester Burton, *Barbara Bodichon* (London: John Murray, 1949), 113.

10 Barbara founded the school with educator, suffragist and activist Elizabeth Whitehead. For more information see Herstein, *Mid-Victorian Feminist, Barbara Leigh Smith Bodichon*, 62–3.

11 Candida Ann Lacey, ed., *Barbara Leigh Smith Bodichon and the Langham Place Group* (New York and London: Routledge & K. Paul, 1987), 1.

To date, Barbara's achievements have been evaluated primarily in a biographical format[12] heavily weighted towards her social work,[13] with a few early feminist readings referencing her artistic aspirations.[14] More recently, the politics surrounding her writing and travel to imperial domains has been analysed unsympathetically within the rubric of trans-imperialism.[15] Still missing in the literature to date is a thorough investigation of her landscape painting as a corpus.[16] This lacuna has much to do with Barbara's indeterminate artistic status as professional or amateur; a circumstance complicated during her lifetime by traditional biases associated with her gender and independently wealthy middle-class status. The latter is summarised somewhat disappointingly by fellow artist-sister, Helen Allingham:

> Madame Bodichon had a very considerable gift for painting: there are some really fine pictures by her; but her many interests, and, perhaps, her independent means and position in society, told against her giving the time and study required to make an entirely successful artist.[17]

12 Burton, *Barbara Bodichon*; Hirsch, *Barbara Leigh Smith Bodichon 1827–1891: Feminist, Artist and Rebel*.

13 Herstein, *Mid-Victorian Feminist, Barbara Leigh Smith Bodichon*; Lacey *Barbara Leigh Smith Bodichon and the Langham Place Group*; Jacqui Matthews, 'Barbara Bodichon: integrity in diversity', in Dale Spender, ed., *Feminist Theorists* (London: The Women's Press, 1983).

14 Whitney Chadwick, *Women, Art, and Society*, 4th edn (1990; London: Thames & Hudson, 2007); Jan Marsh and Pamela Gerrish Nunn, *Pre-Raphaelite Women Artists* (Manchester: Manchester City Art Gallery, 1997).

15 Deborah Cherry, *Beyond the Frame: Feminism and Visual Culture, Britain 1850–1900* (London and New York: Routledge, 2000); Meritxell Simon-Martin, *Barbara Bodichon's Epistolary Education: Unfolding Feminism* (Cham, Switzerland: Palgrave Macmillan, 2020).

16 John Crabbe published a series of articles specifically dealing with Barbara's artistic output in the 1980s. Unfortunately, these essays include little or no documentation of source material. See note 19 for more information on Crabbe.

17 Helen Allingham, H. and E. Baumer Williams, eds, *Letters to William Allingham* (London: Longmans, Green and Co., 1911), 77. This assessment is particularly egregious as it appears in an overview to a collection of letters Barbara wrote to her good friend, the writer William Allingham, edited by his wife and fellow artist sister, Hellen Allingham. The slight is all the more unjustifiable as in the letter to William which follows Bodichon articulates a clear statement of her ambition and

The element of class-snobbism in Allingham's statement relating to Barbara's rank and the acceptance of payment for professional services is clear. This prejudice is more strongly voiced in the observation of another contemporary:

> She made a good deal of money in the course of the year by selling pictures and other things – between 4 & 5 hundred pounds, I think she made last year; and the practice seems to be accepted by her friends – and I know other ladies of fortune who do the same thing. It hardly seems fair, for she takes advantage of her large acquaintance, and her easy establishment, and sells largely to her friends or acquaintance – it seems like entering into rather unfair competition with the mass of struggling women artists who can hardly keep their heads above water.[18]

Should Barbara have declined payment for her work, she would have been comfortably categorised within her own set as an amateur, engaging in the sort of dilettantish women's work that was more socially palatable. The neglect of her artistic output in current assessments can similarly be attributed to historic gender inequality to which the disentitlement vouchsafed by her contemporaries may well have contributed.

The disregard of her peers and the traditional erasure of 'women's work' within the art historical canon are also at play in the fragmented oeuvre that remains today, encumbering an adequate assessment of her productivity. Very few of her exhibition pieces are extant (e.g. Figure 4.1).

Instead, the bulk of what survives takes the form of sketchbooks and a significant number of loosely painted single sheets. The purpose of the latter is not clear. They may have been considered exhibitable, but there

---

dedication to painting: 'I wish you could see my pictures. I have been ambitious and had a disappointment – refused at the R.A. – I sent a monster in oil. I am not disheartened at all and I love my art more than ever – in fact more in proportion to other loves than ever'; July 1862. Allingham and Williams, *Letters to William Allingham*, 78.

18 Cited in Simon-Martin, *Barbara Bodichon's Epistolary Education: Unfolding Feminism*, 234–5. Letter, Elizabeth Blackwell to Emily Blackwell, Braemar House, Belvedere Road, Upper Norwood, 18 January 1875. Blackwell Family Papers, MC 411, Box 6, folder 47. Schlesinger Library, Radcliffe Institute, Harvard University, Cambridge, MA.

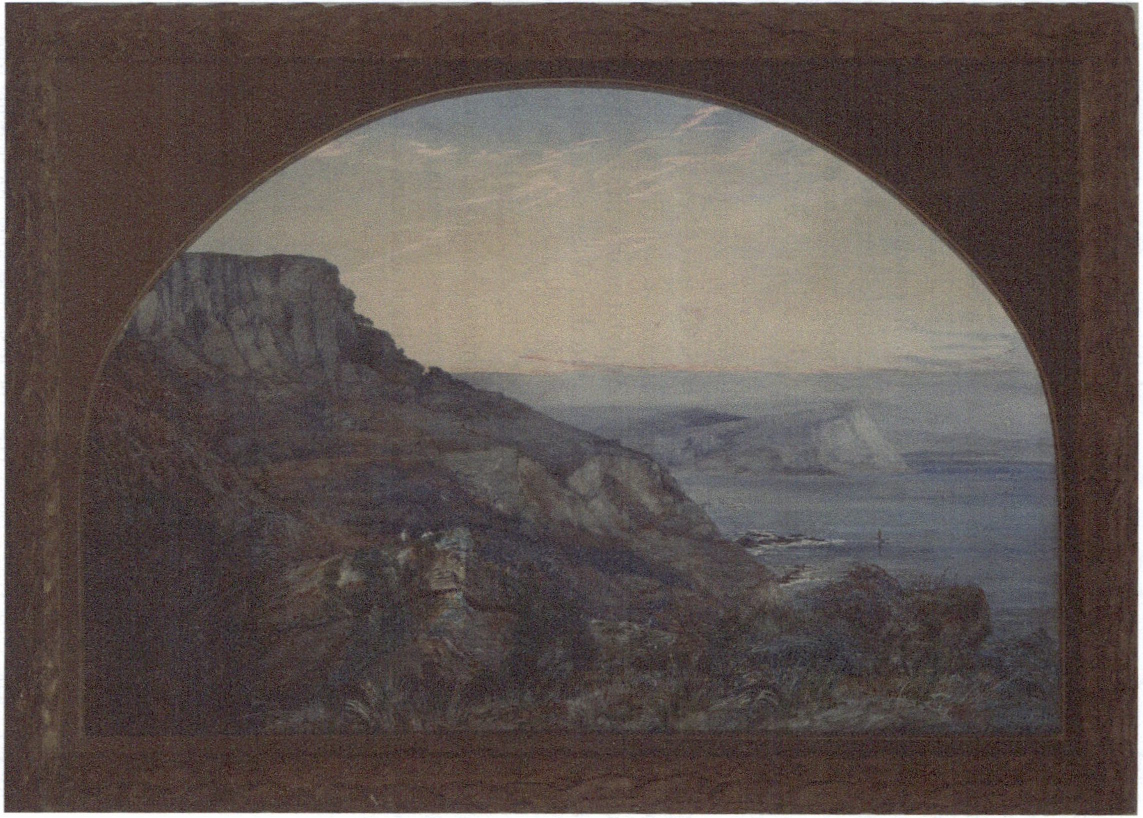

Figure 4.1. Barbara Leigh Smith Bodichon, *Ventnor, Isle of Wight*, 1856, Watercolour and gouache on paper, F.V. du Pont Acquisition Fund, 2016, Delaware Art Museum.

is no indication of title, date or inscription providing confirmation.[19] This dearth of physical evidence of her artistic productivity, in contrast to the rich record of her reform work, has naturally led to the valuation of her politics over her painting.

Gender restrictions in place during the span of her career further encouraged disregard of her artistic achievements. In the ongoing reassessment of female artists, the determination of what constitutes professional status has yet to be codified. Traditional avenues for artistic training were limited for Victorian women, necessitating alternative sources that do not fit comfortably within the roster of assessable bona fides. Sheer determination and consistent pursuit, an exhibition record and evidence of sales are perhaps more accurate markers. Barbara Leigh Smith Bodichon scores well within all.

Excluded by her gender, Barbara could not access the traditionally accepted Royal Academy Schools. Further, the record of her early training is not entirely discernible. As a young woman she was tutored by landscape painter William Henry Hunt, who wintered nearby the family home outside of Hastings. She may have participated in the art classes offered by Eliza Fox,[20] held in the library of her father's home. In 1849 she enrolled in drawing classes offered at Bedford College and taught by Francis Cary. Cary had been the teacher of Leigh Smith's childhood friend Anna Howitt, at Sass's Academy. Through Howitt, she was introduced to Dante Gabriel Rossetti and members of the early Pre-Raphaelite circle, including

19 In the early 1980s amateur historian John Crabbe discovered a cache of paintings and papers by or related to Barbara Leigh Smith Bodichon. Included in this find were a series of scrapbooks including watercolours and pencil and ink wash drawings. Crabbe's archive is now housed in the Girton College Archive, Cambridge. Unfortunately, a number of items were removed from the scrapbooks prior to their arrival at Girton, potentially erasing any chronological order that may have structured the original compilation. It is believed that these scrapbooks were compiled by Bodichon during her later years.

20 In his memoir of his aunt, Francis Jekyll gives an indication of Barbara's early training: 'Her path as a woman student had not been an easy one. She had started, with her friend Eliza Fox, a ladies' class, the first of its kind, for drawing from the undraped model'. *Gertrude Jekyll: A Memoir* (Northampton, MS: Bookshop Round Table, 1934), 94–5.

Elizabeth Siddal, William Holman Hunt, William Stillman, William Bell Scott and William Allingham. In seeking out Rossetti and members of the Pre-Raphaelite Brotherhood, at a moment when they were distinctly avant-garde and therefore on the very fringes of the Victorian art world, Barbara was activating her lifelong empathy for non-conformists. With Rossetti, Howitt and others, Leigh Smith set up the Portfolio Society, a group modelled after the earlier and defunct Cyclographic Society of the Pre-Raphaelite Brotherhood. She was also an early supporter of the relationship between Rossetti and Siddal, entertaining the couple, along with Howitt, at her home in Sussex in 1854, during which portraits of Siddal with an iris in her hair were drawn.[21] She championed Siddal's work, writing to a friend: 'I think Miss S. is a genius and very beautiful and [...] her mind is poetic'.[22]

Barbara began exhibiting in 1850, having two views of north Wales accepted at the Royal Academy.[23] She continued to exhibit at the R.A. as well as at the British Institute, the Royal Society of British Artists, the Dudley Gallery and the Society of Female Artists. In 1857–8 several of her landscapes were included in the exhibition of British Art that toured the east coast of the United States and introduced the Pre-Raphaelites to American audiences. Her work was also featured in a single-artist exhibition at Ernest Gambart's French Gallery in 1859. Of her professional status, Barbara herself had no doubt. Her practice extended throughout her lifetime and was to her mind harmonious with simultaneous reformist

21 A portrait of Siddal drawn at a gathering at Barbara's Sussex home in the spring of 1854, including of Rossetti, Siddal and Howitt, can be found in the Mark Samuels Lasner Collection, University of Delaware Library. See also letter, Rossetti to Ford Madox Brown, [23 May 1854] when he recalled 'B. S., Miss Howitt, and I made sketches of "Lizzie's dear head with iris stuck in her hair"'. William E. Fredeman, ed., *The Correspondence of Dante Gabriel Rossetti*. 10 vols (Cambridge: D. S. Brewer, 2002–15), I:353; no. 54.49.

22 Cited in Hirsch, *Barbara Leigh Smith Bodichon 1827–1891: Feminist, Artist and Rebel*, 50. Papers of Bessie Rayner Parkes, Girton College, Cambridge, 5/173. Hirsch also notes Barbara's empathy with Siddal may well have been grounded in her understanding of Siddal's tenuous social position as artist's model, in relation to her own social ostracism due to illegitimacy.

23 No. 698, *View near Tremadoc, North Wales*; and no. 737, *Dawn – near Manturogg, North Wales.*

activities. The attainment of professional status as an artist was both an act of empowerment and a conscious rejection of convention. As Deborah Cherry has explained, professional artistic practice 'was part of an emerging egalitarian feminist politics'.[24]

Barbara's early embrace of Pre-Raphaelite detail can be seen, for example, in *Ventnor, Isle of Wight* (Figure 4.1), a scene painted on a working holiday with Howitt and described by William Michael Rossetti when exhibited at the Royal Academy in 1856 as a 'capital coast scene [...] full of real pre-Raphaelitism'.[25] The Ruskinian detail of early works such as this, however, gradually waned in favour of a looser, more spontaneous approach derived from study with Camille Corot beginning in 1864. Bessie Parkes explained: 'Mrs. Bodichon is working in a Parisian studio, Corot's; he being an artist on whose instruction she had greatly set her mind; and, though he had never had but three pupils in his life, he has taken her.'[26] Here again, Barbara's determination to seek out the unconventional aesthetic – in the loosely painted plein air scenes of the Barbizon group – suggests a dedication and passion that exceeds amateur dalliance.

Her assimilation of the pastoral softened forms of the landscape enacted by this group of painters (e.g. Figure 4.2) extended over the next several years. She came to know other members of the circle, including Charles-Francois Daubigny, whom she hosted when he fled Paris for England during the Franco-Prussian war.[27]

Given the extent of her reform work, one might assume a preference for scenes of contemporary life aligned with the early works of the Pre-Raphaelite Brotherhood; or the social justice issues addressed by Hubert von Herkomer and other illustrators for *The Graphic*; or even her friend, Anna Howitt, whose *The Castaway* (now lost) exhibited at the Royal Academy in 1855 depicted a fallen woman, perhaps inspired by Rossetti's (unfinished) *Found*. Instead, Barbara chose landscape, a genre which required a hardy

24 Deborah Cherry, *Painting Women: Victorian Women Artists* (London and New York: Routledge, 1993), 28.

25 William Michael Rossetti, 'Art News from England, Letter XVI', *The Crayon* 3/8 (August 1856), 245.

26 Allingham and Williams, *Letters to William Allingham* 82.

27 John House, 'New Material on Monet and Pissarro in London', *The Burlington Magazine* 190/907 (October 1978), 641.

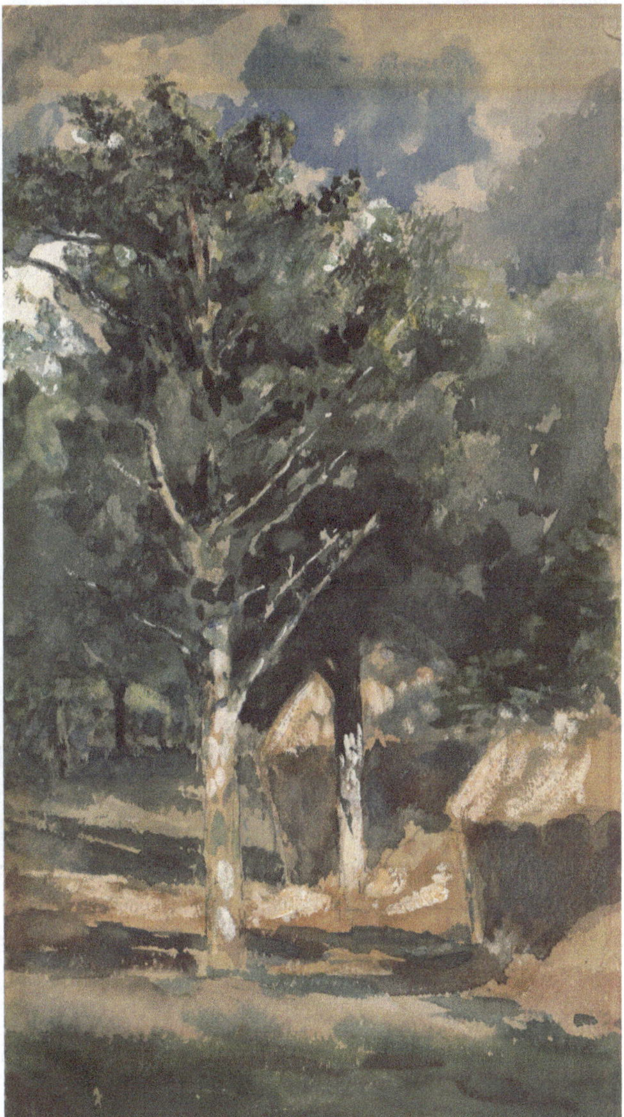

Figure 4.2. Barbara Leigh Smith Bodichon, *Trees with Haystacks,* 1850, Watercolour on paper, Mark Samuels Lasner Collection, University of Delaware Library, Museums and Press.

constitution and distinctly unfeminine attire. Her friend Gertrude Jekyll understood the rigour required of these subjects, which necessitated 'a very determined will and very thick boots. Long hours of exposure to sun and wind are inevitable and free access to nature for months at a time, and a courageous exercise of personal independence.'[28] Barbara's early painting partner Anna Howitt described the difficulty in transporting painting equipment to a selected spot:

> It is altogether a very 'up hill and down dale' sort of business, and so much the more difficult as I have to carry along with me, backwards and forwards, a goodly-sized canvas, the only possible means for the conveyance of which is, so far as I have been able to discover, strapping it over my shoulders and then steadying it with my hands, thus presenting a ludicrous burlesque of a small, very small Samson carrying off the gates of Gaza [...] As for standing-room for your easel there is none — but a mossy tree-stem, round which you can tightly bind your canvas, makes a splendid, most picturesque, appropriate, and comfortable easel.[29]

Barbara seems to have embraced these obstacles, further increasing the degree of difficulty by choosing ever more rigorous destinations for subject matter: 'I must go to some wilder country to paint – because I believe I shall paint well'.[30] She was an inveterate traveller, propelled perhaps by the need to escape from both the weight of the reform work she had taken on as well as the confining gender restrictions of the British middle-class. In these distant lands, unencumbered by societal rules and regulations, she could safely unpack the lack of power she experienced at home. Further, this 'politics of departure' was an act of 'ideological resistance – a self-conscious repudiation and critique of the society left behind – and an opportunity for a new kind of self-construction or self-fashioning'.[31]

28 Jekyll, *Gertrude Jekyll: A Memoir*, 95.

29 Anna Mary Howitt, 'Unpainted Pictures. No. II. Sojourn in the Farm-House by the Sea', *The Crayon* 3/3 (March 1856), 69.

30 Cited in Hirsch 'Barbara Leigh Smith Bodichon: artist and activist', 179. Letter, Bodichon to George Eliot, 14 January 1856. George Eliot and George Henry Lewes Collection, GEN MSS 963, Beinecke Rare Book and Manuscript Library, Yale University.

31 Pauline Nestor, 'Negotiating a self: Barbara Bodichon in America and Algiers', *Postcolonial Studies* 8/2 (2007), 156.

She often travelled with female friends, a pattern that began when, as a young woman, defying social taboos, she and Anna Howitt – two unchaperoned, single women – embarked on an extensive tour of Europe. Similarly, in 1867, she travelled to Spain with novelist George Eliot and author Matilda Betham-Edwards. The latter described the rugged and often dangerous aspects of the trip: 'At that time drivers of the diligence carried firearms, and every inch of the road was beset by dangers of one kind or another, Arab cut-throats and plunderers who if caught were summarily shot down, malaria, and, last but not least, earthquake.'[32]

Barbara was particularly sensitive to autocratic systems of government and extremes of power. She seems to have been drawn to environments of those experiencing tyranny. From Austria she wrote: 'I did not know before, how intense, how completely a part of my soul were all feelings about freedom and justice in politics and government. I did not think, when I was so glad to go into Austria, how the sight of people ruled by the sword in place of law, would stir up my heart, and make me feel as miserable as those who live under it.'[33]

Two noteworthy excursions brought her to domains of particular oppression and disenfranchisement. In 1857 she married French physician and Republican politician Eugene Bodichon. Bodichon was a French colonist of Algeria, where she met him the previous year. The French colonial occupation of Algeria witnessed extreme acts of violence and contestation. Eugene's role in the governance of the colony (as a member of the Chamber of Deputies) placed him at the centre of this subjugation.[34] While it is difficult for present day historians to justify Barbara's attraction to him, it was undoubtedly bolstered by his idiosyncratic character. Within the colony he was appreciated for treating the poor free of charge. He was also 'an advocate of democracy and women's rights in an era dominated by political and social conservatism'.[35] Historically, Barbara's political position,

32 Betham-Edwards, *Reminiscences*, 233.

33 Burton, *Barbara Bodichon*, 33.

34 Eugene published a series of articles which 'delved into nascent theories of scientific racism'; Benjamin Claude Brower, 'Rethinking Abolition in Algeria. Slavery and the "Indigenous Question"', *Cahiers d'études africaines*, 195 (2009), 816.

35 Ibid., 815.

particularly with regard to imperialist politics, although unsubstantiated by surviving primary documentation, has often been assumed by way of marital association.[36] I would suggest, rather, that her role in imperialist subjugation comes under the heading of Michael Rothberg's 'implicated subject', defined as those aligned with power and privilege without being themselves direct agents of harm.[37]

From the time of her betrothal until her husband's death in 1885, Barbara divided her time between Algeria and England. Using their Algiers home, located on the hill of Mustafa Supérieure, overlooking the port as a home base, she continued her habit of arduous excursion, embarking on periodic explorations of the landscape, often in the company of women friends visiting from England.

Directly after their marriage the couple travelled to America, another destination of humanitarian affliction. For eleven months they visited all but one of the fifteen slave states and travelled up the east coast and into Canada as far as Niagara Falls. The trip, taking place just four years prior to the Civil War, was for Barbara an opportunity to view first-hand American enslavement, from which she could draw her own conclusions, parsing out the conflicting reports received at home. While in the south, she viewed a slave auction and interviewed plantation owners, the enslaved, freed slaves and southern belles. In coming to terms with the inhuman suffering she witnessed, Barbara related it to injustices which existed in her own country, noting:

> In these fifteen States of the American Union are 3,700,000 human beings who have no legal rights, no legal rights to their persons or their labour, and who can be sold from hand to hand like horses or dogs. In these fifteen Republican States there are

36 William Gallois, *The Administration of Sickness: Medicine and Ethics in Nineteenth-Century Algeria* (London: Palgrave Macmillan, 2008), 66–92. Along with several other historians, Gallois interprets Barbara's views on racism based on the writings of her husband. Remembering that, at most, she spent only half of each of her married years with Eugene in Algeria (and the remaining campaigning for women's rights in London), I am less comfortable assigning her the beliefs and maxims are those stated by her husband.

37 Michael Rothberg, *The Implicated Subject: Beyond Victims and Perpetrators* (Stanford, CA: Stanford University Press, 2019), 1.

> about 400,000 human beings who have no right to vote, and who cannot mix with the privileged part of the community on any terms of equality; and these are not slaves, but free coloured people [...] In these fifteen Republican States there are from 345,000 to 350,000 men who hold their fellow men in bondage.[38]

On the subject of gender bias, she concluded: 'Slavery is a greater injustice, but it is allied to the injustice to women so closely that I cannot see one without thinking of the other and feeling how soon slavery would be destroyed if right opinions were entertained upon the other question.'[39]

While in America she drew and painted. However, of the few images that remain today (largely in the form of sketch books),[40] as in much of her work as a whole, there is little or no evidence of the human figure, enslaved or free. And yet she wrote prolifically[41] of what she witnessed. In fact, our understanding of Barbara's views on slavery survives by way of her written corpus. These public-facing strongly abolitionist views, however, are nowhere in evidence in her visual production. The finished paintings which Barbara ostensibly created while touring the United States were meant for the market, as indicated by her description of both the beauty and inaccessibility of the southern terrain. She was cognisant of the potential saleability of such scenes, explaining that 'there are great difficulties in getting sketches in America', and concluding that 'mine will be valuable'.[42] The absence of visual renderings of the enslaved, a circumstance of which she was deeply intolerant, suggests perhaps it was off-bounds, an acknowledgement that she would not seek financial gain through the objectification of those struggling under inhumane conditions. She also described

38 Barbara Bodichon, 'Slavery in America', *English Woman's Journal* 2 (October 1858), 94–5.

39 Reed, *An American Diary, 1857–1858*, 63.

40 Sketchbook, hand titled 'B.L.S.B. LOUISIANA./Sketches./1857–8'. Barbara Leigh Smith Bodichon Collection, Gen MSS 119, Beinecke Rare Book & Manuscript Library, Yale University.

41 See bibliography for an abbreviated list of articles on slavery and her observations while traveling in America which Barbara published primarily in the *English Woman's Journal*.

42 Barbara Bodichon, 'Slavery in the South', *English Woman's Journal*, 8/4–6 (October, November, December 1861), 185.

the 'infinite harm […] done by the false representations of travellers',[43] as it encouraged an erroneous understanding of the reality on the ground to audiences abroad.[44]

Tim Barringer has observed of the rise and fall of the landscape genre that it 'seems to have returned to prominence in the fine arts in Britain at moments of enforced insularity'.[45] Viewed from a nineteenth-century feminist perspective, Barbara's habit of carrying small sketchbooks, easily accessed to record views at a moment's notice, could be interpreted as a personal – even subversive – expression of her escape from societal codes of such 'enforced insularity'. The politics in her painted work were personal, a concealed imprinted record of her own. While we are left with minimal evidence of her large-scale exhibited work – work in which she presented her professional ability to the outside world – these numerous surviving sketchbooks (assumedly created for her own reference as aides de memoir) would have been kept nearer to hand, perhaps explaining their retention over time.[46]

In both Algeria and America, the work she created on-site – written and pictorial – has been read as imperialist; as 'pictorializing' the 'oriental',[47] and utilising the disempowered other 'to claim her own […] power to […] pursue intellectual and professional self-fulfilment against gender expectations'.[48] If we assume that all 'creativity [and] cultural production is not insulated from the circumstances of its times', it is not surprising that landscapes of colonised geographical spheres are most often read within

43 Bodichon, 'Slavery in America', 97.

44 See Sarah Thomas, *Witnessing Slavery: Art and Travel in the Age of Abolition* (New Haven, CT: Yale University Press, 2020), in which the author examines the political agenda behind images of the enslaved.

45 Tim Barringer, 'Landscape Then and Now', *British Art Studies*, 10 (Autumn 2018), <https://www.britishartstudies.ac.uk/issues/issue-index/issue-10/landscape-national-contexts>, accessed 25 July 2021.

46 The three surviving Algerian sketchbooks in the collection of the Delaware Art Museum were the property of a descendant.

47 Cherry, *Beyond the Frame*, 80.

48 Simone-Martin, *Barbara Bodichon's Epistolary Education*, 170.

politicising imperial statements of ownership and control over the other.[49] While there is no denying that Barbara's American and Algerian subjects were created within environments of the disenfranchised, I am suggesting here a more personal interpretation, remembering that 'individuals conjure landscape individually. Each inquirer realizes something unique in the concatenation of shapes and forms and spaces and textures ahead or around'.[50]

This is not to argue that Barbara was not a product of her cultural environment, with all the nationalistic, superior and condescending imperialistic attitudes that sanctioned colonisation and oppression which this implies.[51] But this disempowered world into which she was born was one fabricated by men. I am suggesting that her response, which took the form of landscape imagery, may not have been that of the traditional male perspective of a feminised landscape which orientalist historians most commonly document. By placing Barbara's work within the context of her feminist politics and displaced social status, an alternate reading may be more accurate.

The figure in the line drawing *Absorbed* (Figure 4.3), standing with her back to the viewer and immersed in the infinite grandeur of a mountain range, is living within and outwardly discovering a world that heretofore was the vantage of men only. In broaching the gender barrier in inaccessible locations such as this, Barbara experienced an empowerment unattainable within the Victorian societal framework. Her feminist activism was sustained through documentation and evidencing of this personal experience,

49 Michael Rosenthal, 'Introduction', in Christiana Payne and Scott Wilcox, eds, *Prospects for the Nation: Recent Essays in British Landscape, 1750–1880* (New Haven, CT: Yale University Press, 1997), 2.

50 John R. Stilgoe, *What is Landscape?* (Cambridge, MA: The MIT Press, 2015), 17.

51 Barbara's views on race could best be characterised as 'casual racism', a sub-genre applied to Victorians by Carolyn Betensky when she explains: 'When I say that "the Victorians" were racist, I am not saying all Victorians were what we call racist. That would be demonstrably false'. Some show themselves to be 'resolutely opposed to what we could consider racist practices, verbal or otherwise – sometimes, ironically, in the very texts [cited] for their inclusion of racist epithets or stereotypes.' Carolyn Betensky, 'Casual Racism in Victorian Literature', *Victorian Literature and Culture*, 47/4 (2019), 727–8.

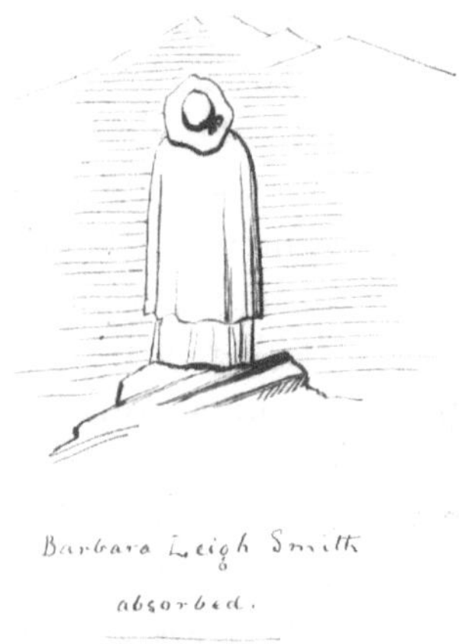

Figure 4.3. Barbara Leigh Smith Bodichon, *Absorbed*, undated, Ink on paper, Personal Papers of Barbara Leigh Smith Bodichon [GBR/0271/GCPP Bodichon], Folder 8–14. The Mistress and Fellows, Girton College, Cambridge.

as manifested in her landscape imagery. These views of previously exclusive, male-only environs pictured an opening of gendered spaces for herself, with the hope of the same for her sisters – an affirmation to all of what could be experienced. The arduous excursions Barbara embarked upon offered the opportunity to set her own limits, not those imposed upon her by the patriarchal time and place in which she lived. In America she marvelled at the forests:

> A new revelation of nature's beauty [...] I never imagined anything like it. Old trees leaning on young trees, the dead prostrate; haughty trees springing straight up to heaven and then spreading out into a fir-like tower – boughs, all of them, covered with this grey garment hanging down straight [...] always beautiful and fantastic, sometimes sublime.[52]

Similarly, in Algeria, undeterred by the relatively inhospitable climate characterised by wind and sand storms, earthquakes, mudslides, floods, droughts, and in Barbara's time, even locusts, she likened it to Heaven,

52 Reed, An American Diary, 1857–1858, 64–5.

describing it as 'ravishingly beautiful [...] The climate is delicious the sea and distant mountains more beautiful than words and pencil can express [...] The place intoxicates me ... I wish I had 100 senses'.[53]

Charges of 'worlding' and 'pictorializing' rely on a rare figural image, *Sisters working in the Fields*, to support the reading.[54] This interpretation, ascribed from a single atypical rendering, ignores the broader spectrum of subjects represented within her oeuvre, including views of England, Wales and Brittany among others.[55] Examined within the entire corpus, imperialist connotations are not convincing. Rather than affirming colonial authority, the variety of geographic locales she pictured might instead be understood as a reflection of the passion with which she pursued her craft – a professional commitment and level of engagement which has been heretofore overlooked, even by feminist historians. If viewed within the drive for artistic excellence, each new environment becomes a set of aesthetic challenges and opportunities – light, colour, topography – to be interpreted. In Spain, for instance, she observed:

> The colours of the landscape are composed of red, yellow, and brown; deserts of sandy space; monotonous and fiery wastes; fortified mud towns, with old churches and convents; then an expanse of wavy ground covered with grey granite rocks like castles or Druidical remains, and forests of small pines, impressive from their multitude and monotony.[56]

Barbara's desire to visualise these various settings is expressed in a varied typology of subject, ranging from individual plant specimens recorded in

53 Letter, 21 November 1856, Bodichon to George Eliot, George Eliot and George Henry Lewes Collection, GEN MSS 963, Beinecke Rare Book & Manuscript Library, Yale University.

54 Cherry, *Beyond the Frame*, 90; or Simon-Martin, *Barbara Bodichon's Epistolary Education*, 226.

55 The image is documentation, and potentially a tribute to the outpost of the Sisters of Charity of the Order of St Vincent de Paul in the village of Marengo which Barbara visited and wrote about in 'Cleopatra's Daughter, Ste Marciana, Mama Marabout, and other Algerian Women', *English Women's Journal* X/60 (1863), 404+.

56 Barbara Bodichon, 'An Easy Railway Journey in Spain', *Temple Bar* 25 (January 1869), 241.

Pre-Raphaelite detail to grand romantic viewscapes. Documented in the previously described small sketchbooks,[57] they align with John Ruskin's belief that to draw a landscape was to know it.[58] For Barbara, to acquire this understanding of place – to internalise it – was to come closer to knowing herself.

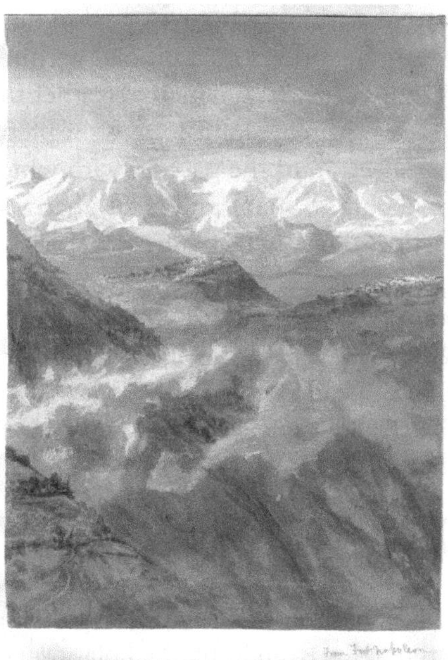

Figure 4.4. Barbara Leigh Smith Bodichon, *From Fort Napoleon*, undated, Watercolour on paper, Personal Papers of Barbara Leigh Smith Bodichon [GBR/0271/GCPP Bodichon], Folder 8–14. The Mistress and Fellows, Girton College, Cambridge.

57 Examples of Barbara's sketchbooks can be found in the collections of the Beinecke Rare Book & Manuscript Library, Yale University; the Yale Center for British Art; and the Delaware Art Museum.

58 For example, in a review of John Brett's *Val d'Aosta* Ruskin remarked, 'And here, accordingly, for the first time in history, we have, by help of art, the power of visiting a place, reasoning about it, and knowing it'; in *Academy Notes*, 1859; republished in Stephen Wildman, ed., *Ruskin and the Pre-Raphaelites: Ruskin's Complete Writings on the Pre-Raphaelites* (London: Pallas Athene, 2012), 204.

The monochromatic *From Fort Napoleon* (Figure 4.4) is a Turnerian capturing of the sublime.[59] In his timeless study of this broad ranging style, Hugh Honor notes: 'that one essential, distinguishing characteristic of Romantic art [is] the supreme value placed by the Romantics on the artist's sensibility and emotional "authenticity" as the qualities which alone confer "validity" on his work [...] the expression of the artist's own personal living experience'.[60]

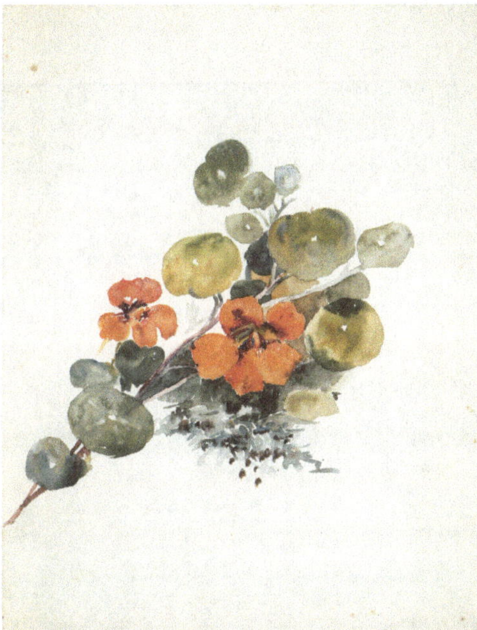

Figure 4.5. Barbara Leigh Smith Bodichon, *Nasturtiums*, undated, Watercolour on paper, Acquisition Fund, Delaware Art Museum.

59 Hirsch first pointed out this Romantic aspect of Barbara's work in 'Barbara Leigh Smith Bodichon: artist and activist', 168.

60 Hugh Honour, *Romanticism* (New York: Harper & Row, 1979), 20.

Grand views such as this could be drawn simultaneously with more focused studies of individual plants, such as *Nasturtiums* (Figure 4.5, potentially drawn from plants in her own garden at Scalands Gate). Within the full range of her work, the singularity of a plant specimen and expansive emotion of breath-taking vistas exist simultaneously as tools for introspection.

In addition, a small number of imagined scenes, often including the presence of otherworldly or spectral elements, have survived, as for instance, *Boats in the Rain* (Figure 4.6).[61]

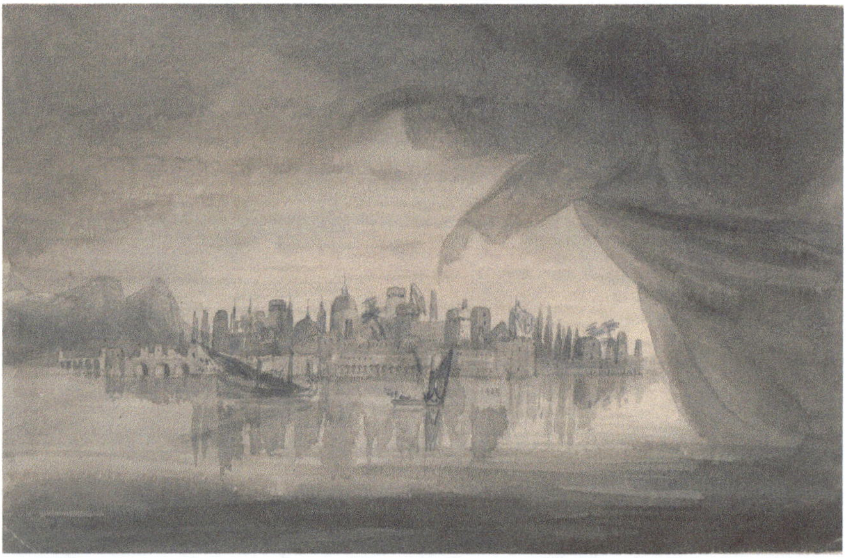

Figure 4.6. Barbara Leigh Smith Bodichon, *Boats in the Rain*, undated, Watercolour on paper, Mark Samuels Lasner Collection, University of Delaware Library, Museums and Press.

61 It has been speculated that the titles for many of the extant watercolours were added by John Crabbe. While generally descriptive, they can be misleading as in the case of this watercolour in which the spectral presence goes unnoted.

This wet-brush composition of an unidentified harbour scene with a city in the background includes a ghostly spectre hovering over the ephemeral surface of the water at night. The God-like figure points downward at the city in a dramatic gesture. It is difficult to know how to interpret this scene. An inscription on the verso reads: 'Dedicated with respect and admiration to one of the most useful of men [Dr] Southwood Smith.' Smith was a physician and advocate for sanitary reform. He was an early proponent of the relationship between environment and illness who campaigned for healthier working conditions, particularly with regard to child labour. He was also a Unitarian, and a strong believer that all would attain salvation.[62] Barbara knew him through friendship with his living partner, the artist Margaret Gillies. Despite Smith's reform work having taken place largely in London, the city depicted evokes a foreign, even eastern port. It is difficult to discern whether the tone is one of well-being – divine protection, as Smith held – or if there is a more sinister message of retribution effected. While grounded in the present through the surviving inscription, it also reflects a fascination with the mystical or even occult that conforms with the Romantic aspect of her aesthetic described above.[63]

Stylistically her brushwork varied – potentially demonstrating a chronological progression – as she moved from the more tightly detailed compositions of early Pre-Raphaelite influence to looser, Barbizon-inspired recordings. *Ventnor, Isle of Wight* (Figure 4.1) is exemplary of the former. Painted in 1856 as she was working on the petition to Parliament for the revision of the Married Women's Property Act, she paused her political reform work to take a painting holiday on the Isle of Wight with fellow painter Anna Howitt. The not-quite bird's eye view is rendered from a location near Luccombe, just to the east of Ventnor, looking northeast across Shanklin bay.[64] Upon close examination, two tiny figures can be glimpsed,

62 See Smith's *Illustrations of the Divine Government*, tending to show that everything is under the direction of infinite wisdom and goodness and will terminate in the production of universal purity and happiness (1816).

63 This mystical element can also be seen in *A Hooded Procession* (undated, watercolour on paper, Mark Samuels Lasner Collection, University of Delaware Library).

64 Despite the seemingly documentary detail, Robin McInnes has identified the headland in the middle distance (which has been placed where it should not be) is Woody Point to the west of Ventnor, transposed for artistic effect.

seated on a rocky outcropping in much the way Barbara must have been situated in order to capture the scene. They are present, but go largely unseen, enveloped within the vastness of the panorama and vegetation – the overlooked, seated on an overlook. For Barbara, the rendering of the landscape was both an act of emancipation and a reminder of the powerlessness of humanity, irrespective of gender, amidst such awe-invoking vistas.

If, indeed, the looser, more abstract renderings of the landscape such as the *View of Scalands Farm* in Sussex (Figure 4.7) came later in life, during and after her training with Corot and the Barbizons in the 1860s, this would correlate to the decade of her most ambitious work for women's rights – the founding of the Kensington Society and subsequent presentation of the first petition for the enfranchisement of women in Parliament (1866) and the opening of Girton College. This view across a valley is painted with a wet brush and broad washes of colour denoting the varied tonalities of the trees and undergrowth, in the middle ground. Looser still is the ephemeral *Trees with Haystacks* (Figure 4.2), in which the light playing upon the surface of tree trunk and haystack are delineated through abstract patterning that is impressionistic, even modern in conception. In works

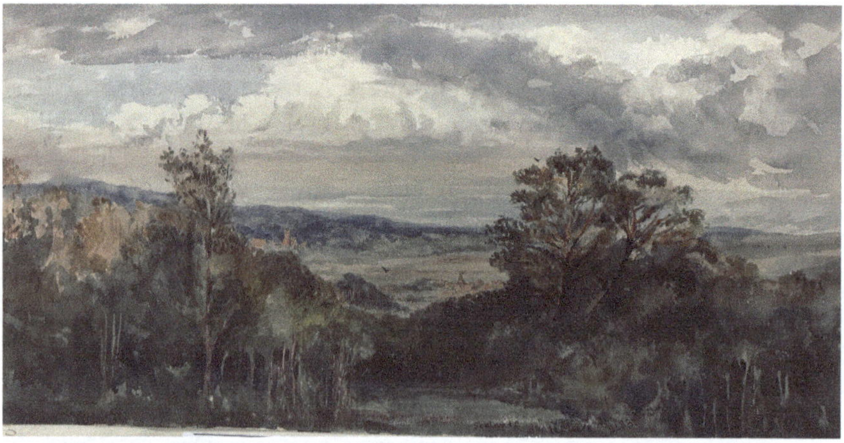

Figure 4.7. Barbara Leigh Smith Bodichon, *View of Scalands Farm*, undated, Watercolour on paper, Personal Papers of Barbara Leigh Smith Bodichon [GBR/0271/GCPP Bodichon], Folder 8–15. The Mistress and Fellows, Girton College, Cambridge.

such as this, Barbara has breached traditional modes of landscape representation for the period. William Michael Rossetti remarked: 'The chief hitch appears to be that her works are not considered sufficiently finished; while she, on the other hand, objects to attempting any finish – and considers it detrimental in her own practice – beyond the point at which she has succeeded in hitting the mark she aimed at.'[65] Barbara's artistic practice, like her campaign for social reform and the rights of women, challenged societal and cultural standards. In scenes such as *Windswept Trees on the Algerian Coast* (Figure 4.8), this loosening of the brush conveys the sheer fury of attempting to capture all she saw and felt in a fervent desire not to

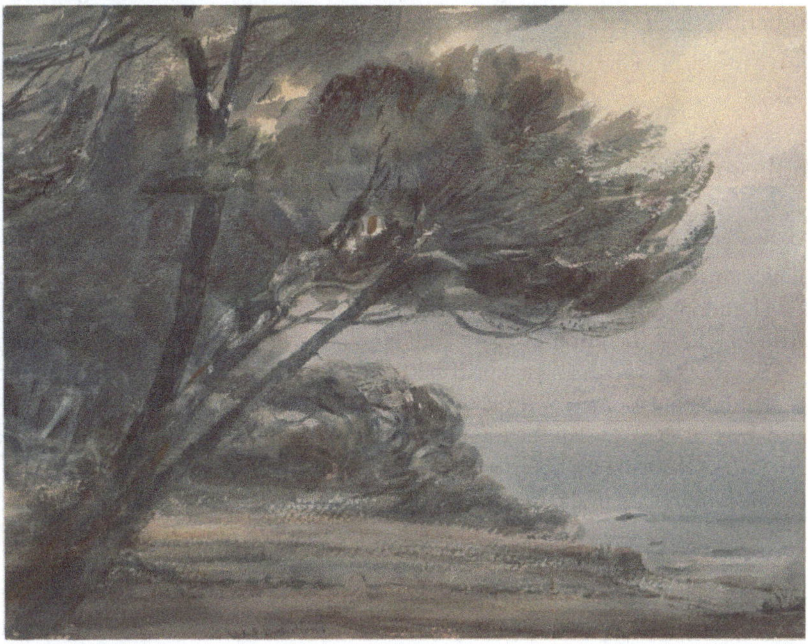

Figure 4.8. Barbara Leigh Smith Bodichon, *Windswept Trees on the Algerian Coast*, undated, Watercolour on paper, Mark Samuels Lasner Collection, University of Delaware Library, Museums and Press.

65 Odette Bornand, ed., *The Diary of W. M. Rossetti 1870–1873* (Oxford: Clarendon Press, 1977), 149.

let it escape her – the momentary exaltation of the wild and windblown freedom from societal stricture.

Barbara's politics and paintings existed on a parallel track, modelling a future of emancipation – the political move towards universal suffrage and an artistic transition from realism to abstraction. Within the historiography, her artistic production, often overlooked in favour of more fully documented accomplishments in political reform, has been cherry-picked to bolster politicised agendas. These investigations have distracted from a serious assessment of the broader spectrum of her oeuvre. Complicated by limited extant examples and impairment of the historical record, and further clouded by historic gender bias, the work of Barbara Leigh Smith Bodichon deserves a fresh evaluation.

Bibliography

Allingham, Helen, and E. Baumer Williams, eds, *Letters to William Allingham* (London: Longmans, Green and Co., 1911).

Barringer, Tim, 'Landscape Then and Now', *British Art Studies*, 10 (Autumn 2018) <https://www.britishartstudies.ac.uk/issues/issue-index/issue-10/landscape-national-contexts>, accessed 25 July 2021.

Betensky, Carolyn, 'Casual Racism in Victorian Literature', *Victorian Literature and Culture*, 47/4 (2019), 723–51.

Betham-Edwards, Matilda, *Reminiscences* (London: G. Redway, 1898).

Bodichon, Barbara, 'Slavery in America', *English Woman's Journal* 2 (October 1858), 94–100.

——, 'Slave Preaching', *English Woman's Journal* 5/25 (March 1860), 87–94.

——, 'Slavery in the South', *English Woman's Journal* 8/44–6 (October, November, December 1861), 111–18, 179–87, 261–66.

——, 'Cleopatra's Daughter, Ste Marciana, Mama Marabout, and other Algerian Women', *English Women's Journal* 10/60 (February 1863), 404.

——, 'Of those who are the property of others, and of the great power that holds others as property', *English Woman's Journal,* 10/60 (February 1863), 370–81.

——, 'An Easy Railway Journey in Spain', *Temple Bar* 25 (January 1869), 542–6.

Bornand, Odette, ed. *The Diary of W. M. Rossetti 1870–1873* (Oxford: Clarendon Press, 1977).

Brower, Benjamin Claude, 'Rethinking Abolition in Algeria. Slavery and the "Indigenous Question"', *Cahiers d'études africaines* 195 (2009), 805–28.

Burton, Hester, *Barbara Bodichon* (London: John Murray, 1949).

Chadwick, Whitney, *Women, Art, and Society* (1990; London: Thames & Hudson, 2007).

Cherry, Deborah, *Painting Women: Victorian Women Artists* (London: Routledge, 1993).

——, *Beyond the Frame: Feminism and Visual Culture, Britain 1850–1900* (London: Routledge, 2000).

Fredeman, William E., ed., *The Correspondence of Dante Gabriel Rossetti*, 10 vols (Cambridge: D. S. Brewer, 1999–2015).

Gallois, William, *The Administration of Sickness: Medicine and Ethics in Nineteenth-Century Algeria* (London: Palgrave Macmillan, 2008).

Herstein, Sheila R, *Mid-Victorian Feminist, Barbara Leigh Smith Bodichon* (New Haven, CT: Yale University Press, 1985).

Hirsch, Pam, 'Barbara Leigh Smith Bodichon: Artist and Activist', in Clarissa Campbell Orr, ed., *Women in the Victorian Art World* (Manchester: Manchester University Press, 1995).

——, *Barbara Leigh Smith Bodichon 1827–1891: Feminist, Artist and Rebel* (London: Chatto & Windus, 1998).

——, 'Bodichon, Barbara Leigh Smith', in *Oxford Dictionary of National Biography* (2007), <https://doi.org/10.1093/ref:odnb/2755>, accessed 15 July 2021.

Honour, Hugh, *Romanticism*. (New York: Harper & Row, 1979).

House, John, 'New Material on Monet and Pissarro in London', *The Burlington Magazine*, 190/907 (October 1978), 636–9, 641–2.

Howitt, Anna Mary, *An Art-Student in Munich* (London, 1853; Boston, MA: Ticknor, Reed, and Fields, 1854).

——, 'Unpainted Pictures. No. II. Sojourn in the Farm-House by the Sea', *The Crayon*, 3/3 (March 1856), 68–70.

Jekyll, Francis, *Gertrude Jekyll: A Memoir* (Northampton, MA: Bookshop Round Table, 1934).

Lacey, Candida Ann, ed. *Barbara Leigh Smith Bodichon and the Langham Place Group* (New York and London: Routledge & K. Paul, 1987).

Marsh, Jan, and Pamela Gerrish Nunn. *Pre-Raphaelite Women Artists* (Manchester: Manchester City Art Gallery, 1997).

Matthews, Jacqui, 'Barbara Bodichon: integrity in diversity', in Dale Spender, ed., *Feminist Theorists* (London: The Women's Press, 1983).

Nestor, Pauline, 'Negotiating a self: Barbara Bodichon in America and Algiers', *Postcolonial Studies*, 8/2 (2007), 155–64.

Reed, Joseph W. Jr *An American Diary, 1857–1858* (London: Routledge & K. Paul, 1972).

Rosenthal, Michael, 'Introduction', in Christiana Payne and Scott Wilcox, eds, *Prospects for the Nation: Recent Essays in British Landscape, 1750–1880* (New Haven, CT: Yale University Press, 1997).

Rossetti, William Michael, 'Art News from England, Letter XVI', *The Crayon* 3/8 (August 1856), 244–7.

Rothberg, Michael, *The Implicated Subject: Beyond Victims and Perpetrators* (Stanford, CA: Stanford University Press, 2019).

Simon-Martin, Meritxell, *Barbara Bodichon's Epistolary Education: Unfolding Feminism* (Cham, Switzerland: Palgrave Macmillan, 2020).

Stilgoe, John R., *What is Landscape?* (Cambridge, MA: The MIT Press, 2015).

Thomas, Sarah, *Witnessing Slavery: Art and Travel in the Age of Abolition* (New Haven and London: Yale University Press, 2020).

Wildman, Stephen, ed., *Ruskin and the Pre-Raphaelites: Ruskin's Complete Writings on the Pre-Raphaelites* (London: Pallas Athene, 2012).

PART II

Poetry and Writing

ROSALIND WHITE

5 'Words Came Slowly One by One from Frozen Lips Shut Still and Dumb': A Reappraisal of the Poetry of Elizabeth Siddal

ABSTRACT

Elizabeth Siddal's poetic voice has often been dismissed for its morbidity. Oswald Doughty spoke of her work as 'sad, sentimental and self-consciously pathetic broodings'.[1] To Rodolphe Louis Mégroz, Siddal's poems 'harp[ed] monotonously' and resemble[d] 'the forced fruit of a fine spirit morbid at the core'.[2] Such sentiment has ensured that Siddal remains an under-theorised voice.

Gathering together the fragments of Siddal's poetry that are available to us, I argue that Siddal's oeuvre actively subverts Pre-Raphaelite aesthetic convention, establishing a parallel between the female body and the poetic form. I take what has been termed the 'Lancelot moment' (the moment in which a masculine observer stands before an insentient female) to trace Siddal's poetic communion with Dante Gabriel Rossetti: exploring how, in a subversive act of poetic ventriloquism, Siddal assumes control of her textual counterpart to restore the insentient female with the poetic power of her own voice.

* * * * *

How does the female poet write in an age in which the active male speaker and the passive, insentient female define poetic convention? As Dorothy Mermin asks, 'if they are the speakers, who are the objects?'[3] Elizabeth Siddal – more so than any other Pre-Raphaelite figure – was defined and confined by such a question. Siddal's poetic afterlife has effectively been

1 Oswald Doughty, *A Victorian Romantic: Dante Gabriel Rossetti* (London: Fredrick Muller, 1949), 291.

2 Rodolphe Louis Mégroz, *Dante Gabriel Rossetti: Painter Poet of Heaven in Earth* (London: Faber & Gwyer, 1929), 59.

3 Dorothy Mermin, '"The Fruitful Feud of Hers and His": Sameness, Difference, and Gender in Victorian Poetry', *Victorian Poetry* 33/1 (1995), 156.

eclipsed by the circumstances of her death and macabre exhumation. As we shall explore, Siddal's extant poetry is imbued with an almost preternatural awareness of this paradigm. Implementing various poetic strategies of anti-representational self-displacement, Siddal subverts the compliance enacted by her textual counterpart. She communes with Dante Gabriel Rossetti as a muse and as a fellow artist, adopting his poetic signature in order to establish a parallel between the female form and the rhythm and contours of his poetry.

Siddal's approach predicates the footsteps of a number of female writers and artists.[4] As Angela Leighton explains, 'the life story [of women in the nineteenth-century] gives way to the story of imaginative creation, which is, very often for Victorian women, a death story'.[5] This convention is of particular pertinence to the historiography of Pre-Raphaelite figures such as Elizabeth Siddal.[6] In *The Pre-Raphaelite Sisterhood* (1985) Jan Marsh explicates the climate that came with living among the Brotherhood:

> While the faces [of women] are seen everywhere – in oil paintings, watercolours, drawings – their voices are never heard. As depicted, they are silent, enigmatic, passive figures, not individuals engaged in activity but objects to be gazed upon by a painter and spectator. True they often stare back, but it is hard to tell what they are thinking and frequently they look away or have their eyes closed.[7]

4 See, for example, Constance Naden's 'Love's Mirror' (1894) or Mary Elizabeth Coleridge's 'The Other Side of a Mirror' (1896). For an overview of the 'ancestry' that shaped female poetic tradition, see Linda Hughes, 'Poetry', in Linda H. Peterson, ed., *The Cambridge Companion to Victorian Women's Writing* (Cambridge: Cambridge University Press, 2015), 89–105.

5 Angela Leighton, *Victorian Women Poets: Writing Against the Heart* (Charlottesville: University of Virginia Press, 1992), 6.

6 There is a wealth of scholarship that explores the mythologising of Siddal's life and death. Notable examples include Jan Marsh, *The Legend of Elizabeth Siddal* (London: Quartet, 1989); Emily Orlando, '"That I May not Faint, or Die, or Swoon": Reviving Pre-Raphaelite Women', *Womens' Studies* 38/6 (2009), 611–46; Alison Hallsal, 'H.D. and the Victorian Spectres of "White Rose and the Red"', *College Literature* 38/4 (2011), 115–33; and Angela Dunstan, 'Stunner: Elizabeth Siddal, the Evolution of a Sensation', in *Literature and Sensation* (Newcastle: Cambridge Scholars Publishing, 2009), 24–33.

7 Marsh, *The Legend of Elizabeth Siddal*, 1.

Just as Elizabeth Barrett Browning's protagonist in 'The Lost Bower' (1857) 'cannot be two people at once, both the questing prince and the dreaming princess, both a poet and his fairy inspiration',[8] Elizabeth Siddal's speaker in her poem 'Love and Hate' pleads with her male counterpart not to 'gaze into [her] face' but to 'turn away [his] false dark eyes', for she can 'neither sing nor pray': his presence becoming 'the poisonous tree that stole [her] life away.' She too longs 'for a place where a woman can situate herself without self-contradiction and in which she cannot just daydream but speak'.[9]

In her recent publication *My Ladys Soul: The Poems of Elizabeth Eleanor Siddall* (2018) – the first to unite Siddal's extant poetry in a single volume – Serena Trowbridge questions the relative obscurity of Siddal's work: asking why is it that 'so few people read [Siddal's] poetry critically'?[10] Indeed, only a small selection of scholars – to date – have critically engaged with Siddal's poetry. Ehnenn (2014) explores Siddal's participation in the balladic tradition; Paxon (2014) points 'to a figurative dismemberment' at work in Siddal's verse; and Hassett (1997) – recognising the 'historical denigration' that Siddal's poetry has faced – sets out to 'modify the perception that [it] is merely personal and gloomily repetitious'.[11] Trowbridge calls for a strain of scholarship that might address this lacuna: work that would give 'critical attention' to Siddal's writing, rather than further sensationalise her 'life story'.[12] A National Trust exhibition at Wightwick Manor,

8 Dorothy Mermin, 'The Damsel, the Knight, and the Victorian Woman Poet', *Critical Inquiry* 13/1 (1986), 65.

9 Mermin, 'The Damsel, the Knight', 65.

10 Serena Trowbridge, ed., *My Ladys Soul: The Poetry of Elizabeth Siddall* (Brighton: Victorian Secrets, 2018), 7. All subsequent references to the differences between Siddal's published poems (edited by William Michael Rossetti) and her original manuscript are noted in this publication.

11 J. R. Enhen, '"Strong, Traivelling": Re-visions of Women's Subjectivity and Female Labour in the Ballad-work of Elizabeth Siddal', *Victorian Poetry* 52/2 (2014), 251–76; Amanda Paxon, 'Love, Dismemberment, and Elizabeth Siddal's Corpus', *Journal of Pre-Raphaelite Studies* 22/2 (2013), 4–23; Constance Hassett, 'Elizabeth Siddal's Poetry: A Problem and Some Suggestions', *Victorian Poetry* 35/4 (1997), 446.

12 Trowbridge, *My Ladys Soul*, 7.

'Beyond Ophelia' – A Celebration of Lizzie Siddal (2018), likewise promised to 'reinstate Lizzie Siddal as an important and influential artist and poet'.[13]

Conventionally, anthologists and literary scholars have positioned Christina Rossetti's 'In an Artist's Studio' (1856) as a direct response to Dante Gabriel Rossetti's art and poetry. Such practices, unwittingly, preclude Siddal from speaking on her own behalf. As Joseph Bristow has noted, a critical focus on Christina Rossetti and Elizabeth Barrett Browning – to the exclusion of other female poets – subsisted in scholarship of the 1980s and 1990s.[14] Though considerable strides have been made since then towards recovering the work of such women, there is still a 'rich abundance' of poems penned by women 'awaiting exploration'.[15] Most conspicuous is the appreciable lack of critical attention devoted to working-class women who took up poetry.[16] Virginia Blain in her anthology of *Victorian Women Poets* (2014) even makes a 'deliberate choice not to include a token working-class poet' in her selection, citing that 'working-class women's verse-making belongs primarily within an oral rather than a written culture'.[17] However, such a categorisation discounts figures like Siddal – muses, mistresses and models who did not move in working-class circles, despite being working-class themselves, and who thus sought solace in written verse when they could not express themselves through spoken word.

Siddal's poetic voice has often been dismissed for its morbidity. Oswald Doughty (1949) spoke of Siddal's work as 'sad, sentimental and self-consciously pathetic broodings'.[18] William Michael Rossetti found 'a wail of pang and pathos' in her poetry.[19] Furthermore, Rodolphe Louis

13 *'Beyond Ophelia' – A Celebration of Lizzie Siddal, Artist and Poet*, Wightwick Manor (2018) <https://www.nationaltrust.org.uk/wightwick-manor-and-gardens/features/a-celebration-of-lizzie-siddal-artist-and-poet>, accessed 1 November 2019.

14 Joseph Bristow *The Victorian Poet* (Oxford: Routledge, 2014), 9.

15 Hughes, 'Poetry', 103.

16 Alison Chapman, 'Introduction', in Alison Chapman, ed., *Victorian Women Poets* (Suffolk: D. S. Brewer, 2003), 2.

17 Virginia Blain, *Victorian Women Poets* (London: Routledge 2014), 3.

18 Doughty, *A Victorian Romantic*, 2.

19 William Michael Rossetti, *Some Reminiscences of William Michael Rossetti*, 2 vols (New York: Charles Scribner's Sons, 1906), I, 196.

Mégroz (1929) wrote that her poems 'harp[ed] monotonously' and resembled 'the forced fruit of a fine spirit morbid at the core'.[20] Such comments echo the nineteenth-century derision conventionally levelled at the 'poetess' or 'woman poet'.[21] These articles conflated what they called 'Poetry in petticoats' with 'poetry on sufferance': 'the morbid fruits' of woman 'essaying to do man's part'.[22] Honesty or candour in a male poet becomes 'too autobiographical' in a female poet; emotion is framed as sentiment, and what might in his work be considered distinctive in hers lacks ambiguity. Unlike Dante Gabriel Rossetti, who was born into a family of poets, artists and scholars – and thus primed to consider himself among them – Elizabeth Siddal did not expressly write with a view to publish her work. Her poems, Serena Trowbridge informs us, survive on 'scrappy, often on torn pieces of paper', in the Ashmolean Museum. Many are hastily written, and thus marred by inkblots.[23] They are personal, honest fragments: written, most likely, as a form of expressive therapy – a means for Siddal to hypostatise her own experience – and give a shape or form to her emotions.[24]

A letter from Siddal to Emma Madox Brown is preserved on the back of an earlier draft of her poem 'it is not now a longing year'.[25] In the letter, Siddal implores Emma to join her 'by the park and library where the buses

20 Mégroz, *Dante Gabriel Rossetti*, 59.

21 Terms like '"female poet", "woman poet" or "poetess" designated a fiercely contested role in the literary market'; such epithets, Susan Brown writes, were 'enabling as well as constraining for women writers in [their] insistence that masculinity and femininity mattered where poetry was concerned'. Brown 'The Victorian Poetess', in Joseph Bristow, ed., *The Cambridge Companion to Victorian Poetry* (Cambridge: Cambridge University Press, 2000), 181.

22 'Poetry in Petticoats', *Scots Observer* (8 March 1890).

23 Trowbridge, *My Ladys Soul*, 96.

24 According to William Rossetti, Siddal's first contact with poetry was similarly emotive. She reportedly developed a love of poetry at a young age after happening upon two of Tennyson's poems, 'on a piece of paper which she brought home to her mother, wrapped round a pat of butter'. See 'Dante Rossetti and Elizabeth Siddal', *The Burlington Magazine for Connoisseurs* 1/3 (1903), 273.

25 Trowbridge, *My Ladys Soul*, 105. Emma was the muse of Ford Madox Brown. After eloping in September 1849, Emma fell pregnant with their daughter, Catherine. Madox Brown delayed any decision to marry Emma until 1853.

stop' so that they may 'have a chat', as she 'would much like to tell [Emma] one or two things'. Such an evasive request (Siddal twice stresses that their meeting is contingent on Emma having 'nothing better to do') gives us an insight into Siddal's personality. She appears to be both desperate to, and wary of, expressing herself. In this context, poetry acts as a means to externalise the self, a therapeutic medium that, unlike speech, can be unanchored from the body. Siddal implements a poetic strategy that would later be adopted by a number of female poets: fulfilling a desire to 'deconstruct the dead self that is a male "opus" [in order to liberate the] living, inconstant self'.[26] Much of Siddal's poems participate in this practice, and in doing so contest the idea that 'the valued space of art [should be] grounded in a feminine body'.[27]

In order for us to trace Siddal's struggle – her aesthetic effort to move from constituent to creator – we must first look to the sources that stifled her subjectivity. Only then can we reach an understanding of the aesthetic confines from which her speakers resist. I therefore want to begin by briefly examining the work of Dante Gabriel Rossetti. Siddal's poetry lies concealed behind the frame of Rossetti's symbolism, like the parallel 'self-same figure' (2) of Christina Rossetti's 'In an Artist's Studio' (1856) 'hidden just behind those screens' (3). Comments from Siddal's contemporaries allude to such a resistance. The poet Algernon Charles Swinburne, for example, makes a conscious effort to imply that Siddal's verse should not be considered a reflection or by-product of Rossetti's work:

> Here is the same note of originality in discipleship which distinguishes her work in art – Gabriel's influence and example [is] not more perceptible than her own independence and freshness of inspiration.[28]

26 Sandra Gilbert and Susan Gubar, *The Madwoman in the Attic: The Woman Writer and the Nineteenth-Century Literary Imagination* (London: Yale University Press, 2000), 19.

27 Lorraine Janzen Kooistra, *Poetry, Pictures, and Popular Publishing* (Athens, OH: Ohio University Press, 2014), 61.

28 Quoted in Rossetti, *Some Reminiscences*, I, 195.

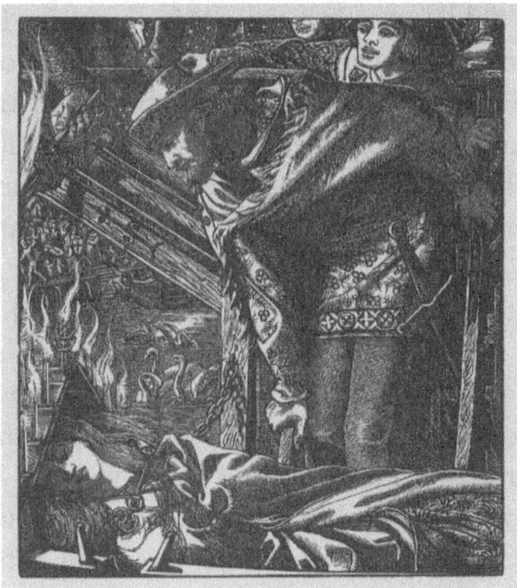

Figure 5.1. Dante Gabriel Rossetti, *The Lady of Shalott*, 1857, from Alfred Lord Tennyson's *Poems* (1903 reissue). Licensed under Creative Commons by The Metropolitan Museum of Art.

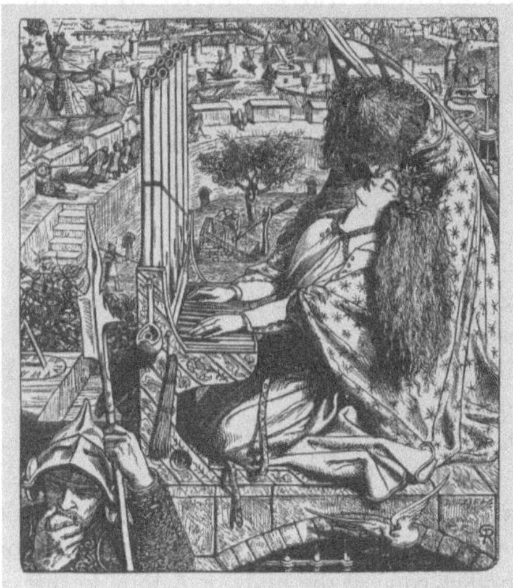

Figure 5.2. Dante Gabriel Rossetti, *St Cecilia or The Palace of Art*, 1857, from Alfred Lord Tennyson's *Poems* (1903 reissue). Licensed under Creative Commons by The Metropolitan Museum of Art.

Most pertinent to Siddal's poetic resistance is a recurring image of Rossetti's that has been termed the 'Lancelot moment'.[29] The moment in which a 'masculine observer stands mystified before a beautiful, insentient feminine body'.[30] This is, of course, exemplified in Rossetti's illustration of this moment for 'The Lady of Shalott' in Edward Moxon's illustrated anthology of *Poems by Alfred Tennyson* (1857) (Figure 5.1). The illustration is an example of what Rossetti describes as an opportunity for the artist to 'allegorize on his own hook'.[31] Extrapolating upon Tennyson's verse – 'He said, "She has a lovely face; / God in his mercy lend her grace, / The Lady of Shalott"' – Rossetti divorces Lancelot's emotions from the text. Time thickens around this verse as the reader, through their engagement with the illustration, lingers on these lines and joins Lancelot in 'reading' his lady's body. Her 'lovely face' is drawn into compositional kinship with the heavenly glow of the candles at the boat's prow as well as the swans at the water's edge. Just as a swan is believed to end its silent life with a beautiful song, the Lady of Shalott, Rossetti suggests, has achieved her artistic zenith in the beauty of her death.

Parallel 'Lancelot moments' occur throughout Rossetti's oeuvre, both before and after Siddal's death.[32] In 'Jenny' (1847–8), Rossetti's male speaker again finds aesthetic transcendence in the idea of beauty quickened by death:

> What, Jenny, are your lilies dead?
> Aye, and the snow-white leaves are spread
> Like winter on the garden-bed.

29 Kathy Psomiades, *Beauty's Body: Femininity and Representation in British Aestheticism* (Stanford, CA: Stanford University Press, 1997), 40; Sullivan Kathryn Kruger, *Weaving the Word: The Metaphorics of Weaving and Female Textual Production* (Selinsgrove, PA: Susquehanna University Press, 2001), 128.

30 Psomiades, *Beauty's Body*, 128.

31 *The Letters of Dante Gabriel Rossetti*, ed. Oswald Doughty and John Robert Wahl, 4 vols (Oxford: Clarendon Press, 1965), II, 97.

32 See also Rossetti's *King Arthur and the Weeping Queens* (another illustration for the Moxon *Tennyson*), in which a group of women gaze upon an insentient male. Notably, their bodies conceal the body of Arthur so that, unlike previous 'moments', the body of the dead is not on erotic display. Moreover, Arthur is gazed at by ten pairs of eyes, as though in order for 'woman' to wield the same sexually charged penetrative gaze as man she must be redoubled.

The poem is presented as a modernised 'Lancelot moment', in which the sleeping beauty is granted aesthetic salvation in lieu of a typical knightly rescue. In another of his illustrations for the Moxon *Tennyson*, 'The Palace of Art'(Figure 5.2), the woman's artistic capabilities (here typified in her somnolent organ playing) are again visually subordinated by the power of her insentient beauty. Early commentators on the illustration noted that 'the man is not an angel but a very flesh and blood man masquerading as angel'.[33] He is often identified as Cecilia's husband Valerian (who, according to legend, allowed her to maintain a vow of chastity in marriage), appearing to her after his martyr's death. The couple achieves a fleshly communion across existential boundaries despite, or perhaps because of, the fact they failed to achieve conjugal union in life. The friction that subsists in Rossetti's work between the body and the spirit, as we shall explore, becomes a subject of frustration in Siddal's verse. Moreover, Siddal takes issue with the bodily display that Rossetti's female figures must carry out to achieve such a paradoxical moment.

Walter Pater, in his appraisal of Rossetti's poems, traces Rossetti's aestheticism to the same wellspring. For Pater, Rossetti's poetic power is both divinely penetrative and, somehow, awakened by the somnolent state of the subject:

> defying distance, and those barriers which are so much more than physical distance – of unutterable desire penetrating into the world of sleep, however lead-bound.[34]

Aestheticism develops an almost necrophiliac strain in Rossetti's work; what is beautiful in life is valued chiefly for its proximity to death. Within the conventions of the 'Lancelot moment', 'the beautiful [insensible female] face is the surface beneath which interpretative failure creates unplumbable depths'.[35] A sense of this ideology can be seen in Rossetti's early sketches, particularly in his sleeping portraits of Elizabeth Siddal.

33 George Layard, *Tennyson and his Pre-Raphaelite Illustrators* (London: E. Stock, 1894), 58.

34 Walter Pater, *Appreciations, with an Essay on Style* (London: Macmillan, 1889), 238.

35 Psomiades, *Beauty's Body*, 40.

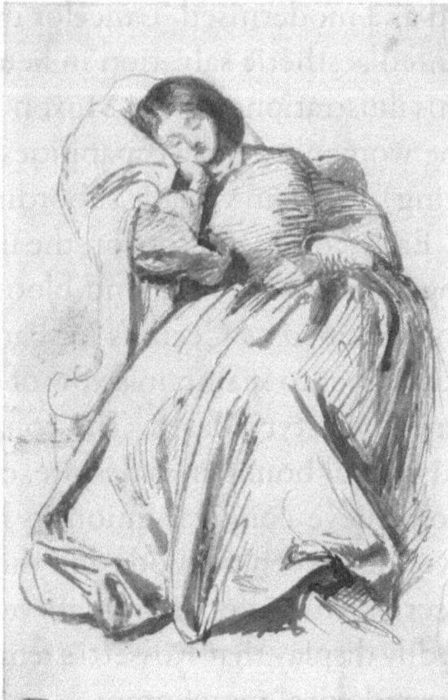

Figure 5.3. Dante Gabriel Rossetti, *Elizabeth Siddal in a chair*, c. 1855, Pen, brown ink & black ink on writing paper, 17.9 × 11.3 cm, Accession no. 1432, The Fitzwilliam Museum, Cambridge. © The Fitzwilliam Museum, Cambridge.

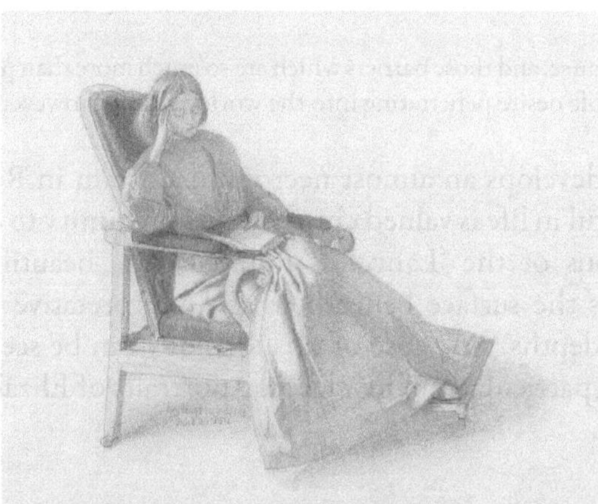

Figure 5.4. Dante Gabriel Rossetti, *Portrait of Elizabeth Siddal, Reading*, 1854, Graphite, pen & Indian ink on paper, 24.2 × 29.0 cm, Accession no. 2155, The Fitzwilliam Museum, Cambridge. © The Fitzwilliam Museum, Cambridge.

Some portraits, in their heavy-lidded haziness, intimate post-coital slumber; others suggest a deathly inertia or a somnambulistic approach to everyday life. In one sketch the act of reading appears to have sent Siddal into an uncomfortable slumber atop a piano. Like Rossetti's *The Lady of Shalott* for the Moxon *Tennyson* (1857), the sleeping woman becomes a cipher; her enigmatic face beckons to be read by a masculine observer. Ford Madox Brown in his diary of 1854 attests to the degree to which Siddal's deathlike demeanour spiritually nourished Rossetti's artistic life:

> Called on Dante Rossetti. Saw Miss Siddal, looking thinner and more deathlike and more beautiful and more ragged than ever [...] Gabriel as usual diffuse and inconsequent in his work. Drawing wonderful and lovely Guggums one after another, each one a fresh charm, each one stamped with immortality.[36]

Many in the Pre-Raphaelite circle framed Elizabeth Siddal as a reclusive figure with a proclivity for introspection. 'Her inner personality', William Michael Rossetti writes, 'did not float upon the surface of her speech or bearing [...] it remained, if not strictly enigmatic, still mainly undivulged'.[37] Charles Rickets similarly described Siddal as 'a ghost in the house of the living':

> I have had her presence in [William] Morris's new Red House described to me as of a delicate wraith, appearing without a word at dinner; rising from among the guests to watch the fire; gliding away silent and unobserved as she had come.[38]

It is through her poetry that Elizabeth Siddal breaks away from this taciturn, disembodied persona, escaping the guise projected onto her – that of 'a pale and lonely figure' who seemed 'to float in an alien air'.[39] In her poem 'Speechless' (written between 1855 and 1857), Siddal transforms the figurative signs of feminine insentience into metaphors of feminine resistance and effectively critiques 'the Lancelot moment' from within its own confines.

36 Quoted in Rossetti, 'Dante Rossetti and Elizabeth Siddal', 292.

37 Rossetti, *Some Reminiscences*, I, 193.

38 Quoted in Marsh, *Legend of Elizabeth Siddal*, 29.

39 Francis Bickley, *The Pre-Raphaelite Comedy* (London: Constable, 1932), 225.

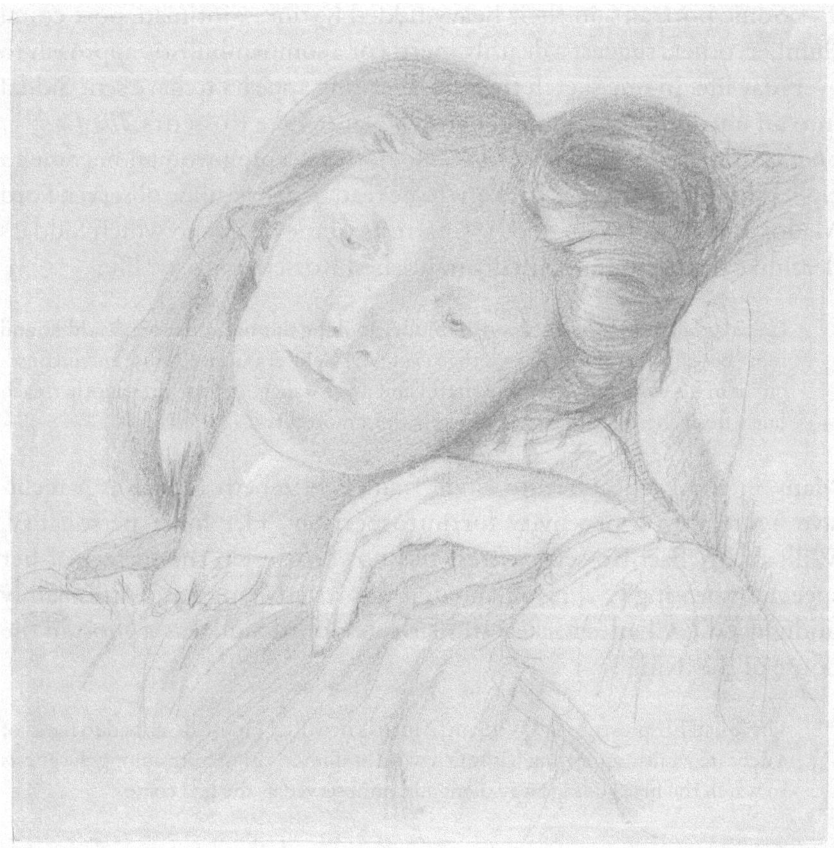

Figure 5.5. Dante Gabriel Rossetti, *Elizabeth Siddal*, 1860, Graphite on paper, 25.8 × 25.2 cm, Accession no. 684, The Fitzwilliam Museum, Cambridge. © The Fitzwilliam Museum, Cambridge.

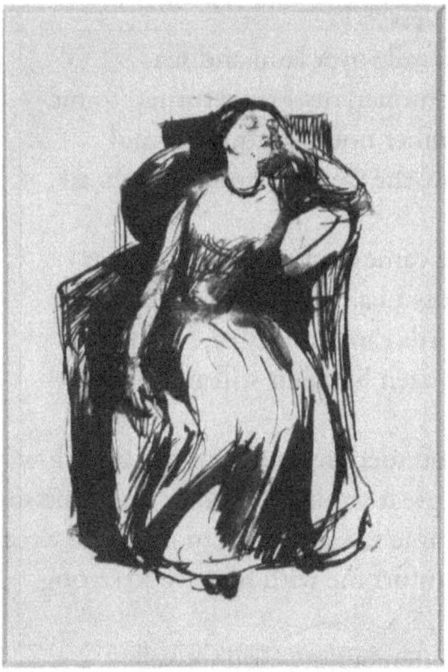

Figure 5.6. Dante Gabriel Rossetti, *Portrait Sketch of Elizabeth Siddal*, c. 1850–60, Pen & brown ink on writing paper, 17.0 × 10.5 cm, Birmingham Museums and Art Gallery. Licensed under Creative Commons by Birmingham Museums Trust.

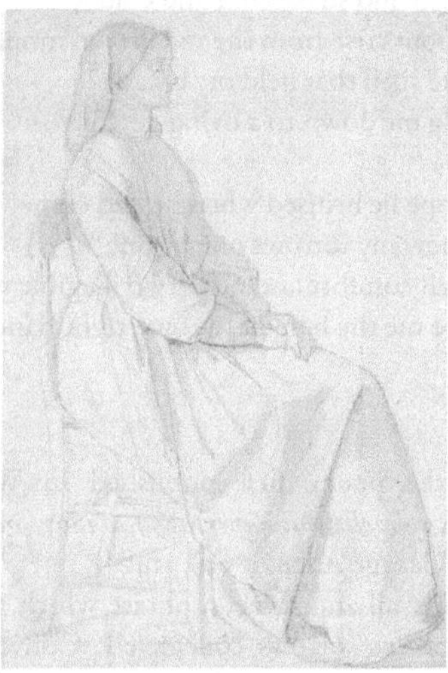

Figure 5.7. Dante Gabriel Rossetti, *Portrait of Elizabeth Siddal*, 1854, Pencil, 17.1 × 11.4 cm, Birmingham Museums and Art Gallery. Licensed under Creative Commons by Birmingham Museums Trust.

'Speechless'[40]
Many a mile over land and sea
Unsummoned my love returned to me
I remember not the words he said
But only the trees moaning over head

And he came ready to take and bear
The cross I had carried for many a year
But words came slowly one by one
from frozen lips shut still and dumb

How sounded my words so still and slow
To the great strong heart that loved me so
Who came to save me from pain and wrong
and comfort me with his love so strong

Ah I remember my God so well
My brain lie dumb in a frozen spell
and I looked away from my lovers face
to watch the dead leaves that were running apace

I felt the wind strike chill and cold
and vapours rise from the red brown mould
I felt the spell that held my breath
Bending me down to a living death

As if hope lie bruised when he had come
who knew my sorrows one by one[41]
and until comfort and pity [two illegible words]
and give me the help of his own right hand[42]

40 William's title for the poem, first published in William Michael Rossetti, *Rossetti: Ruskin: PreRaphaelitism: Papers 1854 to 1862* (New York: Dodd, Mead and Company; London: George Allen, 1899), 154.

41 William's version reads 'all and some', a phrase which suggests the enigmatic 'he' knows all of the speaker's sorrows collectively. Conversely, Siddal's phrase 'one by one' evokes the passage of time and thus intimates that the speaker's lover was not only aware of the speaker's sorrows but was present for or contributed towards them.

42 Siddal, 'Many a mile over land and sea', in Trowbridge, *My Ladys Soul*, 57–8.

The speaker's lover, travelling 'many a mile over land and sea', at first seems to function within the context of the poem as a conventional Rossettian hero. However, Siddal's speaker treats aesthetic love with distrust and suspicion. This is made clear from the antagonistic couplet that opens the poem: 'Many a mile over land and sea / *unsummoned* my love returned to me' [emphasis mine]. Siddal inverts the expected archetype; instead of standing 'mystified before an insentient female body'[43] the male lover is poetically undermined by the wraithlike female narrator: she 'remember[s] not the words he said / But only the trees moaning over head'. As she watches 'the dead leaves that were running apace' – a potent metaphor for the insentient being reanimated by a force outside of their control – the speaker feels the figurative hands of another's will upon her person: 'I felt the spell that held my breath / bending me down to a living death'. This force is at once a psychosomatic, mesmeric and supernatural influence, her 'brain [lying] dumb in a frozen spell', and is implicitly associated with the speaker's lover: the spell taking place as she leans away from him. The speaker's speech patterns – teeth-chattering alliteration and the languorous use of assonance ('words came slowly one by one / From frozen lips shut still and dumb') phonetically mirror her physical state. Her words come 'still and slow' and are uttered at a hypothermic point of figurative death. Thus, from a position usually characterised by beautiful passivity, Siddal's speaker denounces the conventions of aestheticism.

The oppressive atmosphere Siddal describes would have been immediately familiar to those in the Pre-Raphaelite circle. Pater portrays a comparable set of 'conditions' in his appraisal of Rossetti's poetry:

> Here, under this strange complex of conditions, as in some medicated air, exotic flowers of sentiment expand, among people of a remote and unaccustomed beauty, somnambulistic, frail, androgynous, the light almost shining through them. Surely, such loves were too fragile and adventurous to last more than for a moment.[44]

43 Psomiades, *Beauty's Body*, 40.

44 Pater, *Appreciations*, 217.

Pater describes a peculiar vivarium of mystical aestheticism; the 'conditions' do not foster life but seem to suspend the 'frail, androgynous' subjects in a state of somnolent ephemerality: a 'living death'. Robert Buchanan, in his invective against Rossetti, 'The Fleshly School of Poetry' (1871), unwittingly detects the same 'strange' vivaria. He describes the mind of 'Mr. Rossetti as like a glassy mere [housing] weary, wasting, yet exquisite sensuality [...] brooded over by an atmosphere of insufferable closeness'.[45]

Even while paradoxically still alive, Elizabeth Siddal, confined within the gilded Pre-Raphaelite frame of painterly fatality, was already immortalised in death – from Rossetti's divine *Beatrice* (1864–70; Tate, London) to Millais' earthly *Ophelia* (1852; Tate, London), struggling for life amid a proto-Darwinian 'entangled bank'. William Michael Rossetti's monograph of Elizabeth Siddal, notably titled 'Dante Rossetti and Elizabeth Siddal', presents her life primarily as a precursor to her somnolent death: he notes the 'peculiarity' of her 'large lidded' eyes, describes her as 'certainly distant', her 'attitude of reserve, self-controlling and alien from approach', and her conversation as 'scanty; slight and scattered' with 'little to seize hold upon'.[46]

Critics continued to perpetuate this aesthetic narrative of the somnambulatory angel tormented with hysterical melancholy. In 1929, Rodolphe Louis Mégroz intimated that Siddal was little more than a woman

45 Robert Buchanan, 'The Fleshy School of Poetry', *Contemporary Review* 18/3 (1871), 334–50.

46 Rossetti, 'Dante Rossetti and Elizabeth Siddall', 273. Dante Gabriel Rossetti felt a profound sense of guilt about his treatment of Siddall. Shortly after her death, in 1862, his interest in the spirit world took on a new seriousness, when – according to his doctor – he began to receive nightly visitations from his wife at the foot of his bed. The 'spirit' of Elizabeth Siddal appeared in seven of the séances recorded in William's Séance Diary. 'She' was intensively cross-questioned by the Rossetti brothers who were anxious to reassure themselves of her happiness in the afterlife: 'Are you my wife? Yes – Are you now happy? Yes – Happier than on earth? Yes – If I were now to join you, should I be happy? Yes – Should I see you at once? No – Quite soon? – No.' See J. B. Bullen and Rosalind White, *Pre-Raphaelites in the Spirit World: The Séance Diary of William Michael Rossetti* (Oxford: Peter Lang, 2021) and Bullen and White, 'Communication with the Dead: The Séance Diary of W. M. Rossetti', *The Journal of Pre-Raphaelite Studies* 29/2 (2020), 4–11.

'doomed' to 'nervous instability'.[47] Her husband – in stark contrast – is referred to as a man 'who, by the kindest eyes, that are also clear-sighted, can never be seen in too favourable a light'.[48] Even more recent scholarship has projected a fatalistic, romanticised Rossettian frame onto Siddal's life. The editor of *Apollo Magazine*, reviewing the Rossetti exhibition at the Royal Academy in 1973, refers absentmindedly to Siddal as 'a pathetic figure' with a 'rather wishy-washy personality', and suggests, somewhat crudely, that 'it was in keeping with the doomed nature of Lizzie's life that she produced a stillborn child'.[49] Barbara Gates writes in *Victorian Suicide* (1988) that Siddal seemed 'finally to have become obsessed with Ophelia's lot, [and] decided to live – and die – a fiction'.[50] In *Over Her Dead Body* (1992), Elisabeth Bronfen describes Siddal's melancholia as an almost aestheticised force that kept her 'suspended in a position of liminality between life and death'.[51] Bronfen, like the editor of *Apollo Magazine*, goes on to connect such mythologising with Siddal's loss of a child, commenting: 'as if to find an acme to her courtship with death, Siddal gave birth to a stillborn daughter'.[52]

> 'Dead Love'[53]
> Oh never weep for love that is dead
> Since love is seldom true,
> But changes his fashion from blue to red,
> From brightest red to blue,
> And love was born to an early death
> And is so seldom true.
>
> Then harbour no smile on your bonny face[54]
> To win the deepest sigh

47 Mégroz, *Dante Gabriel Rossetti*, 59.
48 Mégroz, *Dante Gabriel Rossetti*, 59.
49 Denys Sutton, 'The Prisoner', *Apollo Magazine* (February 1973), 123.
50 Barbara Gates, *Victorian Suicide* (Princeton, NJ: Princeton University Press, 1988), 149.
51 Elisabeth Bronfen, *Over Her Dead Body* (Manchester: Manchester University Press, 1992), 176.
52 Bronfen, *Over Her Dead Body*, 176.
53 William's title for the poem, first published in *Rossetti: Ruskin: PreRaphaelitism*, 151–2.
54 A subsequent fair copy (held in the Ashmolean Museum) reads 'bonny mouth'. Trowbridge, *My Ladys Soul*, 77.

The fairest words on truest lips
Pass on and surely die,
And you will stand alone my dear,
When wintry winds draw nigh[55]

In anticipation of her aesthetic afterlife, Elizabeth Siddal (the poet) seems determined to liberate the insentient body of Elizabeth Siddal (the muse) from under the trappings of mystical aestheticism. In her poem 'Dead Love', it is not woman who exists in a deathlike stupor but love itself: love is paradoxically 'born to an early death'. Siddal refuses to aesthetically reconcile the sensual and the spiritual; Love, pointedly personified as male, 'changes his fashion from blue to red, / from brightest red to blue'. Aesthetic worship, diminished as the whims of 'fashion', is presented as inherently insincere. As Dinah Roe notes, the 'colour blue is associated with chastity and loyalty whilst red commonly symbolizes passion'.[56] To Siddal, aestheticism rationalises inconstancy. It encourages its devotees to abruptly shift from chaste devotion to intense passion – without a thought for the distress such a sudden change may cause.

Siddal goes on to emasculate the speaker's lover; he is congratulated on his 'bonny face' and referred to repeatedly with diminutive pet names usually reserved for women, such as 'sweet' and 'my dear'. The saccharine sweetness of these epithets creates a purposeful tension with the sharp tone of the poem. This acerbic atmosphere was picked up on by Christina Rossetti, who purportedly found 'Dead Love' 'piquant' and appreciated its 'cool bitter sarcasm'.[57] This sharpness is most palpable in the last stanza:

55 Siddal, 'Oh never weep for love that is dead', lines 1–12 in Trowbridge, *My Ladys Soul*, 76.

56 Dinah Roe, ed., *The Pre-Raphaelites: From Rossetti to Ruskin* (London: Penguin, 2010), 348.

57 Christina Rossetti, quoted in William Michael Rossetti, *Rossetti Papers, 1862 to 1870*, 76–77. See also Christina Rossetti's poem 'After Death', which similarly overthrows the tenets of the 'Lancelot moment'. The insentient female assumes the aesthetic vantage point, while the male mourner is left in the dark: 'he leaned above me, thinking that I slept /and could not hear him'. Her response 'very sweet it is / To know he still is warm though I am cold', carries the same sugary sourness as Siddal's 'Dead Love'. As Trowbridge notes, Christina would have provided Siddal

Sweet, never weep for what cannot be
For this God has not given,
If the merest dream of love were true
Then, sweet, we should be in Heaven
And this is only earth my dear
Where true love is not given

In the last two lines of the poem the speaker's tone shifts; the cynical air that pervaded the poem is supplanted by a peculiar sense of pragmatic sorrow. Such a change poetically denigrates the hyperbolic sentiments of aestheticism. Parallel to this, the word 'heaven' sits in uneasy half-rhyme between two uses of the word 'given', as though purposefully ending the poem with an inelegant sense of tension to reflect the disappointing nature of love: which, far from transcendent, is presented as distinctly earthbound.

'The Lust of the Eyes'[58]
I care not for my Ladys[59] soul[60]
Though I worship before her smile
I care not wheres my Ladys goal
When her beauty shall [lose its wile]

Low sit I down at my Ladys feet
Gazing through her wild eyes,
Smiling to think how my love will fleet
When their starlike beauty dies.

'with her only close female poetic role model' and it is likely that their 'relationship may have been strongly inflected with poetry' (*My Ladys Soul*, 15).

58 William chose the title 'The Lust of the Eyes' for this poem, taken from 1 John 2:16: 'For all that is in the world, the lust of the flesh, and the lust of the eyes, and the pride of life, is not of the Father, but is of the world.' Trowbridge's version of the text, however, is cited here with notes where William's differs.

59 Throughout this poem, Siddal omits the possessive apostrophe for 'ladys'. This may be a conscious omission to underscore the male speaker's perceived ownership of his 'lady'. The lady in question is figuratively (and thus grammatically) detached from her soul, eyes and body.

60 William's adjustment ('I care not *where be* my lady's soul') somewhat softens the male speaker's apathy.

I care not if my Lady pray
To our Father which art[61] in Heaven:
Though for joy in my heart wild pulses play[62]
For to me her love is given.

Then who shall close my Lady's eyes
And who shall fold her hands?
Will any hearken if she cries
Up to the unknown lands?[63]

In this poem (written between 1855 and 1857), the tension between the male speaker's love of beauty and the female subject's love of God is palpably felt (though the speaker himself is impervious to the tension 'gazing *through* her wild eyes'). The union between sensuality and spirituality, so prevalent in Rossetti's work, is severed both thematically and structurally within the poem. Lines that reference the tenets of religion and those that allude to the subject's beauty sit atop one another in poetic friction. While the speaker seeks to aestheticise religion and sanctify love of beauty (he 'worship[s] before her smile'), Siddal's sympathy lies with the subject of the poem, who by becoming an object of aesthetic worship has been stripped of her salvation.

This tension lies not just with the male speaker but also with Rossetti; Siddal makes oblique references to Rossetti's ideology throughout the poem. In 'Nuptial Sleep' (1858), Rossetti compares water droplets, dripping after a storm, to the decelerating pulses of the two lovers' heartbeats after sex; parallel to this, Siddal's speaker dismisses the efficacy of his lady's prayer with the 'joy' of 'heart's quick pulses play' that ensure 'to [him] her love is given'. Likewise, Siddal's line that he 'smil[es] to think how [his] love will fleet / when [her] starlike beauty dies', alludes to Rossetti's 'Blessed Damozel' (first published 1850), whose hair is adorned with seven stars. Walter Pater detects in Rossetti's work a tension between Provençal poetry and Christianity. This friction, personified by Pater as between 'Christ and

61 William alters 'art' (taken directly from the Lord's Prayer) to 'is'.
62 William's version reads: 'but for joy my heart's quick pulses play'.
63 Siddal, 'I care not for my Ladys soul', in Trowbridge, *My Ladys Soul*, 36.

a rival lover',[64] is thus both deconstructed and destabilised in 'The Lust of the Eyes'. For though the female presence remains insentient and does not utter a word, the poem subversively provides a feminine perspective – through the mouth of the male speaker.

'Worn Out'[65]
Thy strong arms are around me love
My hand is on thy breast
Low words of comfort come from thee
Yet my soul is not at rest[66]

For I am but a scared thing
Nor can I ever be
Aught but a bird's whose broken wings
Must fly away from thee

I cannot give to thee the love
I gave so long ago
The love that turned and struck me down
Among the blinding snow

I can but give a tired heart
And weary eyes of pain
A faded mouth that cannot smile
And may not laugh again.

Yet keep thy arms around me love
Until I fall to sleep
Then leave me saying no good bye
Least I might fall and weep[67]

Siddal's poem 'Worn Out' opens with two simple assertions that dramatically undercut the concept of the 'Lancelot moment'. The disparity between the

64 Pater, *Appreciations,* 217.
65 William's choice of title, first published in *Rossetti: Ruskin: PreRaphaelitism*, 156.
66 William's version replaces this line with – the more definitive – 'My soul is not at rest'.
67 Siddal, 'Thy strong arms around me love', in Trowbridge, *My Ladys Soul*, 86–7.

erotic, signified by the lover's 'strong arms' enclosing the female speaker, and the spiritual – 'yet my soul has no rest' – is clearly established. Love becomes a physical force that violently tarnishes the speaker's spiritual purity: a 'love that turned and struck me down / Among the blinding snow'. The Pre-Raphaelite desire for beauty 'quickened by the sense of death' is tragically realised rather than aesthetically glorified: the speaker has 'weary eyes of pain' and 'a faded mouth that cannot smile / And may not laugh again'.[68] As William Michael Rossetti noted (in his preface to the 1901 facsimile of *The Germ*), his brother moved 'towards a more fleshy aesthetic in his later years'.[69] Rossetti revised some of his earlier work, removing religious motifs in an effort to secularise his poetry and disavowing the idea that the Brotherhood 'had anything whatever to do with particular movements in the religious world'.[70] In this context, we can read Siddal's poetic resistance as an attempt to re-establish the 'intimate intertexture' between 'spiritual sense' and 'material form' that guided the Brotherhood in their early years.[71]

Siddal's poems, despite their fragmentary existence, emerge as deeply personal, perceptive critiques of Pre-Raphaelite convention. Unable to remove the motif of the insentient woman from under the gaze of the male poet, Siddal instead strove to 'allegorize on his hook' and occupy his poetic territory.[72] Similarly, Rossetti took up the case of 'Jenny' with supposed unique authority 'not from the distant stand-point of a parliamentary or scientific debate – not from the half-instructed vantage-ground, or rather disadvantage-ground, of a women's-rights council – but from the near position which only one who has seen the inside of Jenny's own room'.[73] Siddal approaches the motif of the 'Lancelot moment' from the position

68 Siddal's poem 'A Year and a Day' speaks of a similar weariness. The poem again reflects upon the concept of a 'living death': ending with the speaker's empty husk left 'there to lie empty of all love Like beaten corn of grain'. A reference, perhaps, to Rossetti's 'Blessed Damozel', whose hair was 'yellow like ripe corn'.

69 *The Germ* (London: E. Stock 1901), 18.

70 Elizabeth Ludlow, *Christina Rossetti and the Bible* (London: Bloomsbury Academic, 2016), 68.

71 See William Michael Rossetti, *The Germ* (London: E. Stock 1901), 18.

72 *Letters*, II, 97.

73 Forman, *Our Living Poets an Essay in Art Criticism*, 208.

of one who has occupied the same aesthetic space. Both 'Jenny's Case' and her 'vengeance' are enacted by their female narrators who appropriate 'the potter's power over the clay'[74] by remoulding and re-contextualising figures of female insentience and subversively leaving their male subjects in the resounding void of 'deep silence', 'remember[ing] not the words [they] said / But only the trees moaning over head'.[75]

Like Rossetti's Lady of Shalott, many of Siddal's speakers find themselves forcibly presented as 'a beautiful object for the contemplation of the multitude'.[76] Upon her death, Siddal's own body was subjected to a comparable moment of sensationalised display.[77] A little-known narrative poem by William Michael Rossetti, 'The Coroner's Inquest', exhumes the details of her death:

> A perfect arch, the forehead undisturbed;
> But the mouth kept its anguish, and the lips,
> Closed after death, seemed half in act to speak. [78]

As Paul Fyfe explains, this poem documented 'the coroner's inquest, which put [Siddal's] body on view; and the newspaper report that circulated the story'.[79] When the poem was later published in the *Broadway Annual* (1868) it was accompanied by an illustration of two men (presumably the jurors) gazing at her corpse in a bedroom.

For too long, critics have operated under the assumption that Siddal would have embraced this kind of literary afterlife, that she would have accepted – or even welcomed – a poem that immortalised her as a figure

74 Dante Rossetti, 'Jenny', in Roe, *The Pre-Raphaelites: From Rossetti to Ruskin*, 181.

75 Siddal, 'Many a mile over land and sea' in Trowbridge, *My Ladys Soul*, 57–8.

76 Psomiades, *Beauty's Body*, 26.

77 William's letters confirm Siddal's corpse was laid out on display for an extended period of time.

78 William Michael Rossetti, 'The Coroner's Inquest', in *The Broadway Annual* (London, George Routledge & Sons, 1867–8), 452, lines 233–46. <http://www.rossettiarchive.org/docs/ap4.b9.1.rad.html#p449>, accessed 5 August 2021.

79 Paul Fyfe, 'Accidental Death: Lizzie Siddal and the Poetics of the Coroner's Inquest,' *Victorian Review* 40/2 (2014), 19. See also 'Death of a Lady from an Overdose of Laudanum', *Daily News* (14 February 1862), 6.

of tragic passivity: her lips 'half in act to speak'. Through her poetry, however, we can begin to understand Siddal as a more complex figure; one who, despite her melancholy, would not have wanted to be remembered as a lifeless *tabula rasa*. Instead, we can come to know her as a subversive poet: who defiantly sought to transmute such an instant of passivity into a transgressive moment that could restore the insentient female with the poetic power of her own voice.

Bibliography

'*Beyond Ophelia* – A Celebration of Lizzie Siddal, Artist and Poet', Wightwick Manor, National Trust (2018) <https://www.nationaltrust.org.uk/wightwick-manor-and-gardens/features/a-celebration-of-lizzie-siddal-artist-and-poet>, accessed 1 November 2019.

Bickley, Francis, *The Pre-Raphaelite Comedy* (London: Constable, 1932).

Blain, Virginia, *Victorian Women Poets: An Annotated Anthology* (London: Routledge 2014).

Bradley, Laurel, 'Elizabeth Siddal: Drawn into the Pre-Raphaelite Circle', *Art Institute of Chicago Museum Studies* 18/2 (1992), 136–45.

Bristow, Joseph, ed., *The Victorian Poet: Poetics and Persona* (Oxford: Routledge, 2014).

Bronfen, Elisabeth, *Over Her Dead Body: Death, Femininity and the Aesthetic* (Manchester: Manchester University Press, 1992).

Brown, Susan, 'The Victorian Poetess', in Joseph Bristow, ed., *The Cambridge Companion to Victorian Poetry* (Cambridge: Cambridge University Press, 2000), 180–202.

Buchanan, Robert, 'The Fleshy School of Poetry', *Contemporary Review* 18/3 (1871), 334–50.

Bullen, J. B., and White, Rosalind, 'Communication with the Dead: The Séance Diary of W. M. Rossetti', *The Journal of Pre-Raphaelite Studies* 29/2 (2020), 4–11.

——, *Pre-Raphaelites in the Spirit World: The Séance Diary of William Michael Rossetti* (Oxford: Peter Lang, 2021).

'Death of a Lady from an Overdose of Laudanum', *Daily News* (14 February 1862), 6.

Doughty, Oswald, *A Victorian Romantic: Dante Gabriel Rossetti* (London: Fredrick Muller, 1949).

——, and John Robert Wahl, eds, *Letters of Dante Gabriel Rossetti,* vol. II (Oxford: Clarendon Press, 1965).

Dunstan, Angela, 'Stunner: Elizabeth Siddal, the Evolution of a Sensation', in Anthony Uhlmann, Helen Groth, and Paul Sheehan, ed., *Literature and Sensation* (Newcastle: Cambridge Scholars Publishing, 2009), 24–33.

Ehnenn, J. R, ' "Strong, Traivelling": Re-visions of Women's Subjectivity and Female Labour in the Ballad-work of Elizabeth Siddal', *Victorian Poetry* 52/2 (2014), 251–76.

Forman, H. Buxon, *Our Living Poets an Essay in Art Criticism* (London: Tinsley Brothers, 1871).

Fredeman, William, Evan, ed., *The Correspondence of Dante Gabriel Rossetti*, vol. VI (Suffolk: Boydell & Brewer, 2002).

Fyfe, Paul, 'Accidental Death: Lizzie Siddal and the Poetics of the Coroner's Inquest', *Victorian Review* 40/2 (2014), 17–22.

Garnett, Henrietta, *Wives and Stunners: The Pre-Raphaelites and Their Muses* (London: Macmillan, 2012).

Gates, Barbara, T, *Victorian Suicide: Mad Crimes and Sad Histories* (Princeton, NJ: Princeton University Press, 1988).

Gilbert, Sandra, and Gubar, Susan, *The Madwoman in the Attic: The Woman Writer and the Nineteenth-Century Literary Imagination* (London: Yale University Press, 2000).

Halsall, Alison, 'H.D. and the Victorian Spectres of White Rose and the Red', *College Literature* 38/4 (2011), 115–33.

Hassett, Constance, 'Elizabeth Siddal's Poetry: A Problem and Some Suggestions', *Victorian Poetry* 35/4 (1997), 443–70.

Hill, George, Birkbeck, ed., *Letters of Dante Gabriel Rossetti to William Allingham, 1854–1870* (London: Fisher Unwin, 1897).

Hughes, Linda, 'Poetry', in Linda H. Peterson. ed., *The Cambridge Companion to Victorian Women's Writing* (Cambridge: Cambridge University Press, 2015), 89–105.

Kooistra, Janzen Lorriane, *Poetry, Pictures, and Popular Publishing: The Illustrated Gift Book and Victorian Visual Culture, 1855–1875* (Athens, OH: Ohio University Press, 2014).

Kruger, Sullivan Kathryn, *Weaving the Word: The Metaphorics of Weaving and Female Textual Production* (Selinsgrove, PA: Susquehanna University Press, 2001).

Law, Alice, 'The Poetry of Christina Rossetti', *Westminster Review* 143/4 (1895), 444–53.

Layard, George, *Tennyson and His Pre-Raphaelite Illustrators* (London: E. Stock, 1894).

Leighton, Angela, *Victorian Women Poets: Writing Against the Heart* (Charlottesville: University of Virginia Press, 1992).
Ludlow, Elizabeth, *Christina Rossetti and the Bible: Waiting with the Saints* (London: Bloomsbury Academic, 2016).
Marillier, H. C., ed., *Dante Gabriel Rossetti, an Illustrated Memorial of His Art and Life* (London: George Bell and Sons, 1899).
Marsh, Jan, *The Pre-Raphaelite Sisterhood* (London: Quartet, 1985).
——, *The Legend of Elizabeth Siddal* (London: Quartet, 1989).
Marshik, Celia, *British Modernism and Censorship* (Cambridge: Cambridge University Press, 2006).
Matthews, Samantha, *Poetical Remains: Poets' Graves, Bodies, and Books in the Nineteenth Century* (Oxford: Oxford University Press, 2004).
Mégroz, Rodolphe, Louis, *Dante Gabriel Rossetti: Painter Poet of Heaven in Earth* (London: Faber & Gwyer, 1929).
Mermin, Dorothy, '"The Fruitful Feud of Hers and His": Sameness, Difference, and Gender in Victorian Poetry', *Victorian Poetry* 33/1 (1995), 149–68.
——, 'The Damsel, the Knight, and the Victorian Woman Poet', *Critical Inquiry* 13/1 (1986), 64–80.
Morris, William, 'Poems by Dante Gabriel Rossetti', *Academy* 8/5 (1870), 199–200.
Orlando, Emily, '"That I May not Faint, or Die, or Swoon": Reviving Pre-Raphaelite Women', *Womens' Studies* 38/6 (2009), 611–46.
Parker, A, 'Expansion and Scholarship in Spain', in Denys Hay, ed., *The Age of the Renaissance* (London: Thames & Hudson, 1967), 221–48.
Pater, Walter, *Appreciations, with an Essay on Style* (London: Macmillan, 1889).
Paxon, Amanda, 'Love, Dismemberment, and Elizabeth Siddal's Corpus', *Journal of Pre-Raphaelite Studies* 22/2 (2013), 4–23.
'Poetry in Petticoats', *Scots Observer* (8 March 1890).
Pollock, Griselda, and Cherry, Deborah, 'Woman as Sign in Pre-Raphaelite Literature: The Representation of Elizabeth Siddall', in Deborah Cherry *Vision and Difference Femininity, Feminism, and the Histories of Art* (London: Routledge, 1988), 128–63.
Psomiades, Kathy, *Beauty's Body: Femininity and Representation in British Aestheticism* (Stanford, CA: Stanford University Press, 1997).
Roe, Dinah, ed., *The Pre-Raphaelites from Rossetti to Ruskin* (London: Penguin Classics, 2010).
Rossetti, Christina, 'After Death' (1862), and 'In An Artist's Studio' (1856), in Simon Humphries, ed., *Christina Rossetti Poems and Prose* (Oxford: Oxford University Press 2008).
Rossetti, Dante Gabriel, 'Body's Beauty' (1881), 'Jenny' (1870), 'A sonnet is a moments monument … ' (1880), 'Nuptial Sleep' (1870), and 'The Blessed

Damozel' (1850), in Jerome McGann, ed., *Dante Gabriel Rossetti Collected Poetry and Prose* (London: Yale University Press, 2003).

Rossetti, William Michael, *The Germ* [Facsimile Reprint] (London: E. Stock 1901).

——, 'Dante Rossetti and Elizabeth Siddal', *The Burlington Magazine for Connoisseurs* 1/3 (1903), 273–95.

——, *Some Reminiscences of William Michael Rossetti* (London: C. Scribner's Sons, 1906).

Sutton, Denys, 'The Prisoner', *Apollo Magazine* (February 1973), 123–7.

Taylor, Beverly, 'Beatrix / Creatrix: Elizabeth Siddal as Muse and Creator', *The Journal of Pre-Raphaelite Studies* 4/1 (1995), 29–50.

Tennyson, Alfred, *Poems by Alfred Tennyson* (London: Edward Moxon, 1857).

Trowbridge, Serena, ed., *My Ladys Soul: The Poetry of Elizabeth Siddall* (Brighton: Victorian Secrets, 2018).

NAT REEVE

6 Queer Tombs and Reframing Doom: Elizabeth Siddal and Georgiana Burne-Jones's Unfinished Collaborative Project

ABSTRACT

Though Elizabeth Siddal and Georgiana Burne-Jones never finished writing and illustrating 'a book of Fairy Tales' together, both made contributions to the project. Its incompleteness opens these contributions to creative readings which foreground the queerness of their relationship with the format in which they do not entirely partake. My chapter explores these multi-disciplinary remnants, focusing on Burne-Jones's drawing *Death and the Lady* (1861) and Siddal's poem 'True Love' (c. 1860–2). Working with queer theory and close reading, I examine the works' responses to the pictorial and literary traditions informing them. The works explore doomed medievalist 'Ladies', overhauling medieval precedents and disrupting ballad narratives to consider how their 'Ladies' might thrive between disaster and consequence. Siddal and Burne-Jones's engagement with impending doom speaks to nineteenth-century (and contemporary) concerns: the works reflect on how to respond to disaster, and whether there are less frightening, more productive ways of framing uncertainty, disruption and incompleteness.

* * * * *

In July 1860, Georgiana Burne-Jones met Elizabeth Siddal. Burne-Jones had encountered Siddal's artworks three years before, at the Pre-Raphaelite exhibition in Russell Place. But in 1860, Siddal showed her work to Burne-Jones in person, specifically 'a design she had just made, called "The Woeful Victory"'.[1] The two planned to write and illustrate 'a book of Fairy Tales' together; though the book was never finished, both 'made' contributions for it, before Siddal's death in 1862 curtailed the idea.[2]

1 Georgiana Burne-Jones, *Memorials of Edward Burne-Jones*, 2 vols (London: Macmillan and Co., 1904), I, 208.

2 Burne-Jones, *Memorials* I, 218.

In this chapter, I focus on two Siddal and Burne-Jones works from the relevant period – which have been identified, by others and by me, as potential contributions to this unfinished project – and, working with queer theory, reveal the queerness of their responses to the literary and pictorial traditions informing them. Siddal and Burne-Jones are an underexplored pairing, but the overlapping groups of the Pre-Raphaelite circle can be fruitfully explored by embracing such neglected groupings, without feeling obliged to centre a Pre-Raphaelite Brother or fit an equivalent male parallel. The incompleteness of – and uncertainty around – their 'book of Fairy Tales' should not prohibit creative study of their works together. Instead, this project's unfinished, ambiguous state creates new opportunities, opening the works to imaginative close readings which foreground the queerness of their relationship with the projected format in which they do not entirely partake. Thinking with the work of queer theorist Jack Halberstam, an awareness of the project's 'failure' (incompletion) 'offer[s] more creative, more cooperative, more surprising ways' of engaging with and close reading the art and poetry.[3] Siddal and Burne-Jones's works revolve around similar ideas, unpicking an incomplete, ill-fated state for its potential and possibilities.

Both works were produced during the years when the 'book of Fairy Tales' was being planned (1860–2). They are some of the only works by Siddal and Burne-Jones which have survived from this period. For Siddal's contribution, I will explore her poem 'True Love' – as Burne-Jones recalls, the book's content was to be 'written' as well as visual.[4] Though none of Siddal's poems are dated, the manuscript of 'True Love' is signed 'EER' (Elizabeth Eleanor Rossetti), suggesting a composition date – or timely redraft – after Siddal's marriage in 1860 and before her death in 1862.[5] 'True Love' is the only poem titled by Siddal and the only one to have a fair copy in her handwriting, indicating preparation for scrutiny by someone other

3 Jack Halberstam, *The Queer Art of Failure* (London: Duke University Press, 2011), 2.

4 Burne-Jones, *Memorials* I, 218.

5 Serena Trowbridge, *My Ladys Soul: The Poems of Elizabeth Eleanor Siddall* (Brighton: Victorian Secrets, 2018), 93.

than herself.[6] The poem's narrator is a bereaved lover at her beloved's tomb, confronting her threatened future in the wake of his death.

> Farewell Earl Richard,
> Tender and brave:
> Kneeling I kiss
> The dust from your grave.
>
> Pray for me Richard,
> Lying alone
> With hands pleading earnestly,
> All in white stone
>
> Soon must I leave thee,
> This sweet summer tide,
> That other is waiting,
> To claim his pale Bride.
>
> Soon I'll return to thee,
> Hopeful and brave,
> When the dead leaves,
> Blow over thy grave,
>
> Then shall they find me
> Close at thy head
> Watching or waking,
> Sleeping or dead.[7]

Burne-Jones, meanwhile, produced visual content. Two of her drawings were connected to the project by Jan Marsh, in the 2019–20 *Pre-Raphaelite Sisters* exhibition which she curated at the National Portrait Gallery. These drawings, done in pen, pencil and ink, are pasted into a

6 William Michael Rossetti, when altering Siddal's poems for posthumous publication, invented titles for them – 'True Love' is the only poem with a title in Siddal's manuscripts. Serena Trowbridge's vital edition of Siddal's poetry removes others' interventions and concentrates on Siddal's content. Other fair copies of Siddal's poems are in the handwriting of William Michael or Dante Gabriel Rossetti.

7 Trowbridge, *My Ladys Soul*, 92. I am grateful to Serena Trowbridge and Victorian Secrets for permission to reproduce the poem in full.

scrapbook and labelled *Death and the Lady*. They are, as Marsh observes, draft illustrations 'intended for woodblock reproduction', with their small size and intricate arrangement of shading lines.[8] I will examine the smaller drawing (Figure 6.1), in which a woman gazes into a mirror, behind which lurks a shadowy skeleton.

These two works share a strong thematic connection – stronger than the contents of an earlier Pre-Raphaelite book project, the 1857 edition of Tennyson's poems, of which Edward Burne-Jones lamented that 'there were so many hands engaged on the pictures as to make it impossible as a book'.[9] Siddal and Burne-Jones are concerned with the predicament of a 'Lady' facing doom – in the skeleton that haunts her room, or the grim fate threatening her at a tomb. Both works preserve a moment of incompleteness, in which the doom has been determined (the skeleton has manifested, Richard is dead), but the consequences have not been fully felt (the lady is alive and the aftermath of Richard's death is yet to unfold). These works move beyond simply dooming their central figures, considering instead how the heroines might position themselves in this space between disaster and consequence. They rethink and reinhabit the doomed position, delving into strategies for enrichment, defiance and survival after the destruction has started.

These works draw on medieval art and ballads alongside modern literary and artistic material, and stand in uneasy relation to the idea of a 'book of Fairy Tales'. Publishing a 'book of Fairy Tales' was a familiar Victorian undertaking: the nineteenth century saw the publication of collections by the Brothers Grimm and Hans Christian Andersen, and the *Thousand and One Nights*. The practice was also common in Siddal and Burne-Jones's social circles. Mary Howitt – mother of Siddal's friend, the artist Anna Mary Howitt – translated Andersen's *Wonderful Stories for Children* in 1846. John Ruskin, Siddal's former patron and friend of the Burne-Joneses, wrote *The King of the Golden River*, published with extensive illustrations in 1860. Edward Burne-Jones provided illustrations for another collection, *The Fairy Family*, in 1857 (in which the written content was, like 'True

8 On the exhibition label in *Pre-Raphaelite Sisters*.

9 Burne-Jones, *Memorials* I, 157.

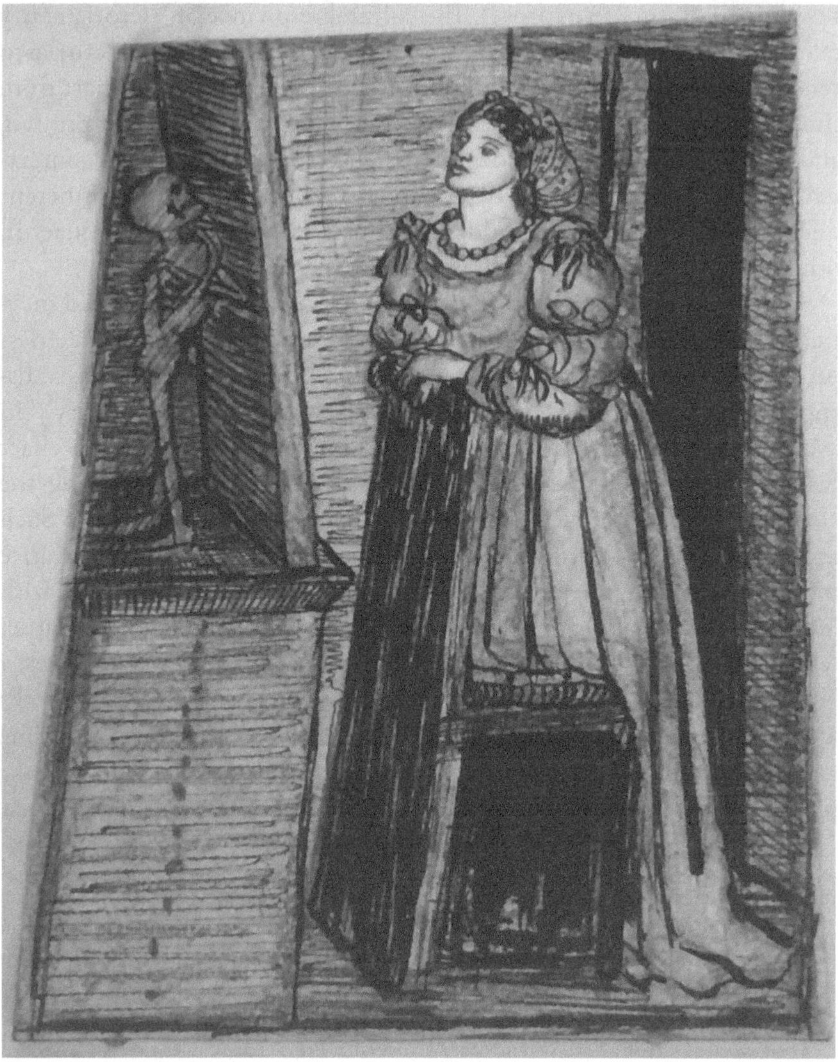

Figure 6.1. Georgiana Burne-Jones, *Death and the Lady*, c. 1861. Reproduced with kind permission from the owner. Photograph by Nat Reeve.

Love', poetry rather than prose). The cultural resonance of Victorian fairy tales has been examined through various critical lenses.[10] But it is crucial to remember that Siddal and Burne-Jones's works are something apart from this tradition. This is not a 'book of Fairy Tales', published and printed, and the artwork and poem under discussion here require a queerer contextualisation. Though there has been important work done on the inherent queerness of the fairy tale, Siddal and Burne-Jones's works are queer in other ways not exclusively connected to the genre.[11]

Their queerness rests on their attempts to let characters avoid inevitably deadly narratives. Lee Edelman builds his conception of queerness on such avoidance, seeing 'the queer' (which I understand here as a disruptive concept) as 'figur[ing] the bar to every realization of futurity'.[12] In avoiding a 'realization of futurity', Siddal and Burne-Jones's works enact Kathryn Bond Stockton's idea of queer 'sideways growth', exploring 'the elegant, unruly contours of growing that don't bespeak continuance'.[13] Such a growth necessarily disrupts the 'continuance' and temporality of narrative movement. Burne-Jones's drawing, as a visual artwork, fills its space with 'sideways growth' and shuns the implicit temporality of its subject matter, whilst Siddal's poem thwarts narrative cues in ways which co-opt and resist both verbal and visual strategies. These works create what Kate Haffey calls 'queer temporalities that stand in clear opposition to [...] normative time frames', 'jam[ming] the mechanisms' of the 'narratives' that (fail to) take place within them.[14] This approach is especially bizarre considering their

10 See Nina Auerbach and U. C. Knoepflmacher, eds, *Forbidden Journeys: Fairy Tales and Fantasies by Victorian Women Writers* (London: University of Chicago Press, 1992), the work of Laurence Talairach-Vielmas, and Caroline Sumpter, *The Victorian Press and the Fairy Tale* (London: Palgrave Macmillan, 2008).

11 See Kay Turner and Pauline Greenhill, eds, *Transgressive Tales: Queering the Grimms* (Detroit, MI: Wayne State University Press, 2012), and Lewis C. Seifert, 'Queer(ing) Fairy Tales', *Marvels & Tales* 29/1 (2015), 15–20.

12 Lee Edelman, *No Future: Queer Theory and the Death Drive* (London: Duke University Press, 2004), 4.

13 Kathryn Bond Stockton, *The Queer Child, or Growing Sideways in the Twentieth Century* (London: Duke University Press, 2009), 13.

14 Kate Haffey, *Literary Modernism, Queer Temporality: Eddies in Time* (London: Palgrave, 2019), 1, 3.

potential future in a 'book of Fairy Tales'. Whilst the fairy tale's 'mode of narrative' can be, as Michael Newton describes, 'fragmented' and 'apparently irrational', these works do not fragment so much as refuse a narrative arc and 'normative time frame' of action and consequence, exploring instead the alternatives which arise between the two.[15]

To create space for such alternatives, Siddal and Burne-Jones's works must confront the hostile precedents which threaten their ladies. I will begin by examining how they do so.

'An Instrument of Self-knowledge'

Skeletons, corpses and living bodies have a long history of sharing the space of the page, the painting or the sepulchre. Burne-Jones's *Death and the Lady* (Figure 6.1) situates itself within a pictorial tradition which began in the late medieval period. The late fourteenth and early fifteenth centuries saw increasing artistic dissemination of the Three Living and Three Dead legend, the introduction of the *transi* tomb (about which more later) and the appearance of the *Danse Macabre*.[16] The Three Living and Three Dead legend, which is depicted on the Camposanto frescoes that inspired the first Pre-Raphaelite Brotherhood, shows three people encountering a triumvirate of corpses, who warn their living counterparts not to forget the transience of life. Like this legend, the *Danse Macabre* took many forms, providing the subject for wall paintings, miniatures and poems. In the *Danse Macabre*, frolicking corpses tug 'human victims' into a dance, warning them that social rank is no protection from death.[17]

15 Michael Newton, ed., *Victorian Fairy Tales* (Oxford: Oxford University Press, 2018), xviii.

16 See Ashby Kinch, *Imago Mortis: Mediating Images of Death in Late Medieval Culture* (Boston, MA: Brill, 2013), 3.

17 Nancy Mandeville Caciola, *Afterlives: The Return of the Dead in the Middle Ages* (London: Cornell University Press, 2016), 227.

Viewers are urged to heed the gambolling cadavers and prepare for a 'good death' with a clean conscience and virtuous lifestyle.

Early pairings of corpses and women preserved this didacticism. In the fifteenth-century poem *Danse Macabre des Femmes*, Death and the dead offer cadaverous insight to female 'victims' in the text, whilst cutting short their occupations in the miniatures.[18] The attack shifts from the women's activities to their vanity in Hans Baldung Grien's painting *Three Ages of the Woman and Death* (1510; Kunsthistorisches Museum, Vienna), in which a naked woman gazes into a mirror, oblivious to the skeleton behind her. The erotic undertones intensify in subsequent depictions of Death and women.[19] 'Death the lover', as Karl Guthke demonstrates, dominated the eighteenth and nineteenth centuries, following the publication of Gottfried August Bürger's ballad 'Lenore', where the eponymous heroine is carried off as the bride of Death.[20] Jan Marsh posits that Burne-Jones's drawings were inspired by 'Death the lover', as depicted in Matthias Claudius's poem 'Der Tod und das Mädchen' ['Death and the Maiden'], in which Death coaxes a woman into his embrace.[21] Yet *Death and the Lady* (Figure 6.1) does not suggest an erotic encounter between woman and skeleton. Instead, Burne-Jones's drawing aligns with earlier pictorial pairings of the dead and the living, where a sense of inevitable doom takes the place of a sexual frisson, the skeleton does not always have to be 'Death' the allegorical figure and the focus is on the self-reflection of the living. Burne-Jones's drawing queers the possibilities offered by these medieval precedents, creating a different perspective on the doomed state and what might be gleaned from it.

Hans Baldung Grien's *Three Ages of the Woman and Death*, like Burne-Jones's drawing, features the cadaver and the woman arranged around a

18 See Ann Tukey Harrison, ed., with a chapter by Sandra L. Hindman, *The Danse Macabre of Women: ms. fr. 995 of the Bibliothèque Nationale* (London: The Kent State University Press, 1994).

19 See Elisabeth Bronfen, *Over Her Dead Body: Death, Femininity and the Aesthetic* (New York: Routledge, 1992).

20 Karl S. Guthke, *The Gender of Death: A Cultural History in Art and Literature* (Cambridge: Cambridge University Press, 1999), 12.

21 On the exhibition label in *Pre-Raphaelite Sisters*.

mirror.[22] The 'three ages of the woman' – child, youth and elderly – cluster as a corpse thrusts an hourglass over the young woman's head. Stefanie Knöll reads this woman, admiring her hair in the mirror, as 'captivated by vanity and self-love', demonstrating 'sin and complete folly' by remaining 'ignorant even of Death' behind her.[23] Accordingly, the living who learn from this grouping are the viewers of the painting, rather than the victim within it. Unlike the non-cadaverous figures in the *Danse Macabre* and Three Living and Three Dead, this woman does not glean any wisdom from her brush with Death in this moment. Instead, her function is to remain oblivious, so that those who look at her might see what she 'ignorant[ly]' misses and educate themselves on her 'sin and complete folly'.[24]

At first glance, Burne-Jones's drawing seems to be moving in a similarly voyeuristic direction. There are, however, crucial differences which disrupt a vanitas approach. Instead of looming behind the woman to convey her 'folly', Burne-Jones's skeleton is hidden behind the mirror. The mirror draws attention to a bigger compositional mirroring: the shape of the skeleton, the mirror and the dresser on which the skeleton kneels reflect both the shape of the woman's chair and the woman's pose, with bent knees, crossed hands and ponderous head-tilt. This mirroring of skeleton and woman, extending into their furniture, accords with a medieval approach. Many depictions of the *Danse Macabre* – including the earliest, the now-destroyed wall painting in the Holy Innocents' Cemetery in Paris – 'juxtapos[e] living and dead' not by having one figure *be* Death, but by making 'both figures […] facets of the same individual'.[25] As Elina Gertsman describes, the fact that the corpses 'double' the living, in the *Danse Macabre* and in medieval art more

22 The painting is available to view on Wikimedia Commons: <https://commons.wikimedia.org/wiki/File:Hans_Baldung_-_Three_Ages_of_the_Woman_and_the_Death_-_WGA01189.jpg>.

23 Stefanie Knöll, 'Death and the Maiden: A German Topic?', in Helen Fronius and Anna Linton, eds, *Women and Death: Representations of Female Victims and Perpetrators in German Culture 1500–2000* (Rochester, NY: Camden House, 2008), 9–27, at 18.

24 Knöll, 'Death and the Maiden', 18.

25 Simona Cohen, *Transformations of Time and Temporality in Medieval and Renaissance Art* (Leiden: Brill, 2014), 83.

broadly, brings an 'uncomfortable intimacy' to the scene.[26] Burne-Jones's skeleton can be read in light of this paradigm: not as 'Death the lover', but as a mirrored double, a 'rotting alter-ego', the lady's 'own personal *mort*'.[27]

Yet Burne-Jones's drawing does not present a straightforward doubling. Her depiction of the doubling dynamic is queer – in Louise Tondeur's words, it 'disrupts' and 'decentres' the normative arrangement – by refusing to balance pictorial priority equally between the woman and her 'personal *mort*'.[28] The drawing unbalances the *Danse Macabre* and contrasts with perhaps the most famous Pre-Raphaelite 'doubling' composition, Dante Gabriel Rossetti's *How They Met Themselves* (1851–64; Fitzwilliam Museum, Cambridge), in which the figures and doubles are of equal size and take up equal space.[29] In *Death and the Lady*, the skeleton's presence suggests the lady's impending doom, but the composition decentres the skeleton, restricting it to a small space in a shadowy corner. Burne-Jones further emphasises the meagreness of the skeletal double with distorted mirroring of the furniture: the mirror and dresser which shadow and squash the skeleton form a reflection of the lady's chair on a massive scale. The lady, meanwhile, is the design's focus – her uptilted head and neck is the lightest point of the picture. We are drawn to her contemplative expression. The result is a composition in which the ominous 'futurity' threatened by the skeleton is both recognised and disrupted. The skeleton lacks spatial prominence, temporal attributes (unlike Baldung Grien's painting, it has no hourglass) and interaction with a 'victim' – the factors which would allow it to assert the threat of impending death over the heroine. The artwork literally thrusts the skeleton into the shadows, so that the lady's look might take priority.

26 Elina Gertsman, *The Dance of Death in the Middle Ages: Image, Text, Performance* (Turnhout: Brepolis, 2010), 27.

27 Michael Camille, *Master of Death: The Lifeless Art of Pierre Remiet, Illuminator* (London: Yale University Press, 1996), 158.

28 Louise Tondeur, 'Elizabeth Siddal's Hair: A Methodology for Queer Reading', *Women: A Cultural Review* 22/4 (2011), 370–86, at 371.

29 There are two versions of *How They Met Themselves* in the Fitzwilliam Museum: a drawing dated 1851–60 and a watercolour c. 1860–64. The date range given above encompasses both.

The pictorial importance afforded to the woman's gaze invites us to wonder what she might be pondering. Now that the expected division of space and the visual cue of the skeleton have been disrupted, potentiality abounds. Unlike her mirror-gazing predecessor, who caresses her hair, Burne-Jones's lady does not make gestures indicative of 'vanity and self-love'. The act of looking into a mirror, moreover, is not exclusively a shorthand indicator of such traits. As Knöll observes, the mirror also 'occurs [in art] as an attribute of Venus and Prudence', becoming 'an instrument of self-knowledge'.[30] Read with this idea in mind, Burne-Jones's design seems to be not so much condemning a vain woman as prioritising her state of reflection, physically and mentally. As Laurence Talairach-Vielmas observes, the 'relationship between [the heroine's] educational journey and the looking-glass that reflects her image' is central to many Victorian fairy tales – for instance, Alice and her looking-glass.[31] Like a fairy tale heroine, Burne-Jones's lady partakes in an 'educational journey' before a mirror, with the scope to ponder more than her 'vanity' or the inevitability of death. Instead, the lady's 'self-knowledge' is queer, 'growing sideways', frustrating the expectations created by the coexistence of mirrors, skeletons and ladies. The design creates a space in which the lady can literally self-reflect – and estrange her self-reflection from us.

The drawing's viewer can see both mirror-images; for us, the skeleton is still present, even if the lady cannot see it. Yet though we have access to this privileged viewpoint, the lady has her own privileges: we cannot know her all-important thoughts. Burne-Jones's lady is not a cautionary tale, operating for the benefit of an observer's education. Her 'self-knowledge' is uncurtailed by temporality and inaccessible to the viewer. Her pondering offers us no answers (though it might offer her some), but it still demonstrates that something different is at work, 'jam[ming]' the direful trajectory suggested by the skeleton. This moment of incompleteness, like the incompleteness of the project itself, becomes a catalyst for new possibilities.

30 Knöll, 'Death and the Maiden', 18.

31 Laurence Talairach-Vielmas, 'Rewriting "Little Red Riding Hood": Victorian Fairy Tales and Mass-Visual Culture', *The Lion and the Unicorn* 33/3 (Sept 2009), 259–81, at 262.

‘Soon I’ll Return’

Whilst Burne-Jones explores strategies for disruption which are grounded in the visual medium, with shrunken skeletons and unrestrainedly thoughtful facial expressions, the threat in Siddal’s ‘True Love’ cannot be visually decentred in the shadows – it must be confronted and cut away. I see this linguistic amputation as a ‘queering act or *process*’, in which the speaker of ‘True Love’ uses her phrasing to ‘creat[e] a possibility for disjuncture’ until the ‘disjuncture’ neutralises an otherwise normative threat.[32]

The threats surrounding ‘True Love’ stem from the poem positioning itself in the world of ballads. Ballads, with their oral folkloric origins, ‘grammar’ of tropes and frequent publication in book collections during the late-eighteenth and nineteenth centuries, seem a parallel genre to ‘book[s] of Fairy Tales’ – indeed, the poetic half-tale half-ballad content of *The Fairy Family*, the collection illustrated by Edward Burne-Jones, shows the blurred boundaries between ballads and fairy tales.[33] Siddal’s descriptions, repeated reworked phrasing and central conceit – a beloved at a tomb – are markedly balladic.[34] One ballad is name-dropped: ‘Earl Richard’, the name of the speaker’s beloved, is also the title of a Border ballad, marked by Siddal in her copy of Walter Scott’s *Minstrelsy of the Scottish Border*.[35] The story of ‘Earl Richard’ speaks to ‘True Love’ – the earl is murdered by his mistress when he courts a new ‘sweetheart’ and a search is undertaken for his corpse.[36] If Siddal’s narrator is Richard’s alternative ‘sweetheart’, her

32 Tondeur, ‘Elizabeth Siddal’s Hair’, 371.

33 Roger deV. Renwick and Sigrid Rieuwerts, eds, *Ballad Mediations: Folksongs Recovered, Represented, and Reimagined* (Trier: WVT Wissenschaftlicher Verlag Trier, 2006), 64.

34 Variants of the ‘Clerk Saunders’ ballad (which Siddal painted in 1857) feature lovers mourning at – or trying to find – their beloveds’ tombs.

35 The marks show which ballads Siddal considered illustrating for another unfinished book project – a ballad collection with Dante Gabriel Rossetti and William Allingham.

36 Walter Scott, *Minstrelsy of the Scottish Border*, vols 3 and 4 (Edinburgh: Adam and Charles Black, 1807), 3.184. Siddal’s copy, in the Fitzwilliam Museum, Cambridge.

vigil takes on a sinister slant, as she mourns in apparent unawareness of his infidelity. But the poem takes no further cues from 'Earl Richard', instead challenging a different deadly narrative.

Siddal's narrator, addressing Richard, describes the threat she faces:

> Soon must I leave thee,
> This sweet summer tide,
> That other is waiting,
> To claim his pale Bride.[37]

The ominous figure of 'That other' has fairy-tale resonance: as Talairach-Vielmas observes, heroines (as in Beauty and the Beast) often 'confron[t]' the 'Other' in the form of a 'monstrous creatur[e]'.[38] Yet the phrase 'That other' also suggests a specific intruder. 'That other', described as what they are not (not Richard), evokes the presence of an absence, a sign given to a blank space – a prerequisite theoretical concept for discussing representations of death.[39] Ashby Kinch sees 'images of death' as 'provisional', struggling to fill 'the aporia […] between us and this unrepresentable event'; 'That other' is a 'provisional' description, acknowledging an 'unrepresentable' subject with its imprecision.[40] The subsequent reference to 'his pale Bride', moreover, tethers 'That other' to an established Death-based trope, the one not depicted in Figure 6.1: 'Death the lover'.

As mentioned, Bürger's ballad 'Lenore' was a populariser of 'Death the lover'. 'Lenore' was translated both by Siddal's husband Dante Gabriel Rossetti, and the editor of *Minstrelsy*, Walter Scott. In Rossetti's translation, Death – disguised as Lenore's husband – summons 'my bride' and declares he has 'come to carry [her] back', whilst her pale 'white hands' are noted.[41] Scott has Death announce 'To-night I ride, with my young bride',

37 Trowbridge, *My Ladys Soul*, 92.

38 Laurence Talairach-Vielmas, 'Beautiful Maidens, Hideous Suitors: Victorian Fairy Tales and the Process of Civilization', *Marvels & Tales* 24/2 (2010), 272–296, at 272.

39 See Camille, *Master of Death*, 56; Kinch, *Imago Mortis*, 276; and Guthke, *The Gender of Death*, 8.

40 Kinch, *Imago Mortis*, 276.

41 Dante Gabriel Rossetti, trans., 'Lenore', *The Rossetti Archive*, <http://www.rossettiarchive.org/docs/1-1844.harvardms.rad.html#1-1844>, 6, 8, accessed 27 July 2021.

as his pale victim twines her 'lily arms' about him.[42] Lenore's Death leads the heroine to her doom: he carries her to a graveyard, reveals his skeletal form and leaves her in her grave, with the dead closing in around her.

Like Burne-Jones's drawing, Siddal's poem must disrupt the threat of a skeleton. But whilst Burne-Jones's skeleton is an ominous double, which can suggest the lady's doom but not actively bring it about, Siddal's skeleton is a separate 'other' with the capacity to evoke 'Lenore' and carry the narrator away to a terrible fate. This direct threat provokes a direct response – a 'queering act', enacted in the poem's phrasing and pacing, which truncates the doom before it can unfold. The lady 'claim[ed]' as a 'pale Bride' reappears immediately in the next line, alone and unclaimed, promising her swift return:

> Soon I'll return to thee,
> Hopeful and brave,
> When the dead leaves,
> Blow over thy grave,[43]

Instead of allowing 'That other' to lead her – both physically, away from Richard's grave, and structurally, by continuing to follow his actions in her narration – Siddal's lady abruptly drops all mention of him from the poem. The 'Soon I'll return to thee' stanza is a cauterising sequel to its immediate predecessor. The seasons change across the two stanzas, drawing boundaries around 'That other' and his curtailed intervention: though he appears in 'summer', he must be gone by autumn, 'When the dead leaves, / Blow' and the lady returns to Richard. 'That other' is also excluded by the line echoes and selective repetitions that shape this stanza. Whilst 'Soon I'll return to thee' echoes the earlier line 'Soon must I leave thee', the three lines that follow hearken back to the first stanza: 'Tender and brave: / Kneeling I kiss / The dust from your grave'. The lines about 'That other' are disregarded by these repetitive strategies; they have no counterparts to develop or echo.

42 Walter Scott, *The Chase, and William and Helen: Two Ballads, from the German of Gottfried Augustus Bürger* (Edinburgh: Mundell and Son, 1796), 32, 31.

43 Trowbridge, *My Ladys Soul*, 92.

By using her words to 'jam the mechanisms' by which 'That other' could 'claim' her, Siddal's narrator escapes a Lenore-like doom. Incompletion is weaponised: the story of 'That other' is left deliberately incomplete so that its ending might be dodged. But the narrator does not curtail the poem to stop this doom – instead, she raises an alternative possibility in its place, which overwrites the expectations of the 'Lenore' trajectory. Though Lenore is carried to a graveyard to face her doom, Siddal's heroine returns to a graveyard to escape hers, specifically to her refuge at Richard's tomb. The tomb, her place of safety, is endowed with new potential – a queer disruption of expected associations which resists the ill-fatedness characterising the tomb in 'Lenore'.

The tomb also plays a major role in Burne-Jones's drawing, which again expands the possibilities suggested by a literary precedent. In these final sections, I will consider how these works explore the tomb's potentiality, driven by the disparate capacities of word and image to reimagine the tomb to diverse ends. The results have much to say to anxieties surrounding incompletion and potentiality in the nineteenth century.

'The Poor Living Corpse'?

Burne-Jones's design disrupts a medieval dynamic between lady and skeleton, but the spatial arrangement also resembles another medieval precedent. *Death and the Lady* twice arranges a figure with clasped hands being pressed down by an opaque rectangle: the back of the woman's chair and the mirror before the skeleton. A black cavity looms behind the lady – if she fell into it, it could be lidded by the chair and the mirror. The overall effect is that of a tomb, specifically a double-decker *transi* tomb. These medieval tombs, an architectural doubling of living and dead, feature two effigies separated by a screen: the person in their finery and the person's skeletal corpse. Alice Chaucer, granddaughter of one of Pre-Raphaelitism's favourite medieval authors Geoffrey Chaucer, has one such tomb in Oxfordshire, as does Henry Chichele, Archbishop of Canterbury, in

Canterbury Cathedral.[44] In the tomb, as in Burne-Jones's design, 'the intact body comes into no visual or physical contact with the decaying *transi* figure; the corpse,' as Gertsman describes, 'although turned towards the *gisant* ["intact" effigy], cannot "see" it through the stone screen that separates them', a 'screen' evoked by Burne-Jones's mirror.[45]

The (*transi-*)tomb-like positioning of figures, surfaces, openings and objects is complemented by another pictorial association with tombs. This association, like Siddal's engagement with 'Lenore' in 'True Love', addresses the fate of a fictional character who bears some resemblance (in this case, visually) to the lady. The look of Burne-Jones's lady gestures towards the hairstyle, headpiece, upper-body pose and dress of the character Clara von Bork from Wilhelm Meinhold's novel *Sidonia the Sorceress* (1847), as painted by Edward Burne-Jones in 1860.[46] Burne-Jones herself modelled for Clara, and her allusion to the character in *Death and the Lady* speaks to her design's interest in the lady's doom and 'self-knowledge', as well as the tomb-like look of the room.

Sidonia the Sorceress was translated into English in 1849 by Jane, Lady Wilde, and was popular with the Pre-Raphaelites. The plot focuses on the malevolent sixteenth-century noblewoman Sidonia von Bork; Clara is Sidonia's cousin, 'learned both in God's will, [and] in all other knowledge', but determined not to face the truth of Sidonia's evil nature.[47] Clara, like Lenore, is doomed to a horrible fate inside a grave: her intelligence (in thwarting Sidonia's plans) and wilful ignorance (of the fact that Sidonia wants revenge) results in Sidonia burying Clara alive. Yet Clara's death sequence is as much about gaining 'self-knowledge' inside the tomb as it is a grisly Gothic demise. Sidonia and Clara converse through the tomb-lid:

44 That Burne-Jones saw these tombs is possible. Canterbury Cathedral influenced the location and design of William Morris's Red House, where Burne-Jones spent the summer of 1860, using it as a base to visit sites in the area (see Burne-Jones, *Memorials*, I, 208–10).

45 Gertsman, *The Dance of Death*, 31.

46 Edward Burne-Jones, *Clara von Bork 1560*, 1860, watercolour and gouache on paper, 34.2 × 17.9 cm, Tate Gallery, London. <https://www.tate.org.uk/art/artworks/burne-jones-clara-von-bork-1560-n05878>.

47 Jane Wilde, trans., *Sidonia the Sorceress* (London: Kelmscott Press, 1893), 61.

> 'Sidonia, by the Jesu cross, I pray thee have pity on me! Save me, save me, I am stifling. Oh, run for some one, if thou canst not lift the lid thyself!'
>
> But the devil made answer to the poor living corpse: 'Dost thou take me for a silly fool like thyself, that I should now undo all that I have done?'
>
> And as the voice went on from the coffin, but feebler and fainter: 'Think on my husband; on my child, Sidonia!'
>
> She answered: 'Didst thou think of that when, but for thee, I might have been a Duchess of Pomerania, and the proud mother of a prince, in place of being as I now am?'
>
> Then all became still within the coffin, and Sidonia sprang upon it & danced, chanting the 109th psalm; and as she came to the words: 'Let none shew mercy to him; let none have pity on his orphans; let his posterity be cut off & his name be blotted out,' there was a loud knocking again within the coffin, and a faint, stifled cry: 'I am dying!' then followed by a gurgling sound, & all became still.[48]

Sidonia fires off questions to provoke Clara into self-reflection ('Dost thou take me for a silly fool like thyself', 'Didst thou think of that'). Clara's reactions indicate the effectiveness of this interrogation. After the first question, her voice and movements become 'feebler and fainter', and after 'Didst thou think of that', 'all became still within the coffin'. The fact that Clara does not die until the second iteration of 'all became still' suggests the first 'still[ness]' is a representation of her self-reflection, generated by the unavoidable truth of her entombment. The paragraph, trapped between the repetitions of the phrase 'all became still', becomes another enclosed space, where Clara's insightful revelation coexists with her ghastly fate.

Burne-Jones's lady is not identified as Clara, in the same way that Siddal's lady resembles fictional precedents without becoming them. These looser links between the drawing, the portrait of Clara and the character's doomed situation allow Burne-Jones to queer Clara's strangely insightful time as a 'living corpse'. This principle can be explained by examining the doors in both artworks. Clara

48 Wilde, *Sidonia*, 221.

and the lady both stand in front of a door: in Edward Burne-Jones's *Clara von Bork 1560*, it leads to a garden, no bigger than Clara's arm. *Death and the Lady*, however, makes the door larger, closer and strips out details, resulting in the tomb-like cavity. The background which functions as set-dressing in the painting becomes, in Burne-Jones's drawing, an inscrutable portal – unfixed to detail and therefore open to possibilities.

Much the same could be said of Burne-Jones's lady. By giving her strong shades of – but no identical resemblance to – Clara, the drawing opens up the novel character's 'stifl[ed]' fate. Clara's 'self-knowledge' has limitations: it is directed by Sidonia, swiftly curtailed by plot temporality and only amounts to a revelation of her own stupidity. Burne-Jones avoids this limited conclusion, presenting a lady acquiring self-knowledge independent from the invasive prompts of onlookers – self-reflection which is linked to but not dictated by the skeleton.

Burne-Jones's drawing embraces the tomb's capacity to provoke insight, but strips away the narrative temporality that binds this insight to a dreadful fate. This approach is 'queer', to follow Carolyn Dinshaw's ideas, 'by virtue of [its] particular engagement with time'; the tomb 'precipitate[s] out of time altogether' to preserve its lady's self-reflecting.[49] The design draws on the capacities of the visual artwork to accomplish this reconfiguration: an artwork considers space as a priority over time, a methodology which allows for the elimination of any temporal element. Thus, the space of 'self-knowledge' for Clara in *Sidonia the Sorceress* – created by a tomb, but curtailed in a paragraph by 'all became still' – literally 'bec[omes] still' in Burne-Jones's drawing. The moment of 'still[ness]' is severed from the onward push of *Sidonia*'s (or any) narrative and preserved in its own right, allowing Burne-Jones's lady her escape. Without temporality, the tomb is simply a space to contemplate, away from the obligation to serve a story and the ending forecast by a *transi* double.

This open situation might have looked very different, had the illustration been contextualised by a complete 'book of Fairy Tales'. Yet the incomplete framework resonates crucially with the design. The project's

49 Carolyn Dinshaw, *How Soon is Now? Medieval Texts, Amateur Readers and the Queerness of Time* (London: Duke University Press, 2012), 4.

unfinished state allows an already queer artwork to remain in Dinshaw's out-of-time 'now' without conceding to an ending.[50] Cut off from a book, and a narrative, which never ended up existing, Burne-Jones's work – like her lady – 'precipitate[s]' away from fixed temporalities and 'foreclosed potentials'.[51] With no solid surroundings in which to situate the design, viewers are encouraged to, as Melissa Gustin describes, 'enter into a slightly altered state to think creatively' – and can explore, alongside the work itself, the idea of reimagining solid surroundings to enable different states of being.[52]

'Watching or Waking, / Sleeping or Dead'

Like the unfinished project, the last stanza of 'True Love' offers something different from a fixed conclusion, reworking a tomb to create an escape – but, unlike Burne-Jones, Siddal avoids doing so in a way which permits any reliance on the visual. Siddal's lady describes what will happen when, having banished the threat of 'That other', she returns to Richard's tomb:

Then shall they find me
Close at thy head
Watching or waking,
Sleeping or dead.[53]

She suggests she will have an audience: 'they' who 'shall […] find' her. 'They' reaches out to include us, the readers, creating 'a queer kind of reading […] where the reader cannot help but be implicated in the text, fulfilling the textual promise' to discover the speaker at the tomb.[54] Yet we

50 Dinshaw, *How Soon is Now?*, 4.
51 Dinshaw, *How Soon is Now?*, 137.
52 Melissa L. Gustin, 'Sporegasbord: Jean-Léon Gérôme's Tanagra and Mushroom Temporalities', *New Directions in Eighteenth- and Nineteenth-Century Art*, season 1 (27 July 2020).
53 Trowbridge, *My Ladys Soul*, 92.
54 Tondeur, 'Elizabeth Siddal's Hair', 373.

are 'implicated' only to become disconcerted. The description of the lady's position atop the tomb is impossible to 'find': she could be 'Watching *or* waking, / Sleeping *or* dead', four options which differ in intention, implication and pose. Dante Gabriel Rossetti rewrote the line after Siddal's death to remove this 'disjuncture', replacing 'waking' with 'fainting' in his fair copy to render more options visually similar – but the original words jar.[55] Siddal, who embraces the likeness between 'fainting' and death in other poems (the speaker of 'O silent wood I enter thee' begs not to 'faint or die or swoon'), did not do so here.[56]

Where Burne-Jones's design grows sideways from motionlessness, drawing potentiality out of a tomb in which 'all became still', Siddal's lady refuses to stay 'still' atop her beloved's tomb. Richard may be an effigy 'All in white stone', but the lady will not become his frozen *transi* double. Though, as Deborah Lutz describes, Victorian literature and funerary practice foregrounded a slippage between living people and effigies, with tomb designers and writers playing on the easy transformation 'from flesh into stone', Siddal's speaker resists this blurring, refusing to let readers 'harde[n]' her in a pose, escaping through the cracks of her confusing description.[57] This resistance also speaks to the 'construction of the self as image' in Victorian fairy tales, where 'heroines [...] are taught to turn their selves into images and to efface their bodies'.[58] But whilst Siddal's speaker may join the ranks of heroines 'effac[ing] their bodies', she also avoids 'turn[ing]' herself into an 'imag[e]', preventing the 'construction' of anything from her physical position. Though the title suggests readers will see 'true love' displayed in the poem, the speaker dodges becoming the ideal's visual exemplar with her multiple-choice anti-conclusion.

Though the methodology differs from Burne-Jones, this final evasion also allows Siddal's lady to escape a doomed fate. There is precedent – and pressure – for a lady at a tomb to die, in 'Lenore' and in ballads more broadly.

55 Trowbridge, *My Ladys Soul*, 93.

56 Trowbridge, *My Ladys Soul*, 72.

57 Deborah Lutz, *Relics of Death in Victorian Literature and Culture* (Cambridge: Cambridge University Press, 2015), 86.

58 Talairach-Vielmas, 'Rewriting "Little Red Riding Hood"', 261.

But 'dead' does not stand alone as the final fate of Siddal's lady. Instead, it is implicated in the chaos of possibilities by the 'or' before it – one of which is 'Watching'. Where Burne-Jones balances the privileges of viewers and lady, letting viewers see the skeleton but not the lady's thoughts, Siddal's speaker strips all visual privilege from the 'they' who 'find' her – 'Watching' them, but not letting them 'watch' her. The differing capacities of word and image enact similar escapes, gaining and losing different aspects in the process.

Again, it is worth remembering that a combination of mediums might have frustrated Siddal's lady's queer escape, had 'True Love' accompanied an illustration in a 'book of Fairy Tales'. Yet evidence suggests this lady's avoidance might not have been compromised. A contemporaneous Siddal drawing, *The Woeful Victory* – the design shown to Burne-Jones – is often linked to 'True Love', as it orbits a similar premise: a lady mourning her beloved and facing the threat of an 'other'.[59] But *The Woeful Victory* does not depict anything which takes place in 'True Love'. If there is a relationship between the two, the design functions as a prequel, depicting the beloved's death at the hands of a (living) rival suitor. Whether or not *The Woeful Victory* was considered for inclusion in the book, or has any link to 'True Love', it is nonetheless significant that it – the only known Siddal artwork created between 1860 and 1862 – does not illustrate this poem, allowing the speaker to perpetually enact her escape from the visual world.

'Shrouded in Incertitude'

Siddal and Burne-Jones's works encourage their heroines to evade disastrous narratives, in which they are marked for doom by tropes, plots,

59 See Jan Marsh, *Elizabeth Siddal: Pre-Raphaelite Artist 1829–1862* (Sheffield: The Ruskin Gallery, 1991), 28, and Trowbridge, *My Ladys Soul*, 93. Elizabeth Siddal, *The Woeful Victory*, 1860, pencil, black and brown ink on paper, 15.6 × 12.1 cm, The Mark Samuels Lasner Collection, University of Delaware. The drawing is available to view online at <https://exhibitions.lib.udel.edu/victorian-passions/exhibition-item/the-woeful-victory-ink-on-paper/>.

precedents and viewers' scrutiny. Burne-Jones's drawing enacts a queer sideways growth, 'jam[ming]' the press of temporality and filling the space between disaster and consequence with possibilities, not all of which are accessible to observers. Siddal's poem's sideways growth is more of a sideways dodge; the lady does not indulge in ambiguous pondering, instead co-opting ambiguity and uncertainty as weapons against anyone wishing to ponder her pose(s). Both works stage, via the methods their mediums allow, a revolt against the voyeuristic learning that comes from watching someone else's doom, against lurking like Lancelot to make reductive pronouncements over women's corpses. Our focus is shifted to responses which decentre disaster and despair; these doomed ladies eschew lamentation for pondering and possibilities. Through this eschewal, the works consider how to respond to the shattering of a stable world.

This idea is one with broader cultural resonance in the nineteenth century. The period saw intense anxiety around a loss of certainty in creative expression, an uncomfortable awareness of symbolic meanings shifting and previous stabilities giving way, as the Romantic past became what poet and critic Matthew Arnold described as an 'unpoetical' Victorian present with uncertain potential.[60] Focus 'shift[ed]', as E. Warwick Slinn observes, from a desire to 'discove[r] completed wholes', to 'structures that stress movement toward an end but where the attainment of that end is shrouded in incertitude'.[61] As Siddal's former patron John Ruskin recounts in *Modern Painters*, the prevalent attitude of nineteenth-century creative work is 'doubtful and indignant [...] anxious or weeping', phrasing reminiscent of the close of 'True Love'.[62] Siddal's earlier work is closely attuned to this fearful doubt, particularly the implicitly ominous future that lurks beyond the interrogative reworkings of old certainties.[63]

60 Lionel Trilling, *The Portable Matthew Arnold* (New York: The Viking Press, 1949), 662.

61 E. Warwick Slinn, 'Experimental Form in Victorian Poetry', in Joseph Bristow, ed., *The Cambridge Companion to Victorian Poetry* (Cambridge: Cambridge University Press, 2006), 46–66, at 48.

62 Philip Davis, ed., *John Ruskin: Selected Writings* (London: Everyman, 1995), 281.

63 See Nat Reeve, '"An Hour Before the Day": the dismembered Book of Hours in Elizabeth Siddal's *Clerk Saunders*', *Word & Image* (in press: DOI 10.1080/02666286.2021.1923316).

Yet the Siddal and Burne-Jones works examined here offer less frightening ways to frame ambiguous potentiality and an 'end [...] shrouded in incertitude'. If nineteenth-century creativity is hurtling towards an impasse, in which symbols lose their meanings and doubt takes the place of certainty, the evasive ladies of this unfinished project suggest that the process of cutting loose past meanings can be freeing, and that uncertainty and incompleteness need not be inherently, prohibitively terrifying and destructive. It is curious that the dogged creativity championed in these works, the result of an initial collaborative endeavour, is ultimately individualistic – the heroines have no access to a community and must work solely with themselves to expand their possibilities. Yet this individuality is more productive for them than the hostile community of characters and precedents in the narratives from which they have escaped. The potentiality of Burne-Jones's design offers something more unfixed and intriguing than the inevitable destruction of its central figure. Siddal's lady cuts ties with old stories and embraces uncertainty without qualms, breaking apart plots and poses which rely on her misfortune. The queer escapes created by Siddal and Burne-Jones – and their ladies – offer a challenge not just to precedents and narrative trajectories, but to the idea that untethering, uncertainty and isolation are detrimental to creativity. As these works and their project suggest, impending doom can also be a starting point.

Bibliography

Auerbach, Nina, and U. C. Knoepflmacher, eds, *Forbidden Journeys: Fairy Tales and Fantasies by Victorian Women Writers* (London: University of Chicago Press, 1992).

Bronfen, Elisabeth, *Over Her Dead Body: Death, Femininity and the Aesthetic* (New York: Routledge, 1992).

Burne-Jones, Georgiana, *Memorials of Edward Burne-Jones* (London: Macmillan and Co., 1904).

Caciola, Nancy Mandeville, *Afterlives: The Return of the Dead in the Middle Ages* (London: Cornell University Press, 2016).

Camille, Michael, *Master of Death: The Lifeless Art of Pierre Remiet, Illuminator* (London: Yale University Press, 1996).

Clark, James M., *The Dance of Death in the Middle Ages and the Renaissance* (Glasgow: Jackson, Son and Company, 1950).

Cohen, Simona, *Transformations of Time and Temporality in Medieval and Renaissance Art* (Leiden: Brill, 2014).

Davis, Philip, ed., *John Ruskin: Selected Writings* (London: Everyman, 1995).

Dinshaw, Carolyn, *How Soon is Now? Medieval Texts, Amateur Readers and the Queerness of Time* (London: Duke University Press, 2012).

Edelman, Lee, *No Future: Queer Theory and the Death Drive* (London: Duke University Press, 2004).

Gertsman, Elina, *The Dance of Death in the Middle Ages: Image, Text, Performance* (Turnhout: Brepolis, 2010).

Gustin, Melissa L., 'Sporegasbord, Jean-Léon Gérôme's Tanagra and Mushroom Temporalities', *New Directions in Eighteenth- and Nineteenth-Century Art*, Season 1, talk given 27 July 2020.

Guthke, Karl S., *The Gender of Death: A Cultural History in Art and Literature* (Cambridge: Cambridge University Press, 1999).

Haffey, Kate, *Literary Modernism, Queer Temporality: Eddies in Time* (London: Palgrave, 2019).

Halberstam, Jack, *The Queer Art of Failure* (London: Duke University Press, 2011).

Harrison, Ann Tukey, ed., with a chapter by Sandra L. Hindman, *The Danse Macabre of Women: ms. fr. 995 of the Bibliothèque Nationale* (London: The Kent State University Press, 1994).

Hartnell, Jack, *Medieval Bodies: Life, Death and Art in the Middle Ages* (London: Profile Books Ltd, 2018).

Howitt, Mary, trans., *Wonderful Stories for Children, by Hans Christian Andersen* (London: Chapman and Hall, 1846).

Kinch, Ashby, *Imago Mortis: Mediating Images of Death in Late Medieval Culture* (Boston, MA: Brill, 2013).

Knöll, Stefanie, 'Death and the Maiden: A German Topic?', in Helen Fronius and Anna Linton, eds, *Women and Death: Representations of Female Victims and Perpetrators in German Culture 1500–2000* (Rochester, NY: Camden House, 2008), 9–27.

Kurtz, Leonard P., *The Dance of Death and the Macabre Spirit in European Literature* (New York: Publications of the Institute of French Studies, 1934).

Lane, E. W., trans., *The Thousand and One Nights; or, the Arabian Nights' Entertainments*, 3 vols (London: John Murray, 1847).

Llewellyn, Nigel, *The Art of Death: Visual Culture in the English Death Ritual c.1500–c.1800* (London: Reaktion Books, 1991).

Lutz, Deborah, *Relics of Death in Victorian Literature and Culture* (Cambridge: Cambridge University Press, 2015).
MacLaren, Archibald, *The Fairy Family: A Series of Metrical Tales illustrating the Fairy Mythology of Europe* (London: Longman, Brown, Green, Longmans and Roberts, 1857).
Marsh, Jan, ed., *Elizabeth Siddal: Pre-Raphaelite Artist 1829–1862* (Sheffield: The Ruskin Gallery, 1991).
——, et al., *Pre-Raphaelite Sisters* (London: National Portrait Gallery Publications, 2019).
Newton, Michael, ed., *Victorian Fairy Tales* (Oxford: Oxford University Press, 2018).
Reeve, Nat, '"An Hour Before the Day": The Dismembered Book of Hours in Elizabeth Siddal's *Clerk Saunders*', *Word & Image* (in press: DOI 10.1080/02666286.2021.1923316).
Renwick, Roger deV., and Sigrid Rieuwerts, eds, *Ballad Mediations: Folksongs Recovered, Represented, and Reimagined* (Trier: WVT Wissenschaftlicher Verlag Trier, 2006).
Rossetti, Dante Gabriel, trans., 'Lenore', *The Rossetti Archive*, <http://www.rossettiarchive.org./docs/1-1844.harvardms.rad.html#1-1844>, accessed 11 August 2020.
Rossetti, William Michael, ed., *Ruskin: Rossetti: Preraphaelitism. Papers 1854 to 1862* (London: George Allen, 1899).
Ruskin, John, *The King of the Golden River, or The Black Brothers* (Boston, MA: Mayhew and Baker, 1860).
Scott, Walter, *The Chase, and William and Helen: Two Ballads, from the German of Gottfried Augustus Bürger* (Edinburgh: Mundell and Son, 1796).
——, *Minstrelsy of the Scottish Border: by Sir Walter Scott, Bart., with his Introductions, Additions, and the Editor's Notes*, vols 3 and 4 (Edinburgh: Adam and Charles Black, 1807). Siddal's copy, in The Fitzwilliam Museum, Cambridge.
Seifert, Lewis C., 'Queer(ing) Fairy Tales', *Marvels & Tales* 29/1 (2015), 15–20.
Slinn, E. Warwick, 'Experimental Form in Victorian Poetry', in Joseph Bristow, ed., *The Cambridge Companion to Victorian Poetry* (Cambridge: Cambridge University Press, 2006), 46–66.
Stockton, Kathryn Bond, *The Queer Child, or Growing Sideways in the Twentieth Century* (London: Duke University Press, 2009).
Sumpter, Caroline, *The Victorian Press and the Fairy Tale* (London: Palgrave Macmillan, 2008).
Talairach-Vielmas, Laurence, 'Rewriting "Little Red Riding Hood": Victorian Fairy Tales and Mass-Visual Culture', *The Lion and the Unicorn* 33/3 (September 2009), 259–81.

——, 'Beautiful Maidens, Hideous Suitors: Victorian Fairy Tales and the Process of Civilization', *Marvels & Tales* 24/2 (2010), 272–96.

Tondeur, Louise, 'Elizabeth Siddal's Hair: A Methodology for Queer Reading', *Women: A Cultural Review* 22/4 (2011), 370–86.

Trilling, Lionel, *The Portable Matthew Arnold* (New York: The Viking Press, 1949).

Trowbridge, Serena, *My Ladys Soul: The Poems of Elizabeth Eleanor Siddall* (Brighton: Victorian Secrets, 2018).

Turner, Kay, and Pauline Greenhill, eds, *Transgressive Tales: Queering the Grimms* (Detroit, MI: Wayne State University Press, 2012).

Wilde, Jane, trans., *Sidonia the Sorceress* (London: Kelmscott Press, 1893).

GLENDA YOUDE

7 Christina and Elizabeth Rossetti: Poetic and Artistic Rivals

ABSTRACT

Christina Georgina Rossetti and Elizabeth Eleanor Rossetti were not only sisters-in-law, but also sisters in ambition. Their relationship was perhaps one of rivalry rather than affection. In this chapter I will examine the complex relationship between Christina and Elizabeth through the correspondence, poetry and art they produced. Christina wrote poetry from an early age and was just 17 years old when her first collection *Verses* was published. Further volumes of poetry appeared during her lifetime, with *Goblin Market* (1862) being the most successful. Her foray into art, however, appeared less successful. Model, muse and eventual wife of Christina's brother Dante Gabriel, Elizabeth was a gifted artist whose work was exhibited alongside that of her male counterparts. Her poetry, however, was only published after her death, severely edited by her brother-in-law, William Michael. Although the women's initial relationship was frosty, the atmosphere softened with Elizabeth's pregnancy and stillbirth. Within less than a year Elizabeth herself was dead, but Christina continued writing and publishing poetry into her sixties. Fate held the final ace: while Elizabeth is remembered for her activities as a model, Christina is heralded as one of the great Victorian poets. Rivals in life, in death they share the same headstone in the family plot in Highgate Cemetery.

* * * * *

Resting in peace together in the Rossetti family grave (Figure 7.4) in the west side of Highgate Cemetery, London, are the earthly remains of Christina Georgina Rossetti (1830–94) and Elizabeth Eleanor Rossetti (née Siddall, 1829–62). Sharing the same headstone, their relationship in life did not always mirror the eternal tranquillity they now enjoy together. Christina and Elizabeth were not only sisters-in-law, but also sisters in ambition, or rivals. They shared a love of reading and writing poetry, producing drawings and watercolours, and both aspired beyond the role of a Victorian 'Angel of the House'.[1] Their association, therefore,

1 Coventry Patmore, *The Angel in the House* (London: Cassell & Company Ltd, 1887 [1854]).

was perhaps founded on rivalry and jealousy rather than affection. In this chapter I will examine the complex relationship between these two ambitious women through the evidence they left behind: the correspondence, poetry and art they produced during their lifetimes. Christina was an avid writer, both of letters and verse, but also drew portraits and sketched illustrations for her work. Elizabeth's literary oeuvre was small in comparison, but her artistic output was much greater.

Regrettably, there is a lack of primary material documenting Elizabeth's thoughts or feelings about her sister-in-law, and only a few of Christina's letters mention Elizabeth. There is no evidence of written correspondence having passed between the two women, but if letters did exist, Dante Gabriel Rossetti would probably have destroyed them all. As Marsh notes: 'On leaving Chatham Place he burnt a great number of letters, in order to destroy all that reminded him of his wife.'[2] Elizabeth's voice, therefore, has effectively been silenced. Her thoughts are known only through the words of others, and from her poems and drawings which Gabriel carefully preserved. Both women used poetry and art as a means of self-expression, and my analysis of their relationship will, of necessity, reflect on the biographical nature of the chosen material. I acknowledge that this may invoke criticism, but I hope it will also provide a positive impetus for discussion and further research into the true relationship between these two women.

The rhythmic flow of poetry appears to have attracted both Christina and Elizabeth from an early age. Although the Rossetti boys, Gabriel and William, attended a local school from 1836, Christina and her sister Maria were home educated and fluent in both English and Italian.[3] Poetry formed part of the Rossetti family heritage, as their father, Gabriele, was a poet and scholar of some note. Christina had a keen ear for language from childhood; her earliest surviving verse, 'To My Mother on her Birthday', was written

2 Jan Marsh, *The Legend of Elizabeth Siddal* (London: Quartet Books, 2010 [1989]), 22.

3 Lona Mosk Packer, *Christina Rossetti* (Cambridge: Cambridge University Press, 1963), 13–14.

when she was 12 years old.[4] At the age of 17, and courtesy of her grandfather's benefaction, her first anthology *Verses* was privately published.[5]

Like Christina, it is believed that Elizabeth also received schooling at home. As the daughter of a cutler who had moved from Sheffield to London, Elizabeth's class status was below that of the Rossetti family, so her education would have been less extensive. Her first encounter with poetry, however, is reported to have been a more dynamic experience than Christina's. William relates an anecdote of how Elizabeth was said to have been introduced to the work of Tennyson 'by finding one or two of his poems on a piece of paper which she brought home to her mother, wrapped round a pat of butter'.[6] It is not known at what age this occurred, but clearly she was old enough to read and appreciate the complexities of the English language as written by the future Poet Laureate.

Both women became inexorably linked to the Pre-Raphaelite circle. Christina was an integral part of the Pre-Raphaelite Brotherhood from its inception, being the sister of two of the seven founding members. She was the only female to contribute to *The Germ*, the journal produced by the Brotherhood in their early days. The first issue, published in January 1850, included her poem 'Dream-Land' anonymously on page 20.[7] The same poem was later republished under her own name in *Goblin Market and Other Poems* (1862).[8]

4 *Christina Rossetti: The Complete Poems*, ed. R. W. Crump, Notes and Introduction by Betty S. Flowers (London: Penguin Books, 2005), introduction xlviii.

5 'Verses/by Christina G. Rossetti, Dedicated to her Mother', *Harry Ransom Center*, The University of Texas at Austin, BK_PR_5237_V4_1847_Copy3_Hanley_001, <https://hrc.contentdm.oclc.org/digital/collection/p15878coll35/id/1916/rec/1>, accessed 31 May 2021.

6 William Michael Rossetti, 'Dante Rossetti and Elizabeth Siddal', *The Burlington Magazine for Connoisseurs* 1/3 (1903), 273.

7 'Pre-Raphaelite Journal, *The Germ*' (C.59.c.19), *British Library*, <https://www.bl.uk/collection-items/pre-raphaelite-journal-the-germ>, accessed 31 May 2021. Christina's later poems in *The Germ* were published under the pseudonym Ellen Alleyn.

8 Christina Rossetti, *Goblin Market and Other Poems* (Cambridge and London: Macmillan and Co., 1862).

Although it is not widely recognised, Christina also inherited her elder brother's love of art. Among her oeuvre (mostly unlocated) she created three watercolour illustrations for 'Dream-Land'.[9] She is also known to have made many more watercolour sketches, including a series depicting her own perception of the goblins in the margins of her manuscript copy of *Goblin Market*.[10] Although none of her drawings were included in any published anthologies of her poetry, this perhaps demonstrates Christina's ambition for future publication.

As Gabriel's sister, Christina was the natural choice for a model in his early Pre-Raphaelite paintings. She sat for the figure of the Virgin in *The Girlhood of Mary Virgin* (1848–9) and *Ecce Ancilla Domini!* (1849–50; both Tate, London). It is not known whether she enjoyed or simply endured the process, but her brother drew and painted many subsequent portraits of her throughout his life. The preparatory sketch for *Ecce Ancilla Domini!* shows Christina seated in a seemingly uncomfortable position, maintaining the pose for the benefit of her brother's art. Christina, therefore, held a respected position as the only established female member of the Brotherhood long before Elizabeth entered the Pre-Raphaelite circle. She clearly wished to participate on equal terms with her male colleagues, demonstrating ambition beyond that of a traditional Victorian woman.

Elizabeth made her first appearance within the group as a model, posing for several members of the Brotherhood, including William Holman Hunt and John Everett Millais, before becoming Gabriel's model, muse and pupil in 1852. There are many versions of the story of how Walter Howell Deverell discovered her working in a milliner's shop.[11] It is more likely, however, that Elizabeth first encountered the Deverells as a dressmaker, visiting Mrs Deverell for measurements or a fitting for a new dress, as suggested in an obituary published in the *Sheffield Telegraph* just a couple of weeks

9 *Complete Poems*, eds Crump and Flowers, 888 ('Dream-Land' note).

10 *Complete Poems*, eds Crump and Flowers, 884–5 ('Goblin Market' note).

11 See, for example, William Holman Hunt, *Pre-Raphaelitism and the Pre-Raphaelite Brotherhood*, 2 vols (London: Macmillan, 1905), I, 198.

after her death.[12] Written by W. I., believed to be William Ibbett, one of Elizabeth's distant relatives from Sheffield, the obituary states that: 'Miss Siddal showed some outlines, designs of her own leisure hours, to Mr D– and he, much pleased with them, introduced them to Mr D– Jnr and the other young artists'.[13] Walter Deverell then persuaded Elizabeth to sit for him for the figure of Viola in *Twelfth Night* (1849–50; private collection), chaperoned by his mother or sisters. Elizabeth's prior interest in art suggests that she too had ambitions above and beyond her position in life.

The exact date when Christina learned of her elder brother Gabriel's new model, and his infatuation with her, remains a mystery. Her younger brother, William, suggests that *Rossovestita* (1850; Birmingham Museums and Art Gallery) was the first watercolour for which Elizabeth sat to Gabriel.[14] He also believes the pair were engaged by the end of 1851, but there is no evidence to support this claim.[15] If this were indeed the case, then Christina would surely have been aware of Elizabeth's existence at that time, but the first documentary evidence of Gabriel mentioning Elizabeth to Christina is found in a letter dating from the summer of 1852:[16]

> Maria has just shown me a letter of yours by which I find that you have been perpetrating portraits of some kind. If you answer this note, will you enclose a specimen, as I should like to see your handiwork. You must take care however not to rival the Sid.[17]

This letter provides evidence not only of Christina's sketching habits, but also that Elizabeth (whose nickname was 'the Sid') was also practising her skills as an artist. There was a stern warning to Christina that she must

12 'The Death of Mrs D. G. Rossetta [*sic*]', *Sheffield Telegraph*, 28 February 1862, cited in Jan Marsh, *The Legend of Elizabeth Siddal* (London: Quartet Books, 2010 [1989]), 157–8.

13 *Sheffield Telegraph*, in Marsh, *Legend*, 157.

14 Rossetti, 'Dante Rossetti and Elizabeth Siddal', 274.

15 Rossetti, 'Dante Rossetti and Elizabeth Siddal', 277.

16 *The Correspondence of Dante Gabriel Rossetti*, ed. William E. Fredeman, 10 vols (Cambridge: D. S. Brewer, 2002–15), I, 197. Letter to Christina, 4 August 1852. 'The Sid', 'Guggum' and 'Gug' were all Gabriel's pet names for Elizabeth, and he also referred to her as both 'Lizzy' and 'Lizzie'.

17 *Correspondence*, ed. Fredeman, I, 197. Letter to Christina, 4 August 1852.

not become too adept at drawing and therefore pose any threat to the supremacy of her brother's new pupil. Was Gabriel trying to incite rivalry between the two women? Perhaps this was intentional, as focusing on their shared artistic interests should have brought them closer together. Furthermore, to ensure his sister was left in no doubt as to the emerging love interest between himself and his new model, Gabriel continued:

> Since you went away, I have had sent me among my things from Highgate a lock of hair shorn from the beloved head of that dear, and radiant as the tresses of Aurora, a sight which may perhaps dazzle you on your return.[18]

At this time, however, it appears that Christina and Elizabeth had not yet met in person, since Gabriel describes the colour of Elizabeth's hair in detail. This would have been unnecessary if a prior meeting had taken place, as Elizabeth's copper-coloured hair would have been unforgettable.

Gabriel's language reveals his true feelings to his sister. In turn he refers to Elizabeth as 'beloved', 'that dear', 'that love' and 'a meek unconscious dove'.[19] This must have been unsettling for Christina, since until then it had been she who had received all Gabriel's attention. After Elizabeth became his pupil and love interest, not just another model, Christina found herself being side-lined, even replaced, both as her brother's model and his confidante. Her elevated position as the only Pre-Raphaelite 'Sister' was being usurped by this newcomer with the red hair. This letter from her brother would surely have wounded Christina emotionally, especially since it followed the breakdown of her own relationship and engagement to Brotherhood member James Collinson.[20]

Once she had begun serious study as Gabriel's pupil, Elizabeth began producing drawings and watercolours from her own ideas. She followed the Pre-Raphaelite style and ethic, illustrating many of the same subjects as her male colleagues, including Tennyson's *The Lady of Shalott* (1853; The Maas Gallery, London). A favourite source of inspiration was the *Minstrelsy*

18 *Correspondence*, ed. Fredeman, I, 197. Letter to Christina, 4 August 1852.

19 *Correspondence*, ed. Fredeman, I, 197. Letter to Christina, 4 August 1852.

20 Jan Marsh, *Christina Rossetti: A Literary Biography* (London: Jonathan Cape, 1994), 113.

of the Scottish Border by Walter Scott, from which she illustrated several ballads. Elizabeth also painted a self-portrait, upheld by William to be 'the most competent piece of execution that she ever produced, an excellent and graceful likeness, and truly good'.[21] She still sat for Gabriel, but her focus was on her own artistic production. Much of her work targeted the blossoming market for book illustration, including working alongside Gabriel for a volume of poetry which William Allingham intended to edit.[22]

Thus, the two women continued to work hard and pursue their own ambitions, possibly fostering an atmosphere of competition, as both wanted to succeed in the male-dominated Victorian society. Their separate paths did not cross until March 1854 when Christina received a surprise invitation to visit her elder brother and his pupil. Rather than writing directly to his sister, Gabriel added the invitation as an afterthought in a letter to William:

> Tell Christina that if she will come here on Thursday, Lizzy will be here & she can also see that Gug's emanations. I shall be glad if she will come, as I have told Lizzy she mentioned her wish to do so.[23]

From this letter it appears that Christina may have requested the meeting, rather than Elizabeth expressing a desire to meet Gabriel's sister. However, the reason for the invitation does not appear to have been social, but more of a business arrangement, since in the same letter to William a prospective volume of Christina's poetry is discussed:

> Allingham has been looking over her poems & is delighted with many of them. I am going to lend them him (trusting in her permission to do so) that he may give his opinion as to which will be the best for a volume. Lizzy will illustrate and I have no doubt we will get a publisher.[24]

21 Rossetti, 'Dante Rossetti and Elizabeth Siddal', 277.

22 *Correspondence*, ed. Fredeman, I, 332. Letter to Ford Madox Brown, 23 May 1854.

23 *Correspondence*, ed. Fredeman, I, 332. Letter to William, 28 March 1854.

24 *Correspondence*, ed. Fredeman, I, 332, Letter to William, 28 March 1854. See also Chapter 9, Laure Nermel, '"Direct and serious and heartfelt": Truth-to-nature in Elizabeth Siddal's creative agency'.

Gabriel, therefore, has assumed that despite the two never having met, both Christina and Elizabeth would meekly accept his plans for them to work together on a publication project, albeit one that would benefit them both. The meeting may not have gone entirely according to plan, as no further mention was made of the proposed volume, and as far as it is possible to establish, Elizabeth did not illustrate any of Christina's poems.

Christina's first impression of the relationship between her brother and his beloved may have inspired a poem she wrote soon afterwards:

'LISTENING' or 'TWO CHOICES'
(Christina Rossetti)

She listened like a cushat dove
That listens to its mate alone;
She listened like a cushat dove
That loves but only one.

Not fair as men would reckon fair,
Nor noble as they count the line;
Only as graceful as a bough
And tendrils of the vine
Only as noble as sweet Eve
Your ancestress and mine.

And downcast were her dovelike eyes,
And downcast was her tender cheek;
Her pulses fluttered like a dove
To hear him speak.

He chose what I had feared to choose –
(Ah, which was wiser, I or he?) –
He chose a love-warm priceless heart
And I a cold bare dignity.

He chose a life like stainless spring
That buds to summer's perfect glow;
I chose a tedious dignity
As cold as cold as snow:
He chose a garden of delights
Where still refreshing waters flow;

I chose a barren wilderness
Whose buds died years ago.[25]

The full poem, as reproduced here, was given the title 'Two Choices' by Christina. Composed in October 1854, it remained unpublished at her death. It was first published in 1896 entitled 'Listening', edited by her brother William to omit the last two stanzas. William explained his actions in his preface to *New Poems*, suggesting that the verses omitted in certain poems 'appear to [him] to represent her less well'.[26]

In the first three stanzas (the edited version), Christina appears to have taken Gabriel's use of 'dove' as a term of endearment for Elizabeth and embellished it to envisage a pair of lovebirds cooing to each other. Meek and subservient, the female hangs onto every word emanating from the male's mouth. Without the last two stanzas the poem presents a view of unity and happiness, a view which William may have thought appropriate given its inevitable biographical interpretation. With his editing hand, however, his sister's true feelings have been erased from public memory. The last two stanzas perhaps reflect Christina's regret at the choice she made in breaking off her own engagement, paired with her envy of her brother's new relationship with Elizabeth. Her pangs of jealousy seem undeniable, and her sorrow when reflecting on her own decision cuts deeply. From Christina's words, the relationship between the two women appears strained.

In April 1855, Elizabeth was introduced to the matriarch, Frances Rossetti. This was not so much a family invitation, but an announcement made in a brief note from Gabriel to his mother:

25 Packer, *Christina Rossetti*, 84–5. The shorter version (as edited by William) appears in Crump and Flowers, *Complete Poems*, 768. The full poem is also reproduced in *Christina Rossetti: Poems and Prose*, ed. Simon Humphries (Oxford: Oxford University Press, 2008), 46.

26 *New Poems by Christina Rossetti, Hitherto Unpublished or Uncollected*, ed. William Michael Rossetti (London: Macmillan and Co., 1896), xi.

Dear Mamma

I write to say I have asked Brown & his wife to accompany Guggum & me to tea at Albany Street to-morrow evening. I don't know yet whether they'll come, but write on the possibility.

Your affectionate son, G.[27]

The timing of this visit is notable. It was the day after John Ruskin had visited Gabriel, viewed Elizabeth's artistic output and made an offer of patronage.[28] Elizabeth, therefore, was now to be a lady of means, and therefore more acceptable as a prospective wife for a budding artist and poet to introduce to his mother. It is also interesting that Gabriel had invited Ford and Emma Madox Brown to join the gathering. Was this to make Elizabeth feel more comfortable, as she had formed a friendship with the Browns? Or was it to diffuse any potential conflict with the Rossetti women? The meeting was bound to be difficult since Gabriel and Elizabeth had been working together unchaperoned for some time, a situation which would have been frowned upon in middle-class Victorian society.

Although there does not appear to be any documentary evidence, Marsh suggests this visit did not go well: 'Miss Siddal […] was shy and stiff, with a silence that seemed frosty rather than dovelike'.[29] Shortly afterwards, Brown revealed in his diary that there was 'a certain coldness' in the atmosphere between Christina and her brother, 'because she and Guggums do not agree'.[30] As Marsh elaborates: 'the chill probably stemmed from Christina's inability to share her brother's high estimate of Miss Siddal's looks and talent'.[31] Was Christina jealous of Elizabeth's recent success in gaining Ruskin's patronage? Elizabeth had achieved much more success in

27 *Correspondence*, ed. Fredeman, II, 32. Letter to Frances Mary Lavinia Rossetti, 13 April 1855.

28 *Correspondence*, ed. Fredeman, II, 32. Letter to Frances Mary Lavinia Rossetti, 13 April 1855.

29 Marsh, *Christina Rossetti*, 170.

30 *The Diary of Ford Madox Brown*, ed. Virginia Surtees (New Haven, CT: Yale University Press, 1981), 155.

31 Marsh, *Christina Rossetti*, 170.

her few years within the Pre-Raphaelite circle than Christina, who at this stage had published nothing commercially.

Conversely, it may have just been awkwardness and shyness from both Elizabeth and Christina. William specifically mentions Christina's diffident nature when discussing her character traits. He also stresses her single-mindedness, which could perhaps also be read as ambition:

> Though shy, and even somewhat nervous, she was of unshaken firmness, making up her mind pretty easily in any crisis of her life, and abiding immovable. The narrow path was the only one for her, and a lion in the same path made no difference.[32]

As twenty-first century readers we have only William's character assessments of both Christina and Elizabeth. While he knew Christina intimately from childhood, he only encountered Elizabeth occasionally. William presents Christina's reserve as 'modesty', a character trait becoming of a young Victorian woman:

> In Christina's character there was great dignity tempered – or rather indeed reinforced – by modesty; and to this her bearing corresponded faithfully. I have already referred to her having been, and this from an early age, rather punctiliously polite.[33]

In Elizabeth, on the other hand, the same characteristic is seen as 'alien':

> She maintained an attitude of reserve, self-controlling and alien from approach [...] she was certainly distant. Her talk was, in my experience, scanty; slight and scattered, with some amusing turns, and little to seize hold upon – little clue to her real self or to anything determinate.[34]

William's assessment of Elizabeth's characterless persona is quite different from the picture she paints of herself in one of her few surviving letters. Writing to Gabriel from the south of France, her account of trying to obtain a letter from the post office on arrival in Nice is humorous and eloquent. She refers to the post office clerk as 'an overdone mutton-chop

32 *The Poetical Works of Christina Georgina Rossetti*, ed. William Michael Rossetti (London: Macmillan and Co., 1904), lxvii.

33 *Poetical Works*, ed. Rossetti, lxvi–ii.

34 Rossetti, 'Dante Rossetti and Elizabeth Siddal', 273–4.

stuck to a gridiron', and describes in closely observed detail the tortuous nature of the whole process.[35]

While there is no record of Elizabeth's feelings about her future sister-in-law, Christina often appears to turn to poetry to express her innermost thoughts. Many scholars have forged biographical links between the observations in her sonnet 'In an Artist's Studio' and her brother Gabriel's relationship with Elizabeth. Written in December 1856, it is most often interpreted as describing Elizabeth in complimentary terms from Gabriel's perspective as the star-crossed artist/lover who ceaselessly paints his beloved:

IN AN ARTIST'S STUDIO
(Christina Rossetti)

One face looks out from all his canvases,
One selfsame figure sits or walks or leans;
We found her hidden just behind those screens,
That mirror gave back all her loveliness.
A queen in opal or in ruby dress,
A nameless girl in freshest summer-greens,
A saint, an angel; – every canvas means
The same one meaning, neither more or less.
He feeds upon her face by day and night,
And she with true kind eyes looks back on him
Fair as the moon and joyful as the light:
Not wan with waiting, not with sorrow dim;
Not as she is, but was when hope shone bright;
Not as she is, but as she fills his dream.[36]

However, it can also be viewed from the opposite angle, that of the writer, Christina. With the lack of real friendship between the two and Elizabeth's supremacy in Gabriel's affections, it is not impossible to imagine Christina grimacing through gritted teeth, her pen held in a vice-like grip as she traced the outlines of her words across her notebook.

35 William Michael Rossetti ed., *Ruskin: Rossetti: Pre-Raphaelitism. Papers 1854–1862* (London: George Allen, 1899), 110–13.

36 *Complete Poems*, eds Crump and Flowers, 796.

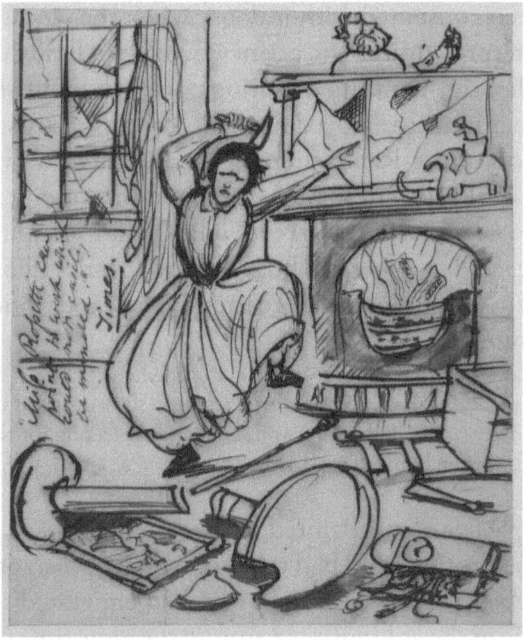

Figure 7.1. Dante Gabriel Rossetti, *Christina Georgina Rossetti (1830–1894) in a Tantrum and destroying the Contents of a Room*, 1862, Pen and brown ink and wash, 39.2 × 33.4 cm, National Trust, Wightwick Manor, Wolverhampton (NT 1287928). © National Trust Images/Derrick E. Witty.

Christina was known to have a fiery temper and was prone to exploding in fits of rage, as evidenced by Gabriel's sketch (Figure 7.1). Here he depicts his sister in the throes of a tantrum, leaping in the air, wildly waving a hammer or mallet in her right hand. A scene of utter destruction pervades the room where everything is smashed and broken. The windowpanes and mirror behind her are cracked, the curtain torn, a table and chair lie broken on the floor and the coils and cogs from the inside of a mantle clock spill out towards the viewer. It is easy to imagine Christina's feelings on her first visit to Gabriel's studio, confronted by a sea of drawings and paintings all featuring Elizabeth. Rereading Christina's words with this heightened level of emotion reveals tones of irritation, of jealousy and possibly even of anger at Elizabeth for having replaced her in Gabriel's life. If Christina had indeed been consumed with jealousy when she wrote 'In an Artist's Studio', the interpretation of the poem would be radically different.

While Christina continued writing poetry without submitting any for publication, Elizabeth enjoyed further success as an artist, participating in an exhibition of Pre-Raphaelite art organised by Brown in 1857 and held at 4 Russell Place, Fitzroy Square, London. Among the works she exhibited were *Clerk Saunders* (1857; Fitzwilliam Museum, Cambridge), which was later sold to American businessman Charles Eliot Norton. Her *Self-Portrait* (1853–4; unlocated) received high praise from the reviewer, Coventry Patmore:

> Her 'Study of a Head' is a very promising attempt, showing great care, considerable technical power, and a high, pure, and independent feeling for that much misunderstood object, the human face divine.[37]

Elizabeth's *Self-Portrait* was painted in the summer of 1853, soon after the members of the Brotherhood had made drawings of each other to send to absentee member Thomas Woolner, who had emigrated to Australia to seek his fortune in the gold rush. At around the same time Christina drew a little-known portrait of her brother William.

Although Marsh suggests Christina possessed 'little natural facility and virtually no "eye" for art', her portrait shows a reasonable amount of skill and marked similarities with the drawing Gabriel made for Woolner (Figures 7.2 and 7.3).[38] William's necktie and jacket lapels appear identical, as if both portraits were drawn from the model at the same time. Is it possible that Christina participated in the portrait exercise with her fellow Brethren? Although sketched from a different angle and technically inferior to her brother's portrait, Christina's drawing provides evidence that she had absorbed the early Pre-Raphaelite outline style and had progressed to learning shading techniques. Her acute eye for detail, present in her poetic language, ensures that almost every hair on William's head is individually defined. The drawing is clearly recognizable as William. Christina's first love was for language and poetry; therefore art may have been a less inspiring

37 Coventry Patmore, 'A Pre-Raphaelite Exhibition', *Saturday Review* 4/88 (1857), 11.
38 Marsh, *Christina Rossetti*, 128.

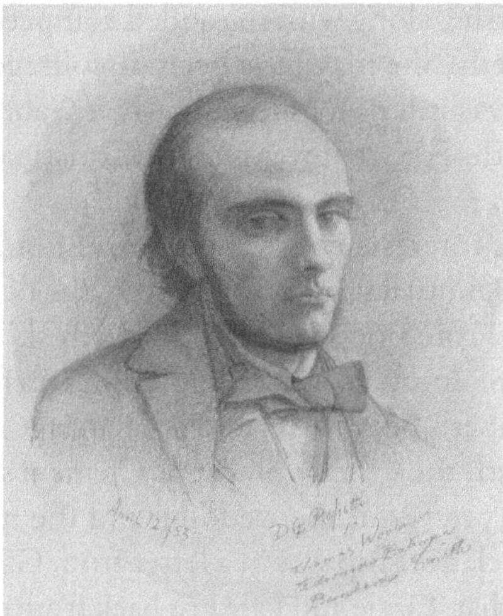

Figure 7.2. Dante Gabriel Rossetti, *William Michael Rossetti,* 1853, pencil and wash, 28.2 × 21.0 cm, National Portrait Gallery, London. NPG 5428. © National Portrait Gallery.

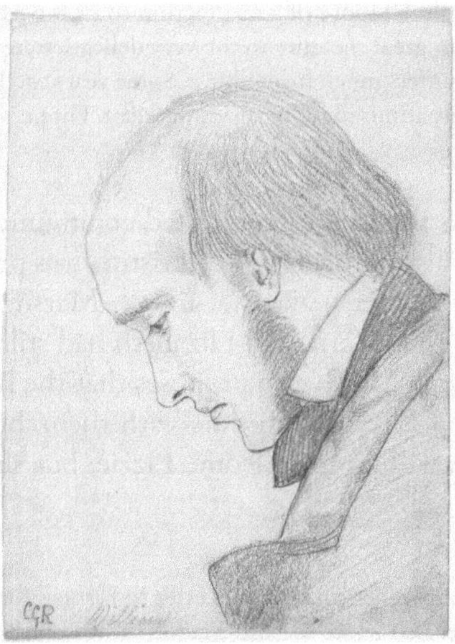

Figure 7.3. Christina Georgina Rossetti, *Portrait of William Michael Rossetti*, c. 1853, Graphite on ivory wove paper, 17.9 × 12.8 cm, Cleveland Museum of Art, Ohio, USA. Purchase from the J. H. Wade Fund 2010.462. Creative Commons Open Access.

career for her to pursue, along with the added competition from both her brother and Elizabeth. She may have been discouraged by criticism and felt that her work was inferior, especially when Gabriel had warned her not to rival Elizabeth. For whatever reason, Christina chose to focus her ambition on poetry.

Sharing similar interests in art and poetry should have created the building blocks for a mutual friendship. Instead, the two women remained distant; Christina wrote poetry while Elizabeth sketched design ideas and produced watercolours. However, circumstances forced change when Christina and Elizabeth became related by marriage on 23 May 1860, as Gabriel and Elizabeth took their vows at St Clement's Church, Hastings. Neither family was present at the wedding and the first Christina knew of her new sisterly relationship was in a letter from Gabriel to her mother heralding the news that 'Lizzie and I are just back from church'.[39] Christina's displeasure at being excluded from the ceremony was evident as she wrote to Lady Trevelyan in August 1860:

> His marriage would be more of a satisfaction to us if we had seen his bride, but owing I dare say in great measure to the very delicate state of her health, we have not yet met. She suffers much from illness. Some years ago I knew her slightly: she was then extremely admired for beauty and talent. I hope we shall be good friends some day.[40]

This letter confirms the lack of continued communication between the two women, while also showing that Christina was prepared to offer the hand of friendship to her new sister-in-law. Marsh suggests (although no source is given) that Maria said Elizabeth had still not visited her in-laws by August 1860.[41] Marsh also proposes that the Rossetti family kept inviting Gabriel and Elizabeth to dine with them, but visits were postponed: 'They were willing to welcome Lizzie, but she did not seem to

39 *Correspondence*, ed. Fredeman, II, 295. Letter to Frances Mary Lavinia Rossetti, 23 May 1860. Gabriel also wrote to Ford Madox Brown on the same day announcing the marriage.

40 *Letters*, ed. Harrison, 137. Letter to Lady Pauline Trevelyan, 17 August 1860.

41 Marsh, *Christina Rossetti*, 251.

want to know them'.[42] As previously mentioned, the first meeting with the Rossetti family had not gone well; nervousness and shyness may have played a part in the delay of facing the inevitable reunion. In addition, Elizabeth's health was inconsistent and building work was being undertaken in Chatham Place to provide more space.[43] However, it appears that family gatherings eventually did take place, as in February 1861 Christina wrote to Mary Haydon: 'My sisterinlaw [*sic*] proves an acquisition now that we know her better; before so very long I hope you will also know her'.[44] Her words suggest that several meetings had taken place by this time and that the atmosphere between the pair had become more relaxed.

Christina had also visited Gabriel and Elizabeth at the expanded accommodation at Chatham Place, as in the same letter she expressed her delight in 'how quaintly and prettily' the drawing-room had been furnished.[45] By this time Elizabeth would have been about six months pregnant, and Christina was about to become an aunt for the first time. It seems, therefore, that the imminent arrival of a new baby had a mellowing effect on the relationship between the two women. Sadly, Elizabeth's baby daughter was stillborn in the late spring of 1861 and Gabriel wrote to inform his mother of the tragedy on 2 May.[46] The joyous prospect of Christina becoming an aunt had vanished, but she seems to have empathised with her sister-in-law. Her poetry appears to express her grief at the loss of her unborn niece as 'Baby lies so fast asleep' and 'A baby's cradle with no baby in it', both published in *Sing-Song* (1872), instantly recall Elizabeth's loss:

BABY LIES SO FAST ASLEEP
(Christina Rossetti)

Baby lies so fast asleep
That we cannot wake her:

42 Marsh, *Christina Rossetti*, 253.

43 *Correspondence*, ed. Fredeman, II, 324–5. Letter to William Allingham, 1 November 1860.

44 *Letters*, ed. Harrison, 142.

45 *Letters*, ed. Harrison, 142.

46 *Correspondence*, ed. Fredeman, II, 353. Letter to Frances Mary Lavinia Rossetti, 2 May 1861.

Will the Angels clad in white
Fly from heaven to take her?

Baby lies so fast asleep
That no pain can grieve her;
Put a snowdrop in her hand
Kiss her once and leave her.[47]

Sing-Song was published as a collection of 'rhymes dedicated without permission to the baby who suggested them', noted by William to be the son of Cambridge mathematician Arthur Cayley, the brother of another of Christina's former suitors, Charles Cayley.[48] Yet the baby in the poem is clearly identified as a girl, suggesting instead that it may be a reference to Elizabeth's stillborn daughter.

There is no record of Elizabeth's own feelings on the loss of her baby, or how deeply it affected her mental health, but her friend Georgiana Burne-Jones describes how she witnessed Elizabeth rocking the empty cradle: 'we found her sitting on a low chair with the childless cradle on the floor beside her [...] she cried with a kind of soft wildness when we came in, "Hush, Ned, you'll waken it!" '[49] These words are mirrored in Christina's poem, 'A baby's cradle with no baby in it':

A BABY'S CRADLE WITH NO BABY IN IT
(Christina Rossetti)

A baby's cradle with no baby in it,
A baby's grave where autumn leaves drop sere;
The sweet soul gathered home to Paradise,
The body waiting here.[50]

47 *Complete Poems*, eds Crump and Flowers, 258.

48 *Poetical Works*, ed. Rossetti, 492.

49 Georgiana Burne-Jones, *Memorials of Edward Burne-Jones*, 2 vols (London: Macmillan & Co. Ltd, 1904), I, 222.

50 *Complete Poems*, eds Crump and Flowers, 230.

The beautiful manuscript of *Sing-Song,* which includes Christina's own sketches illustrating each verse, is held in the British Library, London.[51] This document also shows that despite her lack of artistic success, Christina continued practising her art. Eventually Arthur Hughes was chosen to produce the drawings for the final publication, referring to Christina's manuscript sketches when working on his illustrations.[52]

The change in Christina's relationship with Elizabeth may have prompted her to record her thoughts on her brother's procrastination in committing to marriage. Written in October 1861 but not published until May 1863, 'The Prince who arrived too late' forms lines 481 to 540 of the title poem in *The Princes Progress and Other Poems.* The final poem is a curious amalgamation of two halves. The meter changes between the two sections, creating a disjointed feel, but perhaps reflecting Christina's interpretation of the situation. The first 480 lines were subsequently added in 1865, before publication of the complete poem in the anthology of 1866.

THE PRINCE'S PROGRESS (excerpt)
(Christina Rossetti)

Too late for love, too late for joy,
Too late, too late!
You loiter'd on the road too long,
You trifled at the gate:
The enchanted dove upon her branch
Died without a mate;
The enchanted princess in her tower
Slept, died, behind the grate;
Her heart was starving all this while
You made it wait.

Ten years ago, five years ago,
One year ago,

51 See 'Manuscript of Sing Song, a collection of nursery rhymes by Christina Rossetti', <https://www.bl.uk/collection-items/manuscript-of-sing-song-a-collection-of-nursery-rhymes-by-christina-rossetti>, accessed 24 August 2021.

52 Christina G. Rossetti, *Sing-Song: A Nursery Rhyme Book* with 120 illustrations by Arthur Hughes (London: Macmillan and Co., 1893).

Even then you had arrived in time,
Though somewhat slow;
Then you had known her living face
Which now you cannot know:
The frozen fountain would have leap'd,
The buds gone on to blow,
The warm south wind would have awaked
To melt the snow.[53]

The poem's last stanza conveys the writer's raw emotion at the prince's (Gabriel's?) procrastination:

You should have wept her yesterday,
Wasting upon her bed:
But wherefore should you weep to-day
That she is dead?
Lo, we who love weep not to-day,
But crown her royal head.
Let be these poppies that we strew,
Your roses are too red:
Let be these poppies, not for you
Cut down and spread.[54]

This poem is often read biographically as the references to Elizabeth seem abundant. Christina again uses the symbol of a dove, while the 'enchanted princess' may refer to Ruskin's nickname for Elizabeth as 'Princess Ida' from Tennyson's 'The Princess'. The timeline of ten, five and one year roughly corresponds with Gabriel and Elizabeth's first meeting, the height of their relationship and their period of separation. Poppies represent the source of the opiate laudanum that she became addicted to. The poem also prefigures Elizabeth's death. Was Elizabeth's physical and mental health so bad by October 1861 that Christina saw her death as inevitable? Had the relationship between the sisters-in-law improved so much that Christina now blamed her brother for Elizabeth's deterioration? If the poem was indeed written biographically, Christina's frustration and

53 *Complete Poems*, eds Crump and Flowers, 102–3, lines 481–500.

54 *Complete Poems*, eds Crump and Flowers, 104, lines 531–540.

regret regarding Gabriel's continued deferment of marrying Elizabeth is evident.

Elizabeth's own comment on her marriage has often been associated with her last known drawing, said to have been produced shortly after the wedding.[55] *The Woeful Victory* (1860; The Higgins Art Gallery, Bedford) is a scene depicting the outcome of a medieval duel. The Lady turns her head away in horror as she realises she must marry the knight who has just killed her true love. Are these really Elizabeth's feelings spilling out on to paper? Was the fact that she and Gabriel were now husband and wife so distasteful to her? It seems more plausible that this was just a further exploration of the medieval theme so popular with members of the Pre-Raphaelite circle. Along with Gabriel and Burne-Jones, Elizabeth had previously explored the theme of chivalry in *Lady Affixing a Pennant to a Knight's Spear* (c. 1856; Tate, London, see Figure 9.3). The more confident handling of pencil on paper in *The Woeful Victory* seems to suggest a renewed energy and motivation for pursuing her artistic career, rather than commenting on her personal circumstances.

The relationship which appeared to be blossoming between the two women ended abruptly on 11 February 1862 when Elizabeth died from a laudanum overdose. Gabriel was distraught with grief and guilt. He collected all Elizabeth's drawings together and had them photographed, producing albums of her work which he gave to several of his friends.[56] Conversely, Marsh suggests there was 'no sign that her death caused Maria or Christina any great distress'.[57] Indeed, during the rest of that year Christina continued working hard with Gabriel on the publication of her first anthology, *Goblin Market*. Her poetic ambitions were finally realised late in life; she published several notable poem collections before succumbing to cancer in December 1894. Elizabeth, on the other hand, did not fulfil her potential as an artist or poet. What would she have achieved had she

55 See, for example, Lucinda Hawksley, *Lizzie Siddal: The Tragedy of a Pre-Raphaelite Supermodel* (London: André Deutsch (Carlton Publishing), 2004), 164. After detailing the circumstances leading up to their marriage, Hawksley describes *The Woeful Victory* as being 'aptly named'.

56 See, for example, the extant pages in the Photographic Portfolio, *Ashmolean Museum*, Oxford, Item WA1977.355.

57 Marsh, *Christina Rossetti*, 280.

lived into old age? Would her reputation in the twenty-first century have eclipsed that of Christina?

Conversely, Elizabeth's poetry was unknown during her lifetime, existing only in manuscript form until 1899, when William edited eight poems for inclusion in *Ruskin, Rossetti, Pre-Raphaelitism*.[58] Christina had previously offered to include a selection of Elizabeth's poems as a tribute in *The Princes Progress and Other Poems*, published several years after Elizabeth's death. Writing to Gabriel on 1 February 1865, she asked: 'I wonder if possibly you might ever see fit to let some of dear Lizzie's verses come out in a volume of mine; distinguished, I need not say, as hers: Such a combination would be very dear to me'.[59] On reading the verses, however, Christina declared: 'How full of beauty they are, but how painful: – how they bring poor Lizzie herself before one, with her voice, face and manner'.[60] The proposed inclusion therefore failed to materialise, but Christina's words suggest her posthumous memories of Elizabeth were kind and loving, without a hint of rivalry.

Elizabeth's poetry may have seemed utterly tragic to those reading it in the aftermath of her death, but Christina herself wrote many poems of a similar poignant nature:

LOVE LIES BLEEDING
(Christina Rossetti)

Love that is dead and buried, yesterday
Out of his grave rose up before my face,
No recognition in his look, no trace
Of memory in his eyes dust-dimmed and grey.
While I, remembering, found no word to say,
But felt my quickened heart leap in its place;
Caught afterglow thrown back from long set days,
Caught echoes of all music passed away.

58 Rossetti, *Ruskin: Rossetti: Pre-Raphaelitism*, 150–6.

59 Anthony H. Harrison, ed., *The Letters of Christina Rossetti*, 4 vols (Charlottesville: University Press of Virginia, 1997–2004), I, 224. Letter to Dante Gabriel Rossetti, 1 February 1865.

60 Harrison, *Letters*, I, 252. Letter to Dante Gabriel Rossetti, 6 February 1865.

Was this indeed to meet? – I mind me yet
In youth we met when hope and love were quick,
We parted with hope dead, but love alive:
I mind me how we parted then heart sick,
Remembering, loving, hopeless, weak to strive: –
Was this to meet? Not so, we have not met.[61]

Focusing on love and loss, Christina's words resonate with the transience of love. She tells how Love may cause one's heart to race and music to fill one's senses. Yet Love is fickle and easily turns to loss, leaving only memories. These sentiments are comparable with many of Elizabeth's poems, including the first stanza of 'Dead Love':

Oh never weep for love that is dead
Since love is seldom true,
But changes his fashion from blue to red,
From brightest red to blue,
And love was born to an early death
And is so seldom true.[62]

Elizabeth's language echoes her painterly eye through her colourful choice of words. For her, Love fluctuates from the fiery heat of red to the icy cold of blue. Love's transience is epitomised by Elizabeth's considered use of the word 'fashion'. Notably both narrate from the female perspective, accepting the inevitability of Love's death. Love itself is represented as the male transgressor.

As with Christina's poetry, William edited most of Elizabeth's verses before publication, adding titles which she had seldom included, as well as correcting and inserting punctuation where he deemed it necessary. It was not until 2018, when Serena Trowbridge published *My Ladys Soul*, that Elizabeth's poetry was presented directly from her own words on handwritten manuscripts. Trowbridge offers a detailed analysis of the manuscripts, highlighting William's editing hand and identifying differences

61 *Complete Poems*, eds Crump and Flowers, 204.

62 *My Ladys Soul: The Poems of Elizabeth Eleanor Siddall*, ed. Serena Trowbridge (Brighton: Victorian Secrets Ltd, 2018), 76.

between versions. Subsequently a further publication, *The Poems of Elizabeth Siddal in Context* by Anne Woolley, presents Elizabeth's work in the context of Victorian culture, particularly in terms of the 'duality of love'.[63] Woolley contrasts the physical love found on earth with the spiritual love imagined to exist in heaven. Evidence of this duality is found not only in Elizabeth's work, but also in Christina's, perhaps demonstrating the underlying synergy between their work.

Did the initial rivalry between Christina and Elizabeth help them to achieve the success they desired? Both women appear to have aspired to the same ambition – to become successful in the sister arts of poetry and painting. Their mentor Gabriel provided an excellent role model of what could be achieved. While Christina's success came through painting with words, words provided Elizabeth with the inspiration for her own art, as well as the paintings she modelled for. Perhaps neither really achieved their true ambition as an artist or poet.

Today, Christina is considered one of the greatest poets of the Victorian era. Her poems are well known: 'Remember' (1849) is frequently recited at funeral services; 'A Christmas Carol' ('In the Bleak Mid-Winter', first published 1872) was set to music by Gustav Holst and is a Christmas favourite, while new editions of *Goblin Market* and *The Prince's Progress* are still being published and are now available as eBooks. *The Complete Poems of Christina Rossetti* contains over seven hundred items, ranging from her youthful thoughts to her mature observations, including a large number of poems which remained unpublished until after her death.[64] Conversely, Christina's art has been forgotten. Her drawings are only to be found in private collections or as sketches on manuscripts hidden in the depths of archives.

As a model, Elizabeth lives on in Millais's painting *Ophelia* (1851–2) one of Tate's most popular artworks. The story of how she caught pneumonia after posing for the painting in a bath of water is often retold. Elizabeth is consequently remembered as a model and muse, kept in the public

63 See Anne Woolley, *The Poems of Elizabeth Siddal in Context* (Manchester: Manchester University Press, 2021), Chapter 1.

64 Crump and Flowers, *Complete Poems*.

consciousness by tales of her discovery in a bonnet shop, her untimely death from an overdose of laudanum and the exhumation of her coffin for Gabriel to retrieve the manuscript copy of his poetry, so lovingly placed by her cheek before burial. However, as an artist Elizabeth produced over one hundred drawings and watercolours and wrote at least sixteen poems. Her contribution to the visual development of Pre-Raphaelite art has been overlooked yet is extremely significant.[65] Interest in her career is now blossoming, and she is beginning to regain her rightful place as an important Pre-Raphaelite artist and poet.

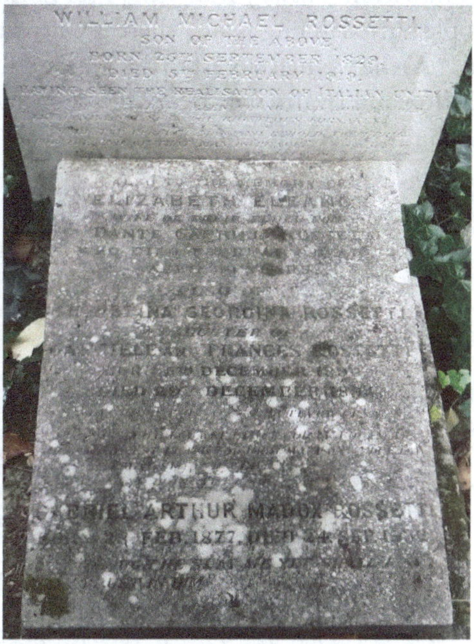

Figure 7.4. Simon Edwards Esq. *Grave of Christina Rossetti [and Elizabeth Rossetti]*, 1 July 2020, Photograph © Simon Edwards Esq. Creative Commons Attribution – Share Alike 4.0 International Licence.

65 Glenda Youde, doctoral thesis 'Beyond *Ophelia*: The Artistic Legacy of Elizabeth Eleanor Rossetti (née Siddall)', University of York, 2022.

In life, the two sisters-in-law faced the same struggles, as independent and ambitious rivals, keen to forge their own careers in an age when Victorian society favoured the 'Angel of the House'. They chose separate creative paths – Christina chose poetry while Elizabeth focused on art – choices which may have helped to diminish the initial rivalry. However difficult their relationship in life, in death Christina and Elizabeth now rest in peace together. The Rossetti grave (Figure 7.4) remains one of the most popular with visitors to Highgate Cemetery, with Elizabeth attracting more attention than Christina, undoubtedly due to the public's ghoulish interest in her exhumation. *History Magazine* lists Elizabeth among the most notable people buried in Highgate, whereas Christina does not even receive a mention.[66] As the women closest to the heart of the Pre-Raphaelite circle, in life ambition and rivalry may have impeded the development of a close friendship, but in death they are inseparable.

Bibliography

Burne-Jones, Georgiana, *Memorials of Edward Burne-Jones*, 2 vols (London: Macmillan & Co. Ltd, 1904).

Crump, R. W. ed., Notes and Introduction by Betty S. Flowers, *Christina Rossetti: The Complete Poems* (London: Penguin Books, 2005).

Fredeman, William E. ed., *The Correspondence of Dante Gabriel Rossetti*, 10 vols (Cambridge: D. S. Brewer, 2002–15).

Harrison, Anthony H., ed., *The Letters of Christina Rossetti*, 4 vols (Charlottesville: University Press of Virginia, 1997–2004).

Hawksley, Lucinda, *Lizzie Siddal: The Tragedy of a Pre-Raphaelite Supermodel* (London: André Deutsch (Carlton Publishing), 2004).

Humphries, Simon, ed., *Christina Rossetti: Poems and Prose* (Oxford: Oxford University Press, 2008).

66 Ben Johnson, 'Highgate Cemetery', *History Magazine*, <https://www.historic-uk.com/HistoryMagazine/DestinationsUK/Highgate-Cemetery/>, accessed 13 July 2021.

Hunt, William Holman, *Pre-Raphaelitism and the Pre-Raphaelite Brotherhood*, 2 vols (London: Macmillan, 1905).

Johnson, Ben, 'Highgate Cemetery', *History Magazine*, <https://www.historic-uk.com/HistoryMagazine/DestinationsUK/Highgate-Cemetery/>, accessed 13 July 2021.

'Manuscript of Sing Song, a Collection of Nursery Rhymes by Christina Rossetti', <https://www.bl.uk/collection-items/manuscript-of-sing-song-a-collection-of-nursery-rhymes-by-christina-rossetti>, accessed 24 August 2021.

Marsh, Jan, *The Legend of Elizabeth Siddal* (London: Quartet Books, 2010 [1989]).

——, *Christina Rossetti: A Literary Biography* (London: Jonathan Cape, 1994).

Packer, Lona Mosk, *Christina Rossetti* (Cambridge: Cambridge University Press, 1963).

Patmore, Coventry, 'A Pre-Raphaelite Exhibition', *Saturday Review* 4/88 (1857), 11–12.

——, *The Angel in the House* (London: Cassell & Company Ltd, 1887 [1854]).

Photographic Portfolio, Ashmolean Museum, Oxford, Item WA1977.355.

'Pre-Raphaelite Journal, *The Germ*' (C.59.c.19), *British Library*, <https://www.bl.uk/collection-items/pre-raphaelite-journal-the-germ>, accessed 31 May 2021.

Rossetti, Christina, *Goblin Market and Other Poems* (Cambridge and London, Macmillan and Co., 1862).

——, *Sing-Song: A Nursery Rhyme Book with One Hundred and Twenty Illustrations by Arthur Hughes* (London: Macmillan and Co., 1893).

Rossetti, William Michael, ed., *New Poems by Christina Rossetti, Hitherto Unpublished or Uncollected* (London: Macmillan and Co., 1896).

——, ed., *Ruskin: Rossetti: Pre-Raphaelitism. Papers 1854–1862* (London: George Allen, 1899).

——, 'Dante Rossetti and Elizabeth Siddal', *The Burlington Magazine for Connoisseurs* 1/3 (1903), 273–95.

——, ed., *The Poetical Works of Christina Georgina Rossetti* (London: Macmillan and Co., 1904).

Sheffield Telegraph, 28 February 1862, 'The Death of Mrs D. G. Rossetta [*sic*]', cited in Marsh, Jan, *The Legend of Elizabeth Siddal* (London: Quartet Books, 2010 [1989]), 157–8.

Surtees, Virginia, *The Diary of Ford Madox Brown* (New Haven, CT: Yale University Press, 1981).

Trowbridge, Serena, ed., *My Ladys Soul: The Poems of Elizabeth Eleanor Siddall* (Brighton: Victorian Secrets Ltd, 2018).

'Verses/by Christina G. Rossetti, Dedicated to Her Mother', *Harry Ransom Center*, The University of Texas at Austin, BK_PR_5237_V4_1847_Copy3_Hanley_001, <https://hrc.contentdm.oclc.org/digital/collection/p15878coll35/id/1916/rec/1>, accessed 31 May 2021.

Woolley, Anne, *The Poems of Elizabeth Siddal in Context* (Manchester: Manchester University Press, 2021).

CAREY GIBBONS

8 'The Result of an Experiment': Evelyn De Morgan and Automatic Writing

ABSTRACT

The Pre-Raphaelite painter Evelyn De Morgan and her husband, the ceramicist and novelist William De Morgan, anonymously published a collection of over 200 of their automatic writing scripts in 1909 under the title *The Result of an Experiment*. Although connections have been made between the Spiritualist-influenced ideas in the De Morgans' writings and the allegorical depiction of spiritual evolution found in many of Evelyn De Morgan's paintings, a closer analysis of the practice of automatic writing is needed to fully understand the link between the messages and the shifting meanings in De Morgan's paintings. The idea of an other-directed, expansive and receptive human body plays against the notion of a body that is dispersed or disrupted in De Morgan's work, reflecting the contemporary tension between the belief that automatic writings were produced through an external spirit agency and the belief that the writings were merely the product of unpredictable, shifting relations of consciousness and control within the self.

* * * * *

The second half of the nineteenth century saw a rising interest in Spiritualism, which involved a belief that the spirits of the dead can communicate with the living through various forms, including séances, table rapping and automatic writing.[1] Although the Pre-Raphaelites have not

1 Useful sources on Spiritualism in Victorian England include Janet Oppenheim, *The Other World: Spiritualism and Psychical Research in England, 1850–1914* (Cambridge: Cambridge University Press, 1985); Roger Luckhurst, *The Invention of Telepathy: 1870–1901* (Oxford: Oxford University Press, 2002); Tatiana Kontou and Sarah Willburn, eds, *The Ashgate Research Companion to Nineteenth-Century Spiritualism and the Occult* (London: Routledge, 2012); Tatiana Kontou, *Women and the Victorian Occult* (London: Routledge, 2015); Alex Owen, *The Darkened Room: Women, Power, and Spiritualism in Late Victorian England* (Chicago: University of Chicago Press, 2004); Alison Winter, *Mesmerized: Powers of Mind in Victorian Britain* (Chicago and London: University of Chicago Press,

traditionally been discussed in relation to Spiritualism, J. B. Bullen has examined Dante Gabriel Rossetti's interest in the spirit world, which was probably initiated by encounters with the artist Mary Anna Howitt, who had been a pupil with Rossetti at Sass's art school and went on to become known for her work as a spirit-drawing medium.[2] After attending public spiritualist sessions, Rossetti began regularly frequenting private séances before organising his own séances in 1865, with the clear intention, as William Michael Rossetti states, of coming 'into communication […] with his wife's [Elizabeth Siddall's] spirit'.[3] According to J. B. Bullen and Rosalind White, these séances 'attracted a number of Pre-Raphaelite artists, their friends, and family members'.[4]

The lives and careers of Evelyn De Morgan and her husband, the ceramicist and novelist William De Morgan, provide further evidence of the Pre-Raphaelites' engagement with Spiritualism. The De Morgans anonymously published a collection of over 200 automatic scripts in 1909 under the title *The Result of an Experiment*. They followed the typical practice of automatic writing, which involved holding a pencil in hand and allowing oneself to become a spiritualist medium, leading to the production of

1998); and Richard Noakes, *Physics and Psychics: The Occult and the Sciences in Modern Britain* (Cambridge: Cambridge University Press, 2019).

2 J. B. Bullen provides an overview of Rossetti's encounters with Spiritualism in 'Raising the Dead: Dante Gabriel Rossetti's "Willowwood" Sonnets', in Matthew Bevis, ed., *The Oxford Handbook of Victorian Poetry* (Oxford: Oxford University Press, 2013), 429–44.

3 William Michael Rossetti, quoted in Helen Rossetti Angeli, *Dante Gabriel Rossetti. His Friends and Enemies* (London: Hamish Hamilton, 1949), 208. Bullen, 'Raising the Dead', 432–3.

4 J. B. Bullen and Rosalind White, 'Communication with the Dead: The Séance Diary of W. M. Rossetti', *The Journal of Pre-Raphaelite Studies* 29 (Fall 2020), 5. William Michael Rossetti's séance diary is currently located in the Angeli-Dennis Collection, Rare Books and Special Collections, University of British Columbia, RBSC-ARC-1009. It is simply entitled 'Memoranda by himself' and records twenty spiritualist séances that took place between 1865 and 1868. A published version of the diary is included in J. B. Bullen, Rosalind White, and Lenore A. Beaky, eds, *Pre-Raphaelites in the Spirit World: The Séance Diary of William Michael Rossetti* (Oxford: Peter Lang, 2022).

writings involuntarily. The writings are believed to have commenced in the 1880s, and both the lengthy period of experimentation and the act of publishing the scripts indicates the importance that the De Morgans attached to them. Anna Maria Wilhelmina Stirling, Evelyn's sister and the biographer of the De Morgans, describes their experience with the practice, noting that 'to the self-constituted mediums it seemed that an influence external to their consciousness evolved every phrase'.[5] Although there is little archival material and primary source evidence about Evelyn's life and work, her acquaintance with the De Morgan family, particularly with William's mother, Sophia De Morgan, an author and Spiritualist, must have contributed to her interest in Spiritualism.[6] Both Sophia's *From Matter to Spirit* (1863) and Evelyn and William's *The Result of an Experiment* adapt to Spiritualism some of the ideas of the eighteenth-century Swedish mystic Emanuel Swedenborg, including the notion of spiritual development and the correspondence between the natural and supernatural realms.

It is also possible that Evelyn was interested in Spiritualism before meeting the De Morgan family. Verses written by her as a child in her exercise book indicate a clear fascination with the supernatural from an early age:

> Hail! Hail! Hail! Hail!
> Thou mighty land
> Where enchantment reigns
> O'er an unearthly band.[7]

5 Anna Maria Wilhelmina Stirling, *William De Morgan and his Wife* (New York: Henry Holt & Co., 1922), 355.

6 In order to distinguish between the different De Morgans discussed and avoid any confusion, I will subsequently be referring to them by their first names. Evelyn left behind no adult notebooks or diaries, and only a few scattered letters survive. The De Morgan Foundation owns childhood notebooks and a teenage diary that belonged to Evelyn. The archives of Wightwick Manor, Wolverhampton, contains a small sketchbook (10 × 15.5 cm) (c. 1877) consisting of approximately 40 leaves, almost all covered with notes and sketches.

7 Mary Evelyn Pickering, December 1868. DMF_MS_006, De Morgan Collection Archive, De Morgan Foundation, London.

Elise Lawton Smith and Judy Oberhausen have observed the relationship between the Spiritualist-influenced ideas in Evelyn and William's automatic writings and the allegorical depiction of spiritual evolution found in many of Evelyn's paintings.[8] Although these scholars' contributions are essential to understanding De Morgan's work, a closer analysis of the process of automatic writing and the notions of the self that developed from the practice is needed in order to fully understand the link between the writings and the layers of meaning within De Morgan's paintings. De Morgan's works reflect the tension between the belief that automatic writings were produced through an external spirit agency, and assertions that the writings were merely the product of unpredictable, shifting relations of consciousness and control within the self. The transmission of messages is never visualised as consistently clear or seamless, and the idea of an expansive, outward-looking and receptive self continually plays against the notion of a self that is unstable and incoherent, with the potential for disruption and dispersion.

Medea

According to Stirling, each evening the De Morgans set aside a quiet time after dinner to practise automatic writing with only a pencil and a sheet of paper.[9] One would place a hand upon the wrist of the other to assist with the transmission. Initially no markings or only meaningless scribbles and scrawls resulted, but as they continued, words began to appear, followed by broken sentences. After months of practicing and persevering, the writings became more legible. The success or legibility of automatic writing experiments was understood to be dependent not only on the

8 Elise Lawton Smith, *Evelyn Pickering De Morgan and the Allegorical Body* (Madison, NJ: Fairleigh Dickinson University Press, 2002). Judy Oberhausen, 'Evelyn De Morgan and Spiritualism', in Catherine Gordon, ed., *Evelyn De Morgan: Oil Paintings* (London: De Morgan Foundation, 1996), 33–52.

9 Stirling, *William De Morgan and his Wife*, 355–6.

practice and perseverance of the medium, but also correlative to the spiritual development of the medium, the identity and force of personality of the controlling spirit and the overall level of correspondence between medium and spirit.

The diverse assemblage of patterns and motifs in Evelyn's *Medea* (1889; Figure 8.1) functions as a kind of metaphor for the results of an automatic writing experiment. Alternating red and blue circular forms appear along the archway, encircled floral forms repeat on the column friezes, a swirling motif is replicated on the stairway and the opus sectile-style floor includes alternating cream and black rectangles and squares. Although the patterns provide a sense of consistency and order within the composition, this is thwarted by the presence of variation and irregularity. For example, the composition contains a profusion of varying types and shades of marble,

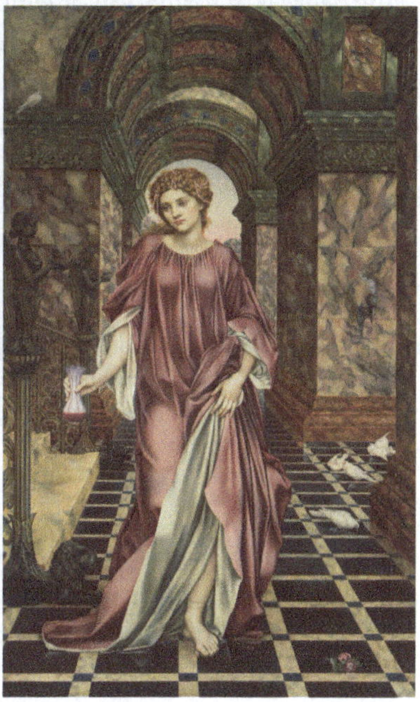

Figure 8.1. Evelyn De Morgan, *Medea*, 1889, Oil on canvas, 148 × 88 cm, Williamson Art Gallery and Museum, Birkenhead. Image © Williamson Art Gallery and Museum, Birkenhead.

a metamorphic rock containing irregularly coloured markings due to the presence of impurities. The regularity of the grid-like floor is counteracted by the marble contained within the structure, with shades of brown, orange, cream and grey blending and fading into one another. Additionally, Medea's carefully constructed hairstyle, consisting of interwoven pearls and braids, plays against the loose strands of hair floating down her neck. The geometry and order within the space, indicated not only by repeating motifs but also by the prominence of edges and borders with crisp, straight vertical and horizontal lines, and the central placement of Medea underneath an arch with columns on either side, is even more apparent in Evelyn's chalk study for the painting (c. 1889; Figure 8.2), suggesting that Evelyn envisioned the painting in terms of an underlying structured system upon which less predictable organic, fluid patterns and forms could be added as contrasting elements. The scene is particularly resonant with the production of automatic scripts with varying degrees of formation or legibility, with order and clarity continually challenged by the potential for irregularity.

The painting incorporates a wide range of materials, including marble, bronze sculpture, white-feathered doves, roses, pearl hair ornaments, smoke emanating from a wall sconce, Medea's lustrous burgundy robe, a glass vial containing liquid poison and Medea's soft, smooth flesh. May Morris might have had the painting in mind when commenting on the attention to detail and texture in Evelyn's work:

> Her pictures have an epic quality and are spacious in conception, while [in her later work] showing an almost exaggerated insistence on decorative detail. They are remarkable for the beauty of drapery design, for drawing vigorous and delicate and for sumptuous colour, for great enjoyment of textures.[10]

Isabel McAllister similarly observed in *The Studio*: 'The distinguishing features of her art were her fine spiritual vision, strong imagination, good composition, and a delight in sumptuous colour, rich textures and draperies'.[11] *Art Journal* specifically noted Evelyn's 'profusion of strange

10 May Morris, quoted in Stirling, *William De Morgan and his Wife*, 192.

11 Isabel McAllister, 'In Memoriam: Evelyn De Morgan', *The Studio* 79/324 (March 1920), 28.

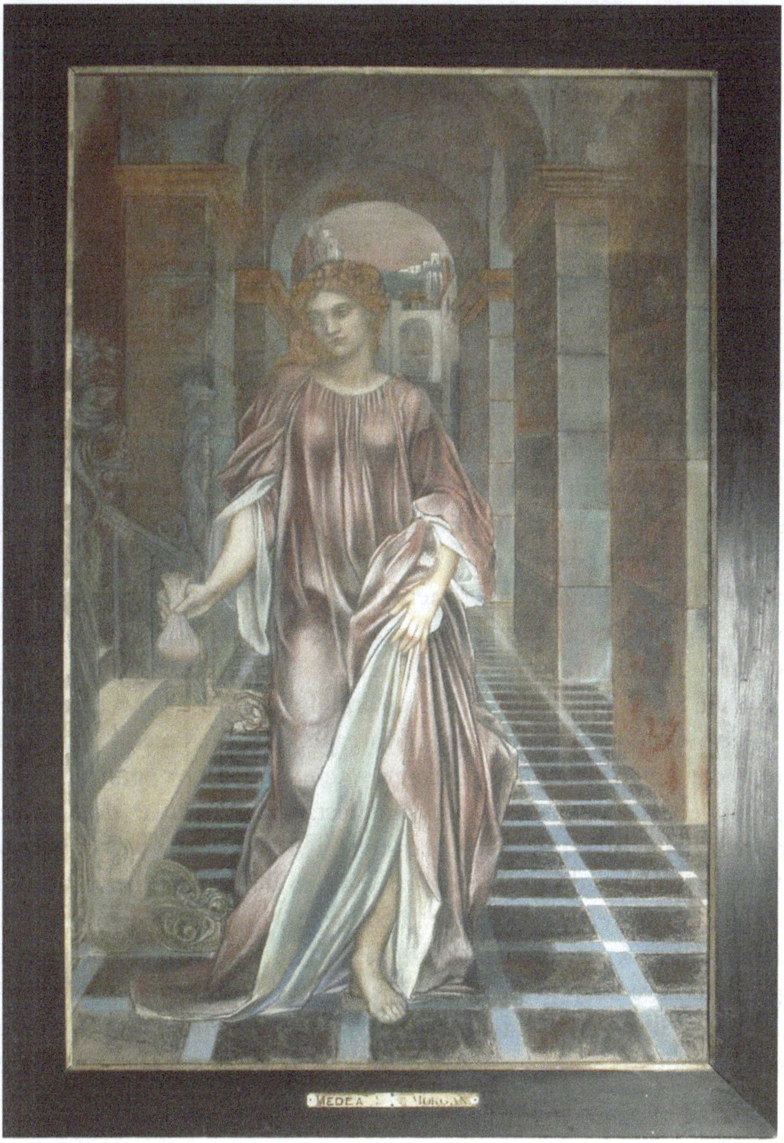

Figure 8.2. Evelyn De Morgan, *Medea*, c. 1889, Pastel on paper, 149.9 × 88.9 cm, Wightwick Manor, West Midlands. Wightwick Manor © National Trust / Sophia Farley and Claire Reeves

[...] detail' in *Medea*.[12] In addition to suggesting Evelyn's interest in the interplay among materials with varying compositions, densities, textures, shapes and colours, the inclusion of the marble, roses, smoke rising into the air and poison, a life-altering and potentially lethal substance, reflect her preoccupation with processes of transition and fluctuation. Despite this, there are consistencies within the composition that provide reassurance and order. Shades of colour are replicated; for example, the poison, the robe and the roses are similar in hue. In addition, the viewer's eye moves diagonally from the single white dove perched near the archway to the group of doves congregating near the marble column. The interplay between consistency and variation forms a parallel with the coherent and incoherent messages produced through automatic writing, with the recognition that legibility exists in varying degrees and depends on a variety of factors and influences beyond one's control. The contrast between the development of legibility and the randomness, sudden movement and intensity of forces beyond one's own will power is described in Ida Ellis's account of one medium's experiment in *Planchette and Automatic Writing* (1904). The medium, writing with a planchette, a flat piece of wood, feels 'a stiffening or contraction in the forearm', and 'a gentle electric current [...] to the finger tips', followed by 'up and down strokes' of the pencil.[13]

Automatic writing involved an interplay between passive and active behaviour, which also finds visual equivalents in Evelyn's painting. Evelyn depicts Medea as caught in a web of circumstances rather than simply an evil sorceress as she had traditionally been portrayed. Medea had become Jason's wife after she helped him capture the golden fleece from her father, and after being betrayed by Jason, she killed Jason's new wife Glauce, Glauce's father and her own two sons that she had by Jason. Evelyn's characterisation appears to have been inspired by that of Ovid in *Heroides XII* (c. 25–16 BCE) and William Morris in *The Life and Death of Jason* (1867), who both portray Medea as a woman of intense love and suffering. Her punishment

12 Claude Phillips, 'The Summer Exhibitions at Home and Abroad', *Art Journal* 52 (June 1890), 166.

13 Ida Ellis, *Planchette and Automatic Writing* (Blackpool: The Ellis Family, Promenade, 1904), 10. Planchettes could be used to facilitate writing.

of Glauce, by sending her a dress and golden coronet covered in poison, is lacking the rage and vengeance often associated with Medea. Morris's poem was quoted in the New Gallery catalogue when *Medea* was first exhibited and makes a statement about her sorrow, presenting her as a tormented soul:

> Day by day she saw the happy time fade fast away;
> And as she fell from out that happiness
> Again she grew to be the Sorceress,
> Worker of fearful things as once she was.[14]

Reviews of the painting noted the uncharacteristic depiction of Medea, with one reviewer observing the lack of ferocity in Medea's face:

> Mrs. Evelyn De Morgan's 'Medea' is a little hard and formal. It is beautiful, and the splendid marble arches and floor – green, blue, purple, and black – are painted with the most scrupulous conscientiousness, and the figure of Medea is finely drawn; her sumptuous red robes are faultless, and the whole thing calculated to win respect and admiration; but no one can accept this pensive young lady as Medea. It is a pretty and rather sad face, but with no potentiality of fierce passion in it.[15]

The pearls in Medea's hair contribute to the portrayal of Medea as a sympathetic figure, as pearls have traditionally symbolised tears. Additionally, the container of poison is held away from Medea, and she looks down and beyond it while her exposed leg and feet seem to express a slight vulnerability, challenging the notion that she is actively engaging in cruel behaviour. One could interpret her state as one of reluctance or compulsion, mirroring the compulsion felt by mediums engaging in automatic writing who lacked conscious control over their activities. One medium describes the feeling as follows:

> My right arm was seized with a convulsive tremor, and though then in a 'positive condition' it refused obedience to my will [...] a pencil and paper were lying on the table. *The pencil came into my hand*: my fingers were clenched on it! An unseen iron grasp compressed the tendons of my arm: my hand was flung violently forward on

14 Patricia Yates, 'Evelyn De Morgan's Use of Literary Sources in her Paintings', in Gordon, *Evelyn De Morgan*, 58.

15 'London Picture Exhibitions', *Birmingham Daily Post* (30 April 1890), 4.

> the paper, and I wrote *meaning* sentences, without any intention, or knowing what they were to be.[16]

This lack of control is echoed in instruction manuals on automatic writing, and the importance of being in a passive frame of mind in order to receive messages is emphasised:

> To develop this power may take a few weeks. Some persons develop sooner than others. It is the best to sit about twice a week. Everything should be quiet, and the mind kept passive. In some instances the spirit communicating has given information on various points, places, and things that were altogether unknown to the medium.[17]

Similarly, Ida Ellis acknowledges how a passive condition can welcome spirits but ultimately lead to the weakening of will power:

> During the condition of passivity, the floodgates are open as it were, to all comers, and the hand is used by the first forcible entity which comes along, whether it be good, bad, or indifferent, but the nervous system of the operator, is so fully drawn upon under these conditions, that it is likely to receive damage by such close contact with powerful occult forces not altogether desirable, yet having sufficient sympathy, to enable such force to make use of the operator's system. When this is the case, the after effects of automatic writing will be decidedly unpleasant, much lassitude and nervous depression being felt, to say nothing of the proportionately weakened will power, according to the time thus spent, and yet the results, so far as the writing itself is concerned, may be varied and interesting, if rambling and inconsistent, in dealing with a subject.[18]

The experience of the medium was not entirely passive, however. The belief that automatic writing could be improved with increased spiritual development, practice and perseverance points to the possibility of obtaining some active control over the production of legibility. Additionally, Ellis states that when the mind is passive, the writings can be full of interest.[19]

16 John S. Adams, *Answers to Seventeen Objections Against Spiritual Intercourse and Inquiries Relating to the Manifestations of the Present Time* (New York: Fowlers and Wells, 1853), 11.

17 Alexander Verner, *Table Rapping and Automatic Writing* (Bolton, 1903), 15.

18 Ellis, *Planchette and Automatic Writing*, 25–6.

19 Ellis, *Planchette and Automatic Writing*, 25.

Writings were also understood to emerge after concentrating the mind. Although these writings were typically less rambling, one needed to be aware that the controlling entity might in fact be the medium's higher self rather than a spiritual agency.[20] Ellis also reminds the reader of the willpower needed to make use of the writing experiments:

> Neither planchette nor automatic writing can infallibly tell what the future holds for anyone. The utmost that can be done in this way, is to point out the possibilities, probabilities, opportunities, and openings likely to arise [...] for the rest, it depends upon the will of each individual concerned as to what use shall be made of such opportunity, or advantage taken of such warning; or whether circumstances shall be allowed to guide the individual instead of being guided.[21]

Furthermore, the messages in *The Result of an Experiment* continually assert the importance of the Will or volition of the medium in order to secure everlasting life. The spirits instruct Evelyn and William to 'work in faith and hope' in order to develop spiritually and break the chain that binds one on earth.[22]

Evelyn's sister acknowledges that the ideas suggested by the automatic scripts may have made such a deep impression on Evelyn and William because they were a 'reflex of their own mentality'.[23] This observation reflects a larger debate that existed as to whether automatic writings were actually produced through an external spirit agency or whether they were merely the product of the unconscious mind. The state experienced during automatic writing was often compared by mediums to a dream state or condition of a passive listener in half-sleep with no conscious control. In *From Matter to Spirit*, Sophia De Morgan acknowledges the potential for automatic writing to be merely a product of the unconscious:

> When involuntary writing is first seen in imperfect mediums, unaccompanied by its more striking allied forms of manifestation, rapping, moving furniture, &c., it

20 Ellis, *Planchette and Automatic Writing*, 26.
21 Ellis, *Planchette and Automatic Writing*, 12.
22 [De Morgan], *The Result of an Experiment* (London: Simpkin, Marshall, Hamilton, Kent, & Co., 1909), 25.
23 Stirling, *William De Morgan and his Wife*, 356.

> is generally thought to be the result either of an uncontrolled self-delusive imagination, or of some undeveloped faculty in the mental nature of the writer akin to that described by some physiologists as unconscious cerebration, or an action carried on in the brain without the knowledge of the mind.[24]

Frederic William Henry Myers, one of the founders of the Society for Psychical Research who experimented with and wrote extensively about the practice of automatic writing, echoes Sophia's belief in its relation to the unconscious, stating, 'Automatic writing in its simplest form is merely a variety of the tricks of unconscious action to which, in excited moments, we are all of us prone'.[25]

Sceptics of Spiritualism, such as the prominent British physiologist William B. Carpenter, held no belief in the supernatural, declaring that automatic writing could be explained by 'unconscious cerebration', or the work of the 'under-stratum' of the mind.[26] Carpenter also argued that much of our mental work was done without consciousness or involvement of the Will, while acknowledging the dynamic, ongoing coordination between mind force, nerve force and motor force even in the most volitional acts.[27] Many other nineteenth-century scientific thinkers posed the unconscious as part of a system in which automatic or involuntary behaviour was intertwined with conscious activity. As Jonathan Miller has observed, there was an increasing emphasis on the importance of the unconscious, as numerous psychologists saw the unconscious as actively generating the processes which are integral to memory, perception and behaviour.[28]

24 [Sophia De Morgan], *From Matter to Spirit. The Result of Ten Years' Experience in Spirit Manifestations. Intended as a Guide to Enquirers* (London: Longman, Green, Longman, Roberts, & Green, 1863), 29–30.

25 Frederic William Henry Myers, 'Automatic Writing, or the Rationale of Planchette', *Contemporary Review* 47 (1885), 235.

26 William Benjamin Carpenter, *Mesmerism, Spiritualism, etc.: Historically & Scientifically Considered: Being Two Lectures Delivered at the London Institution* (London: Longmans, Green & Co. 1877), 139–43.

27 William Benjamin Carpenter, *Principles of Human Physiology* (London: John Churchill, 1855), 552–5, 608–9.

28 Jonathan Miller, 'Going Unconscious', in Robert B. Silvers, *Hidden Histories of Science* (London: Granta, 1997), 1–35.

Myers published numerous papers in the 1880s and 1890s, culminating in the posthumously published book *Human Personality and Its Survival of Bodily Death* (1903).[29] In describing messages which come to the automatist as though from without himself in this publication, Myers asserts that 'their apparent externality does not prove that they have not originated in the submerged strata of his own mind', and 'in most cases' this is what occurs.[30] Myers uses the notion of the 'subliminal self' as a 'limiting and rational hypothesis'.[31] Although communication from the subliminal self and spirit communication seem like conflicting ideas, Myers believes they give support to rather than exclude the other. Myers states: 'If our incarnate spirits can act thus in at least apparent independence of the fleshy body, the presumption is strong that other spirits may exist independently of the body, and may affect us in similar manner.'[32] Acknowledging the possibility of both scenarios, Myers asserts that 'some strain of intelligence, whether without us or within, which is not our conscious waking intelligence of the moment, is in some fashion impressing or informing the conscious self'.[33]

Myers also contrasts the conventional conviction of the self as a fixed, precise and unified entity with the experimental psychologists' new composite or colonial idea of identity characterised by the coordination of constituent elements and states within the self. He attempts to reconcile the two ideas, arguing for the continued existence of the self as a complete, unified personal identity and the notion of a coordinated self, while also

29 Like Evelyn, Myers was influenced by the ideas of Swedenborg, viewing him as the 'true and early precursor of that great inquiry which it is our present object to advance'. According to Myers, for Swedenborg the 'unseen world appeared before all things as a realm of law; a region not of mere emotional vagueness or stagnancy of adoration, but of definite progress according to definite relations of cause and effect, resulting from structural laws of spiritual existence and intercourse which we may in time learn partially to apprehend'. Frederic William Henry Myers, *Human Personality and its Survival of Bodily Death*, 2 vols (London: Longmans, Green & Co., 1903), I, 6.

30 Myers, *Human Personality*, 27.

31 Myers, *Human Personality*, 16.

32 Myers, *Human Personality*, 16.

33 Frederic William Henry Myers, 'Automatic Writing IV', *The Daemon of Socrates* (1888–9), 524.

taking both concepts further. He extends the 'unity of the Ego' concept by stating: 'the Ego can and does survive – not only the minor disintegrations which affect it during earth-life […] but [also] bodily death'.[34] When discussing the coordinated self, he refers to the conscious self as the 'supraliminal self', beneath which exists an unconscious or 'subliminal self', which experiences sensations that cannot be recognised and are outside the margin of consciousness.[35] Cooperation between the two selves is continually taking place, and moments of unconscious intelligence or communications from the subliminal realm are known as 'ripples over the threshold' or 'subliminal uprushes'. The subliminal level encompasses dream states, somnambulism, hypnotism and genius, and can receive information through channels, such as telepathy and clairvoyance, that are not accessible to the supraliminal self. Myers's idea of subliminal consciousness covers all that takes place beneath the ordinary threshold, or outside the ordinary margin of consciousness; according to Myers, it contains:

> not only those faint stimulations whose very faintness keeps them submerged, but much else which psychology as yet scarcely recognizes; sensations, thoughts, emotions, which may be strong, definite, and independent, but which, by the original constitution of our being, seldom emerge into that *supraliminal* current of consciousness which we habitually identify with *ourselves*.[36]

Linking the subliminal self to the spiritual realm, Myers argues for a more comprehensive view of consciousness or a total self that extends beyond the physical or material world, asserting that the self is only revealed in a limited way during life and not fully manifested until after death.[37]

Although Myers and Sophia De Morgan see the 'subliminal self' or unconscious as responsible for much of automatic writing, they acknowledge the interaction between the unconscious and conscious domains. For Myers, automatic writing involves the subliminal or unconscious stratum of the personality conveying messages, either from 'without us or within',

34 Myers, *Human Personality*, 11.
35 Myers, *Human Personality*, 14.
36 Myers, *Human Personality*, 14.
37 Myers, *Human Personality*, 12.

to the supraliminal or conscious stratum, 'impressing or informing the conscious self'.[38] Sophia observes the difficulty of transmitting messages through mediums and the interference by the conscious or 'positive action of the brain', stating, 'We were told that unless the directing power had complete control, the thought uppermost in the medium's mind would be given'.[39] She explains that this made it difficult 'when anything was written by one medium, to repeat it by another', since 'the medium always begins to guess and think whether it is right'.

While the conscious mind could come into play and impact the form and course of a message, the presence of conscious volition was often elusive and unpredictable. Interestingly, Lorraine Daston credits the mathematician and logician Augustus De Morgan, Sophia's husband and Evelyn's father-in-law, with closely identifying volition with chance in his epistemic interpretation of probability. He saw both free will and chance as 'apparent disruptions of the causal order and therefore as kindred classes of events'.[40] Taken in the context of discussions surrounding the origin and nature of automatic writing, nineteenth-century debates about the power of the Will and conceptions of the intermingled, interactive relationship between the conscious and unconscious domains, Evelyn's Medea takes on the qualities of a medium, with the coexistence of active and passive behaviour becoming suggestive of ongoing activity between the conscious or supraliminal self and the unconscious or subliminal self. Medea's dazed or distracted quality is particularly suggestive, indicating that diverted attentiveness or conscious action might coexist with some form of automatic, unconscious behaviour.

Evelyn was familiar with the varied explanations for automatic writing and the shifting meanings and relations which emerge through its practice.[41]

38 Myers, 'Automatic Writing IV', 524.

39 [De Morgan], *From Matter to Spirit*, 39.

40 Lorraine J. Daston, 'The Theory of the Will versus the Science of the Mind', in William Ray Woodward and Mitchell G. Ash, eds *The Problematic Science: Psychology in Nineteenth-century Thought*, (New York: Praeger, 1982), 93.

41 As Emma Merkling has shown, correspondence from the British writer Vernon Lee, a close friend of Evelyn's, suggests that Sophia and Evelyn De Morgan were both acquainted with Frederic Myers. Lee describes a meeting of the Society for Psychical Research (SPR) that she attended in 1885 where she met 'Fred Meyers [sic.] & the De Morgans'. I agree with Merkling's assessment that the 'De

Stirling conveys a sense of Evelyn and William's awareness of the ambiguity associated with automatic writing:

> They recognized that the majority of investigations in Spiritualism were productive of two evils – an incitement to fraud to prey on credulity, and the danger of a loss of mental balance in the participators. Still more they appreciated the fact that all deductions from such experiments must remain largely theoretical, and that the phenomena investigated are open to more than one interpretation. On the other hand, they felt that if any substratum of truth underlay the seeming triviality of much of these phenomena, they did not wish lightly to expose what was sacred to the sneers of the prejudiced.[42]

Morgans' is likely referring to William's mother and sister, Sophia and Mary, with whom Evelyn was close before she married William in 1887; as Merkling argues, 'De Morgans' is unlikely to have referred to Evelyn and William, as Evelyn would not have been a 'De Morgan' at that time and she would probably not have attended such an event publicly, since she was only privately interested in spiritualism. See Vernon Lee, 'Letter to Matilda Paget', 11 July 1885, in Sophie Geoffroy and Amanda Gagel, eds, *Selected Letters of Vernon Lee, 1856–1935* (New York: Routledge, 2017–), Volume II: 1885–1889, edited by Sophie Geoffroy (2021), 60. Emma Merkling, 'Imponderable: Physics, Mathematics, Psychical Research, and Evelyn De Morgan's Spiritualist Art, 1885–1910', PhD diss. (The Courtauld Institute of Art, 2021), 217. Additionally, Merkling observes that Evelyn's sister's publication *Ghosts Vivisected* reveals that Sophia, Myers, and Edmund Gurney, a founder of the SPR, knew each other well enough to have participated in a séance together. See Anna Maria Wilhelmina Stirling, *Ghosts Vivisected: An Impartial Inquiry into their Manners, Habits, Mentality, Motives and Physical Construction* (London: Robert Hale Limited, 1957), 166. As Merkling states, it is likely that Evelyn met Myers through Lee, who knew him well, or Myers's wife, the photographer Eveleen Tennant. Merkling points out that Tennant's sister Dorothy attended the Slade School of Art with Evelyn during the 1870s and that Dorothy and Evelyn exhibited together at the Grosvenor Gallery in 1886. See 'Art Notes and Minor Topics', *Art Journal* 13 (August 1874), 254; Merkling, 'Imponderable', 217. Merkling notes that Lee's letters also suggest that Evelyn attended at least one Tennant family party in the mid-1880s. See Vernon Lee, 'Letter to Matilda Paget', 26 June [1884], in Geoffroy and Gagel, *Selected Letters of Vernon Lee*, Volume I: 1865–1884, edited by Amanda Gagel (2017), 551–2. Evelyn's probable acquaintance with Myers and her interest in spiritualism from the 1880s through the publication of *The Result of the Experiment* in 1909 indicates that she was very likely familiar with his well-known *Human Personality and its Survival of Bodily Death* (1903) and perhaps his earlier published writings on spiritualism and automatic writing specifically.

42 Stirling, *William De Morgan and his Wife*, 355.

Although writings were often understood to be largely products of the unconscious mind, visits by external spirit agencies were still a real possibility. Stirling describes Augustus De Morgan as one of the first men of science in modern times to regard the phenomena of spiritualism with seriousness; he accepted that psychical occurrences are difficult to explain on known materialistic grounds, but believed that 'what their bearing, if any, upon the question of survival and continuity of individuality after death' was left undetermined. His openness to the idea of spirit visitors is reflected in a conversation with Michael Faraday; according to Stirling, when Faraday remarked to Augustus, 'Why, a ghost, sir, is a physical impossibility', Augustus apparently replied, 'Exactly, and for that very reason a psychical possibility!'[43] Mediums provided many plausible reasons why the messages might be the result of an external spiritual agency rather than shifting relations between the unconscious and conscious domains: the opinions expressed in spirit writings might be at odds with one's personal convictions, the prose style might be very different from one's own, the handwriting could be dissimilar, and while writing, one might feel the sense of being propelled by an external force. It was often difficult to determine whether the messages were originating from inside or outside the self, however, as the categories between self and spirit became blurred. Through the process of automatic writing, fluidity and exchange exists between both the conscious and unconscious selves, and between the self and the spiritual realm.

Evelyn suggests the possibility of the self's survival as a spirit after death and the ability to communicate with external spirit agencies through the inclusion of the sky directly behind Medea's head, which alludes to an eternal world beyond. Additionally, the small, winged female statues on the left of the composition appear to be statues of the winged Greek goddess Nike, aligning Medea with strength and victory, while also associating her with the heavens, the domain of both goddesses and spirits. Evelyn captures the expansive idea of subliminal consciousness proposed by Myers, suggesting that this part of ourselves is connected to all that takes place outside the ordinary margin of consciousness, allowing one to

43 Stirling, *William De Morgan and his Wife*, 34–5.

reach beyond the self and functioning as a kind of avenue for transcendent experience. However, Myers's conception of the self as unified, expansive and other-directed is complicated by a coexisting composite notion of self, defined by unpredictable, shifting relations between the supraliminal and subliminal selves. Evelyn's painting functions metaphorically as the results of an automatic writing experiment, capturing the products of the ever-changing, fragile assemblages of human cognition and behaviour.[44] The irregularity associated with this composite notion of identity, as well as the allusions to the mysterious and elusive realm of the spirit, challenge attempts at legibility and order. The difficulty of knowing the origin of the writings adds further confusion; if interpreted as automatic scripts, the elements in Evelyn's composition might derive from the spiritual world; subliminal, unconscious forces; traces of the supraliminal or conscious self; or a combination of these influences. Although *Medea* holds the possibility of connecting with the spirit world and communicating stable and orderly forms, these are continually challenged by visual references suggestive of the uncontrollable forces which challenge attempts at legibility and put any attempt at an organised, unified self in jeopardy. *Medea* contains a kind of decorative grammar, but rather than allowing us to exert mastery over the language produced within the painting, Evelyn suggests that the unpredictable language ultimately constitutes us as subjects. De Morgan's imagery exudes communicative, psychological and spiritual power, as the self is positioned somewhere between legibility and illegibility, possibility and instability.

44 Contemporary audiences would have been sensitive to the potential for imagery to function linguistically. As Johanna Drucker notes, 'The 19th century was […] the period which witnessed the fullscale adoption of the theory of pictorial origins of the alphabetic forms – either linked to hieroglyphic precedents or to the objects associated with the letternames'. Important developments included the deciphering of Egyptian hieroglyphics at the beginning of the century by Jean-François Champollion and the deciphering of Cuneiform at mid-century by Henry Rawlinson. Johanna Drucker, *The Alphabetic Labyrinth: The Letters in History and Imagination* (London: Thames and Hudson, 1999), 239.

Queen Eleanor and Fair Rosamund

Evelyn's *Queen Eleanor and Fair Rosamund* (Figure 8.3) depicts the confrontation between Henry II's wife, Queen Eleanor of Aquitaine and his mistress, Rosamund Clifford. Although the work is undated and was never exhibited during De Morgan's lifetime, it has been assigned a date of c. 1903.[45] According to legend, Henry built his mistress a tower retreat surrounded by a maze, and the queen found her way through the maze to Rosamund by means of a red thread that the mistress had left for the king. Eleanor then presented Rosamund with the option of death by dagger or poison. Nineteenth-century accounts of Eleanor, such as Tennyson's 'A Dream of Fair Women' (1842) and Algernon Charles Swinburne's *Rosamond* (1860), characterised Eleanor as aggressive and evil in contrast to the graceful and innocent Rosamund. Evelyn sets the two women in opposition to each other by contrasting the angular form, jutting profile and forward motion of Eleanor with the soft limbs, oval face and seated figure of Rosamund. The demonic bats, winged reptilian creatures and monkeys around Eleanor contrast with the cherubic putti and transparent white doves near Rosamund. The red thread held by Eleanor divides the

45 Although originally dated as 'probably 1901–02', I have revised the date of the painting to c. 1903 after consulting with Sarah Hardy, Curator of the De Morgan Foundation. It is likely that Evelyn painted *Queen Eleanor and Fair Rosamund* around the same time as *The Love Potion* (1903), given the stylistic and thematic similarities between the two works. Queen Eleanor and the female protagonist in *The Love Potion* are shown in profile, depicted as sorceress-like figures holding glass vials with similarly coloured liquid concoctions (poison v. potion), seemingly both intended to upset the happiness of two lovers. Additionally, the backgrounds of both works feature elaborate wood carving and square frames on the upper right containing lovers embracing – on the terrace within the frame of *The Love Potion* and within the framed stained-glass window of *Queen Eleanor*. Furthermore, a date of c. 1903 for *Queen Eleanor* supports my analysis of the work within the context of the writings of Frederic William Henry Myers. Although Myers wrote about automatic writing prior to 1903, his well-known *Human Personality and its Survival of Bodily Death* was published in 1903.

two women while also symbolically intruding in the space between the two lovers depicted in the stained-glass window above.

Evelyn does not seek to produce a clear confrontation between good and evil, however; she gives the scene a sense of mystery and ambiguity

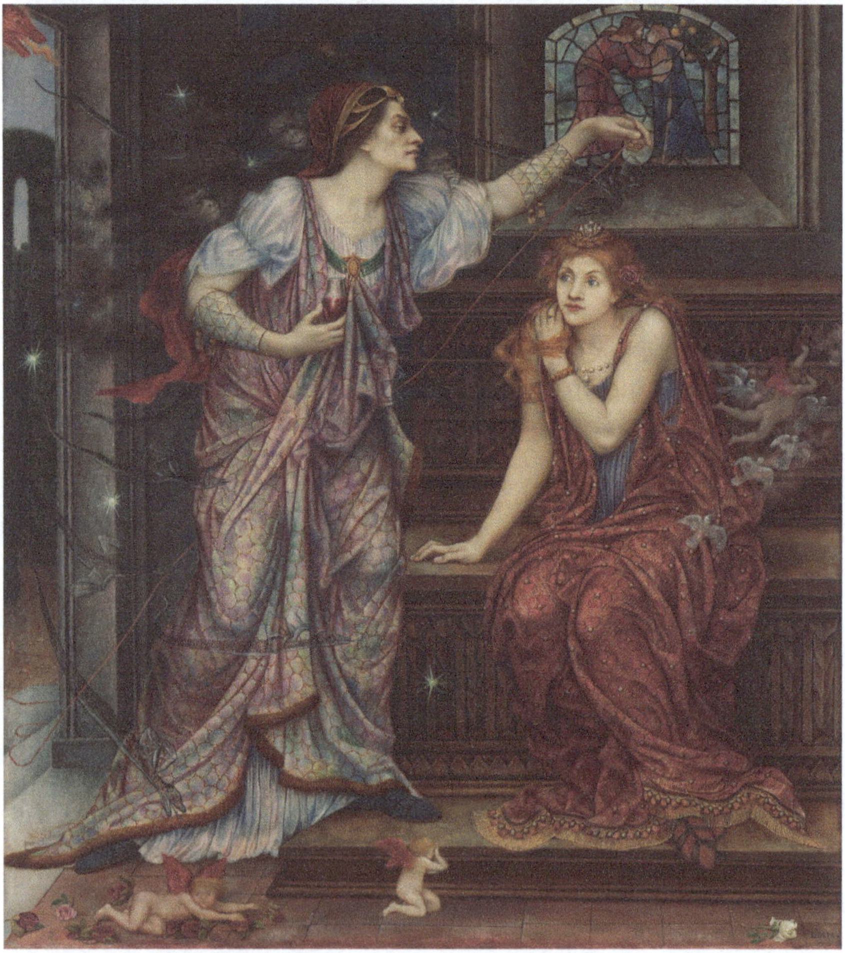

Figure 8.3. Evelyn De Morgan, *Queen Eleanor and Fair Rosamund*, c. 1903, Oil on canvas, Canvas: 75.6 × 66.7 cm, Framed: 96.2 × 87.4 × 8.6 cm, London, De Morgan Foundation © De Morgan Collection, courtesy of De Morgan Foundation.

by aligning love and death, rather than presenting Eleanor's murder of Rosamund as a clear act of cruelty resulting in the disappearance of Rosamund's love. The foreground of *Queen Eleanor and Fair Rosamund* contains both red roses of passion and a single white rose of death. Evelyn was probably familiar with Swinburne's play, *Rosamond* (1860), in which Rosamond approaches death as a new lover:

> Use me the best way found in thee, fair death,
> And thou shalt have a pleasure of mine end,
> For I will kiss thee with a patient lip.[46]

Swinburne also examines the close relationship between love and fear, before overturning expectations of Rosamond by suggesting the vanishing of her fear:

> Fear is a cushion for the feet of love,
> Painted with colours for his ease-taking;
> Sweet red, and white with wasted blood, and blue
> Most flower-like, and the summer-spoused green,
> And sea-betrothed soft purple and burnt black.
> All coloured forms of fear, omen and change,
> Sick prophecy and rumours lame at heel,
> Anticipations and astrologies,
> Perilous inscription and recorded note,
> All these are covered in the skirt of love
> And when he shakes it these are tumbled forth,
> Beaten and blown i' the dusty face of the air.[47]

Evelyn seems to have drawn inspiration from Swinburne's close attention to colour; she uses it as a means of challenging the conventional representations of the two women. Patricia Yates has observed that anyone who looks at *Eleanor and Rosamund* can find an encounter of good and evil, but acknowledges that Evelyn deliberately portrays both women as beautiful.[48] Eleanor's elaborately coloured robe, combining shades of red,

46 Algernon Charles Swinburne, *Rosamond*, in *The Queen-Mother and Rosamond* (London: John Camden Hotten, 1868), 227.

47 Swinburne, *Rosamond*, 184.

48 Yates, 'Evelyn De Morgan's Use of Literary Sources', 71.

pink, purple, yellow and green, presents evil as desirable and enticing, while Rosamund's raised eyebrows indicate that she might be pleasantly intrigued by Eleanor. Apart from the raised eyebrows, Rosamund's overall countenance is rather emotionless, challenging her traditional identification as a victim.

The customary conception of good versus evil between the two women is also questioned by the strange mixture of whimsical and terrifying elements within the composition. The red fire-breathing dragon in the top corner is hardly a threatening creature. Additionally, the reptilian forms seem to initially foreshadow danger and death, but their wings appear almost like hair bows and their transparent, gliding bodies give them a delicate, gentle quality. The bodies of the flying monkeys are cloudy and insubstantial rather than imposing, and their faces appear to be smiling slightly. Two of the cherubs occupy the foreground beneath Eleanor, while a winged reptile enters Rosamund's territory and begins to circle above her head, further overturning a binary division between good and evil. The ambiguity within the scene suggests that Rosamund may not be simply a scared victim but a willing and brave participant in a love that is destructive. Eleanor's extended arm envelops Rosamund, giving her an almost maternal quality which also challenges her traditional evil characterisation. It becomes questionable which woman is responsible for the present scenario, as motives, emotions and actions are called into question. Like Evelyn's Medea, both figures seem to oscillate between passive and active, or unconscious and conscious, states of being. One wonders whether Eleanor has made a conscious, active decision to punish Rosamund, if she is compelled to perform the deadly task or if she is resisting performing the action. Rosamund also confounds any attempt at strict interpretation; one wonders whether she is a passive victim deserving sympathy or a destructive lover.

The elaborate and brightly coloured garments of Rosamund and Eleanor can be interpreted within the context of the passages in *The Result of an Experiment* suggesting the potential for spiritual development in individuals perceived by spirits as bright and vividly coloured. Individuals were classified based on the colour, intensity and blending capability of the flames and atmospheres around them. One spirit writes:

> Of all strange sights the strangest is the flames round human beings [...] They come round people like halos, only fanned by motion [...] Yes, flame in and out, and the colour varies with the health of the person. Intense brightness means death; and dimness health. Brightness also means much in the way of development; the flames brilliant and burning upward indicate high development [...] Also beauty is most usually an accompaniment.[49]

Evelyn seems to be making a statement about the potential for spiritual evolution in both women by depicting them in elaborate, splendidly coloured garments. The robe of Eleanor, the figure one would expect to be lacking in moral character and the ability to develop spiritually, is the most elaborately decorated, with captivating hues blending into one another. Another script discusses the atmospheres around individuals and their potential to blend and unite with those of others:

> I am a spirit not long dead. I only came here a few years ago, and I am still full of wonder at earth; it is so very unlike what I fancied. [...] A strong atmosphere surrounds different people. No one is without, and a most curious thing is the blending of atmospheres. It is not possible to describe [...] Yes, and not only blend but unite at a distance.[50]

Taking the figures of Eleanor and Rosamund within this context, their 'atmospheres' have the potential to blend and unite, further overturning a binary opposition between good and evil and suggesting the potential for the overturning of boundaries and collapsing of identities. The repetition of the red and purple colours appearing in Rosamund's garment within Eleanor's garment, where the colours are blended together, supports the idea of blending atmospheres or identities.

Evelyn attended the Slade School of Art, where she would have been taught the importance of the human form and trained to make individual studies of human figures from life.[51] Yet in this composition, she privileges the interaction between bodies and among elements, including the colours

49 [De Morgan], *Result of an Experiment*, 19–20.

50 [De Morgan], *Result of an Experiment*, 56.

51 Jan Marsh and Pamela Gerrish Nunn, *Pre-Raphaelite Women Artists* (London: Thames and Hudson, 1998), 143.

of the women's clothing, rather than the depiction of individual human figures. The predominance of red in the clothing takes on a new meaning when viewed in relation to the following passage from *The Result of an Experiment*:

> N. is red in her flames; a most peculiar thing, means a very strange sudden growth. I don't think any of her family ever had red flames. (Is it good?) It depends, as it may go either way. No Saint is without them, and great murderers have had them.[52]

This further obscures the notion of a binary division between the two women, suggesting a sense of interchangeability, as they are both shown wearing red, a colour indicative of spiritual growth but representative of both saints and murderers. The profusion of red is accompanied by a large amount of purple, relating to Frederic Myers's discussion of consciousness as a spectrum defined by red and violet, a shade of purple, at either end:

> The limits of our spectrum do not inhere in the sun that shines, but in the eye that marks his shining. Beyond each end of that prismatic ribbon are ether-waves of which our retina takes no cognisance. Beyond the red end come waves whose potency we still recognize, but as heat and not as light. Beyond the violet end are waves still more mysterious; whose very existence man for ages never suspected, and whose intimate potencies are still but obscurely known.[53]

Although Myers acknowledges that the range of human faculty cannot adequately be expressed in linear form, he sees a relationship between a spectrum of light and consciousness, describing the conscious human faculty as 'a linear spectrum whose red rays begin where voluntary muscular control and organic sensation begin, and whose violet rays fade away at the point at which man's highest strain of thought or imagination merges into reverie or ecstasy'.[54] Ordinary consciousness is thus represented by the visible part of the spectrum, while ultra-red and ultra-violet rays extending beyond the red and violet ends of the visible spectrum express a wider range of physiological and psychical activity outside of everyday

52 [De Morgan], *Result of an Experiment*, 173.

53 Myers, *Human Personality*, 17–18.

54 Myers, *Human Personality*, 18.

awareness. Ultra-red rays signify automatic physiological functions, while ultra-violet rays encompass experiences like reverie or ecstasy and are connected with the spirit world, extending towards the possibilities of extraordinary experiences like clairvoyance, telepathy and automatic writing.

The clothing in *Queen Eleanor and Fair Rosamund* can be viewed as reflective of Myers's notions of the spectrum of consciousness, the composite self, marked by continual coordination among levels of consciousness, and the unified self. Although Rosamund is dressed in both vivid purple and red, the dominance of red suggests the presence of the conscious mind, described by Myers as beginning at the point where red rays occur on the spectrum. As discussed, the red and purple shades in Rosamund's garment are incorporated into Eleanor's and blended together, relating to the concept of the 'blending of atmospheres' described in the De Morgans' writings. The blending shades of red and purple within Eleanor's garment also suggest Myers' notion of the composite self, characterised by a sense of interchange and fluidity between different aspects of the supraliminal or conscious realm, signified by the presence of red and purple, and the subliminal or unconscious realm, indicated by the fading, dissolved effect of the colours alluding to the extension into ultra-red and ultra-violet rays at either end of the spectrum. Additionally, the dominance of purple in the garment places Eleanor in greater proximity than Rosamund to the spirit world; although purple or violet represents part of the visible spectrum, it is understood in terms of its closeness to the forms of unconscious activity that extend into the realm of the spirit. The fading, blurred quality of the colour in Eleanor's garment enhances the sense of her proximity to the spirit world, understood to exist at the point where the violet rays on the spectrum fade. The exchange between Eleanor and Rosamund creates a broad, dynamic conception of the self, with an expansive and fluid series of convergences and transformations. Evelyn appears to be suggesting the insufficiency of one material body to fully contain the self, implying that the self is an extended field that moves beyond the human frame and bodily limits. Rosamund and Eleanor form a cohesive yet fluctuating relationship, with Eleanor connected to Rosamund yet also suggesting that which lies beyond Rosamund's conscious awareness and material body. Like Myers, Evelyn suggests that while the self manifests itself through the body, each of us is in fact an extensive entity that cannot be fully contained or understood corporeally. Eleanor seems to represent the unmanifested and elusive part of Rosamund, capable of extending just beyond the violet rays of Myers's spectrum. This sense of correspondence, unity or alignment between a spiritual self and a human self is supported by many of the writings within *The Result of an Experiment*. One spirit remarks on the medium's spirit-matter and their similar place of origin: 'I am certain you are made from other spirit-matter, or you never could have grown like this on your earth, as it is very like ours'.[55] Additionally, the continuity between the earthly and spiritual domains is repeatedly remarked on by messengers. One spirit who professes to have been a great philosopher is asked by the De Morgans if the finding of another world quarrelled with his views, to which he replies, 'No, it extends it on the same lines'.[56]

Like Medea, Rosamund takes on the qualities of an automatic writing medium. The strands of hair wrapped around Rosamund's wrist draw attention to the wrist's important function in automatic writing. Sophia De Morgan discusses the way in which the spirit gives messages to the medium through a spiritual fluid which circulates from the brain through the wrist to the hand.[57] When two people are involved in a writing experiment an influence emanates from the spirit and directs the muscles of the medium as well as the hand of the other individual, which is joined to the hand or wrist of the medium to assist the transmission (Figure 8.4).[58]

Evelyn and William touched wrists during their experiments, supporting the idea that Rosamund might be attempting to make herself a medium through the hair-twirling action around her wrist. The location of Eleanor's hands is also significant within the context of automatic writing. A good spirit was known to influence a medium through the higher portions of the brain, 'namely the organs of veneration, benevolence, ideality, and the intellectual portion', while an evil spirit was known to influence the base of the brain (Figure 8.5).[59] In Evelyn's painting one of Eleanor's

55 [De Morgan], *Result of an Experiment*, 95.
56 [De Morgan], *Result of an Experiment*, 143.
57 [De Morgan], *From Matter to Spirit*, 53–6.
58 [De Morgan], *From Matter to Spirit*, 54–5. [De Morgan], *Result of an Experiment*, xii.
59 [De Morgan], *From Matter to Spirit*, 53.

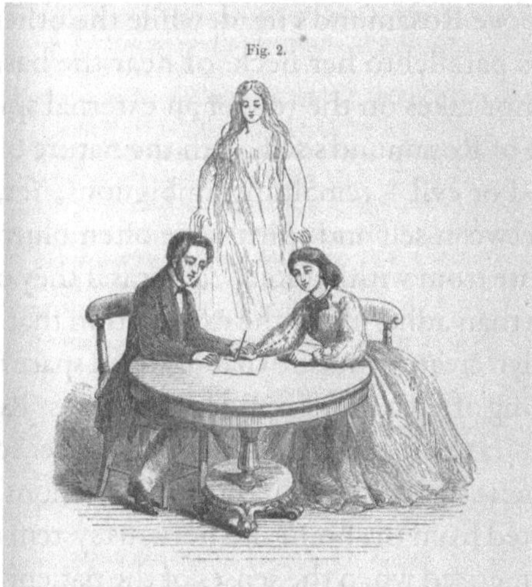

Figure 8.4. Figure 2 in [Sophia De Morgan], *From Matter to Spirit. The Result of Ten Years' Experience in Spirit Manifestations. Intended as a Guide to Enquirers* (London: Longman, Green, Longman, Roberts, & Green, 1863), 55. General Research Division, The New York Public Library.

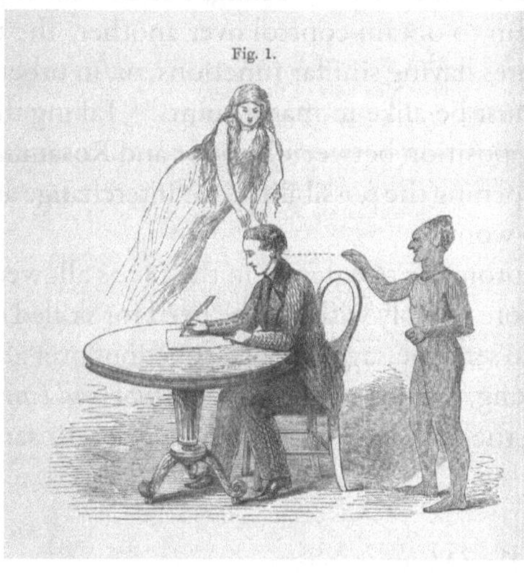

Figure 8.5. Figure 1 in [Sophia De Morgan], *From Matter to Spirit. The Result of Ten Years' Experience in Spirit Manifestations. Intended as a Guide to Enquirers* (London: Longman, Green, Longman, Roberts, & Green, 1863), 54. General Research Division, The New York Public Library.

hands is placed above Rosamund's head, while the other holding the vial of poison remains parallel to her neck, or near the base of the brain. In this context, Eleanor takes on the role of an external spirit agency, rather than an extension of Rosamund's self, with the nature of her influence on Rosamund – good or evil – remaining ambiguous. Yet, as we have seen, the boundaries between self and spirit were often blurred, with writings believed to originate from within often feeling as if they originated outside of the self. Rather than adhering to the expectation that Eleanor exerts an evil influence, Evelyn creates a more dynamic, open space for interpretation.

The positioning of Eleanor's extended arm across Rosamund's head is also significant for its resemblance to a mesmeric pose. Sophia De Morgan refers to the mesmeric state as a 'community of sensations', in which impressions are transmitted from the brain and nervous system of the mesmeriser to that of the mesmerised when the senses of the patient seem to be closed to all external objects. According to Sophia, 'a current of power or influence is established by some mysterious union between the two systems, so that it appears, and probably is the fact, that one nervous force acts equally through both'.[60] She believed the fibres of the brain were responsible for the reception and transmission of feelings and mental impressions, and in order for one brain to obtain control over another, 'the two brains must contain many fibres having similar functions, or, in other words, that the two characters must be alike in many points'.[61] Taking this into account, the traditional opposition between Eleanor and Rosamund is again overturned, further opening the possibilities for interchange and coordination between the two women.

The rise of automatic telegraphy in the 1870s allowed messages to be sent faster and more reliably without the need for skilled operators. It also became possible to send messages in both directions over a single wire simultaneously.[62] The long, red thread in *Queen Eleanor and Fair Rosamund* leads Eleanor through the maze and allows her to reach Rosamund, mirroring

60 [De Morgan], *From Matter to Spirit*, 116.

61 [De Morgan], *From Matter to Spirit*, 116.

62 Tom Standage, *The Victorian Internet: The Remarkable Story of the Telegraph and the Nineteenth Century's Online Pioneers* (London: Phoenix, 1999), 177–81.

the transmission of messages along a telegraph wire.[63] The thread moves behind Eleanor's body, suggesting her openness and expansive potential rather than cutting across her figure. Both women are integral to the process of transmission, and the streams of traffic between them create a powerful network of flux and exchange. Evelyn was likely familiar with Sophia De Morgan's comparison of automatic writing to the operations of telegraphy:

> Many considerations yet remained, and many experiments were still to be tried, before we could have full reason for believing that another intelligence was concerned, or in other words, that an invisible being directed the operations of the telegraphic wire whose mechanism was in our own organization.[64]

63 I explored automatic writing and contemporary technologies of communication, including the telegraph, telephone and typewriter, in relation to De Morgan's work in my MA dissertation, which has formed the basis for this publication. See Carey Gibbons, 'Possibility and Instability in the Paintings of Evelyn De Morgan', MA diss. (Courtauld Institute of Art, 2010). More recently, Clare Pettit has discussed De Morgan's *Moonbeams Dipping Into the Sea* (1900) in relation to the telegraph, writing, 'the linked figures in *Moonbeams* create a kind of "electric chain" or telegraphic cable, their bodies forming the cable core: and the metallic gleam of the paint surface suggesting the conductivity of metals – the copper of their hair, the silver of the sky and the salt water of the sea all replete with possibilities for electrical transmission'. Clare Pettitt, 'Dispersed Consciousness: Evelyn De Morgan's Moonbeams Dipping Into the Sea', in Caroline Arscott and Clare Pettitt, eds, *Victorians Decoded: Art and Telegraphy* (London: The Courtauld Institute of Art, 2016), 88–9. In her recent PhD dissertation, Emma Merkling has paid close attention to *Moonbeams* as well, arguing that the painting is saturated with psychical energy, specifically of the soul or self, envisaged in an etheric register. Merkling also examines De Morgan's work, particularly her infrequently discussed portraits (especially *Portrait of William De Morgan Holding a Vase* from 1909), within the context of Myers's ideas. Although both Merkling and I engage with Myers in relation to the representation of the self in De Morgan's work, I focus on automatic writing, mediumship and telecommunications, while Merkling examines the etherial body and its constitution, with reference to Oliver Lodge, ether, and geometry in addition to Myers. See Merkling, chapter 4, 'The Boundless Surface of the Soul: Ether and De Morgan's Figuring of the Self', in 'Imponderable', 212–78.

64 [De Morgan], *From Matter to Spirit*, 33.

Evelyn could have also been exposed to similar metaphors elsewhere, as Sophia echoes the contemporary tendency to relate the telegraph to the human body by discussing the electric circuitry of the telegraph and the circulatory and nervous systems in comparable terms.[65]

The preface for *The Result of an Experiment* actually draws a parallel between automatic writing and telegraphy, comparing illegible writings resulting from an unstable connection or uncommunicative spirits to a poor telegraphic transmission: '[There] followed long intervals of highly unsatisfactory writing; sometimes accounted for as "the wires having got wrong", or else by the physical condition of the "mediums" making it impossible.'[66] This metaphor conflates the disruptions in telegraphic communication with the disorder and illegibility that could occur through the practice of automatic writing, vividly capturing the sense of being helpless before inescapable forces beyond one's control. Although there was a sense of optimism surrounding the development of communication technologies like the telegraph, this coexisted with continual anxiety. For example, some feared that private affairs might become public through telegraphy. One sender decided not to send a telegram after being informed by a clerk that 'it was impossible to send a message *without [him] first seeing it*'.[67] Spiders were also known to choke up the cups of wire insulators with their webs and nests; the telegraph needles could move in a contrary direction after being demagnetised during thunderstorms; and lightning was even known to blow the telegraph apparatus to pieces.[68] Still, distance was laughed at, and many friendships and even marriages took place between telegraphists after courtships were carried on through the medium of the wire.[69]

65 Laura Otis, 'The Metaphoric Circuit: Organic and Technological Communication in the Nineteenth Century', *Journal of the History of Ideas* 63/1 (2002), 105–28. See also Arscott and Pettitt, *Victorians Decoded* and Jeffrey Sconce, *Haunted Media: Electronic Presence from Telegraphy to Television* (Durham, NC: Duke University Press, 2000).

66 [De Morgan], *Result of an Experiment*, xii.

67 'Curiosities of the Wire', *Chambers's Journal of Popular Literature, Science and Arts* 13/662 (2 September 1876), 566.

68 'Curiosities of the Wire', 567.

69 'Love by Telegraph', *Leisure Hour* 17 (26 December 1868), 822–3.

The late nineteenth century and early twentieth century saw the development of an 'other-directed' person capable of receiving and sending information in ways that were unprecedented. While participating in the circulation of messages, new possibilities emerged for intimacy between humans and between the human, technological and spiritual realms. The communicative potential in Evelyn's painting is accompanied by the potential for 'the wires having got wrong', or glitches in the system that prevent legibility and clarity. Evelyn presents a conception of identity that is expansive and open but also subject to unpredictable, uncontrollable forces and relations within and outside of the self, making coherent and continuous communication and connection challenging. Interestingly, Eleanor and Rosamund do not exchange gazes in Evelyn's painting. Despite the fluid interchange between them, there is also a sense of subjective withdrawal, perhaps symbolising the potential for traditional objective and subjective boundaries to be overturned; the possible breakdowns in one's ability to communicate accompanying the increased possibilities for human connection; or the fear of losing a contained, independent sense of self as movement and exchange beyond the boundaries of the body are embraced. In addition to collapsing the distinctions between Eleanor and Rosamund, layers are formed in the painting by the integration of various forms and substances with different textures and densities. A winged reptile flies across Eleanor's skirt; the smoky, black forms of the monkeys overlap with the architecture; and the air contains sparks, fire and the bodies of creatures with different degrees of transparency. Evelyn pursues the points where matter, life and the supernatural impinge on each other. Promises of intimacy between these realms and the potential for movement beyond the body play against the fear of the disruptions and dislocations that might collapse traditional categories and expose the self's inherent instability and vulnerability.

Conclusion

Through Evelyn De Morgan's work, language enters the realm of imagery, as she envisages systems of transmission and tests the limits of communication. *Medea* and *Queen Eleanor and Fair Rosamund* offer insights into the practice of automatic writing, the content of its messages and the conceptions of the self that emerge through its practice, reflecting the contemporaneous development of a unified model of consciousness supporting the full range of human experience. Automatic writing provides a window into the unconscious or subliminal portions of the mind, extending deep into and even beyond the self. Enabling a rethinking of the borders of consciousness and allowing the limits of the human body to be transcended, the practice opens up the possibilities of survival after death and communication with spirits. A self emerges that is receptive and expansive, asserting itself through not only the practice of automatic writing but also through new technologies of communication which were closely linked to the process. But as the self becomes a space through which information flows, with movement and activity occurring through and beyond the body, the self risks disorder, dispersion and dislocation. Messages with varying degrees of clarity and coherence circulate, capturing the potential for intimate communication, as well as the unpredictable moves and relations within a composite, dynamic self and the elusiveness of the world of the spirit. In Evelyn's work, failures of transmission and instability coexist with the search for new forms of connection during the late nineteenth and early twentieth centuries. De Morgan proposes a world in which we are open yet vulnerable; through the process of automatic writing, the thoughts, feelings and experiences of others are allowed to mirror and overlap with our own in ways that are both thrilling and destabilising.

Bibliography

Adams, John S, *Answers to Seventeen Objections Against Spiritual Intercourse and Inquiries Relating to the Manifestations of the Present Time* (New York: Fowlers and Wells, 1853).

Angeli, Helen Rossetti, *Dante Gabriel Rossetti. His Friends and Enemies* (London: Hamish Hamilton, 1949).

Arscott, Caroline, and Clare Pettitt, eds, *Victorians Decoded: Art and Telegraphy* (London: The Courtauld Institute of Art, 2016).

'Art Notes and Minor Topics', *Art Journal* 13 (August 1874), 254–5.

Bennett, Edward T., *Automatic Speaking and Writing: A Study* (London: Brimley Johnson and Ince, 1905).

Bills, Mark, *Evelyn de Morgan: Drawings and Paintings: 21 September 1996–20 April 1997* (Bournemouth: Russell-Cotes Art Gallery and Museum, 1996).

Bown, Nicola, Carolyn Burdett, and Pamela Thurschwell, *The Victorian Supernatural.* (Cambridge: Cambridge University Press, 2004).

Brandon, Ruth, *The Spiritualists: The Passion for the Occult in the Nineteenth and Twentieth Centuries* (New York: Knopf, 1983).

Bullen, J. B., 'Raising the Dead: Dante Gabriel Rossetti's "Willowwood" Sonnets', in Matthew Bevis, ed., *The Oxford Handbook of Victorian Poetry* (Oxford: Oxford University Press, 2013), 429–44.

——, and Rosalind White, 'Communication with the Dead: The Séance Diary of W. M. Rossetti', *The Journal of Pre-Raphaelite Studies* 29 (Fall 2020), 4–11.

——, Rosalind White, and Lenore A. Beaky, eds, *Pre-Raphaelites in the Spirit World: The Séance Diary of William Michael Rossetti* (Oxford: Peter Lang, 2022).

Carpenter, William Benjamin, *Principles of Human Physiology* (London: John Churchill, 1855).

——, *Mesmerism, Spiritualism, etc.: Historically & Scientifically Considered: Being Two Lectures Delivered at the London Institution* (London: Longmans, Green & Co., 1877).

'Curiosities of the Wire', *Chambers's Journal of Popular Literature, Science and Arts* 13/662 (2 September 1876), 566–9.

[De Morgan, Evelyn and William], *The Result of an Experiment* (London: Simpkin, Marshall, Hamilton, Kent & Co., 1909).

[De Morgan, Sophia], *From Matter to Spirit. The Result of Ten Years' Experience in Spirit Manifestations. Intended as a Guide to Enquirers* (London: Longman, Green, Longman, Roberts, & Green, 1863).

Drucker, Johanna, *The Alphabetic Labyrinth: The Letters in History and Imagination* (London: Thames and Hudson, 1999).

Ellis, Ida, *Planchette and Automatic Writing* (Blackpool: Ellis Family, Promenade, 1904).

Geoffroy, Sophie, and Amanda Gagel, eds, *Selected Letters of Vernon Lee, 1856–1935* (New York: Routledge, 2017–), 2 vols: I, 1865–1884, Amanda Gagel, ed. (2017); II, 1885–1889, Sophie Geoffroy, ed. (2021).

Gibbons, Carey, 'Possibility and Instability in the Paintings of Evelyn De Morgan', MA diss. (The Courtauld Institute of Art, 2010).

Gitelman, Lisa, *Scripts, Grooves, and Writing Machines: Representing Technology in the Edison Era* (Stanford, CA: Stanford University Press, 1999).

——, and Geoffrey B. Pingree, *New Media, 1740–1915* (Cambridge, MA: MIT Press, 2003).

Gordon, Catherine, ed., *Evelyn de Morgan: Oil Paintings* (London: De Morgan Foundation, 1996).

Gurney, Edmund, *Phantasms of the Living* (London: Society for Psychical Research, 1886).

Kittler, Friedrich A., trans. Michael Metteer, *Discourse Networks: 1800/1900* (Stanford, CA: Stanford University Press, 1990).

——, trans. Geoffrey Winthrop-Young and Michael Wutz, *Gramophone, Film, Typewriter* (Stanford, CA: Stanford University Press, 1999).

Kontou, Tatiana, *Women and the Victorian Occult* (London: Routledge, 2015).

——, and Sarah Willburn, eds, *The Ashgate Research Companion to Nineteenth-Century Spiritualism and the Occult* (London: Routledge, 2012).

'London Picture Exhibitions', *Birmingham Daily Post* (30 April 1890), 4.

'Love by Telegraph', *Leisure Hour* 17 (26 December 1868), 822–3.

Luckhurst, Roger, *The Invention of Telepathy, 1870–1901* (New York: Oxford University Press, 2002).

Marsh, Jan, *Pre-Raphaelite Women: Images of Femininity in Pre-Raphaelite Art* (London: Wiedenfeld and Nicolson, 1987).

——, and Pamela Gerrish Nunn, *Women Artists and the Pre-Raphaelite Movement* (London: Virago, 1989).

——, and Pamela Gerrish Nunn, *Pre-Raphaelite Women Artists* (London: Thames and Hudson, 1998).

——, et al., *Pre-Raphaelite Sisters* (London: National Portrait Gallery, 2019).

Marvin, Carolyn, *When Old Technologies Were New: Thinking about Electric Communication in the Late Nineteenth Century* (New York: Oxford University Press, 1988).

McAllister, Isabel, 'In Memoriam: Evelyn De Morgan', *The Studio* 79/324 (March 1920), 28–33.

McCorristine, Shane, *Spectres of the Self: Thinking about Ghosts and Ghost-Seeing in England, 1750–1920* (Cambridge: Cambridge University Press, 2010).

Miller, Jonathan, 'Going Unconscious', in Robert B. Silvers, *Hidden Histories of Science* (London: Granta, 1997), 1–35.
Merkling, Emma, 'Imponderable: Physics, Mathematics, Psychical Research, and Evelyn De Morgan's Spiritualist Art, 1885–1910', PhD diss. (The Courtauld Institute of Art, 2021).
Moses, William Stainton, *Spirit Teachings through the Mediumship of William Stainton Moses* (M.A., Oxon) (London: London Spiritualist Alliance, 1894).
Myers, Frederic William Henry, 'Automatic Writing, Or the Rationale of Planchette', *Contemporary Review* 47 (1885), 233–49.
——, 'Automatic Writing II', *Proceedings of the Society for Psychical Research* 3 (1885), 1–63.
——, 'Automatic Writing III', *Proceedings of the Society for Psychical Research* 4 (1886–7), 209–61.
——, 'Automatic Writing IV. The Daemon of Socrates', *Proceedings of the Society for Psychical Research* 5 (1888–9), 522–47.
——, *Human Personality and its Survival of Bodily Death*, 2 vols (London: Longmans, Green & Co., 1903).
'The New Gallery', *Daily News* (28 May 1900).
'The New Gallery', *Saturday Review of Politics, Literature, Science, and Art* 69/1801 (3 May 1890).
Noakes, Richard, *Physics and Psychics: The Occult and the Sciences in Modern Britain* (Cambridge: Cambridge University Press, 2019).
Oberhausen, Judy, 'Evelyn Pickering De Morgan and Spiritualism: An Interpretive Link', *Journal of Pre-Raphaelite Studies* 3 (1994), 1–19.
Oppenheim, Janet, *The Other World: Spiritualism and Psychical Research in England, 1850–1914* (Cambridge: Cambridge University Press, 1985).
Otis, Laura, 'The Metaphoric Circuit: Organic and Technological Communication in the Nineteenth Century', *Journal of the History of Ideas* 63/1 (2002), 105–28.
Owen, Alex, *The Darkened Room: Women, Power, and Spiritualism in Late Victorian England* (Chicago: University of Chicago Press, 2004).
——, *The Place of Enchantment: British Occultism and the Culture of the Modern* (Chicago: University of Chicago Press, 2004).
Pearsall, Ronald, *The Table-rappers* (New York: St. Martin's Press, 1973).
Phillips, Claude, 'The Summer Exhibitions at Home and Abroad', *Art Journal* 52 (June 1890), 161–74.
Sconce, Jeffrey, *Haunted Media: Electronic Presence from Telegraphy to Television* (Durham, NC: Duke University Press, 2000).
Smith, Elise Lawton, 'Evelyn Pickering De Morgan's Allegories of Imprisonment', *Victorian Literature and Culture* 25/2 (1997), 293–317.
——, 'The Art of Evelyn De Morgan', *Women's Art Journal* 18/2 (1997), 3–10.

——, *Evelyn Pickering De Morgan and the Allegorical Body* (Madison, NJ: Fairleigh Dickinson University Press, 2002).
Sparrow, Walter Shaw, 'The Art of Evelyn De Morgan,' *The Studio* 19 (1900), 221–32.
Standage, Tom, *The Victorian Internet: The Remarkable Story of the Telegraph and the Nineteenth Century's Online Pioneers* (London: Phoenix, 1999).
Stead, W. T., *Real Ghost Stories: A Revised Reprint of the Christmas and New Year's Numbers of the 'Review of Reviews' 1891–2* (London: Grant Richards, 1897).
——, *After Death: A Personal Narrative, New and Enlarged Edition of 'Letters from Julia'* (London: Stead's Pub. House, 1921).
Stirling, Anna Maria Wilhelmina, *William De Morgan and his Wife* (New York: Henry Holt & Co., 1922).
——, *Ghosts Vivisected: An Impartial Inquiry into their Manners, Habits, Mentality, Motives, and Physical Construction* (London: Robert Hale Limited, 1957).
Swinburne, Algernon, *The Queen-Mother and Rosamond* (London: John Camden Hotten, 1868).
Thurschwell, Pamela, *Literature, Technology and Magical Thinking: 1880–1920* (Cambridge: Cambridge University Press, 2001).
Tromp, Marlene, *Altered States: Sex, Nation, Drugs, and Self-transformation in Victorian Spiritualism* (Albany: State University of New York Press, 2006).
Underwood, Sara A. Francis, *Automatic or Spirit Writing with Other Psychic Experiences* (Chicago: T.G. Newman, 1896).
Verner, Alexander, *Table Rapping and Automatic Writing* (Bolton, 1903).
Warner, Marina, *Phantasmagoria: Spirit Visions, Metaphors, and Media into the Twenty-first Century* (Oxford: Oxford University Press, 2006).
Warren, Samuel M., ed., *A Compendium of the Theological Writings of Emanuel Swedenborg* (New York: Swedenborg Foundation, 1974).
Weeks, Charlotte J, 'Women at Work: The Slade Girls', *Magazine of Art* (1883), 324–9.
Wheeler, Michael, *Death and the Future Life in Victorian Literature and Theology* (Cambridge: Cambridge University Press, 1990).
Winter, Alison, *Mesmerized: Powers of Mind in Victorian Britain* (Chicago: University of Chicago Press, 1998).
Woodward, William Ray, and Mitchell G. Ash, eds, *The Problematic Science: Psychology in Nineteenth-century Thought* (New York: Praeger, 1982).

PART III

Female Agency

LAURE NERMEL

9 'Direct and Serious and Heartfelt': Truth-to-nature in Elizabeth Siddal's Creative Agency

ABSTRACT
Elizabeth Siddal's career as an artist and poet has always been associated with that of Dante Gabriel Rossetti; therefore, the theme of nature in her work has been virtually ignored. As a female working closely with the Pre-Raphaelite Brotherhood in their early days, she understood current aesthetic traditions. The Victorian language of flowers is well known, and literature often identified women with plants and flowers. Women artists associated with the PRB in the 1850s often favoured landscape and still-life, genres deemed appropriate to their gender. Elizabeth Siddal was motivated by different aims from most of her male and female counterparts, who studied nature through close examination on the motif. Siddal's settings and botanical elements were indicators of a more suggestive, introspective trend, processed as the site of female subjectivity.

* * * * *

In the memoir devoted to his brother, William Michael Rossetti lists the most emblematic rules of the Pre-Raphaelite programme.[1] Ranking second, the study of nature remained a guiding principle. Traditionally, Pre-Raphaelitism has been described in terms of polarities: naturalism (originated by William Holman Hunt and John Everett Millais) versus revivalism (best represented by Dante Gabriel Rossetti and his followers). In fact, the latter accompanied his associates during the Knole Park expedition of autumn 1850 to Kent, to paint outdoors. However, Hunt remembered how Rossetti 'engaged in a mortal quarrel with some particular leaf which would perversely shake about and get torn off its branch [...] he would put up with no more such treatment [...] stalking back to the

1 William Michael Rossetti, *Dante Gabriel Rossetti: His Family Letters with a Memoir*, 2 vols (London: Ellis and Elvey,1895), I, 135.

lodgings to write and to try designs'.[2] These failed attempts were meant to form the background of *The Bower Meadow* (1850–72; Manchester Art Gallery), but Rossetti did not seem to have had much interest in landscape as a subject matter in its own right.

Because Elizabeth Siddal's career has been so closely related to Rossetti's, the theme of nature in her drawing and writing has received little critical attention. When this has been the case, it was almost always by considering these two modes of creation as disjoined. However, as one of the women best-connected to the initial Brotherhood, Siddal was aware of Pre-Raphaelite motifs and Victorian aesthetic traditions.[3] Meanwhile, a few women associated with the PRB in the 1850s favoured landscape and still-life. This was deemed appropriate for their condition, in contemporary essentialist terminology. Femininity was thought to be morally ordained by nature. Identification of women with plants was customary in literature, maidens and brides being described in terms of floral imagery.[4] This discourse of sexual differentiation established women's creativity as the reflection of some innate biological traits. 'Female art' was codified as innocent, delicate and sensitive, inclined to specific subject-matter. William Michael Rossetti supported these endeavours by arguing that 'a female Fra Angelico, for anything I can see, should surely not be a lusus naturae', that is, an oddity.[5]

At the same time, Pre-Raphaelite ethics of truth-to-nature presented some difficulties for women wishing to record their observations of the

2 William Holman Hunt, *Pre-Raphaelitism and the Pre-Raphaelite Brotherhood*, 2 vols (London: Macmillan, 1905), I, 237.

3 I will be using maiden names, or in any case, surnames related to the artistic identity of these women, as appearing in signatures, correspondence or mentions by fellow painters and writers. Siddal (originally 'Siddall') is often referred to as 'Lizzy', 'Gug' or 'Guggum(s)' in Gabriel Rossetti's letters, her artworks being signed 'E. E. S.' or 'E. E. Siddal' before 1860. Most of the works dealt with in this chapter were produced before marriage.

4 As is the case in John Ruskin's Lecture II 'Of Queens' Gardens' from 'Sesame and Lilies', in *The Complete Works of John Ruskin*, ed. E. T. Cook and Alexander Wedderburn, 39 vols (London: George Allen, 1903–12), XVIII, 109–44.

5 William Michael Rossetti, 'Art News, July 1855', *The Crayon* 2/8 (22 August 1855), 118.

physical world, directly on site. Spaces of femininity were conceived within the limits of the home, a sanctuary preserved from labour and productivity.[6] This division between private and public, interior and exterior, profoundly affected women's experience of the art world. The concept of agency has been the object of much research in gender studies.[7] Creative agency can be defined as the ability to resist or comply with structures of power. Victorian women artists acted upon those through self-fashioning or representational practices (choice of subject matter, composition and medium). Siddal's poetical production, and, to a lesser extent, some of her sketches, have been interpreted as the result of recluse activity, not meant for public consumption: 'none of her associates and friends mention her writing'.[8] However, Siddal's wish for professionalism complicates this idea of the 'separate spheres', as proved by the projects she and Rossetti had in mind:

> Allingham has been looking over her poems and is delighted with many of them. I am going to lend them to him (trustingly in her permission to do so) that he may give his opinion as to which will be best for a volume Lizzy will illustrate & I have no doubt we shall get a publisher.[9]

6 Griselda Pollock articulates the connection between spaces of femininity and nineteenth-century modernity as a keystone to gender relations in *Vision and Difference: Femininity, Feminism and the Histories of Art* (London: Routledge, 1988).

7 See, for example, Griselda Pollock, *Vision and Difference: Femininity, feminism and histories of art* (London and New York: Routledge, 2010 [1988]) and Deborah Cherry, *Painting Women: Victorian Women Artists* (London and New York: Routledge, 1993).

8 Serena Trowbridge, *My Ladys Soul: The Poems of Elizabeth Eleanor Siddall* (Brighton: Victorian Secrets, 2018), 12. See also Jan Marsh, *Elizabeth Siddal: Pre-Raphaelite Artist* (Sheffield: Ruskin Gallery, 1991), 30. Marsh expressed some doubts about Rossetti's awareness of the poems during Siddal's lifetime: 'It is possible that not even Gabriel knew of Lizzie's literary work.'

9 *The Correspondence of Dante Gabriel Rossetti*, ed. William E. Fredeman, 10 vols (Cambridge: D. S. Brewer, 2002–15), I, 332. Letter to William Michael Rossetti, 28 March 1854. In the *Family Letters*, William Michael Rossetti points out that the poems in question are most definitely his sister's. However, the Fredeman edition indicates that Christina Rossetti did not publish any collection between 1847 and 1862 (her own correspondence features very few exchanges with William Allingham). Considering the great amount of editing William Michael Rossetti exerted on his brother's papers – in this letter of March 1854, he erased the part

My aim is to show that Elizabeth Siddal was motivated by objectives which differed from most of her male and female counterparts. These attempted to capture nature through close examination, by travelling and painting from the motif, to assert their status as industrious professionals. Siddal, in order to establish her artistic signature, resorted to other methods and sources of inspiration, later adopted by painters drawn to the subsequent developments of Pre-Raphaelitism. Her settings were indicators of a more suggestive, introspective trend expanding in the 1860s. References to literature evoked a sense of context, as well as impressions of time and place. Exterior space and botanical elements are actually processed as the site of female subjectivity, if not intimacy, in her artistic production.

Siddal's work offers an alternative to the empirical concept of landscape-making, by suggesting a more intimate experience of nature. Her physical immersion takes place not through an exacting system of optical recording, but thanks to the recreation of fleeting sensations and sense of drama. Siddal's focus on the relationships between female characters and the landscape conveyed layered meanings: nature could have been the locus of narrative tension, but the protagonists' emotions were reflected in their surroundings as well.

Gender and the Genre of Landscape

During Victoria's reign, landscape painting was rehabilitated as a noble subject-matter. The deaths of John Constable (1837) and J. M. W Turner (1851) marked a break with ways of representing nature, in line with the sublime and picturesque traditions. Constable and Turner had produced 'pure' landscapes, embracing nature's infinity and unpredictability. They had favoured dramatic effect and large scale. This intensified connection to nature is epitomised in the well-known anecdote of Constable's search

mentioning Christina's desire to 'see that Gug's emanations' – and in view of the strong bond originating between Allingham and Siddal at that time, I believe, like Fredeman, that the writings mentioned are probably Siddal's.

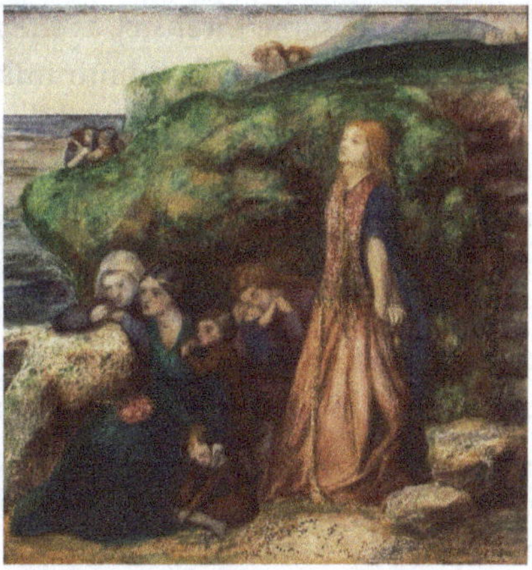

Figure 9.1. Elizabeth Siddal, *The Ladies' Lament from 'Sir Patrick Spens'*, 1856 Watercolour on paper, 24.1 × 22.9 cm, Tate Gallery, London. Purchased 1919. Photo: Tate.

for accurate colours as they are, not according to artificial systems of representation: the painter placed a violin on the lawn, to show his patron George Beaumont that grass was green, not brown.[10] Nevertheless, landscape was not taught at the Royal Academy as a proper genre in the 1850s. Academicians still relied on Joshua Reynolds's precepts, which claimed that 'Nature herself is not to be too closely copied'.[11] Illusionistic devices, such as the single vantage point, gradations from lighter to darker tones and perspective, prevailed.

The Pre-Raphaelites were both drawing from and departing from these notions. They approached nature by spurning standard norms in use.[12]

10 This tale was spread by Constable's friend and biographer, painter Charles Robert Leslie, in *Memoirs of the Life of John Constable*, 1843 (Ithaca, NY: Cornell University Press, 1980), 114.

11 Joshua Reynolds, 'Discourse III', in Robert R. Wark, ed., *Discourses on Art* (New Haven, CT: Yale University Press, 1981), 41.

12 See, for example, Allen Staley, *The Pre-Raphaelite Landscape* (London: Paul Mellon Centre, 2001) and Christopher Newall and Allen Staley, eds, *Pre-Raphaelite Vision: Truth to Nature* (London: Tate Publishing, 2004)

Landscape was treated with the same intensity as the rest of the composition, with bright tints, intricacy of detail and minimum contrast of light and shade. As Hunt recorded in his autobiography, this enabled him to physically engage with the motif: 'directly and frankly, not merely for the charm of minute finish, but as a means of studying more deeply Nature's principles of design, and to escape conventional treatments of landscape backgrounds'.[13] Contrary to Constable and Turner, who sketched outside but completed canvasses in the studio, the PRB were employing the *plein-air* technique: 'to paint an out-of-door picture [...] abjuring altogether brown foliage, smoky clouds and dark corners [...] and with sunlight brightness of the day itself'.[14] Moreover, this empirical attitude echoed the scientific innovations of the time, in the fields of biology, natural history and geology.[15] Artists of the Victorian period were familiar with these developments, as shown by Millais' focus of rocks in his portrait of John Ruskin (1853–4; Ashmolean Museum, Oxford), or in Anna Blunden's coastal seascapes of Cornwall. Blunden's picture thus documents the reflections of the water and the effects of light on the sandstone cliffs, eroded by natural phenomena.

This way of depicting nature departs from the topographical views tackled by previous generations of landscape painters. The extreme precision and visual intensity of Pre-Raphaelite images make them look surreal, let alone discomforting. Even if this new mode of picture-making was condemned in the first place, it is precisely the naturalistic trend that became associated with the group's identity in the minds of contemporaries. From 1851 onwards, the fact that Rossetti had ceased exhibiting in public and that Ruskin had taken the PRB's defence largely contributed to that appreciation. As a fierce advocator of the concept of truth-to-nature, Ruskin had instructed his disciples to 'Go to Nature in all singleness of heart and walk with her laboriously and trustingly, having no other thought but how best to penetrate meaning, rejecting nothing, selecting nothing'.[16]

13 Hunt, *Pre-Raphaelitism* I, 111–12.

14 Hunt, *Pre-Raphaelitism* I, 91.

15 See, for example, John Holmes, *The Pre-Raphaelites and Science* (London: Paul Mellon Centre, 2018).

16 *Complete Works*, ed. Cook and Wedderburn, III, 423. This reflection appeared in the first volume of *Modern Painters*, published in 1843.

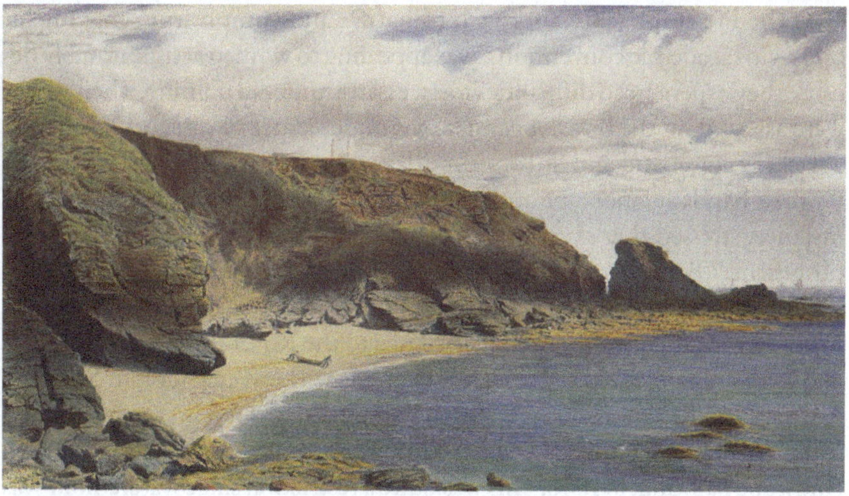

Figure 9.2. Anna Blunden, *View near the Lizard: Polpeor Beach*, 1862, Watercolour on paper, 32.9 × 56.6 cm, The Whitworth Art Gallery, Manchester. Image courtesy of the Whitworth, University of Manchester.

The critic's publications emphasised the need to understand the structure and individual characteristics of each natural form, so that elements of the landscape should form a cohesive whole. Truth-to-nature meant adopting a faithful, uncompromising attitude to one's surroundings that were to be recorded on paper. Besides, Ruskin believed that artists should endorse immediacy of vision with a naive, innocent eye: 'a sort of childlike perception of these flat stains of colour, merely as such, without consciousness of what they signify, or as a blind mind would see them, if suddenly gifted with sight'.[17] He found that Pre-Raphaelitism honoured this spirit, in its 'one principle, that of absolute, uncompromising truth in all that it does, obtained by working everything, down to the most minute detail, from nature and nature only'.[18]

17 'The Elements of Drawing', in *Complete Works*, eds Cook and Wedderburn, XV, 27.

18 'Lectures on Architecture and Painting (Edinburg 1853)', in *Complete Works*, eds Cook and Wedderburn, XII, 157.

The Pre-Raphaelite approach to nature and composition-making, at odds with academic conventions, was appealing to women artists, notably because they experienced difficulties to access institutional training. Their works were assessed on the basis of gender bias under a special category, evaluated as lacking command and finish. Some drawing manuals entreated women to try their hands at landscape and still-life. Jane Wells Loudon's handbook, for instance, stressed that sketching from nature was a ladylike form of accomplishment.[19] Because plant and flower-painting were seen as crafts, however, requiring imitative skills only, its practitioners were considered as amateurs. Moreover, women were barred from entry to the Royal Academy until 1860 and were only admitted to life classes from 1893. The Water-Colour Societies had very few female associates: Helen Allingham was the first to be granted full membership to the Old Water-Colour Society, a body associated with landscape painting, in 1890. This was quite a restriction since watercolour was viewed as particularly appropriate to the female hand. Technically, women were not considered as official members of the Pre-Raphaelite Brotherhood, initially a secret, all-male community. Nevertheless, some were welcome on certain conditions.

Under a female penname, Christina Rossetti published seven poems in *The Germ*; 'Dream Land' explored the journey into some fantasised location. Bessie Parkes had expressed an early interest in these writings: 'Get a sight of *The Germ*, a small publication put forth by a set of crazy poetical young men in London, artists mostly, who call themselves "the Pre-Raphaelian brethren" and seek in all things for the "simplicity of nature" '.[20] Nicknamed 'the Rosa Bonheur of landscape painting' by reviewers, her friend Barbara Smith was proud to announce in 1854: 'Anna Mary says my little oils are very good for first productions from nature. My landscape is very PRB' (see Figure 4.1).[21] The very same Anna Mary Howitt, along with Smith,

19 Jane Wells Loudon, *The Lady's Country Companion or How to Enjoy a Country Life Rationally* (London: Longmans, 1845).

20 Parkes Papers (Cambridge: Girton College), Vol. 6, letter to Kate Jevons, 17 April 1850, cited in Jan Marsh and Pamela Gerrish Nunn, *Pre-Raphaelite Women Artists* (London: Thames and Hudson, 1999), 57.

21 The George Eliot and Georges Henry Lewes Collection (New Haven, CT: Yale University), letter from Barbara Smith to George Eliot, 14 January 1856. Barbara

joined the short-lived Folio Sketching Club, a professional society providing support and mutual emulation, created by Rossetti, Millais, Hunt and their friends. Rossetti greatly admired Smith, whom he called 'quite a *jolly fellow*'.[22] Her boldness described in a letter to his sister implies that she needed to un-sex herself to be accepted by male counterparts on equal terms: 'Ah! If you were only like Miss Barbara Smith […] who thinks nothing of climbing up a mountain in breeches or wading through a stream in none, in the sacred name of pigment'.[23]

The Pre-Raphaelites carefully selected their associates among family members, acquaintances or sweethearts, on the basis of shared affinities. They encouraged untutored ladies who lacked formal education, valuing imaginative potential and originality of expression instead. William Michael Rossetti documented Elizabeth Siddal's limited tuition by his brother, explaining that her peculiar designs coincided with the Pre-Raphaelite agenda:

> In the present day, when vigorous brush-work and calculated 'values' are more thought of than inventiveness of sentiment, her performances would secure little beyond a sneer first, a glance afterwards, and a silent passing-by. But in those early 'Praeraphaelite' days, and in the Praeraphaelite environment, which was small, and ringed round by hostile forces, things were estimated differently. The first question which my brother would have put to an aspirant is, 'Have you an idea in your head?'. This would have been followed by other questions such as 'Is it an idea which can be expressed in the shape of a design? Can you express it with refinement, and with a sentiment of nature […] ?'. He must have put these queries to Miss Siddal practically […] and he found the response on her part such as to qualify her to begin, with a good prospect of her progressing.[24]

Smith and Rosa Bonheur both exhibited at the French Gallery, Pall Mall, founded by Ernest Gambart in 1854. By achieving international fame, Rosa Bonheur provided British women artists with a suitable role model: she depicted outdoor scenes of animals in monumental formats, traditionally used for historical painting.

22 *Correspondence*, ed. Fredeman, I, 294. Letter to Christina Rossetti, 8 November 1853.

23 *Correspondence*, ed. Fredeman, I, 294. Letter to Christina Rossetti, 8 November 1853.

24 William Michael Rossetti, 'Dante Gabriel Rossetti and Elizabeth Siddal', *The Burlington Magazine for Connoisseurs* 3 (1903), 278.

Even within the Pre-Raphaelite circle, women were expected to express delicacy and sensibility in their pictures, not rational knowledge. Ruskin may have supported female creation, but the advice he provided was not always wise, barring artists from wider opportunities to exhibit or gain the attention of other patrons. For example, he recommended Anna Blunden to keep to landscape (Figure 9.2), at a time when narrative subject-matter – which she had treated – was in great demand: 'You must give up figures at once, you will never be able to sell one. In landscape let someone else – any popular hack or an artist – choose your subjects'.[25] It is certain that Pre-Raphaelitism allowed women to secure a professional reputation on the grounds of discipline and earnestness. Nevertheless, it was a style on the margins, whose anomalies were frequently perceived as mistakes. Reviews of Howitt's pictures were not particularly laudatory. The reviews in *The Athenaeum* declared that *The Sensitive Plant*'s 'delicacy of observation has grown almost morbid',[26] while the background of *Queen Boadicea* was compared to a 'wearisome green salad' by the same newspaper, concluding: 'This is botany, not art'.[27]

All in all, the small-to-medium formats of Blunden, Howitt, Siddal and Smith were acceptable because they concurred with gender expectations. Works on paper and drawing materials (pencil, chalks, watercolour) did not require huge studio space and they were easy to transport. Integral to practising landscape *en plein air* and travelling, especially abroad, was a crucial step of artistic education. Thanks to their class and earnings, Howitt and Smith were able to study in Europe. Blunden visited various sites of England and Ireland (Figure 9.2). These cases were by no means common. Women needed to be chaperoned when going out. Long, physical walks were hampered by corsets, crinolines and voluminous skirts.[28] These activities went counter to traditional conceptions of the feminine body as

25 Virginia Surtees, ed., *Sublime and Instructive: Letters from John Ruskin to Louisa, Marchioness of Waterford, Anna Blunden and Ellen Heaton* (London: Michael Joseph, 1972), 140. Letter to Anna Blunden, 6 May 1862.

26 'National Institution of Fine Arts', *The Athenaeum* (21 March 1855), 327.

27 'The Sydenham Picture Gallery', *The Athenaeum* (7 June 1856), 718.

28 See Nina Taylor, '"Too Individual an Artist to be a Mere Echo": Female Artists as Independent Professionals', *The British Art Journal* 12/3 (2012), 55.

domestic and frail. Being ill and from a slightly lower social background, Elizabeth Siddal sat for her female colleagues at the Smiths' farm 'with iris stuck in her dear hair', rather than being included in their country excursions as a fellow art producer.[29]

Inside Out: Domesticating Exterior Space

In Smith's *Ventnor, Isle of Wright* (see Figure 4.1), the distance unfolds before the viewer's eyes through blurry hues, while the foreground is precisely delineated. Other painters associated with the Pre-Raphaelite circle preferred more local views, closer to the capital, where they had relatives or connections they could stay with. Not as socially and physically mobile as Smith, Siddal probably sketched *Landscape with Castle, Tree and Landing Stage (View of Oxford?)* from behind the window of her physician, Henry Acland's house.[30] Similarly, *The Artist's Garden* was made when Rosa Brett lived with her parents from 1851 to 1859.[31] John Brett recorded his sister's dedication to truth-to-nature: 'Rosa has lately made a few – first rate – sketches on Preraffaelite principles'.[32] The representation of familiar, prosaic settings was attractive to women on account of its propriety and convenience. Deborah Cherry has pointed out how landscape-viewing was reshaped as a correct leisure activity for ladies from the urban classes during the Victorian era. Thanks to the expansion of the railway system, the countryside was within easier reach, while illustrated travel literature spread the knowledge of rural scenes to wide audiences.[33]

29 *Correspondence*, ed. Fredeman, I, 353–54. Letter to Ford Madox Brown, 23 May 1854.

30 Elizabeth Siddal, *Landscape with Castle Tree and Landing Stage*, known only from a photograph in the Ashmolean Museum, Oxford.

31 Rosa Brett, *The Artist's Garden*, 1859, oil on board, 15.6 × 14.2 cm, private collection.

32 Diary entry for 30 September 1852, quoted in Newall and Staley, eds, *Pre-Raphaelite Vision*, 50. Family papers unpublished, in possession of the artists' descendants.

33 Deborah Cherry, 'From Towns to Countryside and Seaside', in *Painting Women: Victorian Women Artists* (London: Routledge, 1993), 165–72.

Lovers Listening to Music (Figure 9.7) was completed during one of Siddal's stopovers in Hastings, to which she made several trips on account of health issues. Doctors regularly asked their patients to seek cures in sea-side resorts, whose waters were renowned for their therapeutic qualities. The background of Siddal's drawing resembles Hastings' 'Lovers' Seat' below the edge of the cliff. In his correspondence in July 1855, Rossetti alludes to a design of 'a very dark gipsy looking little girl' with her sister, made 'on the East Hill where there is something which looks off like a ruin' that seems to correspond to the sketch.[34] The sepia ink enabled Siddal to render the various surfaces of natural elements: rough hatchings for the textures of the trees; small, neat touches indicating flower borders and hills. Hastings is the place where Siddal saw the Channel for the first time, in 1852. Her fascination with the aquatic element transcribes in her poetry. The rhyming pattern of 'Now Christ's' opening stanza, taking place on a boat, sounds like the tidal waves of the sea: 'ye save yon bonny shepherd / Sai*l*ing on the sea, / Ten thousand sou*l*s are sai*l*ing there / But they be*l*ong to Thee. / If he is *l*ost then a*ll* is *l*ost / and a*ll* is dead to me'.[35] This effect is reinforced by the use of liquid consonants and the repetition of certain words ('sailing', 'all', 'lost').

As Siddal's patron and benefactor, Ruskin ranked her amongst 'geniuses' like Turner, an artist whose reputation he had largely helped to secure with the publication of *Modern Painters*.[36] Ruskin attempted to direct Siddal towards more majestic scenes: 'Switzerland is all soft and pure air, clear water, mossy rock and infinite flowers – I suppose you like

34 *Correspondence*, ed. Fredeman, II, 51–2. Letter to Frances Lavinia Rossetti, 1 July 1855.

35 I have opted for the versions of the poems published by Serena Trowbridge: *My Ladys Soul* (Brighton: Victorian Secrets, 2018) when they required further analysis. However, their titles have been shortened or simplified from their initial incipits – except 'True Love' (p. 92), the only original title provided by Siddal – in order to make the points discussed more legible and to avoid repeating the first line when this one is quoted. I have adopted a similar transcription for artworks titles, when those are long and mentioned from the second time onwards.

36 *Complete Works*, eds Cook and Wedderburn, XXXVI, 216–17. Letter to Mrs Acland, 10 July 1855.

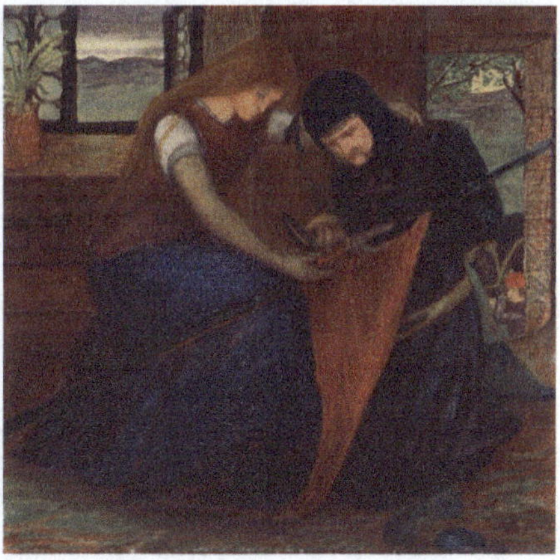

Figure 9.3. Elizabeth Siddal, *Lady Affixing a Pennant to a Knight's Spear*, c. 1856, Watercolour on paper, 13.7 × 13.7 cm, Tate Gallery, London. Bequeathed by W. C. Alexander 1917. Photo: Tate.

that?'.[37] He wished to keep a watch on the places Siddal visited, controlling the potential admiration she might feel for famous sites: 'the whole coast of Genoa, with its blue sea, hills, and white houses, looks to me like a bunch of blue ribands dipped in mud and then splashed all over with lime'.[38] This was motivated by an invasive concern for her health: 'you must get up among the Alps, it will brace you and revive you; and *there* the colour is insuperable'.[39] Ruskin's protégée never applied the Pre-Raphaelite principles in the exacting manner the art critic advocated for. The backgrounds of Siddal's pictures are not precisely located, but are distant evocations of sites she saw or imagined. Jan Marsh has suggested that the hills appearing through the window of *Lady Affixing a Pennant to a Knight's Spear* (Figure 9.3) represent Haddon Hall's surroundings, but there is no sign allowing the viewer

37 *Complete Works*, eds Cook and Wedderburn, XXXVI, 231–2. Letter to Siddal, 27 January–6 April 1856.

38 *Complete Works*, eds Cook and Wedderburn, XXXVI, 231–2. Letter to Siddal, 27 January–6 April 1856.

39 *Complete Works*, eds Cook and Wedderburn, XXXVI, 231–2. Letter to Siddal, 27 January–6 April 1856.

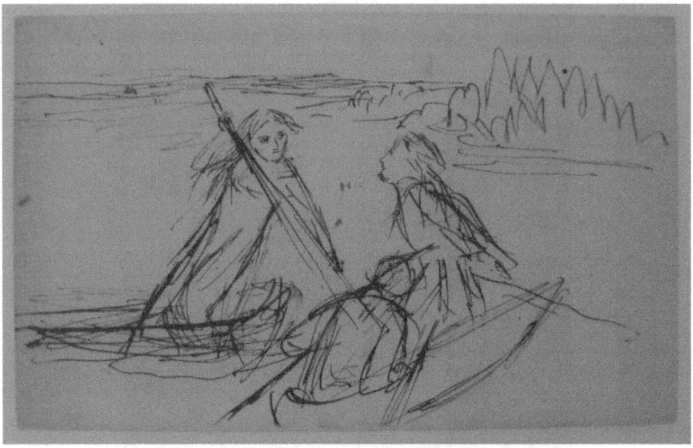

Figure 9.4. Elizabeth Siddal, *Two Men in a Boat and a Woman Punting*, 1850–2, Pen and ink on paper, 11.6 × 18.3 cm, Ashmolean Museum, Oxford. © Ashmolean Museum, University of Oxford.

to recognise the Peak District.[40] The reattribution of the watercolour's date of execution (circa 1856) questions this search for real places, inasmuch as the artist travelled to Derbyshire in 1858.

Botanical and mineral motifs are employed to serve ambivalent means in Siddal's images. Water currents can be associated to danger because of their ability to cause death: the narrator of 'Now Christ' and the eponymous characters of *The Ladies' Lament* (Figure 9.1) are all grieving drowned sailors. Yet, cruising is shown as a peaceful, recreational activity in *Two Men in a Boat and a Woman Punting* (Figure 9.4) and *The Rowing Boat*.[41] In the former, ripples are barely signified, with just a few lines clustered around the barges' hulls. Because of its fluid aspect, ink is an appropriate medium to reproduce the fleeting movement of water. In *The Rowing Boat*, however, Siddal has blended graphite pigments to evoke the quiet surface of the river, leaving ample space for the eye to rest. Siddal's compositions

40 Jan Marsh and Pamela Gerrish Nunn, *Pre-Raphaelite Women Artists* (London: Thames and Hudson, 1999), 117.

41 Elizabeth Siddal, *The Rowing Boat*, pencil on paper, 15.8 × 18.4 cm, private collection. <https://victorianweb.org/painting/siddal/drawings/2.html>.

reveal abrupt disjunctions and angular drawing, features that have been decried and compared to Rossetti's own shortcomings. At the Russell Place Exhibition of 1857, Coventry Patmore judged *We Are Seven* (a cottage girl in a churchyard with mountains, a lake and a waterfall) and the urban subject *Pippa Passes* in these terms: 'Her drawings display an admiring adoption of all the most startling peculiarities of Rossetti's style [...] *We Are Seven* and *Pippa Passes* by the same lady, deserve more notice than we can stop to give them'.[42]

Siddal's rejection of traditional conventions led her to reconfigure pictorial organisation. Watercolour cakes and good quality paper were becoming cheaper in the Victorian era; a wider scope of hues was available, such as Viridian green, Manganese violet and Ultramarine blue.[43] They could be bought at several manufacturers in Central London (Long Acre), where Siddal was accompanied by Ford Madox Brown in April 1855, following the payment of her first allowance by Ruskin: 'Would you have the leisure to go some day with Guggum to Roberson's', asked Rossetti, 'and superintend the purchase of oil-colours and all needfuls for her'.[44] A new technique in vogue was 'stippling', that is, the close juxtaposition of dots next to each other to give the impression of dense patterns and texture modulations. Siddal opted for the placement of larger blocks of pigments instead, many of them unblended, like the compartmentalised panels of stained-glass.[45] This effect was enhanced by her applying paint almost dry on paper and the adding of bodycolour. Mixing watercolour with Chinese white enabled Siddal to create thicker textures and to strengthen the opacity of her tints. This controversial technique went counter to the common use of watercolour, appreciated for its translucent effects and considered as a particularly British form of art.[46]

42 Coventry Patmore, 'A Pre-Raphaelite Exhibition', *Saturday Review* (4 July 1857), 11–12.

43 See Christopher Newall, *Victorian Watercolours* (London: Phaidon Press, 1994), 16.

44 *Correspondence*, ed. Fredeman, II, 31. Letter to Ford Madox Brown, 13 April 1855.

45 Helen Glanville, 'Contemporary Colour Theory', in Stephen Hackney, Jacqueline Ridge and Joyce Townsend, eds, *Pre-Raphaelite Painting Techniques 1848–1856* (London: Tate Publishing, 2004), 33–6.

46 Newall, *Victorian Watercolours*, 13.

Siddal's taste for illuminated manuscripts and the Early Christian masters materialises in her appropriation of optical devices. In *De Pictura* (1435), Alberti had advised artists to conceive the frame of a canvas as an open window to the world. Flemish primitive painters such as Jan van Eyck introduced views onto the exterior to produce a source of light and to add depth. While Siddal's designs concentrate compositional elements in enclosed spaces, she devises windows or glimpses of the outside as thresholds to another world. *Lady Affixing a Pennant* (Figure 9.3) is a relevant comment on gendered relations inscribed in the division of space. The knight, placed towards the open door, is the main character engaging with the exterior, but this might be fatal because he is being equipped for the last fight by his lady, who will wait or mourn for him at home. The companionate demonstration of affection of the two central protagonists is replicated outside, between the squire and the knight's steed. To represent the moors, Siddal uses curves, richly textured hues of green and purple, set up against the browns and stiff lines of the inside.

In her series on *The Eve of St Agnes* (Figure 9.5), the artist conjures up landscape as a site for the female gaze. The figure is in a contorted pose with hands clasped on the windowsill, absorbed in her thoughts. The artist refers

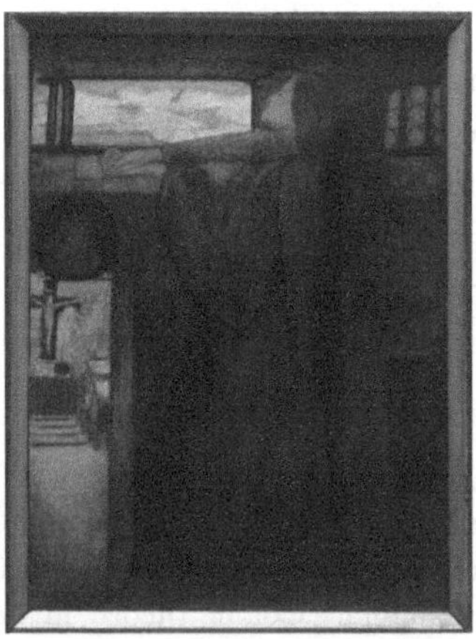

Figure 9.5. Elizabeth Siddal, *The Eve of Saint Agnes*, 1850, Gouache on paper, 16.5 × 12 cm, Wightwick Manor, Wolverhampton. 1889775 © National Trust/ John Pittwood.

to 'The snows [...] sparkling to the moon' of Alfred Tennyson's poem, as St Agnes' feast day takes place in January. Landscape inspires meditation; it becomes a symbol for longing and escapism. Likewise, the external world is a key aspect of *The Lady of Shalott* (1853; The Maas Gallery, London), since it contains the reflections of the scenery that the Lady must replicate on a tapestry. The window on the right displays the close-up of a branch, a row of trees and a distant village. Strangely enough, it does not show Lancelot riding, though his image appears in the mirror on the left. Despite the curse falling upon her, leaving the tower seems a preferrable option for the confined Lady, portrayed as perfectly composed. With these plot twists and the absence of mimetic illusionism, Siddal designates the natural world not solely as the public, male domain, but also as potentially female. Interestingly, Sandra Donaldson has stressed how Siddal 'interacts with the world outside the self, and, in facing nature, she faces her own nature'.[47]

By exposing the limits of precise, painstaking landscape-making in the usual Pre-Raphaelite manner, Elizabeth Siddal establishes connections between iconic figures and the nurturing elements of the landscape. Her three watercolours on the Madonna and Child theme depict the pair in a tender embrace, reaching out for the greenery. The piece depicted in Figure 9.6 portrays young Jesus touching vines reminiscent of *The Girlhood of Mary Virgin* by Rossetti. In the book of John, Christ calls himself 'the True Vine', a device shaped like a cross in both Siddal and Rossetti's pictures, announcing the passion.

Another biblical motif of Pre-Raphaelite imagery is the lily, an emblem of purity and innocence associated with the Virgin, but rearranged as an aspect of some heavenly setting in Siddal's poem 'Life and night': 'Do tall white angels / gaze and wend along / the banks where lilies bend'.[48] Many Victorian artists reconstructed the values usually attributed to plants in contemporary discourse, varying not only by species but by colours too.[49]

47 Sandra M. Donaldson, ' "Ophelia" in Elizabeth Siddal Rossetti's Poem "A Year and a Day" ', *Journal of Pre-Raphaelite Studies* 2 (1981), 128.

48 Siddal, 'Life and night are falling from me', lines 44–7 in Trowbridge, *My Ladys Soul*, 50.

49 Taylor, ' "Too Individual an Artist to be a Mere Echo" ', 56.

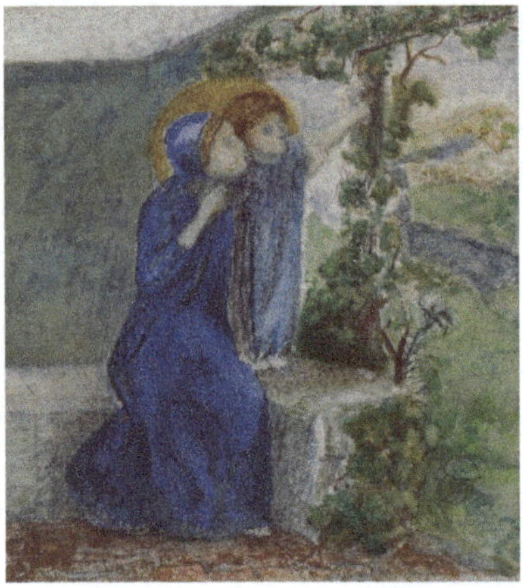

Figure 9.6. Elizabeth Siddal, *Madonna and Child*, 1855–7, Watercolour over pencil on paper, 6.3 × 5.7 cm, Private collection. Photograph: Bonhams.

According to popular beliefs, the 'ferns that cling about' of 'O silent wood' could connote love and sincerity. Therefore, botanical particulars were suffused with multiple meanings. In Siddal's practice, they are meant to contribute to narrative symbolism. She delves on green leaves or grass ('A longing year', 'Now Christ'). Colours possessed emotional values. Blue stood for faith, while red embodied passion and green, hope. Siddal played on this scheme when administered onto the landscape, so that it could echo inner states of the figures' consciousness. The duplicated purple-blue touches on the women's gowns in *The Ladies' Lament* forge a link between them, but with the sea as well (Figure 9.1). The ladies may be outside, but they are waiting for their lovers in vain, as proved by the character on the far left, leaning on the rock for support.

From Walled Garden to the Wilderness: Enchanted or Haunted Woods, Anything but Silent

The quest for a fantasised, ancient place epitomised in Siddal's medieval-inspired imagery owes very much to a shift in the approach to landscape, at a moment of rampant industrialisation and economic growth in Britain. Fellow artist Joanna Boyce, whom Siddal esteemed, enjoyed the North Downs of Surrey because of their relative absence of human activity. So much in fact, that she had a house in Holmbury Hill built, to paint from at leisure: 'they were no visitors or tourists and very few human beings within a mile or two of us'.[50] While in the 1770–1800 period, nature had already been celebrated as a site of retreat, Victorian artists viewed rural areas as shelters from the woes of modern urban life.

Known from a photographic print in the Ashmolean Museum, *We Are Seven* illustrates William Wordsworth's poem of the same name. The main character, with her 'rustic, woodland air' mentions the passing of time punctuated by the deaths of her siblings: 'their graves are green [...] the ground was white with snow'. These pastoral representations of the countryside were constructed as repositories of British heritage. Border ballads were popular during the Victorian era; Siddal possessed a copy of Walter Scott's *Minstrelsy of the Scottish Border*, now in the Fitzwilliam Museum, Cambridge. In 1854, she began selecting ballad subjects to illustrate for the publication of a volume edited by her friend, the poet William Allingham. *The Ladies' Lament* was one of these, telling the story of the best sailor of the land, Patrick Spens, sent to Norway by the King of Scotland to bring his daughter back. Siddal focused on the following lines: 'O lang, lang may the maidens sit / With their goud kaims in their hair / And waiting for their ain dear loves!'. Siddal herself tried to emulate the ballad genre, initially transmitted in oral form and spreading into various versions. She privileged intensity of feeling thanks to short lines, rustic speech

50 *The Boyce Papers: The Letters and Diaries of Joanna Boyce, Henry Wells and George Price Boyce*, ed. Sue Bradbury, 2 vols (Woodbridge: The Boydell Press, 2019), I, 687. Letter from Joanna Boyce to Hennie Moore, 31 August 1858.

and archaisms. Variation and repetition are at the core of her verses, communicated by anaphors or slight modifications of a line from one stanza to the next: 'And mother dear take a sapling twig' and 'And mother dear break a willow wand'.[51] Siddal's narratives are all the more poignant when told by a first-person speaker or through the use of dialogue. She conjures up the experience of multi-sensorial nature, through which a vast range of emotions can be projected. She regularly invokes nature's restorative powers: the narrator of 'A longing year' unites with the 'grassy bed' of the river and the 'voices of a thousand birds' to rest in peace. The perception of natural light seems like a way to enter another realm: 'O mother open the window wide / and let the daylight in'.[52]

Whenever the scene takes place outside, allusions to amorous encounters are either stimulated or negated by contact with the external environment. The beauty of nature seems the perfect setting for *Lovers Listening to Music*. In this case, the landscape is connected to the senses: it is the object of the couple's sight. They are almost hugging, to evoke touch. The two female figures play a stringed instrument at their feet, to allude to hearing. Rossetti frequently visited Siddal when she was away from the city. In the letter to his mother mentioned above, he described how both appropriated the Hastings scenery as a place of sentimental memories, inscribed in their relationship:

> You know no doubt that spot on the East hill where there is something that looks far off like a ruin, but proves if I remember rightly to be nothing but a blocked up door of some kind. On its side Lizzy and I scratched our initials last year – along the corner of one side I think [...] Another place where Lizzy and I scratched our initials was a stone at the Old Roar, a very pretty place indeed and not very far – I forget now in precisely what direction [...] *Our* stone would lie to your right as you stood with your back to the fall.[53]

51 Siddal, 'O mother open the window wide', lines 13 and 21 in Trowbridge, *My Ladys Soul*, 68.

52 Siddal, 'O mother open the window wide', lines 1–2 in Trowbridge, *My Ladys Soul*, 68.

53 *Correspondence*, ed. Fredeman, II, 51–2. Letter to Frances Lavinia Rossetti, 1 July 1855, the possessive pronoun being underlined by Rossetti himself.

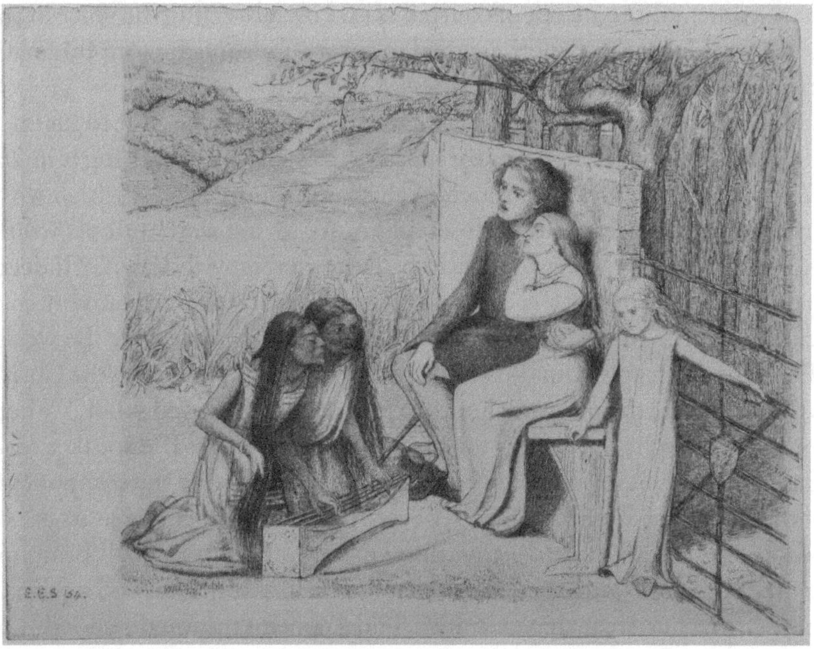

Figure 9.7. Elizabeth Siddal, *Lovers Listening to Music*, 1854, Pen and ink on paper, 29.5 × 23.8 cm, Ashmolean Museum, Oxford. © Ashmolean Museum, University of Oxford.

Siddal's ballads deal with the contradictory reactions provoked by the intensity of love. This is best expressed in 'O god forgive me that I ranged'.[54] The first stanza is the antithesis of the narrator's delusion, invalidating the fulfilment love is supposed to provide. The rest of the storyline is built like a flash-back, returning to the effects of passion unto the 'heart', so entranced that the 'coldest blasts of winter' feel 'like sweet airs in June'. Love is even personified, defying the passing of the seasons and violent meteorological phenomena: 'He calmed the thunder of the storm / and lighted all my ways'. Summer rarely purports positive meanings in Siddal's poetry. The 'sweet summer tide' of 'True Love' is deceptive, because it implies imminent tragedy: 'That other is waiting / To claim his pale Bride'. Siddal challenges

54 Siddal, 'O god forgive me that I ranged', in Trowbridge, *My Ladys Soul*, 63.

the sentimentalist concept of courteous love by subverting the voice of the Romantic heroine in swoon, attuned to nature, for a much more enigmatic attitude to the external world.

Siddal preserved the notion of nature as a secret force, able to lift one's spirit, but also to destroy. Ruskin supports this idea by theorising it in *The Elements of Drawing*: 'how much of all that is round us […] which we at first think we understand, a closer and more loving watchfulness would show to be full of mystery, never to be fathomed or withdrawn'.[55] Indeed, nature is a channel for the expression of the artist's altered states of consciousness. The in-betweenness of spaces such as the forest, or the wood, allows for an escape from life's trials. The 'span of earth' from 'Now Christ' is the site where the mourner hopes to join with her beloved sailor, 'Where some day I might sleep', thus following a cyclical order. The speaker of 'A longing year' is being depicted lying on the ground, while the components of the landscape such as 'The river ever running down between its grassy bed' create the appropriate environment for her repose: 'Shall bring me another dream'. Nature provides a place for self-withdrawal and a form of release. Stefania Arcara has examined Siddal's poems thoroughly, notably by translating them into Italian. Her essay 'Sleep and Liberation: The Opiate World of Elizabeth Siddal' demonstrates how the apparent disembodiment of the sleeping maid is reconstructed to signify female empowerment. By resorting to sleep, she breaks free from the viewer or the reader's perception, preventing her body to become the sight of scrutinised observation. Her fabulous surroundings generate a space for imaginative experiments, substantialised by dreams, apparitions or visons.[56]

More generally, the trope of the magical wood is addressed in Victorian visual culture as the ideal locus of sleeping beauties. This subject-matter, which occupied Edward Burne-Jones during the last stage of his career, was conceived as a series. The first panel, *The Briar Wood* (1874–84), shows not the princess, but the knight discovering the castle's inhabitants under

55 *Complete Works*, eds Cook and Wedderburn, XV, 94.

56 Stefania Arcara, 'Sleep and Liberation: The Opiate World of Elizabeth Siddal', in Béatrice Laurent, ed., *Sleeping Beauties in Victorian Britain: Cultural, Literary and Artistic Explorations of a Myth* (Oxford: Peter Lang, 2015), 105–18.

the spell. According to the tale, the fairy designed a forest of brambles and thorns to protect the princess' sleep. This motif almost fills the whole of the painting's frame. Being Siddal's friend and fellow artist, Burne-Jones had been involved in the second phase of Pre-Raphaelitism initiated by the Oxford Union decoration project depicting scenes from Arthurian legends in 1857. Along with Dante Gabriel Rossetti, Burne-Jones was at the forefront of Aesthetic and Arts and Crafts circles. The landscapes featuring in the works of many artists associated to the Pre-Raphaelites from the 1860s onwards privileged poetical moods and dreamy atmospheres.

Yet, this sense of nostalgia is laden with much more sinister undertones in most of Siddal's works. Nature can be the setting of scenes selected for their dramatic tension, if not their gruesomeness. Siddal was drawn to folksongs, fairy tales and ancient traditions, rather than sources from Greco-Roman literature. Her poetical and pictorial productions expressed a Gothic sensibility, by laying the stress on moments of terror and gloomy atmospheres. She seemed fascinated by spectral creatures inhabiting mysterious forests, designed as liminal spaces between the world of the living and the realm of the dead. She frequently addressed the theme of doomed lovers reunited in the beyond. Siddal's taste for the macabre was not always approved by Ruskin, who tried to have her focus on botany as a more appropriate subject matter: 'you will break off these disagreeable ghostly connections of yours [...] You will see rocks too and heather'.[57] Siddal's patron thought that her peculiar pictures were not even suitable for display. When he wished to have Charles Kingsley adhere to Pre-Raphaelite aesthetics, he pointed out: 'I can show him Miss Siddal's but he *may* think them morbid'.[58]

Indeed, her *Haunted Wood* (Figure 9.8) is the locus of some uncanny phenomena. The female figure faces what looks like a ghost, or her double floating above the ground. Their resemblance is emphasised through the forest of trees, whose vertical lines echo those of the two standing characters.

57 *Complete Works*, eds Cook and Wedderburn, XXXVI, 207–8. Letter to Siddal, May 1855.

58 *Complete Works*, eds Cook and Wedderburn, XXXVI, 190. Letter to Dante Gabriel Rossetti, March 1855.

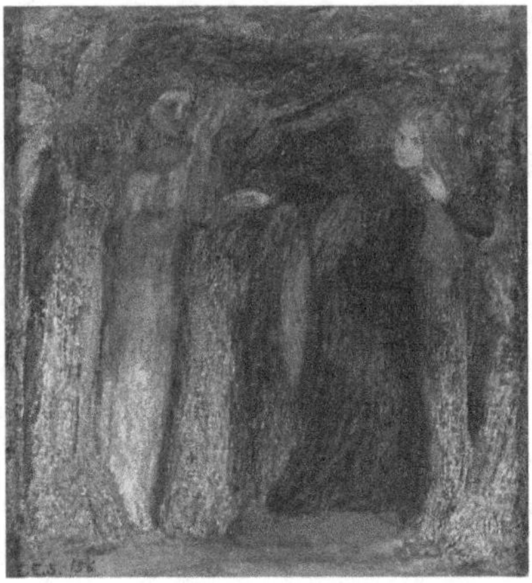

Figure 9.8. Elizabeth Siddal, *The Haunted Wood*, 1856, Gouache on paper, 11 × 12 cm. Wightwick Manor, Wolverhampton. National Trust © National Trust / Paul Highnam.

In ancient folklore, this paranormal encounter is seen as an ill omen. The gouache has been related to the poem 'O silent wood I enter thee' by Trowbridge and others, which may be viewed as paradoxical.[59] On the one hand, the natural environment provides shelter for the speaker's 'heart so full of misery', and it is animated by the fauna and flora's spirits: the 'voices from the trees', the 'ferns that cling' and the 'grey owl'.[60] On the other hand, the narrator uses the lexical field of fear to describe her surroundings: 'darkest shadow', 'gloom', 'frozen'.[61] Siddal's ability to generate ice-cold landscapes in her verse ('Many a mile over land'; 'Life and night') is a means to enhance the gap between the crisp beauty of nature and the speaker's state of mind. In that respect, the yearning for an ominous space has a disquieting effect on the readers.

59 Trowbridge, *My Ladys Soul*, 75.

60 Siddal, 'O silent wood I enter thee', lines 2–4 and 6 in Trowbridge, *My Ladys Soul*, 72.

61 Siddal, 'O silent wood I enter thee', lines 5, 9 and 11 in Trowbridge, *My Ladys Soul*, 74.

The most striking traits of this fusion with nature are expressed in relation to funeral customs, when the body returns to earth. 'O mother' contains particularly gripping images of decay since the narrator is asking her mother to be buried alive. This happens to be done in secret, at night: 'hide me among the graves'. From the third stanza onwards, the daughter alludes to a traditional ceremony that must be performed in order to protect the corpse against the evil eye. 'Bind up my feet' she says, so 'that my spirit many not walk' in the afterlife.[62] She requires the laying of 'a sapling twig and green grass newly mown' too. The fifth stanza insists on these superstitions by specifying the ritual instructions ('three berries red / and pluck them from the stalk, / and burn them at first cockcrow'). Mother and daughter appear like witches knowledgeable in the preparation and dosages of plants.

Siddal's illness may have been one of the reasons preventing her from adopting the *plein-air* technique, but she also deliberately resisted the Ruskinian approach to nature. She subverted and followed bourgeois codes of femininity by insisting on the experience of women inscribed within their environment, made visible in pictorial space. The professional identity Siddal sought was shaped by these representational practices.

As a central creative agent of the Pre-Raphaelite circle, Elizabeth Siddal was engaged in a total form of art, where text and image echoed each other. The groundwork of her pictures was an illustration of stories that appealed to her, the focal point being the intensity of the moment depicted. An equivalent process can be found in her lyrical rhymes. Siddal's concern with narrative still is apparent, but she took her inspiration from British poetry – Romantic or contemporary – traditional ballads and folklore, rather than ancient mythology or classical literature. Compositional devices evoking an impression of space are communicated by synaesthetic effects (shape, line and colour), thus attempting to resonate with the viewer's senses.

In this light, the primeval forests of Elizabeth Siddal's artistic production announce some distinctive characteristics of the Aesthetic landscape. In his memoirs, 'art for art's sake' disciple Walter Crane described the

62 Trowbridge refers to this forgotten burial tradition in her analysis of the poem. Apparently, tying up the feet of the deceased is a way to keep the body to the ground, preventing its soul to wander. See *My Ladys Soul*, 73.

canvasses of Burne-Jones in these terms: 'a glimpse into a magical world of romance and pictured poetry, peopled with ghosts of "ladies dead and lovely knights" – a twilight of dark mysterious woodlands, haunted streams, meads of deep green starred with burning flowers'.[63] This statement could adequately apply to the dreamy atmospheres and claustrophobic settings favoured by Siddal, as well as her disavowal from the modern world, conveying disenchantment and emotional emptiness. It may even be conceivable that aspects of Siddal's work anticipate the Aesthetic Movement, a possibility that has not been considered previously. For these cultural producers, escapism through the arts enabled the constitution of a more desirable environment than reality. Whether it be liminal, a site exploring one's fantasies or emphasising one's feelings, nature is recreated by the powers of imagination, where the artist's personal voice is omnipotent. Towards the end of the nineteenth century, other painters and poets chose to enhance the daunting aspect of the landscape by increasing the defamiliarisation it produces onto the viewer. Elizabeth Siddal's view of nature, therefore, was the expression of a singular Victorian consciousness bordering on fin-de-siècle sensibilities.

Bibliography

Appelbaum Mineola, Stanley, ed., *Lord Alfred Tennyson. The Charge of the Light Brigade and Other Poems* (New York: Dover Thrift Editions, 1992).

Bradbury, Sue, ed., *Joanna, George and Henry: A Pre-Raphaelite Tale of Art, Love and Friendship* (Woodbridge: The Boydell Press, 2012).

Cherry, Deborah, *Painting Women: Victorian Women Artists* (London: Routledge, 1993).

Cook, E. T., and Alexander Wedderburn, eds, *The Complete Works of John Ruskin*, 39 vols (London: George Allen, 1909).

Crane, Walter, *An Artist's Reminiscences* (London: Methuen & Co, 1907).

63 Walter Crane, *An Artist's Reminiscences* (London: Methuen, 1907), 84.

Donaldson, Sandra M., '"Ophelia" in Elizabeth Siddal Rossetti's Poem "A Year and a Day"', *Journal of Pre-Raphaelite Studies* 2 (1981), 127–33.
Fredeman, William, ed., *The Correspondence of Dante Gabriel Rossetti,* 10 vols (Cambridge: D. S. Brewer, 2002).
Gill, Stephen, ed., *William Wordsworth. Selected Poems* (London: Penguin, 2004).
Hackney, Stephen, Jacqueline Ridge, and Joyce H. Townsend, eds, *Pre-Raphaelite Painting Techniques 1848–1856* (London: Tate Publishing, 2004).
Hunt, William Holman, *Pre-Raphaelitism and the Pre-Raphaelite Brotherhood*, 2 vols (London: Macmillan, 1905).
Lasner, Mark Samuels, and Roger C. Lewis, eds, *Poems and Drawings of Elizabeth Siddal* (Wolfville: Wombat Press, 1978).
Laurent, Béatrice, ed., *Sleeping Beauties in Victorian Britain: Cultural, Literary and Artistic Explorations of a Myth* (Oxford: Peter Lang, 2015).
Leslie, Charles Roberts, *Memoirs of the Life of John Constable, Composed Chiefly of His Letters*, 1843 (Ithaca, NY: Cornell University Press, 1980).
Loudon, Jane Wells, *The Lady's Companion* (London: Longmans, 1845).
Marsh, Jan, *Elizabeth Siddal: Pre-Raphaelite Artist 1829–1862* (Sheffield: Ruskin Gallery, 1991).
——, and Pamela Gerrish Nunn, *Pre-Raphaelite Women Artists* (London: Thames and Hudson, 1999).
Motion, Andrew, ed., *Selected Poems by John Keats* (London: Faber and Faber, 2005).
Newall, Christopher, *Victorian Watercolours* (London: Phaidon Press, 1994).
——, and Allen Staley, eds, *Pre-Raphaelite Vision: Truth to Nature* (London: Tate Publishing, 2004).
Pollock, Griselda, *Vision and Difference: Femininity, Feminism and Histories of Art* (London: Routledge, 1988).
Reynolds, Joshua, *Discourses on Art*, 1770, ed., Robert R. Wark (London, New Haven: Yale University Press, 1981).
Rose, Andrea, ed., *The Germ: Thoughts Towards Nature in Poetry, Literature and Art. The Literary Magazine of the Pre-Raphaelites*, 1850 (Oxford: Ashmolean Museum, 1992).
Rossetti, William Michael, *Ruskin, Rossetti. Pre-Raphaelitism: Papers 1854–1862* (London: George Allen, 1899).
——, 'Dante Rossetti and Elizabeth Siddal', *The Burlington Magazine for Connoisseurs* 1/3 (1903), 273–95.
——, *Dante Gabriel Rossetti: His Family Letters with a Memoir*, 1895 (Cambridge: Cambridge University Press, 2012).
Scott, Walter, *Minstrelsy of the Scottish Border: Consisting of Historical and Romantic Ballads, in the Northern and Southern Countries of Scotland, with a Few of Modern Date, Founded upon Local Tradition*, 1802–3, 3 vols (Paris: Baudry, 1838).

Staley, Allen, *The Pre-Raphaelite Landscape* (New Haven: Yale University Press, 2001).

Surtees, Virginia, ed., *Sublime and Instructive: Letters from John Ruskin to Louisa, Marchioness of Waterford, Anna Blunden and Ellen Heaton* (London: Michael Joseph, 1972).

Taylor, Nina. 'Too Individual an Artist to be a Mere Echo: Female Pre-Raphaelite Artists as Independent Professionals', *The British Art Journal* 12/3 (2012), 52–9.

Trowbridge, Serena, ed., *My Ladys Soul: The Poems of Elizabeth Eleanor Siddall* (Brighton: Victorian Secrets, 2018).

ROBYNE CALVERT

10 Dismantling Pre-Raphaelite Dress: Facts and Fictions in Women's Artistic Sartorial Practices

ABSTRACT

Artistic Dress was the Victorian sartorial practice through which individuals communicated their identification with artistic circles, life and philosophies that challenged the boundaries of mainstream ideals. While it is a category that is acknowledged in current fashion histories, Artistic Dress has had limited and at times conflicting treatment, often conflated with other terms like Aesthetic Dress and Dress Reform without clarity or differentiation between them. The term Pre-Raphaelite Dress has also been used to describe this style, especially in relation to the idea that those associated with the Pre-Raphaelite circle often went about publicly in unconventional clothing that expressed their Bohemian lifestyle. This chapter will offer an in-depth discussion of so-called 'Pre-Raphaelite Dress' to scrutinise how and when Pre-Raphaelite women flouted sartorial convention – if they did at all. Focusing on comparative object analysis between images to extant garments, it presents an analysis that re-evaluates key examples – particularly Christina Rossetti, Elizabeth Siddal and Jane Morris – and offers new cases, to conclude that Artistic Dress was rooted in the practice of artists and models styling themselves and their clothes to express artistic fantasies for both creative production and everyday life – rather than the wholesale wearing of alternative garments, as previous scholars (such as Stella Mary Newton) have suggested.

* * * * *

In a letter to his sister dated 10 March 1869, the author Henry James wrote a compelling description of the designer Jane Morris, after visiting her and her husband William Morris at their home:

> Ah, *ma chère*, such a wife! *Je n'en reviens pas* – she haunts me still. A figure cut out of a missal – out of one of Rossetti's or Hunt's pictures – to say this gives but a faint idea of her, because when such an image puts on flesh and blood, it is an apparition of fearful and wonderful intensity. It's hard to say [whether] she's a grand synthesis of all the pre-Raphaelite pictures ever made-or they a 'keen analysis' of her – whether she's an original or a copy. In either case she is a wonder. Imagine a tall lean woman

> in a long dress of some dead purple stuff, guiltless of hoops (or of anything else, I should say,) with a mass of crisp black hair heaped into great wavy projections on each of her temples, a thin pale face, a pair of strange sad, deep, dark Swinburnish eyes, with great thick black oblique brows, joined in the middle and tucking themselves away under her hair, a mouth like the 'Oriana' in our illustrated Tennyson, a long neck, without any collar, and in lieu thereof some dozen strings of outlandish beads – in fine Complete. On the wall was a large and nearly full-length portrait of her by Rossetti, so strange and unreal that if you hadn't seen her, you'd pronounce it a distempered vision, but in fact an extremely good likeness.[1]

James's depiction of Morris is exemplary of both the bohemian impression she gave to her contemporaries, and the romanticised vision we have of her today. At the time of this encounter, she had been married to William Morris for a decade, during which period she became one of the primary faces of Pre-Raphaelitism, particularly as model and muse for Dante Gabriel Rossetti. While James's observations indicate Morris's sartorial eccentricities at home, Pre-Raphaelite artwork has left a skewed impression of the way Pre-Raphaelite women actually dressed, particularly in the early days of this group. This is especially true regarding Elizabeth Siddal, who even in fairly recent scholarship has been credited with starting a specific Victorian fashion trend called 'Pre-Raphaelite Dress'. For example, writing in 1996, Sophia Wilson stated that 'the first women to wear, and therefore promote, Pre-Raphaelite dress were the models of these artists, notably Elizabeth Siddal and Jane Morris'.[2] In 2005, Alice Mackrell made the assertion that the Pre-Raphaelites promoted a particular mode of dress, calling it an 'alternative vestimentary movement' referring to the dresses worn by 'Elizabeth Siddal, herself a Pre-Raphaelite painter and poet, in Dante Gabriel Rossetti's drawings of her'.[3]

1 Henry James, Letter to his sister dated 10 March 1869, in Henry James, *Letters*, ed. Leon Edel (Cambridge, MA: Harvard University Press, 1984), 93–4.

2 Sophia Wilson, 'Away with the Corsets, On with the Shifts', in *Simply Stunning: The Pre-Raphaelite Art of Dressing* (Cheltenham: Cheltenham Art Gallery & Museums, 1996), 20.

3 Alice Mackrell, *Art and Fashion: The Impact of Art on Fashion and Fashion on Art* (London: Batsford, 2005), 88.

These statements are exemplary of the assumption that Pre-Raphaelite women, especially those who sat for Rossetti, wore clothing in their daily lives akin to those in which they sat as art models. These dresses are usually described as being loose in the bodice and sleeves and worn without corsets or crinolines to allow more freedom of movement than more restrictive fashionable dress. The fact that the aforementioned women were skilled seamstresses who made modelling costumes for Rossetti and other artists has reinforced the notion that they must have made similar clothing for themselves that they wore as everyday dress.

While it is true that the Pre-Raphaelites were an important source of inspiration for later Artistic Dress practices, many assumptions about early Pre-Raphaelite clothing are inaccurate. This chapter challenges established notions of how Pre-Raphaelite women (particularly Morris and Siddal) dressed in their early days and argues that the origins of Artistic Dress were much more nuanced than is often reported. It examines the assumption that there was such a style as 'Pre-Raphaelite Dress' in the 1850s and 1860s, analysing frequently cited examples to determine if and how these dresses departed from fashionable clothing. While it has been convincingly shown by some fashion historians that what has been perceived as Pre-Raphaelite Dress was influential to later forms of dressing,[4] there is evidence to show that it was probably not the case that these women wore clothes as some sort of conscious 'movement', as Mackrell's wording implies. Rather, it is more likely that in those early days, such sartorial choices were made for more personal and practical reasons, perhaps related to artistic practice, either for modelling or for physical (work-related) practicalities; comfort; or perhaps even economic reasons. In fact, if any 'fashion statements' were made, it was more likely through the somewhat unconventional (dishevelled) appearance of male artists that may have signified an 'artistic' temperament.[5] Therefore, to understand the reality of Pre-Raphaelite Dress,

4 See Kim Wahl, 'Fashioning the Female Artistic Self: Aesthetic Dress in Nineteenth-Century British Visual Culture' (PhD dissertation, Queen's University, History of Art, 2004).

5 See Robyne Calvert, 'Manly Modes: Artistic Dress and the Styling of Masculine Identity', *Visual Culture in Britain* 16/2 (2015), 223–42.

extant images that are often used as examples of it must be re-analysed, alongside what little we know of the actual attire worn by these women.

What Is Artistic Dress?

Even in recent fashion histories, terms like Artistic Dress, Aesthetic Dress, Pre-Raphaelite Dress and even sometimes Dress Reform, have been often used interchangeably without much clarity on where they overlapped, and where they differed, if at all. These are most often employed to describe sartorial codes in which significant arts practitioners and patrons – particularly those associated with Pre-Raphaelitism, the Arts and Crafts Movement, Aestheticism and Art Nouveau – wore (and at times designed and promoted) clothes that were frequently labelled in contemporary literature as 'artistic' or 'aesthetic'. Such descriptors designated such clothing to be of a unique and creative calibre, but also outside the norm. The terminological problem is not recent, however, and has its roots in the Victorian period itself, as this example from an 1881 article in *The Queen* shows:

> Among the records of fashion during the last few years, one of the most noteworthy is the way in which the apparel variously termed 'Pre-Raphaelite', 'Artistic', 'High Art', or more generally 'Æsthetic', has become a recognised factor in the dress of English women.[6]

The research presented here arises from a larger study of Artistic Dress (1848–1900), for which the following definition was composed:

> Artistic Dress was (and perhaps still is) the sartorial style through which certain individuals – mostly those in artistic circles such as artists, architects, designers, models, and patrons – communicated their identification with aesthetic ideals, life, and philosophies that often ran counter to the mainstream.[7]

6 Anonymous, 'Aesthetic Dress', *The Queen*, 1881, 344.

7 Robyne Calvert, *Fashioning the Artist: Artistic Dress in Victorian Britain 1848–1900* (PhD thesis, University of Glasgow, 2012).

In tracing the chronology of Artistic Dress, Pre-Raphaelitism was examined as one of the founding influences. However, in the years 1848–60, there is scant evidence that Pre-Raphaelite women (those associated with the male artists as models, mistresses and wives) did in fact wear 'alternative vestments' in public. In fact, upon closer inspection of the paintings and drawings that are often cited as examples of Pre-Raphaelite Dress, it becomes clear that where the clothing in question is not meant to be historical costume, the dresses bear much similarity to Victorian fashion. Furthermore, because very little everyday work dress is extant outside of some rare photographs (for it is the fashionable clothing of the wealthy, made of fine fabrics, which is cherished and saved), we have little proof that the everyday clothing worn by these women was in fact any different from that donned by working women throughout Britain, or even middle-class women working in the home.

With the dissolution of the Pre-Raphaelite Brotherhood by about 1855, the Pre-Raphaelite style moved into its second wave, which was predominantly identified with the painting of Rossetti and Edward Burne-Jones; the artists associated with Morris, Marshall, Faulkner and Co. (formed in 1861); and the burgeoning Arts and Crafts movement. Prior to this, sartorial experiments were largely confined to private spaces, notably homes and studios; however, during this second wave we begin to see these artists and models exploring alternative modes of dress in a more public manner, in what will come to be called Aesthetic Dress, or more generally, Artistic Dress. As noted above, the term Pre-Raphaelite Dress has also been used to describe these styles, especially in relation to this idea that those associated with the Pre-Raphaelite Circle often went about publicly in unconventional clothing. What follows is an attempt to clarify what 'Pre-Raphaelite Dress' refers to, and if in fact the term reflects reality in any way.

What Is Pre-Raphaelite Dress?

It is possible to conclude that Pre-Raphaelite Dress was not an actual sartorial movement, but rather is a retrospective term that was adopted nearly three decades after the formation of the Pre-Raphaelite Brotherhood to describe clothing seen first in the images which inspired what we should be more properly calling Artistic Dress. Nonetheless, while the category 'Pre-Raphaelite' was used as a descriptor for art and decoration in this period, one of the earliest print references to 'Præ-Raphaelite Dress' was made by Mary Eliza Haweis in her articles for *The Queen* (1878), a ladies' magazine,[8] and subsequently reprinted and elaborated on in *The Art of Dress* (1879),[9] and a related article in *The Art Journal* (1880).[10] Even in these early days, Haweis indicates semiotic problems with the term:

> In the first place, what is meant by 'Præ-Raphaelitism' in Dress? If one were required to furnish an exact definition of that term it would be very hard; for everybody who catches it up means a different thing. But we may say, in a general way, that the present movement in dress under the above name is gradually spreading; first among art circles who have discovered, then among æsthetic circles who appreciate, the laws which govern beauty; and it represents the common reaction that follows any bad system carried on long [...] But this loose term 'Præ-Raphaelite' is extremely misleading.[11]

This is one of the earliest references to Pre-Raphaelite Dress as a particular sartorial style, and which Haweis herself indicates is unclear. She applies the term to a style which we now label Aesthetic Dress, but which she herself goes on to suggest should rather be called 'Art-Protestant'.[12] She argues that this term is more accurate, as the clothing in question references historic costume from, 'roughly speaking, the period of Edward III's reign, from 1327 to 1377', rather than just costume before the age of Raphael.[13] Although 'Art-Protestant' never really caught on, Haweis's desire to define this style again points to the semiotic confusion of these terms outlined earlier.

8 (Mrs) Mary Eliza Haweis, 'Pre-Raphaelite Dress', *The Queen*, 9 January 1878.

9 (Mrs) Mary Eliza Haweis, *The Art of Dress* (London: Chatto and Windus, 1879).

10 (Mrs) Mary Eliza Haweis, 'The Æsthetics of Dress', *The Art Journal (1875–1887)* 6, New Series (1 January 1880), 129–31.

11 Haweis, *The Art of Dress*, 98.

12 Haweis, *The Art of Dress*, 99.

13 Haweis, *The Art of Dress*, 99.

In the late twentieth century there was limited, sporadic discussion of Pre-Raphaelite Dress in fashion history literature. The early 1970s saw a brief flurry of scholarly activity concerning the Pre-Raphaelites and dress. In 1973, Roger Smith published an analysis of the artist's study of historic fashion, titled 'Bonnard's *Costume Historique* – a Pre-Raphaelite Source Book';[14] and Leonée Ormond gave a lecture on 'Dress in the Painting of Dante Gabriel Rossetti' that was published the following year.[15] Also, in 1974, Stella Mary Newton published *Health, Art and Reason: Dress Reformers of the 19th Century*, which includes a chapter simply titled 'PreRaphaelite Clothing' [*sic*].[16] Generally speaking, these three texts – and particularly Newton's – seem to be the basis for the notion that there was such a phenomenon as Pre-Raphaelite Dress that was worn by members of the Pre-Raphaelite circle even in the early days, and that it was worn by models not just as sitters, but in everyday life. These texts also underpinned the exhibition 'Simply Stunning: the Pre-Raphaelite Art of Dressing' at the Cheltenham Art Gallery & Museums (1996, the only exhibition to date focused on this subject), which was not limited to just the Pre-Raphaelite circle, but also included later nineteenth-century artist-designers such as Kate Greenaway – again pointing to the way in which this term has been used with a broad brushstroke. In fact, the greater proportion of the catalogue essays discuss Aesthetic Dress, rather than specifically the dress of the Pre-Raphaelites.

The Smith and Ormond articles, as their titles suggest, both focus on the use and depiction of costume in the artwork of the Pre-Raphaelite Brotherhood. Smith's research analysed 'Bonnard's *Costume Historique*' as an important source for Ford Madox Brown, Holman Hunt, Millais and perhaps most significantly Rossetti, who we know had his own copy of this expensive two-volume text in his library at his death (along with

14 Roger Smith, 'Bonnard's *Costume Historique* – A Pre-Raphaelite Source Book', *Costume* 7 (1973), 28–37.

15 Leonée Ormond, 'Dress in the Painting of Dante Gabriel Rossetti', *Costume* 8 (1974), 29.

16 Stella Mary Newton, *Health, Art and Reason: Dress Reformers of the 19th Century* (London: John Murray, 1974).

other costume books such as a 1664 edition of *Habiti Antichi*).[17] Smith argued that the engravings in *Costume Historique*, which were by Paul Mercury, were 'greatly admired by the Pre-Raphaelite Brotherhood and appear to have been used extensively as the basis, not only for their mediaeval costumes, but in certain instances, as the basis for whole figures in their paintings and drawings of the 1848–50 period'.[18] Smith compared them to the engravings, tracings made by Brown and Millais as well as drawings made by Hunt and Rossetti, discussing the cut of garments, pose of figures and overall sartorial depictions, showing very clearly how engaged with sartorial research these artists were. While effectively demonstrating the Pre-Raphaelites' deep interest in historical costume, Smith does not discuss any possible real-world manifestations of these costumes as everyday clothing for either themselves or their models.

Ormond's article is much more specific, in that it both focuses on Rossetti's work and uses his correspondence with his assistant Henry Treffry Dunn to discuss actual garments in his personal collection which were used for his models. While the main thread of her argument concentrates on costumes worn for modelling, towards the end of her essay she makes one statement that begins to point towards the blurring of boundaries between modelling costume and dress:

> [Rossetti] wrote of Jane Morris's 'old olive green velvet dress which I painted in that old fiddle picture' [*Veronica Veronese*]. This dress, with full sleeves ruched at the wrists and with a gathered neckline, clearly influenced the so-called aesthetic taste in dress, which swept through London in the 1870s and 1880s.[19]

Ormond's conclusion is significant to understanding how this notion of Pre-Raphaelite Dress has continued, as she is the first modern scholar to point to the influence of Pre-Raphaelite modelling costume on the Aesthetic Dress of subsequent decades, as Haweis and others indicated contemporarily in the nineteenth century. In fact, she makes a sound

17 Anonymous, 'Sale of Rossetti's Library', *Liverpool Mercury Issue 10745* (Liverpool, 19 June 1882).

18 Smith, 'Bonnard's Costume Historique', 2, 8.

19 Ormond, 'Dress in the Painting of Dante Gabriel Rossetti', 29.

conclusion, although she does not note the fact that *Veronica Veronese* was painted in 1872, at a time when Aestheticism was already on the rise; the dress fits that period.

Newton is the first to investigate the subject not just as costume for painting, but as actual sartorial practice. She is the first modern dress historian to draw conclusions connecting what these artists were painting with what their female associates were wearing during these early days of the movement, c. 1850s and early 1860s. She begins by rightfully pointing out that the 'truth-to-nature' strictures followed by the Brotherhood were what drove them to paint from life – including the construction of appropriate clothing for their subject matter to study and paint. Although Smith and Ormond have effectively shown how carefully the Pre-Raphaelites studied costume from pictorial and textual sources, Newton further argued that this would not have been enough to satiate their need for the accurate depiction of light, shape and texture in their images. She also points out the problem of finding authentic period clothing, as 'even surviving garments (few, if any, from periods that the PreRaphaelites [*sic*] were most tempted to paint) were usually shabby and fragmentary'.[20] Millais, for example, was able to find 'a really splendid lady's ancient dress – all flowered over in silver embroidery', about which he commented in a letter: 'I am going to paint it for "Ophelia". You may imagine it is something rather good when I tell you it cost me, old and dirty as it is, four pounds.'[21] It is likely that Elizabeth Siddal posed in this dress, lying in a bathtub (although it is never specifically stated that she was submerged in this dress, Millais' desire to get the proper 'atmosphere and aqueous affects' of the garment floating in the water would make it likely that she was) and famously fell ill when, oblivious in his concentration on his painting, Millais failed to note the lamps which kept the water warm had burned out.[22] The fate of the dress is unknown, but the discovery of it was rare, and as Newton concludes, in addition to the aforementioned secondary sources, '[t]he only expedients

20 Newton, *Health, Art and Reason,* 27.

21 John Guille Millais, *The Life and Letters of John Everett Millais,* 2 vols (London: Methuen & Co., 1899), I, 162.

22 Millais, *Life and Letters,* 144.

left to the Brotherhood, therefore, were [...] to have specially designed clothing made for their sitters to be painted in'.[23] An excellent example of this is the fourteenth-century-style velvet tunic dress worn by Millais' *Mariana*, for which he himself selected the fabric to be made into a dress by his mother for the purpose.[24]

Through reporting these tales in a chapter entitled 'PreRaphaelite Clothing' [*sic*], Newton rightfully draws attention to the actual garments used and worn by models in the paintings, but also inadvertently cultivates a supposition that these were clothes to be worn in everyday situations as well. Subsequent academic and popular discussions pick up on this and go further to state that Pre-Raphaelite Dress was a fashion that departed significantly from fashionable Victorian dress (as Mackrell's quote at the outset suggests) and that it was designed by the artists, made by the models and worn by them in public. Texts which support this idea include Patricia Cunningham's *Reforming Women's Fashion, 1850–1920* (2003);[25] and more recently, Oriole Cullen's definition of Aesthetic Dress in the *Berg Companion to Fashion* (2010), in which she suggests 'The type of dress that emerged was worn by female members of the artists' [Pre-Raphaelite] circle'.[26] The photo she selected to illustrate this entry is that of Jane Morris taken in Rossetti's garden (Figure 10.1, discussed in detail later).

With a close examination of the most frequently cited examples of Pre-Raphaelite women that allegedly wore the clothing in which they modelled – Elizabeth Siddal and Jane Morris – we can begin to see why this is a problematic example. However, to begin examining this possibility, we must look to the earliest model about whom 'Pre-Raphaelite Dress' assumptions have been made: Christina Rossetti.

23 Newton, *Health, Art and Reason*, 27.

24 Millais, *Life and Letters*, 94.

25 Patricia A. Cunningham, *Reforming Women's Fashion, 1850–1920: Politics, Health and Art* (Kent, Ohio: Kent State University Press, 2002).

26 Oriole Cullen, 'Aesthetic Dress', in *The Berg Companion to Fashion*, ed. Valerie Steele (London: Berg, 2010), 7.

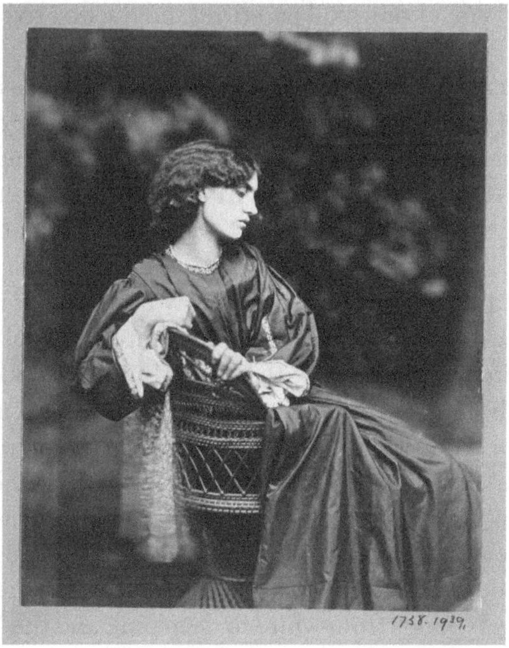

Figure 10.1. John Parsons, *Jane Morris* posed by Dante Gabriel Rossetti, 7 July 1865. Albumen print from wet collodion-on-glass negative, 253 × 200 mm. Victoria and Albert Museum [1738–1939]. © Victoria and Albert Museum.

Christina Rossetti

In her PhD thesis (1990) on Pre-Raphaelite influences on Victorian women's dress, Pamela Radcliffe concluded that 'Dante Gabriel Rossetti created the first "Pre-Raphaelite" dress in his painting, *The Girlhood of Mary Virgin*' (1848–9; Tate, London).[27] The model was Christina Rossetti who, along with her mother who posed for St. Anne, sat for her

27 Pamela Radcliffe, *Pre-Raphaelite Influences on Women's Dress in the Victorian Era* (Tallahassee: Florida State University, 1990), 301.

brother Gabriel's first known oil painting (and the first to be marked with the enigmatic 'PRB' brand).

Radcliffe's assertion is derived from Newton, who stated that she 'almost certainly wore, for the painting, a dress from her own wardrobe, very near in style to what was, twenty years later, to be labelled by fashion journalists, PreRaphaelite dress' [*sic*].[28] Newton does not state any reason or evidence for this assumption; it may be accurate, but an early drawing for *The Girlhood* shows the model in a historic costume of tunic and chemise, suggesting that the model may or may not have sat in the dress we now see.[29] The dress as it appears today is a simple, neutral grey one piece garment, gathered at the waist, with a plain rounded neckline, worn over a white shift. The sleeves are loose and folded back at the cuff to reveal the brown sleeve of an under-dress (which is somewhat incongruous given the white shift showing at her throat). We know that the dress was repainted: first in 1849, before the painting was sent to its new owner, the Dowager Marchioness of Bath; then in 1864, Lady Louisa Fielding, its owner at the time, sent it to Rossetti where the picture was reframed and he 'altered the angel's wings from white to deep pink and the Virgin's sleeves from yellow to brown'.[30] This shows Rossetti's willingness to alter his work for aesthetic reasons, and raises the question of how accurate even the original representation of this garment is. For all that is known, it could be a belted chemise that the artist has chosen to render to appear as a simple dress appropriate to his vision of the chaste Virgin at her embroidery lesson. The natural tone and simple cut breaks from both Victorian conventions as well as the medieval references seen in the sketch, making the garment more timelessly appropriate to a Biblical scene.

Although she claimed that the garment came from Christina's wardrobe, Newton also continues:

28 Newton, *Health, Art and Reason*, 44.

29 See Virginia Surtees, *The Paintings and Drawings of Dante Gabriel Rossetti (1828–1882). A Catalogue Raisonné*, 2 vols (Oxford: Oxford University Press, 1971), I, 10–11 (no. 40a).

30 *The Pre-Raphaelites*, ed. Leslie Parris (London: Tate Gallery, 1984), 64.

> In 1848, when Rossetti was painting his *Girlhood of the Virgin*, this pale grey dress, if worn on the street, would have looked affectedly lumpish and only the quietness of its colour and its complete absence of ornament could have saved it from ridicule, if it was so saved [...] Since this is a 'costume picture' the fact that Christina wore no petticoats beneath her dress could be accepted; in a drawing-room the sharp outline of her knees would have given offence.[31]

This is not to suggest that the dress was *not* a personal garment of Christina's, as that is certainly within the realm of possibility. Earlier drawings made by Rossetti of his sister and other women also show these kinds of garments, such as 'a pen and ink study of 1846 for a *Hermia and Helena* group which Rossetti apparently carried no further'.[32] It is a difficult case to prove. In the end, we simply do not know if this was an actual dress of Christina's, or Rossetti's invention; and though it may be a source of inspiration for later stylistic shifts in fashion, it is perhaps a step too far to label it the first Artistic (or Pre-Raphaelite, or Aesthetic) Dress.

Elizabeth Siddal

Similar conclusions have been drawn about the clothing worn in the drawings Rossetti made of Elizabeth Siddal. That she was a skilled seamstress is well-established; both Marsh and Squire make compelling arguments that it was through her possible work as a dressmaker for Walter Deverell's mother that he first encountered Siddal, not from seeing the 'stunner' in a bonnet shop as is popularly told.[33] But it has been repeatedly assumed that she made and wore dresses similar to those she modelled in,

31 Newton, *Health, Art and Reason*, 30.

32 Newton, *Health, Art and Reason*, 31. For image, see: 'Hermia and Helena', Rossetti Archive, <http://www.rossettiarchive.org/docs/s26.rap.html>.

33 See Jan Marsh, *The Legend of Elizabeth Siddal* (Interlink Pub Group Inc, 2010) and Geoffrey Squire, '"Clothed in Our Right Minds": Some Wearers of Aesthetic Dress', in Geoffrey Squire, ed., *Simply Stunning: The Pre-Raphaelite Art of Dressing* (Cheltenham: Cheltenham Art Gallery and Museums, 1996), 29.

something for which we have little to no factual evidence. For example, Radcliffe makes the following supposition on Siddal's clothes:

> While Rossetti created the prototype of the 'Pre-Raphaelite' dress [in *The Girlhood of Mary Virgin*], Elizabeth Siddall actually made it up and wore it. Rossetti described Lizzie's dressmaking in a letter to his sister in 1852, 'That love has lately made herself a grey dress, also a black one, the first bringing out her characteristics as a "meek unconscious dove", while the second enhances her qualifications as "rara avis in terries", by rendering her "nigro simillima cygno"' (D. G. Rossetti, No. 77, Doughty and Wahl 1965). Furthermore, numerous studies and drawings of her in 1854 and 1855 depict her in this type of dress.[34]

While Rossetti's letter certainly further proves that Siddal made dresses for herself, and perhaps shows us something of the colour and impression left on Rossetti, this statement tells us next to nothing of what these dresses actually looked like. How do we then truly understand how this 'type of dress' appeared? There is also confusion here in terms of the 'creator'. Radcliffe ascribes creative power to Rossetti, leaving Siddal as the 'maker', when from his letter it seems that the dresses were her invention. Radcliffe's assumptions seem to be based on Newton's text, which states:

> Less obsessed with verisimilitude than Hunt, it was Rossetti, nevertheless, who recorded the exact form of dress later to be labelled 'PreRaphaelite' [*sic*]. The form of dress, that is to say, which was certainly worn by Elizabeth Siddal and, a little modified to conflict less with the later fashion, by Jane Morris. Its prototype probably belonged as we have seen, to Christina Rossetti.[35]

Newton then goes on to discuss the series of drawings Rossetti made of Siddal, which are at the heart of this debate on early Pre-Raphaelite Dress. The sketches may be viewed in varying ways: as intimate portraits evocative of a quiet, companionable relationship between the two artists; as preliminary drawings for other works; and, as costume studies, for, as his aforementioned research on historical costume shows, Rossetti fixed

34 Radcliffe, *Pre-Raphaelite Influences*, 302.
35 Newton, *Health, Art and Reason*, 31.

a great deal of interest on the cut of the garments and, in particular, the draping of cloth. His interest in drapery (shared with the other members of the Brotherhood) in fact pays tribute to the Italian masters of whom he was so fond. Newton discusses these images to describe Pre-Raphaelite clothing in the following passage:

> In drawings of Elizabeth Siddal, done in 1855 [...] Rossetti made it clear that not only was Miss Siddal not wearing a crinoline (in fashionable dress approaching its widest span at this date) but that the sleeves of her dress were set well up on to the shoulder, thus giving complete freedom of arm movement. Furthermore the front of her bodice is concealed by an arrangement of drapery probably designed to hide the fact that it was not very tightly laced.[36]

There is no doubt that in Rossetti's drawings she is wearing clothing that seems looser and more comfortable than those generally seen in mid-century fashion plates. Do these dresses depart from all conventions of Victorian dress, or were there perhaps more fashion options for nineteenth-century women than we tend to acknowledge? In a drawing of the artist at her easel (Figure 10.2), Siddal wears a dress with a shoulder seam set low as was typical of the time, but the garment retains the plain appearance and bell sleeve, which has been hallmarked by some as particularly Pre-Raphaelite due to the historicised ideas it evokes. But it is also worth noting that the open bell sleeve, which is seen in many of these drawings, was rather fashionable at the time, as seen in an 1856 fashion plate (Figure 10.3). In fact, Merrifield praised it highly:

> The lines of the sleeves should be flowing; and they are much more graceful when they are wide in the lower part, especially when so open as to display to advantage the beautiful form of the wrist and forearm.[37]

36 Newton, *Health, Art and Reason*, 32.

37 Mary Merrifield, *Dress as Fine Art* (London: Arthur Hall, 1854), 62.

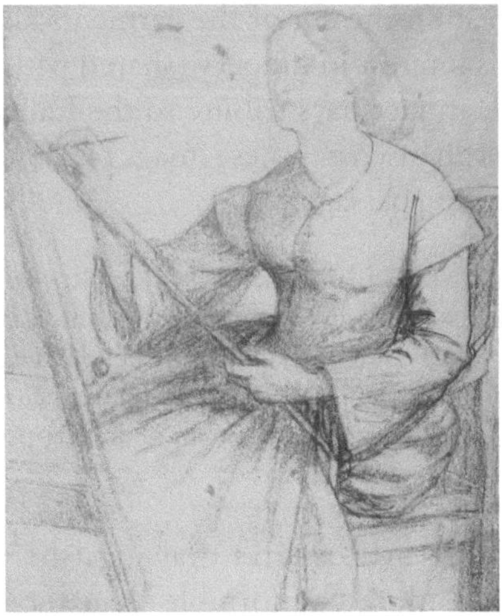

Figure 10.2. Dante Gabriel Rossetti, Photograph of mid-1850s drawing of *Elizabeth Eleanor Rossetti (née Siddal)*, c. 1863. Albumen print, 119 mm × 95 mm, National Portrait Gallery, London [NPG P1273 (2a)]. Photo: © National Portrait Gallery, London. CC-BY-NC-ND 3.0.

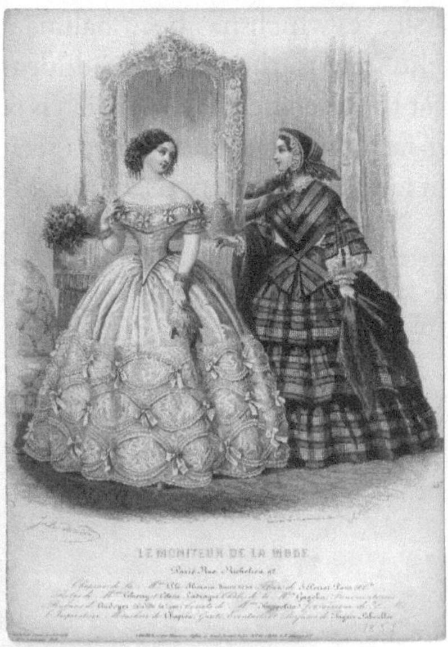

Figure 10.3. French fashion plate of women's day dresses, c. 1855–6. Public domain image courtesy the Costume Institute, Metropolitan Museum of Art, New York. © Metropolitan Museum.

As seen in the same fashion plate, the snug fit of Siddal's bodice is also within the realm of mid-1850s fashionable dress. While Siddal is obviously not wearing hoops, the fullness of her skirt bunched about her suggests that it was designed for fullness in undergarments that would have been provided by petticoats, much like the woman seated in the blue gown in the plate. In a drawing Rossetti made of her at Hastings in 1854 (Figure 10.4), Siddal wears a popular pagoda-sleeved day dress, which, from the fall of the drapery, appears to be of starched muslin. A very similar dress is in the collection of Glasgow Museums, also of muslin but decorated with an indigo roller print pattern (Figure 10.5). Thus in comparing the drawings Rossetti made of Siddal to extant Victorian garments and fashion plates, we can see that while she did seem to prefer styles which adopted loose sleeves and bodices, she wore gowns that were both practical and fashionable, which is unsurprising considering that she was working as a milliner when she first encountered members of the Pre-Raphaelite circle.[38] It is also worth remembering Rossetti's passion for costume, and that these drawings can also be seen as drapery studies that may or may not accurately reflect the actual fit, fall and detail of the fabric Siddal wore.

Furthermore, while the only evidence we have of Siddal wearing 'Pre-Raphaelite Dress' has been interpreted through Rossetti's drawings, there is other photographic and textual evidence to support her wearing mainstream Victorian fashion. In an outing with the Burne-Joneses to the Zoological Gardens, Georgiana Burne-Jones described Siddal as wearing 'a graceful and simple dress, the incarnate opposite of a "tailor-made" young lady'.[39] Upon returning to the Rossettis' rooms at Hampstead that day, Georgiana recalled 'the mass of her beautiful deep-red hair as she took off her bonnet: she wore her hair very loosely fastened up, so that it fell in soft heavy wings'.[40]

38 For further examples, see Calvert, *Fashioning the Artist.*

39 Georgiana Burne-Jones, *Memorials of Edward Burne-Jones*, 2 vols (London: Macmillan & Co. Ltd, 1904), I, 207.

40 Burne-Jones, *Memorials* I, 208.

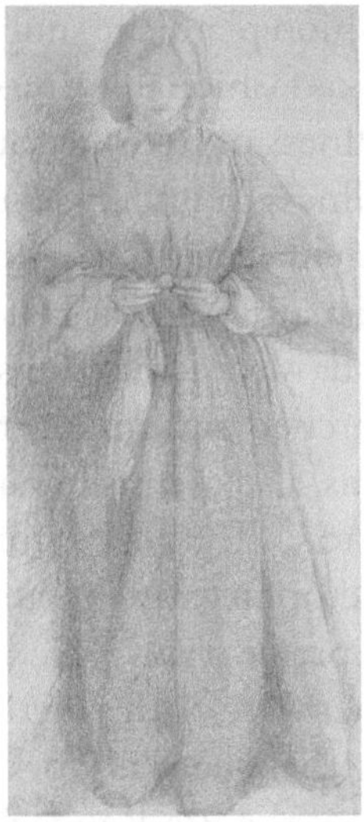

Figure 10.4. Dante Gabriel Rossetti, *Elizabeth Siddal*, c. 1854. Graphite with stumping, on ivory wove paper, edge mounted to off-white wove paper, 26.4 × 11.3 cm. Art Institute of Chicago [1989.472]. CC0 Public Domain.

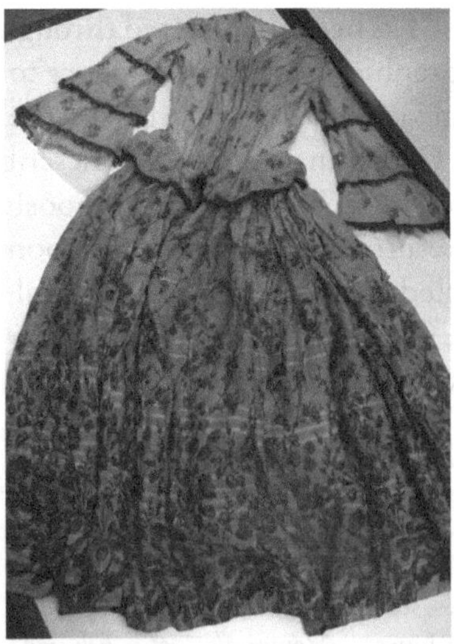

Figure 10.5. Unknown maker, *Day Dress*, c. 1855. White muslin roller-printed with blue flowers and very small dots in background. Glasgow Museums [E.1985.65.4]. © Glasgow Museums.

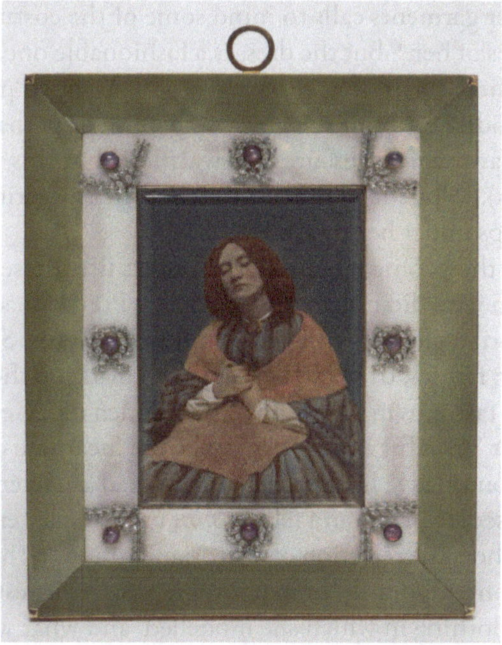

Figure 10.6. Unknown photographer, Elizabeth Siddal, May 1861, Hand coloured photograph, 7.6 × 5.1 cm, The Walters Art Museum, Baltimore. Photo: The Walters Art Museum.

This style can be seen in several of Rossetti's renderings, as well as in the only extant photograph of Siddal, a sombre *carte-de-visite* reportedly taken in May 1861 while she was convalescing, and which was later hand-tinted by Rossetti and given as a gift to Siddal's nurse (Figure 10.6).[41] She holds her hands clasped and has her eyes closed in a manner that is reminiscent of Rossetti's posthumous portrait of her as *Beata Beatrix*.[42] The simplicity

41 Jo Briggs, 'The Making of a Pre-Raphaelite Icon: G. C. Williamson and Walters 38.419', *Journal of the Walters Art Museum* 70/71 (2012–13), 79–88. The identification of Siddal as the sitter in the photograph is still disputed (Briggs, 'The Making of a Pre-Raphaelite Icon', 82).

42 Dante Gabriel Rossetti, *Beata Beatrix*, c. 1864–70. Oil on canvas, 86.4 × 66 cm. Tate Britain, London [N01279].

of the cut of her garments calls to mind some of the costumes in the numerous sketches of her,[43] but the dress is a fashionable one. In addition to the loosely gathered hair, she wears a gown of a striped material, with a high-necked bodice and full skirt over a chemise or perhaps *engageantes* (she wears a shawl which obscures the waistline, but this was probably a two piece dress). While it is difficult to tell if she is wearing a corset, she clearly has hoops under her full skirt.

Although they come late in Siddal's short life, these two examples depict a woman who did not wear loose fitting Pre-Raphaelite Dress, but standard Victorian clothes with proper undergarments. She would have chosen her own fabrics, trim and perhaps even made up these dresses herself, to her own tastes, as many middle-class women did. Georgiana Burne-Jones called her 'graceful and simple' style 'the incarnate opposite of the "tailor made" young lady'; however, this can be read as a reference to Siddal's preference for sedate prints and fabrics *sans* unnecessary embellishments, rather than a wholesale rejection of Victorian fashion.[44] There is no extant data, written contemporarily, or in photographs, to suggest that she wore, in public, the clothing in which she modelled, and what we do have supports the contrary. Additionally, as shown by comparing images of Siddal with extant contemporary garments, her clothing was not just mainstream, but fashionable.

Jane Morris at Tudor House

In 1865, Rossetti arranged for his new favourite model, Jane Morris, to be photographed in the garden of his home Tudor House, in Cheyne Walk, Chelsea. Rossetti set up residence for himself there in 1862 after Siddal's death and, according to Jan Marsh's biography, rather than falling into a deep mourning, he sunk himself into his work, becoming more

43 See Virginia Surtees, *Rossetti's Portraits of Elizabeth Siddal* (Aldershot: Scholar Press (For the Ashmolean Museum, Oxford), 1991).

44 Burne-Jones, *Memorials* I, 220.

productive – and successful – than he had been thus far.[45] In addition to receiving frequent visitors from the artistic world at Tudor House, Rossetti famously kept a menagerie of exotic animals that included racoons, armadillos, peacocks, a white bull (which, according to Ellen Terry, he purchased because it had 'eyes like Janey Morris'),[46] and perhaps most notably, a much beloved wombat. It is uncertain which, if any, of these beasts were milling about the garden when Morris sat for the photographer John Parsons on 7 July 1865, but their presence would have certainly lent something to the exotic atmosphere that was carefully controlled by Rossetti as he directed the poses for these photographs.

These images are often referenced as examples of Pre-Raphaelite Dress, and/or as examples of early 'Aesthetic dressing'.[47] However, Morris was not known to have regularly dressed in an alternative manner, as James suggested, until after the date of these photographs. It may be true, however, that what these images do signal is a transitional time during the rise of the Arts and Crafts Movement (Morris, Marshall, Faulkner & Co. had formed in 1861), in which the associated women – wives and daughters – began dressing in unconventional styles at home, if not amongst their socio-artistic circles. As such, and because these images have become iconic to the wider discussion of Aesthetic/Artistic Dress, they are worth a more detailed analysis.

The main extant source for these images is an album made by May Morris, which is now in the collection of the Victoria and Albert Museum, although there are copies of some of the included photographs in other collections.[48] One point that has not been made clear is that Morris wore at least two different gowns when she posed for the outdoor shots. Perhaps due to the nature of the images – their condition, and the lack

45 Jan Marsh, *Dante Gabriel Rossetti*, 247–8.

46 Dame Ellen Terry, *The Story of My Life* (New York: Doubleday, 1909), 62.

47 Cullen, 'Aesthetic Dress', 7.

48 See also: 'Photographs of Jane Morris, 1865', in Jerome J. McGann, ed., *The Complete Writings and Pictures of Dante Gabriel Rossetti [Rossetti Archive]* (Freely distributed by IATH and the NINES consortium under a Creative Commons License, 2008), <http://www.rossettiarchive.org/docs/sa140.rawcollection.html>, accessed 6 September 2021.

of colour for distinction – this fact has gone largely unnoticed or seems to have been considered irrelevant. However, the two dresses examined here have distinct features that are worth consideration in the context of this discussion.

The first – Dress 'A' (Figures 10.1 and 10.7) – Morris wears in the photographs of her seated in or standing by a wicker barrel chair. It has a loosely fitted bodice that falls in pleats from the shoulder, with a round collar closed around the base of the throat, not outside the typical fashion of this period. One photograph shows the back of the dress clearly, revealing that it is made from a single piece of fabric, making it likely that the bodice fastens in the front, or perhaps even the side. The sleeves are pleated into the bodice at the shoulder joint and are very loose, and the skirt is also very full, with large inverted 'v'-shaped pleats falling from the centre-back and at intervals along the waistline. Both the structure of the bodice and skirt suggest that this gown was designed to be worn with a corset and hoops. Which, from careful examination of the photographs, it appears Morris does not do. In the seated photographs, it is difficult to tell from the sharp bunching of the fabric over her breasts whether she wears stays or not, but certainly the shape of her torso is not tightly compressed at the waist by a boned corset. The skirt falls straight, most clearly seen in the image of her standing with her back to the viewer (Figure 10.7), the fabric creased and clinging closely to her derrière from having been seated. She rounds out this unconventional 'look' by tying a thin cord about her wrists and folding back the loose cuffs around it, and wearing a decorative, embroidered belt (likely her own work) around her waist. Thus, it is the styling of this dress that makes it unusual. Whether this was at the suggestion of Rossetti, or her own choice, is unknown.

The second dress – Dress 'B' (Figures 10.8 and 10.9) – was photographed inside a pavilion erected in the garden and decorated with pillows, rugs and furnishings for an exotic atmosphere.

Dress 'B' is even less structured than Dress 'A', appearing to be a voluminous, satiny floor-length tunic with a train, which Morris wears belted in some images, and loose in others. While the sleeves are similarly pleated into the shoulder and loose, they are fitted from the elbow to wrist. Even so, these dresses could easily be mistaken as the same if we

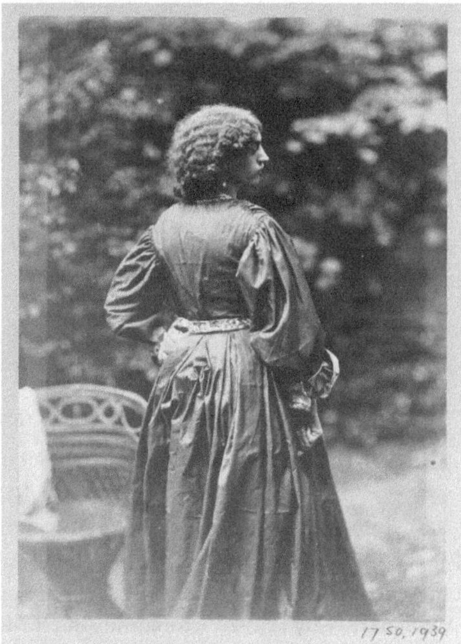

Figure 10.7. John Parsons, *Jane Morris* posed by Dante Gabriel Rossetti, 7 July 1865. Albumen print from wet collodion-on-glass negative, 204 × 140 mm. Victoria and Albert Museum [1750–1939]. © Victoria and Albert Museum.

did not have clear images of the back of both: while Dress 'A' is structured and cut from a single piece, Dress 'B' (Figure 10.9) clearly fastens up the back, probably with buttons, under a covered seam. The clear lack of structure to this dress suggests that it may have been made specifically as a piece of modelling costume, perhaps worn as an under-dress for an Italianate picture such as Rossetti's *La Donna della Finestra* (1879; Harvard Art Museums).[49]

49 (Collection: Fogg Art Museum, Harvard).

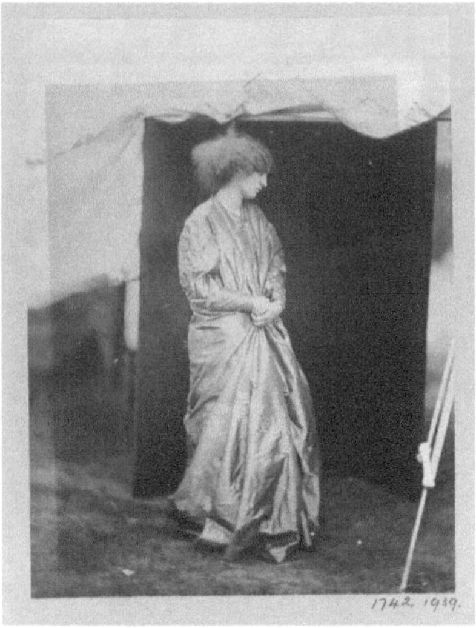

Figure 10.8. John Parsons, *Jane Morris* posed by Dante Gabriel Rossetti, 7 July 1865. Albumen print from wet collodion-on-glass negative, 256 × 203 mm. Victoria and Albert Museum [823–1942]. © Victoria and Albert Museum.

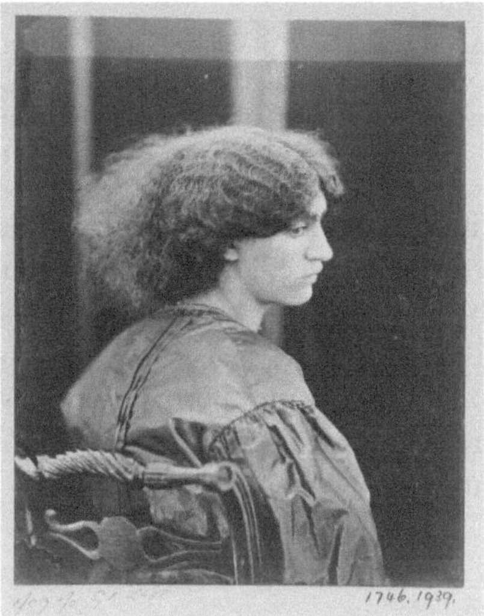

Figure 10.9. John Parsons, *Jane Morris* posed by Dante Gabriel Rossetti, 7 July 1865. Albumen print from wet collodion-on-glass negative, 171 × 133 mm. Victoria and Albert Museum [1746–1939]. © Victoria and Albert Museum.

The supposition that we are seeing Morris in 'snapshots' of her daily life is also highly problematic. Not only were these styled by Rossetti's artistic eye, but they were done so with a very specific purpose: to serve as models for painting. It has been well-discussed that the seated image of Dress 'B', for example, became the basis for *Jane Morris (The Blue Silk Dress)* (1868) (Figure 10.10) which, if the dress is in fact the same one, gives us the colour that we cannot see in the photograph. We also see what I believe is Dress 'A' in a photo taken with her infant daughter May, in which she appears to be wearing it with a crinoline (Figure 10.11). Other extant photos show her wearing dresses with hoops as well.[50]

A further assumption has been made that not only did Morris dress this way in public, but that her clothes were designed by her husband, as suggested by Radu Stern:

> In order to put his theories into practice, [William] Morris probably designed around 1865 a number of loose-fitting dresses for his wife, Jane, which strongly contrasted in their simplicity with the devilishly complicated decoration of contemporary fashion.[51]

Rather than providing evidence to substantiate this claim, Stern includes the following note: 'Though it has not been proven that Morris designed his wife's clothes, it is likely that he did so and persuaded her to wear such dresses'.[52]

50 Three other images – an earlier drawing made by Rossetti in Oxford (1858, National Gallery of Ireland) and two other photographs in the V&A album, probably taken at the same time as the Tudor House garden photos – clearly show Morris wearing fashionable Victorian dress and, in the case of the photos, undergarments: her full skirts are supported by hoops.

51 Radu Stern, *Against Fashion: Clothing as Art, 1850–1930* (Cambridge, MA: The MIT Press, 2005), 5.

52 Stern, *Against Fashion*, 69.

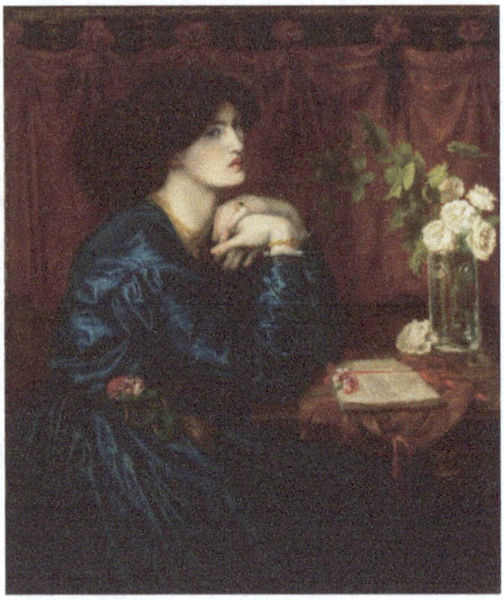

Figure 10.10. Dante Gabriel Rossetti, *Jane Morris (The Blue Silk Dress)*, 1868 Oil on canvas, 110.5 × 90.2 cm. The Society of Antiquaries of London (Kelmscott Manor). © Society of Antiquaries.

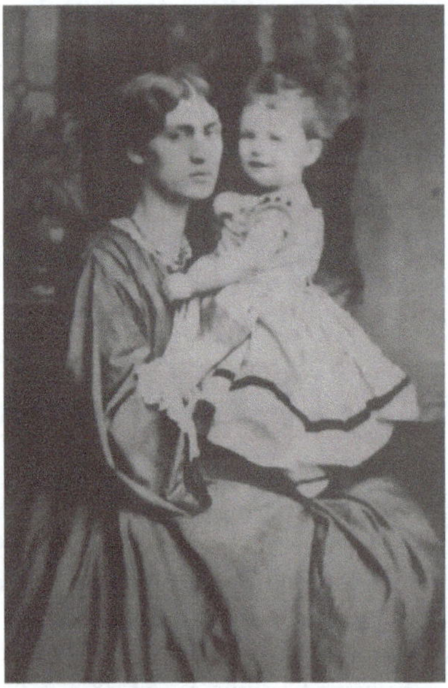

Figure 10.11. Unknown photographer, *Jane Morris holding May Morris*, c. 1865 William Morris Gallery, London Borough of Waltham Forest. Public domain, via Wikimedia Commons.

Why is this likely? It is perhaps just as unlikely, considering that Morris was a skilled dressmaker and embroiderer herself, working in partnership with her husband from the earliest days, for example, on the furnishings for their first home, Red House. Given Morris's class background in comparison to that of her husband, it has been very easy to make presumptions about her education and the degree to which her taste was shaped by the men in her life. However, we cannot presume that she did not design – and prefer – such garments herself; and as seen in the above analysis, we can also see that she wore traditional fashion as well as modelling costume as appropriate.

We likewise cannot presume that Morris was able to influence or promote alternative fashion trends, as Stern's subsequent comment indicates: 'Many other artists' wives were to imitate Jane Morris's example'.[53] It is only in descriptions of seeing her in the context of 'At Homes', or in her own domain, that we hear of her wearing alternative dress. As noted at the opening of this chapter, Henry James visited the Morrises for the first time in 1869, and in addition to being greatly impressed with William Morris's 'superb and beautiful' art objects, he was quite struck by the ethereal and strange visage of Jane Morris. While James no doubt embellished this account for the enjoyment of his sister, certainly he would not have dreamed of such a suggestion were he not to have witnessed it as inspiration. Family photographs from 1874 of her in the garden with the Burne-Joneses (Figure 10.12) later indicate that not only was she wearing loose, comfortable dresses, but Georgiana Burne-Jones, as well as the Morris daughters May and Jenny, were all enjoying the comfort and style of Artistic Dress.

Later in the 1880s, Jeanette Marshall, the daughter of Rossetti's physician, describes her with somewhat less sublime awe than James. She describes Jane Morris's dress as 'sloppy' and on another occasion states she looked 'like a maniac'.[54] These unflattering (and probably unfair) comments

53 Stern, *Against Fashion*, 5.

54 See Zuzanna Shonfield, *The Precariously Privileged: A Professional Family in Victorian London* (Oxford: Oxford University Press, 1987), 117–88; see also chapters four and five; and Charlotte Gere, *Artistic Circles: Design and Decoration in the Aesthetic Movement* (London: V&A Publishing, 2010), 130.

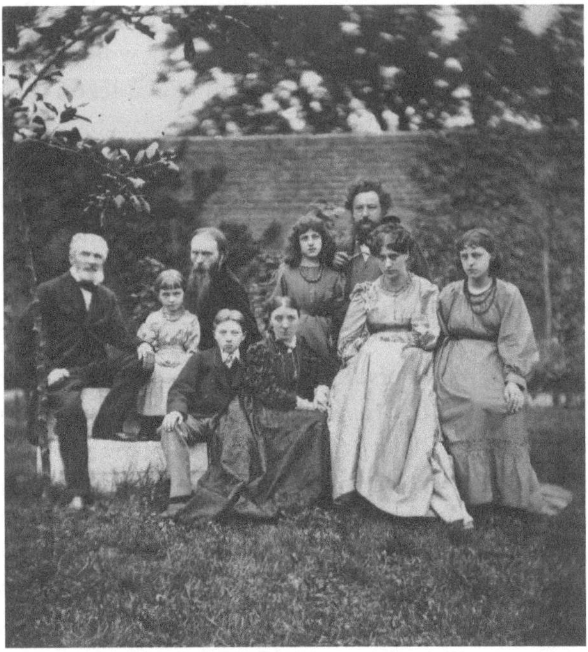

Figure 10.12. Frederick Hollyer, *The Burne-Jones and Morris families*, 1874, sepia-toned platinotype print, 15.0 mm × 13.5 cm, acquired unknown source, 1975 National Portrait Gallery, London, NPG x11881. [NPG x11881]. Photo: © National Portrait Gallery, London. CC-BY-NC-ND 3.0.

illustrate Morris's continued practice of dressing in a manner outside the norm over the next several decades. Thus, while we can certainly say that Jane Morris dressed in an unconventional manner in both the private and in the semi-public sphere, it is again difficult to place the development of Artistic Dress at her feet. However, this style of dressing at home, which slowly emerged into more public realms, helped to cultivate the notion of 'Pre-Raphaelite Dress' that Haweis referred to in the late 1870s.

Conclusion

In her study *Fashion and its Social Agendas: Class, Gender and Identity in Clothing* (2000), Diana Crane observes that '[c]lothing as a form of symbolic communication was enormously important in the nineteenth century as a means of conveying information about the wearer's social role, social standing, and personal character'.[55] Crane discusses the semiology of clothing in the nineteenth century, pointing out that it was not just popular fashion that exerted influence, but also marginal fashion which, if given the proper opportunity and context, may even come to the fore to 'modify or displace' what is considered to be fashionable from a hegemonic standpoint.[56] She clarifies that clothing discourses always include those that 'support conformity to dominant conceptions of social roles and those that express social tensions that are pushing widely accepted conceptions of social roles in new directions'.[57] Although she applies this discussion to dynamics of power and mainstream Victorian women's dress, this idea can be applied across the study of fashion into the present day, most certainly in thinking about trends like contemporary Goth fashion. Crane goes on to explain how these discourses gain mobility and either fail, modify or displace the current hegemonic trend:

> Discourses that express dominant cultural norms and values are supported by more powerful groups, while those that express subculture or marginal norms are supported by minorities and by groups that are in different ways socially marginal, such as intellectuals, artists, and entertainers. Over time, the social impact of each discourse shifts as social and economic changes create a more or less favourable environment for it. The influence of these discourses often depends on factors over which their proponents have little control, such as changes in levels of social mobility, availability of employment for women, and the relative importance attached to work as compared with leisure activities.[58]

55 Diana Crane, *Fashion and Its Social Agendas: Class, Gender, and Identity in Clothing* (Chicago: University of Chicago Press, 2001), 100.

56 Crane, *Fashion and Its Social Agendas*, 99.

57 Crane, *Fashion and Its Social Agendas*, 100.

58 Crane, *Fashion and Its Social Agendas*, 100.

The examples that Crane uses – intellectuals, artists and entertainers – are exactly those who developed the sartorial codes and discourses of Artistic Dress, both as practitioners and commentators. While this research questions the veracity of 'Pre-Raphaelite Dress' as a unique style actively promoted by these artists, the term still exists, and seems to be a retrospective one reflecting the development of new modes of dressing that developed out of Pre-Raphaelite, and Arts and Crafts, approaches to design. Is Pre-Raphaelite Dress itself then a myth, or at least a later reconstruction of a style that was not originally worn by the Pre-Raphaelite Brotherhood and their circle, outside of modelling for artworks? The term was usually used in reference to the dress of artistic and/or aesthetic people, as Haweis declared above, and more particularly in examples of women's clothing. It reflects, perhaps, a crossover between the works of art (and the costumes used for them) and the actual wearing of clothes that attempted to mimic the sensibilities expressed in Pre-Raphaelite art; it is difficult to pinpoint exactly when that happened, but I argue that the assumptions that it was Christina Rossetti and Elizabeth Siddal who began this shift are misapplied.

What Morris's sartorial choices reveal is that modes of artistic dressing developed privately first, amongst circles which were, as Diana Crane suggested, on the margins of society.[59] In the subsequent decades, clothing and art reflect these influences in a more forthright manner. They look back to these images in a self-reflective way, signalling the 'dress of the Pre-Raphaelites' – identified here as the costume in which models posed, and/or wore in the intimacy of their homes – as the point of departure for new sartorial codes that emphasise colour, sumptuous texture, historicity and the natural line of the body. These translate into new fashions that come to be known as Aesthetic Dress from the 1870s to the 1890s.

59 Crane, *Fashion and Its Social Agendas*, 100.

Bibliography

Anonymous, 'Aesthetic Dress', *The Queen* (1881).
——, 'Ladies Dress – Real and Ideal I & II', *The Pall Mall Gazette* (London, 1885).
C. W. [Constance Wilde?], 'Ladies Dress – Aesthetic and Artistic', *The Pall Mall Gazette* (London, 1885).
Calvert, Robyne, 'Fashioning the Artist: Artistic Dress in Victorian Britain 1848–1900', PhD thesis (University of Glasgow, 2012).
——, 'Manly Modes: Artistic Dress and the Styling of Masculine Identity', in *Visual Culture in Britain* 16/2 (2015), 223–42.
Cheltenham Art Gallery and Museums, *Simply Stunning: The Pre-Raphaelite Art of Dressing* (Cheltenham: Cheltenham Art Gallery & Museums, 1996).
Crane, Diana, *Fashion and Its Social Agendas: Class, Gender, and Identity in Clothing* (Chicago: University of Chicago Press, 2001).
Cullen, Oriole, 'Aesthetic Dress', in Valerie Steele, ed., *The Berg Companion to Fashion* (London: Berg, 2010).
Cunningham, Patricia A, *Reforming Women's Fashion, 1850–1920: Politics, Health and Art*, vol. 1 (Kent, Ohio: Kent State University Press, 2002).
Haweis, (Mrs) Mary Eliza, 'Pre-Raphaelite Dress', *The Queen* (9 February 1878).
——, 'The Æsthetics of Dress', *The Art Journal (1875–1887)* 6, New Series (1 January 1880), 129–31.
——, *The Art of Dress* (London: Chatto and Windus, 1879).
James, Henry, *Letters* (Cambridge, MA: Harvard University Press, 1984).
Mackrell, Alice, *Art and Fashion: The Impact of Art on Fashion and Fashion on Art* (London: Batsford, 2005).
Marsh, Jan, *Dante Gabriel Rossetti, Painter and Poet* (London: Orion Books, 1999).
McGann, Jerome J., ed., *The Complete Writings and Pictures of Dante Gabriel Rossetti [Rossetti Archive]*, Freely distributed by IATH and the NINES consortium under a Creative Commons License (2008) <http://www.rossettiarchive.org/index.html>.
Merrifield, Mary, *Dress as Fine Art* (London: Arthur Hall, 1854).
Millais, J. G., *The Life and Letters of John Everett Millais* (London: Methuen & Co., 1899).
Newton, Stella Mary, *Health, Art, and Reason: Dress Reformers of the Nineteenth Century* (London: John Murray, 1974).
Ormond, Leonée, 'Dress in the Painting of Dante Gabriel Rossetti', *Costume* 8 (1974).

Radcliffe, Pamela, *Pre-Raphaelite Influences on Women's Dress in the Victorian Era* (Tallahassee: Florida State University, 1990).
Shonfield, Zuzanna, 'Miss Marshall and the Cimabue Browns', *Costume* 13 (1979), 63–4.
Smith, Roger, 'Bonnard's *Costume Historique*-a Pre-Raphaelite Source Book', *Costume* 7 (1973).
Stern, Radu, *Against Fashion: Clothing as Art, 1850–1930* (Cambridge, MA: The MIT Press, 2005).
Terry, Dame Ellen, *The Story of My Life* (New York: Doubleday, 1909).
Wilson, Sophia, 'Away with the Corsets, On with the Shifts', in *Simply Stunning: The Pre-Raphaelite Art of Dressing* (Cheltenham: Cheltenham Art Gallery & Museums, 1996), 20–7.
Wahl, Kim, 'Fashioning the Female Artistic Self: Aesthetic Dress in Nineteenth-century British Visual Culture', PhD Dissertation (Queen's University, History of Art, 2004).

HELENA COX

11 Alžběta Siddallová and the Czech Rossetti

ABSTRACT

Around 1900, as one of the cultural centres of the Austro-Hungarian Empire, Prague was home to a growing circle of artists admiring the English Pre-Raphaelites. Among them was the painter and etcher Max Švabinský (1873–1963), nicknamed the 'Czech Rossetti'. Although immensely successful as an artist, Max's association with Dante Gabriel Rossetti was mainly based on the enthusiasm of his model and later wife, Ela Švabinská (1878–1967) and her impact on Max's work.[1] Ela first emerged as the artist's model, creating a specific feminine type with a signature look inspired by the Pre-Raphaelites. As Max's wife, Ela became part of a wider artistic circle and devoted herself to an informal study of art history and for short time also painting. Most importantly, Ela compiled a book of memoirs featuring detailed descriptions of her and Max's life and artistic opinions. It is in these memoirs that the couple's admiration for the Pre-Raphaelites comes through strongly and passionately, with Ela being the driving force of this enthusiasm. It is also here that Ela notes that she and Max are being dubbed the *Czech Rossetti and Alžběta Siddallová,* the Czech version of Elizabeth Siddall's name as it sometimes appeared in local art journals.[2] This chapter will use the case study of the Švabinskýs to explore the impact of Siddall and other Pre-Raphaelite women on Max and reflect on how this transformed the Czech reflections of the Pre-Raphaelite movement.[3]

* * * * *

1 I will use first names throughout to differentiate between husband and wife.

2 Siddall's name appeared in several mutations across various journals in the 1890s and 1900s, such as Volné Směry, Rozhledy and books, ranging from Alžběta to Elizabetha to Elisabeth. In this chapter, I am using the spelling with two L's to honour the original spelling of Elizabeth's surname. This is despite the fact that Bohemian journals from around 1900 only ever use the one L and don't recognise Elizabeth as an artist in her own right. To pay homage to her wider personality and talent, I decided to use her original surname Siddall throughout this chapter.

3 This chapter is based on my ongoing PhD research at the History of Art Department, University of York. All translations from Czech are my own unless otherwise stated.

Max Švabinský is amongst the most celebrated Czech artists of the late nineteenth century. His work from the turn of the century until the early 1910s was closely connected to his model, fiancée and later wife, Ela (née Vejrychová). However, her involvement is rarely given much credit – a scenario that will undoubtedly resonate throughout this chapter.

Max was born in the small town of Kroměříž in 1873. He was illegitimate, and legend has it that his mother, steeped in shame, never left the house for the first ten years of Max's life.[4] Allegedly, she only stepped out of her home when 10-year-old Max – deemed a miracle child thanks to his artistic talent – held his first exhibition in the window of the local pharmacy. This anecdote perhaps explains the importance of the role that family played in Max's later life with Ela.

Max first moved to Prague in 1891 to enrol at the Academy of Arts, excellent timing since the Academy had recently undergone a reformation. The upcoming generation of students were blessed with progressive teachers embracing international art trends. This was important as the Prague-based Academy was previously trapped between two opposing tendencies: on the one hand, a desire to formulate an authentically Czech art, liberating the historic Bohemian Lands from the perceived oppression of the Austro-Hungarian Empire; on the other hand, Czech artists desired to emulate international art and prove their connectedness to the latest artistic developments across Western Europe and beyond.

From 1893, the artists Václav Brožík and Vojtěch Hynais were invited to teach at the Prague Academy. Both had lived in France for substantial periods of time and were informed about the latest styles in painting. Hynais especially had the allure of a rebel, as he quickly adopted the French Impressionist style, still novel in the Central-European context. His Impressionist sympathies greatly shaped the young Max, although as he would later confide in Ela, he never fully believed Impressionism was the right way forward. Mediating art trends via Paris, however, remained an important feature of the Bohemian cultural scene.

4 Jana Orliková, *Max Švabinský – ráj a mýtus* (Praha: Gallery, 2001), 6.

Max and Ela first met in 1895 at the National Czechoslavic Exhibition in Prague.[5] She was visiting the exhibition with the rest of her cultured Vejrych family who were well known in the Prague circles. Max immediately bonded with them and together they formed a mutually beneficial arrangement. For the illegitimate Max, the Vejrych family meant stability and acceptance both on a personal level as well as with the Prague cultural milieu. He, on the other hand, embodied what the family lacked: an up-and-coming fine artist. According to the Czech art historian Jana Orlíková, the Vejrychs had utmost regard for Max as a respected personality on the Czech artistic scene, and therefore allowed him to behave in a domineering fashion towards them, and especially to Ela.[6] To what extent this was the case is, however, uncertain. Ela's memoirs, only published in 1962 (decades after the couple divorced), are indeed written in a submissive style, praising Max and his outstanding talent – and yet, they reveal Ela and her family's involvement as crucial to many aspects of Max's artworks, from sewing costumes and sourcing props to finding locations and modelling for the artist. This cooperation had a strong impact on the artwork produced with Ela as Max's main model, creating a specific melancholy figure-type inspired mainly by the work of Dante Gabriel Rossetti and Edward Burne-Jones. Furthermore, not only the artwork but the couple's relationship and creativity dynamics somewhat mirrored aspects of Siddall and Rossetti's private lives.

In her memoirs, Ela reflects on the way that Max was shaping her to fit his vision:

> I was not to be like all the other girls, I had to be 'something different'. Naturally, he was such an outstanding personality with all his talent, and so I had to adapt to that.[7]

5 Czechoslovakia was not established until 1918. The term I used here is used by Czech scholars in the UK when translating the Czech term 'Československá' which literally means 'Czecho-Slavic'. This translation was used in the English article by Marta Filipova which I quote later in my essay.

6 A lecture by Jana Orlíková, Municipal Library at Česká Třebová, 2012: <https://www.youtube.com/watch?v=RSW5rXe3p6Q>, accessed 9 August 2021.

7 Ela Švabinská, *Vzpomínky z mládí* (Praha: SNKLU, 1962), 143.

This statement relates to the late 1890s, a time when Ela started modelling for Max, immediately becoming the key subject of his paintings. Ela's account resonates somewhat with Christina Rossetti's poem 'In an Artist's Studio' and especially with the famous last line: 'Not as she is, but as she fills his dream'.[8]

Ela's memoirs are a true gem of a resource. Perhaps one of the most fascinating passages is where she explains how Max and her family became enamoured with the Pre-Raphaelites.[9] Here, Ela describes how the entire family would eagerly read contemporary Czech magazines and journals such as *Rozhledy*, where articles were published about Pre-Raphaelitism, including translations of Rossetti's poems. While there were numerous articles available in Czech, Ela remarks that Max would also purchase foreign journals and reproductions which were readily available in Prague. Ela's passionate account reflects her emotional involvement with the British movement and a good understanding of their founding aesthetic principles.

Ela is also very eloquent when it comes to describing how Pre-Raphaelite art made her feel:

> I couldn't let go of my passion for the Pre-Raphaelites, I was truly obsessed with them. Again and again with my inner passion, I would dive deep into the reproductions of Rossetti's paintings; I felt there is nothing more magical than the type of his model [...] My heart would tremble with the thought of the magnificent unearthly world of the Pre-Raphaelites. [10]

Although Ela's memoirs were primarily commissioned to celebrate Max's art, it is clear that even in the 1960s she still felt compelled to express the extent to which she and her family adored the Pre-Raphaelites, particularly the works of the later generations. Ela stressed the dreaminess, mysticism and detachment from real life as the most striking features of what she called Pre-Raphaelitism, but what in reality corresponded with the

8 The poem was first published (posthumously) in 1896: Christina Rossetti, 'In an Artist's Studio', in *New Poems by Christina Rossetti, Hitherto Unpublished or Uncollected*, ed. William Michael Rossetti (London: Macmillan and Co., 1896), 114.

9 Švabinská, *Vzpomínky z mládí*, 142–3

10 Švabinská, *Vzpomínky z mládí*, 142–3.

Rossettian branch of Pre-Raphaelitism and later works by Burne-Jones. It does not come as a surprise that these were particularly attractive to Ela, who also notes how Max preferred her to stay away from public life and any friendships with other girls and devote her time to contemplating art instead. As a result, Ela argues that not only herself but the whole of her generation were dreamers. Ela's admiration for dreaminess is also interesting as it taps into a wider phenomenon, mirrored across other countries where the definition varied as to what Pre-Raphaelitism stood for. Bohemian journals around 1900 mostly failed to distinguish between the different generations and strands of Pre-Raphaelitism, and predominantly focused on Rossetti and Burne-Jones as the two major representatives of the movement.

Ela outlines how the main features of the impact of such broadly defined Pre-Raphaelitism on Bohemia comprises a certain type of feminine beauty and symbolic stylisation, fairy-tale motifs and medieval-inspired escapism.[11] Clearly Ela had a good, although not exhaustive, understanding of the Pre-Raphaelites. Her words also confirm that Czech art journals played a pivotal part in circulating reproductions and promoting the aesthetic ideals of British art across Bohemian Lands. This was of course combined with access to international art journals, which were available not only in Bohemia but across the entire Austro-Hungarian Empire and beyond, as recent research on the Polish response to the Arts and Crafts movement confirms.[12]

Furthermore, Ela's account of Pre-Raphaelitism indicates her intense emotional investment in promoting their work in Bohemia and in sharing her views with Max. Ela's memoirs can be problematic to decipher; she often uses submissive statements and refers to Max exclusively as Švabinský, while other members of her family and friends are addressed with their first names. It seems as though Ela is making an exceptional effort to convince her

11 In this chapter, I am using the terms 'Bohemian' and 'Czech' as synonyms. There is a subtle historic difference in these terms, the intricacy of which is beyond the format of this chapter.

12 Julia Griffin and Andrzej Szczerski, eds, *Young Poland: The Arts and Crafts Movement 1890–1918* (Lund Humphries Press, 2020), 30–1.

readers that it was Max who oversaw everything in their lives, from where they travelled, to what Ela wore.[13] Possibly this was because her memoirs were only edited for publication in the 1960s, when Max was enjoying a high status as a 'National Artist'.[14] However, having read Ela's statements about the Pre-Raphaelites, I believe she not only adored the movement, but also used whatever influence she had on Max to make him reflect the Pre-Raphaelite aesthetics in his work.

While in her writing Ela likes to create the illusion of keeping a low profile and following Max's lead, the reality might have been more dynamic. Repeatedly throughout her memoirs, she describes the collaboration that would take place across the entire family whenever Max announced an intention to paint a piece of work with Ela as the main model. Unlike portraits and commissions, which brought Max his income, the paintings that featured Ela were created on his own initiative and were not commissioned by a third party – although they almost always ended up having a very public life and travelling from one exhibition to another. Ela's diary records the process in which Max would choose the theme and the general impression that he intended to create in a painting before tasking Ela's mother and grandmother with sewing the costumes. According to Ela, he would oversee the process, but given Ela's admiration for Pre-Raphaelitism, I envisage her part to be rather more critical in creating the ideal 'setup' for Max's artwork. Ela never mentions how Max arrived at the actual poses she assumes in Max's paintings, which makes me wonder whether it could have been she, rather than he, who found the perfect pose derived from one of her beloved Pre-Raphaelite works. Ela's own agency, however well hidden in her writing, is visible in her passion and knowledge of Pre-Raphaelite art, and in the way she 'feels' herself into the paintings described in her

13 In her memoirs, Ela describes in great detail her journey to Paris in 1899 and how critical Max was of her attire, inspecting and supervising Ela's fashion choices: 'Extremely happy to see each other again. The artist's critical eye immediately focuses on my attire (always so nerve-wracking!) Luckily, this time he was satisfied.' Švabinská, *Vzpomínky z mládí*, 166.

14 'National Artist' is an official, high-ranking award mainly popular during the Communist regime in Czechoslovakia. Švabinský was awarded this title in 1945, as soon as the award was established.

memoirs.[15] She demonstrates both an intellectual and emotional understanding of Pre-Raphaelite works, one that probably surpassed Max's own knowledge. This, however, is something that Ela would never say openly in her memoirs, constructed as a literary monument to Max.

Later in her memoirs, Ela returns to Max's own views on the Pre-Raphaelites: 'this meditative world – turned away from real life and its joys – was not part of his character'.[16] After describing how invested she was in studying the Pre-Raphaelites, Ela's account of Max's lukewarm attitude to their work comes as a surprise. And yet, as will be shown below, Max's work is full of relatively explicit references to the Pre-Raphaelites. I therefore argue that Ela's role in Max's work is much greater than she has been credited for, and that she was far more than 'just a pretty face' coincidentally fitting into the ideal beauty created by the Pre-Raphaelites.

It seems that one of the greatest lessons Max took from the Pre-Raphaelites was the necessity to identify and establish a characteristic look for a single female protagonist appearing throughout various paintings. Unlike Ela, Max himself was probably far less interested in any mythology behind his work. It is therefore not hard to imagine that Ela, vocal about her admiration for Siddall, Rossetti and Burne-Jones, would play a part in styling herself into a reflection of the famed Pre-Raphaelite models.

Confluences and Embraces

For Czech audiences, Max's series of drawings and paintings of 1896, known under the shared title *Splynutí duší (Confluence of Souls)*, remain among the artist's most famous works. Surprisingly, the best-known version of the *Confluence of Souls* – an oil painting from 1896, now in the National Gallery Prague (Figure 11.1) – was not the final version of the

15 Švabinská, *Vzpomínky z mládí*, 142–3.
16 Švabinská, *Vzpomínky z mládí*, 124–5.

composition.[17] As Ela describes in her memoirs, the artist worked on several variants of the subject, the above-mentioned oil version being the first to be completed. However, it was only the ink drawing of the same title that Max considered to be the very final solution to this motif.

The year 1896 saw Max obsessively producing drawings and sketches of Ela, now his fiancée. *Confluence of Souls*, however, transgresses the stage of merely capturing Ela's likeness and presents a truly Symbolist and romantic vision. Her memoirs describe how the artist drew inspiration from their own relationship.[18] According to Ela, the painting depicts the inner dilemma of the artist: symbolically married to his art, but equally attracted to his earthly lover. That is why, she suggests, the young man in the painting seems so tortured and bewildered. A true artist, Ela continues, should live purely for his vision of art.[19] The young man from the painting therefore represents Max, overwhelmed and distracted by his sudden emotional engagement with Ela, feeling obliged to abandon neither his art, nor his love. Having eventually overcome this difficulty, Ela continues in her typical romantic fashion, the two souls merge in their mutual love.

Since Ela's memoirs were edited by Max himself, it is not easy to ascertain to what extent her text is an authentic reflection of the story of the painting, or whether it is a projection dreamt up all those decades later. At the time *The Confluence* was painted, Ela lived with her parents and brother while Max was finishing his final year at the Academy of Fine Arts in Prague. *The Confluence* therefore most likely relates to a time when Ela and Max were falling in love, enjoying their connection on an emotional rather than physical level.

Although the main characters of *The Confluence* bear some physical resemblance to Ela and Max, these are not straightforward portraits. The most striking features of the painting are the man's gazing eyes, staring into the distance. A telling sketch of the man's face was reproduced in the fine art journal *Volné Směry* in 1898, two years after the completion of the

17 [Max Švabinský, *Splynutí duší* [*Confluence of Souls*], 1896, oil on canvas, 68 × 46 cm, National Gallery Prague (O3318).]

18 Švabinská, *Vzpomínky z mládí*, 124–5.

19 Švabinská, *Vzpomínky z mládí*, 124–5.

painting.[20] Traditionally, *The Confluence* was interpreted as an embodiment of Max's interest in the inner life of an individual, where the female figure represents a muse soothing the aching soul of the inwardly tortured artist.[21] However, the exhibition *Mysterious Horizons* at the National Gallery Prague (2014–15) introduced the idea of linking this painting to Edvard Munch's *Vampire* series, begun in 1893.[22] This feeds into the lively interconnection of personalities and artworks across borders that so strongly informed the character of Bohemian art. Munch's *Vampire* series is linked to the Polish poet Stanisław Przybyszewski, who lived in Berlin, published in German and kept in close contact with Czech writers and artists associated with the *Moderní Revue* magazine.[23] Max would have certainly known of Przybyszewski and Munch and the whole debate around the *Vampire* series. The *Confluence* could therefore be viewed as a meeting of two almost opposing trends, the 'dreamy and romantic' style of Pre-Raphaelitism (as described by Ela), mixed with Symbolist German and Nordic influences.[24]

The fact that Max was inspired by the Pre-Raphaelites over forty years after they were originally active creates a fantastic opportunity for a unique mixture of styles. Artworks such as *The Confluence* provide a platform for bringing together the gentleness and historic romanticism of the Pre-Raphaelites with the decadent modern twist, developing on the Continent and especially in the German-speaking cultural domain in the 1880s and 1890s.

20 *Volné Směry*, Issue 7, (1898), <http://www.digitalniknihovna.cz/mzk/view/uuid:b4d091d0-435d-11dd-b505-00145e5790ea?page=uuid:1f8af54d-435e-11dd-b505-00145e5790ea>, accessed 9 August 2021.

21 Hana Volavková, *Max Švabinský* (Praha: Odeon, 1977), 22.

22 Otto M Urban, *Tajemne dálky 1880–1914* (Praha: Arbor Vitae, 2015), 134–7.

23 Piotr Policht, 'Sex, Art and Vampires: The Friendship of Stanisłav Przybyszewski and Edvard Munch', *Culture PL*, 18 June 2020, <https://culture.pl/en/article/sex-art-vampires-the-friendship-of-stanislaw-przybyszewski-edvard-munch>, accessed 9 August 2021; Katherine David-Fox: 'Prague-Vienna, Prague-Berlin: The Hidden Geography of Czech Modernism', *Slavic Review* 59/4 (2000), 751.

24 A connection between Munch and Rossetti was proposed by Robert Upstone in Andrew Wilton and Robert Upstone, eds, *The Age of Rossetti, Burne-Jones and Watts: Symbolism in Britain, 1860–1910* (London: Tate Gallery Publishing, 1997), 284–5.

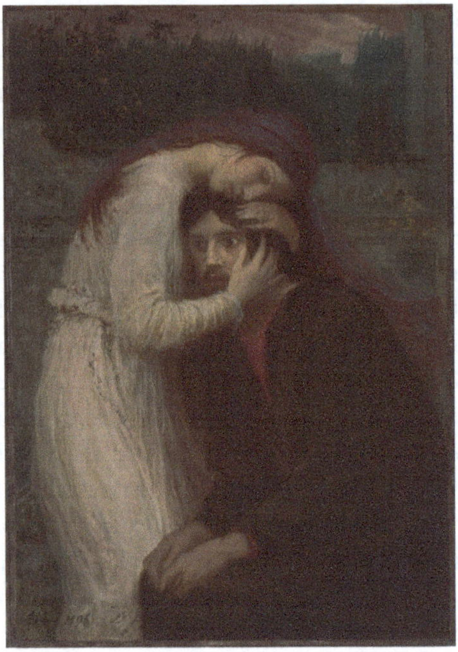

Figure 11.1. Max Švabinský, *Splynutí duší* [*Confluence of Souls*], 1896, oil on canvas, 68 × 46 cm, National Gallery Prague (O3318). Copyright © National Gallery Prague.

In her memoirs, Ela repeatedly mentions Burne-Jones and points out the admiration she and Max had for the artist. The resemblance of Burne-Jones's *Love Among the Ruins* (Figure 11.2) to *The Confluence* (Figure 11.1) has previously been suggested.[25] In Burne-Jones's painting, it is the female figure who casts her deep and unsettled gaze into the distance while embracing her lover with both arms. The young man returns the embrace while resting his head against her forehead, his eyes closed. Burne-Jones's painting is loosely based on Robert Browning's poem of the same name, which ends with the explicit exclamation that 'Love is best'.[26] The couple embrace each

25 Petr Wittlich, *Česká secese* (Praha: Odeon, 1982), 57.

26 Robert Browning, 'Love Among the Ruins', *The Poetry Foundation*, <https://www.poetryfoundation.org/poems/43763/love-among-the-ruins> accessed 21 May 2022.

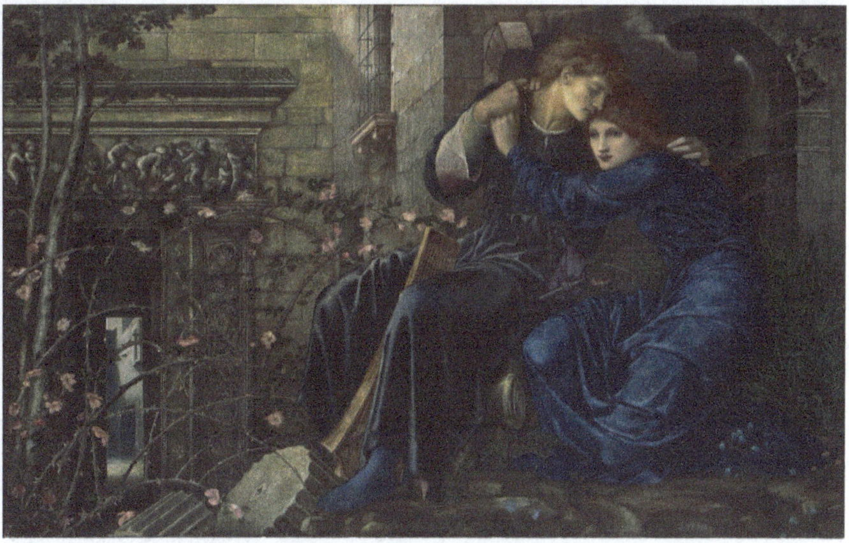

Figure 11.2. Edward Burne-Jones, *Love Among the Ruins*, c. 1873, Watercolour, bodycolour and gum Arabic on paper, 96.5 × 152.4 cm, Private collection. Photo © Christie's Images / Bridgeman Images.

other while resting in their own realms of pensiveness, closed eyes in the case of the man, and the distant look of the woman. Crucially though, *Love Among the Ruins* seems to be celebrating a connection, while *The Confluence* revolves around the young man's gaze, alluding to anything but closeness.

One affinity between the two works is their possible link to the artists' personal lives. *The Confluence* is often seen as an autobiographical depiction of Max and Ela, this view being supported by Ela's memoirs. Burne-Jones's painting is similarly linked to his own passionate (extramarital) love affair with Maria Zambaco. However, it is typical for Max to place his primary focus on the characters portrayed instead of their surroundings. He gives us a glimpse of architecture in the background, and the wall immediately behind the figures seems overgrown with flowering bushes, creating a similar atmosphere to Burne-Jones's ruins. While Max's architectural fragment plays a significant role in the ink drawing, it disappears completely in the oil painting, replaced by a row of coniferous trees or bushes. For Burne-Jones, the architecture depicted takes on a much more elaborate and prominent form, while both works retain a sense of flat pictorial space.

The Burne-Jones painting, however, was not the only influence on Max. He was intrigued by the theme of embracing figures, a topic he continued exploring for several years. Richard Muther's *Geschichte der Malerei* (1894), a popular publication among Czech artists, shows several reproductions of other Pre-Raphaelite artworks which may have fuelled Ela and Max's imagination.[27] Pages 470–1 show the frontispiece of Rossetti's translation of *The Early Italian Poets* (1861) and *Ecce Ancilla Domini* (1849–50; Tate, London) facing each other on opposite pages. These images bring together two distinct features of Max's *The Confluence*: a tender, loving or even passionate embrace, and a sense of distance and apprehension. Rossetti's Virgin Mary certainly embodies fear and distance, with her gaze avoiding the presence of the angel. Perhaps her facial expression and her contrived posture are not that far from Max's young man whose piercing eyes convey nothing but discomfort and angst.

While the Virgin Mary leans away from the approaching angel, in *The Confluence* the 'muse' pulls the young man towards her in an embrace equally as soothing as discomforting. Rossetti's couple from *The Early Italian Poets* shows a composition comprising a seated man and a woman leaning down towards him, not dissimilar to *The Confluence*, although in Rossetti's work the passion is clearly mutual, unlike in Max's. Together, the two reproductions from these pages create a merged image that resonates with Max's masterpiece.

Two years after *The Confluence of Souls*, Max produced an ink drawing, *Radost, radost* (*Joy, Joy*, 1898, Figure 11.3), which was again close to Pre-Raphaelite aesthetics, especially that of Rossetti.[28] The composition shows a pair of lovers indulging in an intense embrace, kissing each other on the

27 Richard Muther, *Geschichte der Malerei im XIX Jahrhundert* (Munich: G. Hirth's Kunstverlag, 1894), 470–1. Available on the Internet Archive, <https://archive.org/details/geschichtedermal03muth_1/page/470/mode/2up>, accessed 9 August 2021. Lenka Bydzovska explicitly mentions the impact of Muther on Švabinský: see Lenka Byždovská, 'Řeč Mlčení', in *Jan Preisler 1872–1918* (Praha: Obecní Dům, 2003), 31.

28 Jana Orliková, *Ráj a mytus* (Praha: Gallery, 2001), 14.

lips as they float among swirling clouds, scattered roses and joyful putti. The lovers bear resemblance to Ela and Max and thus also the central couple of *The Confluence*. The male figure is almost identical, while the female character has lost her powerful long hair to a neat bun. The young man's hair flutters wildly in the wind while the woman's hair remains tidy, as if undisturbed by the joyful swirl. From the worried young man in *The Confluence*, Max has now transformed his avatar to portray himself as revitalised, clutching his beloved without a shadow of doubt. Ela's long hair has been tamed and Max's uncertainties about the relationship cleared.[29] Reinforced by his professional vision, the artist stands energetically in charge of both his talent and his fiancée.

The motif of two lovers floating in their embrace also resonates with Dante Gabriel Rossetti's watercolour *Paolo and Francesca da Rimini* (1855; Figure 11.4).[30] The right-hand section of the composition especially relates to Max's painting. The third part of Rossetti's triptych was originally intended to form the centre of the composition, painted in oil; however, in the end only the watercolour version was completed with Paolo and Francesca flying through hell.[31] Although Francesca's hair plays a far more visually stunning role in the painting compared to Ela's, the depiction of the lovers' intense emotions is strikingly similar. For Max, ink drawing represented the highest technique in *Joy, Joy* – which unlike *The Confluence* was never transformed into an oil painting. Max's main intention for the drawing was publication in the weekly newspaper *Zlatá Praha (Golden Prague)*, which was very popular at that time for combining news and politics with reviews of cultural activities in the municipality. Max originally named the work *The Dream of Young Age*. However, when he showed the drawing to the newspaper's editor and well-respected Czech poet Jaroslav Vrchlický, the poet allegedly sighed 'Joy, joy … !', hence the painting became known under this new title.[32] Vrchlický had an interest in Rossetti himself, which

29 Švabinská, *Vzpomínky z mládí*, 124–5.

30 Wittlich, *Česká secese*, 57.

31 Robert Upstone, *The Pre-Raphaelite Dream: Drawings and Paintings from the Tate Collection* (London: Tate Publishing, 2003), 72.

32 Orliková, *Ráj a mytus*, 14.

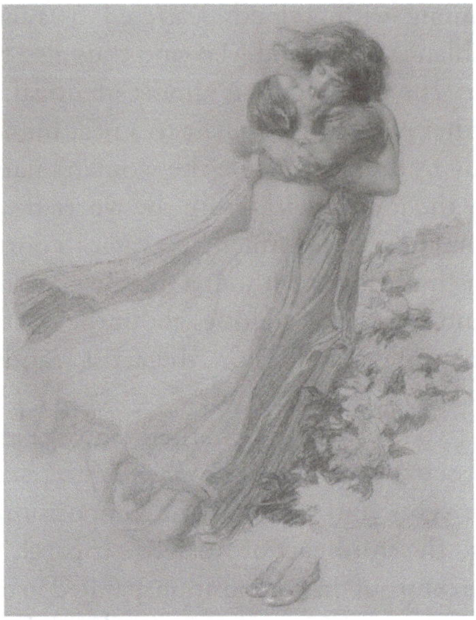

Figure 11.3. Max Švabinský, *Radost, radost - studie milenců* [*Joy, Joy – Study of Lovers*], 1898, charcoal on paper, 68 × 56 cm, National Gallery Prague (K 42911). Copyright © National Gallery Prague.

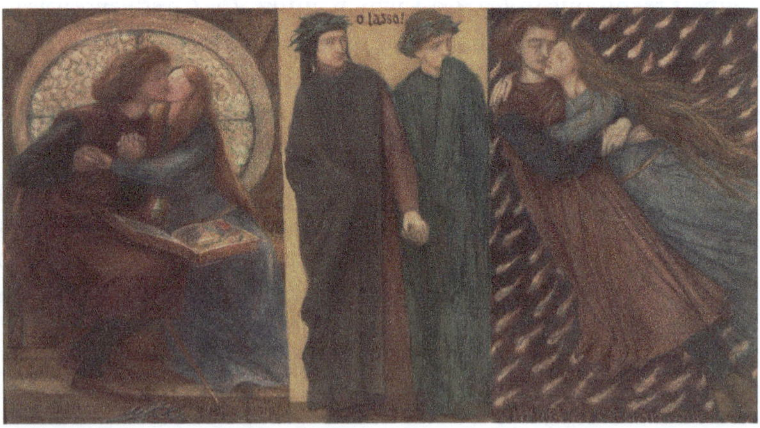

Figure 11.4. Dante Gabriel Rossetti, *Paolo and Francesca da Rimini*, 1855, Watercolour on paper, 25.4 × 44.9 cm, Tate Gallery, London. Purchased with assistance from Sir Arthur Du Cros Bt and Sir Otto Beit KCMG through the Art Fund 1916. Accession #: N03056. Photo: Tate.

he demonstrated in two poems published in 1896, dedicated to Rossetti's paintings *La Bella Mano* (1875; Delaware Art Museum) and *Astarte Syriaca* (1877; Manchester Art Gallery).[33] Vrchlický was exceptionally gifted in his knowledge of languages, translating prose and poetry from a range of languages including English, French, Italian, Spanish and several others.[34]

Max was very fond of the *Joy, Joy* drawing. According to Ela, he decided to show the work to the painter Mikoláš Aleš (1852–1913), an icon of the preceding generation of Czech painters. Ela records how insulted Max felt after Aleš half-jokingly suggested that the composition would have worked better if the young man had 'grasped his young love by her backside'.[35] As this anecdote illustrates, *Joy, Joy* falls within the phase of Max's work inspired by the purity of idealised love.

After their wedding in 1900, there is a notable shift towards intimacy in the way Max portrays Ela. The gentle charcoal and watercolour drawing *Paradisea Apoda* (Figure 11.5) from 1901 captures Ela with – in her own words – 'Rossetti-like lush hair'.[36] In her memoirs, Ela describes how much she desired to pose in Max's studio, but the artist objected. For him, the studio was a place of business and commercial commissions, while his work with Ela focused on what really mattered to him: his artistic expression – art for personal pleasure and self-reflection – which had to be kept separate from the business of the studio. Ela's mother was tasked with sewing a special tunic for the picture, and a bird-of-paradise was bought after whose Latin species the painting was named. The couple adored the bird so much that not only did they keep it, but its purchase started off their large collection of exotic birds and butterflies.

In a much later memoir from 2002 the author, Max's adopted daughter Zuzana Švabinská, recalls:

33 Czech electronic library – full text database of nineteenth and early twentieth century poetry/ Česká elektronická knihovna – plnotextová databáza české poezie 19. a počátku 20. Století: <http://www.ceska-poezie.cz/cek>, accessed 9 August 2021.

34 Věra Menclová, Bohumil Svozil, Václav Vaněk, *Slovník českých spisovatelů* (Praha: Libri, 2000).

35 Švabinská, *Vzpomínky z mládí*, 78. When translating this passage, I decided to go with the term 'backside' as this is a colloquial expression, in line with the Czech humorous original.

36 Švabinská, *Vzpomínky z mládí*, 205.

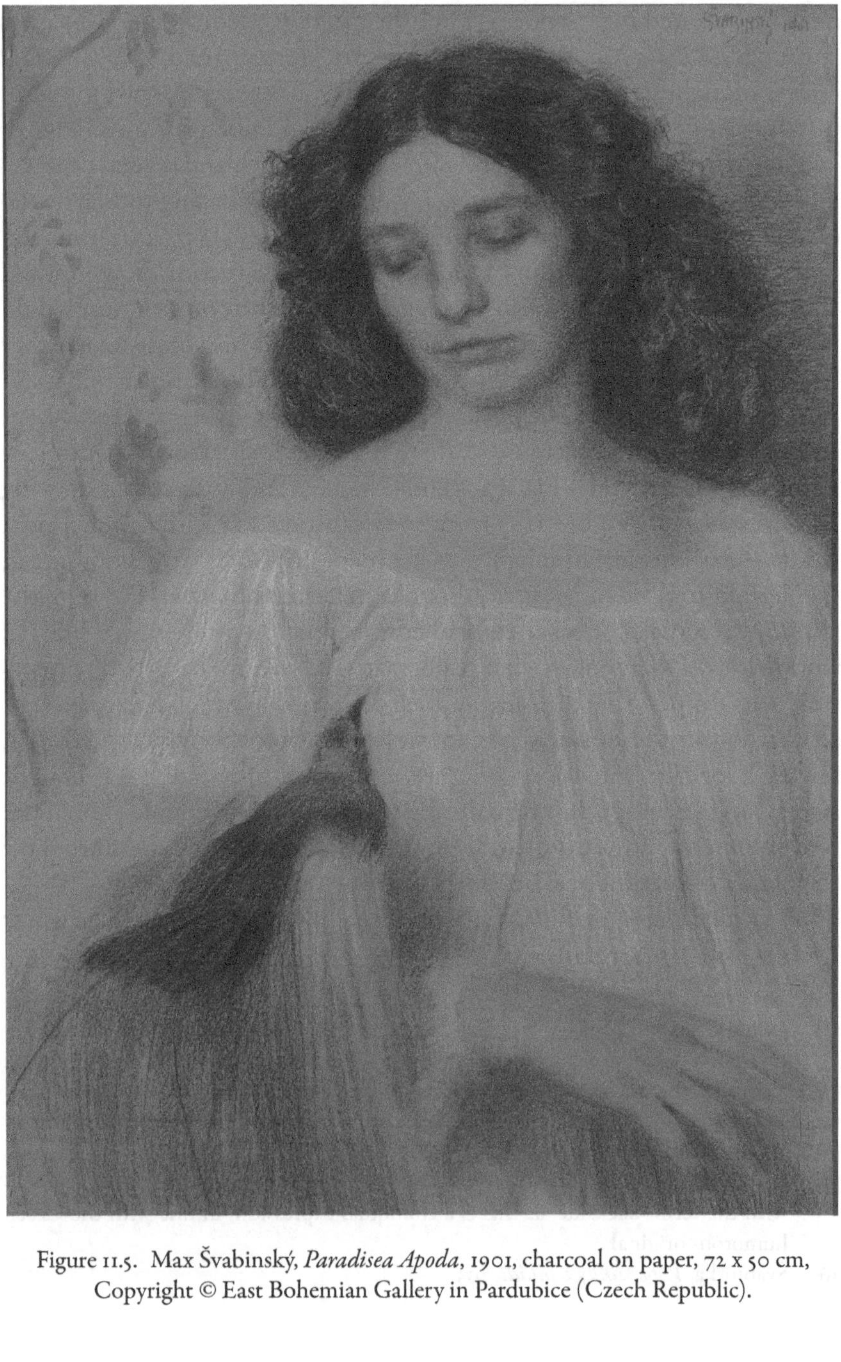

Figure 11.5. Max Švabinský, *Paradisea Apoda*, 1901, charcoal on paper, 72 x 50 cm, Copyright © East Bohemian Gallery in Pardubice (Czech Republic).

> Thinking about muses, next to Beatrice I'm imagining the melancholy Eliška – Elizabeth Vejrychová whom Max so loved to compare to Miss Elisabeth Sidal [sic] from Gabriel Dante Rossetti's paintings. On his painting *Paradisea Apoda,* Max merged the looks of both to such an extent, that we can no longer be sure which of the two it depicts.[37]

Zuzana certainly has a point when saying that the drawing does not focus on capturing Ela's real likeness as much as on merging her looks with those of Siddall. *Beata Beatrix* (1864–70; Tate, London) would be a suitable candidate for a source of inspiration for *Paradisea Apoda*. Following Zuzana's description, Siddall's looks, as well as the entire atmosphere of Rossetti's painting, are not too distant from Ela's melancholy expression.

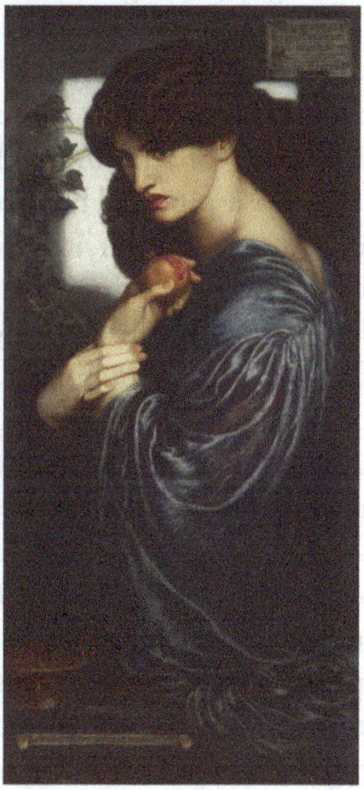

Figure 11.6. Dante Gabriel Rossetti, *Proserpine*, 1874, Oil on canvas, 125.1 × 61.0 cm, Tate Gallery, London. Presented by W. Graham Robertson 1940, Accession #: N05064, Photo: Tate.

37 Zuzana Švabinská, *Světla Paměti* (Academia: Praha, 2002), 209.

However, there might have been more to *Paradisea Apoda* than just Siddall. Although the above quotation explicitly mentions Siddall as the main source of inspiration, I believe that there was a significant proportion of Jane Morris in the drawing too. Rossetti's *Proserpine* exists in several versions, but for this analysis I will focus on the oil painting from 1874 (Figure 11.6). Jane Morris as Proserpine displays the full body of her dark wavy hair, cascading over her shoulders where they meet the neckline of her tunic. Both the waves of hair and the tunic are mirrored in Ela's attire in *Paradisea Apoda*. Depicting Ela's hair in this way is unique in Max's oeuvre and this might be one of his few works where her hair looks so wavy and is not tucked into a bun. In *Proserpine*, a vine of green ivy trails along the left side of the figure. Max reflects this compositional element by featuring some twigs and flowers on the wallpaper to the left of Ela, which is also the most colourful part of the picture.

Known for his lack of sympathy for myth and literature, Max takes Rossetti's composition and transposes it into a neutral space, somewhere between an imaginary realm and contemporary life. Ela's bird-of-paradise replaces the pomegranate of Proserpine and Beatrix's red dove. Rather than a historical symbol or a mythical metaphor, it is reasonable to suggest that the bird-of-paradise stood for a general admiration of nature, of the exotic and the blissful. Shortly after finishing this drawing, Max started to collect exotic birds and butterflies, a passion which later led to his openly erotic series of engravings set in an imaginary exotic paradise, featuring nude portraits of Max and his second wife satisfying their desire for one another.

Paradisea Apoda was probably informed by a series of sources featuring Siddall and Morris from both Burne-Jones's and Rossetti's work. The third volume of Richard Muther's *Geschichte der Malerei im XIX Jahrhundert* presents a handy anthology of paintings and drawings by Rossetti featuring several models, their portraits spread conveniently across several pages almost like a sales catalogue of feminine beauty.[38] With her mother overseeing the costumes and Max composing the artworks, Ela would have been an important active agent in creating this artwork. Max was of course the artist, but Ela's own vision of Pre-Raphaelite beauty, and her agency in embodying this ideal, was equally as essential for their creation as Max's drawing and painting skills.

38 Muther, *Geschichte der Malerei*, 475–83.

Embodying the Countryside

Embodying a Pre-Raphaelite inspired ideal of feminine beauty was only one of Ela's varied roles. In this section I will show Ela in her other incarnation, as a figure symbolising the countryside and more specifically the region of her family's roots. *Chudý kraj (The Poor Region)* is probably Max's best-known work (Figure 11.7). This large-scale oil painting came about as a reaction to the artist's stay in Paris in 1898. Having received a travel scholarship, Max left for Paris with Ela's brother Karel, who was a pianist. Ela was also invited to join for part of the stay. As we know from Ela's memoirs, Max was enchanted by the Impressionists, but he also thought they lacked the rules of classical pictorial composition. Max's great plan was to produce a well-composed painting while combining the Impressionist light style of painting and fully mastering plein-air painting skills.[39] He started to work on the idea of *The Poor Region* towards the end of his Parisian sojourn and began painting as soon as he returned to Prague in 1899.

The idea behind the painting was to create a modern allegory of the Bohemian-Moravian Highlands where Ela's family owned a holiday cottage in the village of Kozlov. It is worth stressing again the utmost importance of Ela and her family for this iconic painting. After meeting Ela, Max visited the cottage on a regular basis and after their marriage in 1900, Ela and Max would spend every summer there. A great number of Max's paintings were conceived during these idyllic holidays. Ela's memoirs repeatedly describe the cottage as a haven for artists and musicians who knew the family and flocked to Kozlov to partake in plein-air painting and musical soirées. Even Ela herself took up painting with lessons from Max during one of the summers and continued her efforts for two years, again following the example of Siddall. Unfortunately, Ela gave up after Max suggested she should paint a plein-air portrait of her friend. Ela felt defeated by this task and never returned to painting again.[40]

39 Švabinská, *Vzpomínky z mládí*, 170.
40 Švabinská, *Vzpomínky z mládí*, 227.

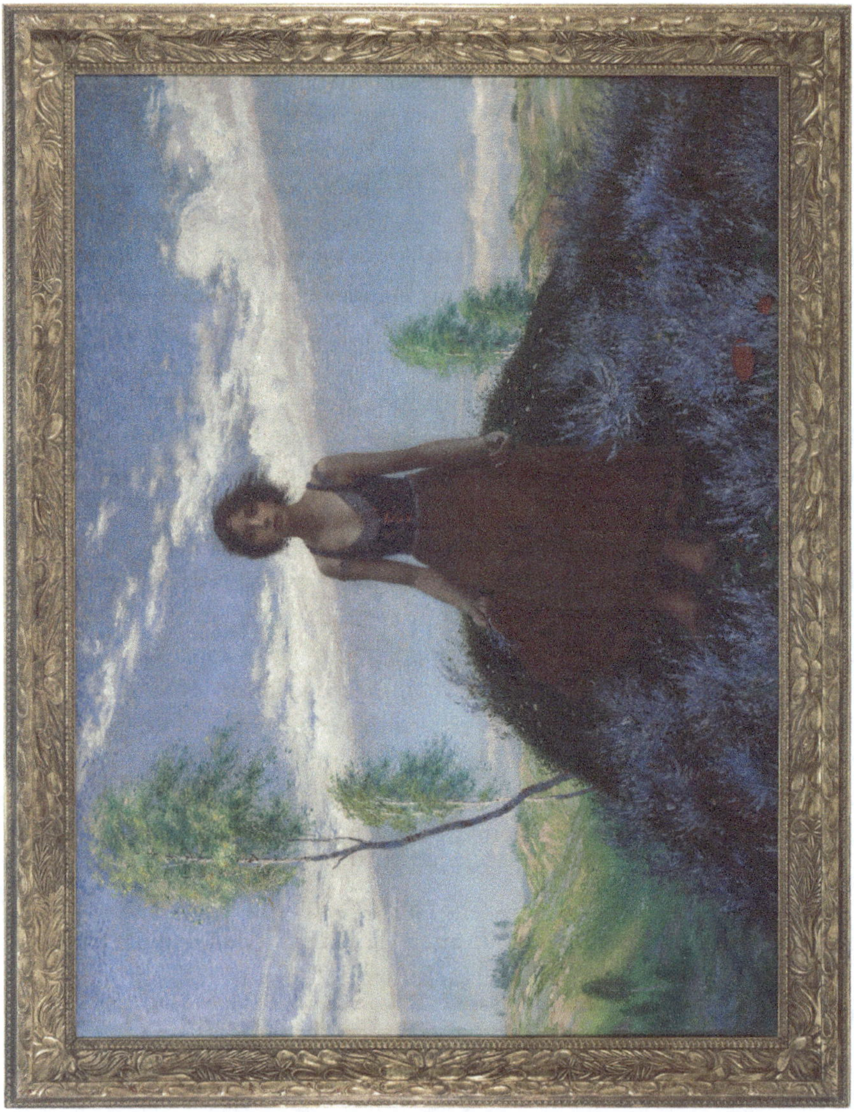

Figure 11.7. Max Švabinský, *Chudý kraj* [*The Poor Region*], 1900, oil on canvas, 179 × 246 cm, National Gallery Prague (O 16459). Copyright © National Gallery Prague.

In contrast to these pastimes, the Bohemian-Moravian Highlands was an area known for the hard lives of its inhabitants with difficult farming conditions and harsh mountain climate. The visual sublime beauty of these lands contrasted with the poor social and economic circumstances of its people. *The Poor Region* was meant to be a celebration of the strength of those who call this region their home, as well as a social criticism of the overlooked harshness of life there.

On one level, *The Poor Region* was a rite of passage for Max. Towards the end of his stay in Paris, he proposed to Ela (after five long years – another intriguing parallel to Rossetti and Siddall's relationship) and negotiated with her family about the practical steps leading to marriage. Max also needed to ensure his mother and grandmother would approve. Ela remarks how he had to make special promises to them that nothing would change in the way he treated them and that he would not shorten the time spent with them to be with his new wife. Painting a tribute to Ela's homeland in the Highlands can therefore be interpreted as a statement of his personal belonging. Although Max always took great care of his mother, it was undoubtedly Ela's family where Max felt true belonging.

It was also in Ela's family where Max would indulge in many discussions about art, including about his English favourites such as Burne-Jones. In her memoirs, Ela recorded how after one of the frequent debates her mother exclaimed in happiness: 'You see, even I now know very well who Rembrandt is, and Rafael, Menzel and Burne-Jones!'[41] It was also Burne-Jones whose work resonated with *The Poor Region*. The seated female figure strikes a similar pose to the beggar girl in Burne-Jones's painting *King Cophetua and the Beggar Maid* (1884; Tate, London).[42] The pose of Ela in *The Poor Region*, as well as her unsettled look towards the viewer, both relate to the beggar maid. Just like a beggar, Ela represents the poverty of her land, its bare and rugged beauty, the hardship of its inhabitants. Burne-Jones shows the King infatuated by the sight of the beautiful maiden. In *The Poor Region*, the viewer is placed in the position of the King, facing

41 Švabinská, *Vzpomínky z mládí*, 108.

42 Volavková, *Max Švabinský*, 26. The resemblance was first noticed by the art historian K. B.Mádl, as Volavková recalls in her monograph on Švabinský.

the seated Ela, and cannot but be charmed by her, as well as unsettled by her poverty. Max makes a powerful statement, merging his admiration for his fiancée with paying respect to the Highlands. With Ela's pose so strongly reminiscent of the beggar maid, the painting can also be read as a tribute to Burne-Jones.

The Industrious Muse (*By the Loom*)

In 1900, the same year as *The Poor Region*, Max experimented with a similarly socially minded theme in his series of drawings and etchings *U stavu* (*By the Loom,* 1900, Figure 11.8). Originally executed as a painting in 1900, *By the Loom* was later exhibited in the United States, where it was later destroyed in an earthquake in San Francisco.[43] This left Max with only the lithograph version of the painting, printed in 1903.

Ela is again the main subject of the lithograph, but this time she is literally interwoven into the item which dominates the entire composition: a large domestic loom. The scene again takes place in the village of Kozlov, the couple's summer residence. Originally a small village hut, the house was extended into a comfortable country cottage, and Max even decorated its façade with a painting of St Wenceslas, the patron saint of Bohemia, in a distinctly Arts and Crafts fashion.[44]

By the Loom is set in an interior of a Kozlov cottage with its low wooden ceilings and religious icon-inspired images on the walls. The room was modelled after the Švabinskýs' neighbours' house in Kozlov, a family of farmers

43 Švabinská, *Vzpominky z mladi*, 214. Ela notes that the painting was exhibited at the American Saint Louis World Fair where it was awarded the Grand Gold Medal. It was then purchased for San Francisco, where it was destroyed in an earthquake. 'We grieved over the painting as if it was a person', Ela concludes.

44 'St Wenceslas receiving gifts' by Max Švabinský and Ela's brother Rudolf Vejrych. Česká Třebová Town Museum. <http://mmct.cz/pristupne-pamatky-chaloupka-maxe-svabinskeho.php>.

who owned the depicted loom. Due to the lack of quality farming land in the Highlands, many families in the region used weaving as their main source of income. Max visited the family and according to Ela's memoirs, he was entranced by the subdued light in the room, and the giant construction of the loom which dominated the whole space.[45] Ela devotes several pages of her memoirs to Max's experience of discovering the loom, and to the fascination stirred among the villagers when Max started working on the painting directly in the neighbours' house. For Max, the loom itself represents what was by 1900 a disappearing industry. Looms like this one would traditionally secure the livelihood of an entire family and would be one of the most common sources of income in the region. With the industrial revolution reaching Bohemian Lands, and with Ruskin's criticism of industrialisation only just becoming discussed among Bohemian intellectuals, Max most probably intended this painting to be a tribute to those values of handicraft and manual production that were mirrored in the work of William Morris, whose designs were reproduced in the art journal *Volné Směry* the same year.

Both Ruskin and Morris were much debated in Czech fine art journals in the year 1900. Their focus on anti-industrialisation and the value of handicrafts and manual production was contrasted with the industrial advancements that were taking place across Austria-Hungary. In the light of these debates, Max's aim to highlight the endangered craft of manual weaving fits within a larger debate, reaching beyond the borders of central Europe and the Austro-Hungarian Empire. With *By the Loom*, Max was joining forces with Morris, Ruskin and the Pre-Raphaelites in making a case for the value of manual craft. Max intuitively continued in the spirit captured in an endearing sketch by Burne-Jones of William Morris from 1880, showing Morris diving into a loom, demonstrating the craft to the public with unhindered passion.[46]

45 Švabinská, *Vzpomínky z mládí* (Praha: SNKLU, 1962), 212–214.

46 Edward Burne Jones, *Caricature of William Morris giving a Lecture on Weaving*, 1888. <https://www.eb-j.org/browse-artwork-detail/MTIwMg==>.

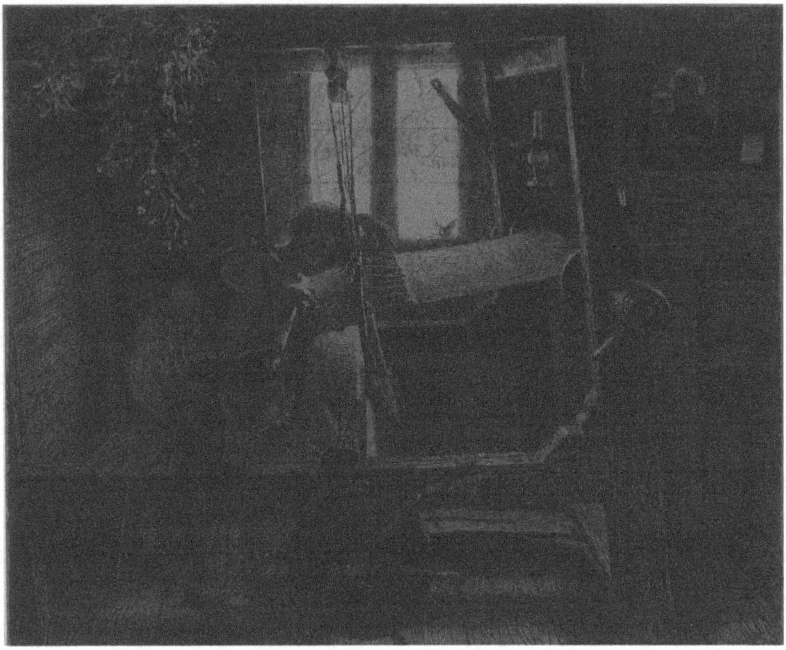

Figure 11.8. Max Švabinský, *U stavu* [*By the Loom*], 1900, Lithograph on paper, 56.2 × 67.3 cm, Moravian Gallery, Brno, inv.no. C4079.

As Ela points out, Max was also inspired by the 'green light' in the room and this was also captured on the painting, which was circular in shape, unlike the lithograph which survives today.[47] Ela further describes how she modelled for the main figure every day throughout the whole summer with many onlookers from the village coming to view the spectacle, fascinated by the fact that a 'noble gentleman from Prague', as Ela states, came to the village to paint an ordinary loom.[48]

Ela describes that her character was meant to look as if she was being lulled to sleep by the sunlight pouring in through the window, leaving the

47 Švabinská, *Vzpominky z mladi*, 213.

48 Švabinská, *Vzpominky z mladi*, 213.

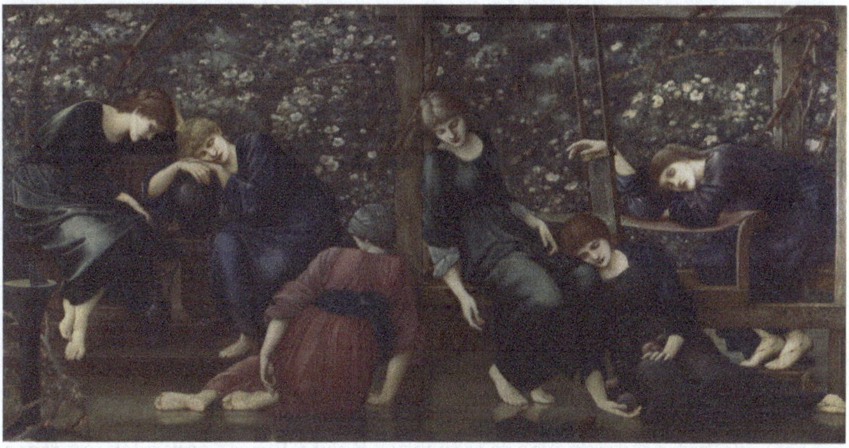

Figure 11.9. Edward Burne-Jones, *The Garden Court*, c. 1894, Oil on canvas, 126.3 × 237.4 cm, Bristol Museum and Art Gallery. © Bristol Museums, Galleries & Archives. Given in memory of Mr and Mrs Francis James Fry by their children, 1930. Bridgeman Images

world of labour behind and drifting off into a land of dreams.[49] This statement resonates with Ela's personal view of the Pre-Raphaelites as being mainly interested in the world of dreams and fantasies. It was this aspect of Pre-Raphaelitism that was closer to Ela's heart than to Max's. I envisage Max being captivated by the imposing structure of the loom, its folk realism and the importance of its role in the villagers' lives. Ela, on the other hand, would be the one to find parallels with Pre-Raphaelite art and especially with Burne-Jones's work, striking a pose almost perfectly copied from his paintings.

Ela's figure in *By the Loom* indeed bears a striking resemblance to Burne-Jones's *The Garden Court* from his *Briar Rose* series, a series of works that span over two decades and encompass three separate series (Figure 11.9).[50]

49 Švabinská, *Vzpominky z mladi*, 213.

50 The watercolour sketch for the painting from the Cleveland Museum dates to 1872: <https://www.eb-j.org/browse-artwork-detail/MjU4Mg==>. The final painting dates to 1894: <https://artuk.org/discover/artworks/the-garden-court-188267>.

Ela is almost a perfect mirror image of Burne-Jones's sleeping maiden, with the loom framing her collapsed body, and her arms and hands stretched out in an almost identical pose. In the watercolour sketch (1872) now at the Cleveland Museum, Burne-Jones seems to have been equally as fascinated by the construction of the loom he depicts as Max was upon seeing the loom in Kozlov. In Burne-Jones's sketch, the straight and sturdy lines of the loom dominate the composition, giving it a geometric grounding. In the final painting, the loom still represents a notable compositional device, slicing the picture into two halves.

When Ela describes how Max was so captivated upon seeing the neighbours' loom, she perhaps means that his fascination originated *because* of these parallels to Burne-Jones' composition. However, with Max's passion for realism, his intention was to transpose Burne-Jones's composition from its fairy-tale dimension back to the reality of contemporary countryside living. This is reflected in Ela's dress, which is based on the local traditional costume.

Max's lithograph sits somewhere between Burne-Jones's fairy-tale and the contemporary reports on the advancements of the textile industry. Images of modern mechanised looms were common in the 1890s in Britain.[51] In Prague, the brewery owner turned museum founder, Vojta Náprstek (1826–1894), promoted industrial advancements in technology with the ultimately charitable aim of liberating women from the ordeal of manual labour at home – something very close to Ela's heart, too. Fuelled by this vision, Náprstek and several of his friends even travelled to London in the early 1860s and purchased several industrial devices. Náprstek's aim was to bring these back to Prague and exhibit them in his planned Industrial Museum, which was finally founded in 1866 and was openly inspired by the Kensington Museum.[52] Náprstek even brought several issues of *The English Women's Journal* from London to Prague and used it as an example of the forward-thinking women who, in his view, even surpassed

51 Kristina Huneault, *Difficult Subjects, Working Women and Visual Culture, Britain 1880–1914* (Farnham, Surrey: Ashgate Publishing, 2002), 164, 171.

52 Milena Secká, *Vojta Náprstek: Mecenáš, sběratel a vlastenec* (Vyšehrad, 2011), 114–18.

their male counterparts.[53] Such a view of female agency must have intrigued the young Ela, who often mentions in her memoirs how life-changing it was when Max hired a maid to help her out with housework and cooking, and only with the maid in the house could Ela enjoy her artistic pastimes.

However, by the year 1900, the debate in Czech cultural circles shifted from the general adoration of technology and its efficiency towards a more critical approach, mainly linked to the loss of traditional skills and crafts in the countryside. As Marta Filipová showed in her paper *Peasants on Display,* Bohemian peasants and country folk were used as a spectacle during the Czechoslavic Ethnographic Exhibition of 1895 (where Ela and Max first met).[54] Given how important a role folklore and traditional designs played in the attempts to formulate the specific character of Czech 'national' art, the booming industrial production directly endangered the very existence of the country-life crafts. This created a problem for those artists and theorists who based their artistic 'Czechness' on traditional crafts linked to the life of peasants and their lifestyle. *By the Loom* can therefore be seen as Max's response to this situation, siding with those Bohemian artists and thinkers who promoted the thoughts of Ruskin and Morris in the Czech press in the 1900s.

While expressing his condemnation of industrialisation certainly played a notable role in the creation of *By the Loom*, Max was also inspired by the visual aesthetics of the Pre-Raphaelites.[55] With both Ela (and Max by proxy) being passionate about Rossetti and Siddall, the comparison lends itself to the series of personal drawings by Rossetti of Siddall sleeping, resting or reading.[56] Like Rossetti, Max would sketch Ela in various poses before deciding on the final composition. While *By the Loom* seems to have been

53 Secká, *Vojta Náprstek,* 122.

54 Marta Filipová, 'Peasants on Display – Czechoslavic Ethnographic Exhibition of 1895', *Journal of Design History* 24/1 (March 2011), 15–36.

55 As Robert Wilkes noticed, there are also strong parallels with Pre-Raphaelite images of *The Lady of Shalott*, specifically those of the Lady weaving in her tower. Ela's pose and facial expression in *By the Loom* even seem to suggest the line 'I am half-sick of shadows' uttered by the Lady in Tennyson's original poem.

56 Virginia Surtees, *Rossetti's Portraits of Elizabeth Siddal: A Catalogue of the Drawings and Watercolours* (Aldershot: Scolar Press, 1991).

inspired by a physical encounter with the instrument in a Kozlov cottage, the composition of the lithograph resembles in many ways *Dante's Dream at the Time of the Death of Beatrice* (1871; Walker Art Gallery, Liverpool) by Rossetti. Here too, the composition is dominated by the angular structure of Beatrice's bed, set in a wooden room with subdued light coming in from an opening above the bed. Beatrice herself is collapsing; while she is falling backwards and life leaves her, her gesture seems as natural as Ela's folding herself over the loom's rim. On the right, the symbolic red dove of Beatrice's life makes its way out of the room. In a similar place in Max's work, we see an outline of an icon-like religious painting, most likely the Virgin and Child. In both compositions, the right-hand side is dedicated to spirituality, and the main character is a collapsing woman, falling into sleep in Max's case, and into eternal sleep in Rossetti's. Both compositions feature candelabra, fixed above Beatrice's bed and above the loom. While Ela notes that the candelabra was part of the neighbour's setting, it is not unthinkable that Max would appreciate the object because it reminded him of Rossetti's painting. Merging the two seemingly opposing tendencies of realism and symbolism is after all a signature style of Max, one that was so strongly informed by Pre-Raphaelite art.

Max's artworks debated in this chapter do not represent an exhaustive account of his work inspired by the Pre-Raphaelites, nor of his extensive oeuvre featuring Ela as the main subject. Ela repeatedly appeared as his model during the 1900s and the early 1910s. This changed when Max fell in love with Anna Vejrychová, the wife of Ela's brother. Max's infatuation was captured in his large statement painting *Ateliér (Studio*, private collection*)* from 1916 which features both women, but where the emphasis is already fully shifted towards celebrating Anna, who was soon to become Max's second wife.

There is a rather astonishing difference between Max's art from around the turn of the century, and his later works depicting his second wife. After leaving Ela in 1919 and finally divorcing her in 1923, Max produced numerous works depicting himself and his new love as Adam and Eve in paradise. As if fascinated with his newly embraced sexuality, the artist indulged in depicting scenes of intense erotic feel, a far cry from the virgin-like decency of his works portraying Ela. This further supports my argument that Ela played a substantial role in the creation of Max's artwork inspired by the Pre-Raphaelites. The artist remained the same, but Max's leaving Ela meant a radical shift in his work – as radical as the role Ela played in constructing his artistic identity.

Ela's presence in Max's life had a profound and transformative impact on his art. Not only was she his main model for over two decades, but as her memoirs uncover, Ela was also instrumental in promoting the aesthetic and poetic ideals of Pre-Raphaelitism which transformed Max's art and echoed through the Bohemian cultural milieu. Her role was layered and complex, ranging from posing to costume design and an active involvement in the entire behind-the-scenes of each painting. Her pivotal role in co-creating the aesthetic concept of Max's artworks comes through clearly in Ela's memoirs, in the passionate accounts of her love for the Pre-Raphaelites and her devotion to the success of Max's art. While Max is considered a household name in the pantheon of Czech artists from the turn of the century, Ela's role does not normally receive much attention. I hope this chapter will contribute towards changing this perception by welcoming Ela to yet another pantheon – that of the many outstanding women models, artists and crafters of the Pre-Raphaelite circles, whose work and thought enriched and transformed the character of the movement and its wider impact in both Britain and the world.

Bibliography

Byždovská, Lenka, 'Řeč Mlčení' in *Jan Preisler 1872–1918* (Praha: Obecní Dům, 2003).

David-Fox, Katherine, 'Prague-Vienna, Prague-Berlin: The Hidden Geography of Czech Modernism', *Slavic Review*, 59/4 (2000), 735–60.

Filipová, Marta, *Peasants on Display – Czechoslavic Ethnographic Exhibition of 1895*, *Journal of Design History*, 24/1 (March 2011), 15–36.

Griffin, Julia, and Andrzej Szczerski, eds, *Young Poland: The Arts and Crafts Movement 1890–1918* (London: Lund Humphries Press, 2020).

Huneault, Kristina, *Difficult Subjects, Working Women and Visual Culture, Britain 1880–1914* (Farnham, Surrey: Ashgate Publishing, 2002).
Menclová, Věra, Bohumil Svozil, and Václav Vaněk, *Slovník českých spisovatelů* (Praha: Libri, 2000).
Muther, Richard, *Geschichte der Malerei im XIX Jahrhundert* (München: G. Hirth, 1893–4).
Orliková, Jana, *Max Švabinský – ráj a mýtus* (Praha: Gallery, 2001).
Rakušanová, Marie, *Bytosti odjinud* (Praha: Academia, 2008).
Rossetti,Christina, 'In an Artist's Studio', in William Michael Rossetti, ed., *New Poems by Christina Rossetti, Hitherto Unpublished or Uncollected* (London: Macmillan and Co., 1896).
Rozhledy - revue umělecká, politická a sociální (Praha: [s.n.], 1897–1909).
Secká, Milena, *Vojta Náprstek: Mecenáš, sběratel a vlastenec* (Praha: Vyšehrad, 2011).
Surtees, Virginia, *Rossetti's Portraits of Elizabeth Siddal: A Catalogue of the Drawings and Watercolours* (Aldershot: Scolar Press, 1991).
Švabinská, Ela, *Vzpomínky z mládí* (Praha: SNKLU, 1962).
Švabinská, Zuzana, *Světla Paměti* (Praha: Academia, 2002).
Upstone, Robert, *The Pre-Raphaelite Dream: Drawings and Paintings from the Tate Collection* (London: Tate Publishing, 2003).
Urban, Otto M, *Tajemné dálky 1880–1914* (Praha: Arbor Vitae, 2015).
Ver Sacrum, 7 (July 1898), 31. <https://doi.org/10.11588/diglit.6363#0231>, accessed 9 August 2021.
Volavková, Hana, *Max Švabinský* (Praha: Odeon, 1977).
Volné Směry – Měsíčník umělecký (Praha: Spolek výtvarných umělců Mánes, 1896 – 1946).
Volné Směry, Issue 7, (1898), <http://www.digitalniknihovna.cz/mzk/view/uuid:b4d091d0-435d-11dd-b505-00145e5790ea?page=uuid:1f8af54d-435e-11dd-b505-00145e5790ea>, accessed 9 August 2021.
Wilton, Andrew and Robert Upstone, eds, *The Age of Rossetti, Burne-Jones and Watts: Symbolism in Britain, 1860–1910* (London: Tate Gallery Publishing, 1997).
Wittlich, Petr, *Česká secese* (Praha: Odeon, 1982).

CHARLOTTE GERE

12 Georgiana, Lady Burne-Jones: A Self-Portrait in the 'Memorials' of Her Husband

ABSTRACT
In her obituary written for *The Times* newspaper by her son-in-law, Edward Burne-Jones's wife Georgiana was completely over-shadowed by her husband. In spite of her independent activities in local government and fund-raising for the philanthropic South London Art Gallery, she is defined solely by her biography of him, published in 1904. In its turn, this literary work, with its inevitable omissions around his romantic relationships, remained the basis for accounts of Burne-Jones himself for some seventy years. However, whether consciously or unwittingly, Georgiana offers the reader a powerful self-portrait, and however delicately expressed, a view of Edward's part in suppressing her personality and ambitions. This chapter disentangles the self-portrait from the story she told of herself as Edward Burne-Jones's wife.

* * * * *

When Georgiana Burne-Jones decided she must be the one to write her husband's celebrated biography (Edward Burne-Jones, 1833–98; begun soon after his death and published in 1904), she cannot have foreseen how it would come to define her.[1] Her 1920 obituary in the *Times* is subtitled 'Pre-Raphaelite Memories'. This anonymous account of her life (in reality of her life as Burne-Jones's wife) is taken, as the writer acknowledges, from the tale

> told by Lady Burne-Jones herself, with incomparable truth, delicacy and skill [...] That book, a labour of love in the fullest sense of the words, is her own best memorial; for it is full throughout of her own living personality. [...] It gives a portrait of its

1 Georgiana Burne-Jones, *Memorials of Edward Burne-Jones*, 2 vols (London: Macmillan & Co. Ltd, 1904). Edward Burne-Jones had spoken to his wife about undertaking this task, but no actual decision was taken until after his death.

> subject, and incidentally of its writer, with an intimacy which is faultless in taste, and with a wealth of detail which never becomes trivial. [2]

Georgiana Macdonald was born in 1840, one of six daughters, and the fourth surviving child of a Wesleyan Methodist minister, the Rev. George Browne Macdonald.[3] His circuits took him every three years to a new parish, and from 1850 to 1853 he was in Birmingham. His son Harry attended the same school as Edward Jones.[4] In 1853, the Macdonald family moved to London and Edward went up to Oxford. His decision to take up art, instead of entering the church, brought him to London and renewed acquaintance with the Macdonalds. Even before their betrothal in 1856 and marriage four years later, Georgie (as she was always known) was committed to Edward; threading through the meticulous reporting, she can be discerned as a remarkable person in her own right.[5]

Inevitably, Pre-Raphaelite romances attract more attention than their domestic arrangements.[6] The term 'stunner', appropriated to describe their

2 'Death of Lady Burne-Jones', *The Times*, (4 February 1920), 17. The author of the anonymous obituary was her son-in-law, J. W. Mackail. Mackail's 'Life' of William Morris had appeared in 1899; to write about Morris is to write about Burne-Jones, and vice versa.

3 The remarkable Macdonald sisters and their distinguished husbands have been much written about: see A. W. Baldwin (Earl Baldwin of Bewdley), *The Macdonald Sisters* (London: Peter Davies, 1960); Ina Taylor, *Victorian Sisters* (London: Weidenfeld & Nicolson, 1967); the most recent group biographical study being Judith Flanders, *A Circle of Sisters: Alice Kipling, Georgiana Burne-Jones, Agnes Poynter and Louisa Baldwin* (London: Penguin, 2001). Although Georgie's sisters are fully present in the *Memorials*, Georgie herself emerges as an individual with her own independent persona.

4 Edward was always known as 'Ned', first Ned Jones and then from about 1860, Burne-Jones, prefixed by his mother's maiden name Coley. The hyphen was not adopted until about 1880, still without any official registration. The change from Jones to Burne-Jones was only made official when he accepted a Baronetcy and took the name Edward Coley Burne-Jones.

5 In this chapter I will refer to Georgiana by the familiar term 'Georgie' as it is how she was always known.

6 Jan Marsh, *Pre-Raphaelite Sisterhood* (London: Quartet, 1985), provides a nuanced account of the circle and the place of the women in it.

beautiful women, was irresistible to mythologising.[7] Represented as oddly one-dimensional love-objects, creatures of painting and poetry, they are hardly real. Patrons came mainly from the prosperous Victorian professional and mercantile spheres; they had expectations of the artist's household but behind a façade of bourgeois respectability, the women, not naturally domesticated, demonstrated ambitions beyond the role of 'Angel in the House' in their choices of husband or lover. With often inadequate domestic help, wives were model, mother, accountant, hostess and housekeeper, managing complex and demanding careers beyond the expectations of middle-class marriage.[8] Negotiating the awkward territory, between the professional and the social, satisfied visitors' imaginative expectations from what was in reality a business. An alternative 'artistic' or Aesthetic ethos flourished under the influence of the women in the studio, in decoration and furnishing, dress and social practices. Edward's studio was to be filled with visitors, and people met there whose paths might never have crossed.

Georgie was not numbered among the 'stunners' (only Edward referred to her thus).[9] She was not inclined to dress artistically; Edward criticised her 'Methodist' gowns and ugly bonnets. Her habit of dressing was plain and neat, but portraits and photographs contradict that grim verdict.

In her earliest portrait, a photograph illustrated in the *Memorials* (Figure 12.1), she wears conventionally suitable dress of a young woman of her class (although only 16, she was a young woman in Victorian eyes). She later adopted a 'Renaissance' model with elaborately ruched sleeves

7 I am indebted to Elizabeth Prettejohn for pointing out to me the earlier usage of the term 'stunner'. Popular literature on the Pre-Raphaelite movement takes it for granted that it always refers to a sexual desirable young woman, but early usage equally applied it to men, from the past (an alternative for heroes) and similarly contemporaries. The earliest citation in the Oxford English Dictionary, of this colloquialism applied to a woman, is in a novel of 1847. It appears that the young men in PRB circles start using it of women later in the 1850s (e.g. George Price Boyce uses it of Jane Burden in his diary for March 1859).

8 See: Charlotte Gere, 'Model Wives and Mistresses', in *Pre-Raphaelite Sisters*, ed. Jan Marsh (London: National Portrait Gallery, 2019), 138–145.

9 Burne-Jones, *Memorials* I, 176. The usage by Edward Burne-Jones to describe Georgiana at a similar date has him adopting the slang of his peer-group, while the connotations may still have been unstable.

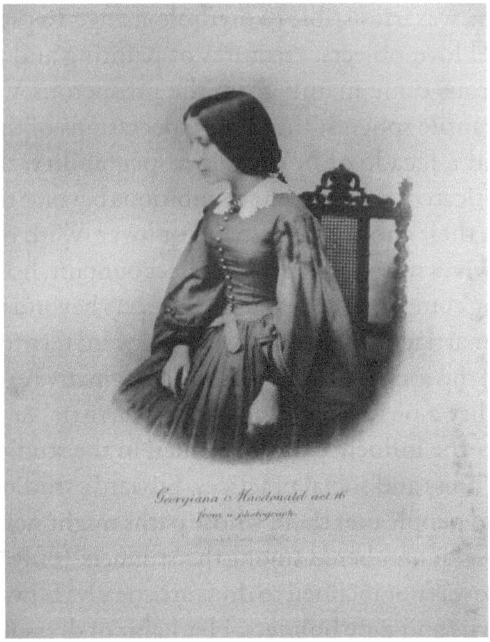

Figure 12.1. *Georgiana MacDonald Æt 16,* from a photograph. *Memorials* I, opposite page 134.

(seen in photographs of the Burne-Jones and Morris families), and a style derived from Holbein's portraits, with a tiny pie-crust frill at the neck. The watercolour portrait by her brother-in-law, Edward Poynter, shows off her artistic taste in her soft white dress.[10] She features less prominently among the Pre-Raphaelite muses than she deserves. Like Edward, she appreciated feminine beauty, and her descriptions of Lizzie Siddal (Georgie uses this spelling of her name) and Morris's future wife, Jane Burden in particular, are very powerful.[11]

10 Edward Poynter, *Georgiana Burne-Jones*, watercolour, commissioned by Rosalind Howard, Lady Carlisle in 1869; see Taylor, *Victorian Sisters*, 1967, illustrated opposite p. 77.

11 The spelling of Siddal with one 'L' adopted here follows the practice adopted in the *Memorials*.

Although always known as Ned, Georgie refers to her husband throughout the *Memorials* as Edward, a practice followed here. Assiduous enquiry and acute observation established the fine details of his birth and boyhood, education and time up at Oxford, where Edward intended to enter the church. As well as relying on her excellent memory, Georgie wrote to a wide circle of friends and associates; the Burne-Jones Papers in the Fitzwilliam Museum give an insight into how she went about this unfamiliar task.[12] At Oxford, Burne-Jones met William Morris, the man who would determine his future life. This led inexorably to Dante Gabriel Rossetti and, with his advice and encouragement, came the entirely impractical decisions to follow careers in art and architecture. They were continually with Rossetti, but knew little of his betrothed, the beautiful red-headed Lizzie. When eventually they met, the tall figure in a 'graceful, simple dress' made a strong impression on Georgie.[13] Something warned her 'of romance and tragedy between her and her husband'.

Georgie paints a portrait in words:

> she wore her hair very loosely fastened up, so that it fell in heavy wings. Her complexion looked as if a rose tint lay beneath the white skin, producing a most soft and delicate pink for the darkest flesh-tone. Her eyes were a kind of golden brown – agate-colour is the only word I can think of to describe them – and wonderfully luminous: in all Gabriel's drawings of her and in the type she created in his mind this is to be seen.[14]

To illustrate the *Memorials*, Georgie chose one of Rossetti's most beautiful pencil portraits, now in the Fitzwilliam Museum (see Figure 5.5).[15] Seeing Lizzie's work on Rossetti's walls and at the Russell Place Pre-Raphaelite exhibition in 1857 perhaps encouraged Georgie's own artistic ambitions.

12 The material for the *Memorials* was passed to the Fitzwilliam Museum. The archive of Burne-Jones's papers comprises extensive correspondence with Rossetti and John Ruskin, notebooks from his student years at Oxford, his account books with Morris & Co., and a handwritten list of all his designs. See also note 87.

13 Burne-Jones, *Memorials* I, 207.

14 Burne-Jones, *Memorials* I, 208.

15 Illustrated in *Memorials* I, opposite page 208. Fitzwilliam Museum, Cambridge, Object no. 684. The drawing was owned by Rossetti's brother William Michael and Burne-Jones's first studio assistant, Charles Fairfax Murray.

Effectively Edward's decision meant that he gave up on being a dutiful son and responsible husband. Mr Jones's framing business was in trouble, financial support from his son would have been very welcome, but all he could promise was 'tin' (Rossetti's word for money) when success came in the future.[16] The outlook was unpromising and he was to experience very great poverty before his career blossomed, but he was sustained by premature and uncritical – but prescient – admiration from Rossetti and John Ruskin and, of course, from Georgie herself.

Georgie introduces herself into the *Memorials* stealthily, noting the arrival, when she was 12 years old, of Ned Jones as a school-friend of her brother Harry in Birmingham. Her emergence as his betrothed in 1856 comes as a surprising development.[17] Edward had found his way to Chelsea, where the family were now living following George Macdonald's posting to London in January, and in the summer, he sought interviews with her father and mother. He had fallen in love with the whole family, his favourite being the second youngest, Louie (Louisa, later Baldwin, mother of the future Prime Minister), but a strong sense of self-preservation made him pick the selfless and faithful Georgie. The interview was a telling preview of their future, as Georgie recalled in the *Memorials*: 'Looking back I feel the deepest respect for my parents because they never discussed with me the "prospects" of my marriage; my father asked Edward no questions about his "position", but, so far as my judgment goes, acted as a minister of the Christian religion should do, seeking nothing but character and leaving the question of fortune to one side.'[18] Edward was at least consistent, never troubling himself about prospects or money. All those matters were left to the anxious attention of Georgie and his most devoted patron, William Graham. Graham helped with his muddled business dealings, negotiating the sale of paintings and putting his financial affairs in order. Edward, dependant on this careful oversight, was devastated by his death in 1885.

16 An experiment with having his father as his framer was unsuccessful and had to be given up.

17 The date of Burne-Jones's first visit to the Macdonald family was 1852 (Burne-Jones, *Memorials* I, 65). The interview with Georgiana's parents took place in 1856, when she was not quite sixteen (Burne-Jones, *Memorials* I, 134).

18 Burne-Jones, *Memorials* I, 134.

Not apparently considered was Edward's persistent ill-health. A running motif throughout his life story, it felled him at inconvenient moments, not least by sabotaging his honeymoon (he collapsed before they had even embarked on the ferry to France, where they had planned to join Rossetti and Lizzie in Paris). Stoical herself but unfailing in outward sympathy for the sufferer, Georgie had an uneasy relationship with poor health. As it happened, she was surrounded by the sofa-bound among family and friends, notably her own sister Louie after her marriage to Alfred Baldwin. Never overtly sceptical, there is an air of puzzlement in some of her reports. Firmly eschewing endless accounts of Edward's illnesses and insomnia, she promised that 'although it was so often a source of suffering and anxiety, I shall say as little as possible, for it has already been dwelt upon, and must take its place as one of the understood influences of his life'.[19]

The exact opposite characterised the marriage of William Morris and Jane Burden, with Jane plagued by ill-health for much of her married life. Eventually, the two who played the role of healthy one, found solace together from their own marital situations. Most surprising in her dealings with sickness, is Georgie's scepticism about Lizzie's ailments: 'The question of her long years of ill-health has often puzzled me; as to how it was possible for her to suffer so much without developing a specific disease'.[20]

Georgie was allowed unusual freedom to associate with Edward and his friends, trusting in her upbringing to guide her. She offers vivid descriptions of the rooms shared with Morris at Red Lion Square and its characterful housekeeper, 'Red Lion Mary' (Mary Nicholson). Mary looked after them amidst the chaotic decoration and furnishing projects and modelled on occasion. A skilled needlewoman, she made costumes to feature in the pictures and later worked on some embroidered hangings for Morris. Georgie's girlhood exposure to thrifty housekeeping and close contact with her mother's two maids, suggests that she appreciated, more clearly than others, Mary's valiant efforts in keeping Red Lion Square rooms afloat, which she addresses in some detail in the *Memorials*.

19 Burne-Jones, *Memorials* II, 3.
20 Burne-Jones, *Memorials* I, 291.

Edward wooed Georgie with books: Fouqué's *Mystic Love* and Rio's *Poetry of Christian Art*, and, of course, Ruskin's works as they appeared. Acquaintance with their hero followed.[21] Ruskin in turn visited Red Lion Square and left with a drawing. Edward was drawing compulsively, recruiting his future family as models. Georgie's face is detectable in scenes of romance and literature. Family and friends people Edward's imagined world, some better likenesses than the portraits with which he struggled later. Pre-Raphaelite artists, in particular, saw the choice of model as having some affinity with the subject. One of Georgie's earliest married tasks was to sit for the 'good' Clara von Bork, while Rossetti's mistress Fanny Cornforth modelled the 'bad' Sidonia.[22] Taken from Meinhold's novel *Sidonia the Sorceress*, Clara is described as 'intelligent, courageous, and faithful, with a quiet, amiable disposition, and of most pious and Christian demeanour'.[23] Possibly a novelty at first, the constant demand to act as models, unpaid and there to hand, was a strain on the wives with their numerous domestic duties having to be suspended.

Georgie was taken to Birmingham to meet Miss Sampson, Edward's devoted nurse and now his father's housekeeper. Her description of the Birmingham home in the *Memorials* corroborates Edward's refrain about the total absence of beauty in his childhood.[24] She barely comments on the contrast between his family circumstances and his privileged education at school and at Oxford, possibly because her brothers partly shared these advantages. She evidently felt obliged to justify his complaints:

> I wish it were possible to explain the impression made upon me as a young girl whose experience so far had been quite remote from art, by the sudden intercourse with those to whom it was the breath of life. The only approach I can make to describing it is by saying that I felt in the presence of a new religion. Their love of beauty did not

21 See, for example, Burne-Jones, *Memorials* I, 141. The visit to Ruskin took place in 1856, and was followed by Ruskin's return visit, at which he took a drawing to show around to friends (Burne-Jones, *Memorials* I, 147).

22 Tate Britain, the pair bequeathed by Walford Graham Robertson, 1948, NO5877-8.

23 Jane Wilde, trans., *Sidonia the Sorceress* (London: Kelmscott Press, 1893), 42. See also Chapter 6, Nat Reeve, 'Queer Tombs and Reframing Doom: Elizabeth Siddal and Georgiana Burne-Jones's unfinished collaborative project'.

24 Burne-Jones, *Memorials* I, 155.

> seem to me unbalanced, but as if it included the whole world and raised the point from which they regarded everything.[25]

Meanwhile, the Macdonald family being established in Chelsea, Georgie enrolled at the Government School of Design, to learn skills helpful in Edward's career.[26] The School, founded in 1842 with the aim of allowing 'young women of the middle class to obtain honourable and profitable employment', was now at Gore House in Kensington.[27] There she studied wood-engraving, for which she

> had a certain deftness of hand, but I did not learn anything vital. Often on the way back Edward met me with flowers, and we walked home together. I had no precise idea of what the profession of an artist meant but felt that it was well to be amongst those who painted pictures and wrote poetry.[28]

The few surviving examples of her work in this medium show sufficient competence to give hope for future employment. The intention was for her to acquire enough skill to engrave her husband's designs.

A visit to Mr and Mrs Archibald MacLaren, at Summertown in North Oxford, concerned Edward's first commission, to illustrate MacLaren's *The Fairy Family: A Series of Ballads & Metrical Tales Illustrating the Fairy Mythology of Europe* (1857). The drawings were begun in 1854 but the project foundered in 1856, and the book was published with just three illustrations. Edward later repudiated this work and Georgie's inclusion of two of them in the *Memorials* poses something of an enigma.[29] It is the more mysterious, because the illustrations are signed 'E. Burne-Jones Del', the hyphenated surname that was not adopted until the 1880s, when Edward had long tried to forget his naïve early efforts. Still in 1904 in the possession

25 Burne-Jones, *Memorials* I, 169.
26 Burne-Jones, *Memorials* I, 142.
27 *The Times*, 18 June 1862.
28 Burne-Jones, *Memorials* I, 142.
29 Burne-Jones, *Memorials* I, illustrated opposite page 120.

of Mabel MacLaren, they were photographed by Emery Walker (Walker & Cockerell) for reproduction.[30]

More pertinently, the connection resulted in one of the few surviving examples of Georgie's art, an illustrated poem or Valentine of 1859, when the author was 19 and its subject 5 years old (Figure 12.2).[31] It is addressed to Mabel, MacLaren's eldest daughter (b.1854), a particular favourite of Edward's, like Louie Macdonald, one of the small girls he was fondly attached to throughout his life. The most substantial of her works to have come to light, it shows aptitude that might have been nurtured. Her designs are more imaginative and original than the usual Victorian amateur production. Both Ford Madox Brown and Ruskin believed in her promise as an artist; perhaps the truth lies somewhere between their faith in her and her own verdict. Like Edward's work at the time, she is influenced by Rossetti.[32]

Georgie persisted with her efforts, attending Madox Brown's studio at 13 Fortess Terrace, Kentish Town in 1858, in order to paint from the model. Brown was encouraging, writing in his diary for 30 January 1858: 'This little girl seems to threaten to turn out an other genious [sic]. She is coming here to paint tomorrow. Her designes [sic] in pen & ink show real intellect'.[33] But this too was barely started before falling foul of illness in his family. Georgie tells of Brown's kindness to her: 'Madox Brown's kindness to me in those early days is one of the delightful recollections belonging to them which nothing can dim'. In the *Memorials*, she quotes a letter from Edward, thanking for his attention to Georgie's art education: 'God bless you, old fellow, how good you are to my Stunner – she does little else but talk about it. There never was any one in all this blessed world half so unselfish as you.'[34]

30 For full details of the collaboration and the later history of the illustrations, see: John Christian, ed., *The Fairy Family* (London: Dalrymple Press, 1985).

31 Georgiana Burne-Jones, *Illustrated Poem titled 'To Mabel'*, British Museum, London, Museum no. 2012,7089.1.

32 For a discussion of her drawing see Dennis T. Lanigan, 'The Bridge of Sighs by Georgiana Burne-Jones (1840–1920): A metaphor for her artistic career', *The British Art Journal* 19/1 (2020), 111–15.

33 *The Diary of Ford Madox Brown*, ed. Virginia Surtees (New Haven, CT: Yale University Press, 1981), 201.

34 Burne-Jones, *Memorials* I, 176.

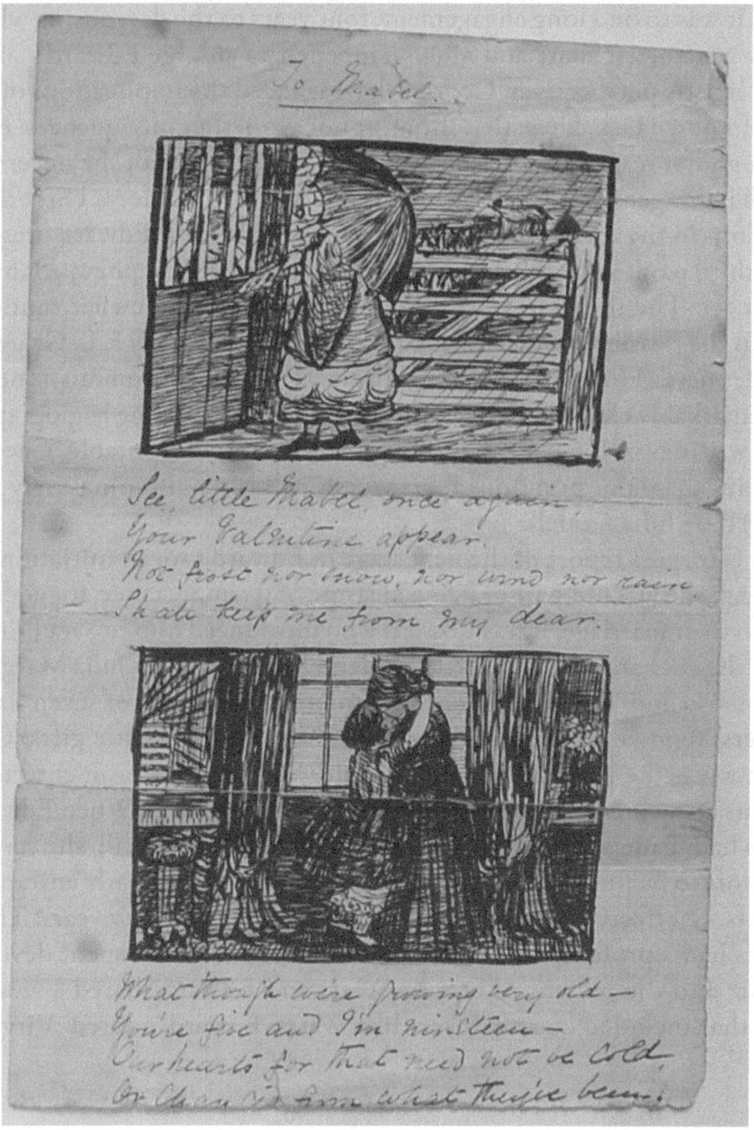

Figure 12.2. Attributed to Georgiana Burne-Jones, illustrated poem titled 'To Mabel'; two of a series of six sketches alternating with verse, depicting a young girl, a baby and an adult woman in various attitudes, on two pieces of paper once joined. c. 1859, Pen and ink, 17.7 × 11.4 cm, British Museum, London. Object no. 2012,7089.1.

It was to be a long engagement, four years to the day, during which they were often apart and much happened to enlarge Edward's social and artistic perspectives. Georgie, having faced the implications of her self-imposed task, knew that she must not avoid the consequences. Even though her respect for her husband was severely tested, she never lost faith in his genius as an artist and his outstanding intellect. Three illustrations in the *Memorials* are of his studios, two with Edward present, the third painted on the day of his death by Georgie's nephew, Ambrose Poynter. The illustrations in the *Memorials* are somewhat random, given the possible material available, but the drawing by F. L. Griggs of 11, Bennett's Hill, Birmingham, appears to have been commissioned.[35] A remarkably clear-eyed portrait resulted, unusual among hagiographic life-writings of the period; although consistently favourable, Georgie was incapable of pompous hero-worship. This is illuminatingly discussed by Julie Codell.[36]

Georgie's report of the next stage in Edward's social initiation, although she was not part of it, is a measure of its importance, for good or ill, to their marriage. It was Rossetti who introduced him to Sara Prinsep and the enchantments of Little Holland House.[37] With Julia Margaret Cameron and Virginia, Countess Somers, she was one of seven Pattle sisters, renowned for their beauty and social and artistic gifts. G. F. Watts was the presiding genius and the Sunday afternoon entertainments attracted politicians and writers as well as artists. When Edward, who had made a favourable impression on Sara, became ill, she carried him off to be nursed back to health there. She had similarly entrapped Watts, so effectively that he stayed for more than twenty years. These visits had a profound effect on Edward's ideal, of a life spent devoted to art and the pursuit of beauty. Watts and Edward shared a view of life that included courtly loves (like Watts, Edward 'adored' Virginia

35 *The Letters of Philip Webb*, ed. John Aplin (Abingdon: Routledge, 2016), IV, 106.

36 See Julie F. Codell, *The Victorian Artist: Artists' Life Writings in Britain, ca. 1870–1910* (Cambridge: Cambridge University Press, 2003), 186–8.

37 Burne-Jones, *Memorials* I, 159.

Somers), nervous illnesses and distaste for the chores of a successful career in art, like portraiture.

The full implications, of Edward's infatuation with the Little Holland House set, became clear to Georgie when she received a visit of 'inspection' by Mrs Prinsep and Lady Somers.[38] She had sensed the change in Edward and was not alone in distrusting the upper-class *laissez faire*, the conversational pyrotechnics and lavish domestic arrangements – 'the very strawberries that stood in little crimson hills upon the tables were larger and riper than others' – that characterised Sara's housekeeping and entertaining. Rossetti came to fear the effect on Ned's health, with reason, for the place was damp and the plumbing primitive. Morris too, disapproved: 'Morris had, generally speaking, a defiant tone towards the fashionable life which existed there'.[39] Georgie struggled, referring to her feelings obliquely in hindsight: 'I could not realize then, as I do now what this visit to Little Holland House must have been to him.' She was referring to the deprived childhood, now more compelling to her as she had experienced the Birmingham household.

The first visit to Little Holland House was quickly followed by the famously flawed project, of decorating the Oxford University Union with murals based on Malory's Arthurian legends. It occupies ten pages of detailed description in the *Memorials*, even though Georgie was not there. That the mural project deserved ten pages of description suggests that Georgie was actively participating in the Pre-Raphaelite myth-making process – the mural project becomes a crucial 'moment' or focal point within the broader Pre-Raphaelite narrative, which can never fail to be mentioned. An Oxford innovation was Edward's decision to grow a moustache and beard, ushering in the look by which he would be recognised in his fame. The dynamics of the group altered; Morris met and fell in love with his future wife. Rossetti hurried to Lizzie's side when she fell ill. Marriages loomed, certain to bring further change to this close-knit group of friends.

38 Burne-Jones, *Memorials* I, 185–6

39 Burne-Jones, *Memorials* I, 183.

Morris married Jane Burden in Oxford in April 1859. Georgie's first sight of Jane made such a deep impression that she dreamed of her that night.[40] The two families were to maintain the closest bond throughout the rest of their lives.

George Macdonald's time in London ended in September 1859 and the family departed to Manchester. Left to Edward, the long engagement might have gone on forever, but Madox Brown intervened. With Georgie away the couple saw little of each other, until, in April 1860, Brown and his wife Emma invited her to stay at Fortess Terrace for a month.[41] Thus, they were able to meet constantly; Edward's prospects had hardly improved and they faced married life with only £30 in hand. True to a vow made at the time of their betrothal, they chose 9 June, its fourth anniversary, as the date for their wedding. Edward's preparations were confined to decorating a sideboard with 'Ladies and animals'; it served them for the rest of their lives.[42]

Her husband having collapsed before reaching their honeymoon destination, they arrived unexpectedly at Edward's untidy, ill-equipped rooms in Russell Place. However, a sturdy oak table designed by Philip Webb was soon joined by chairs and a sofa of panelled wood painted black. Neither Edward nor Georgie had any conception of comfort, the only concession being some unyielding cushions, to Georgie a sinful luxury.[43] Edward's Aunt Catherwood presented an upright piano 'of inoffensive shape' with an unpolished walnut case, which Edward decorated with the disquieting 'Ladies and Death' as well as an early version of his 'Chant d'amour'.[44] Her upbringing in a large family on the tiny stipend of a Methodist minister, taught Georgie how to manage a very frugal household. Mother and sisters cooked, and the family clothes and linen were all sewn at home. Only the

40 Burne-Jones, *Memorials* I, 195.

41 Burne-Jones, *Memorials* I, 202–3.

42 The sideboard was given to the Victoria and Albert Museum by Mrs J. W. Mackail, the artist's daughter Margaret, in 1953, after having been loaned to the break-through exhibition of *Victorian and Edwardian Decorative Arts* held there in 1952: W. 12–1953.

43 Angela Thirkell, *Three Houses* (Oxford: Oxford University Press, 1931), 64.

44 Burne-Jones, *Memorials* I, 207. The piano was presented to the Victoria and Albert Museum by Mrs J. W. Mackail (Margaret Burne-Jones): W.43–1926.

boys went to school; the girls were given the run of their father's library with few of the prohibitions common in a Victorian family. Although probably initiated to keep up with her brothers, Georgie was equipping herself to participate in Edward's literary enthusiasms. Georgie had been preparing herself for Edward since she was 15 years old. Not particularly domestically inclined, she was nonetheless a tower of strength.

Although they were almost penniless in these early married days, soon there was a servant for her to manage – and on occasion misuse; after all, Red Lion Mary had modelled for her artist employers. Georgie teases herself and us as she writes:

> A five or six months' experience of housekeeping in Russell Place did not teach me much, though a couple of small drawings by Edward on the back of my first account-book shew his impression that I practiced housewifery as well as music. [...] I remember thinking it quite natural that in the middle of the morning I should ask our only maid – a pretty one – to stand for me that I might try to draw her; to which she being good-tempered as well as pretty, cheerfully consented.[45]

The pretty maid was Annie West, aged 21, the same age as her mistress. Georgie was fortunate; at 21 this would not have been Annie's first place, so she would have known her duties. The Spartan rooms in Russell Place – shortly after the birth of their first child to be replaced by better quarters in Great Russell Street – were put in order; the Willow-pattern china was regarded in more genteel circles as 'kitchen' ware, but it never occurred to Georgie that their home put them at a disadvantage socially. They were always to be so much visited that, as Georgie relates, an evening when no-one came was an event.[46]

Sole recognition of Georgie's artistic ambitions was a small deal table with a drawer, where she kept her wood-engraving tools. When Ruskin, who had taken a great fancy to Georgie, heard of the plan for engraving Edward's designs, he approved: 'There is just the proper quality of echo in it'; she would not be setting up to rival her husband.[47] That scheme was

45 Burne-Jones, *Memorials* I, 217.
46 Burne-Jones, *Memorials* I, 288.
47 Burne-Jones, *Memorials* I, 233.

soon given up: 'I stopped, as so many women do, well on this side of tolerable skill, daunted by the path which has to be followed absolutely alone if the end is to be reached'. A planned collaboration with Lizzie (married to Rossetti on 23 May), on a book of fairy tales written and illustrated by themselves, stalled. 'Whilst we were in her room she shewed me a design she had just made, called "The Woeful Victory" – then the vision passes.'[48] The one drawing by Georgie, *Death and the Lady* (Figure 6.1), survives, 'but nothing came of it.'[49] 'It is pathetic to think how we longed to keep pace with the men, and how gladly they kept us by them until their pace quickened and we had to fall behind', she added wistfully.[50] Edward's view of female artistic talent – that it did not exist, although possibly exaggerated to provoke – may have stifled ambition in Georgie.[51]

Georgie's duties included reading aloud, and to sing and play, not just for guests, while Edward worked. An important feature of Victorian family life, reading aloud was a bond and a shared experience as much as a chore. At Oxford, discovering books with Morris, Edward's enthusiasms were eclectic: Carlyle and Malory's *Morte d'Arthur*, Dickens and Lane's *Arabian Nights*, as well as the chivalric *Heir of Redclyffe* by Charlotte M. Yonge.[52] Tennyson answered his imaginative needs. Georgie mentions a number of titles and provides a detailed account of the 'happy discovery' of Edward Fitzgerald's translation of *Omar Khayyám*.[53] After the light had gone, Edward worked at stained-glass designs and illustration, so the reading continued into the night. Georgie was less good at being read to, admitting that when Morris was reading poetry or sagas, she had to stick pins in herself to keep awake.[54]

48 Burne-Jones, *Memorials* I, 208.

49 See Jan Marsh ed., *Pre-Raphaelite Sisters* (London: National Portrait Gallery, 2019), 126, illustration 96.

50 Burne-Jones, *Memorials* I, 218.

51 Mary Lago ed., *Burne-Jones Talking: His Conversations, 1895–1898, Preserved by his Studio Assistant Thomas Rooke* (London: John Murray, 1981), 135–6.

52 Burne-Jones, *Memorials* I, 142.

53 Burne-Jones, *Memorials* I, 234–6.

54 Burne-Jones, *Memorials* I, 297.

Marriages prompted schemes for some form of communal living, as a more economical mode of housekeeping. Morris's short-lived occupation of Red House comes closest to realising this aim; its architect, Philip Webb, created a personal 'palace of art', with painted ceilings, walls and furniture and windows filled with stained-glass panels. Planned along with its garden as a single entity, the shared artistic project had roles for everyone. Rossetti and Lizzie, Georgie and Edward would join Morris and Jane, painting walls, ceilings and furniture – largely undertaken by the men – with embroidery, in a Medieval style devised to counter the mechanical aridity of Berlin or counted stitch work, falling to the women. These embroideries, the first things Morris designed for household decoration, required special techniques derived from Medieval ecclesiastical examples. As Georgie wrote: 'Morris was a pleased man when he found that his wife could embroider any design that he made and did not allow her talent to remain idle.'[55] The panels were worked by Jane, her sister Bessie Burden, Georgie and her sister Alice Macdonald. Morris showed Georgie 'what stitches to use and how to place them'.[56] In 1862–3, she painted figures, based on Edward's designs from the *Morte d'Arthur*, onto linen, and began the stitchery. Intended for Great Russell Street and now in the Victoria and Albert Museum, they were never finished.[57]

Philip Burne-Jones was born on 21 October 1861. With the traumatic delivery, Edward was confronted with realities he could not evade. Georgie – whose own temperament was quite un-maternal – knew he was

55 Burne-Jones, *Memorials* I, 218.

56 Burne-Jones, *Memorials* I, 273.

57 Victoria and Albert Museum, Object T. 118–121. The drawings are at the Whitworth Art Gallery. The scheme was originally designed for Burne-Jones's home in 62 Great Russell Street. See T.118 to 120 for other figures in the series. 'A figure of Launcelot, drawn in 1863 by Edward Burne-Jones upon the holland, and embroidered by G. B. J. It was intended for one of a set from the *Morte d'Arthur*, with which we hoped to decorate a room of our own. / Note made by G. Burne-Jones. Feb. 27 '09'. See also Marsh, *Pre-Raphaelite Sisters*, 133, illustration 99. Georgie undertook chores such as tile-painting for the Firm, but her efforts may be masquerading under better-known names. Kate Faulkner, sister of Charles Faulkner, one of the original partners, is credited with most of the ceramic decoration.

not a natural parent, and his remark that 'a painter ought not be married' seems crass, given his dependence on his wife.[58] In the event, his fondness as a father was one of his defining characteristics, and his adoration of his daughter Margaret (born in June 1866) was notorious. His Giorgione-like *Green Summer* was painted at Red House in 1864. Of the eight girls in their idyllic setting, Jane and Georgie were both now mothers. The design recalls Edward's piano panel of 1860, but without the sinister reminder of 'death'. At first the decorating progressed so happily, lightened by pranks and merciless teasing – and caricaturing – of Morris, but it was never completed. Edward made many comic drawings of Morris, dashed off throughout his career, as an ungainly figure of fun, but Georgie thought him handsome.[59] The two illustrated in the *Memorials* show Edward in a sympathetic light, peeping out from behind the great works taken from literature and his imaginary world. The long-term legacy of Red House was Morris's decorating company, to which Edward contributed throughout his career.

A poignant memory of her exclusion after the birth of her first child stayed with Georgie for the rest of her life:

> The difference in our life made by the presence of a child was very great, for I had been used to be much with Edward – reading aloud to him while he worked, and in many ways sharing the life of the studio – and I remember the feeling of exile with which I now heard through its closed door the well-known voices of friends together with Edward's familiar laugh, while I sat with my little son on my knee and dropped selfish tears upon him as 'the separator of companions and the terminator of delights'.[60]

The last phrase is taken from a favourite book, Edward Lane's *Stories from the Thousand and One Nights*.[61]

58 Burne-Jones, *Memorials* I, 230.
59 Burne-Jones, *Memorials* I, 111.
60 Burne-Jones, *Memorials* I, 235.
61 The phrase occurs several times, for example, see Edward Lane, *Stories from the Thousand and One Nights*, The Story of 'Ali Baba and the Forty Thieves' (New York: P. F. Collier and Son, 1909), 444. https://archive.org/details/stories fromthous00lane/page/n9/mode/2up, accessed 24 July 2021. The actual phrase is transposed; in Lane's stories it reads: 'the terminator of delights and separator of companions.'

Georgie's unshakeable belief in redemption might have got her into much more trouble than it did. A scheme to employ Norma, a hired model whom Georgie delicately hints was a prostitute, in the nursery, foundered when Norma herself drew back.[62] This was not to be an isolated example; other attempts to redeem the disadvantaged meant that Georgie made do with often very unsatisfactory help. In return they had to put up with stern readings from Ruskin and Morris, and lectures on politics. Georgie's granddaughter, Angela, recalled other efforts to guide her servants, for their spiritual or political enrichment, notably the garden boy at Rottingdean.[63] Georgie may not have wished to dwell on the less successful.

Georgie saw the end of the Red House idyll in apocalyptic terms: 'Little did any of us think that this would be our last time of careless happiness all together or that illness and death were to be the next experience of the happy party.'[64] Mingled with the horrific premature birth and death of her second son in 1864, while she was almost at death's door herself, is the tragic story of Rossetti and Lizzie's stillborn child and her subsequent death from an overdose of laudanum in February 1862. The new life that began when all hope of the sharing of Red House had been given up, was marked by Edward as 'the end of our first youth'. Their home for the next two-and-a-half years was a fine eighteenth-century house in Kensington Square. Quoting from memory, Georgie recalls the happy atmosphere there in 1865:

> It was a busy household altogether now, and some of the duties that fell to my share were illustrated by Edward in various little family sketches that still exist. The sewing-machine in one of the drawings was a gift from Mr Watts, whose kind imagination realised how many stitches had to be set, and was described by Edward as 'a most clever little thing, that makes dresses and buys the stuff and almost pays for it'.[65]

The sewing-machine was a very generous present, costing £10 to £15, Perhaps Georgie had the recently patented new model by Singer. In 1867,

62 Burne-Jones, *Memorials* I, 262.

63 Thirkell, *Three Houses*, 78.

64 Burne-Jones, *Memorials* I, 281.

65 Burne-Jones, *Memorials* I, 297–98.

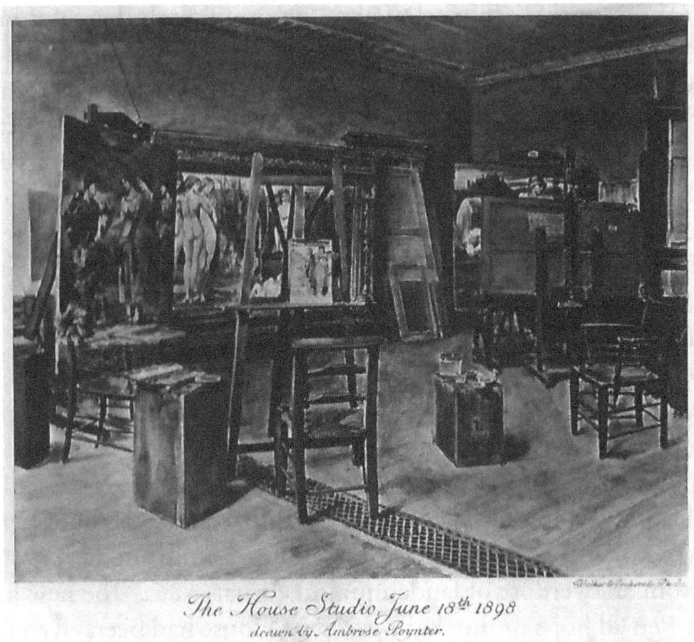

Figure 12.3. *The Studio at the Grange*, 18 June 1898. From a water-colour drawing by Ambrose M. Poynter. *Memorials* II, opposite page 350.

soon after Margaret's birth, they went further west, to The Grange in North End Lane, Fulham, with its large and productive garden.

Edward violently objected to his studio being cleaned, but, with Georgie's connivance, a succession of maids waged clandestine campaigns to outwit him:

> How I hate Spring cleanings; artists ought never to be cleaned – half their vitality goes out of them when they are clean.' He added; 'The glory is too great for me; I don't feel as if I should ever be able to work in it: it would be like trying to paint in a drawing-room'.[66]

66 Burne-Jones, *Memorials* II, 310–11.

Cleaning and white-washing the house-studio at The Grange, led to an attempt to tackle the little studio next door. Edward protested:

> No, I must leave that to take care of itself for a time. The fact is I want a room of this size to paint in, and a rubbish-room seven time larger, and the tidiness of Tadema – then I should do.[67]

Edward's friend, Lawrence Alma-Tadema, was famous for his immaculate studio. Somehow, like much else, this foible was accepted: 'Our life at the Grange lasted thirty years, which were in themselves a second life, for there we finally put away childish things and had our share of sorrow.'[68]

Georgie is more opaque about her cruel betrayal by her husband of just six years. Even more challenging in those days than Little Holland House was the effect of 'a very notable introduction […] to a part of what may be called the Greek Colony in London'.[69] Maria Zambaco (née Cassavetti) is unnamed in the book; she was a sculptor, with whom he conducted a very public affair in 1866, resulting in her attempted suicide and his total nervous collapse.[70] Georgie is discreet about supporters like George Eliot and Rosalind Howard (wife of Edward's patron George, later Earl of Carlisle), in this trial, presenting them as friends of them both. In 1871, Edward's solo trip to Italy gave them time to reflect. Georgie had accompanied him on previous trips but here she reconstructs the journey from sketchbooks

67 Burne-Jones, *Memorials* II, 310–11. Lawrence Alma-Tadema's 'tidiness' was legendary, his immaculate studio inspiring much comment in the many accounts that appeared in contemporary periodicals; see Charlotte Gere, 'The Alma-Tadema's Two Homes in London', in Elizabeth Prettejohn and Peter Trippi, eds, *Lawrence Alma-Tadema: At Home in Antiquity* (Munich, London and New York: Prestel, 2016).

68 Burne-Jones, *Memorials* I, 309.

69 Burne-Jones, *Memorials* I, 303.

70 Mary Seton Watts, who was familiar with the *Memorials* – and may have felt empowered to write her husband's life by Georgie's example – took a similar line, expunging Ellen Terry entirely from her husband's story. She was more ruthless than Georgie, and with less justification, since Watts and Ellen were legally married. 'To what is well known, I wish to add nothing', Mary Seton Watts, *George Frederic Watts: The Annals of an Artist's Life* (London: Macmillan & Co., 1912) I, 221. Another notable absentee from the *Memorials* is Oscar Wilde, once a close friend.

and letters to his assistants, Charles Fairfax Murray and T. M. Rooke. She chose to illustrate this episode with a painting made from a sketch he did after seeing *The Muses on Mount Helicon* in a dream.[71] At that time the illustrations were hard to access and availability would have been of prime importance for the publication.

Edward did not give up Maria – her face haunts his work for years – meanwhile carrying on a succession of courtly pursuits of young women of a higher social class than himself, accompanied by love letters that he barely attempted to conceal.[72] Modern psychology might point to his motherless childhood, and a need for unconditional feminine attention. The sexually charged content of the letters inevitably prompts speculation about the platonic character of these relationships.[73] Some of the women flit uneasily through the *Memorials* – Helen 'May' Gaskell, Mary Gladstone, Frances Graham, Laura Tennant – while some do not. They are featured in *The Golden Stairs* (1880; Tate, London), descending to an unknown destination. Edward harboured an absurd hope that Georgie would become friends with these objects of his adoration, referred to somewhat obliquely in the *Memorials* and slightly more frankly to intimates like Rosalind Howard and George Eliot. Georgie's scrutiny was disquieting: the young Walford Graham Robertson described

71 Burne-Jones, *Memorials* II, illustration opposite page 44.

72 Occasional glimpses of Burne-Jones's intense class-consciousness are a reminder of the journey from motherless son of an unsuccessful carver and gilder in Birmingham, to the Baronetcy engineered by William Gladstone.

73 Penelope Fitzgerald, *Edward Burne-Jones: A Biography* (London: Michael Joseph, 1975), chapter 9, 112–16; Fiona McCarthy, *The Last Pre-Raphaelite: Edward Burne-Jones and the Victorian Imagination* (London: Faber & Faber, 2011), chapter 11, 119–224. The most startling revelations arrived with the publication of many of the letters sent to Helen Mary (May) Gaskell: Josceline Dimbleby, *A Profound Secret* (London: Penguin, 2004). This is now supplemented by Andrew Gailey's biography of Frances Graham, *Portrait of a Muse, Frances Graham, Edward Burne-Jones and the Pre-Raphaelite Dream* (London: Wilmington Square Books, 2020).

> those wonderful eyes of clearest grey [...] their direct gaze would always cause me little sub-conscious heart-searchings, not from fear of criticism or censure, but lest those eyes in their grave wisdom, their crystal purity, should rest upon anything unworthy.[74]

Her eyes dominate Edward's unfinished (and never exhibited) portrait, of Georgie with their two children (begun 1883; private collection).[75] A pansy, for 'thoughts' – *pensées* in French – and enduring love, lies on a copy of Gerard's *Herball*. Morris owned a copy, perhaps it was borrowed from him; it is a reminder of those hours in the studio reading to her husband, shared by the children as soon as they were old enough. Portraits that followed his affair with Maria are among his most ethereal and spiritual, Frances Horner (née Graham), 1879, his daughter Margaret, 1885 and Amy Gaskell (Helen Mary Gaskell's daughter), 1894.

Georgie's view of human relationships was austere and her judgments uncomfortably forthright, but she takes pains to excuse Edward. Maria had 'beauty and misfortune', two things that moved Edward profoundly: 'Indeed his impulse to comfort those in trouble was so strong that while the trouble lasted the sufferer took precedence of everyone else.'[76] The character of their marriage had changed irrevocably, but this accepting carried them through the remaining years: volume II of the *Memorials* covers those years and is partly an apologia for Edward's continuing disloyalties.

Glimpses of Georgie herself are rare – she admitted to finding recent time harder to recall than the distant past. She now appears in the *Memorials* largely through her retelling of Edward's doings. Her withdrawal is a reflection of their deteriorating relationship. Perhaps in the end she no longer cared. She had plumbed the depths of her capacity for grief with the death of her second son long ago, in 1864. The epigraph to Chapter XVI, 'Heart, thou and I are here, sad and alone', is all Georgie allows herself in mourning the loss of the love and trust of their early married life.[77] Thereafter, the

74 W. Graham Robertson, *Time Was* (London: Hamish Hamilton, 1931), 75. In her photograph by Frederick Hollyer, taken just a year before the commencement of the portrait, she shows a more cheerful face.

75 See also Charlotte Gere, 'Portraits', in *Edward Burne-Jones*, ed. Alison Smith (London: Tate Publishing, 2018), 153–4.

76 Burne-Jones, *Memorials* I, 309.

77 Burne-Jones, *Memorials* II, 1.

new volume will change tone. Her intense focus on Edward's early life and his career, and the first years of their marriage, is understandable in light of the extraordinary trajectory, from obscure son of an impoverished frame-maker to one of the most celebrated and decorated artists of his time. The forensic scrutiny of her earlier account is abandoned in favour of other voices, notably the recording of studio conversations by Thomas Matthews Rooke. As she says, when signing off their life up to 1867 at the end of volume I: 'as often as possible I shall let his own voice be heard or his work shall speak'.[78]

Looking back, Georgie was forced to contemplate a merry-go-round of marital dysfunction. Jane Morris admitted she was never in love with her husband, as she confessed to Wilfred Scawen Blunt.[79] In 1859, Rossetti was already in love with Jane and she with him, but it was Morris who had married her. Rossetti, unable to evade his long-time engagement, married Lizzie, and only after her death began the affair with Jane. Morris took refuge with Georgie, his closest confidant until his untimely death.

Writing of Morris's regular Sunday morning visits, she is careful to make clear the distinction between their friendship and the lifelong bond between Edward and Morris: 'Before he left they always either invited me to join them for a little while or else sallied forth from the studio to pay me a call: but it was their hour and power, and I did not proffer my company'.[80]

The 1870s brought difficult separations; the departure of Philip for Marlborough as a boarder in 1874 being perhaps the hardest.[81] Changes to the Morris Firm's partnership, in 1875, were not achieved without bitterness.[82] Edward's support in 1878 for Ruskin, in the infamous trial over Whistler's *Nocturne in Blue and Silver* was ill-judged, a betrayal of his true estimate of Whistler's talent.[83] As Georgie reports: 'By degrees Edward

78 Burne-Jones, *Memorials* I, 308.

79 *The Collected Letters of Jane Morris*, eds Frank C. Sharp and Jan Marsh (Woodbridge: The Boydell Press, 2012), 10.

80 Burne-Jones, *Memorials* II, 5.

81 Burne-Jones, *Memorials* II, 47.

82 Burne-Jones, *Memorials* II, 51–2.

83 Burne-Jones, *Memorials* II, 86.

went more and more in Society'.[84] Until 1885, he had dined two or three times a week with William Graham, and many 'society' invitations were for him alone. Rossetti died in 1882, Graham followed in 1885 and when he was dying Edward sent little paintings to him every day. Edward's father died in 1889. Georgie observed these events with trepidation, knowing the effect they would have on Edward's spirits and health.

His friendship with Morris teetered on the brink, imperilled by his reluctance to become politically involved and his later acceptance of a Baronetcy, but it survived. Morris refused to believe news of the honour, but the bond was too strong for the friendship to be in any real peril. Georgie expresses no opinion of the Baronetcy, although she was reluctant to become Lady Burne-Jones.[85] Edward's excuse, that he did it for Philip, is disingenuous. Surprisingly, no mention is made of the insult to William Gladstone, its instigator, if the offer had been turned down.

In her unsparing truthfulness and moral rectitude, Georgie is a daunting presence, but even she is forced into evasion and subterfuge. With tricky territory to negotiate, she resorted to ruthless suppression of the truth. She borrowed Rooke's notes, but even though she had encouraged Rooke's recording, now she wished to burn them, and although restrained from full-scale destruction, some passages were destroyed.[86] Applied to for correspondence, Frances Horner and May Gaskell offered a selection of harmless notes in playful tone.[87] However, in 1915, while Georgie was still living, Lady Horner circulated a typescript selection, among her friends,

84 Burne-Jones, *Memorials* II, 91.

85 Burne-Jones, *Memorials* II, 240–3.

86 Lago, *Burne-Jones Talking*; for an account of Georgie's treatment of Rooke's manuscript and the burning, see Aplin, *Letters of Philip Webb* IV, letters 952, 960. Charles Fairfax Murray, Burne-Jones's first studio assistant, deplored the evasions: see Fiona MacCarthy, *The Last Pre-Raphaelite* (London: Faber & Faber Ltd., 2011), 517.

87 See also note 12. The letters are embellished with sketches and self-portraits and presented as mock-medieval manuscripts; the pass books with Morris & Co. record their collaboration and their lifelong friendship.

of Edward's letters and notes of his conversations, under the title 'A Book of Beauty'.[88]

Remaking her life in the aftermath of his humiliatingly public adultery, Georgie took up the charitable and political causes unmentioned in her obituary. This was still a largely masculine world; certainly her son-in-law, J. W. Mackail, knew what she was doing, but when he came to write the *Times* obituary, he offered a picture of her at her embroidery, and the short-lived wood-engraving project, as if these few artistic efforts were all she achieved. Perhaps the hand of Margaret or Philip can be detected here, suppressing the formidable and possibly embarrassing campaigner. Her diminutive stature and modest demeanour were misleading (as many had found to their cost), she was an unstoppable force when she chose. Up to a point, Mackail can be forgiven for ignoring the political and charitable activities, since Georgie herself leaves them out of the *Memorials*.

She was an energetic committee member for the founding of the South London Art Gallery in 1887, and from 1894 she was a parish councillor in Rottingdean, where she lived almost all the time after her husband's death. Lady Burne-Jones was the only woman on the ten-seat Parish Council.[89] The South London Art Gallery in Camberwell was no plaything of a Lady Bountiful, achieved against almost insuperable obstacles by a band of powerful men, among them William Gladstone, G. F. Watts, Sir Frederic Leighton and the banker, Sir John Buxton, MP. Edward was a member of the Council and advised on the decoration. Its instigator, William Rossiter was inspired by the Working Men's College, where both he and Edward had taught. The people Georgie encountered represented 1890s philanthropy and the Arts and Crafts generation: Baroness Burdett-Coutts, Alfred Passmore Edwards, Octavia Hill, Walter Crane, Mary Seton Watts, William and Evelyn De Morgan, to name but a few. Georgie wrote

88 See: Evan Charteris, *The Life & Letters of Sir Edmund Gosse* (London: William Heineman, 1931), 378. She later included them in her autobiography, Frances Horner, *Time Remembered* (London, William Heineman, 1933).

89 For an account of her political activities and beliefs, see Isabelle Williams, 'Georgiana Burne-Jones and William Morris: A Subtle Influence', *Journal of the William Morris Society* 12/1 (Autumn 1996), 17–24.

letters to artist friends, soliciting loans of paintings for exhibition.[90] Prone to self-martyrdom and unable to delegate, her effectiveness is in painful contrast to Edward's tinkering with the interior decoration.

She admired the ideas of Mazzini and Ruskin on social reform (writings she would read to bewildered young maids and the gardener's boy), but Edward could not join his wife and his oldest friend in their socialist leanings. It was accepted by all but herself that William Morris loved her, and she shared many of his views, although unable, much to her distress, to follow him into full-blown socialism.[91] For Morris 'she was the woman, that is, whom he trusted as a friend before all others'.[92] By the 1890s, the costs of running their two households in London and Rottingdean had risen alarmingly, and after Burne-Jones's death in 1898, retrenchment took place. Jane Morris wrote to their old friend Cormell Price in July 1898, hoping that Georgiana was managing: 'I trust there is no anxiety of that kind, but they must have lived at enormous expense these last years, and winding up a household is so costly as I experienced. One can't cut things down instantly'.[93]

Her last years are caught in a lively portrait by her granddaughter Angela. A slight figure in unchanging costume of long-skirted black satin or velvet, trimmed with a little lace, welcoming the Mackail children to North End House, Rottingdean.[94] Georgie died on 2 February 1920. Already very frail and deeply upset by the failure of her granddaughter Angela's marriage, she just anticipated the inevitability of having to leave Rottingdean, as she was no longer able to manage her own household. Georgie was a strong and independent woman, characteristics which shine through in her writing. Her legacy lives on in the *Memorials*, still consulted by scholars today for its intimate recollections of life in the Pre-Raphaelite circle.

90 Giles Waterfield, ed., *Art for the People: Culture in the Slums of Late Victorian Britain* (London: Dulwich Picture Gallery, 1994), 20–23.

91 *The Collected Letters of William Morris*, ed. Norman Kelvin (Princeton, NJ: Princeton University Press, 1984–96), I, xxxix.

92 Kelvin, *Collected Letters* I, xxxix.

93 Sharp and Marsh, *Collected Letters*, 315.

94 Thirkell, *Three Houses*, 50.

Bibliography

Aplin, John, ed., *The Letters of Philip Webb*, 4 vols (Abingdon: Routledge, 2016).

Baldwin, A. W. (Earl Baldwin of Bewdley), *The Macdonald Sister* (London: Peter Davies, 1960).

Burne-Jones, Georgiana, *Memorials of Edward Burne-Jones*, 2 vols (London: Macmillan & Co. Ltd, 1904).

Charteris, Evan, *The Life & Letters of Sir Edmund Gosse* (London: William Heineman, 1931).

Codell, Julie F., *The Victorian Artist: Artists' Lifewritings in Britain, ca. 1870–1910* (Cambridge: Cambridge University Press, 2003).

Dimbleby, Josceline, *A Profound Secret* (London: Penguin, 2004).

Fitzgerald, Penelope, *Edward Burne-Jones, a Biography* (London: Michael Joseph, 1975).

Flanders, Judith, *A Circle of Sisters: Alice Kipling, Georgiana Burne-Jones, Agnes Poynter and Louisa Baldwin* (London: Penguin, 2001).

Gere, Charlotte, 'The Alma-Tadema's Two Homes in London', in Elizabeth Prettejohn and Peter Trippi, eds, *Lawrence Alma-Tadema, At Home in Antiquity* (Munich: Prestel, 2016).

Horner, Frances, *Time Remembered* (London: William Heineman, 1933).

Kelvin, Norman, ed., *The Collected Letters of William Morris* (Princeton, NJ: Princeton University Press, 1984–96).

Lago, Mary, ed., *Burne-Jones Talking – His Conversations 1895–1898 Preserved by his Studio Assistant Thomas Rooke* (London: John Murray, 1981).

Lanigan, Dennis T., 'The Bridge of Sighs by Georgiana Burne-Jones (1840–1920). A Metaphor for her Artistic Career', *The British Art Journal* 19/1 (2020), 111–15.

McCarthy, Fiona, *The Last Pre-Raphaelite, Edward Burne-Jones and the Victorian Imagination* (London: Faber & Faber, 2011).

Marsh, Jan, *Pre-Raphaelite Sisterhood* (London: Quartet, 1985).

——, et al, *Pre-Raphaelite Sisters* (London: National Portrait Gallery, 2019).

Robertson, W. Graham, *Time Was* (London: Hamish Hamilton, 1931).

Sharp, Frank C., and Marsh, Jan, eds, *The Collected Letters of Jane Morris* (Woodbridge: The Boydell Press, 2012).

Surtees, Virginia, ed., *The Diary of Ford Madox Brown* (New Haven and London: Yale University Press, 1981).

Taylor, Ina, *Victorian Sisters* (London: Weidenfeld & Nicolson, 1967).

Thirkell, Angela, *Three Houses* (Oxford, Oxford University Press, 1931).

Waterfield, Giles, ed., *Art for the People, Culture in the Slums of Late Victorian Britain* (London: Dulwich Picture Gallery, 1994).

Watts, Mary Seton, *George Frederic Watts, The Annals of an Artist's Life* (London: Macmillan & Co., 1912).

Williams, Isabelle, 'Georgiana Burne-Jones and William Morris: A Subtle Influence', *Journal of the William Morris Society* 12/1 (Autumn 1996), 17–34.

PART IV

Personal Perspectives

BRIAN EATON

13 Fanny Eaton: An Attempt to Discover the Woman behind the Images

ABSTRACT

This chapter describes my personal journey to discover the life of my great-grandmother, Pre-Raphaelite model Fanny Eaton, through census records, family stories and historical data. Describing her mother's journey through slavery to London and Fanny's life thereafter, this chapter examines the story of Jamaican slavery and Victorian attitudes to people of colour. Showing how Fanny survived the hardships of life, it explains how she became a model for the artists of the Pre-Raphaelite circle, including Dante Gabriel Rossetti and Simeon Solomon. Fanny's domestic life with her husband James and her ten children is mentioned, as well as the stories of some of her descendants. Finally, the author questions how Fanny Eaton became lost to the art world and follows attempts to bring her back to prominence.

* * * * *

This chapter is a very personal attempt to recreate the life of my great-grandmother, Fanny Matilda Eaton, a mixed-race woman who stares out at us from so many Pre-Raphaelite paintings. It may appear to be an unusual fit in a collection of academic works as it is not an academic essay on specific artworks, nor even an attempt to discover an artist's thoughts or aims behind a particular painting. Very little is known about Fanny's actual life, therefore in this chapter I will try to address that omission and look behind her soulful eyes. Fanny's story deserves to be told.[1]

Until relatively recently, Fanny was not recognised as an important player in the Pre-Raphaelite art movement. Following research by myself (one of Fanny's many great-grandchildren) and others including Jan Marsh, Pamela Gerrish Nunn, Roberto C. Ferrari and Betty Elzea, Fanny has at

1 First names will be used in this chapter for clarity as I refer to various members of the Eaton family.

last emerged from obscurity into the limelight.[2] She is now widely acknowledged, both within the art world and beyond, to have been an important model for the Pre-Raphaelites and other artists of that period. Her name now appears on numerous internet websites, in magazine articles, and she has even been mentioned in recent television programmes.[3] She now has her own entry in the *Oxford Dictionary of National Biography* – a prospect not even dreamt of a few years ago.[4] Fanny featured significantly in the *Pre-Raphaelite Sisters* exhibition at the National Portrait Gallery in London (17 October 2019 to 26 January 2020).[5] There is even the suggestion that *The Stunner's Opera*, a small theatre production about her which debuted in November 2019, could eventually be performed to a wider audience in major cities.[6]

The question that fascinates me is how Fanny was previously erased from the history of the Pre-Raphaelite movement when her face appears in so many paintings and drawings from that period. My contention is that because she lived in the relative shadows of Victorian England (compared with the other models) it was easy for her to disappear as times changed. Even

2 Jan Marsh, *Black Victorians: Black People in British Art, 1800–1900* (Aldershot: Ashgate Publishing, 2005); Pamela Gerrish Nunn, 'Artist and Model: Joanna Mary Boyce's "Mulatto Woman" ', *Journal of Pre-Raphaelite Studies* 2/2 (1993), 12–15; Roberto C. Ferrari, 'Fanny Eaton: "The Other" Pre-Raphaelite Model', *PRS Review* 22/2 (2014), 3–19; Betty Elzea, *Frederick Sandys, 1829–1904: A Catalogue Raisonné* (Woodbridge, Suffolk, Antique Collectors' Club in association with Norfolk Museums & Archaeology Service, 2001).

3 For example, Stella Halliwell, 'Fanny Eaton: The Forgotten Pre-Raphaelite Stunner', Simple Living Stella (9 January 2012), <https://stellahalliwell.co.uk/pre-raphaelites/fanny-eaton-the-forgotten-pre-raphaelite-stunner/>, accessed 13 May 2021.

4 Roberto C. Ferrari, 'Eaton [née Antwistle/Entwistle], Fanny (1835–1924)', Oxford Dictionary of National Biography, <https://doi.org/10.1093/odnb/9780198614128.013.90000369549>, accessed 13 May 2021.

5 *Pre-Raphaelite Sisters* exhibition curated by Jan Marsh, National Portrait Gallery, London, 17 October 2019 to 26 January 2020; *Pre-Raphaelite Sisters: Making Art*, conference held at the University of York, 12–13 December 2019.

6 *The Stunner's Opera*, Backstage Theatre, Mountview, Peckham, London, 12–16 November 2019. Written by Joanna Harris and Howard Goodall. Directed by Annabel Bolton. Young Fanny played by Jade Kennedy. Mature Fanny played by Sophie Maria Wojna.

her own descendants seem to have been able to 'forget' that she was born in Jamaica and had a career as a model. They have fabricated various family stories to explain their mixed-race heritage, including a Native American link. My quest, therefore, is to discover the real Fanny.

My wife Mary had traced her family in Yorkshire and had found the research very interesting, so we decided to try to trace my family roots. My father had always said that there was a 'Red Indian' (Native American) in our ancestry but would never elaborate on this despite our questions. When the 1881 census was made public in 1999 we went to our local library to see if we could find my family. We found my great grandparents living in London and were amazed to discover that my great-grandmother was named Fanny and recorded as being born in Jamaica – not North America! This information gave us the impetus to find out more about Fanny and her previous life.

My research began with searching for Fanny's birth record. I found that Fanny was born in Jamaica on 23 June 1835, the illegitimate daughter of Matilda Foster, a former slave.[7] The Abolition of Slavery Act became law on 1 August 1834 when the purchase or ownership of enslaved people became illegal in most parts of the British Empire. Fanny was baptised on 15 November 1835 as Fanny Matilda Antvistle, which is assumed to be a misspelling or badly written version of either Entwistle or Antwistle.[8] Another possible explanation is that her mother, Matilda, may have had a heavy Jamaican accent and the surname may have been misunderstood at the baptism ceremony.

Fanny's baptism is recorded as taking place in 'Savanna', but with no further details. The word savanna means grassland, which provides no help in establishing the exact location as there are several places in Jamaica that include the name Savanna. In baptising Fanny, Matilda may have been following a traditional belief held by slaves that baptism made them free. This

7 Birth record for Fanny Matilda Antvistle, 23 June 1835. Jamaica Church of England Transcripts 1664–1880, All Parishes. Baptisms and Births 1835–1849, vol. 3, image 141.

8 Baptism of Fanny Matilda Antvistle, 15 November 1835. Jamaica Births and Baptisms 1752–1920, microfilm 1,291,712, Index 103817-18. St Andrew, Surry, Jamaica.

belief had caused friction between church ministers and slave owners in the past and the planters had even made laws against it. Why did Matilda choose the name Fanny? It may be a coincidence, but the meaning of both her names is significant: Fanny means 'free' and Matilda means 'strong'. I think that Fanny would have needed both these attributes as her life unfolded.

My research from the slave registers held in the National Archives has also identified further details of Fanny's mother. A slave named Matilda was born around 1818 to a woman named Bathsheba on one of the many Foster Estates in Jamaica.[9] This particular register showed that Matilda was passed through the family from Eugene Frederick Foster (or Forster) to John Foster, on Eugene's death. This clearly demonstrates how enslaved people were thought of as possessions rather than human beings. The recording of slaves on slave registers became obligatory leading up to the abolition of slave trading. The Government needed to prepare a system to pay compensation to the powerful plantation owners as this was the only way they would allow slavery to be finally abolished. It was finally agreed to pay the slave owners a total of £20 million in settlement, but the slaves received nothing.[10]

Matilda's father was probably one of the Estate's supervisors, or possibly even another slave, as such relationships were encouraged by the plantation owners as a means of gaining yet more slaves. There were many children of mixed race born to slaves, often involving rape, but there are also stories where the owners acknowledged their offspring and even provided a better life for them. Nathaniel Wells was one such child. Born in 1779, he was the son of plantation owner William Wells and although a slave on the Caribbean Island of St Kitts, he was sent to England to be educated. When the plantation owner died, he left his entire £200,000 fortune to

9 'Slave Registers of Former British Colonial Dependencies, 1813–1834', entry for Matilda Foster, slave in the possession of John Foster, as belonging to the estate of the late Eugene Frederick Foster of Jamaica. Office of Registry of Colonial Slaves and Slave Compensation Commission: Records; Class: T 71; Piece Number: 167, 169, National Archives of the UK, Kew, Surrey.

10 'The Database', Centre for the Study of the Legacies of British Slavery, UCL, <https://www.ucl.ac.uk/lbs/project/details/>, accessed 29 May 2021.

Nathaniel, who freed his mother and other relatives but continued to operate slave plantations.[11]

The Foster (or Forster) Estates were started in 1655 when a Colonel John Forster took part in an 8,000 strong expedition sent out by Oliver Cromwell to obtain land and plunder from the Spaniards to finance his English and Spanish campaigns.[12] They had initially tried to conquer Hispaniola (now Haiti and the Dominican Republic) but were driven off by the Spanish. They then went on successfully to raid a weaker Jamaica and drive the Spaniards off. John Forster was granted land as a reward for his part in this campaign and began growing sugar in 1674. Sugar cultivation is very labour-intensive and although the planters in Jamaica initially used indentured labour from England, they eventually followed the Spanish practice of using slaves brought over from Africa. I think that Matilda's ancestors would have been part of this trade.

Many of the slaves from Africa came through Bunce Island, located off the coast of Sierra Leone, where the slave trafficking was conducted on an industrial scale by various nationalities. Bunce Island was just one of about forty slaving fortresses along the west coast of Africa.[13] It continued to be a slave trading post even after the slave trade was officially abolished. Bunce Island was finally abandoned in 1840 and remained so until being recently rediscovered by American archaeologists. It is now in danger of being washed away by the river, perhaps a fitting end to a place with such a horrible history.

Details of Fanny's father are not recorded on the birth registration and Matilda's choice of this surname is unusual in Jamaica. There is, however, a

11 'Nathaniel Wells, Profile and Legacies Summary', Centre for the Study of the Legacies of British Slavery, UCL (n.d.), <https://www.ucl.ac.uk/lbs/person/view/25474>, accessed 29 May 2021.

12 Timothy Venning, 'Cromwell's Foreign Policy and the Western Design', *The Cromwell Association*, <http://www.olivercromwell.org/wordpress/?page_id=518>, accessed 29 May 2021.

13 See, for example, 'Bloody Bunce: A Legacy of the Transatlantic Slave Trade in Sierra Leone', Royal Historical Society: Historical Transactions (29 October 2019), <https://blog.royalhistsoc.org/2019/10/29/bunce-island-legacy/>, accessed 29 May 2021.

record of the death in Jamaica in 1835 of a 20-year-old soldier named James Entwistle, which is the only evidence found in the Jamaican archives of any person with that or any similar surname.[14] It is possible that he might be Fanny's father, or that somehow Matilda found his name and decided to use it for her child rather than her own slave name. James Entwistle was buried in the Military Cemetery, which is adjacent to the Slave Cemetery in Spanish Town, and Matilda may have seen his name on a visit to the area. Both cemeteries have now been built over, so it is impossible to know if there was any plaque or headstone for James. There are records of other children born to military personnel and slaves so it would not have been unusual for Matilda and James to have had a relationship.[15] The cause of his death is not recorded but many soldiers stationed in the Caribbean died at a young age from tropical diseases. This was especially true of young soldiers who came from poor backgrounds in towns in England and who may have used enlistment in the army to escape these conditions at home.[16]

Following the 1834 Abolition of Slavery Act, many of the former slaves left Jamaica as the economy of the island collapsed. Some would have travelled with their former owners either as house servants or companions. Somehow Matilda and Fanny managed to reach London independently during the 1840s. Matilda then found employment as a laundress and Fanny as a servant, as recorded in the 1851 census.[17] They may have been assisted by the Jamaican Government who were keen to reduce the population of

14 Church of the Latter-day Saints, 'Jamaican Burial Records', Film 1291723, Index Page 112; 1291731, 1826 1836, 1291680, Item 2, No. 88: James Entwistle, 20 yrs, 8th Regiment, Spanish Town, 4th July 1835, Buried – Military Ground by Rev'd L Bowerbank.

15 Examples of other mixed marriages: Mary Jane Seacole (Crimean nurse) was the daughter of James Grant (a Scottish soldier) and a mixed-race woman; Dido Elizabeth Lindsay was the daughter of Sir John Lindsay of the Royal Navy and a freed Spanish slave; Edward Plaice Foster (the same family that Matilda worked for) married a freed slave and had eight children.

16 'The West India Regiments', National Army Museum (n.d.), <https://www.nam.ac.uk/explore/slaves-red-coats-west-india-regiment>, accessed 26 May 2021.

17 1851 Census return for 9 Steven Place, Marylebone, London. HO107/1496, page 16. Mrs McTwistle (sic), Age 37, Laundress Born Jamaica. Fanny Ditto, Age 16, Servant. (Also at this address: Michael Grewby (born Ireland) and family.)

emancipated enslaved people to lessen the burden on the island's economy. In the 1851 census, Matilda claims that she is married. This might just be for the sake of appearance as no record of a marriage can be found in the Jamaican archives or elsewhere. It is probable that she was intimidated by her first contact with a census official in this new country and wanted to give the impression that Fanny was not illegitimate to avoid future repercussions. Whatever the circumstances, Fanny entered the decade that would shape her future life.

Sometime after 1851, Fanny met my great-grandfather, James Eaton, a London cab driver/owner. It is assumed she then left her mother, Matilda, to live with James, as the 1861 census shows Matilda as a lodger living on her own at 32 Cromer Street, Marylebone, London.[18] Matilda was still employed as a laundress; however, she then claimed to be a widow, which she may have thought explained living alone. Fanny and James were also living in Marylebone in nearby Brunswick Street.[19] Life in Victorian London was hard, and unfortunately Matilda was eventually admitted to the St. Pancras Workhouse and died there in 1868.[20] She is buried in a pauper's grave in Islington Cemetery, in North London. James and his parents are also buried in Islington Cemetery, in similar separate pauper's graves.

Like her mother, no record can be found of a marriage between Fanny and James, but Fanny took James's surname and was known as Mrs Fanny Eaton. One could speculate that James's parents, Henry and Mary Ann Eaton, or any of his eight siblings, may have objected to a mixed marriage, but we have no way of knowing. James and Fanny went on to have ten children: Fanny Matilda (born 1858), James Mark (1860), Amelia (1862),

18 1861 Census return for 32 Cromer Street, Marylebone, London. RG9/105, page 18. Matilda Entwistle, Age 45, Widow, Laundress, Born West Indies Jamacia (sic). (Also at this address: Daniel Delworth and family.)

19 1861 Census return for 4 Brunswick Street, Marylebone, London. RG9/105, page 6. James Eaton, Age 24, Cab Driver, Born Middlesex. Fanny, Ditto, Age 26, Charwoman, Born Jamacia (sic). James, Son, Age 1, Born St. Pancras. Fanny, Daughter, Age 3, Born St. Pancras. (Also at this address: Caroline Rodean, Age 34, Mangler, Born St. Pancras and William, Ditto, Son, Age 18, Born St. Pancras.)

20 Certified copy of death certificate for Matilda Entwistle, 13 January 1868. Application number 5325328-1. The General Register Office.

Mildred (1863), Julia (1865), Miriam (1869), Walter (1871), Ernest (1872), Cicely (1877) and the youngest Frank (1879), my grandfather. They raised their ten children in various districts of London before James unfortunately died in 1881 from blood poisoning, probably caused by a horse-related injury.[21]

Sometime in the late 1850s, and well before James's death, Fanny's life changed when she happened to meet someone from the art-world who persuaded her to become a model. William Powell Frith, an artist and lecturer at the Royal Academy of Arts in London, wrote in his autobiography how he found the perfect model for his painting *The Sleeping Model* (1853; Royal Academy, London). He explained: 'Being in the habit of keeping my eyes pretty well open as I walked along the streets, they were one day gratified by the sight of an orange-girl of a rare type of rustic beauty'.[22] Perhaps this was how Fanny was found, by an art teacher looking for interesting or different models for his classes. It is possible she was even spotted by Simeon Solomon, the artist who first drew her in 1859. Solomon attended Sass's Art School (later Cary's School of Art) in Charlotte Street, Bloomsbury, and as he walked to and from the school he would have passed through the area where Fanny lived and worked. I like to imagine that maybe it was her natural hairstyle that attracted him as his first drawings of her seem to concentrate on this feature.

These early drawings of Fanny by Solomon (Figures 13.1 and 13.2) were later used for his painting *Mother of Moses* (1860; Figure 13.3) which was exhibited at the Royal Academy in 1860.[23] Solomon was well known for wanting authentic models for his paintings and must have envisaged Fanny as the ideal model for his biblical works.

21 Certified copy of death certificate for James Eaton. 17 February 1881. Application number 1606345-1. The General Register Office.

22 William Powell Frith, *My Autobiography and Reminiscences* (New York: Harper and Brothers, 1888), 174.

23 Simeon Solomon, *Mother of Moses,* first exhibited 1860, oil on canvas, 61.0 × 50.5 cm, Delaware Art Museum, USA (object no. 1999-1).

Fanny's facial characteristics may have contributed to her popularity as a model. Images show her as having a strong jawbone, high cheekbones and almond shaped eyes, all attractive attributes for a model. Solomon was also part of an informal sketching group with other artists of that period, which may explain how she appears in many other works. The relatively poor artists may have all contributed to pay any modelling fees, as Fanny obviously received payment for her services. The 1860 to 1879 Petty Cash records of the Royal Academy of Arts provide evidence of payment to Fanny for several sittings for their life classes.[24] However, because she appears in so many other paintings, she obviously posed for other artists outside of the Academy. The Royal Academy records also list a 'Miss Eaton' as a model, so perhaps one of her daughters followed her example.

Fanny's career as a model led to her posing for artists who required an Asian, Indian or Middle Eastern figure, but never a Jamaican! It would be interesting to know Fanny's feelings about this disparity. Unfortunately, we have not found any written words from Fanny, or any of her children, as evidence of how they felt about their true slave heritage. Perhaps we can begin to imagine the sadness behind her eyes when we examine the many paintings of her. Is her anguished facial expression in W. B. Richmond's *The Slave* (1886; Tate, London) something the artist asked for? Is she imagining how life must have been for her mother?[25] Is she thinking of how difficult her own life was, especially after James's death? It is interesting to note that the two children depicted in this painting may be Fanny's. Which children would depend on the date she actually modelled for Richmond, although since the work is dated c. 1886 it is most likely to be the two youngest, Cicely and my grandfather, Frank.

24 Mark Pomeroy, Archivist, Royal Academy of Arts, email message to the author, 22 September 2014; details from 'Cash Book of the Royal Academy, 1857–1881' (RAA/TRE/3/13).

25 Willam Blake Richmond, *The Slave*, c. 1886, oil on canvas, 91.4 52.7 cm, Tate, London.

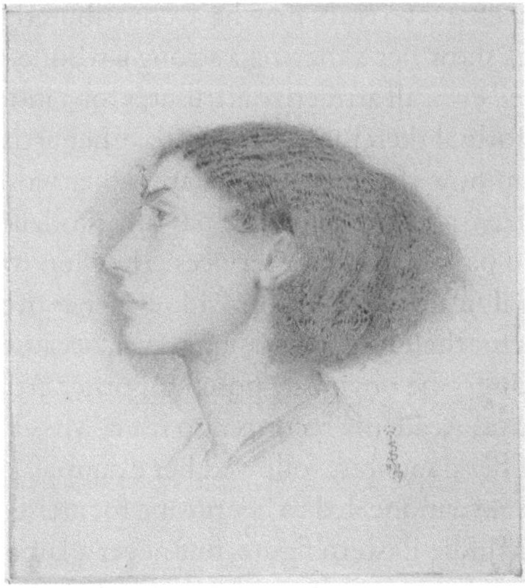

Figure 13.1. Simeon Solomon, *Portrait of Mrs Fanny Eaton, profile left*, 1859, Graphite on paper, 14.9 × 13.1 cm, Fitzwilliam Museum, Cambridge (Accession no. PD.54-1959, Ref. 13633). Photograph copyright © The Fitzwilliam Museum, Cambridge.

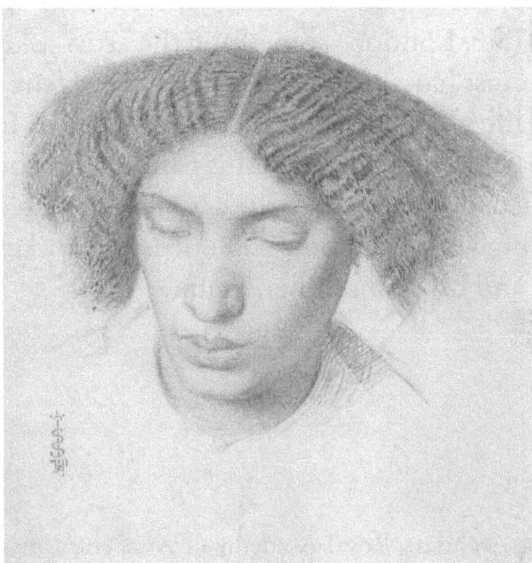

Figure 13.2. Simeon Solomon, *Portrait of Mrs Fanny Eaton*, 1859, Graphite on paper, 14.7 × 13.4 cm, Fitzwilliam Museum, Cambridge (Accession no. PD.55-1959, Ref. 13634). Photograph copyright © The Fitzwilliam Museum, Cambridge.

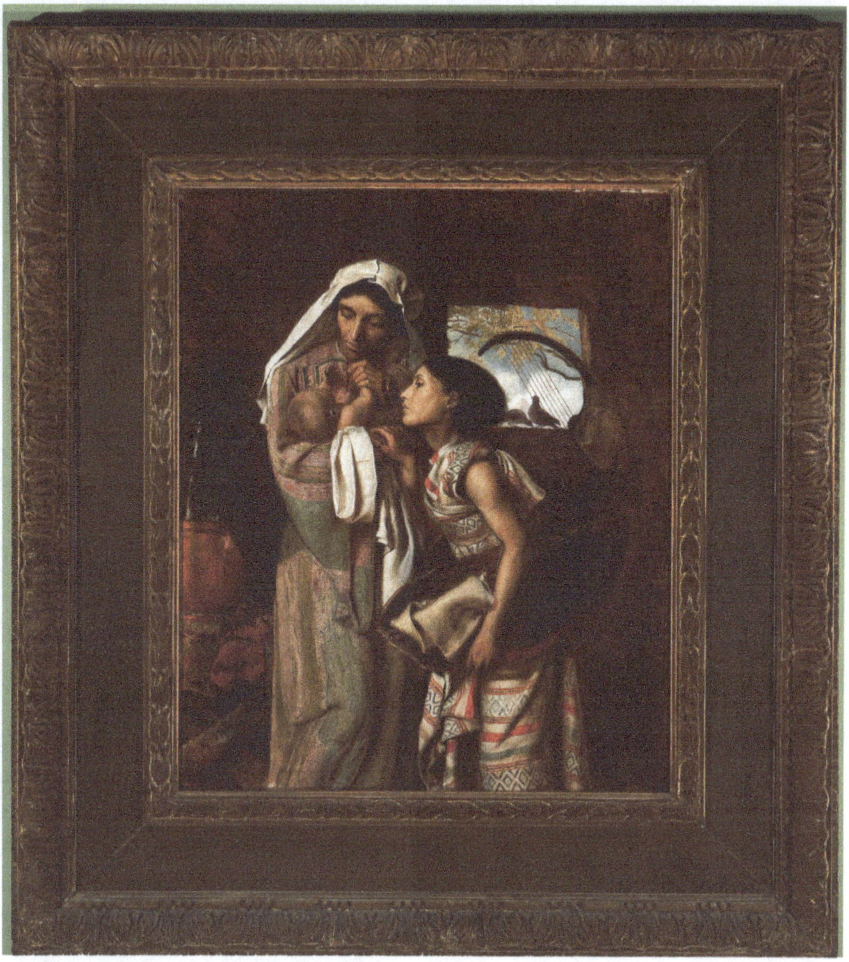

Figure 13.3. Simeon Solomon, *Mother of Moses*, exhibited 1860, Oil on canvas, 61 × 50.5 cm, Delaware Art Museum, Wilmington, USA. Bequest of Robert Louis Isaacson, 1999. © Delaware Art Museum.

In another painting, *Miriam* by Robert Dowling (1864; Warrnambool Gallery, Victoria, Australia), Fanny is depicted crying. Illustrating a scene from the book of Exodus in the Bible, Fanny poses as the mother of Moses at the point when her daughter Miriam is about to take him away and hide him in the bulrushes for safety.[26] Perhaps this soulful expression was easy for her to reproduce, given her own history. Although considered an Australian artist, Dowling was born in England and returned for a period of twenty-seven years between 1857 and 1884. During this time attended Leigh's Academy and exhibited sixteen works at the Royal Academy.[27] It is possible he sketched Fanny at the Royal Academy life classes which he is also believed to have attended.

It is hard to find any paintings or drawings of Fanny that show her smiling. While it is appreciated that many artists at that time wanted her to look wistful or pensive (especially the Pre-Raphaelites), the overall image we are left with is that of a sad woman. Even in Dante Gabriel Rossetti's painting *The Beloved* (1865–6; Tate, London) she appears in the background with a strange look in her eyes.[28] This may not have been Rossetti's intention, but it gives the viewer the impression that Fanny is being excluded.

Albert Moore's *The Mother of Sisera* (1861; Tullie House Museum, Carlisle) really demonstrates how sad Fanny could look.[29] Was this specifically posed for the artist or was it Fanny's natural expression? Is this the look that captured the other artists' attention and gave her so much work in this period? Perhaps it was this sad look that first attracted Solomon to her as a model. His studies of Fanny in the Fitzwilliam Museum in Cambridge (see Figures 13.1 and 13.2) certainly do not show a happy woman. As previously mentioned, he uses these studies for his painting *Mother of*

26 Robert Dowling, *Miriam*, 1864, oil on canvas, 91.0 × 70.5 cm, Warrnambool Art Gallery, Victoria, Australia.

27 'Robert Dowling: Tasmanian Son of Empire', National Gallery of Australia (n.d.), <https://nga.gov.au/exhibition/dowling/default.cfm?MnuID=3&GalID=0>, accessed 12 May 2021.

28 Dante Gabriel Rossetti, *The Beloved*, 1865–6, oil on canvas, 82.5 × 76.2 cm, Tate, London.

29 Albert Moore, *Mother of Sisera*, 1861, oil on canvas, 29.4 × 22.5 cm, Tullie House Museum and Art Gallery, Carlisle.

Moses to depict the deep sorrow of the mother giving up her baby. Possibly the baby in Fanny's arms is her first child, Fanny Matilda, born in 1858, as it would have been difficult to find someone to look after her children whilst being a model. Frederick Sandys captures the same wistful look in his drawing *Study of Fanny Eaton* (1859–60; Art Gallery of New South Wales, Sydney).[30]

Solomon's sister, Rebecca, also uses a sad expression in *The Young Teacher* (1860–1; private collection).[31] Owned by a family from the Isle of Wight, this painting had its first public showing at the *Pre-Raphaelite Sisters* exhibition in 2019 in London. It was given to a member of the family as a reward on her retirement as housekeeper to the original owners. The painting came to the art world's attention when brought to the National Gallery by the family member for an insurance valuation. The sitter was identified as Fanny by Pamela Gerrish Nunn and Jan Marsh.

Even the iconic image of Fanny in Joanna Mary Wells' *Head of a Mulatto Woman* (1861; Yale Center for British Art, New Haven, USA) shows her with a pensive look.[32] Did Joanna ask for this facial expression or did she see in Fanny the ideal model for her project? For this painting, Joanna dressed Fanny in an expensive shawl, perhaps to hide Fanny's working clothes. This painting has an interesting story in that the inscription of the model's name was not clear and the painting was initially thought to be of another Fanny – Fanny Cornforth. However, later research by Nunn and Marsh established that the writing had been obscured and should have read 'Fanny Eaton'.

The most natural representation of Fanny, but still offering a sad expression, appears to be a study by Walter Fryer Stocks (Figure 13.4).

30 Frederick Sandys, *Study of Fanny Eaton*, c. 1859, black and red chalk, pencil on paper, 23.7 × 24.3 cm, Art Gallery of New South Wales, Australia.

31 Rebecca Solomon, *The Young Teacher*, 1861, oil on canvas, 61.0 × 51.0 cm, private collection.

32 Joanna Mary Wells (née Boyce), *Head of a Mulatto Woman*, 1861, oil on paper, 17.1 × 13.7 cm, Yale Center for British Art, New Haven, CT.

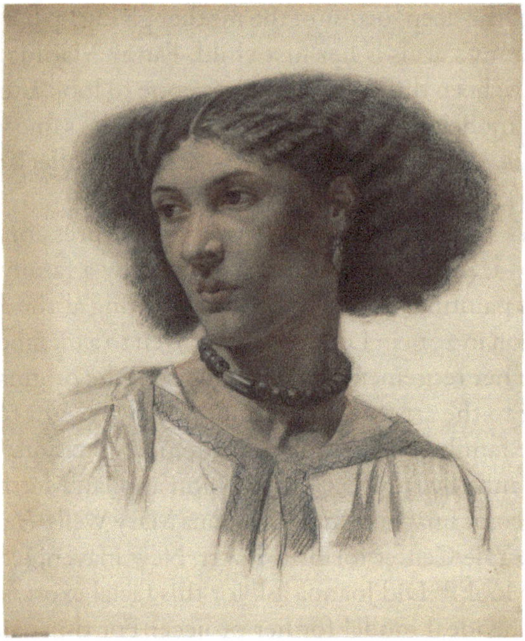

Figure 13.4. Walter Fryer Stocks, *Mrs Fanny Eaton*, c. 1859–60, Black, red and white chalk on cream wove paper, 43.2 × 34.9 cm, Princeton University Art Museum, New Jersey, USA. Museum purchase, Surdna Fund. Object no. 2016-1. © Princeton University Art Museum.

This work also presents an interesting story as the artist is perhaps best known for his landscapes. It was only discovered in 2014 when Rupert Maas, a London gallery owner, bought a collection of the artist's works at auction and found this study of Fanny amongst them. It was purchased by the Princeton University Art Gallery. In my opinion, even though it is not by one of the Pre-Raphaelites, this beautiful drawing most accurately captures the look of a woman who is far away in her thoughts, and perhaps compensates for the lack of any contemporary photographs.

It is sad to think that many of these portraits may in fact show the real Fanny, a sad figure who found life in Victorian Britain extremely hard. Perhaps that is why her children failed to tell their own children of the early career of their grandmother? They had personally witnessed how sad she had been and had seen her struggles first-hand. They had all been very young when Fanny was at the height of her modelling career and perhaps knew little of it. If Fanny experienced any racism or discrimination, it is likely she kept silent rather than burden her children.

These paintings and drawings have allowed me to discover more about the woman who was my great-grandmother. They cannot, however, compensate for the lack of written records, of which there are only brief census details and a few certificates. More frustrating is that there are photographs of some of the other Pre-Raphaelite Sisters from as early as 1865, but no image of Fanny has yet been found. Does this indicate that she was not considered as important by the Brotherhood or their followers? Or had she already slipped from the limelight by the time photography became popular?

Another area to consider is how James would have reacted to his wife becoming a model. Models at that time were thought to be drawn mainly from the prostitute community. James must have wondered what kind of world Fanny had moved into, but perhaps he was persuaded by the prospect of her extra earnings. The Pre-Raphaelite circle would surely have seemed like a different world to Fanny and James. The artists appeared to lead lives that today we would describe as 'Bohemian'. Some of the other models and female artists had personal lives far removed from the working-class life that Fanny led as a mother with ten children. Some even came from wealthy families and moved in the higher levels of society.[33] Many of the other women connected with the Pre-Raphaelites also left records of their lives or works, photographs, and even in some cases their own paintings and books.[34] It is relatively easy to recreate their lives from these records. Regrettably, this is not true of Fanny, who left nothing; therefore research is the only key to unlocking her life.

In the various censuses I have consulted, it is notable that Fanny's occupation is never described as a 'model'. Until 1881, James, as head of the household, may have chosen not to mention her modelling career, probably because of its association with prostitution. In 1861, Fanny's occupation is just listed as a 'charwoman' (cleaning help at another house), even

33 Jan Marsh et al, *Pre-Raphaelite Sisters* (London: National Portrait Gallery, 2019).

34 See, for example, Georgiana Burne-Jones, *Memorials of Edward Burne-Jones* (London: Macmillan & Co., 1904); John Robert Parsons, *Jane Morris posed by Rossetti*, 1865, album of original albumen prints bound in Morris fabric (accession nos. 1736–1752–1939), Victoria and Albert Museum, London.

though Solomon's painting *The Mother of Moses* had just been exhibited at the Royal Academy. She may not have known that her image would be on display, and we can assume that she certainly would not have been able to frequent the art galleries.

In 1871, the entry for her occupation was left blank.[35] However, in the 1881 census, just after James's death, Fanny became the head of the household, yet she still only referred to herself as a 'needlewoman'.[36] She seems to have ceased modelling, even though she was now the main breadwinner. Two of her daughters (Amelia, aged 19, and Julia, 16) were living away from home as servants to ease her burden. By 1891, it appears that Fanny was taking in lodgers (Frederick Rose, Catherine Binless) to help with the finances.[37] Frederick later married Fanny's daughter Mildred in 1893.

It is probable that Fanny (or James) never felt that modelling was a 'proper' occupation, but simply used it just as a way of supplementing James's income as a cab-proprietor. There were so many cabs in London at that time that competition was fierce, and James's income would also have to pay for the upkeep of his horse (horses?) and a licence fee. In 1851, for example, there were over 6,000 licensed cab drivers in London.[38] There

35 1871 Census return for 1 Upper Winchester Street, Finsbury, London, RG10/257, page 60. James Eaton, Age 34, Cab Driver. Fanny, Ditto. Age 35. Fanny, Ditto, Age 14. James, Ditto, Age 12. Amelia. Ditto, Age 9. Julia, Ditto, Age 7. Miriam, Ditto, Age 3. Unnamed, Age 6 months. [Walter?] (All children are noted as being born in Gray's Inn Road. Multiple families are living at this address.)

36 1881 Census return for 191 Lancaster Road, Kensington, London, RG11/33, page 14. Fanny Eaton (Head), Age 44, Needlewoman. James, Ditto (son), Age 21, Carpenter. Fanny, Ditto, Age 23, Dressmaker. Miriam, Ditto, Age 13, Scholar. Walter, Ditto, Age 11, Ditto. Ernest, Ditto, Age 9, Ditto. Cicely, Ditto, Age 5, Ditto. Frank, Ditto, Age 2. (The last three children were born in Kensington. Multiple families are living at this address.)

37 1891 Census return for 36 Woodstock Road, Hammersmith, London, RG12/0039, page 50. Fanny Eaton (Head), Widow, Age 54, Housekeeper. Mildred, Age 28, Dressmaker. Julia, Age 24. Miriam, Age 21 Artists Assistant, crossed out by census official and replaced with 'sculp' (presumably sculptor?). Cicely, Age 14, Mothers keep. (Also at this address Frederick Rose, Age 20, Tailor, Boarder.)

38 Fu-Chia Chen, 'Cab Cultures in Victorian London: Horse-Drawn Cabs, Users and the City, ca. 1830–1914', PhD thesis (University of York, 2013), 23, <https://etheses.whiterose.ac.uk/8047/1/Thesis%20Final.pdf>, accessed 17 May 2021.

was also a male bias in the methods of gathering census data: census officials, including enumerators and civil servants, were predominantly male. Heads of household (normally male) may not have recorded their wives' occupations since the instructions stated that women's work should only be included if it was regular employment. Fanny's modelling career may have been omitted for this reason.[39]

This period of Fanny's life in Victorian England was a time of great change and monumental events. Fanny would have had to negotiate these changes whilst bringing her children up and later, after James died in 1881, face them on her own.

Further problems arrived for James and the other cab drivers when London's first underground line, the Metropolitan Railway Line between Paddington and Farringdon Street, opened in 1863.[40] During this difficult period Fanny seems to have been busy, posing for several artists, including Dante Gabriel Rossetti (*The Beloved*, 1865–6; Tate, London) and Frederick Sandys (*Morgan Le Fay*, 1864; Birmingham Museum and Art Gallery) and the family must have appreciated the extra money that this work raised.

Street demonstrations and meetings were held in support of the cause to free slaves in America. Even if Fanny did not attend these, she must have been aware of the strong feelings on both sides that they generated. Could this be one reason she appears to have moved to a new house so frequently? She was living at different addresses for each census and probably keeping herself in the background where possible. Although she lived in London, Fanny may not have really felt part of 'normal' London life. Conversely, it could just be that Fanny was always looking for cheaper or better accommodation. In the early censuses she was living in multi-occupancy houses, some of which still exist, but by the end of the century she was in single family dwellings.

There were also visits by freed American slaves to rally support which may have made Fanny think of her mother's early life. Matilda must surely have told

39 Edward Higgs, and Amanda Wilkinson, 'Women, Occupations and Work in the Victorian Censuses Revisited', *History Workshop Journal* 81/1 (2016), 17, 20–21.

40 'A Brief History of the Underground', TFL, <https://tfl.gov.uk/corporate/about-tfl/culture-and-heritage/londons-transport-a-history/london-underground/a-brief-history-of-the-underground>, accessed 29 May 2021.

Fanny about her previous life as a slave, if only to explain how and why they had come to England. The best of these orators was said to be Frederick Douglass, a freed slave and abolitionist who drew huge audiences on his second tour of England and Ireland in 1859.[41] He returned home only when abolitionists Anna and Ellen Richardson from Newcastle had raised enough money from public donations to buy his freedom from Thomas Auld, his American owner for twenty years. There was even the prospect of war with America when Union soldiers captured two Confederate diplomats on a British ship bound for Europe in 1861 to seek support for their cause. This became known as the Trent Affair (from the ship's name) but fortunately the two diplomats were later released on the orders of Abraham Lincoln and the tension was reduced.[42]

There were continuing problems in Fanny's birth country even after slavery was abolished. The riots in Jamaica in 1865 started with demonstrations in Morant Bay over the terrible conditions still prevailing for the Black population. However, several prominent people, including Charles Dickens and Alfred Tennyson, and even Pre-Raphaelite patron John Ruskin, praised Thomas Carlyle and joined a society he founded to raise funds in support of his legal fight![43] Surely the Pre-Raphaelite artists would have been privy to Ruskin's opinions? These views would have sat uncomfortably with the artists' use of Fanny as a model. She may have even overheard their conversations on this subject while posing. It is possible they did not know (or consider) that she was Jamaican by birth.

In 1884 there was a meeting at the Guildhall in London to commemorate the fiftieth anniversary of the Abolition of Slavery. Would Fanny have been

41 Hannah Murray, 'Future Visits', *Frederick Douglass in Britain and Ireland,* <http://fredericdouglassinbritain.com/journey/futurevisists/>, accessed 29 May 2021.

42 For full details see Ephraim Douglass Adams, *Great Britain and the American Civil War* (Project Gutenberg EBook #13789), <https://www.gutenberg.org/files/13789/13789.txt>, accessed 19 May 2021.

43 W. F. Finlason, *Justice to a Colonial Governor, or, Some Considerations on the Case of Mr Eyre* (London: Chapman and Hall, 1868). Digital Library of the Caribbean, <https://dloc.com/CA01099980/00001/1j>, accessed 17 May 2021. Thomas Carlyle established the 'Governor Eyre Defence and Aid Committee' to gather funds for Edward Eyre's subsequent trial and to publicise his defence. It attracted many famous people.

aware of this? It is so frustrating that we have been unable to find any writings from Fanny or her ten children to allow us to glimpse their feelings either about these momentous events or the effect on their lives. Fanny's children would have learned to read and write as free education for children became available in Britain for the first time in 1891. Unfortunately, only Frank (now aged 11) seems to be of school age. He and some of the other children had attended school before this (they are noted as 'scholars' on census returns) but how it was paid for is not known. Fanny's grandchildren, however, would go on to benefit from this change in education. One wonders whether they suffered any racism at school if their mixed-race heritage was evident?

In 1899 the Boer War in South Africa began and Fanny's son Ernest, now 27, volunteered for service, was wounded and sent home. None of her other sons seem to have enlisted for this war, but they all served in the next conflict, the First World War. Fortunately, all returned home safely, although we know that Frank, my grandfather, was wounded twice. How did Fanny cope with the extreme danger that all her sons were to experience? At this time, she is recorded as living with her daughter Julia and husband Thomas Powell with their two children.[44] Fanny is noted as a woman of 'independent' means, having returned from the Isle of Wight where she had been a cook for the Hall family, of which little is known.[45] The lack of any photographs of Fanny means that we cannot see how life was treating her. This is possibly an indication that Fanny was not thought to be a noteworthy part of the society in which she lived. Photographs, however, were expensive and Fanny would have needed her earnings simply to survive.

44 1911 Census return for 66 Davisville Road, Hammersmith, London, RG14/schedule 227, Registration District 3, Enumeration District 14. Thomas Powell (Head), Age 52, Carpenter. Julia, Ditto, Age 38. Thomas, Ditto, Age 9. Constance, Ditto, Age 7. Fanny Eaton, Mrs., Age 74, Born West Indies. In this census Fanny states that she completed fifty-four years of marriage with ten children, one dead.

45 1901 Census return for 4 Alexandra Road, St. Helens, Isle of Wight, RG13/1026, page 8. John D. Hall, Age 64, Born London. Fanny Hall, Age 64, Born London. Fanny Eaton, Age 63, Cook/Dom(domestic), Born Jamaica, British Subject. Louisa E. Grant, Age 21, Servant, Born Portsea, Hampshire. (Further research shows that John Hall was a wine merchant on the mainland. It would be interesting to know how Fanny found work on the Isle of Wight with this family.)

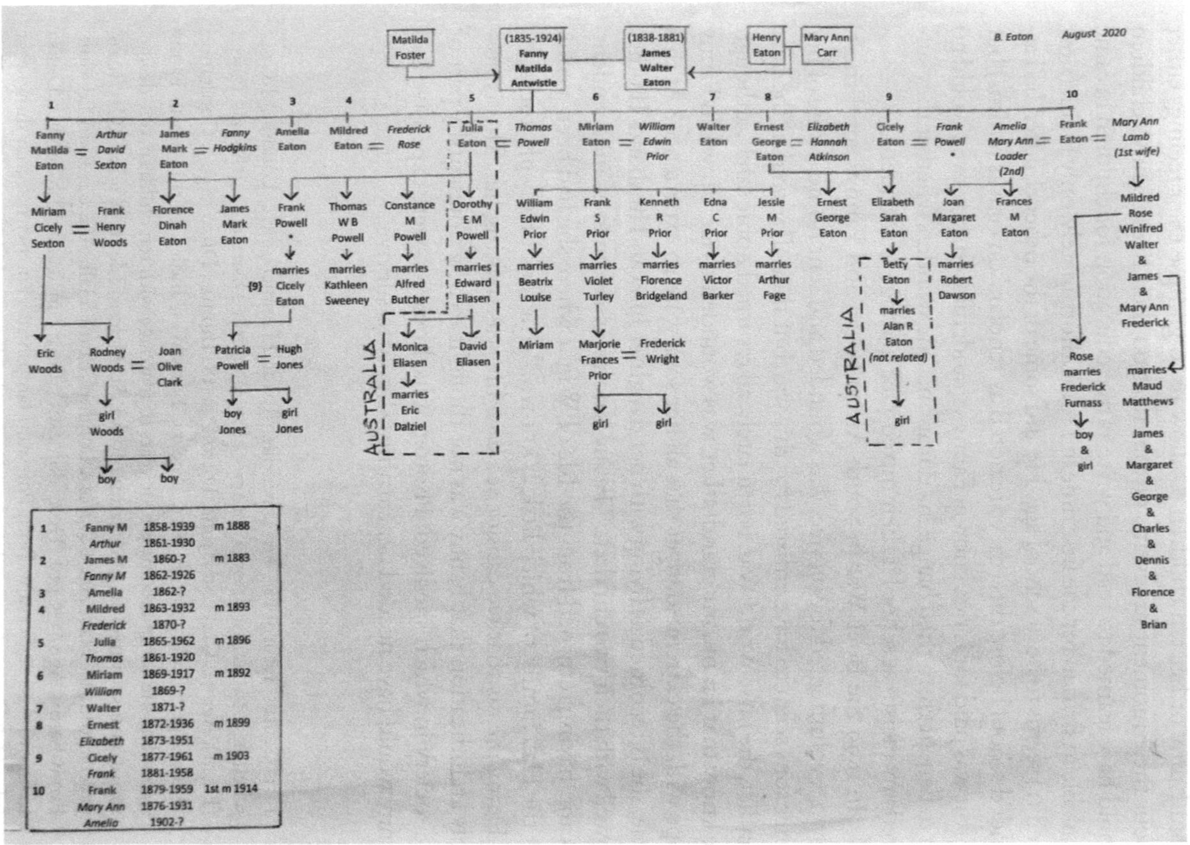

Figure 13.5. The Eaton Family Tree. Copyright © Brian Eaton.

In our efforts to uncover the past we have managed to trace several of Fanny's descendants to try to discover stories from her early life (Figure 13.5). All we have found so far is that every single relative appears to have had Fanny's true story whitewashed from their family history. My own grandfather, Frank, the youngest of Fanny's children, shrouded the story in mystery so that my father claimed we had 'Red Indian' (Native American) blood! As many cowboy and Indian shows came to west London in the late 1800s, my family actually thought for a long time that this might be true. The irony is that there were also many African shows in and around London at the same time. Some members of the family even related stories of an Indian Princess or a Portuguese Lady rather than a working girl. It is my pleasure to correct these inaccurate 'myths'.

Fanny died in Acton, London, on 4 March 1924.[46] She was therefore very much alive when her immediate descendants with their families were living in nearby districts. Apart from her daughter Julie Powell, who she lived with, did she have contact with any of her other children's families? Did they even know of her whereabouts? Now that the true story of Fanny's heritage and struggle has been revealed, we will possibly learn more from as yet untraced relatives. It is difficult to understand why her family chose to ignore her early fame, unless of course it was because of the supposed link between modelling and prostitution. Surely the older children would have known of Fanny's early work as a model? One daughter, Miriam, even claimed to be an 'artist's assistant', even though it was crossed out by the official and replaced with 'sculp'.[47] As previously mentioned, we also know from the Petty Cash Records of the Royal Academy that one daughter actually modelled for their life classes, being listed as 'Miss Eaton', as opposed to when 'Mrs Eaton' was paid for modelling services in 1874, 1875 and 1879.[48]

46 Certified copy of death certificate for Fanny Eaton. 4 March 1924. Application number PAS1068616. The General Register Office.

47 1891 Census return for 36 Woodstock Road, Hammersmith, London.

48 See note 24.

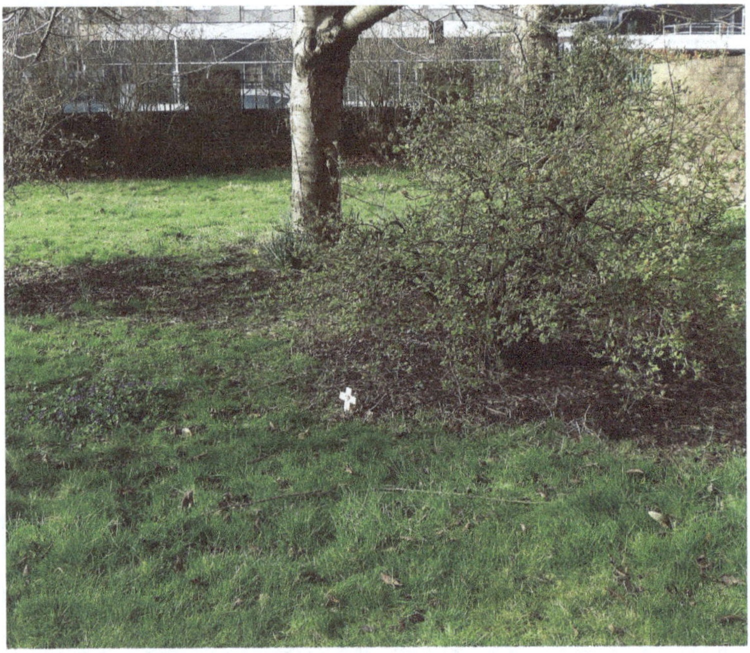

Figure 13.6. Fanny Eaton: Her Final Resting Place in a Common Grave Margravine Road Cemetery, Hammersmith, London. Photograph © Brian Eaton.

After a long search we discovered that Fanny is buried in an unmarked mass pauper's grave in Margravine Road Cemetery, Hammersmith (Figure 13.6), in west London, along with seven other unrelated adults.[49] The only other Pre-Raphaelite Sister to have been buried in a pauper's grave is Fanny Cornforth, who ended her life in Graylingwell Asylum, Chichester and was buried in a common grave in Chichester District Cemetery.[50] The other Sisters were buried in normal churchyard graves, some with

49 Register of Graves, Hammersmith & Fulham Council Cemeteries, Page 321, Letter no. 3.

50 Kirsty Stonell Walker, 'Fanny's Final Farewell', The Kissed Mouth (28 March 2015), <http://fannycornforth.blogspot.com/2015/03/fannys-final-farewell.html>, accessed 21 May 2021.

headstones and some with memorial plaques.[51] It seems a sad ending for Fanny after such a hard life, especially as she is now appreciated by so many people throughout the world who view her image in paintings and drawings in galleries. Unfortunately, without any letters or family papers we can never really know Fanny's thoughts.

Following my extensive research, I am proud to have discovered my true heritage. I am even more proud to tell the story of a child born in the most miserable and unpromising conditions and yet who found a life in a different land and survived, a child who more than lived up to the meaning of her names as 'free' and 'strong'.

The *Pre-Raphaelite Sisters* exhibition in 2019 and subsequent conference were promoted to shine a new light on the many women who inspired the Pre-Raphaelite artists. I hope that my research has helped in that aspiration and that I have succeeded in bringing Fanny Eaton out of the shadows.[52]

Bibliography

'A Brief History of the Underground', TFL, <https://tfl.gov.uk/corporate/about-tfl/culture-and-heritage/londons-transport-a-history/london-underground/a-brief-history-of-the-underground>, accessed 29 May 2021.

Adams, Ephraim Douglass, *Great Britain and the American Civil War* (Project Gutenberg EBook #13789), <https://gutenberg.org/files/13789/13789.txt>, accessed 19 May 2021.

51 The author is delighted to confirm that Hammersmith Council have generously agreed to provide a headstone at Fanny Eaton's grave.

52 Author's Note: I would particularly like to express my appreciation of David Olusoga whose book *Black and British* (Pan Macmillan) has given me a new understanding of life in Victorian England for people of colour. On his recommendation I also read *Staying Power* by the late Peter Fryer (Pluto Press). I would also like to mention the help we have received over many years from the Family History Section staff in Leeds Central Library.

'Bloody Bunce: A Legacy of the Transatlantic Slave Trade in Sierra Leone', *Royal Historical Society: Historical Transactions* (29 October 2019), <https://blog.royalhistsoc.org/2019/10/29/bunce-island-legacy/>, accessed 29 May 2021.

Burne-Jones, Georgiana, *Memorials of Edward Burne-Jones*, 2 vols (London: Macmillan & Co., 1904).

Chen, Fu-Chia, 'Cab Cultures in Victorian London: Horse-Drawn Cabs, Users and the City, ca 1830–1914', PhD thesis (University of York, 2013), <https://etheses.whiterose.ac.uk/8047/1/Thesis%20Final.pdf>, accessed 17 May 2021.

Elzea, Betty, *Frederick Sandys, 1829–1904: A Catalogue Raisonné* (Woodbridge, Suffolk: Antique Collectors' Club in association with Norfolk Museums & Archaeology Service, 2001).

Ferrari, Roberto C., 'Fanny Eaton: 'The Other' Pre-Raphaelite Model', *Pre-Raphaelite Society Review*, 22/2 (Summer 2014), 3–19.

——, 'Eaton [née Antwistle/Entwistle], Fanny (1835–1924)', *Oxford Dictionary of National Biography*, <https://doi.org/10.1093/odnb/9780198614128.013.90000369549>, accessed 13 May 2021.

Finlason, W. F., *Justice to a Colonial Governor, or, Some Considerations on the Case of Mr Eyre* (London: Chapman and Hall, 1868). Digital Library of the Caribbean, <https://dloc.com/CA01099980/00001/1j>, accessed 17 May 2021.

Frith, William Powell, *My Autobiography and Reminiscences* (New York: Harper and Brothers, 1888).

Fryer, Peter, *Staying Power: The History of Black People in Britain* (London: Pluto Press, 2018 [1984]).

Halliwell, Stella, 'Fanny Eaton: The Forgotten Pre-Raphaelite Stunner', *Simple Living Stella* (9 January 2012), <https://stellahalliwell.co.uk/pre-raphaelites/fanny-eaton-the-forgotten-pre-raphaelite-stunner/>, accessed 13 May 2021.

Higgs, Edward, and Amanda Wilkinson, 'Women, Occupations and Work in the Victorian Censuses Revisited', *History Workshop Journal*, 81/1 (Spring 2016), 17–38.

Marsh, Jan, *Black Victorians: Black People in British Art, 1800–1900* (Aldershot: Ashgate Publishing, 2005).

——, et al., *Pre-Raphaelite Sisters* (London: National Portrait Gallery, 2019).

Maynard, Douglas, 'Civil War "Care": The Mission of the George Griswold', *The New England Quarterly*, 34/3 (September 1961), 291–310.

Murray, Hannah, 'Future Visits', *Frederick Douglass in Britain and Ireland*, <http://frederickdouglassinbritain.com/journey/futurevisists/>, accessed 29 May 2021.

Nunn, Pamela Gerrish, 'Artist and Model: Joanna Mary Boyce's "Mulatto Woman"', *Journal of Pre-Raphaelite Studies*, n.s. 2/2 (Fall 1993), 12–15.

Olusoga, David, *Black and British: A Forgotten History* (London: Pan Macmillan, 2016).

'Robert Dowling: Tasmanian Son of Empire', *National Gallery of Australia* (n.d.), <https://nga.gov.au/exhibition/dowling/default.cfm?MnuID=3&GalID=0>, accessed 12 May 2021.

Venning, Timothy, 'Cromwell's Foreign Policy and the Western Design', *The Cromwell Association*, <http://www.olivercromwell.org/wordpress/?page_id=518>, accessed 29 May 2021.

Walker, Kirsty Stonell, 'Fanny's Final Farewell', *The Kissed Mouth* (28 March 2015), <http://fannycornforth.blogspot.com/2015/03/fannys-final-farewell.html>, accessed 21 May 2021.

'The West India Regiments', *National Army Museum* (n.d.), <https://www.nam.ac.uk/explore/slaves-red-coats-west-india-regiment>, accessed 26 May 2021.

HANNAH SQUIRE

14 *Beyond Ophelia* and Wightwick Manor: Collecting and Exhibiting Women Artists' Work at the National Trust

ABSTRACT

As part of Wightwick Manor's *Art and Activism* programme in 2018, an element of the broader National Trust programming to celebrate the centenary of when some women got the vote, I researched and reinterpreted the work of women artists held at Wightwick's collection. I subsequently curated only the second solo exhibition of Elizabeth Siddal's work, entitled *Beyond Ophelia*, which was also the first time all Wightwick's collection of Siddal artworks have been framed and exhibited together. Siddal is primarily remembered as an artist's model, and her work as an artist in her own right has been largely forgotten. The focus of this exhibition was on Siddal's perseverance to achieve a professional status as an artist, and her artistic and poetic output. In this chapter I will discuss the historic context of the collecting habits of Geoffrey and Rosalie Mander, then owners of Wightwick Manor, specifically of Siddal's work. Also to be discussed is the success of this exhibition for the National Trust in engaging the general public and dealing with contemporary issues that are relevant and resonant. Finally, this chapter will also discuss the legacy of this exhibition at Wightwick Manor.

* * * * *

> strangely good, they are – not copies of his own (Rossetti) nor under his influence. [...] her surprising talents – shown in verse as well as drawing.[1]

Rosalie Glynn Grylls (Lady Mander, 1905–88), art and literature historian, Oxford University graduate, writer, lecturer and collector, wrote these words in 1964 about Pre-Raphaelite artist and poet Elizabeth Eleanor Siddal in her biography of Siddal's husband, Dante Gabriel

1 Rosalie Glynn Grylls, *Portrait of Rossetti* (Carbondale and Edwardsville: Southern Illinois University Press, 1964), 53.

Rossetti.[2] A pioneering and influential book, it encouraged a radical re-assessment of Pre-Raphaelite art at a time when it was out of fashion and greatly underappreciated.[3]

Rosalie and her husband, Sir Geoffrey Mander (1882–1962), amassed their collection of Pre-Raphaelite art for their home, Wightwick Manor, Wolverhampton. Inspired by Oscar Wilde's 'The House Beautiful' lecture (1882), the Victorian manor house was built for Geoffrey's parents, Theodore and Flora Mander, by architect Edward Ould.[4] A house of the Aesthetic Movement, though now belonging to the National Trust, it is still full of Pre-Raphaelite, Aesthetic and Arts and Crafts collections, most of which were acquired by Rosalie and Geoffrey to enhance the original character of the Manor.

Given with a financial endowment to the National Trust in 1937, the Manor has been open to the public ever since. As Rosalie remarked, 'The house at once took on new life with its sense of security and we set about acquiring things to add to original treasures'.[5] As the Manders began to form their art collection after the house was given to the Trust, sometimes working with Trust staff members, the Pre-Raphaelite art was therefore acquired for the purpose of going on display for the public. In effect, the Manders created a public art gallery in Wolverhampton dedicated to Pre-Raphaelite art. They were so invested in sharing their home, family history and, more specifically, the artists' work they had collected and the stories and history of the Pre-Raphaelite movement, that the Manders themselves gave tours to visitors and continued to live at Wightwick until their deaths. As Rosalie remarked of Geoffrey, 'he liked to think that the public should enjoy what had been his private property'.[6]

2 Before her marriage to Geoffrey, Rosalie was also a secretary to a Liberal MP and was selected as Liberal candidate for Reading in 1930.

3 Rosalie also wrote many articles about the Pre-Raphaelites, gave lectures and contributed to BBC broadcasts about the artists.

4 Wightwick Manor was built in two stages, beginning in 1887, the family added the east wing in 1892–3. Theodore Mander was a partner in the family business Mander Brothers, which manufactured paint, printing ink and varnish. Stephen Ponder, *Wightwick Manor Guidebook* (Swindon: National Trust, 2016), 3.

5 Ponder, *Wightwick Manor*, 22.

6 Ponder, *Wightwick Manor*, 18.

Rosalie also gave lectures about art history both nationally and internationally, as well as at Wightwick and in Wolverhampton, with a few of the volunteers at Wightwick remembering her passion and vast knowledge. As curator Stephen Ponder remarks in the National Trust guidebook for Wightwick, the Manders' collection shows that their interests lay in an artwork's ability to elucidate something of the 'biographical, historical and literary'.[7] The Manders collected pieces for the stories they could tell about the movement, its influences, ideas and connections, not for their purely visual appeal. I found this particularly fascinating when thinking about Siddal's contributions and the other artworks created by women artists in Wightwick's collection.

Prior to the late twentieth century, there was little interest by museums, galleries or universities in collecting, researching or displaying art created by women.[8] Thankfully, due to the efforts of many dedicated and brilliant feminist art historians including Jan Marsh, Pamela Gerrish Nunn, Deborah Cherry and Griselda Pollock, this really began to change for the Pre-Raphaelite women artists from the 1980s.[9] Yet, in 1961, a few decades before this new scholarly interest in the female Pre-Raphaelite artists flourished, Rosalie and Geoffrey paid a record sum at a Sotheby's auction to acquire a large collection of Siddal's artworks for Wightwick. Jeremy Maas, the art dealer and art historian who was also at the auction, remarked:

> One day at Sotheby's I spotted a parcel of beautiful drawings by Lizzie Siddal, with an estimate, I believe, of about £5. To my (and his) astonishment I was outbid for them by an elderly and distinguished-looking gentleman at about £120, thus creating

7 Ponder, *Wightwick Manor*, 28.

8 See, for example, Germaine Greer, *The Obstacle Race: Fortunes of Women Painters and Their Work* (London: Martin Secker & Warburg Ltd, 1979); Rozsika Parker and Griselda Pollock, *Old Mistresses: Women, Art and Ideology* (London: Routledge & Kegan Paul, 1981), and *Women Artists: The Linda Nochlin Reader* (London: Thames and Hudson Ltd, 2020).

9 For example, Jan Marsh and Pamela Gerrish Nunn, *Women Artists and the Pre-Raphaelite Movement* (London: Sphere, 1989); Deborah Cherry and Griselda Pollock, 'Woman as Sign in Pre-Raphaelite Literature: A Study of the Representation of Elizabeth Siddall', *Art History*, 7/2 (June 1984), 206–27.

> a world record for her work. With sinking heart I asked a porter to slip my card into the parcel. On it I had asked the purchaser to get in touch with me. He, Sir Geoffrey Mander, asked his wife, Lady Mander (Rosalie Glynn Grylls), to seek out the unexpected underbidder to enquire his interest. Most generously they offered to let me buy six of the drawings [...] Thus it was that I met the first of that redoubtable band of ladies who were to contribute so much to pre-Raphaelite studies in the 1960s and '70s.[10]

This quote by Maas is incredibly evocative; it must have been quite a shocking scene in 1961: a bidding frenzy over a Pre-Raphaelite artist's work, and even more so, of drawings by a *female* Pre-Raphaelite artist. Maas's acknowledgement of the importance of Rosalie's contribution to the re-evaluation of the movement's work is also noteworthy. I included this quote and a copy of the auction catalogue entry in the *Beyond Ophelia* exhibition space for visitors to appreciate that these works were pursued by the Manders, who were effectively live-in curators at Wightwick. It is not the case that Siddal's works were bequeathed, as in other collections; the Manders actively sought out and bought these pieces to enhance their collection.[11]

The Manders were primarily interested in procuring works from artists in Rossetti's circle, but this acquisition also speaks to the high regard they had for works by women artists. As the quotation at the beginning of this chapter emphasises, although Rosalie chose to write a biography about Rossetti a few years after this auction, she advocated for the talent of Siddal as an artist and poet in her own right, with her own style and subjects. Unfortunately for Wightwick, as Jeremy Maas explained, the Manders allowed him to purchase from them six of the Siddal drawings they had acquired at the auction: *The Lady of Shalott* (1853; The Maas Gallery), *Study of an Angel* (n.d. private collection), *Angel with Interlocking*

10 Jeremy Maas, 'The Pre-Raphaelites: A Personal View', in *Pre-Raphaelite Papers*, ed. Leslie Parris (London: Allen Lane, 1984), 229.

11 For example, the Ashmolean's collection of Siddal works, which also includes manuscripts of her poetry, was the result of a bequest made by John Bryson (1896–1976), late Fellow and Tutor in English Literature at Balliol College, Oxford (1940–63). Nearly a hundred drawings, mostly by Pre-Raphaelite artists, were donated by him in the 1970s.

Wings (c. 1855; National Gallery of Canada), *The Woeful Victory* (1860; The Higgins Gallery, Bedford), a *Nativity* scene (1860; Wightwick Manor) and one other.[12]

Through researching Siddal's *oeuvre* and the various collections holding her work, I discovered that Wightwick has the second largest public collection of her artworks in the world, with a total of twelve drawings. (The largest collection is held by the Ashmolean Museum, Oxford, with fourteen Siddal artworks.) Wightwick's collection of ten pencil sketches, include the drawings mentioned by Maas that the Manders acquired at auction, and the *Nativity* scene which was bought from the Maas Gallery in the late 1960s.[13] The other two works by Siddal in Wightwick's collection are gouaches, *The Haunted Wood* and *St Agnes' Eve*, which were first on loan from Helen Rossetti Angeli, daughter of Dante's brother William, before being acquired for the collection in the late 1990s and early 2000s.

Art and Activism

Working with Wightwick's collection as a Conservation Assistant, and particularly labouring in the conservation store, cataloguing and storing artworks, I was lucky enough to have access to this incredible collection of Siddal's drawings. Prior to the *Beyond Ophelia* exhibition, just four of her artworks were framed and on display around the Manor. These drawings were normally brought out a few times a year for the House and Collections Manager Helen Bratt-Wyton's informative talks, but otherwise were unseen by many visitors. Of the artworks that were on display, the two gouaches were hung in a narrow upstairs corridor. Visitors often walked past these paintings without noticing them, unless they were pointed out. Even if visitors did want to linger, the opportunity was

12 We believe Lady Mander later bought back the *Nativity* for Wightwick's collection.

13 Of the other five drawings, *The Lady of Shalott* is still in the Maas collection; the remainder are in collections around the world. See Jan Marsh, *Elizabeth Siddal: Pre-Raphaelite Artist 1829–1862* (Sheffield: The Ruskin Gallery, 1991) for more details.

particularly inhibited at busy times, when visitors are quick to traverse this corridor to the nurseries to avoid delaying others. I wanted to change this and have them all prominently displayed together for the first time.

As a feminist art historian, I am fascinated by the collection of women artists' work at Wightwick. During my research I discovered the startling but incredible fact that the Manor includes the work of thirteen professional female artists in its collection, and a total of more than thirty-five works by women – more than the National Gallery in London.[14] It was from this starting point, and knowing that the National Trust were creating a national campaign in 2018, *Women and Power*, to celebrate and commemorate *The Representation of the People Act 1918* – which entitled some women to the vote for the first time in Great Britain and Ireland – that I, with the wider Wightwick team of staff and volunteers, began planning an *Art and Activism* programme of events.

From the 1870s, the Mander family were vocal supporters of women's suffrage. They held Suffragist meetings at Wightwick Manor; fought in Parliament for women's rights, especially for female domestic servants; as well as collecting the work of these women artists. I uncovered the stories of Florence Mander, a Wolverhampton Women's Suffragist Society supporter, who featured in the programming alongside the stories of others including Rosalie Mander. Another woman featured was Princess Sudhira Mander, who trained as a nurse and became a Voluntary Auxiliary Driver (V.A.D.) in London during the First World War. She was honoured with

14 The Manders bought another artwork, *Road to Calvary*, in the 1940s as an artwork by Christina Rossetti, but this attribution was rescinded after subsequent research has revealed it is a copy after an original by Veronese in the Louvre. Dante Gabriel Rossetti visited the Louvre with fellow artist William Holman Hunt in 1849 and was captivated by the work of Veronese. Holman Hunt gives a full account of their trip in *Pre-Raphaelitism and the Pre-Raphaelite Brotherhood*, 2 vols (London: Macmillan, 1905), I, Chapter VIII. However, no specific reference has yet been found of either Christina or Dante Gabriel making copies of this painting, so the attribution has been removed. However, it is still very interesting to know that as well as acquiring collections of Christina's poems for Wightwick's library, the Manders were actively seeking out her work, with National Trust colleagues, to acquire for Wightwick's collection. Therefore, it could be said that the collection was thought to include the work of fourteen female artists.

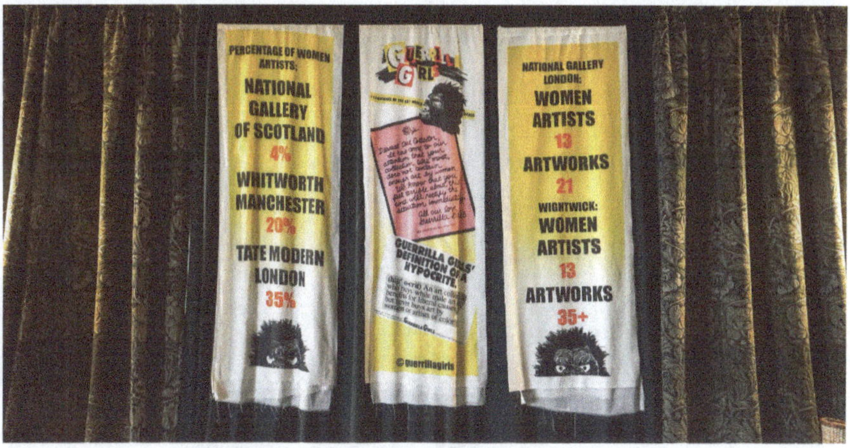

Figure 14.1. A *Guerrilla Girls* inspired banner, Kate Charlesworth, Wightwick Manor, Wolverhampton. Photograph © Lindsey Bucknor.

a medal for her war work. Other characters emerged such as Emma Smith, Wightwick's housekeeper, who attended a lecture by Suffragist writer and activist Sarah Grand, and the stories of female artists such as Lucy Madox Brown, Marie Spartali Stillman, May Morris and Siddal were foregrounded. As part of this theme, I decided to examine both the Mander family's activism and the artists they acquired for their collection, and the interconnectedness of them. Working with Wightwick volunteers, we created a leaflet providing a tour around the manor honouring these women, telling their stories through objects associated with them, explaining their achievements and involvement in advancing women's rights and their place in the political and art worlds.

Another aspect of the *Art and Activism* programming in 2018 was the work created by Wightwick's artist in residence, the illustrator, writer and activist Kate Charlesworth (Figure 14.1).[15] She was inspired by the women of Wightwick's stories and designed art installations – activist banners and

15 Charlesworth had previously created the emotive and powerful illustrations for the graphic novel, *Sally Heathcote: Suffragette* by Mary and Bryan Talbot (London: Jonathan Cape, 2014).

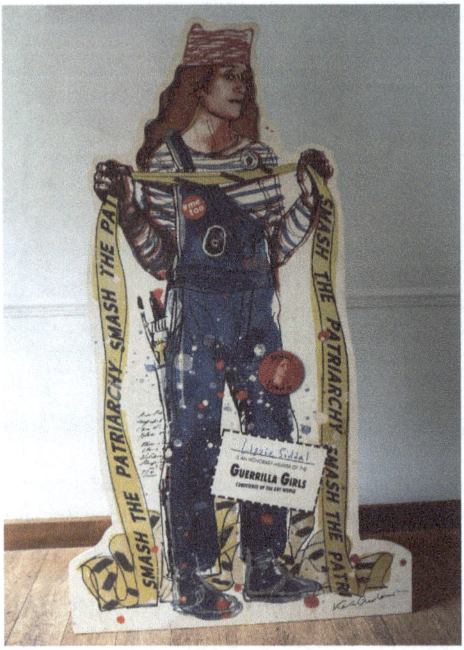

Figure 14.2. *Elizabeth Siddal as a Guerrilla Girl*, Kate Charlesworth, Wightwick Manor, Wolverhampton. Photograph © Beth Squire.

silent companions – around the Manor. Kate related the lives of the artists and Mander family members to stories of gender activism today, including contacting the Guerrilla Girls to use some of their messaging and imagery in the banner images.[16]

One of the silent companions is a reimagining of Elizabeth Siddal as a modern artist (Figure 14.2). Charlesworth cleverly references the famous figure of Millais's *Ophelia* (1851–2; Tate, London), with Siddal's hands raised in the same pose, but subverts this popular narrative by having her wear a pussy hat and dressing her in artist's overalls, as if she were a member of the

16 The Guerrilla Girls were established in 1986 with a mission to bring gender and racial inequality into focus within the greater arts community, something the Manders were also passionate about.

modern Guerrilla Girls. Reiterating themes in the *Beyond Ophelia* exhibition, Charlesworth foregrounds Siddal's incredible artistic achievements and desire to be thought of as a professional artist. Her poetry can also be seen, written in her own hand, behind her legs, and her artist's signature is emblazoned on the waist of her dungarees. The connection between these artists' lives in the past and their relevance and resonance today was an important message to disseminate and worked extremely well with contextualising the exhibition.

Curating *Beyond Ophelia*

I decided that this would provide the perfect opportunity to have all Siddal's artworks in the Mander collection on display. I had never curated an exhibition by myself before, so naively I thought the best place to start was to look at how many previous solo exhibitions of Elizabeth Siddal's work (or exhibitions that featured a number of her works prominently) had been curated. I was astonished to find there had only been one solo exhibition in the 157 years since her death, curated by Jan Marsh at the Ruskin Gallery, Sheffield, in 1991.[17] It seemed long overdue to revisit her work and create an exhibition dedicated to her artistic output. I therefore embarked on curating an exhibition of Siddal's art and poetry, entitled *Beyond Ophelia*.[18] Siddal is primarily remembered as an artist's model and her work as an artist and poet is often ignored. I wanted this exhibition to focus on her desire to be recognised as a professional artist, and to foreground her artistic and poetic output.

17 Jan Marsh's books, research and support were invaluable to me while curating this exhibition, as was her willingness to record the video content included in the exhibition.

18 The title was not my idea, but the idea of a colleague, John Wood. It perfectly encapsulates what I was trying to achieve with the exhibition and coincidentally is also the title of Glenda Youde's recently completed doctoral thesis 'Beyond *Ophelia*: The Artistic Legacy of Elizabeth Eleanor Rossetti (née Siddall)', University of York, commenced January 2014.

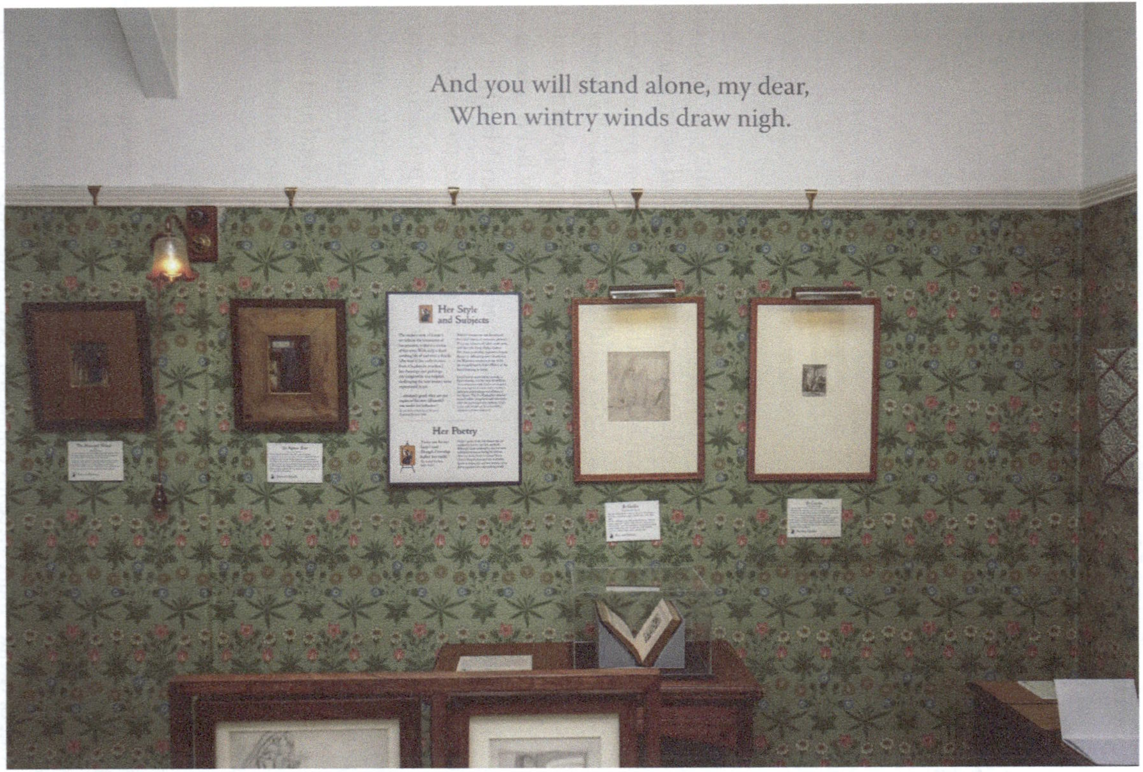

Figure 14.3. View of the *Beyond Ophelia* exhibition, Daisy Room, Wightwick Manor, Wolverhampton. Photograph © Lindsey Bucknor.

Early in the planning stages of this exhibition I decided to root it firmly in Wightwick's unique story. The focus would be on the twelve artworks in Wightwick's collection rather than loaned items. The size of the room was also a deciding factor. We chose an upstairs bedroom, the 'Daisy Room' (Figure 14.3), as an exhibition space, as it was normally roped off and the collection displayed in the room could be moved easily. Not borrowing any artworks also ensured we could keep costs down. We had gratefully received funding from the National Trust Midlands Treasure Houses Innovation fund and from the National Public Programmes team, but it was limited.

I also wanted to ensure that visitors to the exhibition were aware of the role the Manders had played in the reassessment of Siddal's artworks. Incorporated on the *Beyond Ophelia* exhibition panels were quotes (such as the one included at the beginning of this chapter) from Rosalie's book about her opinions of Siddal's art, and portraits of both Geoffrey and Rosalie were on display in the exhibition to explain why this exhibition and collection were at Wightwick. In the interpretation I emphasised that their collection was designed to be shared with everyone, so this exhibition felt like we were continuing in their spirit. A copy of Rosalie's book *Portrait of Rossetti* was also on display in the exhibition for visitors to peruse, as well as her correspondence which showed her research process – including working with Rossetti family members to learn more about Siddal's art, titles, inspirations, provenance and the locations of her artworks.

I made the decision not to include other artists' work in the space and focus purely on Siddal's artistic expression, although a drawing of Rossetti's *St Cecilia* which featured in the Moxon Tennyson was incorporated to highlight the similarities in composition, and the sharing of ideas between the artists.[19] I wanted this space to focus on introducing or reuniting visitors with Siddal's work, inviting their close and undivided attention.

19 I also included a copy of *The Germ* from Wightwick's library in the exhibition, open at the page featuring Walter Deverell's illustration to John Tupper's poem 'Viola and Olivia' from Shakespeare's *Twelfth Night*. Deverell was the first artist Siddal sat for as a model for Viola. This illustration was therefore included, alongside the photo of John Everett Millais' *Ophelia* (incorporated into an interpretation panel) to illustrate the story of the origins of Siddal's artistic career.

During the *Pre-Raphaelite Sisters: Making Art* conference, held at the University of York in December 2019, I was interested to listen to a discussion between Dr Jan Marsh and others, debating the merits of solo exhibitions of women's work in comparison to broader theme-based exhibitions that feature the work of a multitude of women and male artists in dialogue. While I agree that the approach of the *Pre-Raphaelite Sisters* exhibition at the National Portrait Gallery – which incorporated the work of both female and male Pre-Raphaelite artists but focused on examining women's creative involvement – was effective and engrossing, it does not negate the importance of staging solo exhibitions of women's work. Small numbers of Siddal's artworks were included in large survey exhibitions of Pre-Raphaelite art in the twentieth century, but even in more recent events such as the Tate's *Pre-Raphaelites: Victorian Avant-Garde* (2012) or the National Gallery's *Reflections: Van Eyck and the Pre-Raphaelites* (2017–18), her works were never one of the main focuses of the exhibition. The single exception was the aforementioned solo exhibition in 1991 curated by Jan Marsh.[20]

To focus exclusively on Siddal's work, to provide space for intimate engagement with her small-scale drawings and sketches, and place them next to her poems, is another way to encourage meaningful engagement with her art. It also provides an opportunity to dive deeper into her life, her inspirations, how her style evolves, the subjects that matter to her, how she consistently represents the female form, and the statement she is making about women in the Victorian world. We wanted the exhibition goer to focus on Siddal solely and purposely, to put both the spotlight and magnifying glass on her work – especially for the general interest visitors who may not have been familiar with it. Dedicating the space, interpretation and time exclusively to Siddal was a very fruitful experience. Many of the

20 The first solo exhibition of Siddal's work, curated by Jan Marsh, ambitiously brought together most of the art created by Siddal, incorporating thirty-four works, fourteen photographs of unlocated works, a photographic portfolio of her sketches (one of a number compiled by Rossetti after her death), a Gothic-style jewel box which she had helped to decorate, her copy of the Scottish ballads, which inspired four of her art works, and a small group of poems.

visitor cards and interactions I had with visitors, which I will discuss later, reflect an appreciation for focusing on just Siddal and her story, following the narrative of one individual.

The unique visitor journey at Wightwick, in comparison to other museums, also elides any fear of not understanding Siddal in the context of the broader Pre-Raphaelite movement. To reach the Siddal exhibition, the visitor had to walk through many of the rooms in the Manor, filled with Pre-Raphaelite art. It was not possible just to come to see the exhibition, as in other museums that are not in historic homes. Therefore, the visitor would have already soaked up the context of the Pre-Raphaelite movement and the Manders before they reached the exhibition of Siddal's work. By choosing a dedicated space for the exhibition, the Siddal drawings were not lost in grander rooms where one's eye might have been drawn to a larger, colourful oil painting. The visitor was asked to focus on Siddal exclusively for the duration of the exhibition, before returning to the final rooms in the Manor.

This 'solo exhibition' framing also felt very important for the spirit of Wightwick. As mentioned previously, the artworks purchased by the Manders were bought specifically to narrate the stories of the artists – from an early Millais oil painting he made as a teenager, to Burne-Jones sketches for stained-glass window designs, and May Morris's paintings of Kelmscott Manor. As a biographer of the group, Rosalie chose pieces to illustrate their lives and the breadth of their artistic careers. The artworks created by Siddal and bought by the Manders show the different commissions she worked on, her reworking of subjects and compositions, examples of artworks she exhibited and other aspects of her career.[21] They foreground her as an ambitious and dedicated artist.

Beyond Ophelia was aimed at general visitors who may not have previously been aware of Elizabeth Siddal, except perhaps as the 'drowning, mad ginger girl covered in flowers' – as I have heard her described – in

21 As demonstrated by the chapters by Laure Nermel, Nat Reeve, Rosalind White and Glenda Youde in this volume.

Millais's famous painting.[22] To avoid this stereotypical view, I endeavoured to get *Beyond Ophelia* to reinstate her as an important member of the Pre-Raphaelite circle. I did not want to be fixated on the melodrama of her life, which has so often been the focus of discussion. I had to resist the encroachment of my regional colleagues who, while generally helpful and encouraging, disagreed with me and felt that the exhibition focus should have been on Siddal's tumultuous relationship with Rossetti, her overdose and other aspects of her personal life. While this information was available in the exhibition folder, I felt strongly, with the backing of my boss, Helen, that the focus should be on Siddal as an artist and poet and on her creative and professional endeavours, which would have been the case if the exhibition had focussed on Rossetti, or any other male artist. Hence also why I chose to use the professional spelling of her name, with only one 'l', instead of the original family name 'Siddall'. 'Siddal' was the name she used during her lifetime when exhibiting her art.

Video content was an also important aspect of the exhibition. We wanted to reach out to other audiences through the popularity of YouTube and social media as well as including sound within the exhibition space. A colleague, Elizabeth Taylor, and I created two videos, one which features Jan Marsh talking about Siddal and Wightwick's collection, and one a recording of a volunteer reading Siddal's poem 'O Silent Wood', with the background images and noises of the woodland at Wightwick. As poetry is as much an auditory experience as it is a visual one, I felt it was imperative to feature this both in the exhibition space and online. Also, as the poem may relate to *The Haunted Wood*, one of Siddal's art works included in the exhibition, it was beneficial to be able to view the artwork while listening to the poem – to show their interconnectedness in her creativity and artistic expression, despite being separate mediums.

Our major expense for the exhibition was to have frames made for each of the eight drawings in the solander boxes, plus a few extra frames in which to display a couple of Siddal's poems. Extracts from Siddal's poetry were also included in wall quotes, something Geoffrey Mander himself had originally done around the Manor in the 1930s. He featured important

22 Overheard from a visitor at Wightwick, describing Siddal to a friend in 2017, before I began planning the exhibition. I have heard other variations on this theme a number of times over the years as a room guide volunteer.

nineteenth-century poets, including Tennyson. The exhibition was meant to feel like an organic extension of the Manor, something Geoffrey and Rosalie might have created themselves.

For a few of the drawings it was a challenge to work out how to best display them. I had long conversations with Wightwick's works on paper conservator, Graeme Storey, about how we could best exhibit four specific artworks. Siddal sometimes drew on both sides of the paper and not always in the same orientation. Four drawings in Wightwick's collection were double sided, and one of the sheets of paper was turned upside down when she drew on the back. To enable visitors to see the drawings in the correct orientation we had a special wooden frame made for the exhibition – styled to look in keeping with the house and collections. The drawings are encased in secondary wooden frames which are mounted on hinges within the main frame, allowing visitors to turn them in different directions to see both artworks the correct way up (Figure 14.4). The frame was placed in the middle of the room, so visitors could walk round it and appreciate both sides of the paper at the same time. The movement of the frames however also allowed for the future display of the drawings to be flexible – the wooden frame could be placed in front of a wall, and by turning the hinges, both sides would still be able to be viewed. For example, both drawings of *Sir Galahad* could be viewed side by side to compare the compositions. As part of a legacy of this exhibition, these four Siddal drawings, in their unique 'frames within a frame', are still often on display in the Great Parlour.

The exhibition panels focused on Siddal's background and artistic aspirations, her style and subject matter and her poetry. On entering the exhibition space, the first panel made visitors aware of the difficulties of becoming a professional artist in the Victorian art world. The interpretation highlighted how Siddal actively sought out art training, despite not being able to attend the Royal Academy Schools like her male peers, and how she aspired to a professional status, daring to defy gender restrictions. As part of the broader *Art and Activism* programming at Wightwick, we reiterated the difficulties faced by female artists today with ten framed facts on display around the Manor, addressing the statistics of women in the art world and in politics in the twenty-first century.

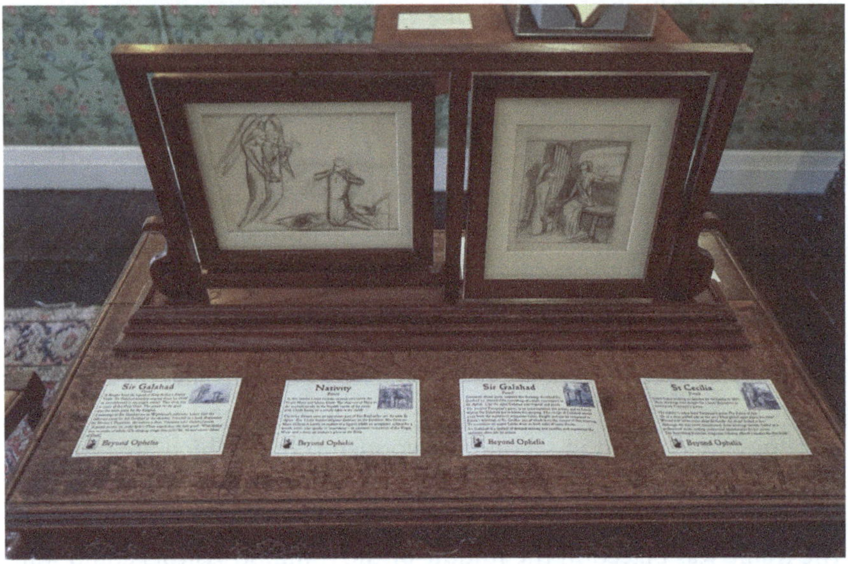

Figure 14.4. The double sided, adjustable frame which now houses four of Siddal's artworks Wightwick Manor, Wolverhampton. Photograph © Lindsey Bucknor.

Comparisons were also drawn between Siddal's career and the modest scale of her artworks and those of another female artist, Evelyn De Morgan, whose expansive oil paintings are also on display at Wightwick – and how the differing contexts of their lives shaped the art works they created.[23] De Morgan was born a generation after Siddal, so she was able to train at the newly opened Slade School of Art and attend life-drawing classes. She benefited from the opening in 1877 of the avant-garde alternative to the Royal Academy, the Grosvenor Gallery, which supported the work of female artists and invited them to exhibit. She was also born into a

23 Building on the legacy of the *Beyond Ophelia* exhibition, I recently curated the new exhibition, *Look Beneath the Lustre* in De Morgan gallery, working with the De Morgan Foundation and its collection. This exhibition examined the stories behind the creative outputs of Evelyn and her husband William De Morgan. Evelyn's struggles as a female artist were explored, together with the relationships that fostered and championed her creativity.

wealthy family, and crucially she had money for art supplies and studio space, unlike Siddal. De Morgan's uncle, John Roddam Spencer Stanhope, was also an artist, and was supportive of her work; historically, having a family member in the profession was crucial for women who had careers as artists, and which Siddal also lacked.

In the wider context of the Manor, it seemed important to contextualise Siddal's art works – small, mostly pencil drawings, simply framed – particularly as visitors would have encountered large, ornately framed, ambitious oil paintings by other women artists earlier on their tour. I wanted to ensure these works felt no less radical or important. The panel interpretation explored the modest size of Siddal's art works, and the reasons why, with prompts for reflection emerging from descriptions of the circumstances which she inhabited as an artist. The first line of the panel entitled *Her Life and Ambitions* reads: 'Born a woman, lower class, with no money of her own, and lacking family connections in the art world, Lizzie's chances of becoming a professional artist were not promising and her choice of career very unusual'.[24] This panel also discussed that despite a short working life of just over a decade (she died in her early 30s from a laudanum overdose), her drawings and paintings are imaginative and original, challenging the way in which women were represented in art. The artworks in Wightwick's collection inform the viewer that Siddal's women are not the sensual, beautiful objects of masculine pleasure one often associates with Pre-Raphaelite art. Instead, they are columns of fabric, with their hands, arms and faces becoming the focus of their bodies. Artistically, the face/head symbolises thought and intellectual engagement, while the hands are the site of artistic creation. Siddal therefore depicts women as creatively and intellectually engaged. She draws powerful, expressive female figures in different guises: whether as the Madonna attentive to her child; the vengeful witch Sister Helen; or the lover listening to music.

24 *Beyond Ophelia* exhibition panel, 2018.

The Artworks and Their Interpretation

The way visitors travelled around the space was something I was very conscious of. The hanging was designed to provide the most striking visual impact to persuade visitors to linger, and to introduce them to Siddal's work in a simple narrative – to entice and not confuse. The two gouaches, the only artworks featuring colour, were positioned in the centre of the room, to draw the eye and visitor into the space. They were both hung next to the board which detailed Siddal's ambition and career, as *The Haunted Wood* was one of the few paintings Siddal had exhibited during her lifetime – at the Pre-Raphaelite exhibition of 1857, organised by Ford Madox Brown at Russell Place, London. As Siddal was the only female artist included in the exhibition, this artwork is vitally important in understanding Siddal's exhibition history.

The Haunted Wood (see Figure 9.8) might also be considered an example of Siddal's influence on Rossetti's compositions. In the exhibition boards I suggested that Rossetti's drawing and later watercolour entitled *How They Met Themselves* (c. 1860–4; Fitzwilliam Museum, Cambridge) may have been inspired by Siddal's *The Haunted Wood*. Wightwick possesses a wardrobe in its collection featuring copies of Rossetti artworks painted by his studio assistant Henry Treffry Dunn. *How They Met Themselves* is included in the wardrobe decoration, and walking past both images every day, opening and closing the house, I realised that there may be a connection between the two. The female figures on the right of the compositions are in a similar pose, reaching out to their counterparts. Doppelgänger imagery can also be found in poems admired by Rossetti and Siddal, such as Elizabeth Barrett Browning's poem *The Romaunt of Margret* (1836).

Another female figure in blue, but alone and contemplative, the composition of *St Agnes' Eve* is more detailed and nuanced. Taken from a Tennyson poem, on the eve of St Agnes' feast day a nun in training contemplates her vows and waits to see her bridegroom. The poet and sister-in-law of the artist, Christina Rossetti, selected this as her favourite piece of Siddal's work and after her brother's death she chose it to hang

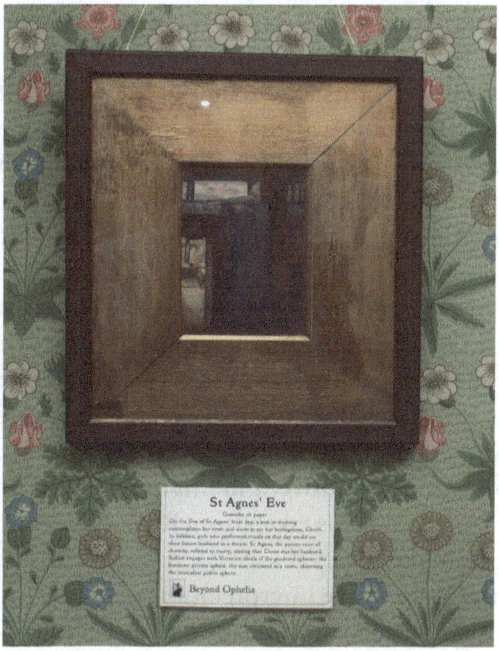

Figure 14.5. Elizabeth Siddal, *St Agnes' Eve* on display in *Beyond Ophelia*, Wightwick Manor, Wolverhampton. Photograph © John Pittwood.

on her wall.[25] This connection between the two artistic sisters-in-law, the regard Christina had for her work, is an interesting detail of the Pre-Raphaelite Sisterhood I wanted to include, and works against the antagonistic or competitive narrative that often is used against women in community.

Once again, a female figure is the prominent feature of the *St Agnes' Eve* (Figure 14.5), with her hands clasped as in prayer and head raised to heaven – the focus on the woman's body being her head (her thoughts) and her hands (for doing/making something). Siddal also engages with Victorian ideals of the gendered spheres: the feminine private sphere, where the nun is cloistered in a room, and the masculine public sphere

25 Marsh, *Elizabeth Siddal: Pre-Raphaelite Artist*, 63.

viewed through the window.[26] Marriage was a perceived preoccupation of women's lives in the nineteenth century. As an alternative, devoting one's life to something else, in this case religion, offered a different path for women, perhaps in the same way that art offered an alternative to Siddal.

Lovers Listening to Music (Figure 9.7), a drawing which Jan Marsh suggests is a fantastical self-portrait of Siddal and Rossetti, was displayed early in the exhibition space.[27] This prominent placement was chosen to enable visitors to understand the elusiveness of Siddal's identity.[28] The interpretation emphasised the importance of this artwork for stressing that Siddal left little written record of her life. She did not write an autobiography or name many of her artworks or poems, therefore we can only speculate on the title and subject matter. What we are able to learn about this drawing is subsequently through the eyes of the two Rossetti brothers. Siddal's own voice is rather elusive, and this drawing is a mystery; the title was not chosen by Siddal but is taken from Rossetti's description: 'the two Egyptian girls playing to lovers'.[29]

However, the focus of the interpretation of *Lovers Listening to Music* was to question whether it was perhaps a representation of Siddal's success in gaining patronage, as well as including a discussion of the subject matter. The Manders focused their attentions on preparatory sketches or drawings that occurred at a key point in the artist's life or showed a stylistic progression, which may explain their purchase of this piece. Rossetti

26 See, for example, Griselda Pollock, 'Modernity and the Spaces of Femininity', *Vision and Difference: Femininity, Feminism and the Histories of Art* (London: Routledge, 1988), Clarissa Campbell Orr ed., *Women in the Victorian Art World* (Manchester: Manchester University Press, 1995) and Susan Casteras, *Images of Victorian Womanhood in English Art* (Rutherford, NJ: Fairleigh Dickinson University Press, 1987).

27 Jan Marsh, *The Legend of Elizabeth Siddal* (London: Quartet Books Limited, 2010), 179.

28 An image of Millais' *Ophelia* and a photograph of Elizabeth Siddal (painted over in gouache, reportedly by Dante Gabriel Rossetti) in the collection of the Walters Art Museum, Baltimore, were also included in the interpretation panel, to create a sense of familiarity with different images of Siddal. The motif of the exhibition, a woman at an easel, was also inspired by Rossetti's drawings of Siddal at work as an artist.

29 Marsh, *Elizabeth Siddal: Pre-Raphaelite Artist*, 45.

showed *Lovers Listening to Music*, among other drawings, to the art critic John Ruskin in 1855 to secure financial support for Siddal. On seeing her work, Ruskin bought it all and offered her an allowance.[30] She used this money to buy paints and brushes of her own.

A section of the exhibition was dedicated to showing how Siddal's creativity in both the mediums of poetry and art, intertwined and informed each other. Poetry was a very important inspiration for Siddal's art. Her drawing of *Sister Helen* is based on Rossetti's poem of the same name. Through this drawing, *Sister Helen* (Figure 14.6), I explored the partnership

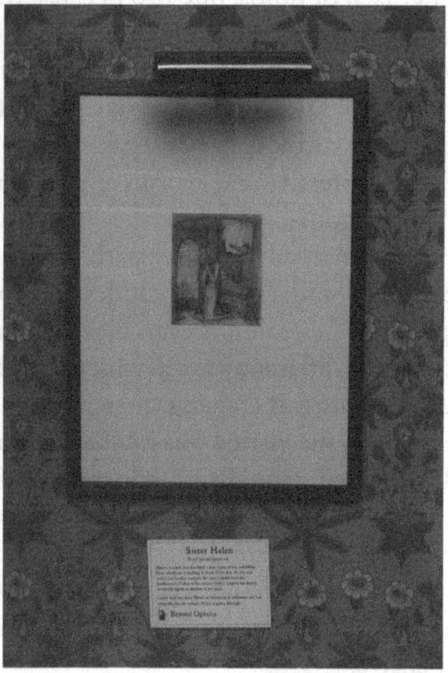

Figure 14.6. Elizabeth Siddal, *Sister Helen* on display in *Beyond Ophelia*, Wightwick Manor, Wolverhampton. Photograph © John Pittwood.

30 *The Correspondence of Dante Gabriel Rossetti*, ed. William E. Fredeman, 10 vols (Cambridge: D. S. Brewer, 2002–15), II, 25–6. Letter to William Allingham, 17 March 1855.

of Rossetti and Siddal and how they mutually inspired each other. A copy of this poem in Rossetti's *Ballads and Narrative Poems* (1893) published by the Kelmscott Press from Wightwick's Library was on display just below the drawing to show these influences.

In this drawing of the witch Sister Helen, who vengefully melts a wax effigy of her unfaithful lover, Siddal does not draw Helen as hysterical or villainous. Instead, she has sympathy for the torture Helen is going through. With very little detail, she manages to evoke so much emotion in Helen's form. The interpretation for this drawing also stressed that Siddal had no consistent art training in figure drawing. This was not only due to her gender and her lack of funds, but also because the Pre-Raphaelites believed that natural talent, imagination and innovation were the most important attributes of an artist. Siddal's study of medieval manuscripts and early Italian art inspired her own expressive naïve style, creating a deliberate awkwardness and stiffness in her figures.[31] Her figures, although naively drawn, are very expressive and evocative, and in many of her drawings women are the protagonists.

Drawings provide a visceral intimacy with an artist's technique. As Wightwick's collection of Siddal's work includes multiple drawings of the same theme, this process of creation is even more apparent and intimate, with visitors able to see the different ways in which sketches of these figures convey emotion and meaning. By having them all framed and on display together for the first time, the visitor was invited to compare and understand what Siddal was striving for. This is apparent in the two versions of *Sir Galahad* in Wightwick's collection. The new hinged frames (Figure 14.7) allow visitors to observe them directly next to each other and compare how Siddal experiments with the depiction of piety in Galahad's pose in prayer, revealing that one appears to show the depiction of shock while the other is more pensive.

Medieval subjects became an important inspiration for the Pre-Raphaelite artists. These drawings of *Sir Galahad* are some of the earliest representations of Arthurian themes in Pre-Raphaelite art – indicating

31 Jan Marsh and Pamela Gerrish Nunn, *Women Artists and the Pre-Raphaelite Movement* (London: Virago Press, 1989), 68.

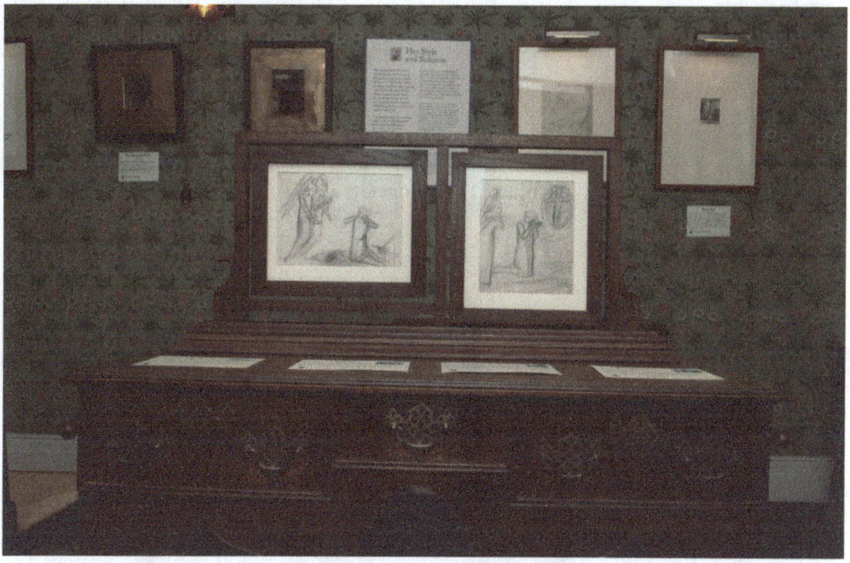

Figure 14.7. Elizabeth Siddal, Two Studies for *Sir Galahad* on display in *Beyond Ophelia*, Wightwick Manor, Wolverhampton. Photograph © John Pittwood.

that Siddal was among the first to develop the idea.[32] In the exhibition interpretation, this exchange of ideas was stressed, showing Siddal's agency and voice, and moving away from the stereotype of the passive model, or the image of the pupil of Rossetti, learning and being inspired by him only.

Both the *Sir Galahad* sketches, as well as the three drawings of *St Cecilia* exhibited, were scenes inspired by Tennyson's poetry. Displaying these sketches in close proximity to each other allowed visitors to see Siddal's thought process while she was working through ideas and compositions. It also emphasised her ambition for professional acknowledgement; these are designs for a potential commission to illustrate the new Moxon edition of Tennyson's poetry, and as Marsh has argued, were probably created some time around 1855 – Moxon's edition was published in 1857.[33] Although

32 Marsh, *The Legend of Elizabeth Siddal*, 187.
33 Marsh and Nunn, *Women Artists and the Pre-Raphaelite Movement*, 68.

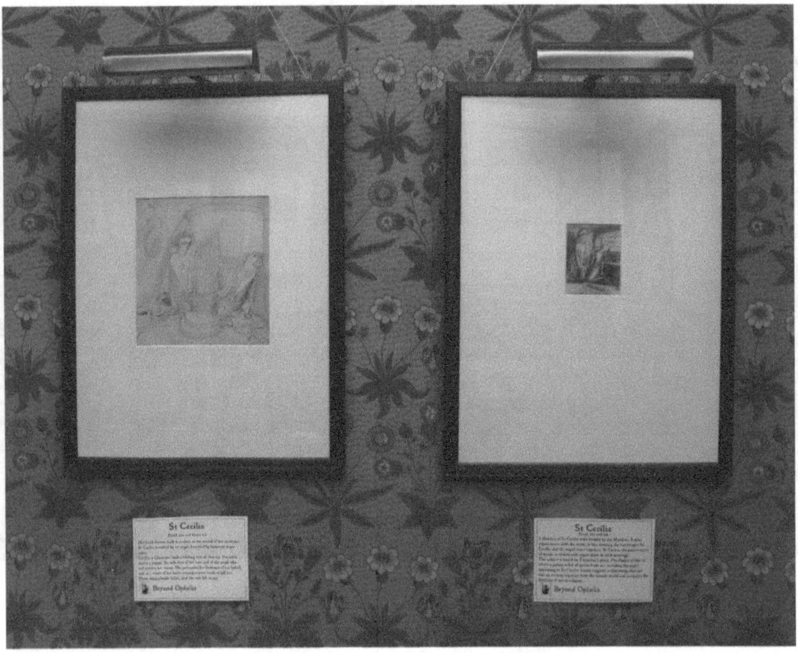

Figure 14.8. Elizabeth Siddal, Two Studies for *St Cecilia* on display in *Beyond Ophelia*, Wightwick Manor, Wolverhampton. Photograph © John Pittwood.

Siddal was never commissioned, these drawings identify her as a professional artist, seizing commercial opportunities for her career and working on her compositions to rework them for publication.

In all three drawings of *St Cecilia* (Figure 14.8), her head is thrown back in ecstasy at the arrival of her protector. The saint, who took a vow of chastity, is visited by an angel heralded by heavenly organ pipes. Below these drawings Wightwick's copy of the Moxon Tennyson was displayed, open at the page depicting Rossetti's illustration of *St Cecilia* for visitors to compare and contrast how Rossetti's later drawing, which was used in the publication, was inspired by Siddal's art. Rosalie (referencing William Michael Rossetti's earlier article about his brother and sister-in-law in the *Burlington Magazine*), wrote in her biography of Rossetti: 'It appears from a collection of Lizzie's drawings that these ideas were hers'.[34] The pose of Rossetti's *St Cecilia*; with her head thrown back, eyes closed in ecstasy, and her hands resting on the organ pipes, is inspired by Siddal's earlier drawings of the saint. Rossetti, however, brings the angel and saint together in a sensual embrace. In the exhibition, I wanted to subvert the narrative where male artists are given credit for women's creativity. Historically, female artists have rarely received the recognition for their own art. Siddal's work has been described as an imitation of Rossetti's, yet, as *St Cecilia* attests, Rossetti drew inspiration from her work.

The final set of drawings on display in the exhibition were three representations of a nativity scene. Having these drawings displayed side by side, the visitor had a window into Siddal's working methods. We can see the decisions she made about the relationship of Christ and Mary in the composition, and how she changed and reworked the idea to show their familial bond and evoke the greatest emotive response in a few strokes of a pencil. Whether to be worked up into watercolours which could be publicly exhibited or sold, or created as designs for book illustrations, the exhibition emphasised that Siddal created her art to be seen and appreciated, she wanted her voice to be heard amongst the canvases of her male peers.

Feedback

Finally, I would like to share some of the feedback received from visitors. The exhibition, and the broader *Art and Activism* programming, was very well attended and shows the appetite for exhibiting the work of Siddal and other female Pre-Raphaelite artists. While we had a great amount of interest and visits from existing audiences, we also drew new audiences to Wightwick, including enquiries from as far away as New York.

We wanted visitors to add their own thoughts to the exhibition, so we created a space where visitors could leave their reflections (Figure 14.9). A single

34 Rosalie Glynn Grylls, *Portrait of Rossetti* (Carbondale and Edwardsville: Southern Illinois University Press, 1964), 44; William Michael Rossetti 'Dante Rossetti and Elizabeth Siddal', *The Burlington Magazine for Connoisseurs*, 1/3 (1903), 295.

question was printed on the top of the comment cards: 'How do you think Lizzie Siddal should be remembered?' Responses were received from children as young as seven, from visitors who had never heard of Siddal before, or those who only knew her as a model to those who had no idea of scale of the collection at Wightwick. Answers included: 'She should be remembered as a talented woman. She should be remembered by one of her pieces of work', by 10-year-old Georgia. Another visitor wrote: 'As an inspiration to women who want to be part or are a part of the Arts. How have I not heard of her before now if she did all this?!'[35] Reflecting on the 2018 political climate, and possibly inspired by the Manders' political engagement in women's rights, another visitor, Neil, wrote: 'By the granting of no-fault divorces in cases of irretrievable marriage breakdown.'[36] I was really inspired by the range of answers and the thoughtfulness of the comments; some people were even

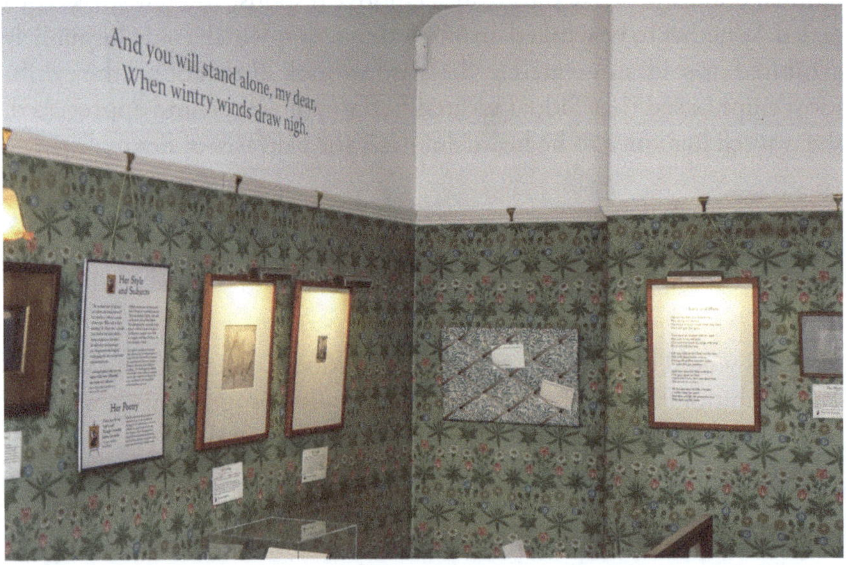

Figure 14.9. Further view of the exhibition space with feedback board for *Beyond Ophelia* Wightwick Manor, Wolverhampton. Photograph © Lindsay Bucknor.

35 All quotes taken from *How do you think Lizzie Siddal should be remembered?* comment cards (Wightwick: National Trust, 2018).

36 This topic gained more media attention in 2018 and is finally coming into force in England and Wales in April 2022.

inspired by Siddal's creativity to provide instead illustrations as their answer to the question.

We also received some excellent reviews and media attention, highlighting the appetite for more exhibitions of this kind. For example, I wrote a piece for the William Morris Society magazine and was interviewed by Serena Trowbridge for the Pre-Raphaelite Society journal *PRS Review*.[37] Jan Marsh wrote an article in *Art Quarterly* about female Pre-Raphaelite artists and featured the exhibition.[38] I was also interviewed in 2019 for the BBC Radio 3 programme *Unearthing Elizabeth Siddal*, where I spoke about the Manders' collection of Siddal artwork, which also led to an increase in visitors to the Manor.[39] The Art Fund, who helped the National Trust acquire *St Agnes' Eve*, also promoted the exhibition, and locally the *Wolverhampton Magazine* ran a four-page feature on the exhibition and Wightwick's wider *Art and Activism* theme.[40]

It has been a privilege not only to share more widely both the incredible collection of Siddal's work at Wightwick and the Manders' dedication in amassing this collection for the nation, but also to foreground Siddal's artistic endeavours. The exhibition still lives on. As part of its legacy, we have added to the digital content on the National Trust Collections website – with more information about Siddal and the Manders' collections online, and more photographs to illustrate the object entries.[41] At Wightwick, more of Siddal's artworks are on display than ever before, with further interpretation, and works by other female artists in the collection have been moved to more prominent positions. Also, in 2020, a book published to

37 Hannah Squire, 'Lizzie Siddal, "her surprising talents – shown in verse as well as drawing"', *The William Morris Society Magazine* (Summer 2018), 3–5. Serena Trowbridge, Exhibition Review: 'Beyond Ophelia', *Pre-Raphaelite Society Review*, 27/1 (Spring 2019), 22–5.

38 Jan Marsh, 'The Popularity of the Pre-Raphaelites', *Art Quarterly* (Autumn 2018), 30–3.

39 Clare Walker, producer, 'Unearthing Elizabeth Siddall', Sunday Feature, BBC Radio 3 (Sunday 13 October 2019).

40 Heather Loat, 'Activism Through Art', *Wolverhampton Magazine* (April 2018), 35–8.

41 <https://www.nationaltrust.org.uk/wightwick-manor-and-gardens/features/the-pre-raphaelite-art-collection-at-wightwick>; <http://www.nationaltrustcollections.org.uk/>.

celebrate 125 years of the National Trust, featuring the top 125 objects, includes, at my suggestion, one of Siddal's art works, *The Haunted Wood*.[42]

To conclude, my aim was for this exhibition to inspire, empower and embolden others. My love of art and passion for the female Pre-Raphaelite artists is due to the time I have spent at Wightwick, and to the incredible stories of the women past and present associated with the Manor. I hope that this exhibition and chapter inspire other women to relentlessly pursue their dreams, the way Siddal has always inspired me.

Bibliography

Brown, David, 'Pre-Raphaelite Drawings in the Bryson Bequest to the Ashmolean Museum', *Master Drawings* 16/3 (1978), 287–93.

Glynn Grylls, Rosalie, *Portrait of Rossetti* (Carbondale and Edwardsville: Southern Illinois University Press, 1964).

Maas, Jeremy, 'The Pre-Raphaelites: A Personal View', in Leslie Parris, ed., *Pre-Raphaelite Papers* (London: Tate Gallery, 1984).

Mander, Rosalie, 'Rossetti and the Oxford Murals, 1857', in Leslie Parris, ed., *Pre-Raphaelite Papers* (London: Tate Gallery, 1984).

Marsh, Jan, *Pre-Raphaelite Sisterhood* (New York: Quartet Books, 1985).

——, *The Legend of Elizabeth Siddal* (London: Quartet Books, 1989).

——, and Pamela Gerrish Nunn, *Women Artists and the Pre-Raphaelite Movement* (London: Virago Press, 1989).

——, *Elizabeth Siddal: Pre-Raphaelite Artist 1829–1862* (Sheffield: Ruskin Gallery, 1991).

Pollock, Griselda; Cherry Deborah, 'Woman as sign in Pre-Raphaelite literature: the representation of Elizabeth Siddall', in *Vision and Difference, Feminism, Femininity and Histories of Art* (London: Routledge, 2003).

Ponder, Stephen, *Wightwick Manor and Gardens Guidebook* (Swindon: National Trust, 2016).

Treuherz, Julian, 'The Pre-Raphaelites and Mediaeval Illuminated Manuscripts', in Leslie Parris, ed., *Pre-Raphaelite Papers* (London: Tate Gallery, 1984).

42 I assisted with research for the text of Siddal's article. Tarnya Cooper, *125 Treasures From the Collections of the National Trust* (Swindon: National Trust, 2021).

Notes on Contributors

ROBYNE CALVERT is a cultural historian with research interests focused on the history of art, architecture and design in Britain. She has researched and lectured in heritage, architecture and design history and theory at Glasgow School of Art; and is also a researcher and visiting lecturer in dress history at the University of Glasgow. She received the Pasold Fund PhD bursary for her thesis 'Fashioning the Artist: Artistic Dress in Victorian Britain, 1848–1900' (University of Glasgow, 2012), and is currently developing this for publication.

HELENA COX (née Gaudekova) is a PhD candidate in History of Art at the University of York. Until 2022, Helena worked as Curator at Beverley Art Gallery, East Riding of Yorkshire Museums, overseeing a collection of late Victorian and Edwardian painting. In January 2022, Helena became the inaugural Art Curator at the University of York where she oversees a collection of over 900 artworks dating from the sixteenth century to the present day. Helena previously worked as a Curator at the National Museum in Prague (Czech Republic) where she researched the Japanese art collection and published two monographs: *Playing All Day Long* (2014), and *Buddhas, Bódhisattvas and Deities – Japanese Buddhist Art from the Náprstek Museum* (2012) and a series of peer-reviewed articles mainly exploring nineteenth century Japanese woodblock prints. Helena's research is focused on intercultural dialogues, such as between Japan and 'Western' culture, and between Austria-Hungary and Britain in the nineteenth century. Helena's research explores the reflection of British art in Bohemia, nowadays the Czech Republic, around 1900. This includes an emphasis on the role of the Pre-Raphaelites in shaping Central European and specifically Bohemian art. As a curator, Helena explores the role of university art collections and exhibitions as a bridge between academia, students and the general public.

BRIAN EATON is the great-grandson of Pre-Raphaelite model Fanny Matilda Eaton. He discovered his great-grandmother Fanny in 2000 while researching his family history after hearing from his father that there was 'Red-Indian' (Native American) blood in the family. That story was untrue, but the discoveries he made were far more exciting. Since then, together with his wife Mary, he has tirelessly researched Fanny and her story to discover as much as possible about their shared heritage.

MARGARETTA S. FREDERICK is the Annette Woolard-Provine Curator of the Bancroft Collection of Pre-Raphaelite Art at the Delaware Art Museum. Dr. Frederick has been integral to the Museum's Bancroft Collection for over twenty years, focusing on women within the Pre-Raphaelite circle. She co-curated (with Jan Marsh) the first retrospective exhibition of the Pre-Raphaelite painter Marie Spartali Stillman (and accompanying co-authored catalogue, *The Poetry in Beauty: The Pre-Raphaelite art of Marie Spartali Stillman*, Antique Collector's Club, 2015) as well as smaller exhibitions featuring May Morris and Barbara Bodichon. Projects currently underway for the future include an exhibition of the work of Evelyn and William De Morgan in fall 2022 with an accompanying book of essays (Yale University Press). She is also co-editing the collected letters of May Morris with Anna Mason.

CHARLOTTE GERE is an exhibition curator and social historian, with an emphasis on women's place in the arts, design and decoration. She has published on Victorian decorative arts, costume, jewellery, homes and gardens and women collectors. She is the author of *Artistic Circles, Design and Decoration in the Aesthetic Movement*, on artists' houses, published in 2010. Recent catalogue essays include studies of Lawrence and Laura Alma-Tadema at home, Edward Burne-Jones portraits, James Tissot's London house and the Pre-Raphaelite Sisters' domestic responsibilities. Co-curator in 2019 of 'At home: royal etchings by Queen Victoria and Prince Albert' at the British Museum.

CAREY GIBBONS is Assistant Professor in the Department of Art History at the University of North Texas. She was the 2021–22 Drawing

Institute Postdoctoral Research Fellow at the Morgan Library & Museum, where she completed research on Pre-Raphaelite drawing and illustration. She received her doctorate from the Courtauld Institute of Art in London, where she wrote a dissertation on the illustrations of Arthur Hughes and Frederick Sandys. In addition to teaching illustration and graphic design history courses at the Pratt Institute and a variety of other institutions, she has acquired curatorial experience at the Columbia Rare Book & Manuscript Library, Fisk University Galleries, and Cooper Hewitt, Smithsonian Design Museum. She is also Digital Art History Editor for *Nineteenth-Century Art Worldwide*.

CAROLINE E. GIDDIS is an art historian specialising in nineteenth-century perceptions of women, proto-feminism and intersections of visual and literary culture, and received her MA from Savannah College of Art and Design in 2020. Caroline recently curated an exhibition at the Delaware Art Museum as its Alfred Appel, Jr. Curatorial Fellow, and is the research assistant working alongside Margaretta S. Frederick on the museum's 2022 exhibition on William and Evelyn De Morgan and its accompanying publication (Yale University Press). She is also an alumna of the 2019 Victorian Society in America's London Summer School, and is the founder of the online arts publication *Tesserae Press*. Caroline's recent work examines the Celtic styles and suffragist motivations of Mary Seton Watts, Phoebe Anna Traquair and other Victorian artists.

SARAH HARDY has been the curator of the De Morgan Foundation since April 2018, following a successful career working as a museum registrar at the British Library and National Gallery. Sarah curated *Sublime Symmetry: The Mathematics Behind William De Morgan's Designs* a touring exhibition which has welcomed 150,000 visitors to date. This sparked her interest in the techniques employed by Victorian artists in their artwork and led her to write the present chapter. Sarah is currently writing on the scientific processes employed by William De Morgan in the creation of his beautiful ceramics for Yale University Press, due 2022. Sarah is Trustee of the William Morris Society and is currently working on an essay on Burne-Jones's visionary illustrations for the Kelmscott Chaucer to be published upon its 125th anniversary in 2021.

LAURE NERMEL is a doctoral candidate focusing on the creative agency of Pre-Raphaelite artist and poet Elizabeth Siddal at Lille University. Her Master's dissertations focussed on Victorian visual arts, enabling her to publish an article in the *Journal des Arts* about fairy painting. She completed her education in Museum Studies at the University of Westminster, by participating in several projects at the Musée d'Orsay, the V&A, Tate and the Museum of London, before mounting her own exhibition "People are Strange/ When You're a Stranger". She is now a licensed tour guide specialised in nineteenth-century visual culture, museum displays and gender issues. In 2021, she contributed to a special issue of the newspaper *Le Monde*, and won the Pickard Essay Prize of the *Pre-Raphaelite Society Review*.

CHRISTIN NEUBAUER is a research assistant and doctoral candidate at the University of Jena, Germany, who received her MAs in History of Art from the University of York and the University of Jena. Her research interests focus on nineteenth-century British art and particularly the art of the Pre-Raphaelites. She examines transnational receptions and is intrigued by issues in reception aesthetics. Forthcoming publications include papers on the construction and perception of rhythm in Heinrich Vogeler's book illustrations, and Germanness in the depiction of Prince Albert in the ITV series *Victoria* and the Neo-Victorian context of his portrayal.

NAT REEVE is an AHRC-funded doctoral candidate at Royal Holloway, University of London, working on everything spectral, queer, medievalist and disruptive in Elizabeth Siddal's art and poetry. They are especially intrigued by Siddal's weird reworkings of medieval objects, persistent destabilisation of visual and literary sources, and shifting attitudes towards nineteenth-century creative practice. Nat was the 2020 Pre-Raphaelite Fellow at the University of Delaware/Delaware Art Museum, and the 2019–20 Co-Director of the Royal Holloway Centre for Victorian Studies. Their debut novel *Nettleblack*, a queer Neo-Victorian adventure, was published by Cipher Press in 2022, with a sequel to come in 2023. Their essay 'Talking to Trees: Elizabeth Siddal and Dante Alighieri' was published in the critical-creative pamphlet *Green Blues* (2020), and they have a forthcoming article in *Word & Image* on Siddal's queer reworking of the Book of Hours.

HANNAH SQUIRE, BA, MRes (University of Birmingham), is an art and literature historian, researcher, writer and curator. She is currently working on an English Literature MA exploring the activism fiction created by members of the Women Writers' Suffrage League in the early twentieth century. Her research interests include women and LGBTQ+ lives in the nineteenth and early twentieth centuries, with a focus on their artistic and literary output. Until 2020, she was Assistant Curator, National Public Programmes at the National Trust, working on national campaigns to create curatorial content focussed on inclusive histories. Before this Hannah worked at Wightwick Manor for over three years, where she curated only the second solo exhibition of Elizabeth Eleanor Siddal's art and poetry, *Beyond Ophelia* in 2018. In 2019 co-curated the *Look Beneath the Lustre* exhibition of Evelyn and William De Morgan's work also at Wightwick. She has been a volunteer at Wightwick for over ten years and is now pursuing some exciting digital projects with the Pre-Raphaelite Society. Hannah is planning a doctorate to further research Wightwick's collection of female artists work, examining how it was described, catalogued, critiqued and collected over the years. Her findings will be compared with the broader history of collecting/curating female Pre-Raphaelite artists' work.

ROSALIND WHITE is a postdoctoral researcher on the 'Finding Middlemarch' project (Royal Holloway, University of London) and on CLiC (Corpus Linguistics in Context) at the University of Birmingham – a project that uses computer-assisted methods to explore nineteenth-century literary texts. Her doctoral thesis (RHUL) interpolated between the history of science and the history of emotions, two interdependent fields that mutually orbit around the same question: what stories emerge from the past when we cease mining it for teleological argument? She co-wrote *Pre-Raphaelites in the Spirit World: The Séance Diary of William Michael Rossetti* (Peter Lang, 2022) and has a forthcoming chapter in

A Cultural History of Insects in the Age of Industry (Bloomsbury Academic, 2022).

ROBERT WILKES is a postdoctoral researcher at the Universidade Estadual de Campinas in Brazil, funded by the São Paulo Research Foundation (FAPESP). He received his doctorate from Oxford Brookes University in 2020 for his thesis on the neglected art and writings of Frederic George Stephens. With Glenda Youde he co-organised the conference *Pre-Raphaelite Sisters: Making Art* at the University of York in December 2019. His current research examines British artists who travelled to Brazil during the nineteenth century. He has published articles in the *Burlington Magazine* and the *British Art Journal* and has contributed essays to *Defining Pre-Raphaelite Poetics* (Palgrave Macmillan, 2020) and *Pre-Raphaelites: Drawings and Watercolours* (Ashmolean Museum, 2021).

GLENDA YOUDE has recently completed her doctorate at the University of York. Her research is focused on the women of the Pre-Raphaelite circle. Her principal area of interest is the neglected artistic legacy of Elizabeth Eleanor Rossetti (née Siddall) and its effect on the visual development of Pre-Raphaelite art. She was a co-organiser with Robert Wilkes of the successful conference *Pre-Raphaelite Sisters: Making Art* held at the University of York in December 2019. She has an essay included in a forthcoming collection examining the life and work of George Price Boyce.

Index

Cultural Interactions
Studies in the Relationship between the Arts

Edited by J.B. Bullen

Interdisciplinary activity is now a major feature of academic work in all fields. The traditional borders between the arts have been eroded to reveal new connections and create new links between art forms. Cultural Interactions is intended to provide a forum for this activity. It will publish monographs, edited collections and volumes of primary material on points of crossover such as those between literature and the visual arts or photography and fiction, music and theatre, sculpture and historiography. It will engage with book illustration, the manipulation of typography as an art form, or the 'double work' of poetry and painting and will offer the opportunity to broaden the field into wider and less charted areas. It will deal with modes of representation that cross the physiological boundaries of sight, hearing and touch and examine the placing of these modes within their representative cultures. It will offer an opportunity to publish on the crosscurrents of nationality and the transformations brought about by foreign art forms impinging upon others. The interface between the arts knows no boundaries of time or geography, history or theory.

Vol. 1 Laura Colombino: Ford Madox Ford: Vision, Visuality and Writing
275 pages. 2008. ISBN 978-3-03911-396-5

Vol. 2 Graham Smith: 'Light that Dances in the Mind': Photographs and Memory in the Writings of E. M. Forster and his Contemporaries
257 pages. 2007. ISBN 978-3-03911-117-6

Vol. 3 G.F. Mitrano and Eric Jarosinski (eds): The Hand of the Interpreter: Essays on Meaning after Theory
370 pages. 2009. ISBN 978-3-03911-118-3

Vol. 4 Grace Brockington (ed.): Internationalism and the Arts in Britain and Europe at the *Fin de Siècle*
368 pages. 2009. ISBN 978-3-03911-128-2

Vol. 5 Gabrielle Townsend: Proust's Imaginary Museum: Reproductions and Reproduction in *À la Recherche du temps perdu*
232 pages. 2008. ISBN 978-3-03911-124-4

Vol. 6 Lennart Nyberg: Bodies of Poems: Graphic Poetics in a Historical Perspective
187 pages. 2009. ISBN 978-3-03911-343-9

Vol. 7 Jeff Adams: Documentary Graphic Novels and Social Realism
214 pages. 2008. ISBN 978-3-03911-362-0

Vol. 8 Caroline Patey and Laura Scuriatti (eds): The Exhibit in the Text: The Museological Practices of Literature
292 pages. 2009. ISBN 978-3-03911-377-4

Vol. 9 Francesca Orestano and Francesca Frigerio (eds): Strange Sisters: Literature and Aesthetics in the Nineteenth Century
324 pages. 2009. ISBN 978-3-03911-840-3

Vol. 10 Carole Bourne-Taylor and Ariane Mildenberg (eds): Phenomenology, Modernism and Beyond
404 pages. 2010. ISBN 978-3-03911-409-2

Vol. 11 Gillian Pye (ed.): Trash Culture: Objects and Obsolescence in Cultural Perspective
264 pages. 2010. ISBN 978-3-03911-553-2

Vol. 12 Carol Adlam and Juliet Simpson (eds): Critical Exchange: Art Criticism of the Eighteenth and Nineteenth Centuries in Russia and Western Europe
420 pages. 2009. ISBN 978-3-03911-556-3

Vol. 13 Kyriaki Hadjiafxendi and Patricia Zakreski (eds): What Is a Woman to Do? A Reader on Women, Work and Art, c. 1830–1890
404 pages. 2011. ISBN 978-3-03911-116-9

Vol. 14 Emma Wagstaff: Writing Art: French Literary Responses to the Work of Alberto Giacometti
227 pages. 2011. ISBN 978-3-03911-871-7

Vol. 15 Linda Goddard: Aesthetic Rivalries: Word and Image in France, 1880–1926
323 pages. 2012. ISBN 978-3-03911-879-3

Vol. 16 Kim Knowles: A Cinematic Artist: The Films of Man Ray
342 pages. 2009. ISBN 978-3-03911-884-7

Vol. 17 Jo Carruthers and Andrew Tate (eds): Spiritual Identities: Literature and the Post-Secular Imagination
248 pages. 2010. ISBN 978-3-03911-925-7

Vol. 18 Giovanni Cianci, Caroline Patey and Sara Sullam (eds): Transits: The Nomadic Geographies of Anglo-American Modernism
350 pages. 2010. ISBN 978-3-03911-949-3

Vol. 19 Nick Havely (ed.): Dante in the Nineteenth Century: Reception, Canonicity, Popularization
343 pages. 2011. ISBN 978-3-03911-979-0

Vol. 20 Phillippa Bennett and Rosie Miles (eds): William Morris in the Twenty-First Century
323 pages. 2010. ISBN 978-3-0343-0106-0

Vol. 21 Simone Francescato: Collecting and Appreciating: Henry James and the Transformation of Aesthetics in the Age of Consumption
217 pages. 2010. ISBN 978-3-0343-0163-3

Vol. 22 Hervé Castanet: Pierre Klossowski: The Pantomime of Spirits
327 pages. 2014. ISBN 978-3-0343-0209-8

Vol. 23 Savina Stevanato: Visuality and Spatiality in Virginia Woolf's Fiction
309 pages. 2012. ISBN 978-3-0343-0241-8

Vol. 24 Paola Spinozzi and Elisa Bizzotto: *The Germ*: Origins and Progenies of Pre-Raphaelite Interart Aesthetics
310 pages. 2012. ISBN 978-3-0343-0298-2

Vol. 25 John Harvey: The Poetics of Sight
330 pages. 2015. ISBN 978-3-0343-0723-9

Vol. 26 Rina Arya (ed.): Contemplations of the Spiritual in Art
264 pages. 2013. ISBN 978-3-0343-0750-5

Vol. 27 Shannon Hunter Hurtado: Genteel Mavericks: Professional Women Sculptors in Victorian Britain
348 pages. 2012. ISBN 978-3-0343-0756-7

Vol. 28 Adrianne Rubin: Roger Fry's 'Difficult and Uncertain Science': The Interpretation of Aesthetic Perception
287 pages. 2013. ISBN 978-3-0343-0791-8

Vol. 29 Harry Heuser: Immaterial Culture: Literature, Drama and the American Radio Play, 1929–1954
374 pages. 2013. ISBN 978-3-0343-0977-6

Vol. 30 Judith A. Kidd: Behind the Image: Understanding the Old Testament in Medieval Art
279 pages. 2014. ISBN 978-3-0343-0993-6

Vol. 31 Outi Remes, Laura MacCulloch and Marika Leino (eds): Performativity in the Gallery: Staging Interactive Encounters
261 pages. 2014. ISBN 978-3-0343-0966-0

Vol. 32 Giovanni Cianci and Caroline Patey (eds): Will the Modernist: Shakespeare and the European Historical Avant-Gardes
306 pages. 2014. ISBN 978-3-0343-1763-4

Vol. 33 Béatrice Laurent (ed.): Sleeping Beauties in Victorian Britain: Cultural, Literary and Artistic Explorations of a Myth 254 pages. 2015. ISBN 978-3-0343-1745-0

Vol. 34 Hyunseon Lee and Naomi Segal (eds): Opera, Exoticism and Visual Culture
299 pages. 2015. ISBN 978-3-0343-1782-5

Vol. 35 Helle Hochscheid: Networks of Stone: Sculpture and Society in Archaic and Classical Athens
519 pages. 2015. ISBN 978-3-0343-0992-9

Vol. 36 Bernard McCarron: The Paradigm Case: The Cinema of Hitchcock and the Contemporary Visual Arts
323 pages. 2015. ISBN 978-3-0343-1780-1

Vol. 37 Terri Mullholland and Nicole Sierra (eds): Spatial Perspectives: Essays on Literature and Architecture
267 pages. 2015. ISBN 978-3-0343-1771-9

Vol. 38 Charlotte Ribeyrol (ed.): The Colours of the Past in Victorian England
318 pages. 2016. ISBN 978-3-0343-1974-4

Vol. 39 Christina Baird: Showcase Britain: Britain at the Vienna World Exhibition 1873
194 pages. 2016. ISBN 978-3-0343-1908-9

Vol. 40 Antony Buxton, Linda Hulin and Jane Anderson (eds): InHabit: People, Places and Possessions
286 pages. 2017. ISBN 978-3-0343-1866-2

Vol. 41 Paola Colaiacomo: Natasha's Dress: Language of Literature, Language of Fashion
296 pages. 2018. ISBN 978-3-0343-2216-4

Vol. 42 Daniela Guardamagna (ed.): Roman Shakespeare: Intersecting Times, Spaces, Languages
286 pages. 2018. ISBN 978-1-78707-967-0

Vol. 43 John Powell: Dancing with Time: The Garden as Art
222 pages. 2019. ISBN 978-1-78997-141-5

Vol. 44 David Maddock: Roger Fry, Clive Bell and American Modernism
273 pages. 2020. ISBN 978-1-78874-927-5

Vol. 45 Béatrice Laurent: Water and Women in the Victorian Imagination
272 pages. 2021. ISBN 978-1-78997-486-7

Vol. 46 Caroline Patey, Cynthia E. Roman and Georges Letissier (eds): Enduring Presence: William Hogarth's British and European Afterlives
Book 1: Aesthetic, Visual and Performative Cultures, 360 pages. Book 2: Image into Word, 350 pages.
2021. ISBN 978-1-80079-155-8

Vol. 47 Jean-Alexandre Perras and Érika Wicky (eds): Mediality of Smells / Médialité des odeurs
416 pages. 2022. ISBN 978-1-78997-606-9

Vol. 48 J. B. Bullen, Rosalind White and Lenore A. Beaky (eds): Pre-Raphaelites in the Spirit World: The Séance Diary of William Michael Rossetti
188 pages. 2022. ISBN 978-1-78997-442-3

Vol. 49 Glenda Youde and Robert Wilkes (eds): Pre-Raphaelite Sisters: Art, Poetry and Female Agency in Victorian Britain
496 pages. 2022. ISBN 978-1-80079-564-8

Printed by
CPI books GmbH, Leck